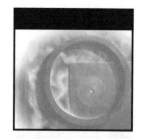

Building Application Frameworks

Object-Oriented Foundations of Framework Design

Mohamed E. Fayad

Douglas C. Schmidt

Ralph E. Johnson

Wiley Computer Publishing

John Wiley & Sons, Inc.

NEW YORK · CHICHESTER · WEINHEIM · BRISBANE · SINGAPORE · TORONTO

Publisher: Robert Ipsen
Editor: Marjorie Spencer
Assistant Editor: Margaret Hendrey
Managing Editor: Marnie Wielage
Text Design & Composition: North Market Street Graphics

This book is printed on acid-free paper. ⊗

This publication is designed to provide accurate and authoritative information in regard to the subject matter covered. It is sold with the understanding that the publisher is not engaged in professional services. If professional advice or other expert assistance is required, the services of a competent professional person should be sought.

Chapter 5, "Visual Builders: Framework Design Issues," reprinted courtesy of *Dr. Dobb's Journal* © 1998. All rights reserved.

Chapter 6, "Usability and Framework Design," reprinted courtesy of *Dr. Dobb's Journal* © 1998. All rights reserved.

Library of Congress Cataloging-in-Publication Data:
Building application frameworks : object-oriented foundations of
    framework design / editors: Mohamed Fayad, Douglas Schmidt, Ralph
    Johnson.
        p.   cm.
    "Wiley Computer Publishing."
    Includes bibliographical references and index.
    ISBN 0-471-24875-4 (alk. paper)
    1. Object-oriented programming (Computer science)   2. Application
software—Development.   3. Computer software—Reusability.
I. Fayad, Mohamed, 1950–   . II. Schmidt, Douglas C.   III. Johnson,
Ralph.
QA76.64.B85   1999
005.1'17—dc21   99-26915
                                                         CIP

Printed in the United States of America.

10 9 8 7 6 5 4 3 2 1

*To the memory of my mom and dad,
to my lovely wife Raefa, to my beautiful
daughters Rodina and Rawan, and to my
handsome son Ahmad.*

–Mohamad E. Fayad

*To Sonja, for helping me appreciate what's
important in life.*

–Douglas C. Schmidt

*To the creators of Simula and Smalltalk,
who were the first to see the vision.*

–Ralph E. Johnson

Contents

Preface   xv

Acknowledgments   xxi

Part One: Framework Overview   1
Mohamed E. Fayad

Chapter 1   Application Frameworks   3
Mohamed E. Fayad, Douglas C. Schmidt, and Ralph E. Johnson

  1.1 What Is an Application Framework?   4

  1.2 Benefits   8

  1.3 An Overview of Widely Used Frameworks   9

  1.4 Classifying Application Frameworks   9

  1.5 The Strengths and Weaknesses of Application
       Frameworks   11

  1.6 Reuse: Components versus Designs   13

  1.7 Application Frameworks versus Other Reuse Techniques   15

  1.8 How to Use Application Frameworks   17

  1.9 How to Learn Application Frameworks   18

  1.10 How to Evaluate Application Frameworks   19

  1.11 How to Develop Application Frameworks   21

  1.12 Organization of This Book   22

  1.13 Summary   23

  1.14 References   24

  1.15 Review Questions   27

Chapter 2   **Frameworks and Patterns: Architectural Abstractions**   **29**
Eyoun Eli Jacobson and Palle Nowack

2.1 Architectural Abstractions   31

2.2 Frameworks   33

2.3 Object-Oriented Patterns   37

2.4 Frameworks and Patterns   46

2.5 Summary   50

2.6 References   52

2.7 Review Questions   53

2.8 Problem Set   54

Chapter 3   **Framework Problems and Experiences**   **55**
Jan Bosch, Peter Molin, Michael Mattsson, PerOlaf Bengtsson,
and Mohamed E. Fayad

3.1 Object-Oriented Frameworks   56

3.2 Examples of Application Frameworks   59

3.3 Problems and Experiences   62

3.4 Summary   78

3.5 References   79

3.6 Review Questions   82

Sidebar 1   **Enterprise Frameworks**   **83**
David S. Hamu

Part Two: **Framework Perspectives**   **87**
Mohamed E. Fayad

Chapter 4   **Simula Frameworks: The Early Experience**   **89**
Jean G. Vaucher and Boris Magnusson

4.1 History of Simula   91

4.2 Basic Concepts of Simula   92

4.3 Standard Simula Frameworks   98

4.4 Other Simulation Frameworks   109

4.5 Simula and Real Time   119

4.6 Other Early Simula Frameworks   130

4.7 Discussion   131

4.8 Summary   136

4.9 References   138

4.10 Review Questions   140

Chapter 5   **Visual Builders: Framework Design Issues**   **143**
Art Jolin, Dave Lavin, and Susan Charpenter

5.1 Parts Can Address Both Sets of Needs   143

5.2 Programmers Connect Part Features to Build
Applications   145

5.3 Making Classes into Parts   145

5.4 Ready-to-Wear Parts versus Tailor-Made Classes   145

5.5 Code Generation Changes the Equation   147

5.6 Giving Up Some Freedom for Convenience   147

5.7 Builders Give You Some Things for Free   148

5.8 A Matter of Degree   149

5.9 Summary   149

5.10 References   150

5.11 Review Questions   150

5.12 Problem Set   150

5.13 Projects   152

Chapter 6   **Usability and Framework Design**   **153**
Art Jolin

6.1 Usability Guidelines   153

6.2 Summary   160

6.3 Review Questions   160

6.4 Problem Set   162

6.5 Projects   162

Sidebar 2   **Viewpoints and Frameworks in Component-Based
Software Design**   **163**
*Paula S.C. Alencar, Donald D. Cowan, Torsten Nelson,
Marcus F. Fontoura, and Carlos J.P. Lucena*

Part Three: Frameworks and Domain Analysis   **167**
Mohamed E. Fayad

Chapter 7   **Deriving Frameworks from Domain Knowledge**   **169**
Mehmet Aksit, Bedir Tekinerdogan, and Francesco Marcelloni

7.1 Description of the Pilot Projects   170

7.2 Modeling Domain Knowledge   172

7.3 Mapping Knowledge Graphs to Object-Oriented
Frameworks   181

	7.4 Evaluation of the Approach and Summary	189
	7.5 References	191
	7.6 Review Questions	194
	7.7 Problem Set	194

Chapter 8   Harvesting Design   **199**
Joan Boone

	8.1 The Harvesting Process	200
	8.2 Identifying Candidates	200
	8.3 Solution Domain Analysis	201
	8.4 Framework Implementation	203
	8.5 Application Development with the Framework	209
	8.6 Summary	209
	8.7 References	209
	8.8 Review Questions	210
	8.9 Problem Set	210

Sidebar 3   Frameworks and Domain Models: Two Sides of the Same Coin   **211**
Giancarlo Succi, Paolo Predonzani, Andrea Valerio, and Tullio Vernazza

Part Four: Framework Development Concepts   **215**
Mohamed E. Fayad

Chapter 9   Reusing Hooks   **219**
Garry Froehlich, H. James Hoover, Ling Liu, and Paul Sorenson

	9.1 Background	220
	9.2 The Hooks Model: An Overview	222
	9.3 Hooking into SEAF	225
	9.4 Summary	232
	9.5 References	233
	9.6 Review Questions	233
	9.7 Problem Set	234
	9.8 Projects	234
	9.9 Appendix: Grammar for Hook Descriptions	235

Chapter 10   A Framework Recipe   **237**
Steven R. Jones

	10.1 The Transition	237

10.2 The Pattern System 241

10.3 Summary 265

10.4 References 265

10.5 Review Questions 266

10.6 Problem Set 266

Chapter 11 Capturing Hypermedia Functionality 267
Alejandra Garrido and Gustavo Rossi

11.1 An Example 268

11.2 The OO-Navigator Architecture 269

11.3 Using the Framework 271

11.4 Describing the Architecture with Patterns 275

11.5 Summary 282

11.6 References 282

11.7 Review Questions 284

11.8 Problem Set 284

11.9 Projects 284

11.10 CASE Tool Appendix 285

Chapter 12 Understanding Frameworks 289
Neelam Soundarajan

12.1 A Simple Model of Frameworks 292

12.2 Behavioral Refinement: From Frameworks
to Applications 293

12.3 Case Study: A Simple Diagram Editor Framework 299

12.4 Summary 305

12.5 References 306

12.6 Review Questions 307

12.7 Problem Set 308

12.8 Projects 308

Chapter 13 Capturing Framework Requirements 309
Granville G. Miller, John McGregor, and Melissa L. Major

13.1 Background 310

13.2 Framework Requirements 311

13.3 Related Work 318

13.4 Summary 320

13.5 References 321

13.6 Review Questions   322

13.7 Problem Set   322

Chapter 14 Managing Class Dependencies   **325**
Andreas Rüping

14.1 Case Study   327

14.2 Classification   332

14.3 Related Work   341

14.4 Summary   342

14.5 References   343

14.6 Review Questions   344

14.7 Problem Set   344

Sidebar 4   Formal Design and Performance Evaluation   **345**
Michael Goedicke and Torsten Meyer

Part Five: Framework Development Approaches   **349**
Mohamed E. Fayad

Chapter 15 Framework Design by Systematic Generalization **353**
Hans Albrecht Schmid

15.1 Framework Design Activities   354

15.2 Application Modeling Activity   355

15.3 Hot Spots and Hot-Spot Specification   356

15.4 Hot-Spot Analysis   359

15.5 Hot-Spot Subsystem   362

15.6 Hot-Spot Subsystem High-Level Design: Mapping
      Characteristics to the Subsystem Structure   365

15.7 Generalization Transformation   367

15.8 Transformations Generalizing the Editor   369

15.9 Summary   373

15.10 References   377

15.11 Review Questions   377

15.12 Problem Set   378

Chapter 16 Hot-Spot-Driven Development   **379**
Wolfgang Pree

16.1 Hot Spots in Whitebox and Blackbox Frameworks   379

16.2 Hook Methods as Elementary Building Blocks
      of Hot Spots   381

16.3 Hot-Spot-Driven Development Process   384

16.4 Summary   392

16.5 References   392

16.6 Review Questions   393

16.7 Problem Set   393

Chapter 17 Structuring Large Application Frameworks   395
*Dirk Bäumer, Guido Gryczan, Rolf Knoll, Carola Lilienthal,
Dirk Riehle, and Heinz Züllighoven*

17.1 Framework Layering in Large Systems   396

17.2 Framework Construction for Large Systems   403

17.3 Related Work   408

17.4 Summary   408

17.5 References   409

17.6 Review Questions   410

17.7 Problem Set   410

Sidebar 5   Framelets—Small Is Beautiful   411
Wolfgang Pree and Kai Koskimies

**Chapter 18 Understanding Macroscopic Behavior Patterns
             with Use-Case Maps   415**
R.J.A. Buhr

18.1 Understanding Macroscopic Behavior Patterns   415

18.2 HotDraw   420

18.3 ACE   428

18.4 Discussion   433

18.5 Summary   437

18.6 References   437

18.7 Review Questions   439

18.8 Problem Set   439

18.9 Projects   439

Chapter 19 Composing Modeling Frameworks in Catalysis   441
Desmond D'Souza and Alan Cameron Wills

19.1 Frameworks—Beyond OOP   441

19.2 Frameworks Build on Types, Refinements,
      and Collaborations   450

19.3 Frameworks with Placeholders   455

19.4 Examples of Frameworks   458

19.5 Summary   458

19.6 References   459

19.7 Review Questions   459

19.8 Problem Set   459

19.9 Projects   459

Sidebar 6   Enduring Business Themes   **460**
Marshall Cline, Mike Girou, and Howard Young

Part Six: Framework Testing and Integration   **465**
Mohamed E. Fayad

Chapter 20 Composition Problems, Causes, and Solutions   **467**
Michael Mattsson and Jan Bosch

20.1 Object-Oriented Framework Examples   469

20.2 Framework Composition Problems   471

20.3 Underlying Causes   476

20.4 From Problems to Causes to Solutions   479

20.5 Summary   484

20.6 References   485

20.7 Review Questions   487

Sidebar 7   Built-In Test Reuse   **488**
Yingxu Wang, Graham King, and Mohamed E. Fayad

Part Seven: Framework Documentation   **493**
Mohamed E. Fayad

Chapter 21 Documenting Frameworks   **495**
Greg Butler and Pierre Dénommée

21.1 Kinds of Framework Reuse   496

21.2 Types of Documentation   497

21.3 Guidelines   501

21.4 Summary   501

21.5 References   502

21.6 Review Questions   503

Chapter 22 Empowering Framework Users   **505**
Jutta Eckstein

22.1 The Aim of Empowerment   505

22.2 Teaching Techniques   506

22.3 Combining the Teaching Techniques   509

22.4 Summary   515

22.5 References   520

22.6 Review Questions   521

22.7 Problem Set   521

Chapter 23 Describing and Using Frameworks   523
Hafedh Mili and Houari Sahraoui

23.1 Requirements   524

23.2 Model   527

23.3 Implementation   539

23.4 Framework Search and Realization   545

23.5 Framework Packaging   552

23.6 Related Work   555

23.7 Summary   557

23.8 References   558

23.9 Review Questions   560

23.10 Problem Set   560

Sidebar 8   Documenting Frameworks: Solitaire Is Not Alone   562
David C. Raines and James C. McKim, Jr.

Part Eight: Framework Management and Economics   565
Mohamed E. Fayad

Chapter 24 Strategic Analysis of Application Framework Investments   567
John M. Favaro and Kenneth K. Favaro

24.1 Software Reuse Economics and Organizational
      Reuse Capability   568

24.2 Strategy: A Value-Based Investment Framework   569

24.3 Finance: Linking Strategy to Value   577

24.4 Summary and Related Work   592

24.5 References   593

24.6 Review Questions   595

24.7 Problem Set   595

24.8 Projects   596

Chapter 25 Evaluating Structural and Functional Stability   599
Jadish Bansiya

25.1 Metrics and OOAF Characteristics Assessment   600

25.2 Framework Stability   601

25.3 Framework Architecture Assessment Method   602

25.4 Summary   611

25.5 References   613

25.6 Review Questions   613

25.7 Problem Set   614

25.8 Projects   615

Chapter 26 Future Trends   617
Mohamed E. Fayad

26.1 Future Research Areas   617

26.2 References   619

26.3 Review Questions   619

Sidebar 9   Framework Maintenance: Vendor Viewpoint   620
Mauri Laitinen

Appendix A   Glossary   625

Appendix B   Index of Authors   635

Index   653

Preface

This book focuses on object-oriented application frameworks (OO application frameworks for short, or OOAF) and is aimed at company decision makers: from the president and vice presidents of a company to software project managers and project leaders, who wish to achieve a large volume of reuse through object-oriented application frameworks. Its purpose is to help the reader understand one of the hottest technologies related to software reuse—*frameworks*—and provide guidelines for making decisions about this technology. It contains our advice and direct experiences in the development and utilization of the framework technology.

Despite dramatic increases in computing power, the design and implementation of complex software remains difficult. Moreover, the growing heterogeneity of hardware/ software architecture and the diversity of operating system and communication platforms make it difficult to reuse existing algorithms, detailed designs, interfaces, or implementations directly. The intensive focus on application frameworks in the object-oriented community offers software developers both a new vehicle for reuse and a way to capture the essence of successful patterns, architecture, components, policies, services, and programming mechanisms. Object-oriented application frameworks are very important for the software industry and academia at this time, when software systems are becoming increasingly complex. We believe that object-oriented application frameworks will be at the core of the leading-edge software technology of the twenty-first century.

There is little guidance for software developers on how to design and build object-oriented application frameworks. This book addresses several problematic topics crucial to the success of object-oriented application frameworks. It presents a complete reference on how to develop a good application framework and provides guidelines for dealing with issues related to application frameworks—such issues as evolving the application framework, protecting your investment, selecting the best framework available, evaluating OO application framework development, documenting the framework, and training on the framework. The book also includes sections on framework metrics, application framework integration and test issues, framework quality issues, and framework documentation issues.

The central claim of this volume is as follows. The OO application framework problems and perspectives are presented and examined with respect to three central themes:

- What makes the development or the adaptation of an OO application framework a mission with a lot of problems?

- How can the development or adaptation of an application framework be accomplished with minimum impact on the cost and schedule?

- Why is it important to buy, instead of developing application frameworks from scratch, and what are the consequences of doing so?

This is a pragmatic book specifically designed to help organizations effectively develop or adapt framework technology in the real world. Comprehensive technical and management guidelines are provided, ranging from specifying framework structures and behaviors to framework economics. Technical issues such as framework concepts, framework architectures, framework domain analysis, framework development, framework documentation, framework testing and integration, framework training, framework economics, and how to utilize frameworks are discussed in detail. Real-world issues such as keeping your expensive framework up to date and ferreting out hidden costs are examined. Limitations such as maintaining frameworks and adding value to your business are treated from a real-world perspective.

Outstanding Features

This book is intended to provide valuable, real-world insight into successful development and/or adaptation of OO application frameworks, by describing the problems with frameworks, explaining the issues related to the development and adaptation of frameworks, and selecting the right methods and tools for building frameworks. All material for the book has been derived from actual experiences, successes, and failures, and is presented in a practical, easy-to-understand manner. This is information that readers can apply today. Key book issues include the following:

- Factors that make the development of and/or adaptation to OO application frameworks a mission with a lot of problems.

- The key application-oriented framework issues.

- How to adapt OO application frameworks with minimum impact on costs and schedules.

- How to provide the right application framework documentation for maximum reuse.

- How to use your large-scale application framework and how to protect your investment.

- How to overcome most of the problems and key issues when developing, adapting, and integrating OO application frameworks.

This book will cover a complete spectrum of framework technology and includes 8 parts with 26 chapters and 9 sidebars. Together, these elements present the *how-to* from real-life application framework developments and adaptations. This book describes complete processes for developing application frameworks, adapting application frameworks, integrating and testing application frameworks, and documenting application frameworks. The reader will learn, in a process-oriented matter, how to:

- Explore and understand OO application framework problems and perspectives.
- Define all the issues related to OO application frameworks.
- Describe guidelines for OO application framework development.
- Insert framework technology into your company.
- Evaluate and select an object-oriented application framework for your domain.
- Evaluate and select the right tools and environments for the development of your application framework.
- Describe the guidelines for selecting the right framework for your domain.
- Describe the framework adaptation process in your company.
- Describe the tracking and controlling of your application framework effectively.
- Discuss the framework training and utilization issues.
- Describe the framework documenting process.

Who Should Read This Book

This volume draws on the experience and collective wisdom of its numerous contributors, to explore problems and present insights into the design, development, and deployment of application and enterprise frameworks. It will prove invaluable to software vendors in building frameworks that are both robust and flexible, to managers in identifying the most appropriate frameworks for the specific enterprise they are engaged in, and to application developers in effectively exploiting frameworks to construct complete applications quickly and efficiently.

This volume, addressing as it does both the fundamental concepts underlying frameworks as well as technological issues, is also exceptionally suitable as a textbook for graduate courses on software engineering with a focus on reuse issues and OO frameworks. Finally, this volume will serve researchers interested in the topic as a unique source of ideas, challenges, and perspectives on OO frameworks.

This book is intended for a broad community of computer and software professionals involved in the management and development of software projects, including company executives, project managers, engineering staff, technologists, software managers, object-oriented business owners, presidents, and CEOs. Software engineers, system engineers, system analysts, software developers, software process groups, contract administrators, customers, technologists, software methodologists, and enterprise program developers will greatly benefit from this book.

Object-oriented practitioners will benefit significantly from discussions of how to:

- Develop an enterprise framework.

- Utilize single and multiple frameworks.

- Document an enterprise framework.

- Integrate multiple frameworks on different levels of abstraction.

Company executives, such as project managers, object-oriented business owners, presidents, and CEOs, will benefit from learning what has been proven to work for others who have developed, utilized, and integrated frameworks in various problem domains. The results described here should save company executives many weeks of experimentation and prevent loss of resources. Company executives will also find discussions related to framework economics, practical tips, and experiences in dealing with OO application frameworks. These are accompanied by assessments of application frameworks.

Software developers (software engineers, programmers, designers), *engineering staffs* (system engineers), and *technologists* will benefit from the insights that are presented here regarding OO application framework architecture, model representation, domain analysis, integration, deployment, administration, and documentation.

Customers and end users are the most important part of any application framework: in particular, an enterprise framework. The belief or attitude that the insights of the customers or users are not the most important information used on a development project will doom software to failure. In this book, end users will gain a sound understanding of application frameworks and why these frameworks are assets to an organization.

Graduate courses on framework technology or advanced software engineering are obvious candidates to benefit from use of this book. Graduate courses on software engineering, object-oriented software engineering, object-oriented distributed computing, and design patterns can use this book as a supplemental text for students, as can courses on system engineering and advanced courses on enterprise developments. Prerequisites include basic knowledge of computing terms and concepts and basic knowledge of software engineering concepts and techniques. This book contains several pedagogical aids:

- More than *178 figures* are used to illustrate concepts and models.

- *Review questions* and *problem sets* are included at the end of each chapter. These are self-study aids designed to test the student's ability to apply the concepts and techniques covered in each chapter.

- *Projects* suitable for teams are also included at the end of most chapters.

- A *glossary* at the end of the book defines all new terms used in the book.

- An *index of authors* at the end of the book lists each author's affiliation, country, primary e-mail address, URL, chapters contributed, and a brief biography.

- An *instructor guide* is also available. The guide describes ways to use this book in different courses, provides a course outline, and supplies an answer key for most of the problems at the end of each chapter.

Acknowledgments

This book would not exist without the help of many great people. I am grateful to all the contributing authors for their submissions and their patience, and to all the reviewers for valuable and useful reviews of the submissions to this book. I would like to take this opportunity to say that I am honored to work with the two editors of this book, Douglas Schmidt and Ralph Johnson, and with all the authors and reviewers. This has been a terrific and enjoyable project because of their tremendous help and extensive patience.

I, along with all of the authors who contributed to this volume, wish to thank all of those who have had a part in the production of this book. First and foremost, we owe our families a huge debt of gratitude for being so patient while we put their world in a whirl by injecting this writing activity into their already full lives. We also thank the various reviewers and editors who helped in so many ways to coordinate this book. We thank our associates, who offered their advice and wisdom in defining the content of the book. We also owe a special thanks to those who worked on the various projects covered in the case studies and examples.

A special thanks to my wife Raefa, my lovely daughters Rodina and Rawan, and my son Ahmad for their great patience and understanding. Special thanks also to my friend Mauri Laitinen for his encouragement and long discussions about the topics and the issues in this book. Thanks to all my students—in particular, Amr Yassin, Jinkun Hu, David Naney, Sanjeev Segan, and Raji Hari, my friend Jun Gu, Marshall Cline, W.T. Tsai, and Yasser alSafadi, for their encouragement during this project, and to the staff of *Communications of the ACM*—my friends Diana Crawford, Tom Lambert, and Robert Fox—for their support.

I am very grateful to the editors at John Wiley & Sons. Thanks to Marjorie Spencer for her belief in and support of the book, to Margaret Hendrey for her patience and sharing in helping to put this text together, and to Marnie Wielage for overseeing the production of such a gigantic project.

Contributor Acknowledgments

Thank you to all the contributors for their tremendous effort and patience in making this volume a reality. Thanks also to all the contributors who participated in the review process for their valuable comments and excellent reviews. This volume provides a unique source of information and a wide spectrum of knowledge intended to aid software vendors, managers, developers, and users in their journey toward managing, developing, adapting, and utilizing application and enterprise frameworks. It is an appropriate book for a variety of graduate courses in advanced software engineering, reuse, framework technology, and more. It is also a single resource for conducting research in component-based reuse and object-oriented application and enterprise frameworks. It was a great honor to work with all of those who contributed. This volume was made possible only by the enormous efforts of the contributors—sincere thanks to all of them is in order. (See the Wiley web page at www.wiley.com/compbooks).

Reviewer Acknowledgments

Special thanks to all the reviewers for their useful reviews, helpful critiques, and pertinent insights that resulted in a clearer presentation and more integrated book than anything I could have produced alone. This manuscript is one of a three-volume set and has been thoroughly reviewed by more than 500 reviewers. Their comments and reviews were invaluable contributions to the making of this book. I am honored to have worked with all of them and their valuable comments have led to improvements in the content and presentation of this book. Thank you all. (See the Wiley web page at www.wiley.com/compbooks.)

Special Acknowledgments

The authors of Chapter 2 (Eyoun Eli Jacobson and Palle Nowack) wish to thank Bent Bruun Kristensen for inspiring and constructive research collaboration.

The authors of Chapter 3 (Jan Bosch, Peter Molin, Michael Mattsson, PerOlof Bengtsson, and Mohamed E. Fayad) wish to thank Christer Lundberg, Lennart Ohlsson, and Mauri Laitinen for their comments on topics discussed in this chapter.

The author of Chapter 6 (Art Jolin) thanks the development teams of all the frameworks whose guidelines and conventions (whether intentional or accidental) were used as examples. Special thanks to Bob Love, who champions many of the guidelines used on the IBM Open Class development team.

The author of Chapter 14 (Andreas Rüping) performed large parts of the work presented in this chapter while working at Forschungszentrum Informatik (FZI), Bereich Programmstrukturen, Haid-und-Neu-Straße 10-14, D-76131 Karlsruhe (Research Center for Computer Science). Several people provided a lot of help during that time. Gerhard Goos encouraged the author to work in the area of object-oriented framework construction and gave much support. Many colleagues, in particular Thomas Lindner, Rainer Neumann, Benedikt Schulz, and Walter Zimmer, provided valuable help throughout many fruitful discussions on various aspects of frameworks. Artur Brauer worked on and implemented the case study. Thanks a lot to all of them! The discussion of related material in workshops at various patterns conferences also provided valuable feedback. Thanks are especially due to Ralph Johnson and Erich Gamma for their comments on the author's patterns workshop contributions. Thanks also to Jens Coldewey for a discussion of the impact that the choice of the programming language has on the techniques described in this chapter.

The author of Chapter 15 (Hans Albrecht Schmid) sends thanks to Clemens Ballarin, Franco Indolfo, Frank Müller, and Jochen Peters, who cooperated with him to build the framework OSEFA, from which the presented design approach evolved; to Jürgen Röder, who helped to prepare this chapter; and to the Deutsche Forschungsgemeinschaft (DFG) for the partial support of the project.

The author of Chapter 18 (R.J.A. Buhr) indicated that this work was funded by NSERC and TRIO. He would like to thank Doug Schmidt for useful discussions and the reviewers of this chapter for helpful comments. Thanks are due to Alex Hubbard for insights into ACE.

The authors of Chapter 21 (Greg Butler and Pierre Dénommée) indicated that this work has been supported by the Natural Sciences and Engineering Research Council of Canada and Fonds pour la Formation de Chercheurs et l'Aide a la Recherche. The authors thank Jeff Poulin and the referees, who provided valuable feedback.

The author of Chapter 22 (Jutta Eckstein) would like to thank Jens Coldewey (her shepherd), Mary Lynn Manns, and Richard Steiger for their input. Additionally, she wishes to thank all the participants of the Writers Workshop at EuroPLoP 1998 in Kloster Irsee, Germany.

PART

One

Framework Overview

Object-oriented application frameworks are a very important issue for the software industry as well as academia at this time when software systems are becoming increasingly complex. We believe that object-oriented application frameworks will be at the core of leading-edge software technology of the twenty-first century. This part provides a complete overview of the application frameworks and other component-based reuse approaches. Part One is made up of three chapters and a sidebar.

Reuse of software has been one of the main goals of software engineering for decades. Reusing software is not simple, and most efforts resulted in small reusable, blackbox components. With the emergence of the object-oriented paradigm, the enabling technology for reuse of larger components became available and resulted in the definition of object-oriented application frameworks. Frameworks attracted attention from many researchers and software engineers, and frameworks have been defined for a large variety of domains. The claimed advantages of frameworks include increased reusability and reduced time to market for applications. Chapter 1 is an introduction and provides complete coverage of application framework issues. Chapter 1 defines application frameworks, provides several classifications of application frameworks, describes the characteristics of application frameworks, discusses the pros and cons of application frameworks, and contrasts the frameworks with other reuse approaches.

Chapter 2 elaborates on the understanding of the term *software architecture* by further developing the concept of architectural abstractions. The principal contributions are a conceptual model of architectural abstractions, an analysis of current pattern approaches, current framework understanding, and a new perspective on both patterns and frameworks as being examples of architectural abstractions. The technical innovation is a characterization of the concept of architectural abstraction in terms of structural characteristics, functionality, abstraction, and reuse.

Chapter 3 discusses the application framework problems based on the authors' experiences. The authors have been involved in the development and the utilization of several object-oriented application frameworks and based on the experiences from these projects, a number of problems related to frameworks are described. The problems are organized according to five categories: framework development, learning, usage, composition, and maintenance. For each category, the most relevant problems and experiences are presented. The goal of this chapter is to help software engineers avoid the described problems and to suggest topics for future research.

Sidebar 1 introduces the object-oriented enterprise frameworks (OOEFs). A new way of developing, deploying, extending, and administering enterprise systems is emerging. These systems either are developed as in-house solutions by organizations that were not satisfied with commercially available options for managing the enterprise or were procured from a small but growing population of enterprise framework vendors. OOEFs should not be confused with middleware and standards for distributed objects (such as Common Object Request Broker Architecture (CORBA) or Distributed Common Object Model (DCOM)). Interoperability represents but a single characteristic of an OOEF. Furthermore, OOEF components may be implemented as vertical CORBA facilities, but this definition alone does not satisfy the requirements of an OOEF either. OOEFs are an emerging discipline of developers and development teams that address reuse in a radical way. OOEFs allow distributed applications to be deployed rapidly with very little coding because applications leverage the framework and the enduring business processes and enduring business themes that are encoded into the framework itself.

Application Frameworks

Computing power and network bandwidth have increased dramatically over the past decade. However, the design and implementation of complex software remain expensive and error-prone. Much of the cost and effort stem from the continuous rediscovery and reinvention of core concepts and components across the software industry. In particular, the growing heterogeneity of hardware architectures and diversity of operating system and communication platforms make it hard to build correct, portable, efficient, and inexpensive applications from scratch.

Frameworks are an object-oriented reuse technique. They share a lot of characteristics with reuse techniques in general and object-oriented reuse techniques in particular. Although they have been used successfully for some time and are an important part of the culture of long-time object-oriented developers, most framework development projects are failures, and most object-oriented methodologies do not describe how to use frameworks. Moreover, there is a lot of confusion about whether frameworks are just large-scale patterns, or whether they are just another kind of component.

Even the definition of *framework* varies. A frequently used definition is "a framework is a reusable design of all or part of a system that is represented by a set of abstract classes and the way their instances interact." Another common definition is "a framework is the skeleton of an application that can be customized by an application developer." These are not conflicting definitions; the first describes the structure of a framework while the second describes its purpose. Nevertheless, they point out the difficulty of defining frameworks clearly.

Frameworks are important and are becoming more important. Systems like Object Linking and Embedding (OLE), OpenDoc, and Distributed System Object Model

(DSOM) are frameworks. The rise of Java is spreading new frameworks like Abstract Window Toolkit (AWT), which is part of the Java Foundation Classes (JFC) and Beans. Most commercially available frameworks seem to be for technical domains such as user interfaces or distribution, and most application-specific frameworks are proprietary. But the steady rise of frameworks means that every software developer should know what they are and how to deal with them.

This chapter compares and contrasts frameworks with other reuse techniques and describes how to use them, how to evaluate them, and how to develop them. It describes the trade-offs involved in using frameworks, including the costs and pitfalls, and when frameworks are appropriate.

1.1 What Is an Application Framework?

Object-oriented (OO) application frameworks are a promising technology for reifying proven software designs and implementations in order to reduce the cost and improve the quality of software. A framework is a reusable, semi-complete application that can be specialized to produce custom applications [Johnson-Foote 1988]. In contrast to earlier OO reuse techniques based on class libraries, frameworks are targeted for particular business units (such as data processing or cellular communications) and application domains (such as user interfaces or real-time avionics). Frameworks like MacApp, ET++, Interviews, Advanced Computing Environment (ACE), Microsoft Foundation Classes (MFCs) and Microsoft's Distributed Common Object Model (DCOM), Java-Soft's Remote Method Invocation (RMI), and implementations of the Object Management Group's (OMG) Common Object Request Broker Architecture (CORBA) play an increasingly important role in contemporary software development.

A framework is a reusable design of a system that describes how the system is decomposed into a set of interacting objects. Sometimes the system is an entire application; sometimes it is just a subsystem. The framework describes both the component objects and how these objects interact. It describes the interface of each object and the flow of control between them. It describes how the system's responsibilities are mapped onto its objects [Johnson-Foote 1988; Wirfs-Brock 1990].

The most important part of a framework is the way that a system is divided into its components [Deutsch 1989]. Frameworks also reuse implementation, but that is less important than reuse of the internal interfaces of a system and the way that its functions are divided among its components. This high-level design is the main intellectual content of software, and frameworks are a way to reuse it.

Typically, a framework is implemented with an object-oriented language like C++, Smalltalk, or Eiffel. Each object in the framework is described by an *abstract class*. An abstract class is a class with no instances, so it is used only as a superclass [Wirfs-Brock 1990]. An abstract class usually has at least one unimplemented operation deferred to its subclasses. Since an abstract class has no instances, it is used as a template for creating subclasses rather than as a template for creating objects. Frameworks use them as designs of their components because they both define the interface of the components and provide a skeleton that can be extended to implement the components.

Some of the more recent object-oriented systems, such as Java, the Common Object Model (COM), and CORBA, separate interfaces from classes. In these systems, a framework can be described in terms of interfaces. However, these systems can specify only the static aspects of an interface, but a framework is also the collaborative model or pattern of object interaction. Consequently, it is common for Java frameworks to have both an interface and an abstract class defined for a component.

In addition to providing an interface, an abstract class provides part of the implementation of its subclasses. For example, a *template method* defines the skeleton of an algorithm in an abstract class, deferring some of the steps to subclasses [Gamma 1995]. Each step is defined as a separate method that can be redefined by a subclass, so a subclass can redefine individual steps of the algorithm without changing its structure. The abstract class can either leave the individual steps unimplemented (in other words, they are abstract methods) or provide a default implementation (in other words, they are hook methods) [Pree 1995]. A concrete class must implement all the abstract methods of its abstract superclass and may implement any of the hook methods. It will then be able to use all the methods it inherits from its abstract superclass.

Frameworks take advantage of all three of the distinguishing characteristics of object-oriented programming languages: data abstraction, polymorphism, and inheritance. Like an abstract data type, an abstract class represents an interface behind which implementations can change. *Polymorphism* is the ability for a single variable or procedure parameter to take on values of several types. Object-oriented polymorphism lets a developer mix and match components, lets an object change its collaborators at runtime, and makes it possible to build generic objects that can work with a wide range of components. Inheritance makes it easy to make a new component.

A framework describes the architecture of an object-oriented system; the kinds of objects in it, and how they interact. It describes how a particular kind of program, such as a user interface or network communication software, is decomposed into objects. It is represented by a set of classes (usually abstract), one for each kind of object, but the interaction patterns between objects are just as much a part of the framework as the classes.

One of the characteristics of frameworks is *inversion of control*. Traditionally, a developer reused components from a library by writing a main program that called the components whenever necessary. The developer decided when to call the components and was responsible for the overall structure and flow of control of the program. In a framework, the main program is reused, and the developer decides what is plugged into it and might even make some new components that are plugged in. The developer's code gets called by the framework code. The framework determines the overall structure and flow of control of the program.

The first widely used framework, developed in the late 1970s, was the Smalltalk-80 user interface framework called Model/View/Controller (MVC) [Goldberg 1984; Krasner 1988; LaLonde 1991]. MVC showed that object-oriented programming was well suited for implementing graphical user interfaces (GUIs). It divides a user interface into three kinds of components: models, views, and controllers. These objects work in trios consisting of a view and a controller interacting with a model. A model is an application object and is supposed to be independent of the user interface. A view manages a region of the display and keeps it consistent with the state of the model. A controller converts user events (mouse movements and key presses) into operations on its model and view. For example, controllers implement scrolling and menus. Views can be nested to form complex user interfaces. Nested views are called *subviews.*

Figure 1.1 shows the user interface of one of the standard tools in the Smalltalk-80 environment, the file tool. The file tool has three subviews. The top subview holds a string that is a pattern that matches a set of files, the middle subview displays the list

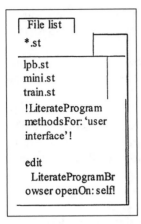

Figure 1.1 The Smalltalk-80 file tool.

of files that match the pattern, and the bottom subview displays the selected file. All three subviews have the same model—a FileBrowser. The top and bottom subviews are instances of TextView, while the middle subview is an instance of SelectionIn-ListView. As shown by Figure 1.2, all three views are subviews of a Standard-SystemView. Each of the four views has its own controller.

Class View is an abstract class with base operations for creating and accessing the subview hierarchy, transforming from view coordinates to screen coordinates, and keeping track of its region on the display. It has abstract and template operations for displaying, since different kinds of views require different display algorithms. TextView, SelectionInListView, and StandardSystemView are concrete subclasses of View, each of which has a unique display algorithm.

As a user moves the mouse from one subview to another, controllers are activated and deactivated so that the active controller is always the controller of the view managing the region of the display that contains the cursor. Class Controller implements

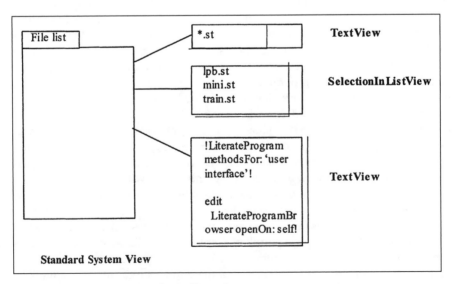

Figure 1.2 Subview hierarchy in file tool.

the protocol that ensures this, so a subclass of Controller automatically inherits the ability to cooperate with other controllers.

Class Object provides a dependency mechanism that views can use to detect when the model's state changes. Thus, any object can be a model. There is also a Model class that provides a faster version of the dependency mechanism at the cost of an extra variable [ParcPlace 1988].

The file tool is a typical Model/View/Controller application that does not need new subclasses of View or Controller. Its user interface consists entirely of objects from classes that are a standard part of the Smalltalk-80 class library. The Smalltalk-80 class library contains several dozen concrete subclasses of View and Controller. However, when these are not sufficient, new subclasses can be built to extend the user interface.

Successful frameworks evolve and spawn other frameworks. One of the first user interface frameworks influenced by Model/View/Controller was MacApp, which was designed specifically for implementing Macintosh applications [Schmucker 1986]. It was followed by user interface frameworks from universities, such as the Andrew Toolkit from Carnegie Mellon University [Palay 1988], InterViews from Stanford [Linton 1989], and ET++ from the University of Zurich [Weinand 1988, 1989]. There are now a large number of commercial user interface frameworks, such as zAPP, Open-Step, and MFCs. Some, like OpenStep's, are a small part of a much more comprehensive system. Some, like zAPP, are designed for developing portable software and shield the developer from the peculiarities of an operating system. Each of these frameworks borrows ideas from earlier systems. Although the differences between the frameworks are due partly to different requirements, sometimes newer systems incorporate better design techniques, and so the state of the art gradually improves.

Frameworks are not limited to user interfaces, but can be applied to any area of software design. They have been applied to very large scale integration (VLSI) routing algorithms [Gossain 1990], to hypermedia systems [Meyrowitz 1986], to structured drawing editors [Beck 1994; Vlissides 1989], to operating systems [Russo 1990], to psychophysiological experiments [Foote 1988], to network protocol software [Hueni 1995], and to manufacturing control [Schmid 1995], to mention a few.

Frameworks do not even require an object-oriented programming language. For example, the Genesis database system compiler is a framework for database management systems (DBMSs) [Batory 1989] as well as a tool for specifying how DBMSs are built from the framework. Genesis does not use an object-oriented language but rather a macroprocessor and conditional compilation to implement an object-oriented design in C.

The important classes in a framework, such as Model, View, and Controller of Model/View/Controller, are usually abstract. Like MVC, a framework usually comes with a *component library* that contains concrete subclasses of the classes in the framework. Although a good component library is a crucial companion to a framework, the essence of a framework is not the component library, but the model of interaction and control flow among its objects.

A framework reuses code because it makes it easy to build an application from a library of existing components. These components can be easily used with each other because they all use the interfaces of the framework. A framework also reuses code because a new component can inherit most of its implementation from an abstract superclass. But reuse is best when you don't have to understand the component you are reusing, and inheritance requires a deeper understanding of a class that is using it as a component, so it is better to reuse existing components than to make a new one.

Of course, the main reason a framework enables code reuse is that it is a reusable design. It provides reusable abstract algorithms and a high-level design that decomposes a large system into smaller components and describes the internal interfaces between components. These standard interfaces make it possible to mix and match components and to build a wide variety of systems from a small number of existing components. New components that meet these interfaces will fit into the framework, so component designers also reuse the design of a framework.

Finally, a framework reuses analysis. It describes the kinds of objects that are important and provides a vocabulary for talking about a problem. An expert in a particular framework sees the world in terms of the framework and will naturally divide it into the same components. Two expert users of the same framework will find it easier to understand each other's designs, since they will come up with similar components and will describe the systems they want to build in similar ways.

Analysis, design, and code reuse are all important, though in the long run it is probably the analysis and design reuse that provide the biggest payoff [Biggerstaff 1996].

1.2 Benefits

The primary benefits of OO application frameworks stem from the modularity, reusability, extensibility, and inversion of control they provide to developers, as described in the following:

Modularity. Frameworks enhance modularity by encapsulating volatile implementation details behind stable interfaces. Framework modularity helps improve software quality by localizing the impact of design and implementation changes. This localization reduces the effort required to understand and maintain existing software.

Reusability. The stable interfaces provided by frameworks enhance reusability by defining generic components that can be reapplied to create new applications. Framework reusability leverages the domain knowledge and prior effort of experienced developers in order to avoid recreating and revalidating common solutions to recurring application requirements and software design challenges. Reuse of framework components can yield substantial improvements in programmer productivity, as well as enhance the quality, performance, reliability, and interoperability of software.

Extensibility. A framework enhances extensibility by providing explicit hook methods [Pree 1995] that allow applications to extend its stable interfaces. Hook methods systematically decouple the stable interfaces and behaviors of an application domain from the variations required by instantiations of an application in a particular context. Framework extensibility is essential to ensure timely customization of new application services and features.

Inversion of control. The runtime architecture of a framework is characterized by an *inversion of control*. This architecture enables canonical application processing steps to be customized by event handler objects that are invoked via the framework's reactive dispatching mechanism. When events occur, the framework's dispatcher reacts by invoking hook methods on preregistered handler objects, which perform application-specific processing on the events. Inversion of control allows the framework (rather than each application) to determine which set of application-specific methods to invoke in response to external events (such as window messages arriving from end users or packets arriving on communication ports).

1.3 An Overview of Widely Used Frameworks

Developers in certain domains have successfully applied OO application frameworks for many years. Early object-oriented frameworks (such as MacApp and InterViews) originated in the domain of graphical user interfaces. The Microsoft Foundation Classes constitute a contemporary GUI framework that has become the de facto industry standard for creating graphical applications on PC platforms. Although the MFCs have limitations (such as lack of portability to non-PC platforms), their widespread adoption demonstrates the productivity benefits of reusing common frameworks to develop graphical business applications.

Application developers in more complex domains (such as telecommunications, distributed medical imaging, and real-time avionics) have traditionally lacked standard off-the-shelf frameworks. As a result, developers in these domains largely build, validate, and maintain software systems from scratch. In an era of deregulation and stiff global competition, however, it has become prohibitively costly and time consuming to develop applications entirely in-house from the ground up.

Fortunately, the next generation of OO application frameworks is targeting complex business and application domains. At the heart of this effort are *Object Request Broker* (ORB) frameworks, which facilitate communication between local and remote objects. ORB frameworks eliminate many tedious, error-prone, and nonportable aspects of creating and managing distributed applications and reusable service components. This enables programmers to develop and deploy complex applications rapidly and robustly, rather than wrestling endlessly with low-level infrastructure concerns.

1.4 Classifying Application Frameworks

Although the benefits and design principles underlying frameworks are largely independent of the domain to which they are applied, we've found it useful to classify frameworks by their scope, as follows:

System infrastructure frameworks. These frameworks simplify the development of portable and efficient system infrastructure such as operating system [Campbell-Islam 1993] and communication frameworks [Schmidt 1997], and frameworks for user interfaces and language processing tools. System infrastructure frameworks are primarily used internally within a software organization and are not sold to customers directly.

Middleware integration frameworks. These frameworks are commonly used to integrate distributed applications and components. Middleware integration frameworks are designed to enhance the ability of software developers to modularize, reuse, and extend their software infrastructure to work seamlessly in a distributed environment. There is a thriving market for middleware integration frameworks, which are rapidly becoming commodities. Common examples include ORB frameworks, message-oriented middleware, and transactional databases.

Enterprise application frameworks. These frameworks address broad application domains (such as telecommunications, avionics, manufacturing, and financial engineering [Birrer 1993]) and are the cornerstone of enterprise business activities [Fayad-Hamu 1999; Hamu-Fayad 1998]. Relative to system infrastructure and middleware integration frameworks, enterprise frameworks are expensive to develop and/or purchase. However, enterprise frameworks can provide a substantial return on investment since they support the development of end-user applications and products directly. In contrast, system infrastructure and middleware integration frameworks focus largely on internal software development concerns. Although these frameworks are essential to rapidly create high-quality software, they typically do not generate substantial revenue for large enterprises. As a result, it is often more cost-effective to buy system infrastructure and middleware integration frameworks rather than build them in-house [Fayad-Hamu 1999; Hamu-Fayad 1998].

Regardless of their scope, frameworks can also be classified by the techniques used to extend them, which range along a continuum from *whitebox frameworks* to *graybox frameworks* to *blackbox frameworks.* Whitebox frameworks rely heavily on OO language features like inheritance and dynamic binding in order to achieve extensibility. Existing functionality is reused and extended by (1) inheriting from framework base classes and (2) overriding predefined hook methods using patterns like the Template Method [Gamma 1995]. Blackbox frameworks support extensibility by defining interfaces for components that can be plugged into the framework via object composition. Existing functionality is reused by (1) defining components that conform to a particular interface and (2) integrating these components into the framework using patterns like Strategy [Gamma 1995] and Functor. Graybox frameworks are designed to avoid the disadvantages presented by whitebox and blackbox frameworks. In other words, a good graybox framework has enough flexibility and extendibility, and also has the ability to hide unnecessary information from the application developers [Yassin-Fayad 1999].

Whitebox frameworks require application developers to have intimate knowledge of the frameworks' internal structure. Although whitebox frameworks are widely used, they tend to produce systems that are tightly coupled to the specific details of the framework's inheritance hierarchies. In contrast, blackbox frameworks are structured using object composition and delegation rather than inheritance. As a result, blackbox frameworks are generally easier to use and extend than whitebox frameworks. However, blackbox frameworks are more difficult to develop since they require framework developers to define interfaces and hooks that anticipate a wider range of potential use-cases [Hueni 1995].

1.5 The Strengths and Weaknesses of Application Frameworks

When used in conjunction with patterns, class libraries, and components, OO application frameworks can significantly increase software quality and reduce development effort. However, a number of challenges must be addressed in order to employ frameworks effectively. Companies attempting to build or use large-scale reusable frameworks often fail unless they recognize and resolve challenges such as *development effort, learning curve, integratability, maintainability, validation and defect removal, efficiency,* and *lack of standards,* which are outlined as follows:

Development effort. While developing complex software is hard enough, developing high-quality, extensible, and reusable frameworks for complex application domains is even harder. The skills required to produce frameworks successfully often remain locked in the heads of expert developers. One of the goals of this theme issue is to demystify the software process and design principles associated with developing and using frameworks.

Learning curve. Learning to use an OO application framework effectively requires considerable investment of effort. For instance, it often takes 6 to 12 months to become highly productive with a GUI framework like MFCs or MacApp, depending on the experience of the developers. Typically, hands-on mentoring and training courses are required to teach application developers how to use the framework effectively. Unless the effort required to learn the framework can be amortized over many projects, this investment may not be cost-effective. Moreover, the suitability of a framework for a particular application may not be apparent until the learning curve has flattened.

Integratability. Application development will be increasingly based on the integration of multiple frameworks (GUIs, communication systems, databases, and so on), together with class libraries, legacy systems, and existing components. However, many earlier-generation frameworks were designed for internal extension rather than for integration with other frameworks developed externally. Integration problems arise at several levels of abstraction, ranging from documentation issues [Fayad-Hamu 1999; Hamu-Fayad 1998], to the concurrency/distribution architecture, to the event dispatching model. For instance, while inversion of control is an essential feature of a framework, integrating frameworks whose event loops are not designed to interoperate with other frameworks is hard.

Maintainability. Application requirements change frequently. Therefore, the requirements of frameworks often change, as well. As frameworks invariably evolve, the applications that use them must evolve with them.

Framework maintenance activities include modification and adaptation of the framework. Both modification and adaptation may occur on the *functional level* (in other words, certain framework functionality does not fully meet developers' requirements), as well as on the *nonfunctional level* (which includes more qualitative aspects such as portability or reusability).

Framework maintenance may take different forms, such as adding functionality, removing functionality, and generalization. A deep understanding of the framework components and their interrelationships is essential to perform this task successfully. In some cases, the application developers and/or the end users must rely entirely on framework developers to maintain the framework.

Validation and defect removal. Although a well-designed, modular framework can localize the impact of software defects, validating and debugging applications built using frameworks can be tricky for the following reasons:

Generic components are harder to validate in the abstract. A well-designed framework component typically abstracts away from application-specific details, which are provided via subclassing, object composition, or template parameterization. While this improves the flexibility and extensibility of the framework, it greatly complicates module testing since the components cannot be validated in isolation from their specific instantiations.

Moreover, it is usually hard to distinguish bugs in the framework from bugs in the application code. As with any software development, bugs are introduced into a framework from many possible sources, such as failure to understand the requirements, overly coupled design, or an incorrect implementation. When customizing the components in a framework to a particular application, the number of possible error sources will increase.

Inversion of control and lack of explicit control flow. Applications written with frameworks can be hard to debug since the framework's *inverted* flow of control oscillates between the application-independent framework infrastructure and the application-specific method callbacks. This increases the difficulty of single-stepping through the runtime behavior of a framework within a debugger since the control flow of the application is driven implicitly by callbacks, and developers may not understand or have access to the framework code. This is similar to the problems encountered in trying to debug a compiler lexical analyzer and parser written with LEX and YACC. In these applications, debugging is straightforward when the thread of control is in the user-defined action routines. Once the thread of control returns to the generated DFA skeleton, however, it is hard to trace the program's logic.

Efficiency. Frameworks enhance extensibility by employing additional levels of indirection. For instance, dynamic binding is commonly used to allow developers to subclass and customize existing interfaces. However, the resulting generality and flexibility often reduce efficiency. For instance, in languages like C++ and Java, the use of dynamic binding makes it impractical to support Concrete Data Types (CDTs), which are often required for time-critical software. The lack of CDTs yields (1) an increase in storage layout (for example, due to embedded pointers to virtual tables), (2) performance degradation (for example, due to the additional overhead of invoking a dynamically bound method and the inability to inline small methods), and (3) a lack of flexibility (for example, due to the inability to place objects in shared memory).

Lack of standards. Currently, there are no widely accepted standards for designing, implementing, documenting, and adapting frameworks. Moreover, emerging industry standard frameworks (such as CORBA, DCOM, and Java RMI) currently lack the semantics, features, and interoperability to be truly effective across multiple application domains. Often, vendors use industry standards to sell proprietary software under the guise of open systems. Therefore, it is essential for companies and developers to work with standards organizations and middleware vendors to ensure that the emerging specifications support true interoperability and define features that meet their software needs.

Some of the problems with frameworks have been described already. In particular, because they are powerful and complex, they are hard to learn. This means that they require better documentation than other systems, and longer training. Moreover, they are hard to develop. This means that they cost more to develop and require different kinds of programmers than normal application development. These are some of the reasons that frameworks are not used more widely than they have been, in spite of the fact that the technology is so old. But these problems are shared with other reuse techniques. Although reuse is valuable, it is not free. Companies that are going to take advantage of reuse must pay its price.

One of the strengths of frameworks is that they are represented by normal object-oriented programming languages. This is also a weakness of frameworks. Since this feature is unique to frameworks, it is also a unique weakness.

One of the problems with using a particular language is that it restricts frameworks to systems using that language. In general, different object-oriented programming languages don't work well together, so it is not cost-effective to build an application in one language with a framework written in another. COM and CORBA address this problem, since they let programs in one language interoperate with programs in another. OLE is essentially a framework based on COM that lets applications be developed in any programming language. Moreover, some frameworks have been implemented twice so that users of two different languages can apply them [Andersen 1998; Eng 1996].

Current programming languages are good at describing the static interface of an object, but not its dynamic interface. Because frameworks are described with programming languages, it is hard for developers to learn the collaborative patterns of a framework by reading it. Instead, they depend on other documentation and talking to experts. This adds to the difficulty of learning a framework. One approach to this problem is to improve the documentation, such as with patterns. Another approach is to describe the constraints and interactions between components formally, such as with contracts [Helm 1990]. But since part of the strength of frameworks is the fact that the framework is expressed in code, it might be better to improve object-oriented languages so that they can express patterns of collaboration more clearly.

1.6 Reuse: Components versus Designs

Frameworks are just one of many reuse techniques [Kreuger 1992]. The ideal reuse technology provides components that can be easily connected to make a new system. The software developer does not have to know how the component is implemented, and the specification of the component is easy to understand. The resulting system will be efficient, easy to maintain, and reliable. The electric power system is like that; you can buy a toaster from one store and a television from another, and they will both work at either your home or your office. Most people do not know Ohm's law, yet they have no trouble connecting a new toaster to the power system. Unfortunately, software is not nearly as composable as the electric power system.

When we design a software component, we always have to trade simplicity for power. A component that does one thing well is easy to use, but can be used in fewer cases. A component with many parameters and options can be used more often, but will be harder to learn to use. Reuse techniques range from the simple and inflexible to the complex and powerful. Those that let the developer make choices are usually more complicated and require more training on the part of the developer.

For example, the easiest way to get a compiler is to buy one. Most compilers compile only one language. On the other hand, you could build a compiler for your own language by reusing parts of the GUN C Compiler (gcc) [Stallman 1995], which has a parser generator and a reusable back end for code generation. It takes more work and expertise to build a compiler with gcc than it does just to use a compiler, but this approach lets you compile your own language. Finally, you might decide that gcc is not flexible enough, since your language might be concurrent or depend on garbage collection, so you write your compiler from scratch. Even though you don't reuse any code, you will probably still use many of the same design ideas as gcc, such as having a separate parser. You can learn these ideas from any good textbook on compilers.

A component represents code reuse. A textbook represents design reuse. The source for gcc lies somewhere in between. Reuse experts often claim that design reuse is more important than code reuse, mostly because it can be applied in more contexts and so is more common. Also, it is applied earlier in the development process and so can have a larger impact on a project. A developer's expertise is partly due to knowing designs that can be customized to fit a new problem. But most design reuse is informal. One of the main problems with reusing design information is capturing and expressing it [Biggerstaff 1996]. There is no standard design notation and there are no standard catalogs of designs to reuse. A single company can standardize, and some do. But this will not lead to industry-wide reuse.

The original vision of software reuse was based on components [McIlroy 1968]. In the beginning, commercial interest in object-oriented technology also focused on code reuse. More recently, pure design reuse has become popular, as seen in the form of patterns [Bushmann 1996; Coplien 1996; Fowler 1997; Gamma 1995; Vlissides 1996]. But frameworks are an intermediate form, part code reuse and part design reuse. Frameworks eliminate the need of a new design notation by using an object-oriented programming language as the design notation. Although programming languages suffer several defects as design notations, it is not necessary (though it might be desirable) to make specialized tools to use frameworks. Most programmers using a framework have no tools other than their compilers.

Reuse (and frameworks) may be motivated by many factors. One is to save time and money during development. The main purpose for many companies is to decrease time to market. But they find that the uniformity brought about by frameworks is also important. Graphical user interface frameworks give a set of applications a similar look and feel, and a reusable network interface means that all the applications that use it follow the same protocols. Uniformity reduces the cost of maintenance, too, since now maintenance programmers can move from one application to the next without having to learn a new design. A final reason for frameworks is to enable customers to build open systems, so they can mix and match components from different vendors.

In spite of all these motivations, the predictions that were made when software reuse was first discussed 30 years ago still have not come true. Reuse is still a small part of most development projects. The one exception is in the world of object-oriented programming, where most environments have at least a user interface framework.

1.7 Application Frameworks versus Other Reuse Techniques

The ideal reuse technique is a component that exactly fits your needs and can be used without being customized or forcing you to learn how to use it. However, a component that fits today's needs perfectly might not fit tomorrow's. The more customizable a component is, the more likely it is to work in a particular situation, but the more work it takes to use it and to learn to use it.

Frameworks are a component in the sense that vendors sell them as products, and an application might use several frameworks bought from various vendors. But frameworks are much more customizable than most components. As a consequence, using a framework takes work even when you are familiar with it, and learning a new framework is hard. In return, frameworks are powerful; they can be used for just about any kind of application, and a good framework can reduce by an order of magnitude the amount of effort needed to develop customized applications.

It is probably better to think of frameworks and components as different, but cooperating, technologies. First, frameworks provide a reusable context for components. Each component makes assumptions about its environment. If components make different assumptions, then it is hard to use them together [Berlin 1990].

A framework will provide a standard way for components to handle errors, to exchange data, and to invoke operations on each other. The so-called component systems such as OLE, OpenDoc, and Beans, are really frameworks that solve standard problems that arise in building compound documents and other composite objects. But any kind of framework provides the standards that enable existing components to be reused.

A second way in which frameworks and components work together is that frameworks make it easier to develop new components. Applications seem infinitely variable, and no matter how good a component library is, it will eventually need new components. Frameworks let us make a new component (a user interface) out of smaller components (a widget). They also provide the specifications for new components and a template for their implementation.

Frameworks are similar to other techniques for reusing high-level design, such as templates [Spencer 1988] or schemas [Katz 1989]. The main difference is that frameworks are expressed in a programming language, but these other ways of reusing high-level design usually depend on a special-purpose design notation and require special software tools. The fact that frameworks are programs makes them easier for programmers to learn and to apply, but it also causes some problems that we will discuss later.

Frameworks are similar to application generators [Cleaveland 1988]. Application generators are based on a high-level, domain-specific language that is compiled to a standard architecture. Designing a reusable class library is a lot like designing a programming language, except that the only concrete syntax is that of the language it is implemented in. A framework is already a standard architecture. Thus, except for syntax and the fact that the translator of an application generator can perform optimizations, the two techniques are similar. Although problem domain experts usually prefer their own syntax, expert programmers usually prefer frameworks because they are easier to extend and combine than application generators. In fact, it is common to combine frameworks and a domain-specific language. Programs in the language are translated into a set of objects in the framework. (See the Interpreter pattern [Gamma 1995].)

Frameworks are a kind of domain-specific architecture [Tracz 1994]. The main difference is that a framework is ultimately an object-oriented design, while a domain-specific architecture might not be.

Patterns have recently become a popular way to reuse design information in the object-oriented community [Coplien 1996; Gamma 1995; Vlissides 1996]. A pattern is an essay that describes a problem to be solved, a solution, and the context in which that solution works. It names a technique and describes its costs and benefits. Developers who share a set of patterns have a common vocabulary for describing their designs and also a way of making design trade-offs explicit. Patterns are supposed to describe recurring solutions that have stood the test of time.

Since some frameworks have been implemented several times, they represent a kind of pattern, too. See, for example, the definition of Model/View/Controller [Bushmann 1996]. However, frameworks are more than just ideas—they are also code. This code provides a way of testing whether a developer understands the framework, examples for learning it, and an oracle for answering questions about it. In addition, code reuse often makes it possible to build a simple application quickly, and that application can then grow into the final application as the developer learns the framework.

The patterns in the book *Design Patterns* [Gamma 1995] are closely related to frameworks in another way. These patterns were discovered by examining a number of frameworks and were chosen as being representative of reusable, object-oriented software. In general, a single framework will contain many of the patterns, so these patterns are smaller than frameworks. Moreover, the design patterns cannot be expressed as C++ or Smalltalk classes and then just reused by inheritance or composition. So those patterns are more abstract than frameworks. Frameworks are at a different level of abstraction from the patterns in *Design Patterns*. Design patterns are the architectural elements of frameworks.

For example, Model/View/Controller can be decomposed into three major design patterns and several less important ones [Gamma 1995]. It uses the Observer pattern to ensure that the view's picture of the model is up to date. It uses the Composite pattern to nest views. It uses the Strategy pattern to have views delegate responsibility for handling user events to their controller.

Frameworks are firmly in the middle of reuse techniques. They are more abstract and flexible (and harder to learn) than components, but more concrete and easier to reuse than a raw design (but less flexible and less likely to be applicable). They are most comparable to reuse techniques that reuse both design and code, such as application generators and templates. Their major advantage is also their major liability; they can be implemented using any object-oriented programming environment, since they are represented by a program.

1.8 How to Use Application Frameworks

There are several ways to use a framework. Some ways require a deeper knowledge of the framework than others. All of them are different from the usual way of developing software using object-oriented technology, since all of them force an application to fit the framework. Thus, the design of the application must start with the design of the framework.

An application developed using a framework has three parts: the framework, the concrete subclasses of the framework classes, and everything else. *Everything else* usually includes a script that specifies which concrete classes will be used and how they will be interconnected. It might also include objects that have no relationship to the framework or that use one or more framework objects, but that are not called by framework objects. Objects that are called by framework objects will have to participate in the collaborative model of the framework and so are part of the framework.

The easiest way to use a framework is to connect existing components. This does not change the framework or make any new concrete subclasses. It reuses the framework's interfaces and rules for connecting components and is most like building a circuit board by connecting integrated circuits or building a toy house from Legos. Application programmers only have to know that objects of type A are connected to objects of type B; they do not have to know the exact specification of A and B.

Not all frameworks can work this way. Sometimes every new use of a framework requires new subclasses of the framework. That leads to the next easiest way to use a framework, which is to define new concrete subclasses and use them to implement an application. Subclasses are tightly coupled to their superclasses, so this way of using a framework requires more knowledge about the abstract classes than the first way. The subclasses must meet the specification implied by the superclasses, so the programmer must understand the framework's interfaces in detail.

The way of using a framework that requires the most knowledge is to extend it by changing the abstract classes that form the core of the framework, usually by adding new operations or variables to them. This way is the most like fleshing out a skeleton of an application. It usually requires the source code of a framework. Although it is the hardest way to use a framework, it is also the most powerful. On the other hand, changes to the abstract classes can break existing concrete classes, and this way will not work when the main purpose of the framework is to build open systems.

If application programmers can use a framework by connecting components without having to look at their implementation, then the framework is a *blackbox framework*. Frameworks that rely on inheritance usually require more knowledge on the part of developers and so are called *whitebox frameworks*. Blackbox frameworks are easier to learn to use, but whitebox frameworks are often more powerful in the hands of experts. However, blackbox and whitebox frameworks are a spectrum, not a dichotomy. It is common for a framework to be used in a blackbox way most of the time and to be extended when the occasion demands. One of the big advantages of a blackbox framework over an application-specific language is that it can be treated like a whitebox framework and extended by making new concrete subclasses.

If a framework is blackbox enough, it is used just by instantiating existing classes and connecting them. Many of the graphical user interface frameworks are like this; most user interfaces contain objects only of existing classes. When this is true, it is usually easy to make an application builder for the framework that can instantiate the components and connect them. This makes the framework even easier to use by novices.

All these ways of using a framework require mapping the structure of the problem to be solved onto the structure of the framework. A framework forces the application to reuse its design. The existing object-oriented design methods usually start with an analysis model and derive the design from it, but this will not work with frameworks unless the framework design informs the analysis model. In spite of the importance of frameworks, most object-oriented methods do not support them very well. One exception is the OORam method [Reenskaug 1996].

1.9 How to Learn Application Frameworks

Learning a framework is harder than learning a regular class library, because you can't learn just one class at a time. The classes in a framework are designed to work together, so you have to learn them all at once. Moreover, the important classes are abstract, which makes them even harder to learn. These classes do not implement all the behavior of framework components, but leave some to the concrete subclasses, so you have to learn what never changes in the framework and what is left to the components.

Frameworks are easier to learn if they have good documentation. Even fairly simple frameworks are easier to learn if good training is available, and complex frameworks require training. But what are the characteristics of good documentation and good training for a framework?

The best way to start learning a framework is by example. Most frameworks come with a set of examples that you can study, and those that don't are nearly impossible to learn. Examples are concrete, thus easier to understand than the framework as a whole. They solve a particular problem and you can study their execution to learn the flow of control inside the framework. They demonstrate both how objects in the framework behave and how programmers use the framework. Ideally, a framework should come with a set of examples that range from the trivial to the advanced, and these examples will exercise the full range of features of the framework.

Although some frameworks have little documentation other than the source code and a set of examples, ideally a framework will have a complete set of documentation. The documentation should explain:

- The purpose of the framework
- How to use the framework
- How the framework works

It is hard to explain the purpose of a framework. Framework documentation often devolves to jargon or marketing pitches. Until people had seen the Macintosh, the claim that Model/View/Controller implemented graphical user interfaces did not make sense, and until people tried to implement one, they didn't understand why they needed help. Often the best way to learn the range of applicability of a framework is by example, which is another reason that it helps if a framework comes with a rich set of examples.

It is also hard to explain how to use a framework. Understanding the inner workings of a framework does not tell an application programmer which subclasses to make. The best documentation seems to be a kind of cookbook [Apple 1986; Johnson 1992; ParcPlace 1994]. Beginning programmers can use a cookbook to make their first applications, and more advanced programmers can use it to look up solutions to particular problems. Cookbooks don't help the most advanced programmers, but most framework application programmers need them.

A lot of framework documentation simply lists the classes in the framework and the methods of each class. This is not useful to beginners, any more than a programming language standard is useful to a new programmer. If the programming environment has a good browser, it isn't much use to anybody. Programmers need to understand the framework's big picture. Documentation that describes the inner workings of a framework should focus on the interaction between objects and how responsibility is partitioned between them.

The first use of a framework is always a learning experience. Pick a small application and one that the framework is obviously well suited for. Study similar examples and copy them. Use the cookbook to see how to implement individual features. Single-step through the application to learn the flow of control, but don't expect to understand everything. The purpose of a framework is to reuse design, so if it is a good framework, then there will be large parts of its design that you can reuse without knowing about them.

Once you've built an actual application, the framework documentation will become clearer. Since the first use of a framework is usually the hardest, it is a good idea to use it under the direction of an expert. This is one of the main reasons that mentoring is so popular in the Smalltalk community; each version of Smalltalk comes with a set of frameworks, and learning to program in Smalltalk is largely a matter of learning the frameworks.

Frameworks are complex, and one of the biggest problems with most frameworks is just learning how to use them. Framework developers need to make sure they document their framework well and develop good training material for it. Framework users should plan to devote time and budget to learning the framework.

1.10 How to Evaluate Application Frameworks

Sometimes it is easy to choose a framework. A company that wants to develop distributed applications over the Internet that run in web browsers will want to use Java and will prefer standard frameworks. A company that is Microsoft-standard will prefer MFCs to zApp. Most application domains have no commercially available domain-specific frameworks, and many others have only one, so the choice is either to use that one or not to use one. But many times there are competing frameworks, and they must be evaluated.

Many aspects of a framework are easy to evaluate. A framework needs to run on the right platforms, use the right programming language, and support the right standards. Of course, each organization has its own definition of *right*, but these questions are easy to answer. If they aren't in the documentation, the vendor can answer them.

It is harder to tell how reliable a framework is, how well its vendor supports it, and whether the final applications are sufficiently efficient. Vendors will not give reliable answers to these questions, but usually the existing customers will.

The hardest questions are whether a framework is suited for your problem and whether it makes the right trade-offs between power and simplicity. Frameworks that solve technical problems such as distribution or user interface design are relatively easy to evaluate. Even so, if you are distributing a system to make it more concurrent and so handle greater throughput, you might find that a particular distribution framework is too inefficient, because it focuses on flexibility and ease of use instead of speed. No framework is good for everything, and it can be hard to tell whether a particular framework is well suited for a particular problem.

The standard approach for evaluating software is to make a checklist of features that the software must support. Since frameworks are extensible, and since they probably are supposed to handle only part of the application, it is more important that a framework be easy to extend than that it have all the features. However, it is easier to tell whether a framework has some feature than to tell whether it is extensible. As usual, we are more likely to measure things that are easy to measure than the things that are important.

An expert can usually tell how hard it is to add some missing features, but it is nearly impossible for novices to tell. So it is best to use some frameworks and develop some experience and expertise with them before choosing one as a corporate standard. If frameworks are large and expensive, then it is expensive to test them, and there is no choice except to rely on consultants. Of course, the consultants might know only one framework well, they might be biased by business connections with the framework's vendor, and they will tend to favor power over simplicity. Every framework balances simplicity with power. Simplicity makes a framework easier to learn, so simple frameworks are best for novices. Experts appreciate power and flexibility. If you are going to use a framework only once, then the time spent to learn it might exceed the time spent actually using it, so simplicity would be more important than power. If you are going to use a framework many times, then power is probably more important. Thus, experts are sometimes less able to make a good choice than novices.

In the end, the main value of a framework is whether it improves the way you develop software and the software you develop. If the software is too slow or impossible to maintain, it will not matter that it takes less time to develop. Many factors go into this: the quality of the framework, tools to support the framework, the quality of the documentation, and a community to provide training and mentoring. A framework must fit into the culture of a company. If a company has high turnover and a small training budget, then frameworks must be simple and easy to use. Unless it repeatedly builds the same kind of applications, it should not be building domain-specific frameworks, regardless of how attractive they might be. The value of a framework depends more on its context than on the framework itself, so there is no magic formula for evaluating them.

1.11 How to Develop Application Frameworks

One of the most common observations about framework design is that it takes iteration [Johnson-Foote 1988]. Why is iteration necessary? Clearly, a design is iterated only because its authors did not know how to do it right the first time. Perhaps this is the fault of the designers; they should have spent more time analyzing the problem domain, or they were not skilled enough. However, even skilled designers iterate when they are designing frameworks.

The design of a framework is like the design of most reusable software [Krueger 1992; Tracz 1995]. It starts with domain analysis, which (among other things) collects a number of examples. The first version of the framework is usually designed to be able to implement the examples and is usually a whitebox framework [Johnson 1997; Roberts 1997]. Then the framework is used to build applications. These applications point out weak points in the framework, which are parts of the framework that are hard to change. Experience leads to improvements in the framework, which often make it more blackbox. Eventually the framework is good enough that suggestions for improvement are rare. At some point, the developers have to decide that the framework is finished and release it.

One of the reasons for iteration is domain analysis [Batory 1989]. Unless the domain is mature, it is hard for experts to explain it. Mistakes in domain analysis are discovered when a system is built, which leads to iteration.

A second reason for iteration is that a framework makes explicit the parts of a design that are likely to change. Features that are likely to change are implemented by components so that they can be changed easily. Components are easy to change; interfaces and shared invariants are hard. In general, the only way to learn what changes is by experience.

A third reason for iterating is that frameworks are abstractions, so the design of the framework depends on the original examples. Each example that is considered makes the framework more general and reusable. Frameworks are large, so it is too expensive to look at many examples, and paper designs are not sufficiently detailed to evaluate the framework. A better notation for describing frameworks might let more of the iteration take place during framework design.

A common mistake is to start using a framework while its design is changing. The more an immature framework is used, the more it changes. Changing a framework causes the applications that use it to change, too. On the other hand, the only way to find out what is wrong with a framework is to use it. First use the framework for some small pilot projects to make sure that it is sufficiently flexible and general. If it is not, these projects will be good test cases for the framework developers. A framework should not be used widely until it has proven itself, because the more widely a framework is used, the more expensive it is to change it.

Because frameworks require iteration and deep understanding of an application domain, it is hard to create them on schedule. Thus, framework design should never be on the critical path of an important project. This suggests that they should be developed by advanced development or research groups, not by product groups. On the other hand, framework design must be closely associated with application developers because framework design requires experience in the application domain.

This tension between framework design and application design leads to two models of the process of framework design. One model has the framework designers also designing applications, but they divide their time into phases in which they extend the framework by applying it and phases in which they revise the framework by consolidating earlier extensions [Foote 1991]. The other model is to have a separate group of framework designers. The framework designers test their framework by using it, but also rely on the main users of the framework for feedback.

The first model ensures that the framework designers understand the problems with their framework, but the second model ensures that framework designers are given enough time to revise the framework. The first model works well for small groups whose management understands the importance of framework design and so can budget enough time for revising the framework. The second model works well for larger groups or for groups developing a framework for users outside their organization, but requires the framework designer to work hard to communicate with the framework users. This seems to be the model most popular in industry.

A compromise is to develop a framework in parallel with developing several applications that use it. Although this will not benefit these first applications much, the framework developers usually help more than they hurt. The benefits usually do not start to show until the third or fourth application, but this approach minimizes the cost of developing a framework while providing the feedback that the framework developers need.

1.12 Organization of This Book

This book is organized into eight major parts: Part One, "Framework Overview," Part Two, "Framework Perspectives," Part Three, "Frameworks and Domain Analysis," Part Four, "Framework Development Concepts," Part Five, "Framework Development Approaches," Part Six, "Framework Testing and Integration," Part Seven, "Framework Documentation," and Part Eight, "Framework Management and Economics."

Part One includes Chapters 1, 2, and 3 and Sidebar 1, and provides complete coverage of application framework issues, defines application frameworks, classifies the application frameworks, describes the characteristics of application frameworks, discusses the pros and cons of application frameworks, and contrasts the frameworks with other reuse approaches. Part One also elaborates on the understanding of the term *software architecture* by further developing the concept of architectural abstractions, and describes the major problems with application frameworks.

Part Two includes Chapters 4, 5, and 6 and Sidebar 2, and discusses several perspectives of application frameworks related to some of the historical application frameworks, describes guidelines for constructing good classes and components for application frameworks, discusses general guidelines for application framework usability, and presents two types of viewpoints: inter- and intra-viewpoints.

Part Three contains Chapters 7 and 8 and Sidebar 3, and discusses the relationships between application frameworks and domain analysis, as well as how to drive application frameworks from domain knowledge.

Part Four consists of Chapters 9 through 14 and Sidebar 4, and discusses several new application framework concepts, such as the hooks approach and framework recipes.

Part Five consists of Chapters 15 through 19 and Sidebars 5 and 6, and discusses framework development approaches, such as systematic generalization, hot-spot-driven development, framework layering, framelets, understanding macroscopic behavior patterns in use-case maps, and composing modeling frameworks in Catalysis, as well as enduring business themes (EBTs).

Part Six is made up of Chapter 20 and Sidebar 7, and discusses issues related to framework testing and integration.

Part Seven comprises Chapters 21, 22, and 23 and Sidebar 8, and covers several topics related to framework documentation.

Part Eight contains Chapters 24, 25, and 26 and Sidebar 9, and covers framework investment analysis, framework structural and functional stability evaluation, framework management, and future research direction in the component-based framework technology.

1.13 Summary

Frameworks are a practical way to express reusable designs. They deserve the attention of both the software engineering research community and practicing software engineers. There are many open research problems associated with better ways to express and develop frameworks, but they have already shown themselves to be valuable.

The articles in this book reinforce the belief that object-oriented application frameworks will be at the core of leading-edge software technology in the twenty-first century. As software systems become increasingly complex, object-oriented application frameworks are becoming increasingly important for industry and academia. The extensive focus on application frameworks in the object-oriented community offers software developers an important vehicle for reuse and a means to capture the essence of successful patterns, architectures, components, and programming mechanisms.

The good news is that frameworks are becoming mainstream and developers at all levels are increasingly adopting and succeeding with framework technologies. However, OO application frameworks are ultimately only as good as the people who build and use them. Creating robust, efficient, and reusable application frameworks requires development teams with a wide range of skills. We need expert analysts and designers who have mastered patterns, software architectures, and protocols in order to alleviate the inherent and accidental complexities of complex software. Likewise, we need expert middleware developers who can implement these patterns, architectures, and protocols within reusable frameworks. In addition, we need application programmers who have the motivation, skills, and training to learn how to use these frameworks effectively. We encourage you to get involved with others working on frameworks by attending conferences, participating in online mailing lists and newsgroups, and contributing your insights and experience.

1.14 References

[Andersen 1998] Andersen Consulting. *Eagle Architecture Specification*. 1998.

[Apple 1986] Apple Computer. *MacApp Programmer's Guide*. 1986.

[Batory 1989] Batory, D.S., J.R. Barnett, J. Roy, B.C. Twichell, and J. Garza. Construction of file management systems from software components. *Proceedings of COMPSAC 1989*.

[Beck 1994] Beck, Kent, and Ralph Johnson. Patterns generate architectures. *European Conference on Object-Oriented Programming*, pp. 139–149, Bologna, Italy, July 1994.

[Berlin 1990] Berlin, Lucy. When objects collide: Experiences with using multiple class hierarchies. *Proceedings of OOPSLA 1990*, pp. 181–193, October 1990. Printed as SIGPLAN Notices, 25(10).

[Biggerstaff 1996] Biggerstaff, Ted J., and Charles Richter. Reusability framework, assessment, and directions. *IEEE Software* 4(2):41–49, March 1987.

[Birrer 1993] Birrer, Eggenschwiler T. Frameworks in the financial engineering domain: An experience report. *ECOOP 1993 Proceedings, Lecture Notes in Computer Science no. 707*, 1993.

[Bushmann 1996] Bushmann, Frank, Regine Meunier, Hans Rohnert, Peter Sommerlad, and Michael Stal. *Pattern-Oriented Software Architecture: A System of Patterns*. Chichester, West Sussex, England: John Wiley & Sons. 1996.

[Campbell-Islam 1993] Campbell, Roy H., and Nayeem Islam. A technique for documenting the framework of an object-oriented system. *Computing Systems* 6(4), Fall 1993.

[Cleaveland 1988] Cleaveland, J.C. Building application generators. *IEEE Software* 4(5):25–33, July 1988.

[Coplien 1996] Coplien, James O. *Patterns*. New York: SIGS, 1996.

[Deutsch 1989] Deutsch, L. Peter. Design reuse and frameworks in the Smalltalk-80 programming system. In *Software Reusability, Volume II*, pp. 55–71, Ted J. Biggerstaff and Alan J. Perlis, editors. Reading, MA: ACM Press/Addison Wesley, 1989.

[Eng 1996] Eng, Lawrence, Ken Freed, Jim Hollister, Carla Jobe, Paul McGuire, Alan Moser, Vinayak Parikh, Margaret Pratt, Fred Waskiewicz, and Frank Yeager. *Computer Integrated Manufacturing (CIM) Application Framework Specification 1.3*. Technical Report Technology Transfer 93061697F-ENG, SEMATECH, 1996.

[Fayad 1996] Fayad, M.E., W.T. Tsai, and M. Fulghum. Transition to object-oriented software development. *Communications of the ACM* 39(2), February 1996.

[Fayad 1999] Fayad, M.E. Application frameworks. *ACM Computing Surveys Symposium*, March 1999.

[Fayad-Cline 1996a] Fayad, M.E., and M. Cline. Aspects of software adaptability. *Communications of the ACM, Theme Issue on Software Patterns* 39(10), October 1996. D. Schmidt, M.E. Fayad, and R. Johnson, guest editors.

[Fayad-Cline 1996b] Fayad, M.E., and M. Cline. Managing object-oriented software development. *IEEE Computer*, September 1996.

[Fayad-Hamu 1999] Fayad, Mohamed E., and David S. Hamu. Object-Oriented Enterprise Frameworks. Submitted for publication to *IEEE Computer*.

[Fayad-Laitinen 1998] Fayad, M.E., and M. Laitinen. *Transition to Object-Oriented Software Development*. New York: John Wiley & Sons, 1989.

[Fayad-Schmidt 1997] Fayad, M.E., and Douglas Schmidt. Object-oriented application frameworks. *Communications of the ACM* 40(10), October 1997.

[Fayad-Tsai 1995] Fayad, M.E., and W.T. Tsai. Object-oriented experiences. *Communications of the ACM*, 38 (10), October 1995.

[Foote 1988] Foote, Brian. Designing to facilitate change with object-oriented frameworks. Master's thesis, University of Illinois at Urbana-Champaign, 1988.

[Foote 1991] Foote, Brian. The lifecycle of object-oriented frameworks: A fractal perspective. Technical Report, University of Illinois at Urbana-Champaign, 1991.

[Fowler 1997] Fowler, Martin. *Analysis Patterns: Reusable Object Models.* Reading, MA: Addison-Wesley, 1997.

[Gamma 1995] Gamma, Erich, Richard Helm, Ralph Johnson, and John Vlissides. *Design Patterns: Elements of Reusable Object-Oriented Software.* Reading, MA: Addison-Wesley, 1995.

[Goldberg 1984] Goldberg, Adele. *Smalltalk-80: The Interactive Programming Environment.* Reading, MA: Addison-Wesley, 1984.

[Gossain 1990] Gossain, Sanjiv. Object-oriented development and reuse. Ph.D. thesis, University of Essex, UK, June 1990.

[Hamu-Fayad 1998] Hamu, David S., and Mohamed E. Fayad. Achieve bottom-line improvements with enterprise frameworks. *Communications of the ACM,* 41 (8), August 1998.

[Helm 1990] Helm, Richard, Ian M. Holland, and Dipayan Gangopadhyay. Contracts: Specifying behavioral compositions in object-oriented systems. *Proceedings of OOPSLA 1990,* pp. 169–180, October 1990. Printed as SIGPLAN Notices, 25(10).

[Hueni 1995] Hueni, Herman, Ralph Johnson, and Robert Engel. A framework for network protocol software. *Proceedings of OOPSLA 1995,* Austin, TX, October 1995.

[Johnson 1992] Johnson, Ralph E. Documenting frameworks using patterns. *Proceedings of OOPSLA 1992,* pp. 63–76, Vancouver, BC, October 1992.

[Johnson 1997] Johnson, Ralph E. Frameworks = (Components + Patterns). *Communications of the ACM,* in Object-Oriented Application Frameworks Theme Issue, M.E. Fayad and D.C. Schmidt, editors, 40 (10), October 1997, 39-42.

[Johnson-Foote 1988] Johnson, Ralph E., and Brian Foote. Designing reusable classes. *Journal of Object-Oriented Programming,* 1(5), June/July. 1988: 22–35.

[Katz 1989] Katz, Shmuel, Charles A. Richter, and Khe-Sing The. Paris: A system for reusing partially interpreted schemas. In *Software Reusability, Volume I,* pp. 257–273, Ted J. Biggerstaff and Alan J. Perlis, editors. Reading, MA: ACM Press/Addison Wesley, 1989.

[Krasner 1988] Krasner, Glenn E., and Stephen T. Pope. A cookbook for using the model-view-controller user interface paradigm in Smalltalk-80. *Journal of Object-Oriented Programming* 1(3):26–49, August/September 1988.

[Krueger 1992] Krueger, Charles W. Software reuse. *ACM Computing Surveys* 24(2):131–183, June 1992.

[LaLonde 1991] LaLonde, W.R. and J.R. Pugh. *Inside Smalltalk Vol. II.* Englewood Cliffs, NJ: Prentice-Hall, 1991.

[Linton 1989] Linton, Mark A., John M. Vlissides, and Paul R. Calder. Composing user interfaces with InterViews. *Computer* 22(2):8–22, February 1989.

[McIlroy 1968] McIlroy, M.D., Mass produced software components. In *Software Engi-*

neering: Report on a Conference by the NATO Science Committee, pp. 138–150, P. Naur and B. Randall, editors. NATO Scientific Affairs Division, 1968.

[Meyrowitz 1986] Meyrowitz, Norman. Intermedia: The architecture and construction of an object-oriented hypermedia system and application framework. *Proceedings of OOPSLA 1986*, pp. 186–201, November 1986. Printed as SIGPLAN Notices 21(11).

[Palay 1988] Palay, A.J., W.J. Hansen, M.L. Kazar, M. Sherman, M.G. Wadlow, T.P. Neuendorffer, Z. Stern, M. Bader, and T. Petre. The Andrew Toolkit—an overview. *Proceedings of the Winter 1988 USENIX Conference*, Dallas, TX, 1988.

[ParcPlace 1988] ParcPlace Systems, Inc. *Smalltalk-80 Reference Manual*. 1988.

[ParcPlace 1994] ParcPlace Systems, Inc. *VisualWorks Cookbook*. 1994.

[Pree 1995] Pree, Wolfgang. *Design Patterns for Object-Oriented Software Development*. Reading, MA: Addison-Wesley, 1995.

[Reenskaug 1996] Reenskaug, Trygve. *Working with Objects: The OORam Software Engineering Method*. Greenwich, CT: Manning, 1996.

[Roberts 1997] Roberts, Don, and Ralph Johnson. *Evolving Frameworks: A Pattern Language for Developing Frameworks*. Reading, MA: Addison-Wesley, 1997.

[Russo 1990] Russo, Vincent F. An object-oriented operating system. Ph.D. thesis, University of Illinois at Urbana-Champaign, October 1990.

[Schmid 1995] Schmid, Hans Albrecht. Creating the architecture of a manufacturing framework by design patterns. *Proceedings of OOPSLA 1995*, pp. 370–384, Austin, TX, July 1995.

[Schmidt 1997] Schmidt, Douglas C. *Applying Design Patterns and Frameworks to Develop Object-Oriented Communication Software* (Handbook of Programming Languages), vol. I. Edited by Peter Salus. New York: Macmillan Computer Publishing, 1997.

[Schmucker 1986] Schmucker, Kurt J. *Object-Oriented Programming for the Macintosh*. Hayden Book Company, 1986.

[Spencer 1988] Spencer, Henry. How to steal code. *Proceedings of the Winter 1988 USENIX Technical Conference*, Dallas, TX, 1988.

[Stallman 1995] Stallman, Richard. *Using and Porting GNU CC*. Boston, MA: Free Software Foundation, 1995.

[Tracz 1994] Tracz, Will. DSSA frequently asked questions. *ACM Software Engineering Notes* 19(2):52–56, April 1994.

[Tracz 1995] Tracz, Will. *Domain Specific Software Architecture Engineering Process Guidelines*, Appendix A. Reading, MA: Addison-Wesley, 1995.

[Vlissides 1989] Vlissides, John M., and Mark A. Linton. Unidraw: A framework for building domain-specific graphical editors. *Proceedings of the ACM User Interface Software and Technologies 1989 Conference*, pp. 81–94, November 1989.

[Vlissides 1996] Vlissides, John M., James O. Coplien, and Norman L. Kerth, eds. *Pattern Languages of Program Design 2*. Reading, MA: Addison-Wesley, 1996.

[Weinand 1988] Weinand, A., E. Gamma, and R. Marty. ET++: An object-oriented application framework in C++. *Proceedings of OOPSLA '88*, pp. 46–57, November 1988. Printed as SIGPLAN Notices 23(11).

[Weinand 1989] Weinand, A., E. Gamma, and R. Marty. Design and implementation of {ET++}, a seamless object-oriented application framework. *Structured Programming* 10(2):63–87, 1989.

[Wirfs-Brock 1990] Wirfs-Brock, Rebecca J., and Ralph E. Johnson. Surveying current research in object-oriented design. *Communications of the ACM* 33(9):104–124, 1990.

[Yassin-Fayad 1999] Yassin, A.F., and M.E. Fayad. *Domain-Specific Application Frameworks*, Chapter 29, Mohamed E. Fayad and Ralph Johnson, editors, New York: John Wiley & Sons, 1999.

1.15 Review Questions

1. What is an application framework?

2. Describe briefly the benefits of application frameworks.

3. Give examples for whitebox, graybox, and blackbox frameworks.

4. Give examples for enterprise frameworks.

5. What are the differences between whitebox and blackbox frameworks?

6. What are the differences between system frameworks and enterprise frameworks?

7. What are the differences between application frameworks and design patterns?

8. What are the differences between application frameworks and software components?

9. What are the differences between application frameworks and class libraries?

10. What are the differences between application frameworks and application generators?

11. State the strengths of application frameworks.

12. State the weaknesses of application frameworks.

13. Explain how to use application frameworks.

14. Explain how to develop application frameworks.

15. Explain how to learn application frameworks.

16. What do the following terms stand for?

    MFC, GUI, ORB, CDT, CORBA, DCOM, EBT, and MVC

CHAPTER 2

Frameworks and Patterns: Architectural Abstractions

Within software engineering in general, *reuse* is considered to be a part of an effective development process. This effectiveness originates from the qualitative and economic benefits reuse accomplishes. Using previously developed and tested components when building an application saves development efforts and reduces the risk of introducing errors into the system. The use of *abstractions* in software development is considered an advantage. Abstractions and abstraction mechanisms make software development easier, because they let the developer work with fewer elements—abstracting from details. This facilitates communication about the software. Furthermore, abstraction facilitates reuse. It is often hard to reuse software designs or implementations directly, because variations in the different application contexts imply that variations of the designs and implementations are likewise needed. When the potential reusable designs and implementations are abstracted from specific contexts and represented by generalized concepts and relations, they typically have much wider application scope.

As means for an effective development process, reuse and abstraction can be applied at many different levels. We are particularly interested in the *software architecture* [Shaw-Garlan 1996] level of design. This level is concerned with the description of elements from which systems are built, interactions among those elements, patterns that guide their composition, and constraints on these patterns. In [Buschmann 1996] software architecture is defined as follows: "A software architecture is a description of the subsystems and components of a software system and the relationships between them. Subsystems and components are typically specified in different views to show the relevant functional and non-functional properties of a software system." In [Kristensen 1996] the notion of *architectural abstractions* is discussed. Software architecture is interpreted as (1) the choice of architectural abstractions and language mechanisms or (2) the use of the chosen elements. With regard to architectural abstractions, no explicit definition is provided. Instead, the set of architectural abstractions is exemplified and divided into various categories. *Design patterns* [Gamma 1995] and *frameworks* [Johnson-Foote 1988] are examples of such categories. The categories are characterized differently in the universe of architectural abstractions according to a set of dimensions. The dimensions include level of abstraction, degree of domain specificity, level of granularity, and degree of completeness.

The notions of *modeling patterns,*[1] *design patterns* [Gamma 1995], and *metapatterns* [Pree 1995] represent different approaches to patterns in object-oriented design. Furthermore, some of these approaches to patterns, together with the notion of *frameworks* [Johnson-Foote 1988], have been proposed as categories of architectural abstractions [Kristensen 1996]. To document the use of a framework, the notion of a *pattern language* has been proposed [Johnson 1992]. Both the idea of a pattern and the idea of pattern languages originate from work within building architecture by Christopher Alexander [Alexander 1977, 1979]. Alexander proposes that a pattern describes a solution to a problem in a context. This notion of a pattern constitutes an *Alexandrian* pattern.

To structure a discussion about this set of concepts, and in order to examine their relationships, we use the ideas of architectural abstractions and Alexandrian patterns as two leitmotifs, as illustrated in Figure 2.1. The goal of this chapter is to elaborate on the conceptual framework associated with the development, documentation, and application of architectural abstractions, exemplified by patterns and frameworks in object-oriented software.

This chapter is organized as follows: *Section 2.1* elaborates on the idea of architectural abstractions. *Section 2.2* and *Section 2.3* survey current framework and pattern technologies, and provide examples of the conceptual framework outlined in *Section 2.1*. *Section 2.4* illustrates the relationships between frameworks and three notions of patterns. Finally, *Section 2.5* provides a summary of the work and results. The empirical foundation for the results described in this chapter is the work documented in [Jacobsen-Nowack 1996], which includes several experiments with framework development, evolution, application, and documentation. Characteristic properties of different types of patterns in the development of frameworks are described in [Jacobsen 1997].

[1]Coad describes *object-oriented patterns* and Fowler describes *analysis patterns*. However, both acknowledge that the patterns are applied in a modeling process [Coad 1992, 1995; Fowler 1997].

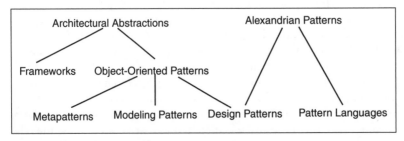

Figure 2.1 The conceptual framework spanned by the two leitmotifs: architectural abstractions and Alexandrian patterns.

2.1 Architectural Abstractions

Reuse and abstraction can be addressed at many different levels and in many different ways in software development. In our study we have come across a statement [Deutsch 1989] that we consider to be essential:

> Interface design and functional factoring constitute the key intellectual content of software and are far more difficult to create or re-create than code.

Agreeing with Deutsch, we believe that software developers should spend substantial efforts on *interface design* and *functional factoring*. Furthermore, we believe that these two issues can be perceived as aspects of *architecture*. According to *Webster's Dictionary*, architecture is "the art or practice of designing and building structures...." In other words, architecture is concerned with the design and building of *structure*—not with the individual building blocks that bring the structures into existence. Interface design of software (classes) is concerned with the external properties of a component as opposed to its implementation. Functional factoring is concerned with the distribution of functionality (responsibility) between the various components. This distribution expresses the logical structure of software.

These two aspects of software resemble the aforementioned notion of structure in conventional architecture. This suggests that software architecture can be perceived as the practice of designing and building logical structures in software. The previously described notions of reuse, abstraction, and architectural abstractions can be used to elaborate the understanding of an architecture concept in object-oriented software development. We consider the following four issues to be characteristic aspects of an architectural abstraction:

Structure. Specifies the interface of a set of basic elements as well as the static and/or dynamic structures that relate them in a composition.

Functionality. Provides useful functionality.

Abstraction. Identifies and names a composition of elements with a certain internal structure and a certain functionality.

Reuse. Can be applied multiple times.

Architectural abstractions support the design and construction of logical structure, which are perceived as the difficult parts of software design. The following describes a conceptual framework related to architectural abstractions. The framework is focused around the notion of a category[2] instead of the general concept. This supports the idea that statements expressed in terms of the conceptual framework can be more specific.

The two main processes associated with architectural abstractions are the application of existing elements and the development of new elements. This is illustrated in Figure 2.2. A category of architectural abstractions is split into the body of knowledge about the underlying concept (category concept) and the set of elements that exemplify the concept (category library). Both are entities that change over time.

---

[2]*Category* refers to the set of architectural abstractions that can be divided into different categories, which are characterized differently in a universe according to a set of dimensions [Kristensen 1996].

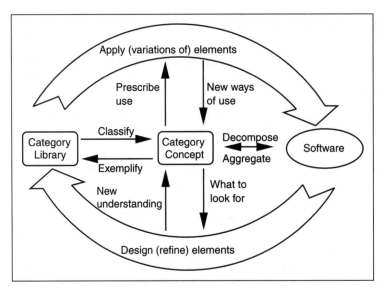

Figure 2.2   Application and development of architectural abstractions within object-oriented software development.

The category library changes when new elements are invented or discovered, or when existing elements are refined. The contemporary library of elements, the contemporary ideas about software in general, and current perceptions of the application and development processes all affect the category concept (illustrated by the arrows pointing into the middle of Figure 2.2). The current understanding of the concept affects how elements are applied when building software, how software is understood, and how new elements are invented (arrows pointing outward). The double-headed arrow between "Software" and "Category Concept" is an implication of the double meaning of *software*. When software is interpreted as basic building blocks (that is, objects), then the category concept is an abstraction of an aggregation of software. When software is interpreted as a (partial) software system, then the category concept decomposes the system into smaller structures. Software plays the opposite role of the category in the two relations. The application and development processes can be mutated in the sense that they can be concerned with the application of variations or with the refinement of existing elements, respectively.

Both frameworks and object-oriented patterns are perceived as categories of architectural abstractions. To be more precise, we perceive the software structure captured by instances of the two ideas as being the real instances of architectural abstractions. But frameworks, modeling patterns, and design patterns are more than this structure (for example, program code, prose, or diagrams). Having noticed the difference, we still denote the complete set of patterns and frameworks as categories of architectural abstractions. Metapatterns are the simplest instances of architectural abstractions in the sense that they are almost pure structure. Modeling patterns, design patterns, and metapatterns are subcategories of the category of object-oriented patterns. The following two sections elaborate on these views.

2.2 Frameworks

This section examines the notion of frameworks [Johnson-Foote 1988] and summarizes its characteristics as a category of architectural abstractions. Since the discussion is presented from the viewpoint of architectural abstraction, this section does not cover issues such as testing for correctness and integration [Mattsson 1999] with other existing code. A framework within an object-oriented design perspective can be perceived as follows:

> **Framework.** A set of cooperating classes that makes up a reusable design for a specific class of software. A framework provides architectural guidance by partitioning the design into abstract classes and defining their responsibilities and collaborations. A developer customizes the framework to a particular application by subclassing and composing instances of framework classes [Gamma 1995].

A framework has a physical representation in terms of classes, methods, and objects. The primary benefit of a framework is not the reusable implementation, but the reusable structure it describes (architectural guidance). A framework describes interface design using abstract classes and it describes functional factoring by specifying responsibilities and collaborations between these. Frameworks are adapted by customizing and extending the structure they provide. The parts in the framework that are open to extension and customization are termed *flexible hot spots* [Pree 1995] (see Figure 2.3).

The hot spots express aspects of the framework domain that cannot be fully anticipated. Hot spots are discovered in the domain analysis or provided by a domain expert. The components to be supplied in the flexible hot spots of a framework can be components from a library belonging to the framework (providing different alternatives), and/or they can be user created.

A framework design provides features at two levels: (1) *domain features*, which are domain-relevant features useful in the applications, made from the framework and (2) features facilitating the adaptation and the evolution of the framework, which we term *structural characteristics*. The structural characteristics include an appropriate arrange-

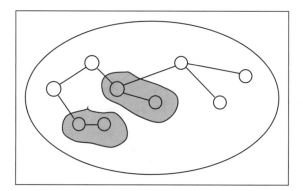

Figure 2.3 A framework describes a predefined overall architecture, consisting of both semifinished and ready-to-use building blocks. The shaded regions are the flexible hot spots of the framework.

ment of both the logical (design) and the physical structure[3] (modules) of the framework. The structural characteristics are especially important because a framework's implementation and design are the actual interface used by the framework users (application developers, programmers). Therefore, the design of a framework's logical structure is essential to the application of the framework. Furthermore, because frameworks are developed in an iterative process, maintainability is an important quality of frameworks. Maintainability also relies on the logical structure of the framework.

A framework is not a pattern—patterns describe ideas and perspectives; frameworks are implemented software. Nor is a framework an application—frameworks do not necessarily provide default behavior; hence, they are not executable programs. They can be perceived as partial designs, because they do not describe every aspect of an application. A framework likewise is not a class library—applications that use classes from a library invoke predefined methods, whereas frameworks contain parts that invoke methods supplied by the user. This *inversion of control* is characteristic for frameworks. Frameworks are complex and interconnected wholes, while libraries (at best) consist of compatible parts.

Frameworks are a complex type of software for three reasons: Frameworks contain abstract designs, frameworks are generally applicable, and frameworks have features at two levels.

2.2.1 Application

From the perspective of being architectural abstractions, frameworks provide reuse at three levels (see Figure 2.4).

The results from a domain analysis include information about concepts, processes, and structures from the domain. A framework implementation and documentation

---

[3]The arrangement of the framework's physical structure, which we have not considered in our work, is concerned with issues relating to programming environments.

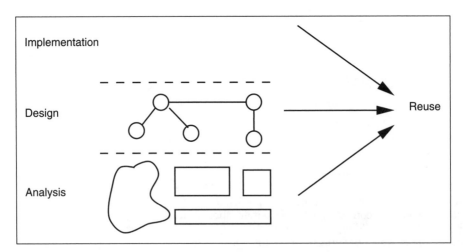

Figure 2.4   Framework use is reuse of analysis, design, and implementation.

describes the domain in terms of this information. The documentation should include an *abstract domain model*. Such a model describes the framework perspective on the given application domain by identifying important abstractions (concepts, processes, and structures) in the domain. As an example, graphical user interface frameworks have an underlying abstract domain model that includes graphical widgets, events, notification mechanisms, pointing, clicking, and dragging. The abstract domain model facilitates thinking about future applications. The resulting structure from a framework design is reused, because applications are built using this structure. The structure includes class hierarchies and patterns for object collaborations. A framework implementation captures elements from both of the aforementioned issues. In addition, some components may already be fully implemented, so they are ready to be composed into an application.

We use the term *framework adaptation* about the process of using a framework to build an application. A framework can be adapted by means of *whitebox* and *blackbox* reuse. The former corresponds to customizing framework classes by specialization, and the latter corresponds to configuring a part of the framework with a (framework-provided) class [Fayad-Schmidt 1997; Johnson-Foote 1988].

A framework should be supplied with different prototypical applications that utilize the various parts of the framework in different ways. From this the framework, the user learns about the framework and how it can be used. Furthermore, a provided application can be copied and modified in the case that it deviates only slightly from the application to be built. This is illustrated in the documentation of the HotDraw framework [Johnson 1992].

2.2.2 Development

The domain analysis provides the framework developer with a detailed understanding of the concepts of the domain and detailed insight into the functionality and flexible hot spots the framework must possess [Pree 1995]. Example applications describe a framework's domain. If no example applications are available (preferably as documented source codes), then prototypes may act as example applications. Framework development is an iterative process and proceeds more slowly than application development. The process demands competent abstractors in order to capture the relevant domain features in the framework: When developing applications, we look for common phenomena in the domain area and abstract them into concepts. When developing a framework, we additionally abstract the found concepts into generalized concepts, which can be used to describe a more general domain. A complete framework analysis and design iteration includes a test, which can be performed by using the framework to implement new versions of the prototype example applications. The test provides information about the usefulness of the framework's structural characteristics. The task of ensuring both domain features and proper structural characteristics in a framework makes the development more complex than application development.

Figure 2.5 illustrates framework development and application as processes within a cycle. The experience gained from using a framework provides information on the framework's domain—for example, the concepts, structures, and processes that constitute, respectively, the center and the periphery of the domain. If the framework adaptation was easy, then the produced application is at the center of the domain. This

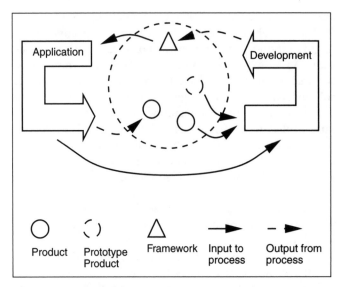

Figure 2.5   The life cycle of frameworks: application and development.

feedback from adapting the framework is a part of the input to the next version of the framework. Another part could be new demands in the domain—for example, new functionality requirements.

2.2.3 Documentation

Frameworks are a complex type of software; hence, the development and application of frameworks are complicated tasks, implying that high-quality documentation is crucial. Framework documentation must support two activities: adaptation and evolution. With regard to the adaptation activities, the documentation should provide information about the framework domain, the purpose of the framework, how to use the framework, and the design of the framework. The documentation should focus on the use of examples in order to make the abstract design more concrete and understandable [Johnson 1992]. An essential aspect of frameworks is their evolution by analysis, design, and test iterations, and the documentation must address this aspect specifically, by documenting the structural characteristics of the framework.

2.2.4 Summary

Frameworks are perceived as a category of architectural abstractions, but not as an Alexandrian pattern. The four aspects of architectural abstractions in relation to frameworks are as follows:

Structure. A framework is a composition of classes, whose collaborations and responsibilities are specified.

Functionality. In order to provide the required domain features, a framework embodies the common functionality of the applications in its domain. Furthermore, in order to be usable in application development, a framework must possess adaptation functionality. An example of the latter is the provision of configurable hot spots.

Abstraction. A framework represents an abstraction of structures and functionality in the domain as generalized structures and functionality. This generalized structure and functionality is named and considered a whole.

Reuse. A framework expresses commonalities among a group of applications and is reusable when developing applications within this group.

Frameworks are software; hence, they are a physical part of and more than just a perspective on the application made using them. When the material in focus is not software, but a domain, then frameworks can be regarded as a specific perspective on the domain.

2.3 Object-Oriented Patterns

This section characterizes the software pattern concept in general and describes and contrasts three approaches toward defining and applying a pattern concept in object-oriented software development: design patterns, metapatterns, and patterns for conceptual modeling.

In general, a pattern is a named perspective on a subject. In order to be relevant, a pattern must express a general recurrent theme that has proved to be useful. Focusing on the analysis, design, and implementation efforts in software development, the subject is a problem domain, a system design, or a program implementation. The subject in Figure 2.6 is a structure diagram with classes, objects, and relationships between them. Other types of subjects could be models of problem domains, interaction diagrams, or source code.

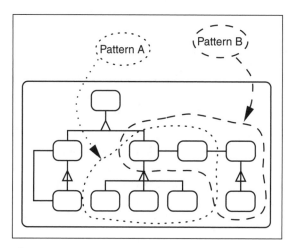

Figure 2.6   Patterns represent different perspectives on a subject.

Applying different concepts of patterns to such descriptions could focus on, respectively, the modeling of structures in a problem domain, the description of object interactions in a design, and the low-level realization idioms in a program implementation. Applying patterns implies that the subject is perceived in a different way as a result of the changed perspective: New and different relations between the participants (objects) constituting the subject are named, abstracted, and made explicit. Patterns can be applied in order to benefit from the functionality they describe and to benefit from their effect in relation to documentation. By documenting in terms of well-defined and high-level structures (like patterns), the complexity of the subject, as well as the amount of documentation needed to describe the subject, is reduced. This relies on the idea of a shared language, where a named perspective can be included in the language, resulting in new possibilities for expression. This means that a collection of patterns (like the design patterns from [Gamma 1995]) can become a vocabulary for experienced developers.

An Alexandrian pattern describes a solution to a problem in a context and connects these three elements. An Alexandrian pattern is *generative* [Beck-Johnson 1994; Coplien 1992] in the sense that the pattern explains the rationale behind its use: *What* design problem is solved by the application of the pattern, and *when* should it be applied? The following uses the prefix term *Alexandrian* when referring to an Alexandrian pattern. Alexander's notion of a *pattern language* [Alexander 1977, 1979] is a more advanced concept than just that of a vocabulary. According to Alexander, a pattern language is a set of related patterns describing how and under which circumstances problems and solutions within a subject are related. The organization of the patterns in the pattern language embodies a specific perspective on the subject in question—typically, how a subject is divided into smaller subjects. Pattern languages have been used for describing software [Johnson 1992]. Another difference between patterns and pattern languages is that the latter typically also are applied to describe perspectives on a process; that is, a process is regarded as consisting of specific subprocesses.

2.3.1 Design Patterns

The motivation for *design patterns* is a desire for reuse of quality designs. The achievement of reuse is envisioned in two ways: (1) by creating a design pattern catalog, like a design handbook, containing numerous problems and corresponding solutions, and (2) by incorporating design patterns into the language in which a designer thinks—a design language. The notion of design patterns is defined as follows:

> **Design Pattern.** A design pattern systematically names, motivates, and explains a general design that addresses a recurring design problem in object-oriented systems. It describes the problem, the solution, when to apply the solution, and its consequences. It also gives implementation hints and examples. The solution is a general arrangement of objects and classes that solve the problem. The solution is customized and implemented to solve the problem in a particular context [Gamma 1995].

A design pattern captures the essence of an idea that experienced designers have reused many times to solve a common problem. The problem is considered generally relevant and the solution is considered generally applicable and flexible. Reuse by design patterns is fine-grained (micro-architecture level [Gamma 1995]), since the design patterns address delimited problems and their solutions involve one to five classes. They are Alexandrian patterns, since they describe problem, context, and solution to a certain extent. They can be reformulated as more generative versions, as described by [Beck-Johnson 1994; Coplien 1992]. The design patterns are divided into three categories: patterns dealing with flexible object creation; patterns dealing with structural aspects of object systems; patterns dealing with behavioral aspects of object systems. A design pattern captures the design idea; it abstracts itself from the specific situation. Therefore, a design pattern is independent of application domains and must be mapped to the specific situation before it can be implemented in specific classes. Some design patterns address the same problem, differing only with respect to their generality. The documentation of design patterns follows a template that addresses the aspects of problem, context, and solution from different perspectives and different abstraction levels.

In [Buschmann 1996] more design patterns are described and a classification system is introduced, consisting of architectural patterns, design patterns, and idioms. The architectural patterns can be applied to the overall organization of a software system, and they are largely influenced by the concept of architectural styles described by [Shaw-Garlan 1996]. They can also be perceived as large-scale versions (with different concerns and goals) of several well-known design patterns. Examples include Layers, Model-View-Controller, and Broker. At the other end of the scale, idioms are small-grained patterns dealing with issues at or a little above the actual programming language level. An idiom typically helps the software developer to maximize the utilization of a specific programming language or environment. Idioms for C++ programming are presented in [Coplien 1992]. Examples include Pointer Counting. In [Beck 1997] a set of idiom-like patterns for Smalltalk programming is presented.

The remainder of this text focuses on the design patterns from [Gamma 1995], partly because the results that concern these design patterns can be generalized to architectural patterns, and partly because we do not want to discuss low-level or language-specific idioms. One language's idiom is another language's mechanism. We present an example of a design pattern (Observer) later in this section.

Application

An application of a design pattern can be brought about for reasons of both documentation and functionality. When the motivation is primarily documentation, the specific design problem is generalized to be an instance of the problem described by the design pattern, and the design is shaped accordingly in order to be documented by the design pattern. The design patterns providing flexibility can be motivated by a need for reuse or a need for facilitating changes. Both needs have variation as their theme. Every design pattern addresses a specific aspect of variation [Gamma 1995]. Flexibility can be achieved by deliberately introducing design patterns to solve a flexibility problem. Alternatively, flexibility can be achieved by iterating over the design. This iteration process can lead to the identification of (unconsciously) applied design patterns. The latter observation illustrates that design patterns really capture design solutions that have proven to be useful, and that the problems they address are common. Therefore the use of design patterns makes software development more efficient, potentially reducing the number of iterations needed. The design pattern catalog in [Gamma 1995] contains a collection of good and relevant examples of problems and solutions, supporting the expression of common problems and the realization of solutions. The design patterns must be understood—they must have become part of one's design vocabulary—in order to be useful.

Consequences of design pattern applications include the following:

- Some required functionality is introduced (typically, flexibility), solving a problem.

- The perception of the domain is affected.

- Rationales for the specific design solutions are manifested and made explicit.

- New terms (design patterns) enter the design language, and the software is understood in these terms.

Development

Development of design patterns emerges from design experience. From sensing that some aspects of previous tasks have something in common, the development of a design pattern proceeds through a crystallizing process, in which the pattern's problem, context, and solution are refined. This process is hard, as finding patterns is much easier than describing them. Describing the structural aspects of the solution of a pattern is the easy part. Defining the problem it solves and the context in which it can be applied is harder [Gamma 1995], but these aspects should be explicitly addressed, because they facilitate communication about, and the application of, patterns.

2.3.2 Metapatterns

The motivation for using metapatterns [Pree 1995] is to provide a means to categorize and describe design patterns on a metalevel, and to support framework construction. The metapatterns are divided into two categories dealing with concepts and compositions of concepts, respectively. The central concepts in metapatterns are defined according to a perspective on class methods. The methods of a class are characterized according to two characteristic method types: *hook* methods and *template* methods. Specific methods are characterized according to subjective perspectives. A specific method can be a hook-method, a template-method, or both—it depends on the method contents and the context. A class that has a template method is termed a *template class*, and a class that has a hook method is termed a *hook class*. Likewise, the notions of template and hook objects are correspondingly defined. The general idea of the template/hook metaphor is that the template method in the template class invokes the hook method in the hook class. A hook method is virtual; it is overruled by additional method declarations in subclasses of the abstract hook class. A hook class can in principle contain several hook methods, which are invoked in turn by the template method.

Each compositional metapattern (on which this discussion will focus) specifies how one template method and one hook method are distributed between classes. The functionality of an individual metapattern specifies a specific variation of the distribution of template and hook methods between classes, where each variation has certain advantages and drawbacks. A metapattern is not a solution to a problem in a context, but a named expression of a class and method relationship in terms of inheritance, reference, template, and hook—it is a name for a specific but generally described implementation structure.

Figure 2.7 illustrates the 1:1 connection metapattern [Pree 1995]. It illustrates that an object of the template class references an object from the hook class. The notation implicitly describes that the template class defines a template method, which contains an invocation of a hook method defined in the hook class. The user of the metapattern provides several different subclasses of the hook class, with different implementations of the hook method. By instantiating one of these different subclasses and assigning it to the template object, the behavior of the template object is configured. Assigning instances of other subclasses to the template object can later alter this behavior.

Other metapatterns define different relationships between the objects and classes: the *unification* metapattern defines the template method and the hook in the same class; the *1:1 recursive connection* metapattern defines the template class as a subclass of the hook class; the 1:1 recursive unification metapattern defines the template method and the hook method as being the same method in the same class, where it is left to the user to provide subclasses that add the required hook flavor. All the 1:1 metapatterns are also defined in 1:*n* variants that can be applied to build trees of objects, instead of chains of objects. The recursive patterns are typically applied to forward messages in a chain (1:1) or a tree (1:*n*), whereas the 1:1 and 1:*n* connection metapatterns are applied to iterate over a finite set of hook methods.

Application

Metapatterns are applied in order to obtain abstract coupling in a design. They (1) provide the ability to treat several objects (a chain or a tree) or a single object uniformly (the recursive patterns) and (2) introduce a lower (more abstract) coupling between classes (the connection patterns) and methods (the unification patterns). Metapatterns are useful when analyzing existing design structures—for example, design patterns; they provide concepts that facilitate discussions about alternative class relations and method types. The application of metapatterns depends on the user's ability to transform the very formal and abstract notions of template and hook relationships into program code that is useful in the particular context. This exemplification process demands good abstractors.

Development

The metapatterns are developed in an analytical manner: basic principles (template and hook) are introduced, and combinations involving inheritance, reference, and the basic principles are analyzed [Pree 1995]. Seven meaningful combinations (selected by the author) constitute the metapatterns. This analytical approach makes the category of metapatterns more complete than the category of design patterns or modeling pat-

Figure 2.7 The 1:1 connection metapattern.

terns. If new metapatterns (in Pree's sense) were to be discovered, it would require a different (extended, replaced, or mutated) conceptual framework from the currently available template/hook metaphor.

Metapatterns and Design Patterns

Figure 2.8 illustrates the roles that metapatterns can have in relation to design patterns. In the common case where a design pattern describes its solution in terms of abstract coupling and the solution has several variations (for example, Observer), then metapatterns illustrate different implementation alternatives for the solution. If the design pattern is simply a trick (for example, Singleton), the metapatterns are not helpful. But, in general, metapatterns assist in design pattern application.

Different design patterns can be applied in order to introduce some functionality into a program. If the functionality is an aspect of abstract coupling, then one of the composition metapatterns can be applied in order to implement the design pattern's solution. Different metapatterns provide different implementation strategies. When developing a design pattern, metapatterns can be used as inspirations for the suggested structure in the solution. Template and hook methods are powerful concepts when describing abstract designs, and design patterns can be expressed in terms of these. The documentation aspect of metapatterns is generally applicable in object-oriented software and therefore also for the implementation of design patterns. However, the effect of using metapatterns is restricted to structural aspects of the solution: classifications of the roles two classes or methods have in relation to each other.

Figure 2.9 illustrates metapatterns and design patterns in relation to problems and solutions in design. A design pattern relates a problem to a solution through a context, whereas a metapattern names certain aspects of a design structure. Metapatterns describe the structure of a design pattern's solution to different extents, by focusing on the purely technical object-oriented mechanisms used to express the solution. This implies that the metapatterns don't describe design patterns on a metalevel; they simply describe aspects of a design pattern's solution. Since the metapatterns are expressed in a more rigid language (basic object-oriented mechanisms) than are design patterns, it is more objectively decidable whether a metapattern is instantiated in some program.

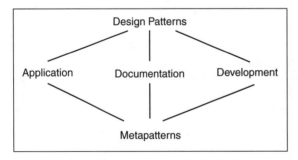

Figure 2.8 Design patterns can be applied, developed, and documented using metapatterns.

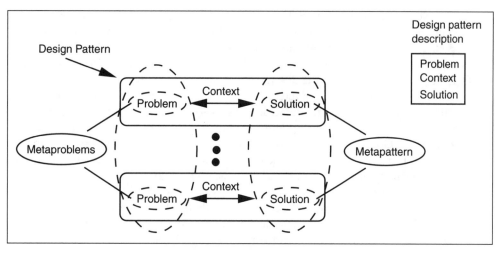

Figure 2.9 Metapatterns describe the structure of a design pattern's solution.

As an example of applying a metapattern to describe a design pattern, Figure 2.10 illustrates how the *1:n connection metapattern* describes the structure of the Observer design pattern. The intent of Observer is to "define a one-to-many dependency between objects so that when one object changes state, all its dependents are notified and updated automatically" [Gamma 1995].

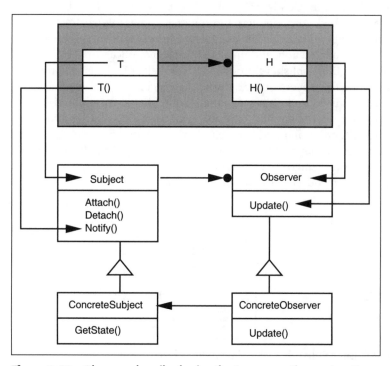

Figure 2.10 Observer described using the 1:*n* connection metapattern.

The Notify method in the Subject class is a template method in relation to the Update method, which is a hook method in the Observer class. Examples of specialized classes (both the template and hook classes) are part of the description of the design pattern, but the metapattern notation omits this part. An additional method, GetState, is also included in the description of the design pattern.

Looking at the description of the Observer design pattern, we see that subjects have functionality for attaching and detaching observers; this is not expressed by the metapattern—only the notification update functionality is expressed by the metapattern. Regarding the Observer design pattern as an expression of the idea that something is a subject that is being observed and the observers are notified of changes to the subject, there can be many implementations of the Observer design pattern. One implementation that differs from the one in Figure 2.10 is a case in which both the notification and observing functionalities are in the same class—that is, the subjects and observers are described by the same class. This implementation, while still being an implementation of the Observer design pattern, is now described by another metapattern, namely, the 1:n *Recursive Unification* metapattern. This is an example of a design pattern that can be described with a different metapattern when implemented differently.

2.3.3 Patterns for Modeling

A modeling pattern is an abstraction of a small grouping of classes that is likely to be helpful again and again in object-oriented modeling—the pattern is likely to be applicable multiple times within a single application, as well as across many different kinds of applications [Coad 1992]. In [Coad 1992] 7 modeling patterns are described, and in [Coad 1995] 31 are described. A modeling pattern names a reusable abstraction over classes, specifies the static structure of the abstraction in terms of method and class relations, exemplifies the abstraction, and provides hints on applicability.

Figure 2.11 illustrates the Publisher-Subscriber pattern. The focus is on broadcast semantics—on modeling that several objects are notified by one object.

A modeling pattern is used as an ideal element—something worthy of imitation—expressing concepts and relations within a problem domain. Modeling patterns are examples of common situations in many problem domains. Modeling patterns are not Alexandrian patterns, even though they are inspired by them [Coad 1992]—they do not explicitly focus on a problem to be solved or a context in which they can be applied. The modeling patterns are concerned with expressing concrete coupling, rather than

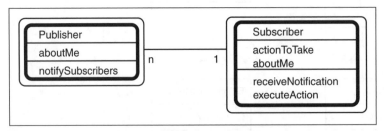

Figure 2.11   The Publisher-Subscriber modeling pattern [Coad 1995].

abstract coupling between classes. Because the patterns are defined in terms of attributes and methods, they are related to design, not purely to analysis, as it is hard to benefit from the use of methods within analysis. The modeling patterns are best suited for the transition from domain analysis to application design. This is because the functionality provided by them is focused around the modeling of concepts and relations from a problem domain—not the provision of flexibility within an implementation (for example, abstract coupling).

In [Fowler 1997] a set of *analysis patterns* is presented. They are applicable in the modeling of business domains such as trading, measurement, accounting, and organizational relationships. Fowler characterizes analysis patterns as "groups of concepts that represent a common construction in business modeling." In many aspects the analysis patterns are a more pure form of modeling patterns than Coad's patterns, in that they deal explicitly with the conceptual modeling of a domain. The applied notation reflects this. The question of how to transform the object-oriented models expressed by the analysis patterns into a design of an information system is dealt with by Fowler in a set of dedicated transformation patterns.

Application and Development

Some modeling patterns can be used both when analyzing a problem in the domain and when designing and implementing the software. Others are difficult to use across analysis, design, and implementation, since object-oriented programming languages do not directly support them. Patterns for modeling focus on the logical structures among a set of domain concepts.

The modeling patterns are found by trial and error and by observation. Experience with the relationships between objects and classes [Coad 1992] and experience with the modeling of different business domains [Fowler 1997] are the major sources for modeling patterns.

Design Patterns and Modeling Patterns

Some modeling patterns and design patterns have similarities. The Observer [Gamma 1995] design pattern and the Publisher-Subscriber [Coad 1995] combination both express that one object notifies several other objects. The modeling pattern focuses on broadcast semantics, while the design pattern expands the focus to include elaboration on the design and implementation.

The general difference between modeling patterns and design patterns is that the design patterns are Alexandrian patterns, and they express their solution in terms of abstract classes, while the modeling patterns are not Alexandrian patterns and are expressed in nonabstract but generally described classes. This difference in the usage of abstract classes reflects different perspectives; modeling patterns focus on modeling (which can be considered part of both analysis and design), whereas design patterns focus on technical design and implementation. This is further supported by the inclusion of sample code, implementation hints, and interaction diagrams in the description of design patterns.

2.3.4 Summary

Considering the four characteristic aspects of architectural abstractions described in *Section 2.2*, we observe the following: Design patterns describe general and reusable solutions to common problems within object-oriented design and implementation. The solutions include descriptions of structures of objects and classes, as well as sample code and implementation hints. The functionality they provide varies from simple tricks to the provision of flexibility in terms of loose couplings between the parts. Used as abstractions, they facilitate communication about problems, designs, and implementations. The design pattern approach is the only approach to object-oriented patterns that can be described as Alexandrian. Metapatterns focus extensively on the description of reusable structural relationships between objects and classes. The different structural relationships provide variations of abstract coupling, which are used to provide flexible implementations. Their use as abstractions is limited to the naming of simple class relationships. Modeling patterns describe structural aspects by specifying class interfaces (that is, methods and attributes), as well as class and object relationships. They provide functionality that has proven to be useful and reusable. The abstractions they provide facilitate communication about object-oriented analysis and design.

2.4 Frameworks and Patterns

This section illustrates the relationships between frameworks and patterns: how patterns are used in the application, development, and documentation of frameworks, and how the domain features and the structural characteristics of frameworks are addressed by patterns (see Figure 2.12).

2.4.1 Design Patterns

Many design patterns are related to abstract coupling or the management of recursive structures, which are issues considered in the more technical phases of design and in

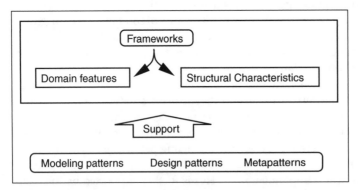

Figure 2.12 Supporting a framework's domain features and structural characteristics with patterns.

the implementation of frameworks. This is the primary focus when using design patterns in the development of frameworks. Because design patterns promote loose coupling between the parts, they make a framework design flexible. To provide flexibility in terms of abstract coupling between the constituent parts, a design pattern is used to design the functional factoring and component interfaces in a part of the framework.

The design patterns address very explicitly the task of providing a framework with structural characteristics. When structuring a framework in terms of design patterns, the framework structure will be made visible because patterns will describe logical units and point out abstract couplings. This is important both for framework adaptation and framework evolution [Beck-Johnson 1994; Gamma 1995]. Design patterns capture many of the structures resulting from refactorings, and using the design patterns can thus avoid some refactorings in later framework design [Gamma 1995]. Design patterns can be used as inspiration when looking for flexible hot spots within a domain. Investigating the information available about problems and context for every pattern in a catalog makes common problems in abstract design visible. The clause "Known Uses" in the description of design patterns mentions examples about the application of the pattern in an existing framework. In general, however, the design patterns are not useful in the domain analysis. This is due to their extensive use of abstract classes and template and hook methods, as well as their elaborate implementation sections—elements of no use when performing domain analysis. The primary role of design patterns is to provide an appropriate arrangement of the components in the framework [Gamma 1995]—in other words, they address the structural characteristics of a framework.

As an architectural abstraction, the design patterns can be used to communicate about the design in terms of entities larger than objects and classes. In addition, information about the context and problems of the solutions is made explicit when communicating in terms of design patterns. Framework developers and users benefit from this when performing framework evolution and adaptation.

A framework that contains design patterns can be understood in terms of these; therefore, when adapting a framework, users can perceive their specific adaptation steps (subclassing or configuring framework classes) as adaptations of small wholes—the involved design patterns—instead of only making new atoms (classes). Users see their adaptations in a perspective larger than that of single classes.

2.4.2 Modeling Patterns

Modeling patterns are useful abstractions when performing domain analysis. If structures within the domain can be expressed with modeling patterns, then these are potential areas for abstract design solutions. The modeling patterns describe ideas and are not very elaborate when considering the actual implementation of the reusable designs. This is due to lack of focus on abstract classes, template and hook methods, and implementation details. In the analysis phase of a development effort this is not crucial because abstract classes are not considered, but when moving on to the more technical design phase the need for abstract coupling within a framework becomes obvious. This implies that modeling patterns are of limited use in connection with framework development because they primarily are intended for expressing an initial domain model and are not concerned with the demanding issues related to the design of a framework's structural characteristics. In summary: The modeling patterns address the domain features of a framework primarily on a conceptual level and secondarily on a design level.

The focus of the modeling patterns as documentation is on expressing the abstract domain model. The concepts underlying the framework are revealed; hence, the framework is easier to apply in application development. The modeling patterns are a means to achieve reuse of the abstract domain model.

The modeling patterns are useful when investigating the framework domain, but in the adaptation process they are not very useful, since they do not express details on the framework design, which is necessary in order to use the framework.

2.4.3 Metapatterns

Metapatterns are not useful in domain analysis, since they are concerned with naming seven structures between two classes and the roles of two methods—they deal with object-oriented mechanisms and are domain independent. The notions of template and hook methods are very powerful in discussions on detailed framework design, which facilitates the communication between the developers. Domain analysis is partly concerned with identifying concepts in the domain and partly with identifying variations (flexible hot spots) within the domain. In [Pree 1995] hot spots are classified and linked to a specific metapattern; thus, the metapatterns have the role as a realization mechanism to a given type of hot spot. Metapatterns address technical design at the level of micro-architecture; they deal with two classes or methods at a time. The metapatterns address the structural characteristics of the framework, both with respect to flexibility and due to the method classifications of template and hook. They also address the issue of a clear and understandable design.

The different ways of realizing flexibility (the different types of hot spots) are classified and linked to a metapattern. The metapatterns can then be used to document how the flexibility is realized by showing the mapping from the specific metapattern to the concrete classes. Hence, the metapatterns are concerned with illustrating technical design and implementation.

The metapatterns help framework users to obtain a clear understanding of the roles (in terms of template and hook) of the components they make—that is, the metapatterns help users to understand the framework's micro-architectures in domain-independent terms (template and hook).

The question of describing whitebox and blackbox reuse in terms of metapattern is not directly related to documentation of a framework, but is more closely related to the process of characterizing frameworks. Framework reuse by inheritance is termed *whitebox* and reuse by configuring is termed *blackbox*. A framework in which whitebox reuse is dominant has many instances of the unification and recursive metapatterns, since these metapatterns rely on inheritance structures. When blackbox reuse is dominant there are many connection metapatterns without recursion, since these metapatterns only rely on abstract coupling. Even if the framework is blackbox, a new hook class will be based on an abstract hook class, and is therefore whitebox reuse. In conclusion, making new parts from the framework will be whitebox reuse; connecting parts, which is to configure a template class with a hook class, will be blackbox reuse.

2.4.4 Summary

This section summarizes and compares the roles of the different patterns in relation to frameworks, focusing on the use of patterns in the application, the development, and the documentation of frameworks (see Figure 2.13).

Development

The modeling patterns are useful for expressing a domain model and less useful when addressing the structural characteristics of a framework. Design patterns address the structural characteristics of a framework and can, in addition, provide inspiration when searching for flexible hot spots. Metapatterns also address structural characteristics, but on a very small scale—two classes or methods at a time.

Documentation

The characteristics of the patterns with respect to development are also valid when considering the roles of the patterns with respect to documentation:

- Modeling patterns are best suited to document the abstract domain model.
- The design patterns document the more technical aspects of the design and, as the only types of patterns, their solution is linked to a context and problem, thus providing documentation for both the *whats* and the *whys* of the design.
- Metapatterns also address the technical design, but on a smaller scale than the design patterns.

Application

The modeling patterns are useful for describing the framework domain, but they are not very useful in the adaptation process, since they do not express details on the framework design. The design patterns are materialized in the framework design; hence, they help users to see their adaptations in a perspective larger than that of single classes. Metapatterns help users to understand the roles of the methods in the framework.

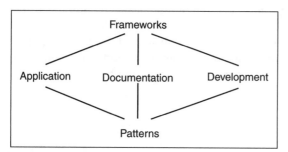

Figure 2.13 Frameworks can be applied, developed, and documented using patterns.

2.5 Summary

This discussion of architectural abstractions concludes with a summary of the *specific categories* of architectural abstractions, which we characterize and compare, followed by a summary of the *concept* of architectural abstraction, which is characterized according to its properties and the processes in which it is involved.

2.5.1 Frameworks

A framework is connected to a specific domain and consists of an abstract domain model, a reusable design, and an implementation of the design. Using a framework is thus reuse at all three levels. Frameworks are a category of architectural abstractions. They specify structure and functionality by their design, they are abstractions over a specific class of software, and they are reusable. A framework provides features at two levels—domain features and structural properties—and this makes frameworks a complex type of software. The complexity of frameworks implies that high-quality documentation is crucial. A pattern language can be used as documentation for framework adaptation. Changing requirements and the complexity of frameworks require that the framework development be an iterative process. From example applications, relevant domain features are abstracted. The experiences of applying the framework, possibly in conjunction with new example applications, are input to the next framework iteration. The structural characteristics of frameworks include the organization of the framework with regard to adaptation, in other words, the provision of flexible hot spots. These characteristics are obtained and refined by the iterative process.

2.5.2 Object-Oriented Patterns

Object-oriented patterns are a category of architectural abstractions. The category can be divided into (at least) three subcategories: modeling patterns, design patterns, and metapatterns. Patterns can be characterized as being Alexandrian, implying that they describe a solution to a problem in a context. Design patterns are the only object-oriented approach considered that has this property. Patterns can be applied in order to obtain all of the four aspects of architectural abstractions: reuse, abstraction, functionality, and structure. Their use as abstractions and as structures supports documentation of systems by decomposing a complex system into logical and comprehensible units. Their property of having reusable functionality makes system development more efficient. Modeling patterns primarily support analysis and design, design patterns support design and implementation, and metapatterns support implementation. Metapatterns can be used to describe the structural part of the solutions of design patterns. They do not describe design patterns on a metalevel.

Patterns and Frameworks

Patterns support the development, application, and documentation of frameworks. Modeling patterns address a framework's domain features by supporting the expression of the abstract domain model underlying the framework. Design patterns address the structural properties of frameworks by supporting the development of the logical structure. Metapatterns address implementation of the flexibility and abstract coupling required in frameworks at a small scale.

Architectural Abstractions

The concept of architectural abstractions facilitates communication about patterns and frameworks in the context of object-oriented software. Architectural abstractions can be categorized, and examples of such categories are frameworks, object-oriented patterns, design patterns, metapatterns, and modeling patterns. An architectural abstraction can be involved in two processes: development and application. The set of desirable properties that make architectural abstractions useful includes reusability, functionality, abstractness, and logic structure. These properties address important problems within software development. The following summarizes the four properties of architectural abstractions as well as the two related processes, including examples from the four categories discussed in this chapter.

Structure

A structure is a specification of the interface of a set of elements as well as the static and/or dynamic relationships between these elements. Frameworks consist of a set of abstract classes that specifies interfaces. The relationships between the abstract classes include association references, aggregations, and specializations. A framework is structured according to flexible hot spots, which provide the structural properties needed to use the framework. Design patterns describe similar configuration of abstract classes and, furthermore, include textual and graphical descriptions of the dynamic patterns of interaction between elements. The structure of a design pattern is described using a generalized example. Metapatterns name and abstract useful structures between two anonymous and generalized abstract classes. Modeling patterns describe structural relationships between concrete classes.

Functionality

The functionality of an architectural abstraction is the set of useful properties that is reused when applying the abstraction. Frameworks provide domain features as reusable code that is useful in all applications within its domain. Design patterns provide functionality varying from simple tricks to different aspects of flexibility. Metapatterns provide the means for organizing a framework as a collection of frozen and hot spots, supporting framework adaptation. Modeling patterns, like design patterns, are based on experience and offer solutions that have proven useful to common modeling problems.

Abstraction

An architectural abstraction identifies and names a composition of elements with a certain structure and functionality. This facilitates communication about designs. A framework provides a set of abstractions that are useful when discussing and describing a domain and is therefore very useful in the analysis and design phase. These abstractions are, furthermore, available as abstract classes in the implementation. Design patterns abstract and name useful designs containing a set of collaborating objects. Metapatterns abstract and name different class relationships based on two important ideas of method roles. Modeling patterns abstract and name modeling patterns of objects useful in both domain modeling (facilitating communication about a domain) and system design.

Reuse

An architectural abstraction can be applied multiple times, requiring different levels of customization and adaptation. Frameworks can be applied in order to build similar applications. When using a framework, one reuses analysis and design information as well as implementation. The designs described by all three pattern approaches must be adapted and translated in a creative process when using the patterns. Current pattern approaches do not support the formalization and automatic instantiation of their abstract designs. Design patterns and metapatterns facilitate the reuse of domain-independent abstract designs involving configurations of classes. Modeling patterns facilitate reuse of generalized object structures.

Development

Development denotes the process of creating an architectural abstraction. Architectural abstractions are conceived from some artifact. The architectural abstraction can be formed in the process of developing an artifact in order to fulfill a set of requirements. The architectural abstraction can also be conceived from an existing artifact, possibly from another context.

Application

Application denotes the process of using architectural abstractions in the development of software artifacts. Different categories of architectural abstractions span different combinations of analysis-, design-, and implementation-focused work. Frameworks span all three areas of work; modeling patterns span analysis and design; design patterns span design and implementation; metapatterns span only the implementation work.

2.6 References

[Alexander 1977] Alexander, C., S. Ishikawa, M. Silverstein, M. Jacobson, I. Fiksdahl-King, and S. Angel. *A Pattern Language*. England: Oxford University Press, 1977.

[Alexander 1979] Alexander, C. *The Timeless Way of Building*. England: Oxford University Press, 1979.

[Beck 1997] Beck, K. *Smalltalk Best Practices Patterns*. Upper Saddle River, NJ: Prentice Hall, 1997.

[Beck-Johnson 1994] Beck, K., and R.E. Johnson. Patterns generate architecture. *Proceedings of European Conference on Object-Oriented Programming* (ECOOP 1994), Bologna, Italy, July 1994.

[Buschmann 1996] Buschmann, F., R. Meunier, H. Rohnert, P. Sommerlad, and M. Stal. *Pattern-Oriented Software Architecture: A System of Patterns*. New York: John Wiley & Sons, 1996.

[Coad 1992] Coad, P. Object-oriented patterns. *Communications of the ACM* 35(9), September 1992.

[Coad 1995] Coad, P., D. North, and M. Mayfield. *Object Models: Strategies, Patterns, and Applications.* Upper Saddle River, NJ: Prentice Hall, 1995.

[Coplien 1992] Coplien, James O.. *Advanced C++ Programming Styles and Idioms.* Reading, MA: Addison-Wesley, 1992.

[Deutsch 1989] Deutsch, L.P. Design reuse and frameworks in the Smalltalk-80 system. In *Software Reusability, Volume II: Applications and Experiences,* pp. 57–71, Ted J. Biggerstaff and Alan J. Perlis, editors. Reading, MA: Addison-Wesley, 1989.

[Fayad-Schmidt 1997] Fayad, M., and D.C. Schmidt. Object-oriented application frameworks. *Communications of the ACM,* 40 (10), October 1997.

[Fowler 1997] Fowler, M. *Analysis Patterns: Reusable Object Models.* Reading, MA: Addison-Wesley, 1997.

[Gamma 1995] Gamma, E., R. Helm, R.E. Johnson, and J. Vlissides. *Design Patterns: Elements of Reusable Object-Oriented Software.* Reading, MA: Addison-Wesley, 1995.

[Jacobson 1997] Jacobsen, E.E., B.B. Kristensen, and P. Nowack. Characterizing patterns in framework development. *Proceedings of International Conference on Technology of Object-Oriented Languages and Systems* (TOOLS PACIFIC 1997), Melbourne, Australia, 1997.

[Jacobson-Nowack 1996] Jacobsen, E.E., and P. Nowack. Patterns and frameworks: Elements of architecture. Master's thesis, Aalborg University, Denmark, 1996.

[Johnson 1992] Johnson, R.E. Documenting frameworks using pattern languages. *Proceedings of Conference on Object-Oriented Programs, Systems, Languages and Applications* (OOPSLA 1992), Vancouver, British Columbia, October 1992, 63-76.

[Johnson-Foote 1988] Johnson, R.E., and B. Foote. Designing reusable classes. *Journal of Object-Oriented Programming* 2(1), January-February 1988.

[Kristensen 1996] Kristensen, B.B. Architectural abstractions and language mechanisms. *Proceedings of the Asia Pacific Software Engineering Conference 1996,* Seoul, Korea, 1996.

[Mattsson 1999] Mattsson, M., J. Bosch, and M.E. Fayad. Framework integration: Problems, causes, and solutions. Accepted for publication to *Communications of the ACM,* 1999.

[Pree 1995] Pree, W. *Design Patterns for Object-Oriented Software Development.* Reading, MA: Addison-Wesley, 1995.

[Schmidt-Fayad 1996] Schmidt. D.C., M.E. Fayad, and R.E. Johnson. Software patterns. *Communications of the ACM,* 39 (10), October 1996.

[Shaw-Garlan 1996] Shaw, M., and D. Garlan. *Software Architecture: Perspectives on an Emerging Discipline.* Upper Saddle River, NJ: Prentice Hall, 1996.

2.7 Review Questions

1. Describe the four characteristic aspects of an architectural abstraction.

2. Characterize frameworks as architectural abstractions by giving examples of the four characteristics.

3. Describe the development of an architectural abstraction in general. Give examples using patterns and frameworks.

4. Describe the application of an architectural abstraction in general. Give examples using patterns and frameworks.

5. What is meant by a framework's domain features?

6. What is meant by a framework's structural characteristics?

7. What is a template method? What is a hook method?

8. Describe whitebox and blackbox reuse of frameworks.

9. Describe the concept of inversion of control.

2.8 Problem Set

1. Compare and contrast patterns and frameworks. How are frameworks and patterns related?

2. Compare and contrast design patterns, metapatterns, and modeling patterns. How are the patterns related?

3. Implement two different instances of the Observer design pattern by applying the 1:n connection metapattern and the 1:n recursive unification metapattern, respectively. Discuss and evaluate the two implementations.

4. Compare and contrast the concepts of Alexandrian patterns and architectural abstractions.

CHAPTER 3

Framework Problems and Experiences

Reuse of software has been a goal in software engineering for almost as long as the existence of the field itself. Several research efforts have aimed at providing reuse. During the 1970s, the basics of module-based programming were defined and software engineers understood that modules could be used as reusable components in new systems. Modules, however, only provided as-is reuse, and adaptation of modules had to be done either by editing the code or by importing the component and changing those aspects unsuitable for the system at hand. During the 1980s, the object-oriented languages increased in popularity, since their proponents claimed increased reuse of object-oriented code through inheritance. Inheritance, different from importing or wrapping, provides a much more powerful means for adapting code.

However, all these efforts only provided reuse at the level of individual, often small-scale, components that could be used as the building blocks of new applications. The much harder problem of reuse at the level of large components that may make up the larger part of a system, and of which many aspects can be adapted, was not addressed by the object-oriented paradigm in itself. This understanding led to the development of object-oriented frameworks (large, abstract applications in a particular domain that can be tailored for individual applications). A framework consists of a large structure that can be reused as a whole for the construction of a new system.

Since its conception at the end of the 1980s, the appealing concept of object-oriented frameworks has attracted attention from many researchers and software engineers. Frameworks have been defined for a large variety of domains, such as user interfaces and operating systems within the computer science domain and financial systems, fire-alarm systems, and process control systems within particular application domains.

Large research and development projects were started within software development companies, but also at universities and even at the governmental level. For instance, the European Union–sponsored Esprit project REBOOT [Karlsson 1995] had a considerable impact on the object-oriented thinking and development in the organizations involved in the project and later caused the development of a number of object-oriented frameworks, for example, see [Dagermo-Knutsson 1996].

In addition to the intuitive appeal of the framework concept and its simplicity from an abstract perspective, experience has shown that framework projects can indeed result in increased reusability and decreased development effort; see, for example, [Moser-Nierstrasz 1996]. However, next to the advantages related to object-oriented frameworks, there exist problems and difficulties that do not appear before actual use in real projects. The authors of this chapter have been involved in the design, maintenance, and usage of a number of object-oriented frameworks. During these framework-related projects several obstacles were identified that complicated the use of frameworks or diminished their benefits.

The topic of this chapter is an overview and discussion of the obstacles identified during these framework projects. The obstacles have been organized into four categories. The first category, framework development, describes issues related to the initial framework design, in other words, the framework until it is released and used in the first real application. The second category is related to the instantiation of a framework and application development based on a framework. Here, issues such as verification, testing, and debugging are discussed. The composition of multiple frameworks into an application or system and the composition of legacy code with a framework is the third category of concern. The final category is concerned with the evolution of a framework over time, starting with the initial framework design and continuing with the subsequent framework versions.

This chapter provides a solid analysis of obstacles in object-oriented framework technology. It presents a large collection of the most relevant problems and provides a categorization of these obstacles. This chapter is of relevance to practitioners who make use of frameworks or design them, as well as to researchers, since it may provide topics to be addressed in future research efforts.

The remainder of this chapter is organized as follows. The next section describes the history of object-oriented frameworks and defines a consistent terminology. Subsequently, *Section 3.2* discusses some examples of object-oriented frameworks in which one or more of the authors were involved, either as designers or as users. *Section 3.3* discusses the obstacles in object-oriented framework development and usage that were identified, organized in the four aforementioned categories. *Section 3.4* summarizes the chapter.

3.1 Object-Oriented Frameworks

Although object-oriented frameworks present a well-known concept in the reuse community, no widely accepted terminology is available. After discussing a brief history of object-oriented frameworks, this section presents the definitions used in the remainder of the chapter.

3.1.1 History of Frameworks

Early examples of the framework concept can be found in literature that has its origins in the Smalltalk environment, such as [Goldberg-Robson 1989] and Apple Inc. [Schmucker 1986]. The Smalltalk-80 user interface framework, Model-View-Controller (MVC), was perhaps the first widely used framework. Apple Inc. developed the MacApp user interface framework, which was designed for supporting the implementation of Macintosh applications. Frameworks attained more interest when the Inter-Views [Linton 1989] and ET++ [Weinand 1989] user interface frameworks were developed and became available. Frameworks are not limited to user interface frameworks but have been defined for many other domains as well, such as operating systems [Russo 1990] and fire alarm systems [Molin 1996b, Molin-Ohlsson 1996]. With the formation of Taligent in 1992, frameworks attained interest in larger communities. Taligent set out to develop a completely object-oriented operating system based on the framework concept. The company delivered a set of tools for rapid application development under the name CommonPoint that consists of more than a hundred object-oriented frameworks [Andert 1994, Cotter-Potel 1995]. The Taligent approach made a shift in focus to many fine-grained integrated frameworks and away from large monolithic frameworks.

Many object-oriented frameworks exist that capture a domain well, but relatively little work has been done on general framework issues such as methods for framework usage and testing of frameworks. Regarding documentation, patterns have been used for documentation of frameworks [Huni 1995; Johnson 1992] and for describing the rationale behind design decisions for a framework [Beck-Johnson 1994]. Other interesting work of a general framework nature is that concerning the restructuring (refactoring) of frameworks. Since frameworks often undergo several iterations before even the first version is released, the framework design and code change frequently. In [Opdyke 1992], a set of behavior-preserving transformations—refactorings—are defined that help to remove multiple copies of similar code without changing the behavior. Refactoring can be used for restructuring inheritance hierarchies and component hierarchies [Johnson-Opdyke 1993].

[Roberts-Johnson 1996] describe the evolution of a framework as starting from a whitebox framework, a framework that is reused mostly by subclassing, and developing into a blackbox framework, a framework that mostly is reused through parameterization. The evolution is presented as a pattern language describing the process from the initial design of a framework as a whitebox framework to a blackbox framework. The resulting blackbox framework has an associated visual builder that will generate the application's code. The visual builder allows the software engineer to connect the framework objects and activate them. In addition, the builder supports the specification of the behavior of application-specific objects.

3.1.2 Definition of Concepts

Most authors agree that an object-oriented framework is a reusable software architecture comprising both design and code, but no generally accepted definition of a framework and its constituent parts exists. Probably the most referenced definition of a framework is found in [Johnson-Foote 1988]:

A framework is a set of classes that embodies an abstract design for solutions to a family of related problems.

In other words, a framework is a partial design and implementation for an application in a given problem domain. When discussing the framework concept, terminological difficulties may arise due to the fact that a common framework definition does not exist and because it is difficult to distinguish between framework-specific and application-specific aspects. In the remainder of the chapter, the following concepts are used: core framework design, framework internal increment, application-specific increment, object-oriented framework, and application. For more debate about the framework definition, please refer to Chapter 1 and [Fayad-Hamu 1999; Fayad-Schmidt 1997].

The *core framework design* comprises both abstract and concrete classes in the domain. The concrete classes in the framework are intended to be invisible to the framework user (for example, a basic data storage class). An abstract class is either intended to be invisible to the *framework user* or intended to be subclassed by the framework user. The latter classes are also referred to as *hot spots* [Pree 1994]. The core framework design describes the typical software architecture for applications in the domain.

However, the core framework design has to be accompanied by additional classes to be more usable. These additional classes form a number of class libraries, referred to as *framework internal increments*, to avoid confusion with the more general class library concept. These internal increments consist of classes that capture common implementations of the core framework design. Two common categories of internal increments that may be associated with a core framework design are the following:

Subclasses representing common realizations of the concepts captured by the superclasses. For example, an abstract superclass Device may have a number of concrete subclasses that represent real-world devices commonly used in the domain captured by the framework.

A collection of (sub)classes representing the specifications for a complete instantiation of the framework in a particular context. For example, a graphical user interface framework may provide a collection of classes for a framework instantiation in the context provided by Windows 95.

At the object level we talk about the *core implementation*, which comprises the objects belonging to the classes in the *core framework design* and *increment implementation*, which consists of the objects belonging to the classes defined in the *internal increments*. Thus, an *object-oriented framework* consists of a core framework design and its associated internal increments (if any) with accompanying implementations. Different from [Roberts-Johnson 1996], where the distinction between the framework and a component library is made, our interpretation of a framework includes class libraries.

Some authors categorize frameworks into *whitebox* and *blackbox* frameworks (for example, [Johnson-Foote 1988]), or *calling* and *called* frameworks (for example, [Sparks 1996]). In a whitebox (inheritance-based) framework, the framework user is supposed to customize the framework behavior through subclassing of framework classes. As identified by [Roberts-Johnson 1996], a framework often is inheritance-based in the beginning of its life cycle, since the application domain is not sufficiently well understood to make it possible to parameterize the behavior. A blackbox (parameterized) framework is based on composition. The behavior of the framework is customized by using different combinations of classes. A parameterized framework requires deep understanding of the stable and flexible aspects of the domain. Due to its predefined flexibility, a blackbox framework is often more rigid in the domain it supports. A calling framework is an active entity, proactively invoking other parts of the application, whereas a called framework is a passive entity that can be invoked by other parts of the application. However, in practice, no framework is a pure whitebox or blackbox framework or a pure calling or called framework. In general, a framework has parts that can be parameterized and parts that need to be customized through subclassing. Also, virtually each framework is called by some part of the application and calls some (other) part of the application.

An *application* is composed of one or more core framework designs, each framework's internal increments (if any), and an application-specific increment, comprising application-specific classes and objects. The application may reuse only parts of the object-oriented framework or it may require adaptation of the core framework design and the internal increments for achieving its requirements.

The presence of reusable frameworks influences the development process for the application. The following phases are identifiable in framework-centered software development:

The framework development phase. This phase, often the most effort-consuming, is aimed at producing a reusable design in a domain. Major results of this phase are the domain analysis model, a core framework design, and a number of framework internal increments, as depicted in Table 3.1. The framework development phase is described in more detail in *Section 3.3.1.*

The framework usage phase. This phase is sometimes also referred to as the *framework instantiation phase* or the *application development phase*. The main result of this phase is an application developed reusing one or more frameworks. Here, the framework user must include the core framework designs or part of them, depending on the application requirements. After the application design is finished, the software engineer has to decide which internal increments to include. For those parts of the application design not covered by reusable classes, new classes need to be developed to fulfill the actual application requirements. We refer to these new classes as the *application-specific increment*. A model for framework usage is outlined in *Section 3.3.2,* and the problem of composing frameworks is further discussed in *Section 3.3.3.*

The framework evolution and maintenance phase. This phase, as all software, will be subject to change. Causes for these changes can be errors reported from shipped applications, identification of new abstractions due to changes in the problem domain, changes in the business domain, and so on. These kinds of issues will be discussed in *Section 3.2.4.*

3.2 Examples of Application Frameworks

The problems and lessons learned that are presented in the next section are based on extensive experience with industry-strength object-oriented frameworks. In this section,

Table 3.1 Framework Development Activities, Software Engineer Roles, and Artifacts

ACTIVITY	THE SOFTWARE ENGINEER'S ROLE	SOFTWARE ARTIFACTS INVOLVED
Framework development	Framework developer	Core framework design Framework internal increments
Framework usage[1]	Framework user[2]	Core framework design Framework internal increments Application-specific increment
Framework maintenance and evolution	Framework maintainer	Core framework design Framework increments

[1]Framework usage is sometimes referred to as *framework instantiation* or *application development*.
[2]By some, the framework user is denoted as *framework reuser* or *application developer*.

the five most prominent frameworks are briefly presented. Several of the frameworks are used in product development, whereas others have not reached that stage yet.

3.2.1 Fire Alarm Systems

TeleLarm AB, a Swedish security company, develops and markets a family of fire alarm systems ranging from small office systems to large distributed systems for multi-building plants. An object-oriented framework was designed as a part of a major architectural redesign effort. The framework provides abstract classes for devices and communication drivers, as well as application abstractions such as input points and output points representing sensors and actuators. System status is represented by a set of deviations that are available on all nodes in the distributed system. The notion of periodic objects is introduced, giving the system large-grain concurrency without the problems associated with asynchronous fine-grain concurrency. Two production instantiations from the framework have been released so far. For more information, refer to [Molin 1996a; Molin-Ohlsson 1996].

3.2.2 Measurement Systems

In cooperation with EC-Gruppen, we were involved in the design of a framework for measurement systems. Measurement systems are systems that are located at the beginning or end of production lines to measure some selected features of production items. The hardware of a measurement system consists of a trigger, one or more sensors, and one or more actuators. The framework for the software has software representations for these parts, the measurement item, and an abstract factory for generating new measurement item objects. A typical measurement cycle for a product starts with the trigger detecting the item and notifying the abstract factory. In response, the abstract factory creates a measurement item and activates it. The measurement item contains a measurement strategy and an actuation strategy and uses them first to read the relevant data from the sensors, then to compare this data with the ideal values, and subsequently to activate the actuators when necessary to remove or mark the product if it did not fulfill the requirements. Refer to [Bosch 1999] for a more detailed description of the framework.

3.2.3 Gateway Billing Systems

Ericsson Software Technology AB started to develop the billing gateway framework as an experiment and it is now used for developing products within the company. The billing gateway framework acts as a mediation device in telecommunication management networks between the network elements generating billing information and the billing systems responsible for charging customers. The framework supports several network communications protocols, both for inbound and for outbound communication. The gateway provides services for processing the billing information (for example, conversion from different billing information formats), filtering of billing information, and content-sensitive distribution of the information. The performance of applications developed based on the framework is of great importance and multithreading is used heavily. Refer to [Lundberg 1996] for a more detailed overview of these issues.

3.2.4 Resource Allocation

The resource allocation framework was part of a large student project (10,000 hours) in cooperation with Ericsson Software Technology AB as a prototype development. The project goal was to develop a framework for resource allocation systems, since a need to develop several similar systems in the domain was identified by the customer. The framework consists of three subframeworks—the core resource allocation framework and two supporting frameworks—handling user interface and persistence through relational databases, respectively. The main part of the generic behavior consists of the general scheme of allocations, in other words, one or several resources could be allocated by one allocator represented by an allocation. The framework user specifies the concrete resources for the application and implements some specific behavior such as editing, storing, and displaying. The framework handles the general business rules, for example, not allowing a resource to be allocated by more than one allocator for overlapping time periods.

3.2.5 Process Operation

In cooperation with researchers from a chemical technology department, one of the authors was involved in the definition of an object-oriented framework for process operation in chemical plants. The goal of the framework was to provide a general frame of reference for all (most) activities and entities in a chemical plant, including sales, planning, process operation, and maintenance. The framework consists of seven concept hierarchies organized into three categories: real-world, coordination, and model structures. The real-world structures are the order structure, material structure, and equipment structure. The model structures are the operation step structure, instrumentation structure, and control structure. The only coordination structure is the equipment coordination structure. These structures describe a considerable part of the domain knowledge for chemical plants as available in the field of chemical technology.

For a concrete plant, the structure hierarchies have to be instantiated based on the actual equipment, orders, materials, and so forth, available in the plant. Due to the size of the framework, parts of it have been instantiated, rather than the complete framework. One experiment has been performed on a batch process application. We refer to [Betlem 1995] for more details concerning the framework.

3.3 Problems and Experiences

As described earlier, three phases can be identified in framework-centered software development: framework development, framework usage, and framework evolution. Each phase is discussed in the subsequent sections. Framework usage, being the most extensive phase, is discussed in two sections, that is, framework usage and framework composition. Framework composition is treated separately since it leads to a number of specific problems.

3.3.1 Framework Development

The development of a framework is somewhat different from the development of a standard application. The important distinction is that the framework has to cover all relevant concepts in a domain, whereas an application is concerned only with those concepts mentioned in the application requirements. To set the context for the problems experienced and identified in framework development, we outline the following activities as parts of a simple framework development model:

Domain analysis. Aims at describing the domain that is to be covered by the framework. To capture the requirements and identification of concepts, the developer may refer to previously developed applications in the domain, to domain experts, and to existing standards for the domain. The result of the activity is a domain analysis model, containing the requirements of the domain, the domain concepts, and the relations between those concepts [Schäfer 1994].

Architectural design. Takes the domain analysis model as input. The designer has to decide on a suitable architectural style to underlie the framework. Based on the selected style, among other considerations, the top level of the framework is designed. Examples of architectural styles or patterns can be found in [Shaw-Garlan 1996] and [Buschmann 1996].

Framework design. The stage in which the top-level framework design is refined and additional classes are designed. Results from this activity are the functionality scope given by the framework design, the framework's reuse interface (similar to the *external framework interface* described in [Deutsch 1989]), design rules based on architectural decisions that must be obeyed, and a design history document describing the design problems encountered and the solutions selected, with an argumentation.

Framework implementation. Concerned with the coding of the abstract and concrete framework classes.

Framework testing. Performed to determine whether the framework provides the intended functionality, but also to evaluate the usability of the framework. It is, however, far from trivial to decide whether an entity is usable or not. [Johnson-Russo 1991] conclude that the only way to find out if software is reusable is to reuse it. For frameworks, this requires the development of applications that use the framework.

To evaluate the usability of the framework, the *test application generation* activity is concerned with the development of test applications based on the framework. Depending on the kind of application, the developer can test different aspects of the framework. Based on the developed applications, *application testing* aims at deciding whether the framework needs to be redesigned or that it is sufficiently mature for release.

Documentation. One of the most important activities in framework development, although its importance is not always recognized. Without a clear, complete, and correct documentation that describes how to use the framework, a user manual, and a design document that describes how the framework works, the framework will be nearly impossible to use by software engineers not involved in the framework design.

The remainder of this section discusses a number of problems encountered during framework development. These problems are related to the domain scope, framework documentation, business models for framework domains, and framework development, as well as to framework testing and releasing.

Domain Scope

When deciding to develop a framework for a particular domain, there is the problem of determining the right size for the domain. On one hand, if the domain is too large, the development team does not have enough experience from the enlarged domain. In addition, it may be difficult to demonstrate the usefulness and applicability of a large domain framework. Also, the (financial) investment in a large framework may be so high that it becomes very difficult to obtain the necessary resources. Finally, the duration of the project may be such that the intended reuse benefits cannot be achieved in a reasonable amount of time.

On the other hand, a smaller domain uses the known experiences in a much more efficient way. One problem is, however, that the resulting framework tends to be sensitive to domain changes. For instance, with a narrow framework, an application may easily expand over the framework boundaries, requiring more application-specific changes to the framework in order to be useful than when the framework would have covered the complete application.

From the preceding, one can deduce that defining the scope of the domain is a decision that must be carefully balanced. One problem is that, because the future is unpredictable, it is very difficult to set clear boundaries for the framework. A second problem is that it is a very natural, human tendency to increase the size of the framework during (especially early) design because a framework that includes yet another aspect seems more useful than one that lacks that aspect (see, for example, [Bosch 1999]).

In addition to these problems, selecting the right domain is a difficult issue. A framework must not be so general that it constitutes overkill for the intended application [Fayad-Hamu 1999]. A one-size-fits-all approach introduces unnecessary risk. The most suitable frameworks for a particular domain will reflect a mature, yet narrow, focus on a particular problem or group of problems [Fayad-Hamu 1999].

Framework Documentation

The purpose of framework documentation is twofold. First, information about the framework design and other related information need to be communicated during the framework development. Second, information on how to use the framework needs to be transmitted to the framework user.

In the first case, it is convenient to rely on informal communication to spread the knowledge about the developed framework. The often small design group uses different ad hoc techniques to exchange information among the individuals in the team. The problem is that these techniques are not very efficient and do not always assure that the correct information is spread.

The second case is more important, since the informal information channels are not available and all information has to be communicated in a way that is possible to deliver with the framework. The current way to do this is by means of different kinds of manuals, using different media. The documentation is usually ad hoc, making it hard to understand and compare. [Johnson 1992] argues that framework documentation should contain the purpose of the framework, information on how to use the framework, the purpose of the application examples, and the actual design of the framework.

For a framework, whitebox or blackbox, users need to understand the underlying principles or basic architecture of the framework. Otherwise, detailed rules and constraints defined by the framework developers make no sense and the framework will probably not be used as intended. Examples of these rules and constraints are cardinality of framework objects, creation and destruction of static and dynamic framework objects, instantiation order, synchronization, and performance issues. These rules and constraints are often implicitly hidden or missing in existing documentation, and they need to be elucidated and documented. The problem is how to convey this information in a concise form to framework users.

A number of methods have been proposed for documenting frameworks. A first example is the cookbook approach, such as in [Krasner-Pope 1988] and [Apple 1989], which are example based, and the metapatterns approach proposed by [Pree 1994]. The pattern approaches provide a second example, in which patterns are used to describe the architecture of the framework [Beck-Johnson 1994; Huni 1995] or the use of the framework [Johnson 1992; Lajoie-Keller 1994]. Finally, a framework description language (FDL) [Wilson-Wilson 1993] can be used that more formally describes, for example, what classes to override and subclass. All approaches address some of the documentation needs, but, we believe, no approach covers all the aforementioned needs for framework documentation. Most of these methods address the issues of purpose, how to use the framework, and the purpose of the example application, but none of these methods address how to communicate the framework design to the user.

There are two more serious problems with framework documentation:

The cost of providing suitable framework documentation is very high. Defining and documenting application frameworks is neither quick nor cheap. The costs of documenting application frameworks can be a high risk. However, it is impossible to extend or customize application frameworks or build new applications without using well-documented frameworks. Defining suitable methods for framework documentation is an important first step. We have found that combining several documentation approaches, such as patterns, hooks, hot spots, examples, and architectural illustrations, was very effective.

A framework documentation standard doesn't exist. Mapping framework documentation approaches to software documentation standards can be difficult. The difficulty is usually traced to the term *standard,* implying that it is "applicable for all frameworks except mine" [Fayad-Laitinen 1998].

Business Models

Even though it may be feasible from a technological perspective to develop a framework for a particular domain, it is not necessarily advantageous from a business perspective. That is, the investments necessary for the framework development may be larger than the benefits in terms of reduced development effort for applications built using the framework. The return on investment from a developed framework may come from selling the framework to other companies, but it often, to a large extent, relies on future savings in development effort within the company itself, such as higher software quality and shorter lead times. One of the main problems for the management of software development organizations or departments is that, to the best of our knowledge, no reliable business models for framework development exist.

A formulation of a business model is given by [Kihl-Ströberg 1995], but this has never been tested in an industrial setting. Other general reuse business models have been proposed by several authors, but none satisfy all relevant requirements as shown in [Lim 1996]. Since no reliable investment models exist, decisions on framework development are often based on gut feeling, with the downside that many framework designs never come to fruition since the technical staff is unable to convince management that framework development would be economically viable.

Another major problem is related to the business culture issues. Business culture can be categorized into several nested and difficult cultures. [Fayad-Laitinen 1998] discuss several tough issues for transition management to object-oriented technology that maps well to application framework and component-based technology. They also state that this culture change will be one of the hardest and longest lasting parts of the transition to a new technology. Once the initial transition is complete, the change will be a continuing part of the business [Fayad-Laitinen 1998].

Framework Development Methods

Existing development methods do not sufficiently support development of frameworks. Framework design introduces some new concepts that need to be covered by the methods, and some existing concepts need much more emphasis. The domain analysis presents problems unlike those of normal application development, for example, behavior and attributes are very likely to change in several cases. The analysis of such behavior and attributes needs to be emphasized in the development model, since it is the nature of frameworks to provide reusable design and implementation that cover the variations—that is, hot spots—in the domain.

During development of the framework, an architecture must be selected or developed. The criteria for a framework architecture are dependent on the domain and the domain variations. The architecture must provide solutions to problems in the domain without blocking possible variations or different solutions to other domain problems. During framework architecture design, decisions need to be made on whether some parts of the framework should be designed as a subframework or if everything should be designed as a single, monolithic framework. Also, interoperability requirements need to be established, for example, whether the framework should cooperate with other frameworks, such as user interface frameworks or persistence frameworks.

In addition to the existing object-oriented design methods [Booch 1994; Jacobson 1992; Rumbaugh 1991], which most often support only inheritance, aggregation, and associations, more emphasis is needed for abstract classes, dynamic binding, type parameterization, hot spots and pre- and postconditions. Abstract classes and dynamic binding represent the way to define and implement abstract behavior that is not emphasized in existing design models. Type parameterization needs support in the methods since this is another useful way of supplying predefined abstract behavior that the framework user then uses by supplying the application-specific parts as parameters. Hot spots are needed to show where the intended framework extensions or application specifics go, and support in the design methods for expressing and designing these is very important. Pre- and postconditions provide the framework developer with the possibility of specifying the restrictions for usage of parts of the framework.

There are other serious issues related to framework development methods:

Application frameworks should be stable over time. Framework stability over time is an important issue. A good framework reflects the concise understanding of the enduring qualities of the business through enduring business themes (EBTs; see Sidebar 6 and [Fayad-Hamu 1999]). EBTs capture abstractions that do not change over time.

Business objects and workflow management and the issue of stability must be considered. The workflow management metaphor provides the necessary modeling capabilities for constructing enduring business processes (EBPs) [Fayad-Hamu 1999] or workflows. Well-designed frameworks should capture the workflows that do not change over time [Fayad-Hamu 1999].

Achieving portability is not a trivial task. Platform independence and portability ensure that the framework supports all the platforms in a given organization. Failing to provide platform independence will diminish the scope of use and acceptance of the framework [Fayad-Hamu 1999].

Verifying Abstract Behavior

When developing a framework, the result must be verified. The current practice is to develop test applications using the framework and then test the resulting application.

In this way most of the core framework design and the framework internal increments can be tested using conventional methods. However, the versatility of the framework cannot be tested by only one application, especially if the application is for test purposes only. Since a framework can be used in many different, unknown ways, it may simply not be feasible to test all relevant aspects of the framework.

Furthermore, testing the framework for errors using traditional methods, such as executing parts of the code in well-defined cases, will not work for the whole framework—for example, using the core framework design. At best, parts of the framework can be tested this way, but since the framework relies on parts implemented by the users it is not possible to completely test the framework before it is released. This is also referred to as the problem of verifying abstract behavior. Standard testing procedure does not allow for testing of abstract implementations, such as abstract base classes.

Framework Release Problem

Releasing a framework for application development has to be based on some release criteria. The problem is to define and ensure these criteria for the framework. The framework must be reusable, reasonably stable within the domain, and well documented. As for reusability, several authors have addressed this issue and in [Poulin 1994] several of the proposed approaches are compared. The conclusion of the research was that no general reusability metrics exist. The problem of determining the stability within the domain is twofold. First, the domain is not stable in itself, but evolves constantly. Second, the issue of domain scope and boundaries, discussed earlier in this section, also complicates the decision on framework release. Deciding whether the framework is sufficiently well documented is hard, since no generally accepted documentation method exists that covers all aspects of the framework, but also because it is difficult to determine whether the documentation is understandable for the intended users.

Releasing an immature framework may have severe consequences in the maintenance and usage of the framework and the instantiated applications.

3.3.2 Framework Usage

Although we have seen that it often is feasible to produce complex applications based on a framework with rather modest development effort, we have also experienced a number of problems associated with the usage of a framework. Before discussing these problems, we believe it is important to provide an outline of how a framework is used. The main purpose of this development method is to relate problems to various activities during the development of an application based on a framework. The method is an adaptation of [Mattsson 1996] and consists of the following activities:

- *Requirements analysis* aims at collecting and analyzing the requirements of the application that is to be built using one or more framework(s).
- Based on the results from the requirements of the analysis, a *conceptual architecture* for the application is defined. This includes the association of functionality

to components, the specification of the relationships between them, and the organization of collaboration between them.

- Based on the application architecture, one or more frameworks are selected based on the functionality to be offered by the application as well as the non-functional requirements. If more than one framework is selected, the software engineer may experience a number of framework composition problems. (These problems are the subject of the next section.)

- When it is decided what framework(s) to reuse, the developer can deduce the application specific that needs to be defined; in other words, the developer specifies the required *application-specific increments* (ASIs).

- After the specification of the ASIs, they need to be *designed* and *implemented*. During these activities, it is crucial to conform to the design rules stated in the framework documentation.

- Before the ASIs and the framework are put together into the final application, the *ASIs* need to be *tested* individually to simplify debugging and fault analysis in the resulting application.

- Finally, the complete application is verified and tested according to the application's original requirements.

The remainder of this section discusses the problems that we identified and experienced during framework-based application development. The problems are related to framework training and learning, the management of the development process, applicability, estimations, understanding, verification, and debugging.

Training and Learning

Learning to use an object-oriented framework effectively can take long time due to the complexity of the framework. Experiences from the use of commercial GUI frameworks such as Microsoft Foundation Classes (MFCs) and MacApp indicate that it takes 6 to 12 months to be productive with the framework [Fayad-Schmidt 1997]. A major reason for this is that a framework is most useful for a developer who understands it in detail. For an in-house developed framework, the learning time can be reduced if one of the framework developers is participating in the application development project and can give hands-on mentoring to the other project members.

Two of the most common training approaches to learning a framework are mentoring and training courses. An advantage with mentoring is that the mentor, one of the framework developers or an experienced user of the framework, is easily available most of the time and can provide information about how to use the framework for particular tasks. However, the problem with the mentor approach is that that kind of highly skilled staff almost always is needed in other projects of higher priority. Regarding training courses, it is extremely important that the application developers be taught concrete application examples, beginning with simple applications and continuing with more and more complex applications that make use of more powerful framework concepts—in other words, a kind of iterative and incremental approach that explains some of the framework's possibilities, uses the framework, explains a little more, uses the framework again, and so on. Thus, this approach illustrates the different possibilities with the framework. A useful approach to organizing the training material is to first describe how to use the framework, to make the framework useful quickly, and not to describe the detailed design of the framework from the beginning. This avoids bothering the framework user with a lot of unnecessary detailed information that is not immediately required for using the framework.

Managing the Development Process

The most important problem of framework-based application development is how to manage the application development process. Development processes for standard applications are well known and have undergone an evolution from ad hoc approaches and waterfall methods to more elaborate models such as spiral models and evolutionary models. We believe that the current state of the art in framework-based application development is still in the ad hoc stage, where an exploratory style of development is used.

The traditional approach for a development process is to start with a specification or description of the work to be done. That specification is used as a base for estimating costs and resources and is also used as an input to design, implementation, and testing. This information is, of course, also needed when a framework-based application is developed, but in the framework case it is much more difficult to explicitly write such a specification. Examples include specifying the new classes that must be implemented and the classes that require adaptation by subclassing.

Applicability of the Framework

One initial difficulty is to understand the intended domain of the framework and its appropriateness for the application under consideration. The challenge here is to be able to make the choice of applying the framework for the application, modifying the framework, if that is an option, or constructing the application from scratch. From an abstract perspective, the question is whether the application matches the domain of the framework. In practice, the question of domain can be rather complex and contains several dimensions. The most obvious dimension of a domain is the functional dimension that corresponds to the way people generally interpret the domain. This dimension defines the functional boundaries of the domain. Another dimension is the underlying hardware architecture. This dimension addresses such aspects as multiprocessor systems versus single processor systems or distribution aspects. A third dimension is the interoperability, under which aspects such as coexistence with other applications are discussed. Issues in this dimension are, for example, whether a particular database engine can or must be used or whether there are any restrictions on the graphical user interface. A fourth dimension incorporates nonfunctional aspects such as performance, fault-tolerance, and capacity. Examples are a framework intended for batch processing and not for real-time data processing and a framework that has an upper limit on the number of items it can handle.

The problem here is to be able to determine, with a reasonable degree of confidence, whether a specific application can be built based on a specific framework and what resources are needed to implement the application-specific increment. It is clear that all dimensions of the domain must be examined. The problem is even more complex if the framework does not support a certain aspect of the application. In that case, the problem is to determine whether it is possible to use the framework at all and, second, to determine the amount of work needed to implement the required application.

Estimations of the Increment

The problem of using frameworks compared to traditional application development is that most of the time spent in such a project could well be spent on understanding the framework, with very little spent on actual coding. From a productivity point of view this may indicate that a framework-based application is slow compared to a traditional approach. On the other hand, complex applications can be built very fast so that real productivity is high. The consequences of traditional estimation techniques based on the number of produced lines of code is inadequate in the framework case. [Moser-Nierstrasz 1996] discuss these problems in more detail.

Another problem is the sensitivity of estimates of the amount of work required for a specific application. Our experience indicates that this is also a well-known effect of tool usage that we refer to as the *90 percent/10 percent rule*, implying that 10 percent of the development time is spent on 90 percent of the application, and 90 percent is spent on the remaining difficult 10 percent of the application. The difference depends on whether a specific feature is supported by the tool (framework). Furthermore, it can be difficult to foresee if a specific requirement is completely supported by the framework. If it is fully supported, the implementation will be fast. On the other hand, if it is not at all supported, a potential implementation can mismatch the intentions of the framework designers and, in that case, the resulting effort can be even larger than with a traditional approach. The conclusion is that the required implementation effort is very sensitive to features close to the domain boundary and the framework boundary.

There is a noteworthy catch when an estimation of the required effort is performed. For an accurate estimation, it is necessary to thoroughly investigate the framework and the application, in order to determine what needs to be done. On the other hand, such an investigation could be the major task of the application development! The same could be true even for traditional application development, but it is much more striking in the framework case.

Understanding the Framework

When a whitebox framework is used, it is necessary to understand the concepts and architectural style of the framework in order to develop applications that conform to the framework. The framework understanding may be a prerequisite for evaluating the applicability of a framework and the amount of required adaptation, and how the adaptation can be carried out. One example of such an important concept could be concurrency strategies adopted by the framework. For example, if the framework is intended for multithreading, then any adaptations must adhere to rules on resource locking and shared variable protection defined by the framework. On the other hand, if a single-thread solution is chosen, the adaptation code must conform to certain timing constraints. Other examples are dynamic memory allocation strategies where it is important that the increment follow the same strategy. Especially in real-time frameworks such as the measurement system or the fire alarm system, it is absolutely necessary that the users understand how external events are processed; otherwise, it becomes very difficult to guarantee any application response time. Many errors can be avoided and the application can be constructed more efficiently if the framework user understands these strategies and styles. One problem is how to obtain this information from, for example, the framework documentation, discussed earlier in the chapter.

An alternative that avoids the understanding approach, or serves as a complement to it, is to explicitly specify the constraints that the framework put on the application. This approach has been proposed by [Mattsson 1996; Molin 1996a].

Verification of the Application-Specific Increment

An application based on a complex framework or based on several frameworks can prove difficult to test. Therefore, it could be advisable to verify the application-specific increment beforehand. For large-scale applications, the increment should be locally certifiable; that is, it should be tested or verified locally without executing the entire application. Such verification must be based on a specification of what requirements the increment needs to fulfill. There are two aspects of verification. The first is a functional verification that verifies that the increment implements the expected behavior of the resulting application. The second aspect is the verification that the increment conforms to the architectural style and design rules imposed by the framework. The trade-off in this case is the amount of effort spent on increment verification compared to the amount of debugging time if problems are detected during the test of the complete application. In cases where straightforward application testing is not sufficient, a more formal increment verification could be useful. These problems have been investigated by [Molin 1996a] and a partial solution has been proposed that suggests verification of conformance to the framework, but not to verify the functionality provided by the increment.

Debugging the Application

Traditional debuggers have problems when debugging programs using libraries. Using single-step methods is impossible, and library calls must be skipped in some way. Normally, there is no automatic support for this distinction of code source. The debugger must manually define which part should be skipped and which routines should be followed through. In some cases, there is an exception raised in the library part, either as a result of bad usage of the library or due to a bug in the library code, and it may be difficult to determine the actual reason for the exception.

Frameworks, and especially blackbox frameworks, have the same problem as libraries. Furthermore, since frameworks often are based on the Hollywood principle, the problems are even more difficult. It can be very difficult to follow a thread of execution that mostly is buried under framework code.

One solution approach, based on the design-by-contract ideas, is to exactly define the interface between the framework and the increment as pre- and postconditions or behavioral interaction constraints [Helm 1990; Lajoie-Keller 1994; Meyer 1992]. Precondition violation causes exceptions to be raised and it can be guaranteed that the framework will never crash as a result of illegal use.

3.3.3 Framework Composition

Traditionally, object-oriented framework-based development of applications takes the approach that the application development is started from the framework and the application is constructed in terms of extensions to the framework. However, this perspective on framework-based development represents only the simplest solution. Often, a framework that is to be reused needs to be composed with other frameworks or with reusable legacy components. Composing frameworks, however, may lead to a number of problems since frameworks generally are designed based on the traditional perspective in which the framework is in full control.

This section discusses the problems related to the composition of reusable components and frameworks with an object-oriented framework. Note that we are concerned with the composition of reusable components and frameworks that were not intended to be composed during their design. This is different from the approach taken in Taligent where mutually compatible frameworks are available that are easy to compose. The composition of reused components that were not designed to work together is much more challenging and it is these kinds of problems that we discuss here.

Architectural Mismatch

The composition of two or more frameworks that seem to match at first may prove to be much more difficult than expected. The reason for that can often be found in a mismatch in the underlying framework architectures. In [Garlan 1995], this is referred to as *architectural mismatch,* in other words, the architectural styles, based on which the frameworks are designed, are different, complicating composition so much that it may be impossible to compose. [Buschmann 1996; Shaw-Garlan 1996] identify several architectural styles (or architectural patterns) that can be used to construct an application. For example, if one of the frameworks is based on a blackboard architecture and the other on a layered architecture, then the composition of the two frameworks may require either substantial amounts of glue code or the redesign of parts of one or both of the frameworks. Lately, an increasing interest in the domain of software architecture is apparent. Explicitly specifying the architectural style underlying a framework design seems to be the first step toward a solution to this problem.

Examples are the resource allocation and the gateway billing frameworks. The resource allocation framework is based on a layered architecture, the typical three-tier structure, whereas the gateway billing framework uses a pipe-filter architecture as its primary decomposition structure. A designer may want to compose the two frameworks to obtain a more flexible gateway billing system where billing applications can dynamically allocate filtering and forwarding resources. However, this will prove to be all but trivial due to the mismatch in the underlying architectural styles.

Overlap of Framework Entities

When constructing an application from reusable components, the situation may occur that two (or more) frameworks are used that, combined, cover the application requirements. In this case, a real-world entity may be represented by both frameworks—for instance, as a class—but modeled from their respective perspectives. Consequently, the representations by the frameworks may have modeled both overlapping and exclusive properties. In the application, however, the real-world entity should be modeled by a single object and the two representations should be integrated into one.

The situation is thus that two frameworks F_1 and F_2 exist that both contain representations of a real-world entity ^{r} in the form of a class C^r_{F1} and C^r_{F2}. The real-world entity has a virtually infinite set of properties P_r, of which a subset is represented by each of the framework classes, that is, $P_{C^r_{F1}} \subset P_r$ and $P_{C^r_{F2}} \subset P_r$, where $P_{C^r_{F1}} \neq P_{C^r_{F2}}$. Integrating these representations can, from a naive perspective, be done using multiple inheritance, that is, the application class C^r_A inherits from both classes C^r_{F1} and C^r_{F2}, thereby combining the properties from these classes, that is, $P_{C^r_A} = P_{C^r_{F1}} \cup P_{C^r_{F2}}$.

In practice, however, the composition of properties from the frameworks classes is not as straightforward as presented here, because the properties are not mutually independent. One can identify at least three situations where more advanced composition efforts are required.

Both framework classes represent a state property of the real-world entity but represent it in different ways. For instance, most sensors in the fire alarm framework contain a Boolean state for their value, whereas measurement systems sensors use more complex domains, for example, temperature or pressure. When these sensors are composed into an integrated sensor, this requires every state update in one class to be extended with the conversion and update code for the state in the other class.

Both framework classes represent a property of the real-world entity, but one class represents it as a state and the other class as a method. The method indirectly determines what the value of the particular property is. For instance, an actuator is available both in the fire alarm and the measurement system frameworks. In an application, the software engineer may want to compose both actuator representations into a single entity. One actuator class may store as a state whether it is currently active or not, whereas the other class may indirectly deduce this from its other state variables. In the application representation, the property representation has to be solved in such a way that reused behavior from both classes can deal with it.

The execution of an operation in one framework class requires state changes in the other framework class. Using the example of the actuator mentioned earlier, an activate message to one actuator implementation may require that the active state of the other actuator class be updated accordingly. When the software engineer combines the actuator classes from the two frameworks, this aspect of the composition has to be explicitly implemented in the glue code.

Composition of Entity Functionality

A typical example of this problem can be found in the three-tier application architecture. A software engineer constructing an application in this domain may want to compose the application from a user interface framework, a framework covering the application domain concepts, and a framework providing database functionality. A problem analogous to the one discussed in the previous section now appears. The real-world entity is now represented in the application domain framework. However, aspects of the entity have to be presented in some user interface and the entity has to be made persistent and suited for transactions. Constructing an application class by composing instances from the three frameworks or by multiply inheriting from classes in the three frameworks will not produce the desired result. State changes caused by messages to the application domain part of the resulting object will not automatically affect user interface and database functionality of the object.

In a way, the behavior from the user interface and database framework classes needs to be superimposed on the object [Bosch 1997]. However, since this type of composition is not available in object-oriented languages, the software engineer is required to extend the application domain class with behavior for notifying the user interface and database classes, for example, using the Observer design pattern [Gamma 1995]. One could argue that the application domain class should have been extended with such behavior during design, but, as mentioned earlier, most frameworks are not designed to be composed with other frameworks but to be extended with application-specific code written specifically for the application at hand.

This problem occurred in the fire alarm framework, where several entities had to be persistent and were stored in nonvolatile memory—an EEPROM. To deal with this, each entity was implemented by two objects: one application object and one persistence object. These two objects were obviously tightly coupled and had frequent interactions, because they both represented parts of one entity.

Hollywood Principle

In [Sparks 1996], the distinction is made between calling and called frameworks. Calling frameworks are the active entities in an application that call the other parts, whereas called frameworks are passive entities that can be called by other parts of the application. One of the problems when composing two calling frameworks is that both expect to be the controlling entity in the application and in control of the main event loop.

For example, both the fire alarm and the measurement system framework are calling frameworks that contain a control loop triggering the iterative framework behavior. If we would compose both frameworks in an application, the two control loops would conflict, leading to incorrect behavior. A calling framework is based on assumptions of execution, which may lead to problems of extensibility and composability. Adding calls in the control loop might be impossible since the inverse calling principle has led designers to assume total control of the execution flow, leaving no means to modify it.

One may argue that a solution could be to give each framework its own thread of control, leading to two or more independently executing control loops. Although this might work in some situations, there are at least two important drawbacks. The first is that all application objects that can be accessed by both frameworks need to be extended with synchronization code. Since a class often cannot be modularly extended with synchronization code, all reused classes must be edited to add this. A second drawback is that often one framework needs to be informed about an event that occurred in the other framework because the event has application-wide relevance. This requires that the control loops of the frameworks become much more integrated than two concurrent threads.

Integrating Legacy Components

A framework presents, among other things, a design for an application in a particular domain. Based on this design, the software engineer may construct a concrete application using framework classes, either directly or indirectly, by inheriting from them. When the framework class contains behavior only for internal framework functionality and not much of the behavior required for the application at hand, the software engineer may want to include existing (legacy) classes in the application that need to be integrated with the framework. It is, however, far from trivial to integrate a legacy class in the application, since the framework depends on the subclassing mechanism. Since the legacy component will not be a subclass of the framework class, typing conflicts result.

To integrate a legacy component, the software engineer is required to create some form of adaptation or bridging. For instance, a class could be defined, inheriting from both the framework class and the legacy class, forwarding all calls matching the framework class interface to corresponding methods in the legacy component. This problem is studied in more detail in [Lundberg-Mattsson 1996] and, as a solution, they propose the use of templates. Their solution, however, requires that the framework be designed using their approach, which is unlikely in the general case.

3.3.4 Framework Evolution and Maintenance

Development of a framework must be seen as a long-term investment and, as such, it must be treated as a product that needs to be maintained. Early in the framework development life cycle, several design iterations are often necessary. An important reason for the iteration is, according to [Johnson-Russo 1991], that a framework is supposed to be reusable and the only way to prove this is to reuse the framework and identify the shortcomings. In [Opdyke 1992], a set of behavior-preserving transformations, or refactorings, has been identified that characterizes the code and low-level design changes that may occur in the iterations. Changes or refactorings related to inheritance hierarchies [Opdyke-Johnson 1993] and component hierarchies [Johnson-Opdyke 1993] are especially of relevance for framework iteration just before releasing the first version of the framework. This iteration between the phases is very frequent and it involves a considerable amount of simple but tedious work that would benefit from tool support.

The correction of an error in the framework is not as simple as one may think. The error should, obviously, be corrected for the current application developed with the framework, but how should the error be handled in the existing applications developed with the framework? The framework development organization has to decide either to split the framework into two separate frameworks that will need to be maintained or to implement a work-around for the current application and live with the maintenance problems for the application.

As described earlier, a framework aims at representing a domain-specific architecture, but, in many cases, it is difficult to know the exact domain boundary that has to be captured. One problem is that business changes in the organization supporting the framework may require that the domain be adapted accordingly. Presently, it is hard to predict how these kinds of business domain changes affect the existing framework.

In the following sections, we discuss the problems of framework change, selection of maintenance strategies, business domain changes, and design iterations.

Framework Change

Imagine the situation in which a fault is found in an application using a framework. Where should the error be corrected? It could be either in the framework or in the application-specific code. If the error is located in the application-specific code, it will be relatively simple to correct. However, if the error is located in the framework, it may be impossible for the framework user to fix the error because of the complexity of the framework (in other words, it is difficult to understand how the framework works) or lack of access to the source code of the framework. Often, the organization has full control of the framework, including the source code, has the ability to correct the error, and does so accordingly. The application will, after the error correction, work as intended, but all existing applications using the framework have not been taken care of in this way. One may wonder whether all applications should be upgraded with the corrected version of the framework, since all are functioning correctly and the error has not (yet) caused any problems. In addition, if one decides to correct the error in the previous applications, there is a potential risk of introducing new faults in these applications. Finally, the cost of upgrading all existing applications is high.

On the first occasion that a real application based on the framework is developed, a number of problems will be found that require changes of the framework. These problems are most easily solved by direct support to the application developers from the framework team [Sparks 1996]. The framework developers then collect all the experiences from the first application and iterate the framework design once more to mature the framework.

However, the identification of errors will not stop after the first application development, and a problem is how to deal with subsequent application developments. It is infeasible to support the application team and redesign the framework over and over again, since the intended reuse benefits will then not be achieved. If problems are encountered when reusing the framework, they are the result of one of two causes. First, the domain covered by the framework is incomplete; in other words, we have failed to capture the domain in our domain analysis. Second, the application does not match the intended framework domain; in other words, we have decided to develop an application whose requirements constitute a bad fit with the domain covered by the framework. In both cases, the framework will generally be changed, forcing the organization to face the problem of selecting maintenance strategies. This is further described in the following section.

Choice of Maintenance Strategy

Given the situation that the framework has changed, either because the domain covered by the framework was incomplete or the current application to be developed is a bad fit with the framework domain, it is necessary to decide whether to redesign the framework or do a work-around for this specific application to overcome the problems.

In the case where we decide to redesign the framework, the current application under development will need to be delayed until a new version of the framework is available. In addition, there will be additional cost for the redesign of the framework that has to be accounted for through more extensive reuse of the framework. A third consequence is that the organization is forced to maintain two versions of the framework: the original, since there may exist applications based on this version, and the redesign, for future applications to be developed. The length of the period during which two maintenance lines need to be supported depends on the expected lifetime of the developed applications and the expected number of applications developed for the original framework version.

In the case of a work-around in the application, there will be no additional maintenance for the framework since there is only a single framework. The maintenance problem will instead occur for the developed application. This maintenance strategy will not be suitable if the application under development will have a long expected lifetime. However, this may be an acceptable situation if it is expected that no similar applications will be developed in the foreseeable future.

In conclusion, the problem of deciding the maintenance strategy is dependent on factors that include time pressure, estimated lifetime for the software involved, and existing and expected future applications. Unfortunately, no clear guidelines exist that support the decision.

Business Domain Change

The framework is developed in a domain that is closely related to the organization's business domain. Unfortunately, the business domain is often weakly defined and not stable over time. Especially when the organization's business domain changes frequently, the framework will be more difficult to reuse and, if not maintained, will be completely useless after a rather short time span. Thus, since the business domain changes, the domain captured by the framework has to be adapted to follow this change, and this affects the existing framework. The probability of business domain change is an important risk factor that must be considered in the investment of the framework development effort.

There are, in principle, three approaches to attacking the problem of business domain change. The developer may define the original framework domain much wider than is currently relevant, assuming that it will capture most future new domain changes. As discussed earlier, there are obvious problems in developing a framework for a large domain. For example, it often is unclear what functionality should be included in the domain to incorporate an existing adjacent business domain or to incorporate a future business domain. Other problems are obtaining funding for a larger framework effort, finding domain expertise for the domain, and verifying framework functionality.

Another approach is to handle the business domain change problem by redesigning the framework such that it covers both the original domain and the new domain. The problem with this solution is that the organization has to support two frameworks with accompanying additional support, maintenance, and costs. Otherwise, the revised framework must be used for new versions of earlier applications, potentially causing major and expensive updates.

A third approach is to reuse ideas from the original framework and develop a framework for the new business domain. One problem with this approach is that the return on investment of the existing framework effort will be less than expected, since most new applications will most likely be in the new business domain. Another problem is that, again, a new framework has to be developed with all its possibilities and, especially, its problems. The main advantage this time around is that developers have (hopefully) learned many lessons from the first framework development.

Design Iterations

It is generally accepted that framework development is an iterative process. Traditional software development may also require this, but iterations are more important and explicit when designing frameworks. The underlying reason, we believe, is that frameworks primarily deal with abstractions, and abstractions are very difficult to evaluate. Therefore, the abstractions need to be made concrete in the form of test applications before they can be evaluated.

There are, in principle, two important problems with the iterations. First, it is expensive and difficult to predict the amount of resources needed for a framework project. The second problem, closely related to the first problem, is that it is difficult to stop iterating and decide that the framework is ready for release. An analogy is possible between these problems and the problems related to software testing. However, some important differences exist, including the fact that design iterations in frameworks are much more expensive than traditional testing. For example, a test case corresponds to an instantiation of a test application. The cost of correcting an error in the traditional system testing depends on where the error was introduced—a coding error could easily be corrected, but design errors or requirements errors are much more expensive. In the framework case, on the other hand, detected errors—that is, situations where the framework was not suitable for a specific test application—may require a redesign of the framework. Not only is such a redesign expensive, but it may also invalidate existing test applications that then need to be modified accordingly.

We have identified three issues that are open for improvement: first, quantitative and qualitative guidelines for when to stop framework design; second, methods that can predict the number of iterations and the corresponding effort involved; and, finally, the need to investigate whether it is possible to evaluate a framework for a specific application without implementing a complete test application.

3.4 Summary

Object-oriented frameworks provide an important step forward in the development of large reusable components, when compared to the traditional approaches. In our work with the frameworks described in this chapter, we have experienced the advantages of framework-based development as compared to the traditional approach of starting from scratch. In addition to our own positive experiences, others, such as [Moser-Nierstrasz 1996], have identified that the use of object-oriented frameworks reduces the amount of effort required for application development and can be a productive investment.

However, as we report in this chapter, a number of problems and hindrances that complicate the development and use of object-oriented frameworks still exist. These problems can be divided into four categories:

Framework development. Problems in the development of a framework are related to the domain scope, framework documentation, business investment models for framework domains, and framework development methods, as well as framework testing and releasing.

Framework usage. The user of a framework has problems related to managing the framework development process, deciding whether a framework is applicable, estimating the development time and size of application-specific code, understanding the framework, verifying the application-specific code, and debugging.

Framework composition. In case the application requires multiple frameworks to be composed, the software engineer may experience problems with respect to mismatches in the architectural styles underlying the frameworks, the overlap of framework entities, the composition of entity functionality, possible collisions between the control flows in calling frameworks, and the integration of legacy components.

Framework evolution and maintenance. Being long-lived entities, frameworks evolve over time and need to be maintained. The framework development team may experience problems with handling changes to the framework, choosing the maintenance strategy, changes of the business domain, and handling design iterations.

The experiences and problems reported in this chapter are relevant for both software engineers and researchers on object-oriented reuse. Based on this chapter, practitioners should be able to avoid the problems that some of their predecessors have experienced. In addition, this chapter could be used as an agenda for researchers on object-oriented software development or on software reuse in general.

3.5 References

[Andert 1994] Andert, G. Object frameworks in the Taligent OS. *Proceedings of Compcon 1994.* Los Alamitos, CA: IEEE CS Press, 1994.

[Apple 1989] Apple Computer Inc. *MacAppII Programmer's Guide.* 1989.

[Beck-Johnson 1994] Beck, K., and R. Johnson. Patterns generate architectures. *Proceedings of the 8th European Conference on Object-Oriented Programming,* Bologna, Italy, July, 1994.

[Betlem 1995] Betlem, B.H.L., R.M. van Aggele, J. Bosch, and J.E. Rijnsdorp. *An Object-Oriented Framework for Process Operation.* Technical report, Department of Chemical Technology, University of Twente, 1995.

[Booch 1994] Booch, G. *Object Oriented Analysis and Design with Applications,* 2nd ed. Redwood City, CA: Benjamin/Cummings, 1994.

[Bosch 1997] Bosch, J. Composition through superimposition. In *Object-Oriented Technology–ECOOP1997 Workshop Reader,* J. Bosch, S. Mitchell, eds., LNCS 1357. Springer-Verlag, 1997.

[Bosch 1999] Bosch, J. Measurement systems framework. In *-Domain-Specific Application Frameworks*, M. Fayad andR. Johnson, editors. New York: John Wiley & Sons, 1999.

[Buschmann 1996] Buschmann, F., R. Meunier, H. Rohnert, P. Sommerlad, and M. Stahl. *Pattern-Oriented Software Architecture: A System of Patterns.* New York: John Wiley & Sons, 1996.

[Cotter-Potel 1995] Cotter, S., and M. Potel. *Inside Taligent Technology.* Reading, MA: Addison-Wesley, 1995.

[Dagermo-Knutsson 1996] Dagermo, P., and J. Knuttson. *Development of an Object-Oriented Framework for Vessel Control Systems.* Technical Report ESPRIT III/ESSI/DOVER Project #10496, 1996.

[Deutsch 1989] Deutsch, L.P. Design reuse and frameworks in the Smalltalk-80 system. In *Software Reusabilit, Volume II,* T.J. Biggerstaff and A.J. Perlis, editors. Reading, MA: ACM Press/Addison-Wesley, 1989.

[Fayad-Hamu 1999] Fayad, M.E., and D. Hamu. Object-oriented enterprise frameworks. Submitted for publication to *IEEE Computer,* 1999.

[Fayad-Laitinen 1998] Fayad, M.E., and M. Laitinen. *Transition to Object-Oriented Software Development.* New York: John Wiley & Sons, 1998.

[Fayad-Schmidt 1997] Fayad, M.E., and D. Schmidt. Object-oriented application frameworks. *Communications of the ACM,* October 1997:32–38

[Gamma 1995] Gamma, E., R. Helm, R. Johnson, and J.O. Vlissides. *Design Patterns: Elements of Reusable OO Software.* Reading, MA: Addison-Wesley, 1995.

[Garlan 1995] Garlan, D., R. Allen, and J. Ockerbloom. Architectural mismatch or why it's so hard to build systems out of existing parts. *Proceedings of the 17th International Conference on Software Engineering,* Seattle, WA, April 1995.

[Goldberg-Robson 1989] Goldberg, A., and D. Robson. *Smalltalk-80: The Language.* Reading, MA: Addison-Wesley, 1989.

[Helm 1990] Helm, R., I.M. Holland, and D. Gangopadhyay. Contracts: Specifying behavioural compositions in object-oriented systems. *Proceedings of ECOOP/OOPSLA 1990,* Ottawa, Canada, October, 1990.

[Huni 1995] Huni, H., R. Johnson, and R. Engel. A framework for network protocol software. *Proceedings of the 10th Conference on OOPSLA,* Austin, TX, July 1995.

[Jacobson 1992] Jacobson, I., M. Christerson, P. Jonsson, and G. Övergaard. *Object-Oriented Software Engineering: A Use Case Approach.* Reading, MA: Addison-Wesley, 1992.

[Johnson 1992] Johnson, R.E. Documenting frameworks with patterns. *Proceedings of the 7th Conference on Object-Oriented Programming Systems, Languages and Applications,* Vancouver, Canada, October 1992.

[Johnson-Foote 1988] Johnson, R., and B. Foote. Designing reusable classes. *Journal of Object-Oriented Programming* 1(2), June 1988.

[Johnson-Opdyke 1993] Johnson R.E., and W.F. Opdyke. Refactoring and aggregation. *Proceedings of ISOTAS 1993: International Symposium on Object Technologies for Advanced Software,* 1993.

[Johnson-Russo 1991] Johnson, R.E., and V.F. Russo. *Reusing Object-Oriented Design.* Technical Report UIUCDCS 91-1696, University of Illinois, 1991.

[Karlsson 1995] Karlsson, E.A., editor. *Software Reuse: A Holistic Approach.* New York: John Wiley & Sons, 1995.

[Kihl-Ströberg 1995] Kihl, M., and P. Ströberg. The business value of software development with object-oriented frameworks. Master's thesis, Department of Computer Science and Business Administration, University of Karlskrona/Ronneby, Sweden, May 1995 (in Swedish).

[Krasner-Pope 1988] Krasner, G.E., and S.T. Pope. A cookbook for using the Model-View-Controller user interface paradigm in Smalltalk-80. *Journal of Object-Oriented Programming* 1(3), August–September 1988.

[Lajoie-Keller 1994] Lajoie, R., and R.K. Keller. Design and reuse in object-oriented frameworks: Patterns, contracts and motifs in concert. *Proceedings of the 62nd Congress of the Association Canadienne Française pour l'Avancement des Sciences,* Montreal, Canada, May 1994.

[Lim 1996] Lim, Wayne. Reuse economics: A comparison of seventeen models and directions for future research. *Proceedings of the International Conference on Software Reuse,* Orlando, FL, April 1996.

[Linton 1989] Linton, M.A., J.M. Vlissides, and P.R. Calder. Composing user interfaces with interViews. *IEEE Computer* 22(2), February 1989.

[Lundberg 1996] Lundberg, L. Multiprocessor performance evaluation of billing gateway systems for telecommunication applications. *Proceedings of the ICSA Conference on Parallel and Distributed Computing Systems,* pp. 225–237, September 1996.

[Lundberg-Mattsson 1996] Lundberg, C., and M. Mattsson. 'Using legacy components with object-oriented frameworks. *Proceedings of Systemarkitekturer 1996,* Borås, Sweden, 1996.

[Mattsson 1996] Mattsson, M. Object-oriented frameworks—A survey of methodological issues. Licentiate thesis, LU-CS-TR: 96-167, Department of Computer Science, Lund University, 1996.

[Meyer 1992] Meyer, B. Applying design by contract. *IEEE Computer,* October 1992.

[Molin 1996a] Molin, Peter. *Verifying Framework-Based Applications by Conformance and Composability Constraints.* Research Report 18/96, University of Karlskrona/Ronneby, 1996.

[Molin 1996b] Molin, Peter. *Experiences from Applying the Object-Oriented Framework Technique to a Family of Embedded Systems.* Research Report 19/96, University of Karlskrona/Ronneby, 1996.

[Molin-Ohlsson 1996] Molin, Peter, and Lennart Ohlsson. Points & deviations: A pattern language for fire alarm systems. *Proceedings of the 3rd International Conference on Pattern Languages for Programming,* Paper 6.6, Monticello, IL, September 1996.

[Moser-Nierstrasz 1996] Moser S., and O. Nierstrasz. The effect of object-oriented frameworks on developer productivity. *IEEE Computer Theme Issue on Managing Object-Oriented Software Development,* Mohamed E. Fayad and Marshall Cline, editors. September 1996:45–51.

[Opdyke 1992] Opdyke, W.F. Refactoring object-oriented frameworks. Ph.D. thesis, University of Illinois at Urbana-Champaign, 1992.

[Opdyke-Johnson 1993] Opdyke, W.F., and R.E. Johnson. Creating abstract superclasses by refactoring. *Proceedings of CSC 1993: The ACM 1993 Computer Science Conference,* Indianapolis, Indiana, February 1993.

[Poulin 1994] Poulin, Jeff. Measuring software reusability. *Proceedings International Conference on Software Reuse,* Rio de Janeiro, November 1994.

[Pree 1994] Pree, W. Meta patterns—A means for capturing the essentials of reusable object-oriented design. *Proceedings of the 8th European Conference on Object-Oriented Programming*, Bologna, Italy, July, 1994.

[Roberts-Johnson 1996] Roberts, D., and R. Johnson. Evolving frameworks: A pattern language for developing object-oriented frameworks. *Proceedings of the Third Conference on Pattern Languages and Programming*. Allerton Park, IL, September 1996.

[Rumbaugh 1991] Rumbaugh, J., M. Blaha, W. Premerlani, F. Eddy, and W. Lorensen. *Object-Oriented Modeling and Design*. Englewood Cliffs, NJ: Prentice Hall, 1991.

[Russo 1990] Russo, V.F. An object-oriented operating system. Ph.D. thesis, University of Illinois at Urbana-Champaign, October 1990.

[Schmucker 1986] Schmucker, K.J. *Object-Oriented Programming for the Macintosh*. Hayden Book Company, 1986.

[Schäfer 1994] Schäfer, W., R. Prieto-Diaz, and M. Matsumoto. *Software Reusability*. Ellis-Horwood Ltd., 1994.

[Shaw-Garlan 1996] Shaw, M., and D. Garlan. *Software Architecture: Perspectives on an Emerging Discipline*. Upper Saddle River, NJ: Prentice Hall, 1996.

[Sparks 1996] Sparks, S., K. Benner, and C. Faris. Managing object-oriented framework reuse. *IEEE Computer Theme Issue on Managing Object-Oriented Software Development*, Mohamed E. Fayad and Marshall Cline, editors. September 1996:53–61.

[Weinand 1989] Weinand, A., E. Gamma, and R. Marty. Design and implementation of ET++, a seamless object-oriented application framework. *Structured Programming* 10(2), July 1989.

[Wilson-Wilson 1993] Wilson, D.A., and S.D. Wilson. Writing frameworks—Capturing your expertise about a problem domain. Tutorial notes, *8th Conference on Object-Oriented Programming Systems, Languages and Applications*, Washington, DC, October 1993.

3.6 Review Questions

1. Define the following: architectural mismatch, Hollywood principle, framework gap.

2. Describe briefly the following application frameworks: fire alarm systems, measurement systems, gateway billing systems.

3. Name all the application frameworks in this chapter.

4. Classify these frameworks according to the [Fayad-Schmidt 1997] classification.

5. What are the purposes of framework documentation?

6. List the ways of documenting frameworks.

7. List and explain the major obstacles in framework documentation.

8. List the problems and the causes of framework integration.

9. List the problems and causes of framework evolution.

10. Suggest solutions to three problems in this chapter. Explain your solutions.

SIDEBAR 1
ENTERPRISE FRAMEWORKS

Object-oriented enterprise frameworks (OOEFs or enterprise frameworks) are becoming strategic assets for organizations across all business sectors. Evidence of this is reflected in the recent entry of flexible and extensible products for enterprise resource planning (ERP), manufacturing execution systems (MES), product data management (PDM), and other commercially available, framework-based business applications. Despite improvements in computing power and software development tools, the design, implementation, and maintenance of complex systems remains difficult, expensive, and risky. This sidebar identifies the conditions that contribute to system complexity and risk, introduces the terminology and characteristics of enterprise frameworks, and describes how these frameworks provide the essential tools needed to mitigate complexity and risk throughout the life cycle of complex business systems [Hamu-Fayad 1998; Fayad-Schmidt 1997].

The increase in complexity and risk involved in enterprise systems is related to two factors. The first factor is the velocity of business. The increasing velocity of business and industry refers to the need to provide highly personalized products and services in an increasingly competitive marketplace where differentiation is the key to success. Increasingly, companies have identified that products and services tailored to the individual customer ensure competitive advantage. However, it is also recognized that highly specialized software solutions are required to support a highly customer-tailored business model [Baumer 1997].

The second factor contributing complexity and risk is the growing heterogeneity of systems architectures. The heterogeneity of systems architectures refers to the complexity of hardware and software systems. This complexity results from rapid changes in technology as well as the heterogeneity of architectures that results from acquisitions and mergers.

Information technology gives us tools for creating new products and services and increased productivity. The increasing demand for these products and services, and for greater productivity, places further demands on information technology. This cycle contributes to an increase in the velocity of business—the speed at which businesses reinvent themselves, their processes, and their product and service offerings. The result is unprecedented demand for integrated enterprise systems and applications that are capable of modeling the rapid changes in business policies.

Companies have invested heavily in information technology products and services to maintain a strategic and competitive position in the marketplace. Over time, legacies are created both in hardware and software, resulting in heterogeneous systems. This is compounded by the frequency of acquisitions and mergers. While we may debate the economic and social impacts of acquisitions and mergers, the technological ramifications are the battlefield of the CIO and the information technology (IT) staff. In the wake of the changes that occur every day, IT operatives must map out a plan of attack and then adjust as the battlefield evolves.

These conditions compound the complexity and risk already present in the business systems life cycle. Enterprise frameworks are designed to provide a full complement of tools to match up against this complexity, while mitigating risk through flexibility. A

Continues

framework is a semicomplete application that can be specialized to produce custom applications [Fayad-Schmidt 1997]. An enterprise framework is a software product with a well-defined, highly structured and documented architecture.

Enterprise frameworks are domain-specific frameworks, which expose a rich set of semantics and modeling paradigms for developing and extending enterprise applications. The remainder of this sidebar focuses on the principal characteristics of enterprise frameworks and describes how these features mitigate the complexity and risk associated with business systems today.

SB1.1 Characteristics of Enterprise Frameworks

A good framework provides mature runtime functionality within a specified domain. Frameworks require relatively little code to meet user requirements. Therefore, the design and implementation of the framework must reflect a strong understanding of the domain. The most suitable framework for a particular application domain reflects a narrow focus on a particular group of problems. For instance, frameworks for shop floor control expose a mature model for Work-in-Progress tracking (WIP), equipment tracking and preventative maintenance, statistical process control, data collection, and so on.

An OOEF contains the business objects and enduring business themes (EBTs), which accurately reflect the specific domain serviced by the framework. Hence, a shop floor control framework for petrochemical processing cannot satisfy the runtime requirements for a molded plastics operation or a pharmaceutical products manufacturer. A business objects catalog contains ready-to-use objects, which are used to extend the framework. The EBT is concerned with a business issue, namely, what is being done, while the business objects are concerned with the implementation, that is, how it is being done, as shown in Sidebar 6.

Software is often extended in ways its developers have not anticipated. An OOEF is not intended to be used like an application. Instead, an OOEF is the basis for constructing and delivering business applications that are highly tailored to a specific domain. Extensibility and tailorability ensure that the framework may adapt new constructs and more accurately model a specific business. Extensibility is achieved through broad support for object-oriented constructs such as polymorphism, inheritance, encapsulation, reuse, and persistence.

Well-designed frameworks capture the enduring business processes (EBPs) or workflows that are fundamental to the target application domain. These enduring processes capture workflows that do not change over time. They are concerned with the high-level sequence of what is done (the top-level state diagram). One benefit of the workflow paradigm is that the same workflow metaphor also provides a means for instantiating those detailed and dynamic business processes that are concerned with the step-by-step sequence of activities used to complete a task. Workflow management streamlines the complex interactions between objects that are found in large-scale object-oriented applications. Workflow mechanisms also minimize the need for custom code writing and emphasize reuse [Prins 1996].

OOEFs require platform independence. In addition, they must support integration of multiple application frameworks and legacy components. When frameworks are narrow in focus, support for integration is critical, because it is often necessary to integrate several best-of-breed frameworks or legacy components to produce a top-to-bottom solution. For instance, a manufacturing corporation must integrate an ERP framework, an MES framework, a warehouse management system (WMS), and other components to assemble its complete business systems. OOEFs provide a model for distributed objects, such as object request brokering, distributed message passing, and remote procedure calls/remote method invocation. The distribution models enforce scalability; as more users (clients) are added to the system, additional server instances are added to improve throughput. Another important aspect of the distribution model is that object definitions or structure are preserved across the transport, eliminating the need for the numerous data translation layers found in legacy systems.

OOEFs must provide mature development, testing, deployment, modeling, and maintenance tools. The framework must provide an integrated development environment (IDE), which supports a rapid application development (RAD) approach. The better the integration of the IDE with the framework, the more likely it is that the framework developer will be successful. The development of rapid prototypes is essential when responding to the frequent changes in business processes. It provides the best opportunity to get feedback validating the design of system enhancements. Mature modeling tools are also critical. If the modeling tools are not mature, then the framework will prove inadequate. Framework adequacy ensures the goodness of fit of the framework. Therefore, the framework should integrate extensive modeling adequacies [Fayad 1994]:

Descriptive. The ability to visualize and monitor objects in the framework.

Synthetic. Integrated problem resolution, thereby improving maintainability.

Analysis. Integrated validation and verification tools.

Blueprint. Integrated specifications and configuration management.

Notational. Presentation constructs facilitating ease of graphical user interface (GUI) modifications.

Procedural. Recognition and search capabilities.

Contractual. Client or user-friendly tools for modeling system behavior.

Scalable. Constructs supporting partitioning, composition, and access control.

Administrative. Includes installers, launch/shutdown, database management, and so on.

Documentation is key to the success of an enterprise framework. It is the single most distinguishing characteristic of a high-quality software product. Many mature frameworks may lack in one or more of the characteristics described here, but mature documentation ensures that a framework gets used. High-quality documentation ensures that rigorous design and implementation standards are reflected in all of the application content built with the framework. Therefore, mature framework documentation ensures reuse and

Continues

maintainability. In short, framework documentation describes the purpose of the framework, how to use the framework, and the detailed design of the framework [Johnson 1992].

SB1.2 Summary

Object-oriented framework technologies are becoming mainstream [Schmidt-Fayad 1997]. OOEFs offer a streamlined and flexible alternative to traditional tools and applications. OOEFs embody the enduring themes and processes of a particular business domain, while providing the flexibility to model the rapid changes in business practices, which are required to stay competitive. OOEFs enable a company to create a strategic advantage over its competitors and, therefore, they become the cornerstone of an organization's systems engineering activities.

SB1.3 References

[Baumer 1997] Baumer, D., G. Gryczan, R. Knoll, C. Lilienthal, D. Riehle, and H. Zullighoven. Framework development for large systems. *Communications of the ACM* 40(10), Theme Issue on Object-Oriented Application Frameworks, M.E. Fayad and D. Schmidt, editors. October 1997: 52–59.

[Fayad 1994] Fayad, M.E. Object-oriented software engineering: Problems and perspectives, Ph.D. thesis, University of Minnesota, 1994.

[Fayad-Schmidt 1997] Fayad, M., and D. Schmidt. Object-oriented application frameworks. *Communications of the ACM* 40(10), October 1997:32–38.

[Hamu-Fayad 1998] Hamu, D.S., and M.E. Fayad. Achieving bottom-line improvements with enterprise frameworks. *Communications of the ACM* 41(8), August 1998: 110–113.

[Johnson 1992] Johnson, R. Documenting frameworks using patterns. *Proceedings of OOPSLA 1992,* Vancouver, Canada, 1992, 63–76.

[Prins 1996] Prins, R. *Developing Business Objects.* New York: McGraw-Hill, 1996.

[Schmidt-Fayad 1997] Schmidt, D., and M.E. Fayad. Building reusable OO frameworks for distributed software. *Communications of the ACM* 40(10), October 1997: 85–87.

PART

Two

Framework Perspectives

Part Two contains three chapters and a sidebar. Part Two discusses several perspectives of application frameworks related to some of the historical application frameworks, describes guidelines for constructing good classes and components for application frameworks, discusses general guidelines for application framework usability, and presents both inter- and intra-viewpoints.

Chapter 4 describes some of the earliest object-oriented application frameworks on record. These were written in the 1960s and 1970s using Simula, the language that invented objects classes, inheritance, and virtual binding. Although many of the concepts introduced by Simula have now been integrated into the current generation of object-oriented languages, many useful features of Simula were never widely discussed and are still overlooked. The chapter starts out with a brief overview of the language, its history, and its principal features including coroutine sequencing. Then, it presents a sequence of frameworks that allows Simula, a general-purpose programming language, to describe and program increasingly complex parallel systems. Although Simula frameworks have been developed in other areas, it is in the area of parallel programming that Simula, initially developed for simulation, has the most to offer. This area is also of particular interest for today's multitasking environments. First, the chapter describes the two standard frameworks furnished with every Simula system, which provide for list processing and discrete event simulation. Then, the chapter introduces other frameworks developed independently of the Simula team, which add to the ability to simulate parallel systems. These include GPSSS for queuing models and the UMxx series for the modeling of operating systems. Finally, the chapter shows that Simula's elegant notation is not limited to simulated parallelism. Several frameworks that extend Simula's process scheduling to real time are presented. In particular, the chapter describes how SimIOProcess, from the Lund Simula Library, handles preemption and IO interrupts. The chapter then explores another unusual aspect of Simula. Inheritance between objects is a key concept in the use of frameworks, but Simula extends the concept by allowing a program to inherit from a class. The chapter also describes some early Simula-inspired research that illustrated the usefulness for frameworks of allowing inheritance between methods. Finally, the chapter concludes with some lessons that can be drawn from these pioneering efforts.

Chapter 5 discusses guidelines for constructing classes and components to be used by a visual builder. Early object-oriented class libraries were designed to deliver as much function as possible. Design standards evolved to meet the needs of programmers who wrote every line of application code themselves. Today, an increasing number of application programmers use visual builders (and, to a lesser extent, wizards) to generate much (but rarely all) code. This code also makes use of class libraries. In this environment, however, programmers tie together classes by interface, with a minimum of handwritten code. Good framework design must now address the needs of visual programmers as well as those of direct coders. This chapter describes design issues from which these requirements diverge.

Chapter 6 discusses general guidelines for framework usability. User interface (UI) usability has received much attention from the computer science community, but little formal attention has been paid to the usability of application programming interfaces (APIs) such as in class libraries and frameworks. Programmer productivity is claimed as a key benefit of frameworks, but productivity hinges on how easy they are to learn and use. Taking the general guidelines of UI usability as an outline, we have pulled together guidelines for framework usability that practitioners actually use. These guidelines have been arrived at over time during development of commercial class libraries and frameworks.

Sidebar 2 describes two types of viewpoints, called *inter-* and *intra-viewpoint* representations. A key consideration of viewpoints is that multiple viewpoints must present the same system consistently. The sidebar describes a viewpoint in terms of an object-oriented model, because of the rich constructs provided by this form of design language. The concepts associated with viewpoints are still evolving. For example, the Unified Modeling Language (UML) uses intra-viewpoints, while the Open Distributed Processing (ODP) Standard uses inter-viewpoints.

Simula Frameworks: The Early Experience

As Santayana once said, "Those who cannot remember the past are condemned to repeat it." It is thus interesting to consider early frameworks written in Simula, the language that precipitated the invention of the concepts of object-oriented programming, more than 30 years ago. In the present context, Simula is particularly important because it was specifically designed to support *frameworks*, or *application-oriented extensions* as they were then called. The reason for this was that the language was created under contract (with Univac) for a *simulation* language. As it turned out, the language designers, inspired by the elegance of Algol 60, did not produce a specialized language restricted to simulation. Rather, they designed Simula as a minimal addition to Algol that allowed the language to be extended with the concepts and operations pertinent to any given application areas. The *minimal* addition included all the basic concepts of object-oriented programming objects such as classes and inheritance. This not only permitted the designers to meet their contractual obligation by providing the language with a standard library containing two frameworks, Simset for list handling and the Simulation for discrete-event simulation, it also allowed some basic features of the language, such as text handling and files, to be specified and implemented as classes.

To underscore Simula's contribution to object-oriented programming, here is a list of the new concepts introduced by Simula:

Objects. Runtime entities combining data (or state) attributes with characteristic operations. Designed to represent real-life objects, Simula's objects are also capable of independent actions in parallel with other objects. In this, Simula went further than what is nowadays considered to be an object, and these objects might now be termed processes or threads.

Classes. The type definition for objects with identical attributes. Declaring classes rather than individual objects allows the dynamic creation of an indeterminate number of instances as well as semantic verification of many operations.

Inheritance. The ability to specify that a subclass is a specialization of a more general class. Simula supports single inheritance.

Virtual methods. A method specified in a general class but meant to be implemented or redefined in more specific subclasses. This is the basis of polymorphism.

References. A controlled pointer that is guaranteed to designate an object of a given class or subclass (or none).

Type system. Inheritance and references together define a hierarchical type system, based on name equivalence, where each class defines a type.

Simula was also a pioneer in the successful implementation of concepts that had been proposed previously but not implemented or implemented in more limited ways. This includes *garbage collection,* which had been used for Lisp but with a limited number of predefined data structures, and *coroutines* [Conway 1963] and *processes* [Knuth-McNeeley 1964], which had never been implemented in a general-purpose language.

Although many of the object concepts introduced by Simula have found their way into current object-oriented languages, many useful features of the language were never widely discussed and are still overlooked. Of particular interest for today's multitasking environments, is Simula's *expressiveness* in the area of parallel programming. The raison-d'être of a simulation language is the modeling of parallel activity and from the first, Simula objects were active interacting entities, based on the process concepts introduced by Dijkstra [Dijkstra 1968]. As a result, Simula programs for typical parallel situations, such as producer/consumer synchronization or semaphore implementation, are short and highly legible; very close to the pseudocode found in OS textbooks.

It is enlightening to contrast Simula's approach to object-oriented programming with the solutions offered by the current set of C-based languages such as C++ and Java. In artificial intelligence, progress is often ascribed to the interplay between two opposing approaches, usually described as the "neats" versus the "scruffies." Simula, which is a direct descendent of Algol, can be viewed as representative of the "neat" European tradition, inspired by theory and concerned with elegance, generality, and verification. In contrast, popular American languages such as C and C++ which developed in a more ad hoc fashion in response to pragmatic concerns such as runtime efficiency and hardware access, could be considered "scruffy." Each family of languages has particular advantages for the creation of frameworks and it is important to be aware of alternatives. To illustrate these alternatives, we shall sometimes compare Simula with Java, the current front-runner of the C school, which has adopted several "neat" concepts such as garbage collection and references.

Since so little has been published about Simula and its applications, this chapter starts out with a brief overview of the language and its history. It also provides many bibliographic references, and many of the examples, frameworks, and references can be found on the Université de Montréal Simula web page (www.jsp.umontreal.ca/~simula/).

This chapter presents various Simula frameworks developed over the years. First, it examines the two standard frameworks furnished with every Simula system: Simset and Simulation. Then it considers other frameworks for simulation developed independently of the Simula designers. These include GPSSS for queuing models and the UMxx series for the modeling of operating systems. After that, it describes some frameworks that apply to real-time systems. Finally, it shows the usefulness of allowing inheritance between methods. In the discussion section we summarize the usefulness for frameworks of the language mechanisms particular to Simula and compare this with the situation in Java.

4.1 History of Simula

Simula was designed in 1967 in Norway by O-J. Dahl and K. Nygaard [Dahl 1970]. This language, known as Simula 67, superseded a previous effort by the same authors called Simula-1 [Dahl 1968; Dahl-Nygaard 1966]. In retrospect, this similarity of names was unfortunate because, whereas Simula 1 was a dedicated simulation language, Simula 67 was radically different: It was a general-purpose language—a superset of Algol 60—with classes, objects, and coroutines, which was *also* superbly suited to discrete-event simulation. Simula incorporated several interesting ideas by C.A.R. Hoare, notably those on *records* and record subclasses [Hoare 1968] as well as some ideas on parallelism by Dijkstra [Dijkstra 1968].

An important reference for Simula is the 1978 ACM conference entitled "The History of Programming Languages" [Nygaard-Dahl 1981], where Simula was showcased as one of a select dozen historically significant programming languages. Apart from these 1978 papers, there are few easily available documents describing the language. To add to the confusion, the article on Simula published in the authoritative CACM [Dahl-Nygaard 1966] describes Simula-1, the simulation-oriented precursor to the object-oriented Simula 67. Complete description of the language and its implementation was available as internal reports from the Norwegian Computer Center [Dahl 1970; Dahl-Myhrhaug 1973], but for many years these were not publicly available. The scarcity of documentation, compounded by the fact that the language was created in a remote country with financing from Univac, a company that went into eclipse, may go a long way toward explaining the general lack of knowledge about Simula. In his 1994 overview of Simula, Magnusson comments further on this point. The best early description of Simula's capabilities can be found in Dahl and Hoare's contribution to a book on the emerging field of structured programming [Dahl-Hoare 1972]. In the ensuing fad for goto-less programming, the *macro* structuring aspects inherent in the object approach of Simula were overlooked in favor of *micro* structuring of code as presented in such languages as Pascal. For a historical perspective on the events and political infighting surrounding the development of the language, refer to Jan Holmevik's paper issued from his Ph.D. dissertation [Holmevik 1994].

Currently the definitive reference for the language is published by the Swedish Standards Institute [SIS 1987]; but this slim volume is available only through national standards institutes. Starting with this publication, the official name of the modern language became (plain) Simula. Examination of the 1987 standard also reveals that the modern language is essentially unchanged from that initially designed 20 years previously. The changes consisted mainly of extensions to the standard libraries and clarification of arcane details in the standard. Old programs would continue to work.

Several books have been written on Simula, but many of the older ones are now out of print. The most recent is an introductory programming text written by Kirkerud [Kirkerud 1989]; unfortunately, it skips over several more advanced parts of the language. In particular, it leaves out any mention of the two standard *frameworks* present in the language: Simset and Simulation. These are better described in an older book by Franta [Franta 1977], which deals mainly with the application of Simula to simulation; however, 20 pages are devoted to the basic language and a further 50 on the Simset and Simulation frameworks. This book also includes extensive Simula material from Vaucher dealing with the GPSSS simulation framework [Vaucher 1971] and techniques for advanced scheduling [Vaucher 1973; Vaucher-Duval 1975]. Other books, now out of print, include a textbook by the initial implementation team [Birtwistle 1973] and a more recent volume by Rob Pooley [Pooley 1987]—now available on the web.

Good short overviews of Simula are also available. The earliest is by Jean Ichbiah [Ichbiah-Morse 1972], who implemented Simula for CII, in France, then went on to design ADA. There are also good introductions by Magnusson, the implementer of the Lund compilers, in [Magnusson 1994a] and in [Meyer 1988]. Other papers that concentrate on the *implementation* of Simula include [Madsen 1995; Magnusson 1994b; Papazpglou 1984].

Scandinavian research and development of object-oriented languages did not stop after the implementation of Simula. Kristen Nygaard has remained active in the development of OO languages, being one of the architects of Beta [Madsen 1993; Vaucher 1979] and now involved in the GOODS conceptual platform [Nygaard 1997]. A good review of post-Simula object-oriented research in Scandinavia can be found in the 1993 summary of the Mjølner Project [Knudsen 1994].

Simula has influenced, directly or indirectly, many succeeding generations of OO languages. In particular, experience with Simula during his Ph.D., led Stroustrup to introduce objects into C and create C++. The most recent C mutation, Java [Arnold-Gosling 1996], integrates even better the basic ideas of Simula (single inheritance, garbage collection, and references) with some additional features of its own.

4.2 Basic Concepts of Simula

Though Simula was created over 30 years ago, Simula programs are still easy to read and understand. This is because Simula was designed as a superset of Algol 60, the most advanced algorithmic language at that time, and Algol traits are present in many modern languages. Secondly, the object concepts first introduced by Simula have percolated into most current OO languages.

Simula objects are defined through class declarations with a syntax chosen to resemble that of procedures. The class body, most often a "begin . . . end" block, can contain local declarations as well as instructions. Local *variable* declarations represent object attributes and the local *procedures* and *functions* are the object's methods.

Like procedures, classes can be declared to have parameters (essentially instance attributes whose initial value must be specified at object creation time) and statements, which are executed when an object is created. Often these statements are used with the parameters to initialize the object state much as a constructor method in Java or C++; but more generally, the instructions in a class body represent a scenario or sequence of actions that an active object will execute during its active lifetime—possibly in parallel with the actions of other active objects.

The following example shows the declaration of a Person class, which has two data attributes, names and creationDate, and one method, descrip. Names is specified as a parameter, and a value will have to be provided when the Person is created. The method descrip returns a text with a person's name and class. It is specified to be virtual; that is, it can be redefined in subclasses and the most specific version will always be used. By default, methods are not virtual and follow traditional rules of visibility whereby names declared in subblocks or subclasses are not directly visible. This is different from Java, where all methods are virtual, but attribute visibility is the same as Simula's.

```
Boolean trace;

class Person (names);
      text     names virtual:
      procedure descrip is text procedure descrip ;;
begin
      text creationDate;

      text procedure descrip ;
          descrip :- "Person " & names;

      creationDate:- datetime;
      if trace then
          outtext("*** Creation: " & names);
end;
```

Objects are created through a new operation, and references to objects are kept in *reference* variables. By default, all attributes and methods are accessible from outside the object through dot notation; however, it is possible to protect local names from either the outside or from subclasses with hidden and protected specifications. Now we show the creation of a Person object and access to its creationDate. This creationDate is initialized by the object itself executing its code body upon creation with new.

```
ref(Person) P;
P :- new Person("John Brown");
outtext( P.creationDate );
```

The concept of references (typed pointers) was first suggested by C.A.R. Hoare [Hoare 1968], but implementation was hardly obvious, especially when inheritance and subclasses are added. To do so safely requires garbage collection as well as initializing all pointers to none upon block entry. Simula was the first language to implement and use references (it also initializes all variables to neutral values such as none, zero, or false).

4.2.1 Inheritance

Simula supports single inheritance denoted by *prefixing*: using the name of the super-class as a *prefix* to the subclass declaration. The effect of inheritance was defined as a textual concatenation of all the class elements, including parameters, attributes, and code. For code, there is a special mechanism that will be used extensively later: a special keyword *inner* is used to denote where to place the subclass code in the super-class's body. In the following example, B is declared to be a subclass of A.

```
class A (A_pars...);          A class B (B_pars...);
begin                         Begin
    A_attributes...;              B_attributes...;
    A_code1...;                   B_code...;
      inner                   end;
    A_code2... ;
end;
```

The effect is that B objects act as if they had been defined as follows:

```
class B (A_pars, B_pars...);
begin
    A_attributes...;
    B_attributes...;

    A_code1...;
      B_code...;
    A_code2... ;
end;
```

The next example shows the declaration of two subclasses of Person: Employee and Customer. Customer is a minimal subclass, adding no new elements; but in Simula's name-based type system objects of this class can be distinguished from objects of class Person. Employee is more consequent; it adds two attributes: salary and empNum. Salary will be initialized on creation; it is also *protected*—that is, invisible from outside the class; empNum is initialized by the code body that also increments a global counter of employees.

```
integer empCount;

Person class Customer; !empty body;  ;

Person class Employee (salary);
    real salary;
protected
    salary;
begin
    integer empNum ;
    real procedure pay;
        pay := salary;
    text procedure descrip ;
        descrip :- "Employee " & names;
```

```
        empNum := empCount := empCount+1;
    end;
```

To allow the hidden salary to be accessed, Employee declares an accessor method: pay. It also redefines the virtual procedure descrip. The following shows examples of the creation of an Employee and a Customer as well as access to the methods. Note that, to create an Employee, we must provide two actual parameters: names for Person and salary for Employee.

```
ref (Person)   Tom ;
ref( Employee) Dick;
Tom  :- new Customer( "Tom Thumb");
Dick :- new Employee( "Dick Tracy", 250 );
outtext ( Dick.descrip ); outimage;
outtext ( Tom.descrip );
```

4.2.2 Nested Classes

Simula differs from most modern OO languages in that class declarations may be nested; that is, classes may contain other class declarations. Another way in which Simula goes further than other OO languages is in permitting inheritance, not only between classes but also between classes and program blocks. In *Section 4.7.2*, we will argue that the concept should be extended even further, showing that inheritance between procedures would allow easy and safe implementation of mutual exclusion between parallel tasks.

One principal use for nesting is to hide uninteresting, technical classes, and another is to create packages of related classes, procedures, and variables that can then be inherited as one package by application programs. In our example, we could group together our three class declarations and the two global variables into one Personnel class:

```
class Personnel (trace);  Boolean trace;
begin
    integer empCount;

    class Person (names);  ... ;
    Person class Employee (salary ); ... ;
    Person class Customer; ... ;
    ...
end;
```

A user program would then inherit these declarations through prefixing. Since execution of a block is akin to the creation of an object, a list of actual parameter values follows the prefix name. In our case, for a program with trace facilities:

```
Personnel (true) begin
    < ...user program...>
end
```

Most often, in a given application there is only one instance of a package class, but the generality of Simula classes is such that there could be more. For example, one could envisage a multifirm system with multiple Personnel objects. Some researchers have explored and used these capabilities for multilevel simulations [Einarson 1997; Islo 1997]. A practitioner and ardent advocate of this approach is Dr. Evzen Kindler from Charles University in Prague [Kindler 1995a, 1995b].

4.2.3 Simula Particularities

As could be seen from the early examples, Simula syntax differs in some interesting ways from current languages. This is because it is a direct descendant of Algol and retains much of its ancestor's concern with formalism. For example, Simula keeps the mathematical meaning of equality for the "=" operator and uses":=" for assignment. It goes further in distinguishing between value assignment (":=") and reference assignment (":-"). In the same way, Simula distinguishes between testing for equality of content ("=") and identity ("= ="). These distinctions are particularly important when dealing with objects (for example, strings) where both operations are meaningful.

Simula also provides an interesting decision statement: It is the Inspect statement, which not only can discriminate depending on object class but also opens an object much like Pascal's *with*. Given the Personnel classes described here, the following is a bit of code that checks on the class of object pointed by the reference Tom, declared as ref(Person), and then accesses its pay attribute directly:

```
inspect Tom
    when Employee do TotPay := TotPay + pay
    otherwise outtext("Tom is not an Employee");
```

However, the most obvious difference from most current OO languages is that Simula objects have code bodies and can operate as independent parallel entities. This is not surprising when we remember that Simula was designed to model dynamic systems, and objects were meant to describe active processes. At the most basic level, Simula objects function as coroutines. This means that an object can pause and pass control to another object. Later, when it is resumed, it will continue from where it left off. Benefiting from automatic memory management and garbage collection, objects can pause and resume in the middle of recursive calls (and there is no need for the programmer to estimate stack sizes). Note that coroutine objects work in pseudo parallel (one at a time) and that there is no preemption; the only way for control to leave an object is if the object explicitly passes control to another (or if it terminates). However, given coroutines, it is possible to implement frameworks that provide preemption, as discussed in *Section 4.5.3*.

4.2.4 Coroutine Sequencing

Coroutines represent the first step in achieving lightweight multitasking. They can also be used in their own right to solve problems that are otherwise hard or clumsy to describe. The basic coroutine sequencing primitives are resume, detach, and call. In the first language definition, the call primitive was missing; it was added in 1977. Initially, some aspects of coroutine sequencing were not specified, but benefiting from Wang's research on coroutine sequencing [Wang-Dahl 1971], the semantics were clarified in the 1987 Simula standard [SIS 1987]. Roughly:

resume. Transfers control from the executing object, which will be halted, to another object which will continue from where it had previously halted.

call. Like resume, transfers control to another object, which will continue from where it was previously halted; also causes the called object to be attached to the caller.

detach. Halts execution and returns control to either (1) the creating object (if the object has just been created with new and is active for the first time), or (2) the caller (if it was attached), or else (3) the main program. Note: An object that executes detach is no longer attached.

These scheduling instructions are essential to the coding of any type of higher-level scheduling algorithm. Frameworks will often adopt one of two styles of control based on the use of either call+detach or resume+detach. In the first case, one particular object plays the role of a scheduler passing control to each object in turn; here, detach acts as a return and is the inverse of call. In the second style, based on resume, control is passed directly from one object to another. It is more complex, in that scheduling is distributed and performed by the object giving up control.

Here we will illustrate their use for a conceptually simple task that combines recursion with the need for independent loci of activity. The task is the merging of the node values in two ordered binary trees.

Traversing a tree with a recursive procedure is one of the classic algorithms of computer science. The basic pattern is shown here.

```
procedure traverse(T); tree T;
if T <> none then
begin
    traverse(T.left);
    traverse(T.right);
end;
```

Furthermore, extracting the node values in preorder, inorder, or postorder can be achieved putting the output operation before, between, or after the recursive calls. Now consider the merging of the key values of *two* binary trees, as shown in Figure 4.1.

What is required is two recursive traversers active at the same time returning the values from each tree one by one under the control of a merge algorithm. The solution in Simula is shown in Figure 4.2.

For each tree, we create a Traverser object that executes a recursive traversal of its tree. But after obtaining each value it detaches and returns control to the calling point. This enables the merge loop in the main program to compare the next value from both trees, print the smallest, and resume the relevant traverser to find its next value. The while-loop can be seen as a (simple) scheduler of the two traverser objects based on Val.

There are many situations where coroutines can usefully provide independent tasks without the scheduling overhead of thread packages or operating system processes.

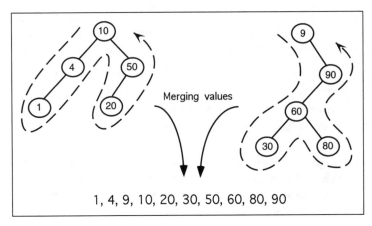

Figure 4.1   Merging the values from two binary trees.

Coroutine primitives are the software equivalent of hardware instructions for context switching such as LoadPSW or interrupts, where one task is suspended and another continues. Even for frameworks where more complex scheduling or real parallelism is required, it is useful to have coroutine sequencing as a fundamental mechanism from which other forms of scheduling can be expressed or implemented.

4.2.5 Simula and Frameworks

The distinction between a framework and a mere library of classes is generally accepted to hinge on the presence of *inverted control*, in other words, the possibility that code in the framework may call code in the user part.

In primitive languages, this is implemented with callbacks, that is, procedure parameters. In most OO languages, the only way to achieve inverted control is through *virtual* procedures—procedures declared and invoked in the framework, but whose actions can be redefined by the user. Simula has virtual procedures, but there is also the *inner* mechanism (described in *Section 4.2.1*), which has the same characteristics of the framework calling user code. The only other language with this mechanism is Beta, described more fully in [Hedin-Knudsen 1999].

The advanced frameworks presented later were chosen to illustrate either inverted control or the handling of parallelism.

4.3 Standard Simula Frameworks

Simula is a general-purpose language that provides superb facilities for simulation by means of two object-oriented frameworks: Simset for list handling and Simulation for discrete event simulation. These are defined formally in the language standard and are a required part of any Simula system. Standard Simula systems also rely on OO frameworks to provide even more basic facilities. In particular, the framework for input/output is interesting in that file and text classes are integrated so well that many users are not even aware of the objects involved.

```
% Treemerge.sim:
%    A program that merges the values from two binary trees
%    using both coroutines and recursion.

begin
   class BinaryTree;
   begin
      ref(BinaryTree) left, right;
      integer          key;
   end;

   class Traverser (T);   ref(BinaryTree) T;
   begin
      integer Val;

      procedure traverse(Node);  ref(tree) Node;
      if N=/= none then
      begin
           traverse( Node.left );
           Val:= Node.key ;
           detach;
           traverse (Node.right) ;
      end;

      traverse(T);
      Val := MAXINT;     ! sentinel  ;
   end -- Traverser --;

   ref (BinaryTree) tree1,
             tree2;
   ref (Traverser) trav1,
                trav2;

   <..... initialization of tree values ..... >

   trav1 :- new Traverser( tree1);
   trav2 :- new Traverser( tree2);

   while trav1.Val <> MAXINT and
         trav2.Val <> MAXINT
   do
      if trav1.Val < trav2.Val
      then begin
         outint(trav1.Val,5);
         call(trav1);
      end
      else begin
         outint(trav2.Val,5);
         call(trav2);
      end
end
```

Figure 4.2   Merging two binary trees with coroutines.

Here, however, we shall concentrate on Simset and Simulation. Both frameworks use the previously described mechanisms. Each consists of a single packaging class that contains all the component classes, procedures, and variables, and an application program obtains these capabilities by using the framework name as a prefix to the program.

4.3.1 Simset (1967)

Simset implements two-way circular lists with distinct Head objects. List members are defined as subclasses of a Link class that provides references to the previous and succeeding list members as well as the usual methods to insert and remove objects from lists. Figure 4.3 shows the structure of such lists.

The list handling facilities are provided through three classes embedded in the Simset packaging class. These classes: include Head for lists and list methods (such as first), Link for list members and their methods (such as into(List)), and a common superclass, Linkage, which provides the links needed by both Head and Link objects. Whereas the Head class corresponds to concrete useful objects, the Link class is *abstract* in the sense that it will never be used on its own; it is meant to be used as a prefix for more particular objects that will be put in lists. A simplified implementation of Simset is shown in Figure 4.4 (the actual class is not much larger: only 80 lines of code).

Even in such a simple framework, there are a few subtle points. To ensure the integrity of lists, the linking pointers (actually called SUCC and PREDE) are hidden from the user, who can access only read-only functions: suc and pred. The protected attribute in the Linkage class ensures that the references cannot be accessed remotely and the hidden declarations in Link and Head prevent access from subclasses.

These same pointers, SUCC and PREDE, are initialized by default to none in Link objects, but they are set to point to their containing object for new Heads, thus maintaining the circularity.

Note also that the suc function returns none for the successor of the last element of a list, even though the SUCC reference does indeed point to something—the list Head. This simplifies the coding of iterations over the elements of a list, stopping when the next element is none. The symmetric function pred operates in the same way; however, there is a function, prev, that returns the value of PREDE without testing the class of the reference. This allows the head of a list to be obtained from a member.

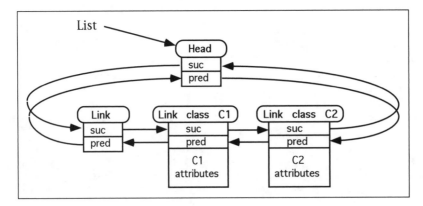

Figure 4.3   Structure of Simset lists.

```
class Simset;
 begin

    class Linkage;
    protected SUCC, PREDE;
    begin
      ref(Linkage) SUCC, PREDE;

      ref(Link)    procedure suc ;
         SUC:- if SUCC in Link
                   then SUCC
                   else NONE;
      ref(Link)    procedure pred; ...;
      ref(Linkage) procedure prev; ...;
    end;

    Linkage class Head;
    hidden SUCC, PREDE;
    begin
      ref(Link) procedure first ; ...;
      ref(Link) procedure last  ; ...;
      boolean   procedure empty ; ...;
      integer   procedure cardinal;..;
                procedure clear ; ...;

      SUCC :- PREDE :- this Head;
    end;

    Linkage class Link;
    hidden SUCC, PREDE;
    begin
     procedure into    (L); ref(Head) L ; precede(L);
     procedure precede(ptr); ref(Linkage)ptr;
      begin out;
      if ptr=/=none and then ptr.PREDE=/=none then begin
        SUCC:-ptr;
        PREDE:-ptr.PREDE;
        PREDE.SUCC:-ptr.PREDE:-this linkage end
      end precede;

     procedure follow (X); ref(Linkage) X; ...
     procedure out     ;...
    end;
 end;
```

Figure 4.4 The Simset framework.

Finally, the reader will notice that LINKed elements have only one SUCC and one PREDE pointer. Thus they can be in only one list at a time, and the standard makes clear that when a user tries to insert into a list an object that is already in a list, the object is automatically removed from its old list.

Simset Example

Following is a program that uses a list to store characters read from the standard input, so that it can print them out in reverse order. Characters are represented by the Link class Elem, declared with a character as a parameter to simplify the creation of the list. The code body of Elem objects also automatically places newly created objects on the list.

```
Simset begin

    ref( Head ) list;
    ref( Elem ) P;

    Link class Elem( C ); character C;
    begin
        into (list );
    end;

    list :- new Head;

    while not endfile do
        new Elem( inchar );

    P :- list.last;
    while not P == NONE do
    begin
        outchar(P.C);
        P :- P.pred;
    end;

end
```

Comments

With only three classes and 12 methods, Simset is a minimal framework by today's standards, but in 1967 it was thought revolutionary for the following reasons:

Programmers were used to packages of *mathematical* functions where the emphasis was on algorithms such as matrix inversion. It was unusual to have a package that concerned itself with data structures.

It was considered *big*. In a time when large computers had 64 Kbytes of memory, the Simset framework seemed unduly wasteful of memory. For example, all linked elements were automatically given *two* pointers, when many applications could have worked just as well with singly linked lists (like LISP). Furthermore, Simset included 12 functions, when any given problem probably only needed 4 or 5. Again, a waste of memory.

It was unusual for language features to be described in terms of the language itself. This, however, was a boon to both implementers and users since many obscure points of behavior (for example, what happens when a user tries to make an object *follow* another that is not in a list?) could be clarified by looking at the code.

In retrospect, Simset proved an excellent framework for all kinds of applications. It was used as for queues, stacks, sets, and ordered event lists. It also served as a model for similar packages in Algol, Pascal, and even FORTRAN, which were then used to implement more complex Simulation packages [Vaucher 1984]. All in all, Simset is probably the oldest and most reused framework of any object-oriented language.

4.3.2 Simulation (1967)

Simulation is a framework that was developed along with the original language to allow it to handle the discrete event Simulation [Birtwistle 1973; Franta 1977]. Basic to this kind of simulation is the notion of *event*: a change in system state considered to be instantaneous. Simulation provides a Process class that is used to specify sequences of events for the active entities in a system. It also implements a notion of simulated time as well as a scheduling mechanism to order process events according to the time at which they are required to occur.

A discrete event simulation program does not seek to emulate the real system exactly; it merely keeps track of the events and the time at which they occur. Often, as long as it does not impact on other activities, activity in a system is modeled by doing nothing at all. Thus events allow complex parallel systems to be simulated with a minimum of computational work.

For example, consider a repair shop with two workers. The first worker is assigned a task that takes 75 minutes and is scheduled to start at 9:15. The second worker starts at 10:00, doing a job that takes 40 minutes. This system could be modeled with the following minimal program:

```
start:      clock :=  0:00 ;   busy1 := busy2 := false;
event1:     clock :=  9:15 ;   busy1 := true;
event2:     clock := 10:00 ;   busy2 := true;
event3:     clock := 10:30 ;   busy1 := false;
event4:     clock := 10:40 ;   busy2 := false;
end_of_day: clock := 17:00 ;
```

Note that simulated time bears no relationship to real time or to computer execution time. In the program, it takes as much computation effort to go from 10:30 to 10:40 as it does to go from 10:40 to the end of the day at 5:00. Furthermore, the same program could be used to model the construction of a cathedral between the years 915 and 1040. Simulation time merely serves to determine the order in which the events from various processes should be executed.

When modeling a complex parallel system, it is useful to concentrate on the active objects, described as processes, and to provide them with a code body that gives the sequence of events they execute during their existence. The correct interleaving of the events from various processes is left up to the central scheduling mechanism. In a process-oriented simulation [Franta 1977], this example would be specified as follows (in pseudocode):

Process Worker1	Process Worker2
wait until time = 9:15	wait until time= 10:00
busy1 := true	busy2 := true
wait 75 min	wait 40 min
busy1 := false	busy2 := false

Note that the scenario for each process is structured as an alternation of active phases (events), which take zero simulated time, separated by *wait* periods when the process state does not change and time can advance. Simula objects operate as coroutines and control can pass out of an object to execute events in other objects before *resuming* the original object to execute the next instruction in its scenario. This means that it is relatively easy to interleave events with multiple processes and simulate parallel activity. However, to schedule events in proper time sequence, an additional mechanism is required.

To sequence events according to event time, simulation packages rely on an agenda; that is to say, an ordered list of event notices where each notice records the simulated time at which a given process should resume its activity. Scheduling operations operate by inserting, deleting, and moving notices in the list. There is also a protocol whereby all scheduling operations finish by updating the clock and passing control to the next process in the list. The event list has been given various names such as *future event list, agenda* or *ready queue*. In Simula, it is called the sequencing set (SQS) but we prefer the generic term *event list*. Figure 4.5 shows the state of an event list for the repair shop example at two points in the execution.

Initially, the event list contains one notice for each process: worker 1 scheduled to start at 9:15 and worker 2 scheduled for 10:00. The hollow arrowheads at the side of each process represent the reactivation point where the process will resume execution. Initially, the scheduler would set the clock to 9:15 and resume worker 1 to carry out the first event: Set busy1 to true and then "wait 75 minutes." This waiting would be implemented by incrementing the event time for Worker 1 to 10:30 and moving it to the correct position in the list (after Notice 2). Like all scheduling operators, the wait operation would terminate by passing control to the first event in the list (Notice 2).

When using the Simulation framework, a programmer never accesses the event list directly; neither does the programmer use the coroutine primitives resume, call, or detach; all sequencing is achieved through a few scheduling statements and procedures, the most important of which is the activate statement, which has several variants. For example:

activate Fred at 50   schedules process Fred at simulated time 50

activate Fred delay 50   schedules Fred for 50 time units from *now*

The variant "activate Fred" places an event notice for Fred immediately before the notice currently at the head of the list (with the same time). This means that the process scheduling Fred momentarily gives up control to execute the next event for Fred.

Other scheduling primitives include hold(dt), which causes the executing process to sleep for *dt* simulated time units and passivate, whereby an active process can stop its own execution indefinitely.

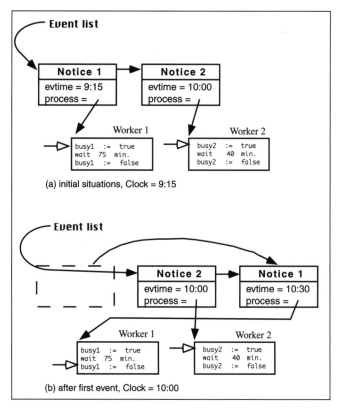

Figure 4.5 Scheduling simulation events.

The Simulation framework also implements two very important mechanisms. First, there is a global function, current, which returns a reference to the currently executing process. Second, the main program can be scheduled just like any other process. Exactly how this is done will be shown in the section describing the implementation.

Simulation Example

The following example shows the use of Simulation. The example shows customers arriving into a system (every 5 minutes on the average) where they spend 20 minutes and then leave. N indicates the number of customers in the system; U is a seed for the uniform random number generator. To show how the model performs, a second Spy process is defined, which prints out the number of customers at regular intervals.

The simulation is started by the main program, which creates and starts the first customer. Thereafter, each arriving customer schedules the arrival of the next. After creating the first customer, the main program suspends itself for 100 minutes. (Note that we have used the same operation, hold, for the main program as for the Client Process.) After this time the main program resumes operation and passes through its final end, and execution terminates.

```
Simulation begin

    integer U,N;

    Process class Client;
    begin
        activate new client delay uniform(0,10,U);
        N := N+1;
            hold( 20 );
        N := N-1;
    end;

    Process class Spy;
    while TRUE do
    begin
        outint(time,5); outchar(':'); outint(N,5); outimage;
        hold(5);
    end;

! --- Main Program --- ;

    U := 1231;
    activate new Spy;
    activate new Client;

    hold( 100 );
    outtext("--- the end ---");

end
```

An excerpt of the following output shows the number of customers increasing, to stabilize around 4 or 5.

```
    0:      0
    5:      1
   10:      2
   15:      3
    . . . . .
   70:      5
   75:      4
   80:      5
   85:      4
   90:      6
   95:      5
--- the end ---
```

Note the simplicity of this program, yet it describes a situation with two kinds of entities where the number of active processes is dynamic and unknown a priori. The clarity of the program contrasts interestingly with the verbose and opaque code of even the simplest examples of parallel programming written in Java [Lea 1997].

Implementation of Simulation

An interesting thing about Simula is that its defining document [SIS 1987] specifies many of its features by giving equivalent pseudocode in Simula itself. The specification of class Simulation amounts to only about 120 lines of code, and the brevity and clarity of the specification are a tribute to the descriptive power of the language and the conceptual integrity of its features. Figure 4.6 gives a simplified version of the Simulation class.

Simulation inherits its list handling capability from Simset. The event list, SQS (for *SeQuencing Set*), is presented as a Head object. Process objects inherit from Link and can thus be placed in lists. To simplify the description, we have omitted event notices and act as if process objects were scheduled by placing them directly into the SQS list. The body of the Process class shows that, initially, process objects execute detach and thus do not start executing the user-defined body until they are scheduled; furthermore, once the user-defined code is ended, processes passivate themselves and any further attempt to schedule them leads to error.

The two functions that follow the Process declaration are particularly interesting. They reflect an *invariant* of the framework that the currently operating process is at the head of the event list. Current is therefore not a variable but a function denoting the process at the head of SQS. Similarly, there is no separate Clock variable: Simulation time is given by the event time of the current process. The so-called simulation monitor or simulation algorithm previously discussed reduces to a single statement: "resume (current)," which is executed after any alteration of SQS. This technique of equating the current process with the one at the head of the readyQ can eliminate many sources of error in operating system environments.

Next in the description comes the passivate procedure, which just removes the current process form SQS and goes on to the next event with "resume (current)." (Note that the values returned by the two invocations of current will be different.)

The operation of the activate statement is described by the activate procedure. It sorts the process PROC into SQS according to the scheduled time T and gives it control in case it is now current. The hold procedure can then be described in terms of the activate procedure.

The description of the last class MainProcess is particularly interesting. As shown in the examples, it is useful to be able to schedule the main program exactly like any other process. To this end, Simulation provides a global reference Main, which points to a process object that serves as a proxy for the main program. This special object is the only instance of the class MainProcess, which just loops on the single operation, detach. This object can be scheduled in SQS or activated directly. Since the execution of detach by any object resumes the main program, scheduling Main is equivalent to scheduling the main program.

Comments

The simulation class allows the specification of independent processes that need have no knowledge of each other. Each process schedules its own events and the use of an ordered event list automatically ensures that events from various processes are merged correctly. Note that the Simulation framework completely shields the user from the basic coroutine primitives: resume, call, and detach, which are conceptually replaced by activate and passivate.

```
Simset class Simulation;
begin

    ref(Head)      SQS ;

    Link class Process;
    begin
        real evtime;
        detach;
        inner;
        passivate;
        ERROR;
    end  -- process --;

    ref( process ) procedure current;
        current :- SQS.first;

    real procedure time;
        time := current . evtime;

    procedure activate_ ( Proc,T);
            ref(process) Proc;
            real      T;
    begin
        Proc.evtime := T;
        ... insert Proc into SQS according to  T ...;
        resume(current);
    end;

    procedure hold (DT);  real DT;
            activate_( current, Time+DT);

    procedure passivate;
    begin
        current.out;
        resume(current);
    end;

    ref(Process)     main;

    Process class MainProcess;
            while true do detach;

    SQS :- new head;
    main :- new MainProcess;
    activate_ (main, 0);

end  -- Simulation --;
```

Figure 4.6 The Simulation framework.

4.4 Other Simulation Frameworks

Although Simula provides all the language features and scheduling primitives required for many types of simulation, it remains a general-purpose language and not a specialized package. For any given area, it is useful to have a dedicated simulation package with more specialized objects, operations, and reporting facilities. In this section, we present early simulation frameworks that extended Simula's capabilities.

4.4.1 GPSSS (1971)

Simulation is often applied to queuing models where processes compete for *resources* and have to wait in queues when the resources they need are in use—a typical example is a model of supermarket checkout lines. In this type of model, time scheduling is not enough; there must also be predefined objects to represent resources as well as operations to seize and release them. Furthermore, it is important to be able to gather statistics on resource utilization and waiting times.

Probably the best-known package for queuing simulations is GPSS, a discrete-event simulation system developed by G. Gordon of IBM [Gordon 1975]. GPSS views systems in terms of active entities—called *transactions*—flowing from one work area to another. It provides a set of predefined objects and a set of operations (function blocks) on those objects. Resources are represented by *facilities* (unit resources) and *storages* (groups of identical resources). Other object types include groups to represent transaction batches, *regions* (called *queues*) to get statistics on transit times, and *histograms*. GPSS also provides priorities, multiple runs, and generalized conditional scheduling.

In a typical model, transactions are created by a Generate operation and are said to *flow* from function block (operation) to function block until they reach a Terminate block, which removes them from the system. Some operations, like Advance, model the passage of time (much like Simula's Hold); others like Seize or Release model the occupation of a resource with the possibility of a delay if the resource is occupied. Here is an example of a simple GPSS program for a queue.

```
GENERATE 5,0      { generate one transaction every 5 time units }
SEIZE SERVER      { occupy facility named server}
ADVANCE  4,1      { delay t time units, with t uniformly distributed
                    between 3 and 5 }
RELEASE SERVER
TERMINATE 1       { kill transaction and increment transaction
                    count }
START  200        { run the simulation until 200 transaction finish  }
```

The language is restrictive but the brevity of typical models indicates that the choice of basic objects and operations is well founded. Of particular use to the modeler is the automatic printing of statistics at the end of the simulation.

One of authors had used GPSS before coming into contact with Simula. This prompted him to design a Simula extension that would provide the same objects and statistics as GPSS while retaining the general algorithmic capability of Simula. The framework was called GPSSS [Vaucher 1971]. The scheduling core of GPSSS was implemented in about 400 lines of Simula, but procedures for error reporting and statistics add another 400 lines. Details on implementation and use of GPSSS can also be found in Franta's book on simulation [Franta 1977].

GPSSS is significant in that it represented the first time an outsider, distinct from the designers of Simula, had exploited the potential of an object-oriented language to create a useful and nontrivial application framework. The GPSSS mechanism for time delays is already part of the standard Simulation framework and needs no further explanation. We will consider only the operation of facility and storage resources:

Facility. A single nonshareable resource that can be occupied by only one transaction at a time. A facility is thus busy (if occupied) or not busy. A transaction requests a facility by flowing into a Seize block and releases it by executing a Release block. Transactions attempting to seize a busy facility become blocked and are placed in a first-in, first-out (FIFO) queue associated with the facility resource. When a Release is executed, the next waiting transaction, if any, occupies the facility and can continue its progress through the model.

Storage. A resource with a capacity greater than one. Portions of the capacity can be allocated to (that is, be occupied by) different transactions. A transaction requests a portion of the capacity by flowing through an Enter block and releases an occupied portion by flowing through the Leave block. Both Enter and Release blocks have a parameter indicating the number of resource units required or released. Entering transactions whose requirements cannot be met are made to wait in a queue. Whenever a transaction Leaves, all waiting transactions are given a chance to obtain their requested resource units.

Implementation

GPSSS is implemented as a class prefixed by Simulation, thus inheriting the event list for the passage of time as well as Simset's lists. An outline of the implementation is shown in Figure 4.7. It includes the declarations for three relevant classes: Facility, Storage, and Transaction. It also includes lists (FacilityQ and StorageQ) where created resource objects (subclasses of Link) will place themselves. This allows the report generator to print statistics on all the created resources.

The Facility class has two local variables: a pointer to the current occupier (or "none" if idle) and a list for waiting transactions. The body takes care of initialization: creating the input queue and placing the newly created facility into FacilityQ. Storages are declared in the same way as facilities.

The Transaction class contains most of the methods describing interaction between transactions and resources. We show only two, for *seizing* and *releasing* a facility, and omit all code dealing with statistics or error control. In GPSSS, we adopted a more systematic naming convention for resource operations: seize/release is replaced by enter_facility and leave_facility; similarly, for storages, we use the terms enter_storage and leave_storage.

```
Simulation class Gpsss ;
begin
   ref (Head) facilityQ, storageQ, ... ;

Link class Facility (id) ;  text id;
begin
   ref(head) inq ;
   ref(transaction) occupier ;

   inq :- new head ;
   into (facilityq);
end facility definition ;

Link class Storage (id, capacity) ;
   text id; integer capacity ;
   ...;

Process class transaction ;
begin
   procedure enter_facility (f) ; ref (facility) f ;
   inspect f do
      if occupier == none then
         occupier :- this transaction
      else begin
         into (inq) ;
         passivate ;
         this transaction . out
       end  ;

   procedure leave_facility (f) ; ref (Facility) f ;
   inspect f do begin
      occupier :- inq.first ;
      if occupier == none
         then < update facility statistics...>
         else activate occupier delay 0 ;
   end ;

   procedure enter_storage (s, units); ... ;
   procedure leave_storage (s, units) ; ... ;

end class Transaction ;

procedure standard_report ; ... ;

! ********** INITIALIZATION ************* ;

   facilityq :- new head ;
   storageq :- new head ;
   ....
      INNER ;
   standard_report ;

end Gpsss ;
```

Figure 4.7   The GPSSS Framework.

Basically, if a facility is free (it has no occupier), an entering transaction reserves the facility by assigning a reference to itself as occupier; otherwise, it places itself in the facility queue and goes to sleep. It is the responsibility of transactions leaving a resource to wake up the next transaction waiting for it. The provision of pairs of methods such as enter_facility/leave_facility is fairly typical for resources, be they named facilities as in GPSS or *semaphores* and *monitors* in OS applications. There are many different ways in which these could be implemented, but they must always be designed in tandem.

The last interesting thing to consider in the GPSSS class is its code body: It is composed of two parts separated by the keyword Inner. The first part takes care of initialization, such as creating the resource queues; Inner then passes control to the user program that uses GPSSS. When the user program terminates, control then returns to GPSSS, which prints out the final statistical summary of resource use. The possibility to have terminating actions in addition to initialization is obviously quite useful in this case.

GPSSS Example

The following program shows the use of GPSSS for a queuing situation similar to that given previously for Simulation. The difference is that customers queue up for a single teller, whereas before they entered and left without requiring a resource. Furthermore, the package will automatically provide statistics on the occupation of the teller. Note also that, since a user framework such as GPSSS is not part of the standard library, it is compiled separately and declared to be an external class.

```
external class Gpsss;

Gpsss begin
    Transaction class Client;
    begin integer i;
        activate new Client delay uniform(0,10,U);
        N := N+1;
        enter_facility(teller);
            hold(uniform(0,10,U));
        N := N-1;
        leave_facility(teller);
    end ;

    Transaction class Spy;
    while TRUE do
        begin integer i;
            outInt(Time,5); outText(": ");
            for i := 1 step 1 until N do outchar('X');
            outimage;
            hold(5);
        end ;

    integer i,n;
    ref(Facility) teller;
```

```
       teller :- new Facility("Teller");
       activate new Spy;
       activate new Client at uniform(1,10,U);
       hold(50);
end
```

The output of execution is shown as follows. The trace of N, the number of customers in the system, printed by the Spy object, shows the increasing congestion (as expected with an average occupation time equal to the interarrival time) and the report shows the overall teller utilization to be 83 percent.

```
 0:
 5:
10: X
15: XX
20: XXX
25: XX
30: XXXX
35: XXXX
40: XXX
45: XXXX


*************************  -version 5.1-
***    montreal  gpsss   ***
***  simulation_report   ***
*************************


pass =  1
start time =      0.00
end   time =     50.00


* facilities *
*************

                    avg.    avg.time
             entries contents transit status

Teller             7     0.83    5.90    busy

* no storages *
```

Comments

The GPSSS framework was obviously useful for simulation, but its deeper significance was in the development of specialized objects and algorithms for synchronization. When we turned to the modeling of operating systems, it was quite easy to adapt the GPSSS class descriptions into objects relevant to operating systems. For example, GPSSS *facilities* operate exactly as *binary semaphores* and GPSSS *storages* are analogous to *general semaphores*. There is also a strong structural analogy between the simulation Event List and the OS ready_queue.

4.4.2 Modeling Operating Systems (1981)

In his textbook on operating systems, Alan Shaw [Shaw 1974] included the description of a student project to accompany the course. It involved writing a complete multi-tasking operating system on top of a simulated centralized batch computer. The students first had to write the simulator, including peripheral devices, then implement the OS. Early in the 1980s, we adopted this case study for the one-term OS course at the University of Montreal; however, we decided to give students a head start by providing a Simula framework that described the hardware components and the environment. The students would extend this framework to implement their own operating system including a file system, a command language interpreter, multiprogramming, and spooling. Through the years, there were several variants of these frameworks (UM81, UM82, and so on), which came to be known as the UMxx series.

Figure 4.8 shows a typical configuration for the simulated computer. It consisted of a central processing unit (CPU), memory, 2 disks, a printer, a timer, and 10 telecommunication lines through which users can submit jobs remotely. Direct memory access (DMA) allowed IO to proceed in parallel with the CPU. User programs were coded in machine language with a minimal set of 9 instructions chosen to provide a mixture of compute-bound and IO-bound jobs. These included load, store, add, branch, and supervisor calls to do IO or halt. Machine registers included an instruction counter (IC), an accumulator, and base/limit address registers.

As described initially by Shaw, the machine was a typical early batch computer with jobs submitted through a card reader. As the years went by, we upgraded the model but always had to compromise between realism and complexity to maximize the pedagogical benefit of the project. For example, we tried paging but found that our simulated jobs didn't run long enough to allow realistic comparisons of various page replacement algorithms. The idea of remotely submitted jobs was, again, a compromise between batch and interactive computing. In our model, the system can set and alter the number of users, but there is no flow control. All connected users follow the same script: They wait a random time then submit the next job in a predetermined set of jobs. Once a user starts to submit a job, data is sent at a steady rate and will be lost if the operating system does not react fast enough to empty the receiving buffers.

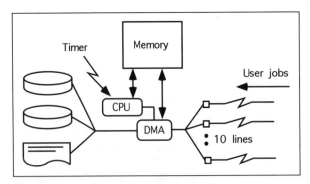

Figure 4.8   The UMxx hardware.

To make things more interesting, the objective of the project was not only to handle jobs correctly but also to maximize profit. An accounting formula was given and students tried to optimize multiprogramming and parallel activity to run the maximum number of jobs during a simulated period of 24 hours.

The challenge to the teachers was to implement a realistic environment. We wanted to confront the students with the two kinds of parallelism encountered in actual operating systems: (1) the *real* parallelism between the CPU, the users, and the peripherals and (2) the *simulated* parallelism between system tasks sharing a single CPU. We also wanted to provide the same primitives operations for task switching as are found in modern systems so that the students would have to implement their own basic scheduling tools and use them to develop higher-level tools such as semaphores and monitors as the course progressed.

Implementation

Simula turned out to be an ideal vehicle for such an assignment. First, all components capable of real parallel activity were implemented as Simulation processes. Second, operating system (time-shared) parallelism was achieved by having the single CPU process act as *current* for all simulated computer activity—much in the same way the MainProcess object acted as a proxy for the main program in the Simulation framework. This required use of the coroutine primitives, Resume and Detach, and showed the usefulness of having various levels of scheduling primitives.

To reflect the context switching instructions present in modern computers, we provided Process Control Block (PCB) objects and a single LoadPCB instruction. A PCB can store the contents of all pertinent hardware registers, such as the instruction counter (IC), the addressing registers (Base and Limit), and the mode (user/supervisor) bit. In other words, a PCB can store a process state so that a process can be stopped and resumed later. Execution of a LoadPCB(X) instruction loads all system registers from the X, effectively switching the CPU from its current task to that represented by X. We also implemented a dual mode of operation. In *user* mode (as determined by the mode bit), the CPU functions as a machine language interpreter, executing user instructions in the simulated memory; in *supervisor* mode, the CPU directly resumes the PCB objects. This allows the students to implement their OS as Simula objects (subclasses of PCB) and procedures.

We also provided *privileged* instructions such as StartIO, whereby a student could initiate data transfer between peripherals and central memory. Finally, we implemented an interrupt system to inform the hardware of various events such as end_of_IO or timeouts or runtime errors. We also provided an interrupt vector: a global array of PCB pointers, each of which associated to a particular type of interrupt. An interrupt causes a LoadPCB instruction to be executed on one of these PCBs. On start-up, the student's OS has to initialize the array with his or her own supervisor mode PCBs (interrupt handlers).

The students are thus isolated from both Simulation operations (such as hold) and coroutine primitives (such as resume). In this framework—as on a real machine— they start with the strict minimum (LoadPCB) and have to implement everything else.

Obviously, it was quite useful to have a simulation language to simulate the basic hardware and environment; but this was not the major advantage of using Simula. What was really useful was the combination of object orientation and the correct primitives for coroutine control. This enabled our students (with our guidance) to implement and apply all the scheduling tools described in the literature.

Use

Students using the UMxx framework would need to build up their operating system in layers. At the most basic level, they would have to implement process scheduling with a ReadyQ and procedures to insert and remove processes and, most important, a dispatching operation to pass control to the next ready process (in the following, it is called SelectNextProcess). Typically, the necessary code would look like the following:

```
ref (Head) ReadyQ;

procedure SelectNextProcess;
    loadpcb(ReadyQ.first);

procedure Schedule(P); ref(Pcb) P;
if P =/= none then
begin
    P.into(ReadyQ);
    SelectNextProcess;
end;

procedure Wait_in(Q); ref(Head) Q ;
begin
    readyQ.first.into(Q);
    SelectNextProcess;
end;
```

On this base they would normally build more sophisticated operations. For example, the following code shows the ease and clarity with which Dijkstra's general semaphores could be implemented (along with the wait and signal operations).

```
Head class Semaphore (n); integer n;
    begin end;

procedure wait (s); ref(Semaphore) s;
    if s.n > 0
        then s.n:= s.n-1
        else Wait_in( S );

procedure signal (s); ref(Semaphore) s;
    if not s.empty
        then  Schedule( s.first );
        else s.n := s.n+1;
```

Allocators

With semaphores, students could then implement resource allocators. A good example is the generic allocator shown in the following, which manages resources that are requested and returned one unit at a time like disk sectors, file descriptors, or memory buffers. It combines a list to store available resources with a semaphore to synchronize access. Two methods are provided: the get method used to obtain one unit of the resource and the put method used to return a unit.

```
class  Allocator;
protected
    available, list;
begin
    ref(Semaphore) available;
    ref(Head) list;

  ref(Link) procedure get;
  begin
    ref(Link) p;

    wait(available);
    get:- p:- list.first;
    p.out;
  end;

    procedure put (res) ; ref(link) res;
    begin
       res.into ( list );
       signal ( available ) ;
    end;

    available :- new Semaphore(0);
    list:- new Head;

  end  ** allocator **;
```

This generic allocator would be used in close to a dozen cases in one of our typical student programs.

Conditional Scheduling

For more complex synchronization, such as waiting for multiple resources of different types, programming with semaphores or monitors proves quite complex, and *conditional* scheduling is often the best answer. In simulation, this takes the form of a Wait_Until (Boolean expression) statement. The conditional critical regions proposed by Brinch-Hansen are an example of this kind of scheduling in the OS area [Brinch 1973]. In the 1970s, we studied several ways to implement Wait_Until efficiently [Lapalme-Vaucher 1981; Vaucher 1973; Vaucher-Davey 1978], and this was also the subject of Lapalme's Ph.D. thesis. Excerpts of this work are also available in [Franta 1977].

With conditional scheduling, the responsibility for deciding whether to proceed or to wait is left to the requesting process. The trick is to allow this process to check its condition whenever there is good reason to suspect that the condition may have changed. One implementation used in UMxx assumed that all interacting methods and variables are located in one object: a Wait_Class object. Processes waiting for their condition to be true are placed in a local wait queue and a check procedure is provided that should be called at the end of any method that changes the object state. The following description shows the implementation. We rely on Simula's Name parameter mode (same as Algol's), but the same thing could be implemented via macros.

```
class Wait_Class ;
begin
      ref (head) WaitQ;

      procedure Check;
      while not WaitQ.empty do
         WaitQ.first.into(readyQ);

      procedure wait_until( B ); name B; Boolean B;
      while not B do
         Wait_in( WaitQ);

      Queue :- new head
end;
```

The next example uses the Wait_Class to implement the synchronization (only) for an allocator like a GPSS storage, where one may request and return several units.

```
Wait_Class class Block_Alloc (avail); integer  avail;
begin

      procedure GET (n); integer n;
      begin
         wait_until(avail>= n );
         avail:= avail- n;
      end;

      procedure PUT (n); integer n;
      begin
            avail:= avail+ n;
            Check;
      end;

end Block_Alloc ;
```

Comments

The UMxx framework served in various forms every year from 1981 to 1994, at which time, the curriculum was changed and the emphasis switched to advanced Unix features. In one term, with the UMxx environment, students would generally succeed in getting their operating system to run, although their systems usually retained mysterious bugs. A classic bug that occurred year after year was IO interrupts being received by the wrong job when priorities were introduced. Most often, this was a result of not respecting the invariant that the current operating process should be at the head of the ReadyQ, forgetting to call SelectNextProcess at the end of a scheduling operation. Simply, what would happen is as follows: If a task unblocks as the result of a signal on a semaphore that has a higher priority than the current task, it would place itself at the head of the ReadyQ in front of the current task and succeeding operations such as wait would passivate the wrong task. The UMxx environment allowed many hard lessons on the difficulty of programming in a parallel environment to be learned—better these toy systems should fail than ones built later in the outside world.

In conclusion, the object and process facilities of Simula allowed us to provide students with objects implementing the latest concepts discussed in OS texts but rarely available in programming languages. These included semaphores, monitors, critical regions, and WaitUntil primitives. The UMxx environment allowed students to come to grips with the pitfalls of parallel programming and resolve these with structured tools and clean architectures.

4.5 Simula and Real Time

From the preceding presentation of frameworks using simulated time, it is apparent that they share many constructs with real-time packages. For example, the concept of process with scheduling operations (activate, passivate, hold, wait) and a scheduler working on a queue of processes. Furthermore, it is often striking, when looking at a simulation model, how much of the code would seem to be useful for implementing a real controller for the simulated system. There are also, of course, differences. A control system interacts with the physical world through input/output signals, while a simulation model for such a system interacts with additional code, which imitates the environment; the simulation model works in *simulated* time, whereas interacting with physical reality must be done in *real* time, often with demands on response times. Finally, in a simulation model, control can pass from one component to another only at specific programmed scheduling points (in operations such as passivate, hold, and wait); whereas, a real-time system need interrupts—at unpredictable times—in order to react to external signals. But even so, the similarities have led several researchers to look into creating frameworks for real-time applications based on Simula's simulation capability.

These frameworks have taken two different approaches. The first is to directly use the concepts of Simulation, but to offer a second implementation with different semantics adapted to work in real time rather than in simulated time. The second approach is to implement the process and synchronization concepts known from concurrent and real-time programming (semaphore, monitor, message passing, and so on) by using the basic scheduling facilities in Simula (detach/call/resume).

4.5.1 Simulation for Real Time

Jacob Palme, an enthusiastic advocate of the successful DEC10 Simula system, made a proposal, as early as 1975 [Palme 1975], to add a real-time framework to Simula. In his paper, he pointed out that there is a large class of *soft* real-time applications that can benefit from a process-based architecture, but that don't need interrupt facilities. These are interactive systems where the response time required is relatively large compared to the typical time for processing an event or a transaction. Typical examples include database applications where a single system manages the data and services on several terminals in parallel. In a modern context, many servers in client/server applications fit the picture as well as clients connected to many servers. The paper thus concludes that, for these interactive applications, interrupt facilities are not strictly needed, while the possibility of structuring a system as a set of processes (one for each terminal/user) has big advantages.

Having only explicit scheduling points and no interrupts or preemptive scheduling has the big advantage of not having to deal with the problems of concurrency (such as mutual exclusion and deadlocks). In the (rare) cases of transactions with long processing times, the programmer will need to insert rescheduling (yield) points to share the CPU and allow other processes to advance. When using Simulation, this yielding takes the form of calls to Hold(0). Only at these explicit points need the programmer worry about interaction between processes.

The chapter also points out the value of the safety aspects of Simula in this kind of interactive application. The execution of a Simula program is always well defined—it may end up in an execution error reported by the runtime system, but it can never *run wild*. Finally, the chapter points out that simulation can be an effective way to prototype real-time systems and basing a real-time framework on class Simulation makes development by partial simulation possible.

Problems to Be Solved

The chapter identifies a couple of shortcomings in Simula that militate against development of this kind of application.

Input/output. The standard framework for input in Simula, in particular class Infile is missing facilities for *interrupt handling*, for example, mechanisms for a process to detect that input is available. The basic input mechanisms (Inimage) in class Infile blocks the entire program when no input is available.

Garbage collection. The stop-the-world garbage collectors popular at the time were a potential problem for interactive use. Fortunately, the size of primary memory in the 1970s was so small that it turned out not to be a severe problem. The chapter notes that with 50 Kbytes on an IBM 370 mainframe typical of the period, a garbage collection cycle would take 20 to 70 milliseconds and thus go unnoticed. The chapter notes that if shorter times were needed, the garbage collector would have to be rewritten in an incremental way. It is interesting to note that development since then [Hudson-Moss 1992; Ungar 1987] has come up with solutions that offer the same times on modern machines, but with primary memories measured in megabytes rather than kilobytes. There is even development of garbage collectors for hard real-time applications [Magnusson-Henriksson 1995].

Proposal

The solution proposed in the chapter is formulated as an addition to the Simulation framework and is surprisingly short. It contains a new subclass of class process, TerminalProcess, with a parameter to an Infile object and a special queue, TerminalQueue.

In order to solve the blocking IO problem, a TerminalProcess must call Wait(TerminalQueue), with the semantics that it will be passivated if there is no data until input is available in its Infile object. Passivation means that the next process is scheduled in its place. An additional operation, DataReady, makes it possible to explicitly check if input is possible.

For synchronization with real time, the chapter suggests a simple solution. It requires the ability to Sleep for a given (real) time interval—a standard procedure found in all operating systems. Users implement Simulation's scheduling primitives as if simulated time were real time. To synchronize real and simulated time, it is sufficient to add *one* clock process, which calls Sleep(DT) whenever it calls Hold(DT). In the simplest and most inefficient case, this clock would cycle in 1-second increments:

```
Process class clock;
while true do
begin
    hold(1); sleep(1);
end;
```

A smarter technique would be to compare real and simulated time and to *sleep* for the difference. The synchronization could be turned on and off explicitly, offering the possibility to run the program (faster or slower) in a simulated environment and in this way support the idea of development from simulation to the real thing.

Applications

The chapter contains several examples: a database system with several users, which behaves differently if the user responds quickly or slowly; a conversational time-sharing system; and a robot control application. Here we will show a slightly edited version of a system handling dialog with several terminals:

```
Simulation begin
   Terminal_Process class Terminal (FileSpec);
         text FileSpec;
   begin
      procedure OpenTerminal; ···;
      procedure ReadInputAndProduceAnswers; ···;

      OpenTerminal;
      while true do
      begin
         Wait(TerminalQueue); ! Wait for input on my file;
         ReadInputAndProduceAnswers;
      end;
   end --- Terminal ---;
```

```
   ! Main program - acts as a process of its own;
while true do
begin
   text procedure ReadDialogForUser; ...;
   text NewUser;
   Wait(TerminalQueue); ! Wait for input on SysIn;
   NewUser:- ReadDialogForUser;
   Activate new Terminal(new Infile(NewUser), NewUser);
end - starting new terminal -;
end;
```

Implementation

The framework was implemented in the LIBSIM library of the DEC-10 implementation of Simula, but the proposal never made it as an official change of the Simula standard. The framework was used for development of several large interactive systems including the KOM system, also developed by Palme, quite a popular Swedish online news system at the time.

4.5.2 Class Realtime

This framework was developed at the Norwegian Computing Center as an extension of the class Simulation. It was initiated as part of a project to implement an X25 DTE protocol in Simula [Belsnes-Løvdal 1977]. The objective was similar to that of the previous project: using the same code in both a simulation of the system and in the actual implementation. The code was explicitly structured to make this practical. In the simulation, the code that would go into the final implementation was clearly separated from the code that simulated its environment. Furthermore, the interfaces were designed to fit the situation in the real system. In this way the implementation of the X25 protocol could be developed and tested offline on a large computer with debugging aids. After switching to the actual target computer and exchanging the code to simulate the environment with an interface to the HDLC line, it was finally debugged in a very short time. Maintenance could be aided by collecting data during actual execution of the system and then having the data drive a simulation with the very same code.

With this development process in mind, the project elected to develop an alternative framework for Simulation, with the same interface but with different semantics. This new framework was called Realtime. The implementation strategy followed the one previously outlined. In Realtime, time is made to follow real time by inserting appropriate delays at scheduling points, before handing control to the next process. Input/output was handled in a pragmatic way, handling only I/O in connection with the network. Input and output requests (Receive/Transmit) are implemented to passivate (block) the calling process until the network is ready for the operation. Also in this application, it was sufficient to rely on explicit scheduling points and to avoid interrupts and preemptive scheduling. An unusual feature of the framework was a facility for deadline scheduling of low-priority background processes. These would call the operation Timeshare(t), where t should be the time it would need to reach its next call to Timeshare or another scheduling point. Control would be given to the process only when no high-priority process would need to execute before t has elapsed.

In a Unix setting, the facilities added in this framework were easily mapped to the operating system services: Select (for the TerminalQueue) and Sleep (for synchronizing with real time). From a framework point of view, it illustrates how a model developed for one domain can be reused and expanded to use in a different domain. Both this framework and Palme's show that a framework for real time without preemption can be quite useful if used with some care. Furthermore, these experiments show that real-time frameworks can be implemented in Simula with minimal and standard operating system services.

4.5.3 SimIOProcess: Real Time with Interrupts

Simula's Simulation is a very useful framework for process scheduling, but it is possible to implement others. The basic scheduling primitives Detach/Call/Resume used to implement Simulation are also available to the programmer who can thus define new process concepts and scheduling mechanisms. Defining a framework for real time as opposed to simulated time is thus tempting. Inspiration came both from the work by Per Brinch-Hansen on Concurrent Pascal [Brinch 1977] and from Niklaus Wirth's work on Modula [Wirth 1977]. Note that both these languages appear to have been influenced by Simula: There is a limited class concept in Concurrent Pascal and, in Modula, the operation Resume has semantics similar to the operation with the same name in Simula. It is thus interesting to see how the work done in these systems can be mapped back to Simula.

First efforts in this direction, class C_P_System [Magnusson-Löfgren 1981], were already reported in 1981. Then it was suggested that a new pair of scheduling primitives CoStart/CoStop be introduced as alternatives to Call/Detach, but with the possibility of managing interrupts and preemptive scheduling. As work continued with this approach, it was found that the same things could be achieved by retaining Call/Detach and allowing an *implicit* Detach in a single interrupt procedure. The current implementation of this idea, called SimIOProcess [Magnusson 1995], is available as part of the Lund Simula distribution.

This framework consists of three essential classes: IOProcess, of which users define subclasses with action sequences, ProcessManager, a singular class scheduling IOProcess objects, and BasicProcess Event (with subclasses), for event-based communication. There are two additional classes in the framework, Semaphore and Monitor, but these are defined on top of the others and included in a system only if actually used.

Figure 4.9 shows a simplified version of the classes IOProcess and ProcessManager, so we can explain how they interact.

This extract shows one typical way to organize process scheduling in Simula. Upon creation, objects are immediately detached. The operation Start inserts them into the ReadyQ in priority order. The heart of the scheduler lies in the Run procedure of the ProcessManager. Run repeatedly selects processes one by one from the ReadyQ and activates them with the coroutine primitive call. Control returns to the scheduler by a process executing detach—when it hits a Stop (or finishes). If an IOProcess is interrupted (as discussed subsequently) or the operation ReSchedule is called, it will be reinserted into the ReadyQ and thus placed after other processes with the same (or higher) priority. This scheme thus supports strict priority scheduling with round robin for a process with the same priority.

```
Link class IOProcess(PMG); ref(ProcessManager) PMG;
begin
    integer Priority;
    integer State,
            SReady=1,   SStop=2, SWaiting=3,
            SDelayed=4, STerminated=5;
    State:=SStop; ! Initially Stopped.;
    Detach; ! Initial detach - return to after the corresponding 'new'.;
    Inner; ! Takes execution to user-defined code in subclass(es)
            of IOProcess.;
    State:=Sterminated; ! Will prevent erroneous scheduling after death.;
    out;                    ! Remove this object from the PMG ReadyQ;
end --- IOProcess ---;

class ProcessManager;
begin
    procedure Start(P); ref(P) IOProcess;
    begin
        P.State:=P.SReady;
        P.SortInto(ReadyQ); ! P available for scheduling.;
    end - Start -;

    procedure Stop;
    begin! CurrentProcess is already placed in some waiting Q, and
        ! no longer in ReadyQ.;
        CurrentProcess.State:=CurrentProcess.SStop;
        CurrentProcess.Detach; ! Takes execution to just after 'call';
    end -Stop -;

    procedure ReSchedule;
        CurrentProcess.Detach; ! Allow other process to execute;
    procedure SetTimeSlice(T); real T;
        TimeSlice:=T;

    procedure Run;
    begin
        while not ReadyQ.Empty do
        begin
            CurrentProcess:-ReadyQ.First;
            EnableAlarm(TimeSlice); ! See below.;
            Call(CurrentProcess); ! Takes execution to after the
            ! last executed 'detach' in the selected process.;
            if CurrentProcess.Status=CurrentProcess.SReady then
                CurrentProcess.SortInto(ReadyQ); ! Round robin;
        end;
        ...
    end - run -;

    real TimeSlice; ! in seconds ;
    ref(IOProcess) CurrentProcess;
    ref(PriorityQ) ReadyQ;
    ReadyQ :- new PriorityQ; ! Subclass of Head with sorting
                                'into' operation;
end --- ProcessManager ---;
```

Figure 4.9 Managing processes in SimIOProcess.

In order to complete the overview we have to answer the following questions:

- How are interrupts and preemptive scheduling handled, and, as a consequence, how is mutual exclusion guaranteed in the kernel itself?

- How does one implement synchronization primitives such as Semaphores, Monitors, and Events?

- How is I/O handled?

- What happens when the ReadyQ is empty and the loop in Run terminates?

Interrupts and Preemptive Scheduling

Let us first consider the implementation of time-sharing with quantum interrupts. When a timer interrupt occurs, we would like control to return to the scheduler, which could then give control to the next ready process. As already stated, control is passed from a process back to the scheduler by having the process execute detach. The problem is that the detach has to be written explicitly in the code in advance. This problem is solved by having an interrupt mechanism (in Unix, Alarm) that actually performs a detach on an object as if it was written in the code. This implicit detach can thus be executed potentially anywhere in the program. To know which Process to detach, the interrupt routine consults the reference, InterruptProc, which always points to the currently active IOProcess. Figure 4.10 shows the routines that implement timer interrupts. These use the Unix utility Alarm(T, AlarmRoutine), which has the effect that the AlarmRoutine is executed as an interrupt after time T. The implementation of AlarmRoutine thus takes a little bit of tricking behind the scene since it is executing as an interrupt where the environment is different from the usual execution of procedure calls. Apart from this implementation consideration, the rest is pure Simula. The procedures are placed as operations in class ProcessManager.

To maintain integrity of the synchronization primitives, it is necessary to ensure mutual exclusion by temporarily suspending interrupts. This is accomplished by the Enable/Disable procedures simply by modifying the contents of the InterruptProc reference.

Handling Input/Output and Delays

The ProcessManager interacts with IOProcesses in terms of Events. An IOProcess can indicate which input events it will accept (for example, EnableInputEvents) and it can wait for them with a call to WaitEvent, at which point it is removed from the ReadyQ. When input arrives, the ProcessManager will send the waiting process an InputAvailableEvent, which has the effect that the process is moved back to the ReadyQ. Input (and output) events in modern interactive environments are typically from Window Managers or Sockets communicating with other programs (on the same or other machines), but in a control situation the same mechanism could be used for other input/output devices.

Event handling is implemented as two operations in class IOProcess: WaitEvent and PutEvent. It is shown in Figure 4.11.

```
ref(IOProcess) InterruptProc;
Boolean        Pending;

procedure EnableAlarm(T); real T; ! Order an interrupt after time T.;
begin
     Pending:=False;
     InterruptProc:-CurrentProcess;
     Alarm(T,AlarmRoutine); ! Unix utility ;
end -- EnableAlarm--;

procedure AlarmRoutine;
begin
     inspect InterruptProc do
     begin
          InterruptProc :- None;
          this IOProcess.Detach;
     end
     otherwise
          Pending:=true;
end --- AlarmRoutine  ---;

procedure Disable;
     InterruptProc:-none;

procedure Enable;
begin
     if Pending then
          CurrentProcess.Detach ! Delayed Interrupt;
     else
          InterruptProc:-CurrentProcess;
end;
```

Figure 4.10   Handling timer interrupts.

Most of this code is similar to an implementation of a Semaphore (with the length of the Event-queue as the counter). The only tricky part is to make sure that interrupts are disabled over the critical parts. The ProcessManager enables interrupts when giving control (through Call) to an IOProcess. This is why there are fewer Enables than one might expect and there is an additional Disable after Detach.

An IOProcess can also delay its own execution for a period of (real) time (for example, DelayTime). As a result, the process is removed from the ReadyQ. When the time has passed, the ProcessManager will put it back into the ReadyQ.

Empty ReadyQ

When the ReadyQ is empty this means that there are no more ready processes to execute. In a simulation, the scheduler would then terminate execution since nothing else could ever happen. In a real-time framework, it means that the program should be sus-

```
Link class IOProcess(PMG); ref(ProcessManager) PMG;
begin
     ... as of above ...

     ref(BasicProcessEvent) procedure WaitEvent;
     begin
          PMG.Disable;
          if Events.Empty then
          begin
               State:=SWaiting;
               Out; ! leave the ReadyQ;
               Detach; ! Block this process;
               PMG.Disable;
          end;
          WaitEvent:-Events.First;
          Events.First.Out;
          PMG.Enable;
     end - WaitEvent;

     procedure PutEvent(E); ref(BasicProcessEvent) E;
     begin
          PMG.Disable;
          E.Into(Events);
          if State=SWaiting then
          begin
               State:=SReady;
               PMG.Start(this IOProcess);
               PMG.Reschedule; ! if started process has higher
                                        prio.;
          end
          else
               PMG.Enable;
     end -- PutEvent --;

     ref(Head) Events;
     Event :- new Head;
end --- IOProcess ---;
```

Figure 4.11   Handling events in SimIOProcess.

pended, waiting for something to happen. This may be the passage of time, so a process that is delayed now should be executed. It might also be that input arrives on an input channel and a process that is servicing it should be inserted into the ReadyQ.

Delayed processes (which have called DelayTime or DelayUntil) are kept in a queue (sorted after time) and moved back to the ReadyQ when the time has expired. The ProcessManager also keeps track of which process is servicing which file so it could be sent appropriate events.

In a Unix implementation the situation of an empty ReadyQ maps exactly to a call of the Unix utility Select. This takes the files we are interested in and a maximum time as parameters and will block the entire Unix process until input is available and/or the maximum time has passed.

Timeslice and Preemptive Scheduling

In class ProcessManager the operation SetTimeSlice can be used to define the length of the quanta given to each process. If this is set to zero the result is that preemptive scheduling is turned off. Since a concurrent program should be correct in every possible execution order, it should also work when interrupts are turned off (although real-time constraints might not be fulfilled). This can be a very useful debugging aid since in this way the execution order is more predictable. It also illustrates how narrow the line is between what is considered a concurrent program and a sequential one. Here the same program can be executed in both ways.

Synchronization

SimIOProcess also provides the traditional OS synchronization tools: Semaphores and Monitors. The following shows the outline of these classes. Note the convenient modeling of Conditions as nested classes. The correct implementation of these primitives for real time in SimIOProcess must deal with some interesting problems. This includes keeping all waiting queues sorted according to priority (rather than using FIFO). Furthermore, the implementation of Monitor handles the problem of priority inversion through dynamic priority inheritance.

```
class Semaphore(PMG,S); ref(ProcessManager) PMG;
                        integer S;
begin
    procedure Wait; ···
    procedure Signal; ···
end --- Semaphore ---;

class Monitor(PMG); ref(ProcessManager) PMG;
begin
    procedure EnterMonitor;
    procedure ExitMonitor;
    class Condition;
    begin
        procedure Await;
        procedure CauseOne;
        procedure CauseAll;
    end -- Condition;
end --- Monitor --;
```

The implementation of these two classes is based entirely on the two operations, Start and Stop, and the ReadyQ. An interested user could develop other synchronization primitives in the same way. Monitor is an abstract class that users will extend to create their own objects with appropriate operations. To ensure mutual exclusion, these operations in the subclasses should start with a call to EnterMonitor and finish with a call to ExitMonitor, as illustrated in the following bounded buffer example.

```
Monitor class Buffer(Size); integer Size;
begin
     procedure Put(Item); text Item;
     begin
          EnterMonitor;
          while Count=Size do NonFull.Await;
          B(Inp):-copy(Item);
          Inp:=mod(Inp+1,Size); Count:=Count+1;
          NonEmpty.CauseOne;
          ExitMonitor;
     end - Put -;
     text procedure Get;
     begin
          EnterMonitor;
          while Count=0 do NonEmpty.Await;
          Item:-B(Outp);
          Outp:=mod(Outp+1,Size); Count:=Count-1;
          NonFull.CauseOne;
          ExitMonitor;
     end;
     integer array B(0,Size-1);
     integer Inp, Outp,Count;
     ref(Condition) NonFull, NonEmpty;
     NonFull:- new Condition;
     NonEmpty :- new Condition;
end --- Buffer ---;
```

Applications

The SimIOProcess framework has been used extensively and applied to different problems. It has been used for graphical user interfaces based both on X11 and on the Macintosh. It has also served for teaching real-time programming and operating systems. In an earlier version, it was used to implement operating systems from scratch for Data General Eclipse 16-bit machines.

In the GUI area, processes are used extensively. In the X11 implementation, an IOProcess is used to take care of the input socket from the X-server. There are also other classes designed to work with sockets. The framework thus supports implementation of servers (serving multiple clients) and clients that connect to several servers. Furthermore, each window is implemented as a process to make the windows behave as parallel, independent objects in the user interface. These processes are scheduled without preemption since their actions are usually short and this option removes a large volume of synchronization code.

A similar framework for the Macintosh had the interesting property of providing a process concept on a machine without preemptive scheduling. The aspect of safety previously mentioned was extremely useful when developing for the Macintosh, a system with no memory protection; programming errors were captured and reported rather than resulting in a bomb.

Conclusions

We have presented frameworks for real-time applications in Simula based on two slightly different approaches. In both cases they explore the facilities in Simula to provide inverted control through the class body and the inner mechanism. This mechanism seems to provide for the global event loop what virtual binding provides for procedure calls.

The second framework also demonstrates a third way to use the basic scheduling primitives in Simula, besides for arbitrarily scheduled coroutines, and Simulation where scheduling is after event-time; in the SimIOProcess framework processes are scheduled after priority.

4.6 Other Early Simula Frameworks

This section offers pointers on some interesting object-oriented frameworks created before objects became fashionable, that is, before 1986 and the first ECOOP and OOPSLA conferences.

4.6.1 SIMDBM (1975)

This framework implemented a network-oriented (CODASYL) database management system and included several utility programs to define schemas, to query, and to maintain the database. It was developed by K. Mäkilä at the Swedish Institute of National Defense [Mäkilä 1975] and served as an administrative database in the early 1980s at the Université de Montréal. It was also used for a large distributed project 10 years later. Though it does not deal with parallel programming, we mention it as an example of a well-designed durable framework. This software has been used on many different machines (DEC10, CDC Cyber, Vax, HP Apollos, Sun, and SGI) and the bulk of the source code has been unchanged for over 20 years. It is interesting to think of how much software written with today's object-oriented languages will still be usable in 10 years (or even next year with frequent version changes).

4.6.2 DISCO (1978)

DISCO was a large framework for the time (2100 lines of Simula). It was designed for simulations that involve both continuous activity described by differential equations as well as discrete changes. DISCO was implemented as an extension (subclass) of Simulation. For continuous evolution, the inner mechanism was used in conjunction with coroutine scheduling to evaluate the differential equations at intervals determined by integration control routines and even backtrack in time if errors proved too large. This example illustrates once again the usefulness of low-level scheduling to implement frameworks with different forms of scheduling.

4.6.3 DEMOS (1979)

DEMOS, Discrete Event Modeling On Simula, was a complete industrial strength simulation package (2600 lines of code) inspired by GPSSS and written by Graham Birtwistle [Birtwistle 1979].

4.7 Discussion

We have presented a series of frameworks written in Simula over the last 30 years. The examples were chosen to illustrate the appropriateness of Simula's basic concepts and syntax in the area of parallel programming. It is now time to draw some lessons from these applications.

First, a distinguishing feature of Simula objects is that they have code bodies and can operate as independent parallel entities. This maps well with modern concepts of parallel agents and processes interacting in distributed systems. Furthermore, inheritance between Simula classes also means that code (behavior) can be inherited, and previous sections have exploited Simula's inner mechanism, which allows inverted control whereby user code is executed under framework control. In the next section, we further explore the benefits that would arise from extenuation of these concepts.

Second, we note that our frameworks dealt with various forms of parallelism by implementing a diversity of scheduling mechanisms. That such a variety of schedulers could be programmed is a testament to the correct choice of basic context switching operations in Simula, namely, the coroutine operations of call, detach, and resume. In *Section 4.7.2*, we will also show that, given the ability to *nest* frameworks, it is even relatively easy to combine different parallel schedulers.

Third, we compare our scheduling mechanisms with those provided by Java, a language that stresses its ability to handle parallelism with its concept of threads. This was difficult to do because, in contrast to the Simula clear code model, Java does not have a precise, legible specification of its behavior.

This leads us to propose a clear hierarchy of parallel behavior distinguishing among coroutines, threads, processes, and tasks.

4.7.1 Code Inheritance and *inner*

Simula allows classes to inherit code, and this feature was used by both Simulation and SimIOProcess to implement inverted control. In the early 1970s, the first author realized that code inheritance between *procedures* combined with the inner mechanism, was a powerful mechanism [Vaucher 1975] that could be used in many situations. This was underlined by showing the ease with which operating systems concepts such as semaphores [Dijkstra 1968], mutual exclusion, and monitors [Hoare 1974] could be described and implemented, given procedure inheritance.

The Simula property that was highlighted in the chapter was the inner mechanism, whereby the code of a subprocedure is executed at the point at which the *inner* keyword appears in the body of the superprocedure. This means that a protocol for actions can be defined where a specific prologue is executed *before* the user's code and some other instructions are executed *after*.

This is a typical pattern in parallel programming for coding *critical sections*, where a locking mechanism is used to ensure exclusive access to shared variables. The user must execute some entry code *before* accessing the variables, with the possibility of having to wait if another process is already in the section; and the access must be released on exit. Assuming that we have semaphores with wait and signal operations, critical sections are usually coded as follows:

```
Semaphore mutex1 init 1;
...
wait (mutex1 );
    < operations on some shared variables >
signal (mutex1 );
```

This is the behavior that is required in Java when the keyword *synchronized* is used. Given procedure inheritance, we could define this behavior with the following Synchronized procedure, which implements the entry and exit protocol for a critical section protected by a semaphore S:

```
procedure Synchronized (S); ref (semaphore) S;
begin
    wait (S);
        inner;
    signal(S);
end;
```

Procedures inheriting from Synchronized would automatically inherit the property of exclusive access. In the following examples, we first show a Synchronized procedure, then a Synchronized code section, both of which access variables protected by the semaphore mutex1.

```
ref(Semaphore) mutex1;

Synchronized (mutex1) procedure updateR1;
begin
   < code which accesses variables of region 1  >
end;

mutext1 :- new Semaphore(1);
...
Synchronized (mutex1) begin
   < user code which accesses variables of region 1  >
end;
```

The effect is that the user code is automatically bracketed by the wait and signal operations of the Synchronized prefix, thus ensuring correct synchronization. What is interesting here is that *prefixed procedures* would allow unambiguous specification of exactly what the Java synchronized modifier does and would give a model for its implementation.

Furthermore, having this useful mechanism available in the language would allow the user to use it for other purposes. This is the route taken in Simula's successor, Beta

[Madsen 1993]. But Beta goes much further than what is proposed here, in that both procedures and classes have been unified into one construct: the *pattern*.

4.7.2 Combining Frameworks

One of the problems with many frameworks is that they implement a form of central control that often revolves around a global *event-loop*. Combining two such frameworks that both insist on being the master is nontrivial. The aforementioned frameworks, built on the Simula sequencing primitives, turn out to be easy to combine. For example, suppose we have a simulation model and want to have it drive an animation in real time. We thus want to combine the Simulation framework with the SimIOProcess framework.

A simulation program is typically written with a main program containing Hold(SimulationTime) after the initialization of the model (and before code to print out gathered statistics). The framework SimIOProcess contains mechanisms for real time and they can be utilized in the Simulation model in the following way:

```
IOProcess class SimulationAnimation;
begin

    Simulation begin
        Process class P1;      ··· the definition of the model
        Activate new P1;      ··· initialization of the model, creating
                                    and activating SIMULATION processes.
        real SpeedFactor;  ! Ratio of clock-time to simulated time.;
        ! Hold(SimulationTime) — replaced below;
        while EvTime<SimulationTime do
        begin
            DelayTime((NextEvent.EvTime-Time)*SpeedFactor );
            ReActivate this MainProgram after NextEvent;
        end;
    end - Simulation block -;
end
```

Technically, the solution is thus to embed the whole Simulation model in an IOProcess and to schedule the model represented by its main program in real time. The Simulation-Animation object becomes active each time the simulation time advances and makes sure that it is synchronized with clock time. This is very much as described for the Simulation-based real-time frameworks previously mentioned. Note that the processes in the simulation model will continue to be scheduled by the simulation system just as before, and that they will not interrupt each other. The SimulationAnimation object will be scheduled by the ProcessManager (in SimIOProcess) and might be interrupted to execute other IOProcess objects (for example, other objects of class SimulationAnimation), but this does not risk the integrity of the Simulation system—it will be continued exactly where it was interrupted. If different IOProcess objects wish to communicate, mutual exclusion Semaphores, Monitors, or message passing will have to be used.

An animation will typically use a graphical interface and we could use the GUI framework for Xlib briefly mentioned before. This package takes the form of one IOProcess object, EventManager, which waits for events from the X-server on a socket.

In this type of application, each window is also a WindowProcess. When an X-event becomes available, the EventManager determines which window it is targeted for and schedules that process for execution. Again we have a process of one system acting as a scheduler at the next level.

So far, in this example, we thus have three different systems with different processes scheduled by different mechanisms.

- At the top level we have IOProcess objects scheduled in real time according to priority.

- In the Simulation model, we have Process objects scheduled according to simulated time.

- In the GUI system, WindowProcesses are scheduled in response to input events.

We can easily imagine adding even more process-based frameworks. For example, the coroutines for traversing trees might be useful in the Simulation model, creating a situation with three nested systems.

We hope that this example will show the power of being able to define process scheduling in the language itself. In this case, all the various schedulers were programmed using the fundamental coroutine operations of Call, Resume, and Detach; and the resulting systems of processes could be combined, in parallel or nested, without interfering with each other.

The only other object-oriented language that has taken the same route is Beta, where the primitives Resume and Suspend correspond to Call and Detach in Simula (unfortunately, the definition of Suspend follows the old version of Detach with dynamic binding), and a framework similar to SimIOProcess has been implemented in Beta. This approach of providing access to low-level scheduling primitives in the language is in strong contrast to the situation in languages that have only a single higher-level mechanism built in. In such systems, it is sometimes possible to use the process mechanism for a purpose for which it was not intended, such as using concurrent processes for discrete event simulation; but since there is only one implicit (and inaccessible) ReadyQ, it cannot be used for the original or some other purpose at the same time. The elegant possibilities of combination we have demonstrated here are thus not possible.

4.7.3 Simula versus Java

This chapter has concentrated on Simula's forte: programming parallel applications (both simulated and real) and has shown that, far from being dated, this 30-year-old language still surpasses most current OO languages. It is thus interesting to compare Simula to Java, a language that advertises its ability to handle parallel activity through its concept of threads.

The framework provided by Java threads appears to be close to the facilities provided by the SimIOProcess, although exact comparison is difficult since there is no equivalent to the Simula framework's precise description—in Simula—of its semantics. In both systems, users assume that scheduled processes are kept in a ReadyQ, sorted by priority. In both systems, there are mechanisms for preemptive scheduling via interrupts, as well as opportunities to voluntarily give up control. A difference is that SimIOProcess, intended for real-time applications, interprets priorities very strictly to guarantee response times, whereas Java has a more relaxed attitude. Table 4.1 compares the primitives in the order in which they apply as a parallel activity is created, interacts, and dies.

The meaning of the Scheduling operations is that a process/thread is placed into (or moved out of) the ReadyQ. In SimIOProcess, synchronization is provided through objects such as Semaphores and Monitors, whose behavior is implemented in terms of the more primitive Stop and Start. In Java, the equivalent operations (synchronized, Wait, Notify) are implemented as special cases, although there is no reason why they could not be implemented (or at least defined) in terms of suspend and resume.

In environments where there is no preemption or interrupts, Java threads can also be compared to the framework provided by the Simulation class. Again, the user assumes that scheduled processes are kept in an ordered list. There is an obvious difference in the interpretation of the ordering value: It represents priority in Java and future event time in Simulation, but aside from that, the scheduling operations are remarkably similar. In this situation the only way that a thread (or process) can lose control is if it decides to stop execution (wait/passivate), schedules another process with a higher priority than its own (activate P), or skips its turn voluntarily (yields = hold(0)). Equivalencies are shown in Table 4.2.

In terms of pure scheduling, it would appear that one can do similar things in both Java and Simula. However, there are two important differences.

First, one aspect that stands out with Simula is the clarity of the specification. Although, the semantics of each scheduling operation are explained in words, wherever possible, a new language feature is explained by giving the equivalent code (written in Simula itself). This is possible because there are two levels at which scheduling can be described: the basic *coroutine* level (resume, call, and detach) and that of processes (for example, hold). This allows process scheduling to be specified in terms of the coroutine operations and auxiliary structures like the event list. In Java, there are no scheduling operators more primitive than those for threads. As a result, the workings of Java scheduling are described in words and remain mysterious.

Table 4.1 Java versus SimIOProcess

JAVA	SIMIOPROCESS	MEANING
new+start()	new+Start	init+scheduling+call
suspend(), wait(), synchronized	Semaphore/Monitor calls using Stop	detach+descheduling
resume(), notify(), *synchronized*	Semaphore/Monitor calls using Start	scheduling+call
yield()	ReSchedule	detach+reschedule+call
sleep()	DelayTime()	detach+deschedule and reschedule+call
top(), run finish	Terminate, Kill, body finish	deschedule, terminate

Table 4.2   Java Thread versus Simulation Class

JAVA	SIMULATION	MEANING
new+start()	new+Activate P	detach+scheduling+resume
suspend(),wait()	Passivate	descheduling+resume
resume(),notify()	Activate	schedule+resume
yield()	Hold(0)	reschedule+resume
sleep()	Hold(t)	reschedule+resume
stop()	Terminate	descheduling, terminate

Second, Java's syntax and choice of basic objects (without Simula's code bodies) mean that parallel programs require a complex mixture of classes, interfaces, and operations. The simplicity of the Simula programs presented here contrasts interestingly with the verbose and opaque code of even the simplest examples of concurrent programming written in Java [Lea 1997].

4.7.4 Levels of Parallelism

Comparing the various frameworks for parallel programming reveals the fact that there are several levels of *parallel* programming. Recognizing and naming these parallel entities at each level would help in comparing language features. The levels that we have identified are as follows:

Coroutines. Supports independent threads of execution, but sequencing operations (resume and call) require explicit references to other coroutines, such as resume(Fred).

Threads (Simulation Process). Coroutines plus an ordered global list of scheduled objects so that scheduling is indirect, such as passivate.

Processes (IOProcess). Threads with preemption and interrupts for real-time operation.

Actually, one could think of further levels such as OS tasks with independent address spaces or multiprocessor systems, but the three identified here would seem to be appropriate concepts for a programming language. In this chapter, we have shown how, in Simula, levels 2 and 3 could be implemented in terms of level 1.

Other languages, such as Java, could benefit from this layered structure, but this would require both coroutine and coroutine scheduling.

4.8 Summary

This chapter describes some of the earliest object-oriented frameworks on record. These were written with Simula, the language that enabled the invention of objects. We have concentrated on Simula's forte: programming parallel applications (both simulated and real) and we hope to have shown that, far from being dated, this 30 year old language still surpasses most current OO languages.

First, we presented standard frameworks delivered with Simula systems that implement pseudoparallelism and allow simulation of complex systems. Then we considered other frameworks that implement progressively more complex scheduling schemes. These include GPSSS for queuing models and the UMxx series for the modeling of operating systems. Finally, we showed that Simula's elegant notation was not limited to *simulated* parallelism. Several frameworks that extend Simula's abilities to real time were presented. In particular, we showed how SimIOProcess handles preemption and IO interrupts.

Several features, particular to Simula, are key to the successful implementation of these frameworks. First, Simula objects have a code body that specifies the actions that an object will perform during its active lifetime. Second, an object can function as a coroutine with its own thread of control so that its actions can be interleaved with those of other objects. This provides simulated parallelism and is the first step toward achieving lightweight multitasking. Simula also provides three operations to transfer control between coroutines: Call, Resume, and Detach. Finally, there is the possibility of nesting class declarations. Given these features, it is possible to schedule parallel processes in many different ways. The combination of elegant syntax and correct primitives means that the description in Simula of these scheduling mechanisms is highly legible and the code can be used directly in specifications.

We also discussed code inheritance and the way it could be used with Simula's inner mechanism to achieve inverted control. We showed how an extension of this mechanism, allowing inheritance between procedures, could facilitate the safe implementation of mutual exclusion.

In the area of parallel programming, we compared Simula and its frameworks to Java, the object-oriented language most in the news recently. We concluded that there are (probably) equivalent scheduling operations in both. However, we could not be sure because Java lacks Simula's precise specification of its operations. Simula provides code describing exactly the mechanics of its scheduling based on the coroutine primitives: Call, Resume, and Detach. Without these, Java must resort to a vague description in English. Java is also a moving target: In JDK 1.2, basic scheduling primitives (suspend and resume) are marked as "deprecated" and will be removed in some future release. Unfortunately, this is a step away from providing support for Simula-type coroutines in Java.

Java can match Simula for the implementation of any *one* application framework; however, we showed that, in Simula, it was particularly easy to *combine* quite diverse frameworks.

Comparison of these various modes of parallel operation led us to suggest a hierarchy of three levels of parallel behavior: coroutines, threads, and processes. Availability in a language of the most primitive level, coroutines, is a prerequisite to the implementation (or description) in the language itself of the other two.

Simula invented objects, but it was left to subsequent—mainly American—languages like Smalltalk, C++, and Java to promote and carry out the object revolution. The implementers of these languages had their own views on object technology and their languages concentrated on different language features. It was therefore interesting to look at frameworks written 10 or 20 years ago in the original OO language, Simula.

This exercise has shown that Simula's design choices in the area of concurrent programming are still quite pertinent today. There are still lessons to be learned and concepts to be borrowed.

4.9 References

[Arnold-Gosling 1996] Arnold, Ken, and James Gosling. *The JAVA Programming Language.* Reading, MA: Addison-Wesley, 1996.

[Belsnes-Løvdal 1977] Belsnes, D., and E. Løvdal. Use of simulation techniques in actual network implementation. *EIN Symposium on Simulation and Modeling of Data Networks*, Oslo, Norway, September 1977.

[Birtwistle 1973] Birtwistle, Graham M., Ole-Johan Dahl, Bjørn Myhrhaug, and Kristen Nygaard. *SIMULA Begin.* Lund, Sweden: Studentlitteratur, 1973.

[Birtwistle 1979] Birtwistle, G.M. *Discrete Event Modelling on Simula.* New York: Macmillan Press, 1979.

[Brinch 1973] Brinch-Hansen, Per. Concurrent programming concepts. *ACM Computing Surveys* 5(4):223–245, 1973.

[Brinch 1977] Brinch-Hansen, Per. *The Architecture of Concurrent Programs.* Englewood Cliffs, NJ: Prentice Hall, 1977.

[Conway 1963] Conway, M.E. Design of a separable transition-diagram compiler. *Communications of the ACM* 6(7), July 1963:396–408.

[Dahl 1968] Dahl, Ole-Johan. Discrete Event Simulation Languages. In *Programming Languages*, F. Genuys, editor. London: Academic Press, 1968.

[Dahl 1970] Dahl, O-J., B. Myhrhaug, and K. Nygaard. *SIMULA-67 Common Base Language.* Oslo, Norway: Norwegian Computer Centre, 1970.

[Dahl-Hoare 1972] Dahl, Ole-Johan, and C.A.R. Hoare. Hierarchical program structures. In *Structured Programming.* London: Academic Press, 1972.

[Dahl-Myhrhaug 1973] Dahl, Ole-Johan, and Bjorn Myhrhaug. *SIMULA Implementation Guide.* Oslo, Norway: Norwegian Computing Center, 1973.

[Dahl-Nygaard 1966] Dahl, O-J., and K. Nygaard. SIMULA—An Algol based Simulation Language. *Communications of the ACM* 9(9), September 1966: 671–678.

[Dijkstra 1968] Dijkstra, E.W. Co-operating sequential processes. In *Programming Languages*, F. Genuys, editor. London: Academic Press, 1968.

[Einarson 1997] Einarson, Daniel. Passing control over nested quasi-parallel systems. *ASU Newsletter* 24(1), January 1997:1–9.

[Franta 1977] Franta, W.R. *The Process View of Simulation.* Operating and Programming Systems Series edition. North-Holland, 1977.

[Gordon 1975] Gordon, Geoffrey. *The Application of GPSS V to Discrete Event Simulation.* Englewood Cliffs, NJ: Prentice Hall, 1975.

[Hedin-Knudsen 1999] Hedin, Görel, and Jorgen L. Knudsen. Language support for application framework design. In *Object-Oriented Application Frameworks*, Mohamed E. Fayad, R. Johnson, D. Schmidt, editors. New York: John Wiley & Sons, 1999.

[Hoare 1968] Hoare, C.A.R. Record handling. In *Programming Languages*, F. Genuys, editor. London: Academic Press, 1968.

[Hoare 1974] Hoare, C.A.R. Monitors: An operating system structuring concept. *Communications of the ACM* 17(10), October 1974:549–557.

[Holmevik 1994] Holmevik, Jan Rune. Compiling SIMULA: A historical study of technological genesis. *IEEE Annals of the History of Computing* 16(4):25–37, 1994.

[Hudson-Moss 1992] Hudson, Richard L., B. Moss, and J. Eliot. Incremental collection of mature objects. *Proceedings of the International Workshop on Memory Management*, St. Malo, France, September 1992.

[Ichbiah-Morse 1972] Ichbiah, J.D., and S.P. Morse. General concepts of the Simula 67 programming language. *Annual Review in Automatic Programming* 7: 65–89, 1972.

[Islo 1997] Islo, Henry. Special number on models within models. *ASU Newsletter* 24(1), January 1997.

[Kindler 1995a] Kindler, Eugene. Simulation of systems containing simulating elements. *Proceedings of the European Simulation Multiconference*, Prague, Czech Republic, June 5–7, 1995.

[Kindler 1995b] Kindler, Eugene. Tutorial on Mejtsky's diagrams. *ASU (Association of SIMULA Users) Newsletter* 23(1), January1995:18–43.

[Kirkerud 1989] Kirkerud, Bjorn. *Object-Oriented Programming with SIMULA*. Reading, MA: Addison-Wesley, 1989.

[Knudsen 1994] Knudsen, J.L., O.L. Madsen, M. Lofgren, and B. Magnusson, eds. *Object-Oriented Environments—The Mjolner Approach*. Englewood Cliffs, NJ: Prentice Hall, 1994.

[Knuth-McNeeley 1964] Knuth, D.E., and J.L. McNeeley. SOL—A symbolic language for general-purpose systems simulation. *IEEE Transactions on Electronic Computers* EC-13(4): 409–414, 1964.

[Lapalme-Vaucher 1981] Lapalme, G., and J. Vaucher. Une implantation efficace de l'ordonnancement conditionnel. *RAIRO-Informatique* 15(3): 255–285, 1981.

[Lea 1997] Lea, Doug. *Concurrent Programming in Java: Design Principles and Patterns*, *The Java Series*. Reading, MA: Addison-Wesley, 1997.

[Madsen 1993] Madsen, Ole Lehrmann, Birger Møller-Pedersen, and Kristen Nygaard. *Object-Oriented Programming in the BETA Programming Language*. Reading, MA: Addison-Wesley, ACM Press, 1993.

[Madsen 1995] Madsen, O.L. Open issues in object-oriented programming: A Scandinavian perspective. *Software-Practice & Experience* 25(Suppl 4)(4): 3–43, 1995.

[Magnusson 1994a] Magnusson, Boris. An overview of Simula. In *Object-Oriented Environments: The Mjolner Approach*, J. Knudsen, M. Lofgren, O. Lehrmann-Madsen, and B. Magnusson, editors. Englewood Cliffs, NJ: Prentice Hall, 1994.

[Magnusson 1994b] Magnusson, Boris. Simula runtime system overview. In *Object-Oriented Environments: The Mjolner Approach*, J. Knudsen, M. Lofgren, O. Lehrmann-Madsen, and B. Magnusson, editors. Englewood Cliffs, NJ: Prentice Hall, 1994.

[Magnusson 1995] Magnusson, Boris. *Using the SimIOProcess Library on Unix Systems*. Lund, Sweden: Lund Software House AB, 1995.

[Magnusson-Henriksson 1995] Magnusson, Boris, and Roger Henriksson. Garbage collection for control systems. *IWMM 1995, International Workshop on Memory Management*, Kinross, Scotland, September 1995.

[Magnusson-Löfgren 1981] Magnusson, Boris, and Mats Löfgren. An extension of Simula for concurrent execution. *Proceedings of the 9th Simula Users' Conference,* Geneva, Switzerland, 1981.

[Mäkilä 1975] Mäkilä, Kalle. *A CODASYL-type DBMS system in SIMULA.* Swedish Research Institute of National Defense, 1975.

[Meyer 1988] Meyer, Bertrand. *Object-oriented Software Construction,* Englewood Cliffs, NJ: Prentice Hall, 1988.

[Nygaard 1997] Nygaard, Kristen. GOODS to appear on the stage. *ECOOP 1997—Object-Oriented Programming,* Jyväskylä, Finland, June 1997.

[Nygaard-Dahl 1981] Nygaard, K., and O-J. Dahl. The development of the SIMULA language. In *History of Programming Languages,* R. Wexelblat, editor. Academic Press, 1981.

[Palme 1975] Palme, Jacob. Making SIMULA into a programming language for real time. *Management Datamatics* 4(4), 1975.

[Papazpglou 1984] Papazpglou, M.P., P.I. Georgiadis, and D.G. Maritsas. An outline of the programming language SIMULA. *Computer Languages* 9(2):107–131, 1984.

[Pooley 1987] Pooley, R.J. *An Introduction to Programming in SIMULA.* Oxford, England: Blackwell Scientific Publications, 1987.

[Shaw 1974] Shaw, Alan C. *The Logical Design of Operating Systems.* 1st ed., Englewood Cliffs, NJ: Prentice Hall, 1974.

[SIS 1987] SIS 1987. Data Processing—Programming Languages—SIMULA. Stockholm, Sweden: Swedish Standards Institute, 1987.

[Ungar 1987] Ungar, David. *The Design and Evaluation of a High Performance Smalltalk System.* Cambridge, MA: MIT Press, 1987.

[Vaucher 1971] Vaucher, J. Simulation data structures using SIMULA67. *Proceedings 1971 Winter Simulation Conference,* New York, 1971.

[Vaucher 1973] Vaucher, J. A WAIT-UNTIL algorithm for general purpose simulation languages. *Proceedings 1973 Winter Simulation Conference,* San Francisco, CA, 1973.

[Vaucher 1975] Vaucher, J. Prefixed procedures: A structuring concept for operations. *INFOR* 13(3): 287–295, 1975.

[Vaucher 1979] Vaucher, J. BETA: un successeur à SIMULA pour la programmation des systèmes. *BIGRE* 15:4–10, 1979.

[Vaucher 1984] Vaucher, J. Process-oriented simulation in standard PASCAL. *SCS Multiconference on Simulation in Strongly Typed Languages,* San Diego, CA, February 1984.

[Vaucher-Duval 1975] Vaucher, Jean, and Pierre Duval. A comparison of simulation event list algorithms. *Communications of the ACM* 18(4), April 1975: 223–230.

[Wang-Dahl 1971] Wang, A., and O-J. Dahl. Coroutine sequencing in a block structured environment. *BIT* 11(4): 171, 425–449.

[Wirth 1977] Wirth, Niklaus. MODULA: A language for modular multiprogramming. *Software—Practice and Experience* 7(1), January 1977: 3–35.

4.10 Review Questions

1. Name three Simula frameworks.

2. Define according to Simula: objects, classes, inheritance, virtual methods, and type system.

3. Write examples of Simula's code for the following concepts: objects and classes, inheritance, and nested classes.

4. Describe briefly the following: GPSSS and Simset.

5. What are the challenges of building simulations for real-time systems?

6. Describe briefly the following: Class Realtime and SimIOProcess.

7. Describe briefly: DISCO, SIMDBM, and DEMOS.

8. What are the differences between Simula and Java?

Visual Builders:
Framework Design Issues

Early object-oriented class libraries were designed to deliver as much function as possible. Design standards evolved to meet the needs of programmers who wrote every line of application code themselves.

Today, an increasing number of application programmers use visual builders (and, to a lesser extent, wizards) to generate much (but rarely all) code. This code also makes use of class libraries. In this environment, however, programmers tie together classes by interface, with a minimum of handwritten code. Good framework design must now address the needs of visual programmers as well as those of direct coders. This chapter describes design issues where these requirements diverge.

5.1 Parts Can Address Both Sets of Needs

A *part* (sometimes called component) is a class with special characteristics to support visual programming and code generation. Well-designed parts comply with a simple but powerful interface protocol. A Java Bean is one example of a part, but there are also part protocols for Smalltalk and C++; the latter two, however, are not as standardized across vendors as the Beans interface in Java.

The *part interface* is composed of three clearly defined programming interface *features*: *attributes*, *actions*, and *events* (JavaBeans uses the terms *properties*, *methods*, and *events*) [JavaBeans]. These features correspond to a natural way of viewing objects: their data, the behaviors they can perform, and their response to internal changes. This protocol addresses the general format of the programming interfaces, not the specifics of implementation behind the interface (see Figure 5.1).

The *attribute interface* provides access to selected properties of a part. The attribute interface can be used to return the value of a property as an object, to set the value of a property, and to notify other parts when the value of a property changes. The class designer is not required to supply a complete attribute interface for a property. For example, a property might be read-only, in which case the part's attribute interface would not support the ability to set the property's value.

The *action interface* provides access to selected behaviors of a part. Actions represent tasks that the part supports, such as displaying itself or adding an object to a collection of objects. The class designer implements this interface in a part by supplying a public member function or method.

The *event interface* provides a means to notify other parts that something has changed within a part. Events can be signaled when changes in state occur, such as when a push button is clicked or when a window is opened, or when thresholds are reached, such as when the balance in a bank account goes negative. Events can also be signaled when the value of a part's attribute changes, such as when money is deposited into or withdrawn from a bank account. Events appear as messages broadcast to all parts that are registered as being dependent on the occurrence of the event.

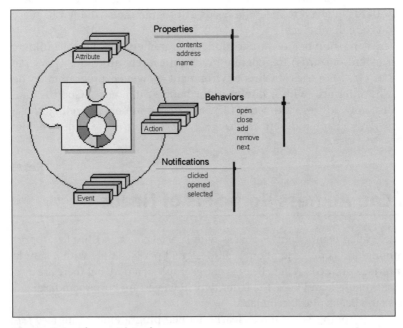

Figure 5.1 The *part* interface.

5.2 Programmers Connect Part Features to Build Applications

With visual builder technology, application programmers can connect parts to build larger composite parts or entire applications. Typical visual builders enable programmers to make several kinds of connections. Each part can support multiple connections. In most builders, connections are an implementation of the Observer design pattern, where one class observes what happens to another class [Gamma 1995]. In Java, this pattern is embodied in the listener interfaces. The following kinds of connections are typically supported:

Event-to-action. These connections execute an action when a certain event occurs. The action (a specially-marked method) can have parameters. These parameters are attributes or literals. An example is connecting the clicked event from a push button to the clear action on a text entry field.

AttributeChangeEvent-to-action. These connections start an action when an attribute changes value. An example is connecting the street attribute change event of an address to the enable action on a save push button.

Attribute-to-attribute. These connections link two attributes (data values) together so that they always stay the same. An example is connecting the street attribute in an address part with the text (contents) attribute in a text entry field.

Event-to-script. These connections cause a script to run whenever a certain event occurs. The script is defined in the native language used (Java, C++, or Smalltalk), either as a method attached to the part class or as custom logic attached to the connection class.

5.3 Making Classes into Parts

One major difference between parts and classes is that parts can notify other parts about changes to themselves, triggering other processing. This distinction is lessening as some more advanced classes add this capability. Implementing notification in classes is the first and key step toward enabling a class for visual programming. The absence of notification limits the kinds of connections that can be made to a class.

Using a sample part from the VisualAge Java product (from IBM), Figure 5.2 shows how notification was added to the Address class to signal when the value of street was changed [VisualAge].

5.4 Ready-to-Wear Parts versus Tailor-Made Classes

The most widely felt difference between parts and classes is related more to usage than to design. Visual programmers work better with self-contained, ready-to-use classes as

```
public class Address implements java.lang.Cloneable {
String fieldStreet = "";
protected transient java.beans.PropertyChangeSupport propertyChange =
new         java.beans.PropertyChangeSupport(this);
String fieldState = "";
String fieldCity = "";
String fieldZipCode = "";
. . .
/**
 * Sets the street property (java.lang.String) value.
 * @param street The new value for the property.
 * @see #getStreet
 */
public void setStreet(String street) {
     /* Get the old property value for fire property change event. */
     String oldValue = fieldStreet;
     /* Set the street property (attribute) to the new value. */
     fieldStreet = street;
     /* Fire (signal/notify) the street property change event. */
     firePropertyChange("street", oldValue, street);
     return;
}
. . .
}
```

Figure 5.2   Code enabling class Address for notification.

parts. Such a class might have a large number of configuring options, but it doesn't use ancillary classes to perform its function (as far as the visual programmer can see), nor do you subclass it in order to use it. An example of such a part class is a telephone entry-field class. The class validates text entered against the specified pattern for a phone number. It has built-in support for drag/drop and substring selection. All attributes, events, and actions for this part are reflected in this class (regardless of the other classes it might use internally).

On the other hand, a direct coder is more comfortable with extending the function of a simple class by subclassing it or (better) by combining it with other classes using composition. An example here is a simple text entry field class that can be optionally combined with a class for pattern filtering, one for drag/drop and one for text selection. In this example, the text entry field acts as a *view,* while the classes providing additional function act as *controllers.*

The class designer can construct a part by preassembling classes using the same techniques direct coders use. Alternatively, the part can be integrated with the builder such that the builder assembles the classes according to a part configuration set by the visual programmer.

5.5 Code Generation Changes the Equation

A more subtle difference between parts and classes relates to design. The main factors in measuring good traditional framework design are:

Ease of coding. Is it easy for the programmer to write code using the framework? Do many classes have to be derived and many methods overridden? Is there unnecessary duplicate code for the programmer to write?

Performance and size. Does the resulting application run fast? Is the resulting application suitably small in memory and disk footprint?

Robustness. Has the framework code been thoroughly tested to ensure that it does not introduce errors into the resulting application?

With a visual builder added to the equation, class designers can give significantly less weight to ease of coding, because code for derived classes and overrides is generated. What impact remains relates to the usability of the builder: How much configuration information must the programmer supply in order for the builder to generate code correctly? How easy is it to supply that information? The programmer must also be able to debug, document, and manage the code once it is generated.

Framework designers can actually use code generation technology to their advantage. Consider the design of a data class, that is, one whose primary purpose is to encapsulate data and control access to it. It is otherwise impossible to design an abstract base data class that provides significant inheritance to its subclasses. Even in Java, it is awkward to always return an Object and expect the caller to interrogate it to determine its actual class.

Every concrete data class has at least a pair of accessor functions (get and set) for each accessible property. If the class supports persistence, the designer must write functions to stream properties in and out. Scripting support might require additional accessor functions. All these accessor functions might take different input arguments; they might or might not return a value or object, depending on the property. Accessor logic might vary greatly. No abstract class design can account for all these situations. However, a visual builder can generate code for all cases, given a few bits of information by the visual programmer. In this respect, visual builders provide better support (to designers as well as programmers) than C++ templates or Java introspection.

5.6 Giving Up Some Freedom for Convenience

Visual builders impose some standards on classes to ensure that the generated code works correctly. Frameworks designed for use with a visual builder must adhere to these standards in order for the builder to use them. Some of these standards limit the design of a class, at least the part exposed to the visual builder.

In strongly typed languages like Java and C++, builders have a difficult time (without also being compilers) of ensuring that the connecting of two attributes will compile correctly. To help the builders, actions must support a larger variety of argument types for a given function, by means of overloading. This also ensures that the builder can match up return types and argument types. In C++, this even includes accepting arguments of type AClass and type AClass* (pointer to AClass); it might be trivial for a human being to dereference the input argument, but to some builders it is not.

For example, a visual builder user may wish to connect a "dialNumber" action with an attribute for the number to be dialed; in the builder-generated code the attribute becomes the argument to the dialNumber method. The attribute may be of type int (5551212) or type string ("555-1212") or type PhoneNumber. Since types are one of the things that visual builders try to hide from the user, a good dialNumber action will be able to accept any of the three attributes, while rejecting (at build time) an attribute of type "Address." This requires (in most languages) three different versions of the method dialNumber, or four if you are using C++ and wish to allow PhoneNumber and PhoneNumber*. A direct coder could write "dialNumber(aPhoneNumber.asInt( ))" but a visual builder is not intelligent enough to know what to do.

There is much less difficulty in this area with Java, which has introspection (the ability to ask a class about its methods and their parameters) and does not have a distinction between references and pointers.

Without default constructors, visual builders cannot always generate the correct code. Again, this is because no visual builder is as intelligent as a human being. An experienced programmer can often (but not always) find a harmless constructor to call instead of a default one. This constructor may take arguments that can be given dummy or innocuous values. For example, a graphical user interface (GUI) frame window part may insist on at least a parent window. An experienced programmer might know that the system desktop window can be used if no other parent is known. It is always better for the class designer to predefine a default value, which means that the class can support a default constructor.

Parts must support certain methods and patterns of arguments on those methods, especially for basic tasks like positioning, copying, or connecting parts. A direct coder can always read the manual and find some way to accomplish the task. However, consistency and coverage in the methods supported improve usability even for direct coders.

5.7 Builders Give You Some Things for Free

Some standards that parts must follow result in added functionality essentially for free. A builder can protect visual programmers from name changes designers might make in later releases. The names of attributes, events, and actions as seen by the visual programmer can be mapped to the actual method names of the part. This second level of indirection is resolved at code generation time, so there is no performance impact in the resulting code. By default, the names are the same. If there is, for example, some future change to the framework method-naming standards, code can be regenerated to the new interfaces without impacting the visual programmer's implementation.

A builder can give every multiargument method a more flexible syntax without extra effort by the class designer. Some visual builders enable member function arguments to be specified in any order and any combination desired. This is a huge advantage in Java, which currently does not support default parameter values. The class designer does not have to write another variant of a method for every possible ordering and combination of the arguments. The builder rearranges the arguments and supplies defaults to fit the existing overload. This is resolved at code generation time, so there is no impact in the resulting code.

5.8 A Matter of Degree

Many design principles are similar for both builder-oriented and direct-use frameworks, differing only in the degree to which they must be applied. All class designers should have the goal of reducing complexity in the framework structure: reducing the number of classes that must be used and of member functions that must be overridden or called to accomplish some task. In direct-use frameworks, this relates mainly to the learning curve. In builder-oriented frameworks, this also relates to the amount of screen real estate. The complexity of a builder work environment is strongly affected by the number of objects on the work surface (the screen). Usually, the upper limit here is even lower than the one imposed by a learning curve.

This limit on interface complexity also extends to the number of connections between parts on the screen. This corresponds to the number of methods that are called within a block of code. The upper limit for builder connections is much lower than the upper limit on the number of method calls a direct developer can juggle mentally while editing code. Builders uses various layering techniques to reduce the number of connections the user must deal with visually at any given moment. Component architectures, where a single object encapsulates and visually hides a group of subobjects and the connections between them, might also help. It is certainly easier to mentally deal with a modest number of connections when they are portrayed visually as opposed to a series of possibly nested method calls as seen in a simple editor. Visual builders have a real challenge to make more complex logic just as easy to deal with visually.

5.9 Summary

Although there are many principles in common between classes and parts, there are significant differences that framework designers should take into account when creating parts to be used by a visual builder. The following is a summary of the items to ensure that classes work well with a visual builder:

- Change classes to parts by implementing event notification.
- Create more self-contained, ready-to-use parts.
- Follow the standards (default and copy constructors) required or recommended by the visual builder.
- Provide common actions or attributes in the part to reduce the number of connections that need to be made. Test and use parts with the visual builder to ensure that the number of connections have been minimized.
- Make parts easy to use by providing default parameters and supporting multiple data types as input to actions and attributes.

5.10 References

[Gamma 1995] Gamma, Erich, Richard Helm, Ralph Johnson, and John Vlissides. *Design Patterns: Elements of Reusable Object-Oriented Software.* Reading, MA: Addison-Wesley, 1995.

[JavaBeans] JavaBeans API, JavaSoft, on the Web at http://java.sun.com:80/beans/index.html.

[VisualAge] VisualAge Visual Builder is part of VisualAge for C++, VisualAge for Smalltalk, and VisualAge for Java, available from IBM Corporation, on the Web at www.ibm.com/ad.

5.11 Review Questions

1. What are the three features that make up a part interface? Relate each one to a language feature or concept in Java programming.

2. The most common way to reuse a class in a visual builder is to subclass it (True/False).

3. What is the major design difference between parts and classes? Is there reason to believe this will change in the future?

4. Name three typical kinds of connections and explain in general terms how each works.

5. What special consideration must be given to constructors of classes destined to become parts used by visual builders?

6. Of the three design factors—ease of coding, performance and size, and robustness—which one can visual builders worry less about and why?

7. What programming concept, represented as a certain kind of language statement by hand-coders and as a certain kind of graphic element by visual builders, is more limited (in how many such can statements/graphics be used before the programmer becomes confused with the complexity) in visual builders than in direct coding?

5.12 Problem Set

1. Using any development environment you choose (simple editor to an elaborate IDE), write a class with at least three instance variables. Two of those instance variables should have both a setter and a getter method, and the third should only have a getter method. The class should also have at least three methods that are neither setters nor getters but perform some (simple) function; for example, one method could examine the current time and return true if the value is even or false if the value is odd. One method should return nothing, one should return a Boolean, and one should return a reference to an object (a nonprimitive) already defined in whatever framework or class library comes with the compiler chosen by the instructor. Give the class only a constructor that takes parame-

ter(s), no parameterless (default) constructor; this will cause difficulty later, but experiencing this difficulty is part of the learning. Compile and test the class to ensure that it works.

Next, using a visual builder chosen by your instructor (one that supports a parts-type architecture, such as the one in IBM VisualAge C++ or VisualAge Java[1], or Symantec VisualCafe—formerly just Cafe[2]), convert your class into a part usable in that visual builder. Add at least one event to this part; it can be a simple one, such as an event that fires when one of the instance variables is changed. Follow the guidelines included with the visual builder; in the case of Java-based builders, the guidelines are the JavaBeans architecture (simplified, thank goodness—the Beans specification is more than 100 pages) and Java Beans serve the role of "parts." Upon completion, demonstrate that you can add an instance of your part to the visual builder work surface[3], make connections to its actions and attributes, and make connections from its events to other parts that come with the visual builder. *Hint*: If you use existing visible parts within a frame window, the testing and demonstration are much easier, since this simple GUI directly displays the test results.

The instructor should have demonstrated how to bring up the visual builder as well as where to find the tool/dialog(s) that help you through the process of converting a class to a part. Learning how to use the tool/dialog(s) is up to you and is part of the problem. You should not have knowledge of the tool/dialog(s) at the time you first write the class; part of the learning process is to see firsthand how a hand-written class can differ from the requirements of a parts architecture.

Estimated time to complete: 3–4 hours total. 2–3 hours to write the class and convert it to a part, 1 hour to create the testing/demo application with the visual builder and to fix final bugs.

2. Demonstrate a specific example where a visual builder's code generation capability reduces the amount of code a direct coder would have to otherwise write. Describe a specific example of your own choosing, where a set of (10 or less) values or choices made by the user would allow builder logic to produce at least 100 lines of source code (embodied in as many classes and methods as you like). An abstract parent class (or Java interface) or use of C++ templates must be incapable of producing the same code; that is, it must not be a simple matter of substituting the user-supplied values into a canned block of code. Look for cases where a particular user value causes very different kinds of code to be generated.

The solution to this problem should include a general description of the code to be generated, a list of the values/choices to be made by the user, and pseudocode for the actual generation logic showing how each value/choice controls the specific code generated.

Estimated time to complete: 2 hours.

---

[1]See www.software.ibm.com/ad and click on the node you want from the list on the left.

[2]See www.symantec.com/domain/cafe/vc4java.html.

[3]You should have difficulty doing this because of the lack of a default constructor on your class. Add a default constructor to the part and you should see how the difficulty goes away.

5.13 Projects

Project 1: Read and familiarize yourself with the JavaBeans specification (java.sun .com/beans/). This document is (at the time of writing) the only existing widely accepted standard for the parts concept in any language. Although only accepted as a standard for the Java language, the basic design points could apply equally well to any other OO language. Understanding it will give you a deeper understanding of the parts concept in general.

Project 2: Using a tool that supports the creation of JavaBeans via a wizard or Smart-Guide, use the tool to create a variety of Beans. Using a compatible visual builder, combine those beans with others to create a medium-complexity application. See when (or if) you encounter places where you must go back to writing code directly, augmenting existing beans, in order to achieve some bit of function in your application. IBM VisualAge Java or VisualAge C++ is such a tool.[4]

Project 3: Using the visual builder tool you used in the "Problem Set," examine the code generated by that tool. Try to understand what the generated code is doing. Often, the tool documentation doesn't describe what generated code does; this is seen as part of the internals of the tool.

---

[4]See www.software.ibm.com/ad and click on the node you want from the list on the left.

Usability and Framework Design

As programmers are expected to do more and more development in less and less time, we can no longer afford to deal with colorful idiosyncrasies that interfere with getting the job done. The usability of frameworks is being placed on an equal footing with their raw functionality and the speed of the resulting code.

6.1 Usability Guidelines

Using the general guidelines of user interface (UI) usability as an outline, this chapter presents a set of rules for framework usability (they actually apply to class libraries as well). These guidelines have been arrived at over time during actual class library and framework development by a variety of practitioners (some have even been carried over from procedural development). These guidelines are not about writing efficient code, although they don't make your code any less efficient. Nor are these guidelines about writing easy-to-maintain code, although they may provide that as a side effect. These guidelines are about making it easier for programmers to learn your frameworks—and to write good programs with them.

6.1.1 Keep It Simple

When designing frameworks, your primary goal should be to have as few classes, methods, and parameters as possible to achieve the function you are providing. The number of classes and methods relates neither to the quality of design nor necessarily to functionality. Bragging on size is an admission of failure in design; developers are rightly balancing the appearance of rich function with the learning curve of a large framework. If you have to brag, do so on what can be done with the framework.

However, you shouldn't write huge methods just to reduce the total. The flexibility benefits of small methods must be balanced against the cost of learning many methods. One way to reduce the number of methods is to keep some of them private. Better still, isolate and remove useless methods entirely.

Cognitive scientists discovered years ago that the human mind can typically deal with seven (plus or minus two) unrelated items (digits in a phone number, words in a random list, and so on) at a time. More complex data is best handled as hierarchies, where each level has this magic number of nodes. This cognitive ideal is sadly too much to ask of frameworks. However, you can keep things simpler by organizing classes into a number of smaller, relatively separate, frameworks. The IBM Open Class library[1] in VisualAge C++, for example, has one framework for creating GUI-control-based interfaces, and another for drawing lines, circles, text, and the like.

While it must be as easy to work with the frameworks together as separately, it's important that users can learn them separately. This is possible only if the frameworks are truly separate. For example, frameworks should not use each other's classes as parameters or return values except in those few places necessary to make them work together. In the case of Open Class, the connection point is that the *context* used by the drawing classes can be obtained from a window object in the GUI library. This is the only place the two frameworks refer to each other, but it is enough to allow integration.

In frameworks, a number of classes usually interact to accomplish a given task; this set of classes is called a *clique*. Experienced practitioners minimize the number of classes in a given clique, especially the number the user must derive from to accomplish the clique's task. For example, Liant's C++/Views framework[2] has a menu clique that consists of only VMenu, VMenuItem, VpopupMenu, and method (see the guideline on consistent capitalization), with VOrdCollect as an optional fifth class. This clique is even within the seven-plus-or-minus-two ideal.

6.1.2 Help the User Be Productive Quickly

You might expect that helping users quickly become productive refers to product installation and initial configuration (setup). However, other aspects come to mind if we think of setup in the more general sense.

For starters, you should minimize the classes that must be subclassed before they can be used (this style of framework is sometimes called *blackbox*). Every subclass is another class the user must document (at least internally) and maintain (probably forever). Every additional subclass may even need to be defined in, and managed by, a code-control library (which must be accounted for in the compile-build process). It is easier for developers to find the class they want and instantiate it, than to pause, write a subclass, implement some method overrides, and go back to the original problem they were trying to solve.

[1] Open Class is part of VisualAge for C++, IBM Corporation.

[2] C++/Views, Liant Software Corporation.

For those classes that are intended to be subclassed, you should minimize the number of methods that must be overridden to accomplish the job. This does not mean that you want to forbid developers from overriding other methods in special situations, nor mash several methods together just to reduce the method count. The goal is to keep them to a minimum without violating the other usability guidelines.

6.1.3 Identify the Tools for a Task

It should be clear to users what items they need to perform a given task. Therefore, you should clearly identify those classes that are purely for your internal implementation and that you don't want to ship in your final product (unless you include source code). For example, some practitioners include a comment such as //**NOSHIP*** INTERNAL USE ONLY in C++ headers and document what this comment means. In this way, if you find yourself accidentally exposing one of these headers, the chance of catching the error somewhere prior to product shipment is much better.

You should also clearly identify the classes that must be subclassed to do a particular task and the methods within those classes that must be overridden. A number of frameworks, including Microsoft's MFC,[3] Borland's OWL,[4] and IBM's Open Class, have identified certain methods as *advanced* or *implementation*, or some other magic word indicating to the developer that this method is not used in the typical situation (but may be for more unusual ones). It appears unavoidable that there be such methods; this is especially true in frameworks, where, by definition, your classes interact in semiprivate ways. How you will inform the developer should be planned from the beginning.

6.1.4 Use Real-World Knowledge to Speed Understanding

The ability to transfer knowledge from the real world to a computer interface helps a user to instantly understand how to use (at least parts of) a system. This is equally true for programming interfaces. The main way knowledge transfer takes place here is in naming conventions for classes and methods.

Pick class and method names from the domain to which this library applies. If you are writing a financial-analysis class library, classes named StockPortfolio and MarginAccount are reasonable (not to mention obvious).

Less obvious are the guidelines involving natural language syntax in naming. Generally, name classes with nouns and methods with verbs or verb phrases. The goal is to achieve a sort of object-action reverse English sense out of the resulting source code, such as file->print() or aCollection sort. Smalltalk is famed for its elaborate pseudo-sentences, such as "aTextTool align:aString at:aPoint showFrom:N," which tells a text-drawing tool to align the beginning of a string at a specified point on the screen and show it from the Nth character to the last character.

In most cases you cannot make a class or method name too long. Modern editors and IDEs virtually eliminate typing-time concerns, and names using complete words

---

[3]MFC is part of Visual C++, Microsoft Corporation.

[4]OWL is part of Borland C++, Borland Corporation.

are easier to spell correctly than abbreviations. (There are obvious exceptions for widely used acronyms or abbreviations such as "TCP" or "Mac.") If you follow the previous natural syntax guidelines and the subsequent consistency guidelines, a longer name is often easier to remember than a short one.

For example, consider the method name unsetf( ). This is a method on the ios class (itself not a model of clarity). ios is part of the AT&T C++ library for stream *I/O*. unsetf is the method used to remove previously set data format flags and restore the prior flags. The "f" made that perfectly clear, right?

Smalltalk is not immune to poor method naming. The Collection class method inject:into: sounds understandable. Unfortunately, it doesn't inject anything into anything. What it does do is let you iterate through a Collection, processing each element in turn. The processing is done via a block of code, and the block also has access to the results of the prior iteration of processing. This makes it easy to bubble-sort a collection, for example. Apparently, the name was chosen because it rhymed with sibling methods select, collect, detect, and reject. Enough said.

6.1.5 Be Consistent

As users begin to learn your framework, you want the knowledge to build up as quickly as possible. The key to this is consistency. Establish standards for how to handle similar situations and stick to them. For header file names (in languages that have them), for instance, establish a convention for deriving the 8.3 file name from the name of the key class or classes declared therein. For example, irect.hpp is a good name for the header file in which class IRectangle is declared. It is less obvious that COLE-TemplateServer is found not in afxole.h but in afxdisp.h.

Some frameworks establish class naming conventions using prefixes. Open Class prefixes all of its classes with "I," while MFC uses "C" and C++/Views uses "V." The obvious benefit here is to avoid name clashes when several libraries are used in the same application. There is an ANSI standard in the works to give separate name spaces for different libraries (and thus frameworks).

Should you capitalize class names? Each word in a class name? Should you capitalize method names? Each word (after the first) in a method name? There is no consensus on this issue among practitioners. Within the Smalltalk and Java worlds, classes are word-wise capitalized and methods are lowercased with subsequent words capitalized. Rogue Wave[5] Open Class and C++/Views follow this same convention in C++, while MFC and Borland capitalize methods. Whatever you do, decide on it and be consistent or you will earn the wrath of developers constantly mistyping initial letters.

Accessors are methods that set the value of some data in an object or that return the current value. Often, 30 percent or more of a class's methods are accessors. Consistency here yields great benefits in interface usability. The majority of C++-based frameworks use either the getAbc/setAbc scheme or the abc/setAbc scheme, where Abc is the data item. Unfortunately, it is not enough for a clear consensus. In Smalltalk, the convention (well established) is that a method abc with no parameter *gets* the value, while abc: with a parameter *sets* the value. In Java, the getAbc/setAbc is not only a nearly universal convention, but the JavaBeans component standard requires this scheme. The

[5]Rogue Wave, Rogue Wave Software.

point is, as long as you are self-consistent, and maybe even consistent with the other libraries your developer audience likes, you should be okay.

There are similar conventions for some other method categories. The two most common ones are isAbc and asAbc. If your class has states that it can be in (such as enabled/disabled or visible/hidden), you should have methods isEnabled and isVisible, which return true or false. The choice of which Boolean state to use in the method name (isVisible or isHidden) is made based on which state developers would most often expect to be true; in this way, their "if" clauses are most likely to stay simple with no confusing negative logic.

The asAbc convention is used for methods that return this object in a different form. For example, the Java 1.1 and 1.2 frameworks have an asString method on the root Object class. Another example is the Smalltalk String class, which has methods such as asLowerCase and asInteger. Given that the developer knows a desired type, he can make a good guess as to the proper method to call. That is, after all, the goal behind the goal of library usability is: Design things so the developer can guess the right class, method, or whatever without reading the documentation. We rarely read it anyway.

6.1.6 Don't Make Things *Almost* the Same

If two things appear identical, they should *be* identical; otherwise, make them appear clearly different. Anyone who remembers file selection dialogs before the advent of a system standard will recognize the importance of this guideline. There is universal agreement on this principle in UI circles; there should be in framework circles as well, particularly as applied to class and method naming. Among current practitioners there is wide but not universal agreement (yet).

To illustrate, here are a couple of bad examples. The ios class uses the >> operator to extract data from a stream. For example, aStream>>doc; extracts data from aStream and places it in the variable doc. On the other hand, aStream>>dec; appears the same but does a completely different thing. It turns out that "dec" is a special keyword signifying "decimal," and this statement sets the mode of aStream to decimal. A better solution would be to have a decimalMode (spell it out!) method that sets the mode, and leave the operator to what it does best.

The choice is not always that obvious. The Taligent AE framework had its own I/O stream classes, used for (among other things) persistent storage of objects. TModel was a class that was expected to stream itself out and back in on demand. It is true that when TModel streamed itself out, it was not quite the same thing as a TStream object streaming via the >> operator. Therefore, it might not be wise to use the same >> operator in TModel. The choice made by Taligent was to instead use a >>= operator. According to our guideline, a better choice would have been streamToStore or something distinctively different.

In general, operator overrides should be carefully considered. Operators like + and > come to us from the world of mathematics with concrete meanings. According to the guideline on real-world knowledge, supporting these operators for nonmathematical objects (where it makes sense) is a fine idea. However, programmers who first began making up new operators (such as >>) opened a Pandora's box, which is only now being hammered shut by the OO community. If you find yourself tempted to make up a new operator, think it through very carefully, consider all the ramifications, and, if it still seems like a good idea, bang your head against a wall until the temptation passes.

Almost the same doesn't just apply to operators. Don't get carried away with polymorphism to the point where you are stretching the original meaning of the method name. It makes sense to rotate a page of text 90 degrees. It may even make sense to rotate a video clip. But what does it mean to rotate a sound clip 90 degrees? The fact that you can make up some strange waveform manipulation algorithm is beside the point; the typical developer won't know what you mean.

6.1.7 Design to Prevent User Errors

Some languages are more ripe for developer errors than others, but they all could use some help. As in GUIs, the ultimate goal is to make it impossible for the user to make an error in the first place.

For those languages that use includes, multiple include protection is a must. Most people have found that this simple device is even simpler to manage by always naming the protect variable the same as the include file name. In C++, an include file iframe.hpp would look like this:

```
#ifndef _IFRAME_
#define _IFRAME_
... body of include ...
#endif // _IFRAME_
```

In this way you don't even have to worry about keeping track of the #define labels.

Passing or returning a reference instead of a pointer (a distinction made in some C-derived OO languages, such as C++) can avoid certain errors. By definition, a reference always points to *something*. If you always have something to return (that is, never a null pointer), then using a reference is a good choice to improve usability; the caller never has to worry about a jump to zero.

Regardless of whether you return a reference or a pointer, you are taking a usability risk in non-garbage-collecting languages like C++. You must clearly communicate the lifetime of the object being referred to and who is responsible for destroying it. Use of a pointer (or reference) to an object that has secretly been destroyed is one of the most common and difficult-to-catch errors a developer can face. A memory leak, caused when no one destroys an object, is just as bad.

So, what is the guideline? Use naming conventions, if possible, to consistently cue developers regarding ownership. For example, Taligent uses an *adopt and orphan* convention. Any method that returns an object Xyz and wants the caller to take delete responsibility for that object is named OrphanXyz; the receiver (the callee) is being asked to orphan the returned object. If delete responsibility remains with the receiver, the method is named GetXyz. Likewise, a method that takes an object as an argument and where the caller wants the receiver to take delete responsibility for the object is named AdoptXyz(anXyz). Otherwise, it is called SetXyz(anXyz). There is support for this convention; however, most frameworks have yet to address this situation, so there is no consensus at this time.

6.1.8 Try to Have a Default Value or Behavior

If simpler is better, then a method with no parameters is the best method to have. One way to get more of them is to support default values for parameters. Even in languages such as Java, which make it difficult to support default values, you should take the time to write the necessary constructor variants. What makes a good default depends on the class and method, so there are no easy answers here. Talk to your developer-users.

Default behaviors apply to any abstract "implemented by subclass" method in your Smalltalk classes (similar in intent to a pure virtual function in C++ or a Java interface). Because the subclass may not actually override the inherited method, your framework should, if possible, perform some reasonable default behavior. Only if there is no reasonable default should you instead throw an error. C++ and Java are a bit nicer here, in that an abstract function that your developer forgets to override results in a compiler error.

This guideline also applies to a class or, more specifically, to a newly created object (instance) of a class. Any object should be as fully formed and ready to use as possible before it is returned to the caller. This makes it easier for developers to get an initial prototype of their application up and running and to gradually add code as they learn. The design of some distributed object systems as well as some component architectures have led to the use of an initialize method that must be called following creation of the object; an object is not ready to use until both the constructor and the initialization method have run. Although there may be good technical reasons for this separation, the usability problems it introduces should not be ignored. In some of these systems, the initialize method is called automatically, thus eliminating the usability concern.

6.1.9 Be Modeless

User interface designers agree that designing a system with modes is usually asking for trouble. Whatever mode the system is in, the user invariably wants to perform some task in another mode. The solution is to keep user operations atomic and to design the system to be modeless.

This is a general feature of human thinking, not confined to GUIs. We often need to be doing several things at once, or we are interacting with several other processes at once. The best design in a framework, then, is a modeless one. Keep methods atomic and independent. As much as possible, developers should be able to call the methods in whatever order they like. Take, for example, a File class. One design would require developers to first call "open" before calling "read." A better design would automatically do an open if a read was called first. Even if you are a layer on top of a truly modal base (such as in the File example), it does not mean you must be modal.

6.1.10 Immediate and Reversible Results

In UI design, users should be able to immediately see the results of an action and should be able to undo that action. In frameworks, the equivalent also applies. When developers call a method to set a value, a subsequent get should return the new value. If there is any reason for a delay (such as for time lag due to distribution across systems), the get method must account for it in some way. As distributed object-oriented systems become more commonplace, there will be more need for standards for asynchronous methods. These will have to balance the improved usability of synchronous behavior (or the appearance of synchronous behavior) with the benefits of distributed systems.

Reversible also applies to class libraries. This can be achieved by having a resetAbc method along with the set and get methods. A reset method is not always needed. If the original value of this attribute is convenient to keep around (small, not shared), then the developer can reset by calling setAbc with the original value. However, there are some attributes where this is not so easy. Add a reset method in these cases. Also, there are cases where you need to set a complex group of attributes that together define the state of the object. If there is a clearly defined default state for the group, it may be awkward to keep around all the individual attributes you have changed. For example, a printer usually has defaults for font, page size, layout, and many other attributes. Having a resetToDefault method would allow all the attributes to be reset at once.

6.1.11 Documentation for Developers

Documentation of frameworks usually consists of brief notes on a per-class, per-method level. The best practitioners understand that the most important thing to document in a framework is the interactions between classes. These interactions, after all, are what differentiate a framework from a simple class library. I have found that the most usable frameworks document these interactions, often in a task-based or *cookbook* format. Task-based documentation often crosses the lines between separate frameworks within a product, so general prose descriptions of the individual frameworks are also very useful.

In some cases, the behavior of a framework reflects one or more of the standard design patterns as documented in *Design Patterns* by Gamma et al. or some other book. In this case, stating this in your documentation will give developers an instant understanding of your goal for this framework. Give them a reference to the pattern itself, in case they have not heard of it yet.

6.2 Summary

Training yourself and your team to apply these guidelines will take time. Deciding how they apply to a particular situation is not always cut and dried, and the discussion will also take time. Only part of this time will be regained later in your development cycle. The result, however, as shown by some of the commercial frameworks mentioned here, is greatly improved usability. Developer-users are recognizing that this saves them time in their development cycles. And that, after all, is the whole purpose of frameworks.

6.3 Review Questions

1. The number of classes and methods in a framework is typically a direct measure of the functionality and quality of design; as the number increases, the functionality and quality of design increases (True/False).
2. It is easier for your developer-user to learn several smaller but relatively independent frameworks than to learn a single closely-integrated framework (True/False).

3. A design goal for frameworks is to:
   a. Maximize the number of classes that can be derived from, to maximize the flexibility of the framework.
   b. Minimize the number of classes that can be derived from, to maximize the ease of learning and usage of the framework.
   c. Keep the number of classes that can be derived from in any given clique or subframework at or near the 7-plus-or-minus-2 guideline.

4. Documentation for classes in a framework should:
   a. Differentiate between those classes commonly used, those used only for unusual situations, and those only used internally by the framework.
   b. Not differentiate between commonly used classes and less commonly used classes; only the developer understands his or her own needs and thus how commonly a class is likely to be used.

5. The length of class names and method names should be
   a. No longer than 10 to 15 characters, to avoid typing overhead and unnecessarily increasing executable size.
   b. Long enough to ensure that the name is unique within the framework.
   c. Long enough to ensure that most users will understand what the class or method does.
   d. At or near the 7-plus-or-minus-2 guideline.

6. Each clique or subframework within a framework should use a separate convention for whether class and method names are capitalized, whether words in a method name are capitalized, and so on. This makes it easier for the developer to know to which clique or subframework a given class or method belongs (True/False).

7. If your language has the ability to overload operators:
   a. Use it rarely if ever. Operators are often misunderstood as to their purpose.
   b. Make use of it when possible. Operators are an easy-to-remember way to implement function for a class (one picture [operator] is worth a thousand words).

8. Polymorphism is a powerful OO technique. It is good design to reuse the same method name across different classes:
   a. Even if the function being performed is not conceptually the same as that for the other classes; the unique class name tips off the developer, while the familiar method name is easier to remember than defining yet another unique method name.
   b. Only when the function being performed is conceptually the same as for the other classes; the developer is expected to ignore the unique class names and assume like-named methods perform conceptually like functions. The additional unique method names the developer must learn because of this design restriction is an accepted side effect.

9. Write typical multiple-include protection statements for a C++ header file named foo.hpp. For those unfamiliar with the C++ language, the statements available to you include the following:

```
#define   ...somename...    // defines a name (hereafter, the name exists)
#undefine ...somename...    // removes a defined name (hereafter, the name
                            // no longer exists)
```

```
#ifdef   ...somename...      // if (one of a pair of statements)
#ifndef  ...somename...      // if not (one of a pair of statements)
#endif                       // closing statement of the pairs above
```

10. The purpose of the adopt/orphan naming convention is to:
    a. Cue your developers as to who is to own the instance of a class being referred to; the class name includes "adopt" if the owner is to be the caller (the one calling methods on the instance).
    b. Cue your developers as to who is to own the instance of a class being referred to; the method name includes "adopt" if the owner is to be the receiver (the one being passed the instance).
    c. Cue your developers as to who is to own the instance of a class being referred to; the method name includes "orphan" if the owner is to be the receiver (the one being passed the instance).
    d. Cue your developers as to who is to own the instance of a class being referred to; the class name includes "orphan" if the owner is to be the caller (the one calling methods on the instance).

11. Regarding default parameter values, good design practice is to:
    a. Avoid default parameters, since the only way to ensure that you are doing what the developer intends is to obtain all values from him or her.
    b. Supply default parameter values whenever possible, since the fewer parameter values the developer needs to supply, the easier the method is to use.

12. Describe what it means for a method to be modeless.

13. What is the important area of framework documentation that is often left out?

6.4 Problem Set

1. Write a set of classes that demonstrate the BREAKING of the guidelines in the reading. You may skip guideline 1), since it would take too much time to write enough classes to break the guideline. For guideline 11), a successful example does not have to include documentation for all your classes, only one particular class or set of classes.

   For those guidelines that actually describe several related guidelines, you may pick any one of the related guidelines you wish and use it in your example code. It is acceptable to use pseudocode in the implementation (if one is needed) of a method.

   Estimated time to complete: 2 hours.

6.5 Projects

Project 1: Examine a framework of your choice and document two examples of each guideline, one example following the guideline and the other example breaking the guideline. Suggested frameworks include:
   a. Sun's Java frameworks (written in Java), especially java.awt, java.sql, java.io, and/or java.beans.
   b. Microsoft's MFC (written in C++).
   c. IBM's VisualAge C++ OpenClass (written in C++).

SIDEBAR 2
VIEWPOINTS AND FRAMEWORKS IN COMPONENT-BASED
SOFTWARE DESIGN

Separation of concerns is a well-established principle in software engineering that uses abstraction to hide complexity. The importance of this principle increases dramatically as new technologies are introduced and as software applications and, in particular, frameworks, become more complex. Mastering the inherent complexity in the organization and design of object-oriented frameworks makes it necessary for developers to deal with an increasing number of concerns that need to be separated.

Current frameworks involve a basic concern and a number of special-purpose concerns. The basic concern is represented by the fundamental computational algorithms that provide the essential functionality relevant to an application domain, and the special-purpose concerns relate to other software issues, such as user interface presentation, control, timing, synchronization, distribution, and fault tolerance. Special-purpose concerns are extensions to the basic functionality that fulfill special requirements of the application, or enhance, manage, or optimize the basic algorithm. Separation of these concerns localizes the different kinds of information in the software descriptions, making them easier to write, understand, reuse, and modify.

The identification of the concerns relevant to a particular application and the definition of mechanisms to separate them has been an old challenge. As Dijkstra states: "The crucial choice is, of course, what aspects to study 'in isolation,' how to disentangle the original amorphous knot of obligations, constraints and goals into a set of 'concerns' that admit a reasonably effective separation . . ." [Dijkstra 1976].

Typical approaches to integrate concerns into the basic concern usually intertwine the fundamental algorithm with the special concerns. However, there are several problems that arise from this approach, including the following: First, there is very little design or code reuse because all concerns have to be dealt with at the same time and at the same level; second, it is difficult to design, codify, understand, maintain, and evolve systems in which all the concerns are strongly coupled.

To avoid strong coupling and promote design and code reuse, we separate the various concerns of the frameworks through *viewpoint* concepts throughout the design process. A viewpoint is a view of a system from a suitable perspective where we focus on a specific set of concerns. We could view a distribution system framework from a user or supplier perspective, or from the business rules that have been implemented. In contrast, we could also view a framework from a structural, functional, or sequencing perspective. In the first case, we are examining the system from the functionality presented to the external world, while in the second case, we are examining the different relationships of the same aspect of the system.

The two types of viewpoints are called *inter-* and *intra*-viewpoint representations, respectively. A key consideration of viewpoints is that multiple viewpoints must present the same system consistently. We choose to describe a viewpoint in terms of an object-oriented model, because of the rich constructs provided by this form of design language. The concepts associated with viewpoints are still evolving. For example, the Unified Modeling Language (UML) uses intra-viewpoints, while the Open Distributed Processing (ODP) Standard uses inter-viewpoints.

Continues

In order to keep the concerns separated, we use a relationship called *views-a* [Alencar 1998; Cowan-Lucena 1995]. Views-a can be used to model the connection between classes or components, often called *glue.* Using this abstraction to model, glue allows the software developer to visualize the assembly operation more clearly. Normally, the glue would be buried in a complex programming structure that would obscure its real purpose.

The views-a operation has well-defined properties or semantics [Alencar 1998]. We characterize the relationship between viewer (also called Abstract Design Views or ADV) and viewed (also called Abstract Design Objects or ADO) objects based on a set of primitive semantic properties. A rigorous definition of such properties, which can be seen as a formal model for gluing object-oriented components, is provided in [Alencar 1998].

The views-a properties include the ones shown in Table SB2.1.

Table SB2.1 Views-a Properties

1. **Identity:**
Viewed and viewer have different identities.

2. **Cardinality:**
The general cardinality is m viewers for one viewed.

3. **Creation/deletion:**
A viewed can outlive its viewers; a viewer cannot outlive its views.

4. **Singularity/multiplicity:**
A viewed can have different viewers.

5. **Vertical consistency:**
Views viewing the same state of a viewed must be consistent.

6. **Horizontal consistency:**
A viewed and a viewer object must be consistent.

7. **Visibility:**
A viewed object does not know its viewers.

The views-a operation can be implemented in terms of one of the standard object-oriented design patterns [Gamma 1995] such as the observer, mediator, or state. We choose the appropriate design pattern by comparing each design pattern with the views-a properties required in a specific design. For example, the observer or mediator pattern would be chosen to implement views-a if the viewed state of an object is changing and consistency among the viewed and viewers must be ensured over time. We have demonstrated the mapping of the views-a operation into different design patterns.

We propose a model for framework development based on viewpoints that includes the following five steps.

1. Determine the viewpoints of an application through viewpoint analysis where we can see each viewpoint as a subframework.

2. Determine the classes within a subframework and the subframeworks of an application that deal with the basic and the special concerns.

3. Glue both the classes within a subframework and the subframeworks together to create a complete application—the glue semantics is characterized by the views-a operation. Prebuilt components can also be connected to frameworks by using this glue model.

4. Map the glue into design patterns—the required views-a semantics is used to guide the selection of appropriate design patterns. Object-oriented descriptions of the applications are produced.

5. Transform the resulting object-oriented design into "real" components—the interface and functionality of some components from an object-oriented perspective are described and the corresponding transformations are developed.

We have partially tested each of these steps by describing aspects of several applications. First, as a preliminary investigation, we have considered a case study that dealt with the NACHOS file system. In this case [Alencar 1997b], there are two viewpoints: one for concurrency and one for large extensible files. Other case studies dealt with a process life-cycle application [Alencar 1998], a web-based education software system based on viewpoints [Alencar 1998], and hypermaps [Alencar 1997a].

We believe that our proposed approach to component-based design can be used even when the software developer uses ad hoc methods. We have found through experimentation that using some of the steps to analyze a design in progress clarifies many of the design decisions in the context of separation of concerns. Furthermore, an approach to framework development based on viewpoint concepts definitely improves the organization and leads to better-designed frameworks.

SB2.1 References

[Alencar 1997a] Alencar, P.S.C., D.D. Cowan, C.J.P. Lucena, and M.A.V. Nelson. An approach to hypermap-based applications. *Proceedings of the 2nd International Symposium on Environmental Software Systems (ISESS 1997)*, pp. 244–251, Whistler, BC, April 28–May 2, 1997.

[Alencar 1997b] Alencar, P.S.C., D.D. Cowan, C.J.P. Lucena, and T. Nelson. Viewpoints as an evolutionary approach to software system maintenance. *Proceedings of the International Conference on Software Maintenance,* Bari, Italy, October 1997.

[Alencar 1998] Alencar, P.S.C., D.D. Cowan, and C.J.P. Lucena. A logical theory of interfaces and objects. Revised for *IEEE Transactions on Software Engineering*, 1998.

[Cowan-Lucena 1995] Cowan, D., and C. Lucena. Abstract data views: An interface specification concept to enhance design., *IEEE Transactions on Software Engineering*, 21(3), March 1995.

[Dijkstra 1976] Dijkstra, E.W. *A discipline of programming.* Prentice-Hall, Englewood Cliffs, NJ, 1976.

[Gamma 1995] Gamma, E., R. Helm, R. Johnson, and J. Vlissides. *Design Patterns: Elements of Reusable Object-Oriented Software.* Reading, MA: Addison-Wesley, 1995.

PART

Three

Frameworks and
Domain Analysis

Part Three contains two chapters and a sidebar. Domain analysis is a fundamental process for systematic software artifacts reuse. Domain analysis process has three major activities:

Domain context analysis. Identifies the scope of the domain, analyzes the knowledge source and produces a context diagram.

Domain abstraction modeling. Identifies the right domain components and their data, behavior, and interaction models.

Domain architecture. Generates the backbone of the application framework.

Chapter 7 discusses how to drive application frameworks from domain knowledge. Although a considerable number of successful frameworks have been developed during the last decade, designing a high-quality framework is still a difficult task. Generally, it is assumed that finding the correct abstractions is very hard, and therefore a successful framework can only be developed through a number of iterative (software) development efforts. Accordingly, existing framework development practices span a considerable amount of refinement time, and it is worthwhile to shorten this effort. To this end, this chapter aims at defining explicit models for the knowledge domains that are related to a framework. The absence of such models may be the main reason for the currently experienced extensive refinement effort. The applicability of the approach is illustrated by means of three pilot projects. This chapter indicates that some aspects of domain knowledge could not be directly modeled in terms of object-oriented concepts. The chapter describes an approach, the pilot projects, the experienced problems, and the adopted solutions for realizing the frameworks. This chapter concludes with lessons learned from this experience.

Chapter 8 discusses the harvesting process of the application framework design. The design of application frameworks employs both problem and solution domain analysis. By analyzing existing solutions, one can harvest design and code that can be refined for reuse in new frameworks.

The steps of the harvesting process are identification of existing solution candidates, analysis of their domains for similarities and variations, and framework implementation. This chapter describes how this process was used to evaluate several solutions from different industry domains to produce a general-purpose framework for application task management.

Sidebar 3 discusses the relationship between frameworks and domain abstraction and architecture models. Frameworks and domain models are closely related. The behavior and usability of frameworks depend on their capability to fit different requirements. Frameworks originate from the analysis of domains and are designed to support the development of new applications. A domain model is a general representation for many applications in a problem domain; these applications may be only potential and still to be developed. The core of frameworks and of domain models is (1) to describe commonality and variability and (2) to support the management of the different parts in similar products coming from the same domain. Framework development and domain analysis and engineering (DA&E) have the same economic justification: They exploit the economies of scope arising from the reuse of the assets in the domain. This sidebar outlines how DA&E can positively support the production of frameworks and focus on Sherlock, an object-oriented DA&E technique targeted to the development of frameworks.

Deriving Frameworks from Domain Knowledge

Object-oriented frameworks offer well-defined infrastructures for a family of applications [Johnson 1988]. Frameworks have to be tailored to the specific needs of a particular application setting, mostly through subclassing and/or compositions, preferably with minimal effort. In comparison with developing dedicated software, developing frameworks may provide long-term benefits such as enhanced productivity, reduced maintenance costs, improved consistency, and better integration of software components [Taligent 1996].

Although a considerable number of successful frameworks have been developed during the last several years [Huni 1995], it is generally agreed that designing a high-quality framework is still a difficult task [Roberts 1996; Taligent 1996]. Several methods have been proposed to support the development of frameworks. For example, in [Taligent 1996], first the primary abstractions are derived from the requirement specification document and the related solutions. Second, the interactions of clients with frameworks are defined. Finally, frameworks are implemented, tested, and refined.

In [Roberts 1996], a pattern language is proposed for developing frameworks. The assumption made here is that primary abstractions are very hard to find, and therefore a successful framework can be developed only after a series of (software) development efforts. First, it is advised to implement three applications that could be derived from the framework to be developed. Second, as a generalization of these applications, a *whitebox* framework has to be developed. A whitebox framework is structured primarily by inheritance relations. Due to the heavy use of inheritance, it requires understanding the implementation details of the used classes. Once a whitebox framework is understood sufficiently, it can be converted to a *blackbox* framework, which is based primarily on compositions. Composition-based frameworks require less knowledge of the implementation of reused classes, provide runtime adaptability, and can be easily tailored by *composing objects* rather than programming new subclasses.

A similar approach is taken in [Huni 1995], where a whitebox communication framework was converted to a blackbox framework. This was possible because a considerable amount of experience was gained through the application of the initial framework. The design makes extensive use of composition-based design patterns [Gamma 1995].

It is clear that existing framework development practices span a considerable amount of refinement time, and it is worthwhile to reduce this effort. The main reason for this extensive refinement is the lack of an integrated approach to model domain knowledge related to the framework and to map the identified domain models into an object-oriented framework. For this purpose, this chapter aims at finding answers to the following questions: First, would it be possible to identify and model the necessary domain knowledge for supporting framework development? The absence of such a model may be the main reason for an extensive refinement effort. Second, what might be the obstacles that one experiences in mapping domain knowledge into object-oriented frameworks? Finally, what kind of research activities would be needed to address the identified problems, if any? This chapter presents our approach and findings in this experimental research. The applicability of our approach is illustrated by means of three pilot projects.

The chapter is organized as follows: The following section describes the initial requirements for the pilot projects. *Section 7.2* explains how the related domain knowledge is identified and modeled. *Section 7.3* describes the realization of the frameworks and the experienced problems in mapping domain knowledge into object-oriented concepts. *Section 7.4* evaluates the approach, presents the lessons learned, and gives conclusions.

7.1 Description of the Pilot Projects

In the following sections we describe the initial requirements for the pilot projects.

7.1.1 Transaction Framework

Our first pilot project aims at designing an object-oriented atomic transaction framework to be used in a distributed car dealer management system.[1] Data and processing in a car dealer management system are largely distributed and therefore *serializability* and *recoverability* of executions are required. Using atomic transactions [Bernstein 1987], serializability and recoverability for a group of statements can be ensured. Serializability means that the concurrent execution of a group of transactions is equivalent to some serial execution of the same set of transactions. Recoverability means that each execution either completes successfully or has no effect on data shared with other transactions.

A car dealer management system is a data-intensive system that involves several applications with varying characteristics, operates in heterogeneous environments, and may incorporate different data formats. To achieve optimal behavior, each of these

[1]This project is carried out together with Siemens-Nixdorf Software Center and supported by The Dutch Ministry of Economical Affairs under the SENTER program.

aspects may require transactions with dedicated serialization and recovery techniques. This requires transactions with dynamic adaptation of transaction behavior, optimized with respect to the application and environmental conditions, and data formats. The adaptation policy, therefore, must be determined by the programmers, the operating system, or the data objects. Further, reusability of the software is considered as an important requirement to reduce development and maintenance costs.

7.1.2 Image Processing Framework

At the Laboratory for Clinical and Experimental Image Processing, located at the university hospital of Leiden, an image processing system is being developed for the analysis of the human heart [Zwet 1994]. Up to now, image processing algorithms have been implemented at the laboratory using procedure libraries. For example, assume that the application of three image processing algorithms algorithm$_1$, algorithm$_2$, and algorithm$_3$ on the input image produces the output image:

```
outputImage = algorithm3 (algorithm2 (algorithm1 (inputImage)));
```

The result of the first algorithm is the input parameter of the second algorithm, and the result of the second algorithm is the input parameter of the third algorithm. Here, all cascaded input-output values must be compatible. Procedures, however, are largely dependent on the representation of the input and output values [Wegner 1984]. This is problematic due to the large number of different representations for images.

In object-oriented modeling, algorithms could be defined as operations of a class, and the structure of an image could be encapsulated within the private part of the class. By sending cascaded messages, the user can transform images subsequently:

```
outputImage = ((inputImage.algorithm1).algorithm2).algorithm3;
```

Here, inputImage receives the message algorithm$_1$, which results in a new image that receives the message algorithm$_2$, and so on. Provided that each image understands these messages, one may apply the algorithms to images in any order. This means, however, that each image must define all the required image processing algorithms, which may demand a large number of method definitions.

The image processing framework must be expressive enough to construct virtually any image processing algorithm that can be used for medical imaging. Effective code reuse can simplify implementation of image processing algorithms and decrease the maintenance costs.

7.1.3 Fuzzy-Logic Reasoning Framework

For several years, we have been carrying out research activities in formalizing object-oriented software development processes [Aksit 1996]. One of the problems in modeling a software development process is to represent design inconsistencies and uncertainties. As a result of our research, we concluded that fuzzy-logic theory [Dubois 1980] might be useful for this purpose. For the practical implementation of our ideas, we decided to build a fuzzy reasoning framework [Broekhuizen 1996].

A fuzzy reasoning system is characterized by two basic features. First, it has the ability of deducing a possibly imprecise but meaningful conclusion from a collection of fuzzy rules and a partially true fact. Second, rules and facts are codified in a natural language.

Consider, for example, the following rule: "If an entity is relevant in the problem domain then select it as a class." Two-valued logic forces the software engineer to make abrupt decisions, such as, "the entity is relevant" or "the entity is not relevant." The software engineer may, however, conclude that the entity partially fulfills the relevance criterion and may prefer to define the relevance of an entity, for instance, as substantially relevant. A fuzzy reasoning system can accept input values such as fairly, substantially, and the like, and reason, for example, about the relevance of a class. In fuzzy logic, these values are generally represented as partially overlapping sets.

The design of the fuzzy-logic reasoning framework involves a number of considerations. First, fuzzy logic may be based on different implication operators. Second, in fuzzy reasoning, the semantics of the connectives AND and ALSO can be interpreted in various ways. Third, the framework must provide both goal-driven and data-driven reasoning. Fourth, since contextual information plays a significant role in a software development process, the rules must be dynamically adapted to the changing context. Finally, the framework must be able to execute two-valued logic–based reasoning as well.

7.1.4 Comparison of the Pilot Projects

The required features of these frameworks are quite different because they relate to different application domains. The key characteristics, however, are quite similar. Each framework must support different kinds of implementations. For example, the transaction framework must provide different serialization techniques, the image processing framework must be able to support several image processing algorithms, and the fuzzy-logic reasoning framework must be able to implement different implication rules. In addition, for all frameworks, adaptability and reusability are important concerns.

7.2 Modeling Domain Knowledge

We first model the top-level structure of frameworks using the so-called knowledge graphs [Bakker 1987]. Second, we refine each node within a top-level knowledge graph into a subknowledge graph called a knowledge domain. Finally, we identify which nodes in a knowledge domain can be included together in the top-level knowledge graph. In the following sections, these steps will be described in more detail.

7.2.1 Identification of the Top-Level Knowledge Graph

Figure 7.1 shows a knowledge graph, which represents the related background for building a simple motorized vehicle. This graph consists of four nodes: Engine, Chassis, Brake, and Wheels. The relations represent the direct dependencies between the nodes. For example, Engine rotates Wheels; Brake stops Wheels; Chassis carries Engine, Wheels, and Brake.

Finding the top-level knowledge graph of a framework requires searching the related literature and finding similarities among various publications. Each node refers to a concept that is indispensable for a given framework. The minimum configuration of a framework can be found by gradually excluding concepts until essential characteristics of the framework are left. For example, concepts that can be considered as a part of another concept are excluded from the top-level knowledge graph.

This approach to representing knowledge fits in with the human way of thinking and reasoning. In the area of knowledge representation and expert systems, the techniques of *frames* [Minsky 1975] and *semantic networks* [Levesque 1979] can be considered as the underlying techniques required to construct knowledge graphs.

A number of systems have been developed for knowledge acquisition and representation. The KADS system [Wielinga 1992], for example, provides three *categories* called *domain knowledge, inference knowledge,* and *task knowledge,* in which the expertise knowledge is analyzed and described. The KARL system [Fensel 1995] was based on the principles of the KADS system, with an emphasis on formalizing expertise models and making them operational. The basic idea behind these systems—knowledge acquisition through model construction—is similar to our approach in constructing knowledge graphs. Most of the features of these systems, such as complex inference mechanisms, however, were not needed in our approach. Therefore, we preferred to adopt a much simpler knowledge representation model.

The following subsections describe the identification of the top-level knowledge graphs of our three pilot projects.

Transaction Framework

A considerable number of textbooks and articles have been written on atomic transactions [Bernstein 1987]. After analyzing and comparing the literature, we noticed that most publications adopt a similar structure. Figure 7.2 shows a top-level knowledge graph for transaction systems.

The node Transaction represents a *transaction block* as defined by the programmer. The node TransactionManager provides mechanisms for initiating, starting, and terminating the transaction. It maintains the data objects that are affected by the transaction. If a transaction reaches its final state successfully, then the node TransactionManager sends a

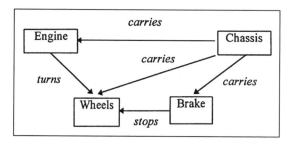

Figure 7.1 The top-level knowledge graph of a simple vehicle framework.

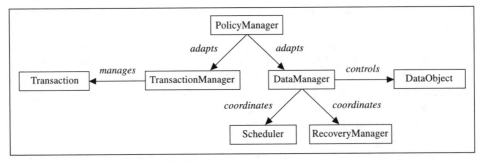

Figure 7.2 The top-level knowledge graph for the transaction framework.

commit message to the corresponding data objects to terminate the transaction. Otherwise, an abort message is sent to all the data objects to undo the effects of the transaction.

The node PolicyManager determines the strategy for optimizing the transaction behavior. In most publications, PolicyManager is included in TransactionManager. However, we considered transaction policies as a different concern and therefore defined it as a separate node. The node DataManager controls the access to its DataObject and includes the nodes Scheduler and RecoveryManager. The node Scheduler orders the incoming messages to achieve serializability. Scheduler may include deadlock avoidance and/or detection mechanisms. The node RecoveryManager keeps track of changes to the data object to recover from failures.

Image Processing Framework

The image processing framework must be capable of expressing virtually any image processing algorithm suitable for medical imaging. Therefore, we had to search for techniques that could cover the area of image processing. After a thorough literature survey, we came across the theory of *image algebra,* which is capable of expressing *almost all* image-to-image transformations [Ritter 1990]. The top-level knowledge graph of the image processing framework is derived from this theory, as depicted in Figure 7.3.

The image processing framework consists of *coordinate* and *value* sets. Images can be expressed as a composition of these two sets. The theory of image algebra introduces the concept of image templates. A template is a specific image pattern, which is used to implement image algebra operations such as rotation, zooming, and masked extraction.

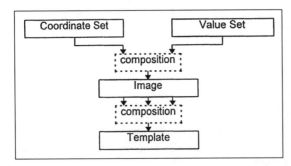

Figure 7.3 The top-level knowledge graph for the image processing framework.

Using image templates, an image processing algorithm can be defined as:

```
anOutputImage = anInputImage.anAlgebraicOp(aTemplate)
```

Here, anOutputImage represents the resulting image, anInputImage is the image to be processed, anAlgebraicOp is one of the basic operations defined by image algebra, and the argument aTemplate represents the algorithm to be applied on anInputImage. If templates can easily be derived from the user requirement specifications, this approach overcomes the problem of defining a large number of operations for each image, as only a few algebraic operations are required.

Fuzzy-Logic Reasoning Framework

A large number of publications have been written on fuzzy-logic reasoning (for example, [Dubois 1980; Turksen 1993]). After investigating the available literature, we concluded that the knowledge graph shown in Figure 7.4 conforms to the concepts in most of these publications.

We selected the so-called *generalized modus ponens* (GMP) as the basic inference mechanism because of its common usage in the literature. In the most general form, the GMP may be expressed as follows:

For a given rule R = "If A then B," and a fact A', the conclusion B' is equal to A' ○ R, where ○ is a composition relation between the fuzzy sets corresponding to A' and R.

In Figure 7.4, the node Fuzzy Inference Element implements the inference mechanism. This element contains Rule, Fact, GMP, and Conclusion. During the initialization phase, the nodes Rule and Fact communicate with the node Linguistic Variable to create a representation of themselves in terms of fuzzy sets. These fuzzy sets are provided to the node GMP, which carries out the inference process and generates a conclusion. The node Conclusion combines all the outputs of the related GMP nodes using the connective ALSO. The result of this combination, expressed in terms of fuzzy sets, may be defuzzified by the node Linguistic Variable. The defuzzification operation converts the fuzzy set into a crisp value or approximates it to a linguistic value. In case of a goal-driven inference, the node Linguistic Variable requests the node Conclusion to provide

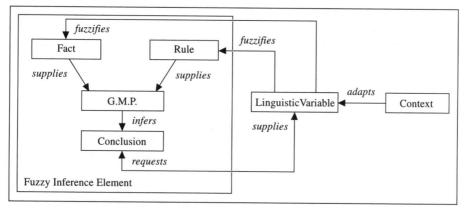

Figure 7.4   The top-level knowledge graph for the fuzzy-logic reasoning framework.

a value. In case of a data-driven inference, however, the node Conclusion delivers directly a value to the node Linguistic Variable.

Specific to our framework is the node Context. As specified in the initial requirement specification, the validity of rules used in a software development process largely depends on changes in the context. An explicit formulation of the effects of the context is therefore mandatory. The node Context is an instance of the entire fuzzy reasoning framework shown in Figure 7.4. Context reasons about the context information and may request to the node Linguistic Variable to modify the meaning associated with the linguistic values. Notice that the node Context may also include a subnode Context, thereby allowing specification of the effects of the context on a context, and so on. If the node Context is omitted, then the interpretation of linguistic values is fixed and cannot be changed dynamically.

7.2.2 Refinement of Top-Level Knowledge Graphs into Knowledge Domains

The next step is the refinement of each node in the top-level knowledge graph into a subknowledge graph called *knowledge domain*. The nodes within a knowledge domain correspond to a particular specialization in the domain and the relations typically represent generalization and specialization relations. For example, the node Engine in Figure 7.1 may correspond to a subknowledge graph including the nodes Combustion Engine, Gasoline Engine, Diesel Engine, and so on.

When a framework is instantiated as an application, each node in the top-level knowledge graph corresponds to a specialization of the related knowledge domain. For example, while building a specific vehicle, the node Engine will refer to a particular engine type, such as Combustion Engine. In our approach, therefore, an application is a composition of specializations from related knowledge domains.

Transaction Framework

To refine the top-level knowledge graph of the transaction framework shown in Figure 7.2, we investigated publications related to each node. We organized the available information for each node as a graph structure. Shortly, the node TransactionManager includes transaction management, and several different commit and abort protocols. The node Scheduler relates to concurrency control and deadlock detection techniques. The node RecoveryManager includes several recovery techniques.

In this section, for illustration purposes, we show in Figure 7.5 the specialization hierarchy of schedulers. More detailed information can be found in [Tekinerdogan 1994].

Node UniversalScheduler represents the common characteristics of all schedulers. Node SerialScheduler allows only one transaction at a time to access the object. The other schedulers use various mechanisms to preserve consistent access to the object. Node LockingScheduler represents schedulers that synchronize access to the object by using locking mechanisms in case of conflicting operations. Node Timestamp-OrderingScheduler orders operations from transactions according to the transactions' timestamps. This node can be further specialized by using the Thomas-Write rule (TWR) to omit a late write operation, which would not have any effect at all. Node

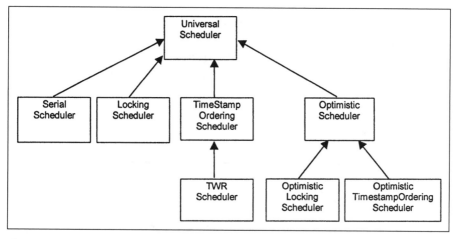

Figure 7.5 The refinement hierarchy of schedulers.

OptimisticScheduler orders conflicting transactions only at commit time. Optimistic schedulers may either use timestamp ordering or locking mechanisms to preserve consistency.

Schedulers may abort or delay conflicting operations of transactions. In case of delaying schedulers, operations of two different transactions may cause a deadlock because they are mutually waiting for each other. In order to resolve the occurred deadlock, schedulers may use deadlock avoidance and deadlock detection techniques [Bernstein 1987]. Therefore, a specialization hierarchy for deadlock handlers has been modeled as well.

Image Processing Framework

We show two related refinement hierarchies from the image processing framework:

The node Image defines functional dependencies between coordinate and value sets. Similarly, the node Template defines functional dependencies among images. Further, this node includes knowledge about image processing algorithms. Template is a specialization of Image. Further, Template is classified in InvariantTemplate and VariantTemplate.

The nodes Coordinate and Value Sets represent homogeneous sets, that is, all the set elements belong to the same type. These nodes are therefore specializations of set theory, as defined by node Set. By defining a small number of primitive algebraic operations on homogeneous sets, different image processing algorithms can be easily defined, as shown in Figure 7.6.

Fuzzy-Logic Reasoning Framework

We briefly summarize the nodes from Figure 7.4 and then look at the knowledge domain for rules in particular. The node Linguistic Variable represents a specialization of language theory. Its knowledge domain therefore includes the definition of a (small)

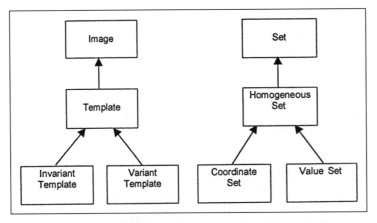

Figure 7.6 The main refinement hierarchies for image algebra.

language with its syntax and semantics. The node Fuzzy Inference Element relates to two theories: logic theory and fuzzy set theory. During a reasoning process, the nodes Fact, Rule, GMP, and Conclusion interact with each other. All these nodes adopt fuzzy sets as a common data structure to exchange information. The node Rule defines a rule. Further, it contains the definition of the implication operator and connective AND as a fuzzy relation and a fuzzy conjunction, respectively. The node Generalized Modus Ponens implements the *compositional rule of inference* as a *composition* between two relations. The node Conclusion implements the aggregation operation as an intersection or union between fuzzy sets. In the literature, several implementations of fuzzy implications, conjunctions, compositions, intersections, and unions have been proposed.

We only show the refinement hierarchy for rules in more detail. Node Rule defines the common characteristics for all the possible types of rules. After examining the related literature, we concluded that the types of rules can be grouped in three categories: FuzzyConjunction, FuzzyDisjunction, and FuzzyImplication implications. The

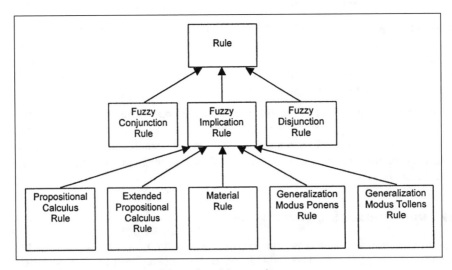

Figure 7.7 The refinement hierarchy of fuzzy rules.

latter can again be refined into five families: PropositionalCalculus, ExtendedPropositionalCalculus, Material, GeneralizationModusPonens, and GeneralizationModusTollens rules. The hierarchy in Figure 7.7 reflects this organization.

Overview of the Related Knowledge Domains

Table 7.1 shows the related knowledge domains of the pilot projects. It has been an extensive amount of work to find out the related knowledge domains from the literature. Nevertheless, for each domain, we could extract the information necessary to define a stable framework infrastructure.

7.2.3 Defining Constraints and Adaptability Space

In the final step of our approach, we identify which nodes in a knowledge domain can be included together into the top-level knowledge graph. A set of semantically

Table 7.1 Summary of the Related Knowledge Domains

PILOT PROJECT	NODE	RELATED KNOWLEDGE DOMAINS	REFERENCES
Transaction Framework	TransactionManager	Commit and abort protocols	[Elmagarmid 1992]
	PolicyManager	System performance control, reliability modeling techniques, and decision making	[Agrawal 1987]
	Scheduler	Concurrency control and deadlock detection techniques	[Bernstein 1987]
	RecoveryManager	Recovery techniques	[Bernstein 1987]
Image Processing Framework	Coordinate Set and Value Set	Set theory, mathematical domains, algebra	[Ritter 1987a,b]
	Template	Function theory, image representation techniques, algebra, image processing	
Fuzzy-Logic Reasoning Framework	Linguistic Variable	Language theory, fuzzy set theory	[Zadeh 1973, 1996]
	Fuzzy Inference Element	Fuzzy set theory, logic theory	[Dubois 1980; Klir 1988]

correct alternatives determines here the *adaptability space*. Each alternative defines which specializations from different domains enforce constraints on each other, when they are included within the same framework. For example, in building motorized vehicles, a specific chassis structure must be suitable to the power of the engine used. Additional user-defined constraints may be added, for example, to restrict the scope of the framework.

Transaction Framework

In the Transaction Framework, the interaction protocols between the nodes in Figure 7.2 determine compatibility constraints between the specializations of the corresponding knowledge domains. For example, the commit and abort protocols of TransactionManager must be understood by the corresponding DataManager. If the protocols of TransactionManager are changed, then the protocols of the DataManager must be changed accordingly. If the transaction behavior is dynamically changed, for instance by the operating system, then the nodes Scheduler and RecoveryManager must be adapted accordingly.

In addition to interaction compatibility requirements, there may be restrictions on the composability of components. For example, the nodes Scheduler and Recovery-Manager are in some cases dependent on each other [Weihl 1989]. Therefore, not every node of the knowledge domain Scheduler can be combined with all nodes of the knowledge domain RecoveryManager. Finally, the different serialization protocols adopted by scheduler nodes may be incompatible with each other [Guerraoui 1994].

Image Processing Framework

There are two important constraints for the elements of coordinate and value sets. First, these sets must be homogeneous. Therefore, a coordinate set must contain only, for instance, coordinates of a specific dimension type such as the frequency domain. Similarly, a value set must contain only values of a given type such as Boolean values for black-and-white images.

Second, there may be some ordering relations among the elements of a set. For example, in a two-dimensional spatial representation, the adjacent coordinates correspond to the image samples that are also physically adjacent to each other.

Further, additional constraints are imposed by the algebraic operations. An algebraic operation between two images, for instance, may be performed only if both images have exactly the same coordinate set.

Fuzzy-Logic Reasoning Framework

The nodes of the top-level fuzzy-logic reasoning graph, as defined by Figure 7.4, can be considered as specializations of some aspects of fuzzy-set theory. Theoretically, we can select each combination of specializations for implementing the reasoning process. For instance, in the node Rule, the connective AND, and the implication operator may be interpreted as a fuzzy conjunction, which uses the minimum operator, and the Mandami's implication operator [Mandami 1977], respectively. The node GMP may be implemented by the max-min compositional rule of inference defined by Zadeh [Zadeh 1973]. The node Conclusion may implement the connective ALSO as a fuzzy union, which uses the maximum. Not all the possible combinations, however, can produce logically meaningful conclusions [Marcelloni 1996; Turksen 1993]. This means that fuzzy set theory is constrained by the logic theory in the fuzzy logic domain.

Overview of the Constraints and the Adaptability Space

As illustrated by Table 7.2, all three frameworks require interaction and composability constraints to guarantee correct behavior. These constraints define the adaptability space of each framework.

7.3 Mapping Knowledge Graphs to Object-Oriented Frameworks

Mapping knowledge graphs to object-oriented frameworks does not happen without cost. *Section 7.3.1* discusses all the problems that we experienced during mapping the knowledge graphs into object-oriented concepts. *Section 7.3.2* discusses and compares the major characteristics of the implementation of three frameworks: transaction, image processing, and fuzzy-logic reasoning frameworks.

7.3.1 Experienced Problems

During the mapping of knowledge graphs to object-oriented frameworks, we experienced a number of problems because not all the elements of the knowledge graphs could be directly mapped into the object-oriented concepts. As a consequence, we were, for example, forced to represent some elements in the implementation of opera-

Table 7.2 Required Adaptability and Internode Constraints

PILOT PROJECT	REQUIRED ADAPTABILITY	INTERNODE CONSTRAINTS
Transaction framework	Scheduling and recovery concepts.	Intradata manager (scheduler and recovery) and interdata manager.
Image processing framework	Different coordinate and value types, a large possible number of templates in eight categories.	Sets must be homogeneous, ordering of elements in sets, type compatibility restrictions imposed by algebraic operations, eight categories of templates.
Fuzzy-logic reasoning framework	Several implementations of fuzzy reasoning, language used in the rules.	Rule, generalized modus ponens, and conclusion are constrained by each other by logical soundness, rules and facts constrained by the linguistic variable.

tions of objects instead of adopting explicit representations. This may reduce adaptability and reusability of frameworks. The following sections explain some significant problems that we experienced during the development of the frameworks.

Dynamically Changing Implementations

In many situations, the implementation of an object may not be fixed but can change at object initialization or execution time because of improvement and/or evolvement requirements. Improving can be necessary, for example, to optimize time and space performance of objects. Evolving is required for dealing with open-ended behavior of real-world systems.

In all the pilot projects, dynamically changing implementations are required. For example, in the transaction framework shown in Figure 7.2, the nodes Scheduler and RecoveryManager have to be adapted dynamically with respect to changing application and/or system conditions. Most transaction systems are distributed and long-lived. During the life cycle of a transaction system, new commit and abort protocols, serialization, and recovery algorithms may be introduced to cope with the changing demands of applications and system architectures.

In the image processing framework, dynamically changing implementations are required mainly for improving time and space performance of algorithms. For example, implementing a spatial image as a matrix may not be space efficient if the matrix is sparse. On the other hand, matrix representation can be time efficient for certain algorithms since each image element can be directly accessed.

In the fuzzy-logic reasoning framework, a particular implementation of the nodes from the knowledge graph affects the results of the reasoning. The type of application and the input values generally determine such a choice. Therefore, only at runtime is it possible to determine the implementation, which allows the inferring of the desired conclusions. For most fuzzy-logic reasoning systems, instantiation of implementations during object creation would be satisfactory. For reasoning systems with learning behavior, however, the implementation may change dynamically.

The Bridge or Strategy patterns [Gamma 1995] can be used to define objects with dynamically changing implementations. In these patterns, different implementations are represented as objects. Now let us assume that C_d is the class that requires a dynamic implementation. Therefore, C_d encapsulates its implementation object O_i. Here, O_i implements the methods m_1 to m_n. C_d declares these methods at its interface, but redirects the requests for these methods to O_i by invoking the corresponding methods on O_i. For example, C_d implements the method m_1 in the following way:

```
Cd::m1(arguments)
    return Oi.m1(arguments);
```

Provided that all the implementation objects implement the methods m_1 to m_n, one can change the implementations of class C_d by assigning a new implementation object O_{new} to O_i.

```
Oi := Onew ;
```

Here, the implementation of the class C_d is changed to O_{new}. Notice that the implementation object O_i behaves like a superclass because all its methods are visible at the interface of the class C_d. Changing the implementation is equivalent to changing the superclass of the object.

There are, however, a number of problems with this approach. First, class C_d must declare all the methods $m_1 \ldots m_n$ explicitly. If n is large, this can be a tedious and error-prone task, particularly if O_i inherits a lot of methods defined in its superclasses. Second, the Bridge and Strategy patterns cannot be used for evolving systems. The precise set of methods and their arguments has to be fixed when class C_d is defined since C_d has to declare all the dynamically changing methods explicitly. Third, although the implementation object behaves like a superclass, it cannot polymorphically refer to the encapsulating object (instance of C_d) through self-calls. This is similar to the self problem as defined in [Lieberman 1986].

An alternative to the pattern approach is the delegation mechanism [Lieberman 1986]. If an object cannot respond to a particular request of a client, then it delegates this request to one or more *designated* objects. One of the designated objects may execute the request on behalf of the object. Further, the designated object can refer to the object by calling on the pseudovariable self. Delegation is similar to inheritance; the designated object behaves like the superclass of the object. Delegation can express dynamic implementations if an object delegates the requests, which it cannot respond to, to its internal implementation objects. Delegation, therefore, eliminates the need of declaring the dynamically changing methods explicitly and can support the evolution of the implementation objects. Further, delegation solves the self-problem by providing the pseudovariable self. The conventional delegation mechanism, however, cannot enable or disable the delegation process, for example, based on a condition of the delegating object. This may be necessary, for example, if the implementation of an object has to be adapted based on a state of that object. In the pilot applications, we found a conditional delegation mechanism useful in adapting the behavior of an object in a well-defined manner. The State Pattern [Gamma 1995] does not provide an adequate solution for this problem because it has the similar limitations as the Bridge or Strategy pattern.

In our prototypes, we have implemented the conditional delegation pattern using the so-called Dispatch filter [Aksit 1992a]. Dispatch filter affects the incoming messages to the object that it is attached to and thereby can implement a conditional delegation mechanism.

Difficulties in Expressing Knowledge Specializations Using Class Inheritance

In our approach, the related knowledge domains are identified and represented by using generalization and specialization relations. We experienced that the generalization-specialization hierarchies as defined in the knowledge domains cannot always be directly mapped to the object-oriented inheritance hierarchies.[2]

Generally, object-oriented inheritance semantics are defined as inheritance of methods and instance variables from one or more superclasses by one or more subclasses. A

[2]In [Aksit 1992b], this problem was termed *arbitrary inheritance*.

subclass may add new methods and instance variables and override existing methods. These semantics cannot always represent complex generalization, specialization, and diversification relations among knowledge domains.

In the transaction framework, for instance, the PolicyManager chooses a particular policy by applying several different rules and constraints. In a generalization-specialization hierarchy of PolicyManagers, gradually more rules and constraints are added. Mapping this hierarchy to a class-inheritance structure is far from trivial.[3]

In the fuzzy-logic reasoning framework, the language-based specifications of linguistic variables require a grammar specification for parsing. In the generalization-specification hierarchy of the knowledge domain LinguisticVariable, the definitions of linguistic variables are refined and extended in specialization classes. This is represented as an extension of the grammar rules. It is not possible to map this grammar-based hierarchy directly onto a class-inheritance hierarchy.

Implementing a dedicated inheritance mechanism as a framework feature can solve the problem of representing knowledge specializations. In [Aksit 1990], for example, a grammar inheritance mechanism is presented as a structural organization of grammar rules by which a grammar inherits rules from supergrammars or may have its own rules inherited by subgrammars.

Architectural Constraints

As discussed in *Section 7.2,* a number of constraints must be enforced on the top-level knowledge graph. For example, nodes from different knowledge domains may not be composed arbitrarily. We consider the enforcement of such constraints as fully distinct and independent from the application behavior.

In the Transaction Framework, for instance, many different specializations are available for both the nodes Scheduler and RecoveryManager. One of the main reasons for separating the Scheduler and RecoveryManager is that these are largely orthogonal. This allows choosing independent specializations. However, in a number of cases, these domains are *not* orthogonal: Adopting a particular type of Scheduler excludes certain types of RecoveryManager. This implies that whenever the composition is changed, the consistency of the new composition must be checked. Although the verification may involve interactions with multiple objects, its specification must be modular so that it can be adapted and reused separately from the application classes.

The enforcement of constraints on composition is typically achieved through type-checking mechanisms: By specifying a particular type for each of the components, we can ensure that only specialization of that type will be used as components. However, when several components and complex rules determine the constraints on composition, a more powerful type-checking mechanism than subclassing and/or signatures is needed.

---

[3]Note that it *is* usually *possible* to implement an object-oriented application that provides correspondence to a domain knowledge hierarchy. However, this may require the creation of additional structures and interactions because a one-to-one mapping is impossible. Usually those additional structures have a negative impact on the adaptability and extensibility.

In general cases, the main difficulty is that constraint specifications are required to be modular, but at the same time the enforcement of constraints may be needed at many different locations and circumstances.

To solve these problems, in the pilot projects we have adopted metalevel objects that monitor and control the compositional structure of the architecture [Aksit 1993].

Other Difficulties

In this section, we briefly mention two other relevant issues that we had to deal with in realizing the frameworks. We refer to the first issue as the *multiple views* problem. In the transaction framework, for example, the application objects that are involved in a transaction should be accessed in two distinct ways with respect to the type of client. The application-specific functionality should be invoked by other application objects (*user view*), whereas the data management functionality, such as locking or recovery methods, should be used by the transaction framework (*system view*). The enforcement of such distinct views, which is important for preserving consistency, cannot be expressed in a convenient way by the conventional object model. The multiple views problem has been addressed in more detail in [Aksit 1992a, 1992b].

The second issue has been referred to as the *shared behavior affected by shared state* problem. This problem is encountered whenever a particular state shared by multiple objects affects the behavior shared by these objects. Sharing of behavior is usually achieved by a code reuse mechanism such as inheritance. Class inheritance cannot, however, adequately deal with a shared state that is encapsulated under the shared behavior. This is because each instance of a class in a class hierarchy has its own encapsulated state. Using an external server object for retrieving the shared state weakens encapsulation. In addition, the polymorphic variable self refers to the server object but not to the object that provides the shared behavior (the self problem [Lieberman 1986]).

In the transaction framework, for example, all TransactionManager objects share the behavior of the PolicyManager. The method chooseScheduler is implemented by PolicyManager and reused by TransactionManager. A PolicyManager object collects all kinds of relevant system parameters and stores them in its instance variables. Here, the shared method chooseScheduler is affected by the shared state system parameters. The delegation mechanism can be used to solve this issue, as described in more detail in [Aksit 1992b].

Table 7.3 provides an overview of the pilot projects, showing where certain difficulties were encountered, with a brief description of the area.

7.3.2 Implementation of the Frameworks

Table 7.4 summarizes the most important characteristics of the implementation of the three frameworks. Here, the column Language indicates the programming language used in the implementation. The column Inheritance and Number of Classes gives the number of classes defined within a specific inheritance hierarchy. The column Time Spent shows both the design effort and the implementation effort. The design effort indicates the total time spent in defining the knowledge graphs and designing the

Table 7.3 Pilot Projects versus Problems

PILOT PROJECT	DYNAMIC IMPLEMENTATIONS	INHERITANCE VERSUS KNOWLEDGE SPECIALIZATIONS	CONSTRAINTS	MULTIPLE VIEWS	SHARING BEHAVIOR AND STATE
Transaction framework	Scheduling, recovery	Policy manager	Data manager	User-system views	System parameters
Image processing framework	Alternative implementations	No	Value and coordinate sets	No	No
Fuzzy-logic reasoning	Fuzzy-logic implementation	Linguistic variables	Operator types	Linguistic variables	No

Table 7.4 Implementation Aspects of the Frameworks

PILOT PROJECT	LANGUAGE	INHERITANCE AND NUMBER OF CLASSES	TIME SPENT	REFERENCE
Transaction framework	Smalltalk	Scheduler hierarchy: 8 Deadlock hierarchy: 7 Recovery hierarchy: 9 Other: 20	Design = 6 months Implementation = 1 month	[Tekinerdogan 1994]
Image processing framework	C++	Single-inheritance hierarchy: 20	Design = 6 months Implementation = 2 months	[Vuijst 1994]
Fuzzy-logic reasoning framework	Smalltalk	Rule hierarchy: 8 Linguistic variable hierarchy: 4 Membership functions hierarchy: 8 Linguistic value hierarchy: 10 Other classes: 29	Design = 6 months Implementation = 1 month	[Marcelloni 1997]

framework. The implementation effort shows the time spent for coding and testing the framework. Finally, the column Reference shows where more details about the design and implementation of the frameworks can be found.

Transaction Framework

The transaction framework has been implemented using the Smalltalk language. To change the implementations of Scheduler and RecoveryManager, we implemented a delegation mechanism on top of the Smalltalk language. Each delegated message is *reified* and represented as a first-class object. This *message object* can be treated and manipulated like other objects. In the literature, this concept is known as *message reflection* [Ferber 1989]. By changing the attributes of a message object (in particular, the receiver of the message) and reactivating it again so that a real message invocation is created from the object, a delegation mechanism can be realized.

In the implementation of the Transaction Framework, constraints on object interactions and compositions are defined in separate constraint classes. To enforce a constraint, the messages that may violate the constraints are reified and redirected to the constraint objects. After verifying the validity of message invocations, the messages are reactivated again. If the constraints are violated, an exception is raised.

The prototype is currently running on a single machine. To implement the framework we mapped each node within a knowledge domain into a class. The implementation consists of 44 classes. Each knowledge domain is represented by inheritance hierarchies. The framework consists of three major inheritance hierarchies.

In the current prototype, class TransactionManager implements a single commit/abort protocol. Class PolicyManager adopts a simple policy management strategy. Our future work includes the implementation of different protocols and an expert-system–based PolicyManager. In addition, the transaction system will be ported to a distributed system platform so that it can be used within the implementation of the car dealer management system.

Image Processing Framework

The image processing framework has been implemented using the C++ language. Each node of a knowledge domain is mapped into a C++ class. Similar to the transaction framework, interaction and composability constraints are enforced by defining metalevel classes, and reifying and redirecting the messages that may violate the constraints to these classes.

Currently, classes Coordinate Set, Value Set, Image, and Template are fully implemented. As an example, we implemented three templates: a low-pass filter, a Fourier transform, and image histogram templates. We also defined a method to guide the software engineer in creating templates conveniently [Vuijst 1994].

Fuzzy-Logic Reasoning Framework

The fuzzy reasoning framework has been implemented in the Smalltalk language.

In the framework, class LinguisticVariable has two major methods for the fuzzification and defuzzification process. At the moment, we have implemented only the most common defuzzification strategies by using a Strategy Design Pattern. Class Linguistic-Variable is the root of the inheritance hierarchy in which each subclass implements a different linguistic variable.

Rules are organized in an inheritance hierarchy that was shown in Figure 7.7. Class Fact is composed of one or more instances of class Proposition. The classes Proposition and Rule inherit from class FuzzySet, which encapsulates class MembershipFunction. We have defined eight types of membership functions. The node GMP is implemented as a method of class Rule as it can be considered as an operation executed by the rule when a fact is provided to the rule. So far, we have only considered the generalized modus ponens as a fuzzy reasoning mechanism. We intend to investigate other possibilities such as the *syllogisms* proposed by Zadeh [Zadeh 1985]. Further, we will implement more defuzzification strategies and membership functions. Alternative implementations of the generalized modus ponens that can be used with particular implication operators and fuzzy sets are being analyzed (see [Lazzerini 1997]). Such implementations allow for considerable performance improvements.

Comparison of the Implementations

All three implementations have been derived directly from the respective knowledge domains. In addition to adopting standard object-oriented models and design patterns, delegation and message reflection techniques were implemented to increase software adaptability and reusability. In all the pilot projects, the designers were not experienced in the corresponding domains. Therefore, they spent a considerable amount of their time in understanding the related domain knowledge.

7.4 Evaluation of the Approach and Summary

The main claim of this chapter is that the framework refinement through iteration effort may be reduced considerably by modeling the related domain knowledge explicitly. In other words, blackbox frameworks can be derived directly by composing a number of specializations from the related knowledge domains. To verify this claim, we proposed a framework development approach based on modeling domain knowledge and carried out three pilot projects.

We extensively tested these frameworks from the perspective of robustness and adaptability. For example, we tested the transaction framework for dynamically changing serialization and recovery semantics. In addition, to test our implementations on unforeseen changes, we asked students to apply and extend the frameworks by using, if possible, techniques different from those already implemented. For example, in [Visser 1994], students successfully extended the knowledge domain Scheduler with a hierarchical locking scheme that was not considered initially in the transaction framework [Tekinerdogan 1994].

Our conclusion is that modeling domain knowledge explicitly may reduce the number of iterations and the amount of refinement time required for achieving stable, robust frameworks. However, we experienced some problems when we tried to map domain knowledge to the object-oriented model. Our findings are summarized by the following items:

Specific inheritance semantics are necessary for certain knowledge domains. The method and attribute inheritance mechanism as defined by most object-oriented models are not always suitable to model generalization/specialization relations of the knowledge domains. In this case, the extension of the object-oriented model with some dedicated *specification inheritance* mechanism is required to solve this in a modular and maintainable way. An example of such an approach is the grammar inheritance mechanism [Aksit 1990].

Conditional delegation is needed. As discussed in *Section 7.3.1*, we found the delegation mechanism quite necessary in defining adaptable software systems. For example, delegation can help in improving several design patterns such as Bridge because it supports evolution of interfaces. In addition, delegation techniques can help dealing with the "shared behavior affected by shared state" problem (see *"Other Difficulties"*). We do not, however, consider delegation as a replacement of inheritance or class concepts. Delegation, inheritance, and class concepts can coexist together. A major problem of the conventional delegation mechanism is that the delegation relations of an object cannot be controlled, for example, based on a state of the object. We, therefore, extended the conventional object model using Dispatch filters [Aksit 1992a].

Enforcing constraints is essential, but not fully supported yet. To instantiate and manage a dynamically evolving application while preserving its robustness, high-level mechanisms to enforce the semantic constraints of that application are required. Strongly typed languages aim at detecting semantic errors as early as possible. We experienced, however, that type-checking mechanisms of current strongly typed object-oriented languages are not sufficient; type-checking rules, in general, fail in detecting the complex interaction and composability constraints of objects. A possible approach to solving this problem is to introduce metalevel objects, which monitor and control the compositional structure of the application. To this aim, we used metaobjects called Abstract Communication Types [Aksit 1993]. However, in our current implementations, metaobjects to enforce constraints only offer runtime verification.

Further research is needed in object-composition techniques. In an architectural description, knowledge domains may model different aspects such as real time, synchronization, and coordinated behavior. It has been shown by a number of publications that, although separation of concerns is an essential concept for improving robustness, adaptability, and reusability, composing separated concerns such as real time and synchronization is far from trivial [Aksit 1996; Bergmans 1996; Kiczales 1997; Nierstrasz 1995]. Since frameworks can be considered as a composition of specializations from knowledge domains, we think that research activities for enhancing the composability capabilities of object-oriented models can be of great help; highly composable object models would improve the adaptability and reusability factors of frameworks [Bergmans 1997].

In our own work, to separate concerns from each other, we developed the composition-filters model [Aksit 1992a, 1993, 1994]. Composition filters extend the conventional object model in a modular and composable way. A modular extension means that the basic characteristics of the underlying language model remain the same. A composable extension means that various filters can be attached to the same object independently, because filters are semantically orthogonal to each other. For example, dynamic delegation and constraint enforcement can be added to an object by simply attaching a Dispatch and a Meta filter together.

Software artifacts must be recorded, related, and integrated. During the software development process, from domain analysis to coding, lots of information was generated and processed and different kinds of models were built. These *software artifacts* were recorded in various formats, from informal textual information to executable object-oriented programming concepts. We found it extremely difficult to record, trace, and relate all the artifacts, although we used object-oriented CASE environments, hypertext-like tools, and modern programming environments.

To overcome these problems, during the last several years we have been carrying out research activities in modeling software artifacts and design environments. Basic concepts underlying this research are to make each software artifact self-contained, with its own intelligence in the form of rules, and active in the sense that each artifact will initiate activities to keep the software system under development correct and up-to-date. Further, we apply fuzzy logic techniques to define rules, since this allows expressing design heuristics in a more accurate way than traditional two-valued logic [Aksit 1996].

Most of these problems can be attributed to the lack of expressiveness of the object-oriented model. By adopting the solution approaches as described for each of the preceding items, we were able to successfully realize the pilot frameworks. In conclusion, we are convinced that the approach described in this chapter allows the reduction of the traditional number of refinement steps by developing frameworks directly from domain knowledge.

7.5 References

[Agrawal 1987] Agrawal, R., M. Carey, and M. Livney. Concurrency Control Performance Modeling: Alternatives and Implications. *ACM Transactions on Database Systems,* 12(4), December 1987, pp. 609–654.

[Aksit 1990] Aksit, M., R. Mostert, and B. Haverkort. *Compiler Generation Based on Grammar Inheritance.,* Memoranda Informatica 90-07, University of Twente, The Netherlands, February 1990.

[Aksit 1992a] Aksit, M., L. Bergmans, and S. Vural. An object-oriented language-database integration model: The composition-filters approach. *ECOOP 1992 Conference Proceedings,* Utrecht, The Netherlands, June 1992, LNCS 615, pp. 372–395. Springer-Verlag, 1992.

[Aksit 1992b] Aksit, M., and L. Bergmans. Obstacles in object-oriented software development. *OOPSLA 1992 Conference Proceedings,* ACM SIGPLAN Notices 27(10), October 1992: 341–358.

[Aksit 1993] Aksit, M., K. Wakita, J. Bosch, L. Bergmans, and A. Yonezawa. Abstracting object interactions using composition-filters. In *Object-Based Distributed Program-*

ming, ECOOP 1993 Workshop, Kaiserslautern, Germany, July 1993, LNCS 791, pp. 152–184, R. Guerraoui et al., editors. Springer-Verlag, July 1993.

[Aksit 1994] Aksit, M., J. Bosch, W. van der Sterren, and L. Bergmans. Real-time specification inheritance anomalies and real-time filters. *ECOOP 1994 Conference Proceedings,* Bologna, Italy, July 1994, LNCS 821, pp. 386–407. Springer-Verlag, 1994.

[Aksit 1996] Aksit, M. Separation and composition of concerns. *ACM Computing Surveys.* 28(4), December 1996: 148–162.

[Bakker 1987] Bakker, R. Knowledge graphs: Representation and structuring of scientific knowledge. Ph.D. thesis, University of Twente, Department of Computer Science, The Netherlands, 1987.

[Bergmans 1996] Bergmans, L., and M. Aksit. Composing Real-Time and Synchronisation Constraints. *Journal of Parallel and Distributed Computing* 36:32–52, 1996.

[Bergmans 1997] Bergmans, L. An introduction to composability issues. *Proceedings of the ECOOP Workshop on Composability Issues.* In *Special Issues in Object-Oriented Programming,* pp. 75–80, M. Mühlhäuser, editor. 1997.

[Bernstein 1987] Bernstein, P.A., V. Hadzilacos, and N. Goodman. *Concurrency Control and Recovery in Database Systems.* Reading, MA: Addison-Wesley, 1987.

[Broekhuizen 1996] Broekhuizen, P. FLUENT: A fuzzy logic user environment for an OO fuzzy logic reasoning framework. Master's thesis, University of Twente, The Netherlands, 1996.

[Dubois 1980] Dubois, D., and H. Prade. *Fuzzy Sets and System.* Burlington, MA: Academic Press, 1980.

[Elmagarmid 1992] Elmagarmid, A., editor. *Database Transaction Models for Advanced Applications.* San Mateo, CA: Morgen Kaufmann, 1992.

[Fensel 1995] Fensel, D. *The Knowledge Acquisition and Representation Language, KARL.* Norwell, MA: Kluwer Academic Publishers, 1995.

[Ferber 1989] Ferber, J. Computational reflection in class-based object-oriented languages. *OOPSLA 1989 Conference Proceedings,* ACM SIGPLAN Notices 24(10), October 1989:317–326.

[Gamma 1995] Gamma, E., R. Helm, R. Johnson, and J. Vlissides. *Design Patterns: Elements of Reusable Object-Oriented Software.* Reading, MA: Addison-Wesley, 1995.

[Guerraoui 1994] Guerraoui, R. Atomic Object Composition. *ECOOP 1994 Conference Proceedings,* Bologna, Italy, July 1994, LNCS 821, pp. 118–138. Springer-Verlag, 1994.

[Huni 1995] Huni, H., R. Johnson, and R. Engel. A framework for network protocol software. *OOPSLA 1995 Conference Proceedings,* Austin, Texas, July 1995, pp. 358–369.

[Johnson 1988] Johnson, R., and B. Foote. Designing Reusable Classes. *Journal of Object-Oriented Programming,* June/July 1988: 23–35.

[Kiczales 1997] Kiczales, G., J. Lamping, A. Mendhekar, C. Maeda, C. Lopes, J-M. Loingtier, and J. Irwin. Aspect-oriented programming. *ECOOP 1997 Conference Proceedings,* Jyväskylä, Finland, June 1997, LNCS 1241, pp. 220–242. Springer-Verlag, 1997.

[Klir 1988] Klir, G.J. and T.A. Folger. *Fuzzy Sets, Uncertainty and Information.* Toronto: Prentice-Hall, Canada Inc., 1988.

[Lazzerini 1997] Lazzerini, B., and F. Marcelloni. Improving performance of MISO fuzzy systems. *Second International ICSC Symposium on Fuzzy Logic and Applications ISFL 1997,* Zurich, Switzerland, February 12–14, 1997, pp. 82–88.

[Levesque 1979] Levesque, H., and J. Mylopoulos. A procedural semantics for semantic networks. *Associative Networks,* Findler, editor. 1979, pp. 93–119.

[Lieberman 1986] Lieberman, H. Using prototypical objects to implement shared behavior. *OOPSLA 1986 Conference Proceedings,* ACM SIGPLAN Notices 21(11), November 1996:214–223.

[Mandami 1977] Mandami, E.H. Application of fuzzy logic to approximate reasoning using linguistic synthesis. *IEEE Transactions on Computer.* C-26(12):1182–1191.

[Marcelloni 1996] Marcelloni, F. On inferring reasonable conclusions for fuzzy reasoning with multiple rules. *Proceedings of IPMU 1996,* Granada, Spain, July 1–5, 1996.

[Marcelloni 1997] Marcelloni, F. and M. Aksit. *The Design and Application of an Object-Oriented Fuzzy-Logic Reasoning Framework.* Draft paper, University of Twente, 1997.

[Minsky 1975] Minsky, M. A framework for representing knowledge. In *The Psychology of Computer Vision,* pp. 211–277, P. Winston, editor. New York: McGraw-Hill, 1975.

[Nierstrasz 1995] Nierstrasz, O., and D. Tsichritzis, editors. *Object-Oriented Software Composition.* Upper Saddle River, NJ: Prentice Hall, 1995.

[Ritter 1987a] Ritter, G.X. and P.D. Gader. Image Algebra Techniques for Parallel Image Processing. *Journal of Parallel and Distributed Computing,* Vol 4, 1987, 7–44.

[Ritter 1987b] Ritter, G.X., M.A. Shrader-Frechette, and J.N. Wilson. Image Algebra: A Rigorous and Translucent Way of Expressing All Image Processing Operations. *Proceedings of the 1987 SPIE Tech. Symp.,* Orlando, FL, May 1987.

[Ritter 1990] Ritter, G.X., J.N. Wilson, and J.L. Davidson. Image Algebra: An Overview. *Computer Vision, Graphics and Image Processing* 49(3):297–331.

[Roberts 1996] Roberts, D., and R. Johnson. *Evolving Frameworks: A Pattern Language for Developing Object-Oriented Framework.* At st-www.cs.uiuc/edu/users/droberts/ evolve.html, 1996.

[Taligent 1996] Taligent white papers. At www.taligent.com, 1996.

[Tekinerdogan 1994] Tekinerdogan, B. The design of an object-oriented framework for atomic transactions. Master's thesis, University of Twente, Department of Computer Science, The Netherlands, 1994.

[Turksen 1993] Turksen, I.B., and Y. Tian. Combination of rules or their consequences in fuzzy expert systems. *Fuzzy Sets and Systems* 58:3–40.

[Visser 1994] Visser, B.S., M. J. Evers, and C.W. van den Ende. A multi user software development environment framework in Smalltalk. Design project, University of Twente, The Netherlands, November 1994.

[Vuijst 1994] Vuijst, C. Design of an object-oriented framework for image algebra. Master's thesis, University of Twente, Department of Computer Science, The Netherlands, 1994.

[Wegner 1984] Wegner, P. Capital-intensive technology and reusability. *IEEE Software,* July 1984:7–45.

[Weihl 1989] Weihl, W.E. Local Atomicity Properties: Modular Concurrency Control for Abstract Data Types. *ACM Transactions on Programming Languages and Systems* 11(2), April 1989, 249–282.

[Wielinga 1992] Wielinga, B.J., A.Th. Schreiber, and J.A. Breuker. KADS: A modelling approach to knowledge engineering. *Knowledge Acquisition* 4(1), March 1992:5–53.

[Zadeh 1973] Zadeh, L.A. Outline of a new approach to the analysis of complex systems and decision processes. *IEEE Transactions on Systems, Man, and Cybernetics* SMC-3(1), January 1973:28–44.

[Zadeh 1985] Zadeh, L.A. Syllogistic reasoning in fuzzy logic and its application to usuality and reasoning with dispositions. *IEEE Transactions on Systems, Man, and Cybernetics* SMC-15(6), November/December 1985:754–763.

[Zwet 1994] van der Zwet, P.M.J. Work breakdown structure knowledge guided image processing. Internal memo, LKEB, University Hospital, Leiden, 1994.

7.6 Review Questions

1. Define the modeling domain knowledge process.

2. What is a knowledge graph? Provide an example.

3. Describe the knowledge graphs of the following frameworks: transaction framework, Image Processing Framework, and Fuzzy-Logic Reasoning Framework.

4. Define with examples: domain, frames, semantic networks, domain knowledge, inference knowledge, and task knowledge, adaptability space, self-call, self-problem, conditional delegation mechanism, architectural constraints, and multiple views.

5. What are object decomposition techniques? Provide examples.

6. Discuss the following statements:

   ▪ Specific inheritance semantics are necessary for certain knowledge domains.

   ▪ Enforcing constraints is essential, but not fully supported yet.

   ▪ Software artifacts must be recorded, related, and integrated.

7.7 Problem Set

Sorting is the process of arranging items "in order." The arrangement of items is undertaken so that computations may be more effective and efficient. Different sorting algorithms exist in the literature. First let us consider a well-known sorting algorithm, called Bubble-Sort, which is given in the following Bubble-Sort example:

```
sort
    temp: Element; i,j,length : Integer;
    length:=self.size;                    "Range"
    for i:=1 to length-1 do
      for j:=length downto i+1 do
          if self.compare(          "Compare"
              col at(i), col at(j))          "Indexing"
          then begin
              temp:= col at(i);
              col at: i put: j.          "Update"
              col at: j put: i
                        end;
        end;
      end;
  end;
```

This sorting algorithm swaps two elements if they are not in order in the collection. First the size of the collection is determined after which each element from the beginning is compared with one of the remaining elements in the collection. The second while loop starts the iteration from the last element in order to restrict the number of needed swaps, in case of forward iteration.

The sorting algorithm SwapSort uses the forward iteration mechanism, but is further the same as BubbleSort.

Another sorting algorithm is Select-Sort, which selects each time the smallest element in the collection and swaps this with the (selected) element in front of the collection. The sorting algorithm CardSort looks like SelectSort, but CardSort does not swap the elements, but replaces the order of each element each time. The Select-Sort algorithm is faster than Bubble-Sort.

7.7.1 The Approach

The approach for deriving frameworks from knowledge domain is summarized in Figure 7.8. On the left side of the figure the basic steps are shown. On the right side are the deliverables of each step.

The first step is the solution domain analysis in which the related theory in the literature is searched and expressed in reusable knowledge model, called knowledge graphs. This top-level knowledge-graph actually represents the global architecture of the final framework. The knowledge graph consists of nodes which represent specific concepts.

The second step includes the refinement of these nodes in the knowledge graph and produces a taxonomy for the corresponding knowledge domain model node only. The top-level architecture will consist of specialization of these knowledge domains.

The third step is the analysis on compatibility between the different specializations of knowledge domain models. This will visualize the total adaptability space of the

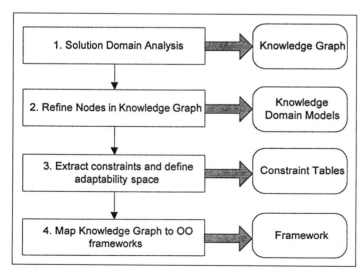

Figure 7.8 The approach for deriving frameworks from domain knowledge.

framework. This is expressed in compatibility tables that show the compatibility relations between different nodes.

The last step is the mapping of the knowledge graph and the sub-knowledge graphs to the object-oriented framework.

The following assignments are organized around these steps.

1. Define Top-Level Knowledge Graph

In this assignment you need to define the knowledge graph for sorting architecture. For this you need to do some literature study. Use the following domain analysis steps:

1. Identify knowledge sources that describe sorting algorithms in more details. These can be books, journal publications, presentations, etc. Ensure that the knowledge sources are reliable and reflect the consensus of the basic scientists on that topic. Write down your identified knowledge sources in a table.

2. Extract the essential knowledge about sorting from these sorting domain knowledge sources. Try to understand the essence of sorting using this knowledge.

3. Abstract the collected knowledge and try to find commonalties and differences of different sorting algorithms by comparing them. Look for concepts that appear in all sorting algorithms. Look for concepts that are variable.

4. Using the classification and abstracted knowledge define a common canonical knowledge model expressed as a top-level knowledge graph of the sorting architecture.

5. Validate your top-level knowledge graph by checking if different sorting algorithms can be explained using your model.

2. Refining Knowledge Graph

You will now focus on each node apart in the top-level knowledge graph. For this you need practically to follow the same domain analysis steps as for the top-level knowledge graph.

1. Extract the essential knowledge about a single node in the top-level knowledge graph.

2. Abstract the collected knowledge and try to define classifications of the specializations of the node. You may for example have a node called Comparison, and different specializations of this node. Use OO standard analysis techniques for identifying generalization-specialization relations.

3. Describe your classifications as sub-knowledge graphs in which the nodes represent specializations of the node in the top-level knowledge graph, and the arrows represent generalization/specialization relations.

3. Defining Adaptability Space

Now that you have completed the knowledge modeling phase, you need to analyze the compatibility relations between the different nodes in the top-level knowledge graph. This may again be found in the literature.

1. Now look at your knowledge sources again and try to extract the compatibility constraints between the different nodes. Specify the compatibility relations in tables with the following table format.

	NODE B	NODE 1	NODE 2	...	NODE N
NODE A					
NODE 1					
NODE 2					
...					
NODE M					

Hereby the table represents the relations for two different nodes called node A and node B in the top-level knowledge graph. The top row represents the different specialization of Node B, whereas the left column represents the specialization of node A. A cross (+) in the field of the table represents that the two nodes may not be included together in the top-level knowledge graph.

You may need more tables to express the constraints between the different nodes.

4. Map Knowledge Graph to OO Frameworks

The last step includes the mapping of the knowledge graph to the object-oriented frameworks. This will be done by considering the quality criteria adaptability, performance, and reusability. The knowledge graph will first be mapped to object-oriented design constructs, and then to object-oriented programming constructs.

Mapping to Design

1. In OOD, concepts are mapped to classes. The nodes in the top-level knowledge graph represent well-defined concepts. For each node in the top-level knowledge graph define a class.

2. Define class hierarchies for each node of the top-level knowledge graph.

3. Map the different concept relations in the top-level knowledge graph to associations relations in OOD.

4. Complete your object model by searching for fundamental attributes of the classes.

5. How do you realize run-time adaptability in OOD?

6. How do you realize compile-time adaptability in OOD?

7. By using the top-level knowledge graph of the sorting algorithm, draw four class diagrams, with the following adaptability requirements:

   ■ The first diagram should model run-time adaptability for all nodes.

   ■ The second diagram should model run-time adaptability for some nodes and compile-time adaptability for other nodes.

- The third diagram should model compile-time adaptability for all the nodes.
- The fourth diagram should provide no adaptability.

8. Explain why the most adaptable solution has a trade-off with the reusability requirement.

9. How do these four solutions affect the performance?

Mapping to Implementation

1. How do you implement run-time adaptability in OOP?

2. How do you implement compile-time adaptability in OOP?

3. Implement the design of the framework in any object-oriented programming language. Make sure that you implement also the generalization-specialization relations.

4. Try to implement different sorting applications by customizing your framework.

CHAPTER 8

Harvesting Design

Framework design begins with domain analysis—the problem domain is analyzed to create a new design and the solution domain is analyzed to understand how the problem has already been solved. Solution domain analysis is advantageous for two reasons:

- Solutions that have been deployed in production environments are likely to have addressed a broad range of design issues.

- A deployed solution is a good source for design and code reuse.

On the other hand, solutions may be too implementation-specific so as to inhibit code or design reuse. The objective of harvesting from existing solutions is to extract as much design and code as possible that can be refined for reuse.

This chapter describes the harvesting process and how it was used to design and develop an application framework. The development of the framework originates with an effort to harvest components from a patient record system. The first harvesting candidate selected for implementation was an infrastructure framework that provides task management services for an application. The framework addresses a common problem in application development—how to organize, present, and manage a single, controlling application that has multiple subapplications, or tasks. Because this problem had been solved on several other projects, the harvesting effort benefited greatly from the availability of multiple solutions. Although the solutions were implemented for different domains (medicine, insurance, network management), each required similar infrastructure code to manage the various application tasks.

The steps of the harvesting process—candidate identification, solution domain analysis, and framework implementation—are the topics of this chapter.

8.1 The Harvesting Process

The first step of the harvesting process is identification of appropriate candidates. The primary source for the harvesting effort was a recently completed patient record system. This system was especially valuable because it was developed by a small team that had worked together on several other object-oriented applications. The infrastructure code in the patient record system represented a refined solution to the task management problem because it evolved through the development of several applications.

Since the objective was to develop a framework that was reusable across industry domains, generalization of function was essential. Four candidate projects were selected, two in the insurance domain and two in the network management domain. After the candidates were identified, we began the analysis phase, where each source was evaluated for:

- Any functionality related to task management
- Abstractions employed to solve task management functions
- Similarities in the abstractions

The generalizations derived from this analysis established the foundation for the design phase during which the object model and architecture were defined. The framework design includes both *blackbox* components and *whitebox* interfaces. The former are fully functional components with implementations that do not have to be understood by the developer. The latter interfaces are defined to permit flexibility and function extensibility by the developer.

The final phase of harvesting is implementation. The effort relied primarily on design harvesting with a refined implementation using Smalltalk. The framework consists of collaborating Smalltalk classes that provide the task management services. In addition, the framework provides a generic application shell that can be customized using visual programming. The following sections of this paper discuss the development phases in more detail.

8.2 Identifying Candidates

In addition to the patient record system, four Smalltalk projects were selected as candidates for solution domain analysis. Three of the projects were developed through customer engagements and two were produced as IBM products:

- Proof-of-concept patient record system that supports the creation and browsing of patient record information at a regional medical center
- Customer service system for an automobile insurance company that provides policy and billing support

- Claims handling system for an insurance company
- Product for modeling the configuration and performance of network hardware and software
- Product for managing inventory and assets in a communications network

Although each system supports different domains, they are similar in their underlying application architecture. Each defines a single controlling function that manages the organization and presentation of the various subapplications, or tasks. The graphical counterpart of the controller function is a main window or shell, and the tasks are typically represented by secondary windows, or *views*. For example, in the patient record system there are tasks and corresponding views, to search, create, browse, and summarize a patient record.

8.3 Solution Domain Analysis

The objective of the analysis phase is to identify the task management–related functions required by each solution domain and the abstractions employed to provide them. It is important to understand both the similarities and the variations across domains. The similarities provide the basis for generalization and the variations are valuable for fine-tuning the design.

Six abstractions that were common to each project are summarized in the following sections.

8.3.1 Application Shell

This abstraction represents the main window, or *shell*, that is displayed when an application is started. Task views are typically displayed within the physical boundaries of the shell.

8.3.2 Application Descriptor

This abstraction defines the nonvisual characteristics of the application. These include static attributes such as defined tasks and start-up tasks, as well as dynamic attributes such as currently active tasks and the current user.

8.3.3 Task Manager

This abstraction defines the controller function for the application. It provides the services for activating and deactivating tasks, navigating among currently active tasks, and managing interactions among active tasks.

8.3.4 Task Descriptor

This abstraction defines the graphical characteristics, or presentation view, of a task. Additionally, it may include information about the domain objects associated with its initialization and preconditions for its activation.

8.3.5 Task List

This abstraction is a collection object that contains the currently active tasks, usually defined in activation order.

8.3.6 User

This abstraction is not defined by each system and is found only where a logon function is required. The user object defines a userid and password for verification and, optionally, customization information for specifying task presentation preferences.

These abstractions are good candidates for generalization because they suggest common functions that should be available in a general-purpose task management framework. At the same time, the variations in their implementations provide insight into how some elements of the design should be defined to permit flexibility and extensibility by the application developer. For example:

>**The systems vary in the *number of tasks* that can be active concurrently.** The network performance modeling product probably has the simplest application architecture because it allows only one task to be active at a time. The network planning product, at the other extreme, allows users to open as many task windows as the system environment will permit. The framework must be able to accommodate either the single or multitask approach.

>**The systems vary in the *relationship between tasks and domain objects*.** Generally, a given task is associated with a specific domain object—the task may manipulate multiple domain objects, but there is usually a primary one that populates its view, such as a hospital patient or insurance policy. In the patient record system, only one patient can be viewed at a time; there may be multiple tasks with different views of the same patient, but only one patient is active at a time. In contrast, the insurance customer service system permits multiple tasks on multiple policies simultaneously. Again, the framework must support either approach.

>*Navigation* **refers to the selection of an active task for viewing.** Both the patient record system and the network performance modeling product support guided navigation in a hierarchical manner. The other systems permit the user to navigate among task views in an arbitrary manner. The framework supports both sequential navigation through the active task list and arbitrary selection from a task list window.

>**Most of the systems supported *multiple views* of the same object, which means changes must be propagated if a view changes an object.** The framework uses a dependency manager abstraction to handle consistency across views and the dispositioning of views as a single *unit of work*. For example, the patient record system supports several views to collect patient demographic information. When the user selects *ok* to complete a record update, the resulting behavior is to save all of the changes in the views and then close them as a single unit of work. Table 8.1 summarizes the variations across the candidate domains.

These variations may appear subtle, but design decisions that strongly favor one approach over another may greatly restrict the general usefulness of the framework. It is in these areas that the design must balance flexibility with built-in function.

Table 8.1 Variations across Solution Domains

	PATIENT RECORD	INSURANCE	NETWORK PLANNING	NETWORK PERFORMANCE MODELING	FRAME-WORK
Number of Active Tasks	Multiple	Multiple	Multiple	Single	Multiple
Number of Domain Objects	Single patient	Limited policies	Multiple networks	Single model	Multiple
Navigation	Guided	Arbitrary	Arbitrary	Guided	Arbitrary
Multiview Update	Yes	Yes	Yes	No	Yes
Units of Work	Yes	Yes	No	No	Yes

The generalizations that were derived from the abstractions during the analysis phase were:

Task initialization and activation. Assuming that a task roughly equates to a window, a task can be initialized with default settings and/or a domain object before activation.

Task disposition. A task can be deactivated with or without accepting changes to its state, or it can accept changes to its state without deactivation.

Task interaction. Change notification should occur when a task modifies a domain object shared by multiple tasks. Tasks in a unit of work should be dispositioned at the same time.

Task navigation. Multiple tasks can be active simultaneously and the user should be able to navigate among them in a simple and arbitrary manner.

These generalizations provide the foundation of the framework design and define the scope of services made available to a business application. The next section discusses the refinement of these generalizations into an object model and architecture.

8.4 Framework Implementation

Designing a framework that is both reusable and useful is a balancing act. A design that attempts to maximize reuse by generalizing function for any application architecture may provide little substantive function. Conversely, a framework that provides rich and robust services may prove to be too restrictive or complex for broad reuse. In order to maintain balance in the task management framework design, several guidelines were used:

- Abstractions that are very similar across the solution domains are candidates for blackbox components.

- Abstractions that are similar in purpose but variant in implementation are candidates for whitebox interfaces to permit customization and extensibility.

- Minimal assumptions are made about the graphical representation or internal logic of a task.

- The objective is a simple public interface so that developers are more likely to use the framework as is.

The analysis phase identified the major abstractions of the framework. The methodology of the design phase was to evaluate the scenarios found in each solution domain as a means to refine and enhance the abstractions. A summary of the most significant scenarios associated with each generalization follows:

TASK INITIALIZATION AND ACTIVATION

- Create the view for a task.

- Initialize the view with default settings.

- Initialize the view from a domain object.

- Open the view for display.

- Show the view for an active task that is not currently displayed.

- Close the view and destroy (nondomain) resources associated with the task.

TASK DISPOSITION

- Process an OK request that saves domain object changes and closes the task's view.

- Process a cancel request that closes the task's view without saving domain object changes.

- Process an apply request that saves domain object changes without closing the task's view.

TASK INTERACTION

- Register a task for notification.

- Notify all tasks that reference a domain object when that object is changed.

- Notify all tasks that are registered as observers of some subject.

- Register a task as a member of a unit of work.

- Propagate disposition changes to all tasks in a unit of work.

TASK NAVIGATION

- Navigate backward in the active task list by hiding the currently displayed task view, and displaying the view for the task that was activated prior to the current task.

- Navigate forward in the active task list by hiding the currently displayed task view and displaying the view for the task that was activated after the current task.

- Display the view for the first task in the active task list, the *home* task.

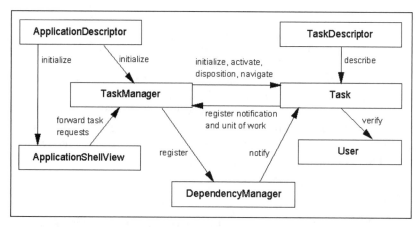

Figure 8.1   Object model overview.

Using the abstractions found during analysis and the scenarios identified during design, an object model was developed. Figure 8.1 illustrates the classes and primary collaborations in the model.

The following sections describe each class in more detail, including the purpose of each class, its major responsibilities and collaborations, and any issues that had to be resolved during the design.

8.4.1 ApplicationDescriptor

This class defines the general characteristics of an application and provides framework initialization for an application. In terms of the Model-View-Controller (MVC) model proposed by Reenskaug [Reenskaug 1995], this class provides the model and controller functions at the application level. The view for the application is defined separately in the ApplicationShellView class. An instance of the ApplicationDescriptor is a blackbox component with a public interface for defining application parameters.

The responsibilities of the class are to initialize the framework, open/close the shell, and provide housekeeping functions when the shell is closed.

The ApplicationDescriptor collaborates with the ApplicationShellView to open and close the shell. The class also collaborates with the TaskManager to run any start-up options specified in the application parameters.

8.4.2 ApplicationShellView

This class is a visual part that is the generic shell, or main window, for an application. It defines the basic features of a shell: title bar, menu bar, tool (or task) bar, status bar, and a large area for displaying views. The shell is an example of a class that exhibits both blackbox and whitebox characteristics. The navigation and disposition buttons, for instance, are available to each task as a component. Activation buttons and the menu bar are examples of interfaces that must be modified or extended by the developer.

An important objective of the shell design was to impose as few restrictions as possible on its contents and layout since every business application has different requirements. The only required subpart is the view area—its geometry may be changed, but it cannot be deleted from the shell. Although this one requirement may prove too restrictive for some applications, we believe that it is compatible with a large class of business applications that are sometimes called *form-based.*

The responsibilities of the shell are to create itself, to respond to user requests, and to size task views appropriately in the designated view area.

The shell collaborates with the ApplicationDescriptor to open/close itself, define the application parameters, and to initialize the framework. The shell also collaborates with the TaskManager by forwarding to it any user requests for activation, navigation, and disposition of tasks.

8.4.3 TaskManager

The TaskManager class is the focal point of the framework because it provides most of the services that are available to the tasks in an application. This class is an example of a Mediator design pattern [Gamma 1995] because it encapsulates knowledge about how tasks interact with each other and with other framework components. In terms of the MVC model, the TaskManager is the controller—it receives and dispatches all of the task-specific requests and maintains the separation between application- and task-level responsibilities. The TaskManager is a blackbox component with a public interface for its services.

The responsibilities of this class are to create and initialize task views; open/close and show/hide views; process disposition and navigation requests; register tasks for notification and unit-of-work membership; and propagate dispositions to tasks in a unit of work.

The TaskManager collaborates with the ApplicationDescriptor to run start-up options specified in the application parameters. It collaborates with the TaskDescriptor and Task classes to create, initialize, open/close, and show/hide views; it also collaborates with the DependencyManager for task registration.

8.4.4 TaskDescriptor

The TaskDescriptor class defines nonvisual information about a task. There is one TaskDescriptor for each Task, where a Task instance corresponds to a developer-defined visual part. The primary responsibility of this class is to maintain a separation between the visual part for a task and any nonvisual information that is needed to manage it. For instance, this class associates a domain object with a task that can be used for initialization. This class collaborates with the TaskManager and has no public interface.

8.4.5 Task

Task is an abstract class that defines the behavior needed by any visual part that uses the framework. This class is an example of a whitebox interface because the developer must extend (or subclass) this class to define a task. The framework assumes that the developer uses visual programming to build parts that define the user interface and business logic for the task. By subclassing the Task class, the task inherits behavior needed to obtain TaskManager services. The subclassed instance may extend the initialization and disposition services.

The responsibility of this class is to collaborate with the TaskManager by forwarding requests for services from subclassed instances.

8.4.6 DependencyManager

This class defines two types of dependencies among tasks. A notification dependency exists when tasks that are viewing the same domain object want to be notified of any changes to the object. A unit-of-work dependency exists when two or more tasks are to be treated as a single entity when a disposition request is sent. This class is an example of an Observer design pattern [Gamma 1995] because it manages the one-to-many relationships between tasks that are required for notification and units of work. There is no public interface for this class.

The responsibilities of this class are to record the dependency relationships and propagate notifications.

The DependencyManager collaborates with the TaskManager to process the notification and unit-of-work registrations. It also collaborates with the Task class to send notifications.

8.4.7 User

The User class provides a proxy interface for verification of userids and passwords when an application requires logon services. The class assumes that user information is obtained from an existing source that is external to the application. The class serves as a placeholder for those services that can access user information. This class collaborates with a sample logon task that is provided with the framework.

The classes defined in the final object model differ somewhat from the abstractions identified during the analysis phase. The first deviation is the refactoring of the TaskDescriptor abstraction into nonvisual and visual classes—TaskDescriptor and Task. As previously noted, the rationale for this decision was to maintain a separation between the nonvisual information needed to manage a task and the visual part defined by the developer. This approach supports the design guideline for minimizing assumptions about the graphical representation or internal logic of a task.

A second deviation is the omission of a TaskList abstraction in the object model. In the patient record system, some of the descriptive information about a task is defined in its TaskList abstraction, the StackEntry class. In the framework, all of the descriptive information has been consolidated in the TaskDescriptor class; hence, there is no need for a separate class to define the TaskList. It is modeled as an OrderedCollection instance variable in the TaskManager class.

The third deviation is the inclusion of a DependencyManager class in the object model. The capabilities of this class are present in the solution domains, but not necessarily as a separately identifiable abstraction. For instance, notification dependencies can be implemented using the built-in dependency mechanism in the Smalltalk Object class. The unit-of-work relationships among tasks are often implemented by the individual tasks themselves. There were several reasons for creating the DependencyManager class:

- The notification and unit-of-work capabilities both manage one-to-many dependency relationships among tasks; therefore, this was a good candidate for abstraction.

- The Smalltalk dependency mechanism is limited to one type of dependency per object. The DependencyManager provides a more general-purpose solution that allows any number of dependency types to be associated with an object.

- By using the DependencyManager to define units of work, a task no longer has to maintain explicit knowledge about those tasks it interacts with.

In the next section, we provide an overview of the implementation and describe how a developer might use the framework services.

8.4.8 Implementation

A more detailed view of the framework's object model is illustrated in Figure 8.2. Each box represents a class with a list of its instance variables and the significant public protocol. Classes that are connected by an arrow indicate an inheritance relationship.

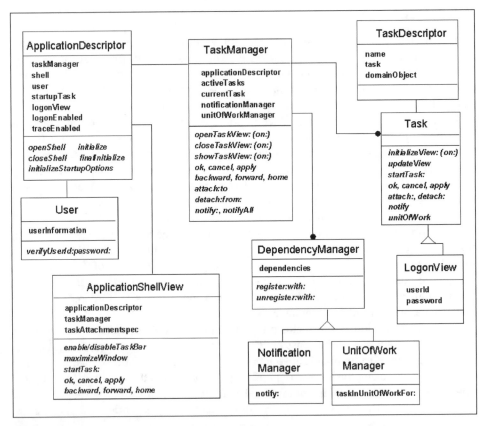

Figure 8.2   Detailed view of the object model.

8.5 Application Development with the Framework

In a visual programming environment, the developer produces visual parts that represent application tasks. These parts must be defined as subclasses of the Task class to inherit the framework services. Tasks are activated by sending a startTask message to the TaskManager with the class name of the visual part as the argument. Primary tasks that are frequently performed can be associated with the shell by using the Composition Editor to make a connection between the activating widget and a script that sends the startTask message to the TaskManager. Tasks can also be activated from other tasks by sending the same message. The framework does not impose any restrictions on the number or ordering of activated tasks; however, only one task window is visible at a time.

Disposition messages such as OK, Cancel, and Apply, can be activated from predefined buttons on the shell tool bar. If one of these is selected by the user, the message is sent to the TaskManager, which forwards it to the currently visible task for processing. For example, if the user selects OK, the current task processes the message first—presumably, to perform functions such as data validation and applying domain object updates to the database or other persistence mechanism. On completion, the TaskManager regains control and closes the view for the task.

Task dependencies are determined by the developer and are defined by the protocol inherited from the Task class. Notification and unit-of-work dependencies are defined by attach and unitOfWork messages, respectively. If a task changes an object that has multiple viewers, it sends a notify message to the TaskManager, which, in turn, forwards the request to the NotificationManager (subclass of the DependencyManager). When a disposition message (ok, cancel, apply) is sent, the TaskManager collaborates with the UnitOfWorkManager (subclass of DependencyManager) to request a list of all tasks in the current unit of work. The disposition message is then sent to all tasks in the list.

8.6 Summary

The harvesting and design effort described in this paper produced an initial version of the task management framework. Because the design was derived from existing solutions, it is anticipated that the framework will be more readily usable than if it was developed from scratch. However, truly viable frameworks are never actually completed—they evolve. The next step is to ensure that the framework is incorporated into customer engagements and products, with the expectation that the next version will provide more, and better, services.

8.7 References

[Gamma 1995] Gamma, E., R. Helm, R. Johnson, and J. Vlissides. *Design Patterns: Elements of Reusable Object-Oriented Software.* Reading, MA: Addison-Wesley, 1995.

[Reenskaug 1995] Reenskaug, T. *Working with Objects*. Upper Saddle River, NJ: Manning/Prentice Hall, 1995.

8.8 Review Questions

1. Define the steps for harvesting design and code from existing solutions.

2. What is solution domain analysis and why is it useful for framework design?

3. Abstractions that are common across multiple solution domains are good candidates for generalization. Why?

4. Abstractions that are similar in purpose but have varying implementations are good candidates for whitebox interfaces. Why?

5. What kind of relationships does the DependencyManager class support?

8.9 Problem Set

1. The User class in the task management framework provides an interface for services that access user information. If a user management function was to be included with the framework, what functions should be supported? Would these functions be implemented as blackbox or whitebox components, and why?

2. A trace function that records task behavior would be a useful utility to add to the framework. Describe how you would extend the framework object model to include this function.

3. Discuss the advantages and disadvantages of separating visual and nonvisual information about an application task.

4. Describe other task management functions that could be added to the framework by subclassing the DependencyManager class.

SIDEBAR 3
FRAMEWORKS AND DOMAIN MODELS:
TWO SIDES OF THE SAME COIN

Frameworks and domain models are close relatives [Arango 1993]. The behavior and usability of frameworks depend on their ability to fit different requirements. Frameworks originate from the analysis of domains and are designed to support the development of new applications. A domain model is a general representation for many applications in a problem domain; these applications may be only potential and still to be developed.

The core of frameworks and of domain models is (1) to describe commonality and variability and (2) to support the management of the different parts in similar products coming from the same domain.

Framework development and domain analysis and engineering (DA&E) have the same economic justification: They exploit the economies of scope arising from the reuse of the assets in the domain.

In the following, we outline how DA&E can positively support the production of frameworks. We focus on Sherlock, an object-oriented DA&E technique targeted to the development of frameworks.

SB3.1 A Two Step Approach to Requirements

Sherlock manages variable parts of requirements for products in two steps.

The first step is the analysis of the applications the framework should support. These applications are analyzed from the user's perspective with use cases [Jacobson 1997]. The description of each application is a complete use case.

The second step analyzes the applications transversally. It focuses on their mutual relations in terms of commonality and variability. A *common use case* describes commonality. A common use case is a *very general* use case. Variability is expressed through variation points. A *variation point* is a feature that (1) conceptually belongs to all the applications in the domain and (2) can be implemented in different ways in different applications. A *variant* is a way to implement a variation point [Jacobson 1997].

SB3.2 A Brief Example of Variation Points and Variants

Consider a sample domain comprising real-time signal processing applications. Assume that there are three applications at hand. Step 1 of Sherlock requires the development of a use case for each application:

An embedded controller for control systems. It processes signals in a control loop.

A multichannel voice processor for echo cancellation. The application complies with the standards for digital telephony.

Continues

A software module for audio reverberation on personal computers. It requires two high-fidelity processing channels and complies with the techniques that allow integration in a modular environment, e.g., libraries and plug-ins.

Step 2 requires extracting a domain use case with commonality and variability. Using the available information and other implicit reasonable hypotheses, we write a common use case as follows: "The application runs on a hardware/software platform, performing real-time processing of data. Data are organized in channels and run at a given sampling rate."

The variation point chart includes the variation points—*VP*, and the variants—v, that we have extracted (see Figure SB3.1).

The variation points may be constructed iteratively when new applications are discovered or the already available ones are analyzed more in depth. For instance, we could discover a new variant, spectrum equalization, for VP2 (type of processing). Moreover, we could consider a new application: processing of video streams. This could lead to a new variation point—VP5, Data dimension—with the following variants: scalar for what we had so far, 2-dimensional, and *n*-dimensional (see Figure SB3.2).

Not all variation points and variants need to be implemented. Some of them can be technologically too expensive or unattractive. In our example, 2-dimensional data would be unattractive and *n*-dimensional data too expensive.

VP1: Hardware and software platform v1-1. Embedded for control systems v1-2. Embedded for telephony v1-3. PC environment
VP2: Type of processing v2-1. Control system processing v2-2. Echo cancellation v2-3. Audio reverberation
VP3: Number of channels v3-1. One v3-2. According to standards, more than eight v3-3. Two
VP4: Sampling rate v4-1. KHz range v4-2. 8 KHz v4-3. 44.1 KHz

Figure SB3.1 Variation point chart.

VP5: Data dimension
v5-1.   Scalar
v5-2.   2-dimensional
v5-3.   *n*-dimensional

Figure SB3.2   New variation point.

SB3.3 Framework Architectures to Support Variation Points

Frameworks deliver components and architectures. Components are software assets written in a given language. Architectures organize components in a logical way [Fayad-Schmidt 1997; Garlan 1995]. Software can be viewed from several perspectives; each perspective has an associated architecture to describe it [Bass 1998]. Architectures give the overall view of how components work and interact, and provide application developers with the rules for composition of components.

Sherlock produces frameworks that are described by at least three architectures: functional, class, and dynamic.

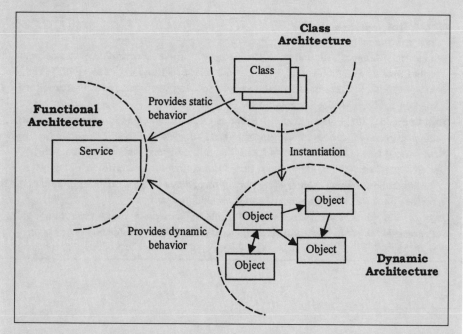

Figure SB3.3   Interactions of the three framework architectures.

Continues

SIDEBAR 3
FRAMEWORKS AND DOMAIN MODELS:
TWO SIDES OF THE SAME COIN *(Continued)*

The *functional* architecture considers the services provided by applications. The architecture is layered and services belong to layers; the layers are *environment, domain-specific, application-specific*. The environment layer wraps low-level and platform-specific features. The domain-specific layer contains services common to all the applications. The application-specific layer contains services specific to individual applications. Variability is provided through *composition between* services and through *customizability within* services.

The *class* architecture represents the static relations between classes. Variability is provided through parameters, method overloading, inheritance, virtual methods, interfaces, multiple inheritance, templates, aggregation, delegation, and network combination. Unified Modeling Language's (UML) class diagrams are the tool to represent the class architecture [Fowler 1997].

The *dynamic* architecture considers the relations and interactions between objects. Objects are instances of classes. This architecture represents data and control flow of running applications. Variability is provided in two ways: (1) object state and (2) interaction, timing, and synchronization.

Classes and objects contribute to implement services. Figure SB3.3 presents how the three framework architectures interact.

SB3.4 References

[Arango 1993] Arango, G. Domain analysis methods. *Software Reusability*, W. Schaeffer, R. Prieto-Diaz, and M. Matsumoto, editors. New York: Ellis Horwood, 1993.

[Bass 1998] Bass, L., P. Clemens, and R. Kazman. *Software Architectures in Practice*. Reading, MA: Addison Wesley Longman, 1998.

[Fayad-Schmidt 1997] Fayad, M., and D. Schmidt. Object-oriented application frameworks. *Communications of the ACM* 40(10), October 1997.

[Fowler 1997] Fowler, M. *UML Distilled*. Reading, MA: Addison Wesley Longman, 1997.

[Garlan 1995] Garlan, D., R. Allen, and J. Ockerbloom. Architectural mismatch or why it's hard to build systems out of existing parts. *Proceedings of the 17th International Conference on Software Engineering*, Seattle, Washington, April 1995.

[Jacobson 1997] Jacobson, I., M. Griss, and P. Jonsson. *Software Reuse. Architecture Process and Organization for Business Success*. Reading, MA: Addison Wesley Longman, 1997.

PART

Four

Framework Development Concepts

Part Four consists of six chapters and a sidebar, and discusses several new application framework concepts, such as the hooks approach and framework recipes.

Chapter 9 discusses the hooks approach for reusing and utilizing object-oriented application frameworks. Object-oriented frameworks can be complex. Often, considerable time is needed to understand the framework, including not only what the framework does, but also how to use it. Techniques for documenting the design of a framework already exist, but less work has been done on documenting how to use the framework. This chapter discusses the notion of hooks as a means of representing knowledge about the places in a framework that can be adapted by application developers to produce an application from the framework. They have applied the concept to the Size Engineering Application Framework (SEAF) project. By describing the hooks, implicit knowledge about how to reuse the framework is made explicit and open to study, refinement, or use. Having this knowledge available can make frameworks easier to reuse, since developers need not spend the time deriving the knowledge themselves. With hooks, a template is provided to describe the hooks and to capture all of the relevant knowledge in a form that provides guidance to application developers. This chapter discusses the model of hooks as a means of capturing knowledge about how to reuse the framework, reports on our experience with hooks in the SEAF project, and gives some initial assessment of the notion of hooks.

The goal of Chapter 10 is to describe a proven technique that software architects can use in creating the foundation of an application architecture. The technique is presented as a recipe that includes seven individual patterns as the raw ingredients and a series of steps or guidelines for combining the patterns to create a flexible application framework. Architects can use the recipe to gain insight into a subset of the challenges of building robust technology solutions. These architectures are crucial to the successful adoption of new technologies that are ultimately used to support the ongoing business of an organization. The main contribution of this work is a self-contained pattern system that builds upon the growing catalog of design patterns available to software developers and that is open to extension and customization. The technical innovations of this work are that framework-based development is encouraged as a means to resolve the various issues surrounding application architecture design. Both inheritance-based and delegation-based framework approaches are provided in the recipe's solutions in addition to a design patterns approach to describing frameworks. This work continues in that vein.

Chapter 11 addresses lessons learned from and experience in the design and implementation of an object-oriented application framework (OO-Navigator) that allows the addition of hypermedia functionality to an object-oriented application. First, this chapter discusses what it means to combine navigation with more conventional computations. Next, the architecture of the OO-Navigator framework is presented. This chapter briefly describes the use of the framework by showing how its components are instantiated and plugged into application objects. The framework's architecture is then exposed in terms of design patterns. Finally, some further work is discussed.

Chapter 12 describes how to understand application framework behavior and defines a trace-based approach for specifying the behavior of the framework. When designing a framework F, the designer abstracts certain key methods of certain key classes of the framework, leaving them as virtual functions (in C++ terminology). One of the most important contributions that F makes to the final application built on F is the flow of control implemented in the nonvirtual functions of F; this relieves the application builder from having to worry about this important and difficult issue. An application builder who builds a complete application A using F refines the abstract base classes of F by providing specific bodies for the virtual functions, thus implementing specific behaviors. This chapter uses the term *behavioral refinement* to characterize this type of refinement. This chapter addresses several important questions, such as how do we understand the behavior—specifically the flow-of-control behavior—implemented by the framework code, how do we understand the behavior implemented by the method bodies defined in the application code, and how do we combine these to obtain an understanding of the behavior of the entire application?

Chapter 12 describes a trace-based approach for specifying the behavior of the framework, in particular the control flow. The particular refinement that an application builder implements is captured in an appropriate refined specification of the respective virtual functions of F. This chapter then shows how this refined specification can be combined with the specification of the framework to arrive at the behavior of the entire application. This chapter illustrates this approach on a simple diagram editor framework.

Chapter 13 describes how to capture application framework requirements. Application frameworks have become a widely used foundation for system development. Although refactoring existing class structures and architectures is the preferred technique for developing a framework, numerous business pressures have resulted in the need to identify and capture requirements for a framework in the beginning of the development process. This chapter describes use case assortment, a framework requirements capture and tracing technique. The technique refactors a use case model that represents requirements for an application. The refactored use cases then provide framework requirements that allow the application to be developed from a framework. The technique is illustrated by examples taken from the telephony domain.

The goal of Chapter 14 is to classify and describe techniques for managing class dependencies in frameworks. Class dependencies occur when different hot spots within a framework aren't independent of each other, but the flexibility offered by one hot spot reduces the flexibility offered by others. A classification is presented that introduces four categories of techniques for managing class dependencies: closely coupled classes, consistent object creation, data-driven classes, and metalevel configuration. Several techniques from each category are presented, and their advantages and disadvantages are discussed. A framework for interactive and animated presentations on the web is presented as a case study.

Sidebar 4 describes an example for developing and evaluating application frameworks based on a formal architecture description language.

Reusing Hooks

An application framework provides a generic design within a given domain and a reusable implementation of that design. An object-oriented application framework presents its generic design and its reusable implementation of a system through a set of classes and their collaborations [Beck-Johnson 1994]. Applications are built from frameworks by extending or customizing parts of the framework, while retaining the original design.

Frameworks solve larger-grained problems than individual components, making the effort of finding and reusing them much more cost-effective than for small components. Due to the potentially large size and complexity of frameworks, even well-designed frameworks, the time required to understand how to use the framework can be significant. To be cost-effective, it should take substantially less time to understand and reuse a framework than to build an equivalent application without the framework.

To aid in framework reuse, we have developed the notion of *hooks* as a means of representing knowledge about the places in a framework that can or should be changed or augmented by application developers to produce an application from the framework. Hooks focus on how the framework is intended to be used, and provide an alternative and supplementary view to the design of the framework. A hook may involve something as simple as inheriting from an existing class in the framework, or as complex as adapting the interaction of a large number of classes within the framework. Each hook captures the relevant knowledge of some potential use of a framework in a form (template) that provides guidance to application developers. The *framework builder*, who is the most knowledgeable about the framework, defines the hooks and through them passes on his or her knowledge to the application developer. In this way, the framework builder can tell the application developer what needs to be completed or extended in the framework or what choices need to be made about parts of the framework in order to develop an application using the framework.

There are several novel contributions of the hooks approach. First, hooks present a structured and uniform method to allow the framework builder to be more precise about how the framework is intended to be used. By describing the hooks, implicit knowledge about how to use the framework is made explicit and open to study, refinement, or reuse. Having this knowledge available can make frameworks easier to reuse, as developers need not spend the time deriving the knowledge themselves. Having this knowledge available can also lead to better-designed frameworks, as it gives framework builders a means of examining and refining how the framework can be used. Second, the type system for hooks catalogs many of the ways in which changes can be made to a framework and how they can be supported.

Last, but not least, the hooks model provides a number of characterizations for each hook (for example, the requirement, the use area, the adaption type, the participants), which makes it easier for application developers to find the hook they need from the database of all the hooks for a framework. This is especially useful for frameworks having many places of potential reuse or that are open for refinement. Application developers will not have to read through all of the hooks to begin to gain an understanding of the framework and which hooks to use.

Our notion of hooks is being evaluated in the context of the Size Engineering Application Framework (SEAF) project, a joint effort with Teledyne Fluid Systems–Farris Engineering, to develop an engineering tool for the sizing and selection of pressure relief valves [SEAF 1997]. This project involves two orthogonal application frameworks. One deals with persistent object management and user interface support (as two subframeworks that collaborate extensively), while the other deals with support for engineering calculations.

The rest of the chapter proceeds as follows. *Section 9.1* briefly overviews the related work and the background research on techniques for documentation of application frameworks. We discuss the notion of hooks as a means of capturing knowledge about how to reuse the framework and survey the basics of the hooks model in *Section 9.2*. *Section 9.3* presents our experience with hooks in the SEAF project and gives some initial assessment of applying the hooks model. *Section 9.4* is a summary.

9.1 Background

Frameworks can be quite complicated and difficult to understand. Properly documenting a framework is important in order to ease its understanding and use. Johnson proposes that framework documentation needs at least three parts: one describing the purpose of the framework, one describing how to use the framework, and one describing the design of the framework [Johnson 1992].

Several approaches to framework documentation have focused on the design of the framework. Some approaches that have been used are providing multiple views of the design, using exemplars, and using design patterns. Campbell and Islam propose a six-view approach to documenting the design, which includes documenting the classes, but also documenting the relationships between classes [Campbell-Islam

1992]. Exemplars [Gangopadhyay-Mitra 1995], which consist of a concrete implementation provided for all of the abstract classes in the framework along with their interactions, provide another means of understanding the design of frameworks.

Design patterns [Gamma 1995] are a popular means of both building and describing frameworks. [Beck-Johnson 1994] have used design patterns to help show how the architecture of the HotDraw framework is derived. Since design patterns are often flexible and extensible, using them to design a framework can lead to more flexible and extensible frameworks. Design patterns are also useful for describing the design of the framework and showing the decisions that were made regarding the design. Using commonly known design patterns can also help developers understand the framework by serving as a common vocabulary between the framework builder and the application developer.

[Pree 1995] uses metapatterns to both design and document the hot spots of a framework. The hot spots are the flexible or incomplete places within a framework. Each hot spot tends to have several hooks within it. Many design patterns can be broken down into a group of metapatterns. The metapatterns document the design of a particular hot spot in terms of the relationship between template classes that encapsulate some standard functionality within the framework and hook classes to be filled in by application developers that have methods for extending that functionality.

All of the design-oriented approaches provide excellent means of documenting the design. They were, however, not targeted for explicitly capturing the purpose of a framework nor how the framework should be used. For example, they show classes and their interactions, but not the ways in which those classes can be used or adapted to build applications from the framework.

Less work has focused on the purpose and intended use of frameworks. Two such approaches are cookbooks and patterns. The cookbook in [Krasner-Pope 1988] consists of a general description of the purpose of the Smalltalk Model-View-Controller (MVC) framework, the major components of the framework, and their roles, and follows with a number of examples to illustrate how the components can be used. It is presented as a tutorial to learn the framework. A different type of cookbook found in [VisualWorks 1995] focuses on specific issues such as how to create an active view in MVC. Each entry in this cookbook defines a problem to solve and then gives a set of steps to follow along with some examples for solving the problem. Johnson's patterns [Johnson 1992] fall roughly into the same category as a cookbook, documenting the purpose and use of a framework as well as a little of the design. Each pattern describes a problem that application developers will face when using the framework, gives general narrative advice and examples about ways to solve the problem, summarizes the solution, and refers to related patterns. All of these techniques rely on narrative descriptions that may be imprecise or incomplete.

Hooks focus on the intended use of the framework, much like cookbooks or motifs, but do not focus on the design like design patterns or exemplars. Hooks provide an alternative view to design documentation, but they are meant to augment, rather than replace other types of documentation. Examples and design documentation are important in terms of learning and using a framework. Examples capture specific uses of the framework. Design documentation presents the design and even the reasons why a particular design was chosen. Hooks show how and where a design can be changed. They present knowledge about the usage of the framework.

9.2 The Hooks Model: An Overview

A hook is a point in the framework that is meant to be adapted in some way, such as by filling in parameters or creating subclasses. Each hook description documents a problem or requirement that the framework builder anticipates an application developer will have and provides guidance about how to use the hook and fulfill the requirement. Each description typically focuses on a small requirement. For more complex problems, a group of hooks can be provided with each focusing upon a smaller problem within the larger, more complex problem.

Each hook details the changes to the design that are required, the constraints that must be adhered to, and any effects upon the framework that the hook will impose. Only the information needed to solve the problem is provided within the hook. Developers are then able to quickly understand and use the hook. Once the correct hook has been found, an application developer uses the hook simply by performing all of the changes within the changes section of the hook in the order given.

Hooks are meant to be used for developing applications from a framework, not developing new frameworks from old ones. Selecting options, filling in parameters, or extending the framework for a particular application are all hooks. However, refactoring an existing framework is beyond the scope of hooks.

9.2.1 Hook Descriptions

Each hook description is written in a specific format made up of several sections. The sections detail different aspects of the hook, such as the components that take part in the hook (participants) or the steps that should be followed to use the hook (changes). The sections serve as a guide to the people writing the hooks by showing the aspects that should be considered about the hook and helping to ensure that all relevant information is included. The format in which hooks are described helps to organize the information and make the description more precise and less ambiguous than pure English narrative. Each hook description consists of the following parts:

Name. A unique name, within the context of the framework, that identifies the hook.

Requirement. A textual description of the problem the hook is intended to help solve. The framework builder anticipates the requirements that an application will have and describes hooks for those requirements.

Type. An ordered pair consisting of the method of adaption used and the amount of support provided for the problem within the framework.

Area. The parts of the framework that are affected by the hook.

Uses. The other hooks required to use this hook. The use of a single hook may not be enough to completely fulfill a requirement that has several aspects to it, so this section states the other hooks that are needed to help fulfill the requirement.

Participants. The components that participate in the hook. These are both existing and new components.

Changes. The main section of the hook that outlines the changes to the interfaces, associations, and control flow among the components given in the participants section.

Constraints. Limits imposed on the hook or on the use of the hook.

Comments. Any additional description needed.

Not all sections will be applicable to all hooks, in which case the entry not required is simply left out. For example, a hook that does not use any others will have no Uses declaration. Concrete examples of hook descriptions will be given in *Section 9.3*.

9.2.2 Characterizing Hooks

Hooks are currently categorized by the following two characterization types (recall the Type description of a hook in Section 3.1). The first characterization, the *method of adaption*, indicates the type of change that the hook uses, such as enabling a feature within the framework, removing a default feature, or adding a completely new feature. The second characterization, the *level of support*, indicates how much support the hook provides for the adaption within the framework. The method of adaption used is distinct from the level of support provided for the changes. For example, removing a feature may be well supported and simply require turning off a switch in the framework, or it may be less well supported and require the modification of one or more methods.

A hook's method of adaption quickly gives an application developer an idea of what the hook does. Its support type indicates how difficult the hook may be to use. Each type indicates the issues that both the hook writer and the application developer must consider. For example, removing a feature will often have an impact on other features of the framework.

Method of Adaption

There are several ways that a developer can adapt a framework, and each hook uses at least one of these methods:

- Enabling a feature
- Disabling a feature
- Replacing a feature
- Augmenting a feature
- Adding a feature

The two most common methods are enabling a feature and adding a feature, and these are examined in this chapter. The others are more fully described in [Froehlich 1997]. *Enabling* a feature involves activating features that are a part of the framework but may not be a part of the default implementation. Hooks of this type often involve using prebuilt components that come with the framework that may be parameterized. The hook needs to detail how to enable the feature, such as which components to select for inclusion in the application, which parameters to fill in, or how to configure a set of components. The constraints imposed by using the feature, such as excluding the use of another feature, are also contained in the hook.

Unlike enabling a feature, where the developer is using existing services, possibly in new ways, *adding* a feature involves adding something that the framework wasn't capable of before. These additions are often done by extending existing classes with new services or adding new classes, and adding new paths of control with the new services. The hook shows what new classes or operations are needed, where to integrate them into the framework and how they interact with old classes and services. The framework builder may also provide constraints that must be met by the new class or service and may limit the interfaces that the new class can use to interact with the framework.

Level of Support

Another important aspect of hooks is the level of support provided for the adaption within the framework. There are three main levels of support types for hooks:

- Option
- Supported pattern
- Open-ended

The *option* level provides the most support and is generally the easiest for the application developer to use. A number of prebuilt components are provided within the framework and the developer simply chooses one or more without requiring extensive knowledge about the framework. Most often, components are chosen to enable features within the framework or to replace default components. The hook describes the options and how the chosen option(s) can be inserted into the framework. Often, this insertion should be obvious and can potentially be handled automatically.

At the *pattern* level, the developer supplies parameters to components and/or follows a well-supported pattern of behavior. The simplest patterns occur when the developer needs to supply values or parameters to a single class within the framework. The parameters themselves may be as simple as base variables or as complex as methods or component classes. Some common tasks may require the collaboration of multiple classes, and may also have application-specific details. For these, a collaboration pattern is provided, which the developer follows to realize the task. Using a pattern hook requires more knowledge about the framework than does using an option hook, but since it is well supported within the framework, the developer does not usually need to worry about unwanted interactions or require a deep understanding of the design of the framework.

It is at the *open-ended* level that hooks are provided to fulfill requirements without being well supported within the framework. Open-ended hooks involve adding new properties to classes, new components to the framework, new interactions among components, or sometimes the modification of existing code. The knowledge about the framework required to use open-ended hooks is generally greater than with the other two support types. Since they are open-ended, the developer has to be more careful about the effects changes will have on the framework.

In the next section we report our experience with the hooks model in the SEAF project and illustrate the roles of hook characterization types in guiding the reuse of application frameworks by examples taken from our experience with SEAF.

9.3 Hooking into SEAF

The Size Engineering Application Framework (SEAF) project is focused in part on the reengineering and redevelopment of the Size Master-Plus engineering software package for sizing and selecting pressure relief valves. The project involves the collaboration of Teledyne Fluid Systems–Farris Engineering in Edmonton and researchers in the Software Engineering Research Laboratory at the University of Alberta. To support current and future product development, two frameworks have been built. The first is the user interface and persistence framework, which is responsible for coordinating the interaction between an application's user interface, the underlying database of information, and actual calculations embedded in the application. The second is the engineering framework, which provides a worksheet model that guides the engineer through a complex calculation, reminding them of important steps, ensuring that key decisions and subcalculations are made in the proper order, and recording the process for future review. The two frameworks are fully integrated and together form the basis for developing future size engineering packages. The hooks model was developed in parallel with the SEAF application frameworks. As a test of the capabilities of the hooks model, we chose an interesting portion of the engineering framework in which to retroactively apply the model.

9.3.1 The Engineering Application Framework

The core of the SEAF engineering framework is a hierarchically organized set of calculations called a *worksheet*. Each worksheet captures all of the possible calculations that are relevant to the problem domain. The purpose of the framework is to help the user fill in the parameters of the worksheet and then perform the calculations. In this sense, each engineering tool is a very sophisticated spreadsheet, where each cell can contain an entire spreadsheet. But the framework provides more, in the form of *wizards* that encapsulate common design workflows through the worksheet.

Each wizard provides a view on the worksheet that exposes only the data that is necessary to the task at hand. However, a worksheet can have a number of wizards active concurrently, and they could share common data. Thus, one function of the engineering framework is to support concurrent access to common data. In other words, we have a small database manager inside each application that manages access to the worksheet contents. Because it is simple, yet rich, we will use this aspect of the framework to illustrate hooks.

Worksheets and Data

A worksheet uses *calculations* to manipulate *data elements*. No calculation is allowed to directly manipulate a data element—it must always go through an *accessor*. Accessors allow controlled reading and writing of properties of the data element. Accessors also mediate database activities such as write locking and the attachment of handlers for *change events*.

The relationship between data elements and accessors is essentially the same as between the subject and observer in the observer design pattern described in [Gamma 1995]. The difference is that observers must communicate with the data through the accessors. This controlled interface enforces certain framework policies such as no fetching if invalid data and no write access to locked data.

Figure 9.1 gives a heavily sanitized UML [Booch 1996] class diagram for this part of the engineering framework. It contains the two base classes TDataElement and TDataAccessor. The data element and accessor classes are always friends. The class diagram contains a simple dimensioned numeric data element, TNumData and its accessor TNumAcc. A TNumData is a floating-point number plus a base dimensional unit (for example, meters). It also incorporates the concept of display units that are compatible with the base units (for example, feet). TNumData and TNumAcc are produced by using the hooks given later in this section.

Although not illustrated, there can be many different types of accessor to the same data element, perhaps for enforcing restricted access or increased functionality. For example, a user might want an accessor that did conversions from one unit to another.

We use *properties* (as in Eiffel or Object Pascal) to encapsulate the get and set methods for attributes. Unless qualified, properties are read/write. We have omitted many features from the class diagram, such as basic aspects like the identity and structural

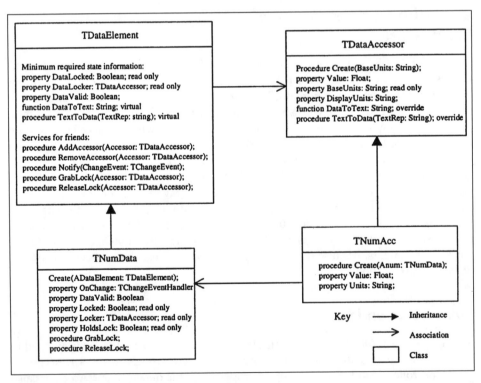

Figure 9.1   Data element and accessor pattern.

context of the data element and the callbacks that lock holders get when another accessor wants them to release the lock.

All data elements support basic locking services, conversions to and from text representations, a change notification mechanism, and the important engineering notion of whether the data element actually contains valid data. This is all provided by TDataElement. Access to these basic services is provided by TDataAccessor.

Change events are propagated via the OnChange property of a TDataAccessor. The engineering framework can pass change information to the handler—for example, the magnitude of the change or a list of all the components in an aggregate that changed.

Orthogonal to the description of the design, the description of the hooks shows how the classes and collaborations within the design can be extended or modified to produce an application from the framework. The hooks show how the framework is intended to be used. One of the requirements that we anticipate that application developers using the framework will have is the need to create a new type of data element and its associated accessor, such as TNumData and TNumAcc in Figure 9.1. There are actually three hooks involved in defining a new data element. The main hook, New Data Element, uses two other hooks, New State and New Accessor, to detail all of the actions required to define the new type.

```
Name: New Data Element
Requirement: A new type of data is required for calculations.
Type: Enabling, Parameter Pattern
Area: DataElement
Uses: New Accessor, New State
Participants: TDataElement, // The data type base class.
     NewDataElement // The new data type to be created.
Changes:
     new subclass NewDataElement of TDataElement
     NewDataElement.Create()
          extends TDataElement.Create()
     New State[DataElement = NewDataElement]
     New Accessor[DataElement = NewDataElement]
     NewDataElement.DataToText overrides TDataElement.DataToText
          returns String
     NewDataElement.TextToData overrides TDataElement.TextToData
```

There are only two participants in the New Data Element hook: TDataElement, which is the base class from which the new type will be derived, and NewDataElement, which represents the new data element. NewDataElement does not correspond to any existing class within the framework, but merely represents the new class to be created. When the hook is used, NewDataElement is replaced with the actual name of the new class. These participants are used in the changes section of the hook. First, the new subclass is created and a construction method Create defined for it. Next, the New State and New Accessor hooks are used to create the actual data fields within the data element and the accessor for the data element. Finally, the methods DataToText and TextToData are overridden to provide a means of serializing the data element for the purpose of storing and retrieving the data type in persistent storage.

When developers use this hook, they are essentially filling in a template or, in other words, providing parameters to customize a standard pattern. In this case, the parameters are methods to be overridden and the results of other hooks. For this reason, the hook is said to have the type pattern. The method of adaption is enabling as this particular hook uses the existing capabilities of the framework. The actual extensions are encapsulated in another hook, New State.

```
Name: New State
Requirement:
      New state information is needed for a type of data element.
Type: Adding, Open-Ended
Area: DataElement
Participants: DataElement
Changes:
      repeat as necessary
            new property DataElement.newproperty
```

The New State hook is used by the New Data Type hook to actually define the data fields for the new data element type. The fields are called properties that can be either base (simple variables) or calculated values. As many of these properties can be added as desired. As with the New Data Element hook, this hook operates on data elements and so refers to the DataElement area of the framework. The hook is open-ended, as there is no limit to the number or type of properties that can be added to the class. Since new properties are being added, the method of adaption is adding.

For every new data element that a developer creates, one or more new accessors must be created as well. The New Data Element hook uses the New Accessor hook to show how to create the new accessor.

```
Name: New Accessor
Requirement:
      A new accessor is needed for a new type of data element.
Type: Adding, Pattern
Area: DataElement, Accessor
Participants: TDataAccessor, NewAccessor, DataElement, TDataElement
Changes:
      new subclass NewAccessor of TDataAccessor
      NewAccessor.Create(DataElement) extends
            TDataAccessor.Create(TDataElement)
      repeat as necessary
        new property NewAccessor.newproperty where
            read of newproperty maps from set of DataElement.property
            write of newproperty maps into set of DataElement.property
```

The New Accessor hook also uses the adding method of adaption, since it adds new properties to the accessor class. However, the choices of properties are limited to ones reflecting the actual properties within the data element that the accessor is being created for. The statement for adding the properties is given in a repeat statement of the changes section. New properties of NewAccessor must map to and from the properties that are being accessed in DataElement.

Using Accessors

Figure 9.2 is a collaboration-style diagram that shows a typical use of data elements and accessors. The worksheet contains a local data element Temp and a subcalculation that contains a local data element X. An accessor is needed for every scope in which we wish to use the data. Thus, some accessors cross structural boundaries. For example, Temp has three accessors: one locally in the main body of the worksheet, one in a sub-calculation, and one external to the worksheet in a user interface form. The notes on the figure illustrate how the various services are used.

Within the framework, accessors have two distinct roles. Inside a worksheet, the accessors and change events drive the evaluation mechanism. We use spreadsheet semantics—that is, when a data element changes, it triggers the reevaluation of all downstream data elements. Unlike spreadsheets, worksheet calculations cannot contain cycles, so their updates always terminate.

The Access Data Element hook is provided for connecting the users of data (such as the form) to the actual data elements. The hook involves the collaboration of several classes, the DataElement, the actual Accessor, and the Caller that wishes to access the data. The collaboration is a standard pattern built into the framework and so the hook is an enabling pattern.

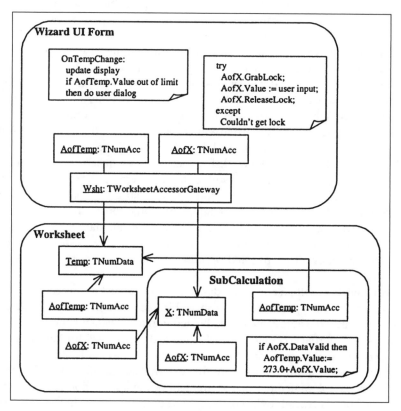

Figure 9.2 Example of using the data element and accessor pattern.

Name: Access Data Element
Requirement:
   A class needs access to an internal data element and needs to
be notified when the data element changes.
Type: Enabling, Collaboration Pattern
Area: Accessor
Participants:
   DataElement, // The data to be accessed.
   Accessor,   // The mediator between the DataElement and the caller.
   Caller   // The class that needs notification of changes.
Changes:
   Caller -> Accessor.Create(DataElement)
        // Create accessor and add to accessor list.
   new operation Caller.Update
        // Do actions upon notification here.
   Accessor.Onchange -> Caller.Update <provided>
   Caller -> read and write Accessor.Property
Constraints:
   Accessor and DataElement are of compatible types.

The actual changes specified by the hook description involve the Caller creating the new Accessor for the DataElement, which automatically adds the Accessor to the DataElement's accessor list. To be notified of changes, the Caller must provide an Update method that will be called by the Accessor. The Update method can be given whatever name is desired (for example, OnTempChange, as in Figure 9.2). To retrieve or modify values within the DataElement, the Caller must use the property access methods provided by the Accessor. One constraint is placed on the hook, stating that the actual Accessor and DataElement classes used in the hook must be of compatible types (that is, TNumData and TNumAcc must be used together).

Outside the worksheet, the accessors mediate the views and controllers of the worksheet. Thus, in Figure 9.2, the wizard graphical user interface (GUI) form is notified of changes in Temp, and also attempts to alter the value of X. Accessors from outside the worksheet need to first access the worksheet before they can access its components. In this case, we do not want them to have the same change notification behavior as the accessors inside the aggregate. They should have changes signaled only when the aggregate as a whole has completed changing and is in a consistent state. For example, once the worksheet change events have ceased causing calculation reevaluation, then the change event is propagated to the accessor outside the worksheet. (In fact, there may be no change event propagated because the data element returned back to its starting value.)

The worksheet is itself an aggregate data element, and so has an accessor, Wsht. All external accessors must pass through Wsht, which acts as a gateway that defers their change events until the aggregate has stabilized into a consistent state.

The hook for external accessors is nearly identical to the hook for internal accessors, reflecting the fact that to application developers the two mechanisms appear the same. The key difference is in the requirement that external accessors have different change notification behavior. Matching the requirement of the application to the service provided by the hook is crucial to the successful use of frameworks. In this case, using an internal accessor where an external one is required will cause incorrect behavior in the application. There is an additional hook, not detailed here, for creating new data aggregates, which is similar to the New Data Element hook but also requires the gateway accessor policy for propagating change events outside of the aggregate to be defined.

Name: Access Data Aggregate
Requirement:
      Some class needs access to a data element within an aggregation of elements and needs to be notified of a change to that element after all internal changes to the aggregate have been made.
Type: Enabling, Collaboration Pattern
Area: Data Management
Participants:

```
    DataAggregate     // The container data element
    DataElement,      // The data within the aggregate to be accessed.
    GatewayAccessor,  // An accessor to DataAggregate
    Accessor,         // The mediator between the DataElement and the
                      // caller.
    Caller            // The class that needs notification of changes.
```

Changes:

```
    Caller -> GatewayAccessor.CreateComponentAccessor(DataElement)
    new operation Caller.Update  // Do actions upon notification here.
    Accessor.OnChange -> Caller.Update <provided>
    Caller -> read and write Accessor.Property
```

Constraints:

```
    Accessor and DataElement are of compatible types.
    Caller.Update called only when all data elements within the
aggregate have changed.
```

The Access Data Aggregate hook provides the same mechanisms as the Access Data Element for notifying the Caller of changes and for allowing the Caller to get and set values within the DataElement. However, the GatewayAccessor is called to create the external accessor. The constraint that the Accessor and DataElement are of compatible types is still present, but one additional constraint is added, stating that the Update method of the Caller is invoked only when the aggregate as a whole has completed changing.

9.3.2 Experience

We have found that applying the hooks model to a framework has several benefits. The precise and structured description provided by hooks can help clarify understanding and prevent incorrect use of the framework by application developers. For example, in an earlier version of the framework, a narrative description of how to use internal accessors was provided and used in developing the current SizeMaster application. However, since the description did not clearly state the requirement that the accessors to aggregates fulfilled, and the developers did not clearly state the application requirements, the accessors were used incorrectly and caused a flaw in the application. Discovery of the error also caused external accessors to be added to the framework.

Describing the hooks for the engineering framework before developing the application also would have caught the need for external as well as internal accessors. Writing the hooks forces the framework builder to state precisely how some part of the framework should be used. By forcing a walkthrough of the intended use of the framework, defining hooks can help to expose deficiencies within the framework. When the hook for internal accessors was written, it became clearer that external accessors were needed.

Finally, writing hooks also exposes unnecessarily complex structure within the framework and forces the framework builders to either justify the complexity or to rethink it. While the proper hooks for using the framework may exist, those hooks may be complex or difficult to use. Often a complex hook or set of hooks is a reflection of needlessly complex structure within the framework. In an earlier version of the framework, the state (the properties) of a data element was part of a different class. Deriving a new type of data element then involved inheriting from three different classes (state, data element, and accessor) and creating a complex pattern of interactions between the three. After attempting to describe the hooks for it, the structure was streamlined to the current and easier-to-use version. Ease of use is one of the desirable features of frameworks, and describing hooks can help expose where the use of the framework can be simplified.

9.4 Summary

We have discussed the hooks model as a means of capturing knowledge about how to reuse the framework. The hooks model presents a structured approach to modeling the knowledge about the reuse properties of a framework. Each hook describes one aspect of the intended use of the framework and identifies the places in a framework that can or should be changed or augmented in the development of an application. By describing the hooks, implicit knowledge about how to use the framework is made explicit and open to study, refinement, and reuse. Our experience with SEAF demonstrates that having knowledge about how a framework is intended to be reused is vital to the successful (cost-effective) use of a framework. Without it, application developers must synthesize the reuse knowledge implied in a framework design by examining architectural descriptions, source code, and examples, before they can use the framework. Similarly, without a structured means of describing the properties of reuse of a framework, framework builders can only rely on informal narratives. These descriptions may be imprecise or incomplete, and inadequate for passing on to application developers the knowledge of what needs to be completed or extended in the framework or what choices need to be made about parts of the framework in order to use the framework effectively.

We have chosen the SEAF frameworks to gain some initial experience in applying the idea of hooks developed in [Froehlich 1997]. This work has helped to validate our views that structured and precise descriptions are needed to communicate the intended use of the framework to application developers. We have also found that simply specifying the hooks helps to expose deficiencies or overcomplexity in the design of the framework. The idea of hooks will continue to be refined based on our continued experience.

There are a number of areas of future work related to research involving hooks. First, tool support involves both finding the appropriate hook for a given application requirement, and then applying the framework extensions within the hook. Hooks at the option and pattern levels are well-defined and can be partially automated by asking the application developer for the option desired or the parameters to fill in and then performing the appropriate actions automatically to incorporate those options into the framework.

Second, hooks are currently text based, but a more graphical definition can be developed for incorporation into graphical object-oriented diagrams as well as the proposed tools. Third, operators on hooks can be defined. Structured means of adding new hooks by application developers, modifying existing hooks, or even applying hooks will aid in the use and management of collections of hooks. Finally, we are interested in the area of framework evolution and how hooks affect evolution. The hooks themselves may indicate when a framework should evolve. If the hooks defined are not being used, then the framework may need to be rethought. Additionally, as more information and experience is gained about a framework and what it can be used for, the framework might evolve to change open hooks into pattern hooks or even option hooks.

9.5 References

[Beck-Johnson 1994] Beck, K., and R. Johnson. Patterns generate architectures. *Proceedings of ECOOP 1994*, pp. 139–149, Bologna, Italy, July 1994.

[Booch 1996] Booch, G., I. Jacobson, and J. Rumbaugh. *The Unified Modeling Language for Object-Oriented Development.* Rational Software Corporation, *www.rational.com/uml*, 1996.

[Campbell-Islam 1992] Campbell, R.H., and N. Islam. A technique for documenting the framework of an object-oriented system. *Proceedings of the 2nd International Workshop on Object-Orientation in Operating Systems,* Paris, France, September 1992, pp. 288–300.

[Froehlich 1997] Froehlich, G., H.J. Hoover, L. Liu, and P. Sorenson. Hooking into object-oriented application frameworks. *Proceedings of the 1997 International Conference on Software Engineering,* pp. 141–151, Boston, Massachusetts, 1997.

[Gamma 1995] Gamma, E., R. Helm, R. Johnson, and J. Vlissides. *Design Patterns: Elements of Reusable Object-Oriented Software.* Reading, MA: Addison-Wesley, 1995.

[Gangopadhyay 1995] Gangopadhyay, D., and S. Mitra. Understanding frameworks by exploration of exemplars. *Proceedings of 7th International Workshop on Computer Aided Software Engineering (CASE-95),* pp. 90–99, Toronto, Canada, 1995.

[Johnson 1992] Johnson, R. Documenting frameworks using patterns. *Proceedings of OOPSLA 1992,* pp. 63–76, Vancouver, Canada, 1992.

[Krasner-Pope 1988] Krasner, G.E., and S.T. Pope. A cookbook for using the Model-View-Controller user interface paradigm in Smalltalk-80. *Journal of Object-Oriented Programming* 1(3), August-September 1988: 26–49.

[Pree 1995] Pree, W. *Design Patterns for Object-Oriented Software Development.* Reading, MA: Addison-Wesley, 1995.

[SEAF 1997] SEAF Project, unpublished, www.cs.ualberta.ca/softeng/SEAF/project.html, 1997.

[VisualWorks 1995] *VisualWorks Cookbook,* Release 2.5. Sunnyvale, CA: ParcPlace-Digitalk Inc., 1995.

9.6 Review Questions

1. Define the following terms: framework builder, the open-ended level, accessor pattern.

2. Describe the hooks approach, and provide an example.

3. What are the two characterization types of the hooks?

4. Describe the five methods of adapting a framework.

5. Show an example of using data element and accessor pattern.

6. List and describe future trends with hooks.

7. What is a hook?

8. Who defines the hooks?

9. What is the difference between applications and frameworks?

10. What kind of documentation is needed for frameworks?

11. What do application developers need to know in order to use a framework?

12. What types of hooks are easiest to use? What types are the most flexible?

13. Why does SEAF use two different frameworks?

14. Why does SEAF require two different types of accessors?

15. Why are there two hooks for creating new Data types in SEAF—New Data and New State?

9.7 Problem Set

Some of the questions and projects require access to the Client-Server Framework (CSF), which can be found through the Software Engineering Research Laboratory World Wide Web page at the University of Alberta (www.cs.ualberta.ca/~softeng/).

1. Pick any Unix client-server pair (for example, ftp) and describe how you would build it using CSF.

2. Identify areas of the CSF that would need to change to adapt to a different connection mechanism, such as RMI, CORBA, RPC, or Jini.

3. Evaluate the strengths and weaknesses of building an application using a framework such as CSF as opposed to building it without the framework. Evaluate from the point of view of both an application developer and a manager.

4. Pick a framework (for example, MFC, Delphi, HotDraw, Java AWT) and give examples of several hooks of different types.

9.8 Projects

Some of the questions and projects require access to the Client-Server Framework (CSF), which can be found through the Software Engineering Research Laboratory World Wide Web page at the University of Alberta (www.cs.ualberta.ca/~softeng/).

1. Use CSF to construct a simple client-server application such as a web browser or ftp client and evaluate the use of the framework in terms of:

   Ramp-up time to learn the framework.

Changes required to the architecture of the framework.

Points where the framework had to be extended but no hook was available versus the number of hooks used (hacks-to-hooks ratio).

2. Given an application constructed from a framework, describe the new hooks needed to build that application. Does the framework need to evolve in order to add the new hooks?

9.9 Appendix: Grammar for Hook Descriptions

```
<hook> ::=<name>
          <requirement>
          <type>
          <area>
          [<uses>]
          <participants>
          [<constraints>]
          [<comments>]

<name> ::= Name: <string>
<requirement> ::= Requirement: <string>

<type> ::= Type: <method>, <level>
<method> ::= enabling | adding | replacing | augmenting | disabling
<level> ::= <option> | <pattern> | open-ended
<option> ::= single option | multi-option
<pattern> ::= parameter pattern | collaboration pattern | pattern

<area> ::= Area: <string> [, .., <string>]

<participants> ::= Participants : <identifier> [<type>] [<style>] [, ..,
    <identifier> [<type>] [<style>] ]
<type> ::= set of <identifier> [, .., <identifier>] |
    sequence of <identifier> [, .., <identifier>]
<style> ::= new | exists

<uses> ::= Uses: <hook name> [, .., <hook name>]

<changes> ::= <statement> [, .., statement>]
<statement> ::= <loop statement> |
    <hook statement> |
    <new element statement> |
    <method statement> |
    <modify statement> |
    <participant statement> |
    <option statement> |
    <behavior statement>

<loop statement> ::= <loop id> <statement> [.. <statement>]
<loop id> ::= repeat [as necessary] | forall <var> in <set>
```

```
<hook statement> ::=          <identifier> = <hook name> "[" <identifier>
"]" |
     <hook name> "[" <identifier> = <rhs> [, .., <identifier> = <rhs>]
"]"

<new element statement> ::= [new] subclass <identifier> of <identifier>
|
     [new] property <qualified identifier> <whereclause> |
     [new] operation <qualified identifier>
<whereclause> ::=
     read of <identifier> maps from [set of] <qualified identifier> |
     write of <identifier> maps into [set of] <qualified identifier>

<method statement> ::= <qualified identifier> <method operation>
               <qualified identifier> [<return expression>] |
     <qualified identifier> <return expression>
<method operation> ::= copies | specializes | overrides | extends
<return expression> ::= returns <string> |
     returns [set of | sequence of] <rhs>

<modify statement> ::= remove code '<string>' [, .., '<string>'] |
     replace '<string>' with '<string>'

<participant statement> ::= fill in <identifier> [, .., <identifier>] |
     <identifier> add <set>

<option statement> ::= choose <identifier> from <set>

<behavior statement> ::=
     synchronization ( <qualified identifier>, <qualified identifier> [,
               .., <qualified identifier> ) [in <qualified
identifier>]
               [provided]|
     [control flow] <qualified expression> -> [<read/write>]
               <qualified expression> [provided]
<read/write> ::= read | write | read and write

<rhs> ::= <identifier> |
     <set> |
     instance of <var> [[of | with] <attribute> <var>] |
     <loop id> <rhs>

<set> ::= <var> | ( <identifier>, <identifier> [, .., <identifier>] )

<var> ::= <identifier> | <qualified identifier>
<attribute> ::= <identifier>
<qualified identifier> ::= <identifier>.<identifier>

<constraints> ::= Constraints: <string> [, .., <string>]

<comments> ::= Comments: <string>
```

CHAPTER 10

A Framework Recipe

10.1 The Transition

To support their business and to remain competitive within a dynamic marketplace, organizations are often motivated to adopt and embrace new technology platforms. A compelling example of such a platform is the Internet and its lure of electronic commerce. Another is Java and its ease-of-use, portability, and mobility.

Organizations should plan for such an adoption by first creating a solid foundation for that technology such that, over time, many applications can be built in a consistent manner and can leverage a standard set of common services (security, persistence, logging, and so on). By investing in a robust infrastructure that harnesses the power of the chosen technology, organizations will better prepare for creating and maintaining suites of applications that support their business [Fayad-Laitinen 1998]. This technology foundation is often referred to as an *application architecture*.

As those who have succeeded can testify, building an application architecture is not a trivial task. It typically requires months of intense domain analysis supported by a series of design iterations. To assist in this challenging endeavor, a growing number of proven, repeatable solutions are available to application architects. Software professionals have been providing design patterns [Gamma 1995] and, more recently, framework [Pree 1996; Roberts-Johnson 1997] and architectural patterns [Buschmann 1996, Shaw-Garlan 1996] that reflect successful experiences in constructing robust solutions. Patterns and their more tangible incarnation, frameworks, are ideal vehicles for sharing valuable architectural knowledge. The Framework Recipe seeks to contribute to that effort by providing software developers with a head start in crafting a robust and flexible foundation for adopting new technology platforms. Note that the framework introduced here is domain-independent and addresses common technical challenges. Additional analysis and design are required to fit it to the needs of a specific organization.

This chapter presents a system of patterns that apply to the design and development of an application architecture. While these patterns can be used independently, they are most effective when used together to create a powerful framework for application development. Utilizing these patterns as a collective set is herein referred to as a *recipe.* This recipe assists in understanding the overall pattern system and prescribes a procedure for applying the patterns in the proper order. This recipe has been successfully proven over the past few years to create solid application foundations for many large organizations adopting C++ and Java.[1]

10.1.1 Tracking a Real-World Example

In exploring this system of patterns, we employ a running concrete example to provide additional context for each pattern and to show how related architectural obstacles can be addressed by this recipe. In our example, an organization has chosen to adopt and embrace the Java platform by creating an application architecture to support the development of one or more of its forthcoming business systems. A Java development team has been assembled to build a prototypical application for internal use. The target application is used to schedule meeting or conference rooms in the various buildings on the organization's campus. The scheduling application was selected because it uses the same client-server-style architecture as other business systems that will be built on the Java platform. In completing the prototype, the organization expects to address and solve the technical challenges it will encounter with its other business applications.

10.1.2 Architecture Derives from Experience

The key to building and extending an architecture lies in understanding the individual components in a system and the relationships, dependencies, and interactions among those components. It is equally important to understand the patterns that guide the organization of the components and the forces that result in the selection of the patterns themselves. Patterns serve as a good head start for architects but do not fully compensate for the actual experience of having done it before. Learning from experience is what prevents developers from repeating the same mistakes. More specifically,

---

[1]The author has created application frameworks based on these and other patterns for an options clearing system (The Options Clearing Corporation), a web-based retirement services management system (The Northern Trust Bank), an employee time-tracking system (Abbott Laboratories), a help-desk system (SPS Payment Systems), and a content-management system (Banta Integrated Media). Other applications at these companies have since been built and deployed using the same underlying architecture.

experience is what enables an architect to know which questions to ask during the architecture design phase. Asking the right questions at the right time is one of the most important steps in defining the appropriate solution.

The following list of questions is part of a much larger set that highlights separate but related concerns that often arise during the development of a new enterprise-scale architecture. The questions are derived from practical project experience. One might argue that just knowing to ask these types of questions can be valuable in itself, but ultimately what is needed are real solutions. The patterns in the Framework Recipe provide the answers to these questions as a way to share architectural experience.

The Java development team in our example has many issues to contend with in building a robust application architecture, including error handling, security, persistence, client-server communication, transactional integrity, scalability and performance, and redundancy and availability. This pattern system does not address all these issues; however, the team can make significant progress in their effort by finding answers to the following questions.

How will the architecture provide a flexible and consistent program configuration mechanism that can support all phases of application development and deployment?

> Developers can increase the flexibility of applications by replacing hardcoded values at compile time with values that are obtained dynamically at runtime through some external configuration source. The core Java library provides a basic approach to obtaining configuration values that can be used to configure applications at runtime. But Java's Properties for stand-alone programs and HTML parameters for embedded applets are not even accessed in a consistent way, requiring programs to use separate interfaces for leveraging the same basic architectural service. For our development team, this means increased learning curves and contending with at least two different configuration models.

How will multiple applications in a system employ a straightforward and consistent message-logging strategy?

> Like most robust programs, Java applications require the ability to route text-based messages through a variety of output mechanisms (for example, shell consoles, status bars, pop-up dialogs, persistent files, databases). Each of these mechanisms is supported in Java, but each has its own unique interface and requires specialized programming. To leverage any one of these techniques, the development team must learn multiple interfaces for achieving what amounts to the same functionality.

How can an application itself be accurately represented in the various object models and reap the same benefits of inheritance, encapsulation, and polymorphism?

> Applet is a prominent class in the Java programming model. There is no corresponding class for stand-alone applications, however, and this can lead to confusion about the most appropriate place to start developing nonvisual applications. The development team cannot find the base Application class for

their Java programs. More specifically, they are unsure about which class in their object model will contain the main( ) routine.

How can the architecture provide and enforce a common programming model for large systems comprising tens or hundreds of applications?

The Applet programming model is captured succinctly in just four life-cycle methods: init( ), start( ), stop( ), and destroy( ). The Java development team is certain that this programming model does not fit the nonvisual, server programs in their prototype. They do recognize the value in following a consistent model but are unsure about how to proceed.

How can the architects build flexibility into the architecture up front so that they can globally introduce anticipated improvements and/or new requirements in later iterations?

As the Java platform expands, existing applications may need a way to leverage the newer components and services. The development team is interested in upcoming features such as drag-and-drop, security, or printing. They are looking for a way to ensure that new functionality can be easily inserted into all applications at any time down the road.

Within an application class hierarchy, how can derived application classes at all levels participate in flexible initialization and shutdown routines?

Constructors have a unique call-chaining feature in most object languages where base class constructors are guaranteed to be called before derived class constructors. This valuable property could prove useful at other critical states of an application's life cycle. The Java development team would like to provide that same feature at any point in their application hierarchy.

How does the development team properly segregate the different kinds of applications in the system and capture the unique information and behavior associated with each?

Java has proven to be useful in creating a wide variety of applications from client-server to publish/subscribe to mobile agents. The development team recognizes that the scheduling prototype may represent only a subset of the application architectural styles for their Java platform [Shaw-Garlan 1996]. They are looking for a way to capture the similarities and differences associated with each major type of application in the architecture.

10.1.3 Disclaimer

The patterns in this system may seem intuitive; however, the fact that they have been used to identify architecture-specific deficiencies in the Java platform serves to demonstrate their inherent value, especially for the inexperienced developer. You are free, of course, to ignore some or all of the patterns presented here and are otherwise encouraged to share your own experiences in a similar fashion. Note, too, that using this recipe does not guarantee success for your particular effort, nor is it intended to provide any shortcut for project schedules other than the time savings reaped from an approach based on pure trial and error.

10.2 The Pattern System

No single design pattern is sufficient for designing an entire application architecture—which is perhaps the realm of architectural patterns [Buschmann 1996, Shaw-Garlan 1996]. More often, many patterns will come into play during the architecture design stages and there is inherent value in understanding how these patterns are related. What is most valuable is not a loose collection of patterns but a formal system of patterns that are intended to work together to solve a set of related problems [Gamma 1995]. This chapter describes such a pattern system. The underlying context is the design and implementation of an application architecture. Each pattern in the system brings the architect further from the blank page to a coherent, flexible, and robust solution.

The Framework Recipe is a metaphor for constructing an initial application architecture. It describes the ingredients first, the seven individual patterns, and a set of instructions or guidelines for blending them to create an application framework. Similar to recipes for cooking, there are some opportunities in this system for personal creativity and improvisation. Indeed, not all of the ingredients (patterns) are required to produce a robust application architecture. Thus readers may choose to develop their own particular variations on the recipe that produces the best results for their respective business scenarios. The Framework Recipe simply provides the standard directions for obtaining what has proven to be a successful solution.[2]

10.2.1 Pattern 1: Configuration Framework

In this section, the configuration framework pattern is explained.

Problem

How do you provide a flexible and consistent program configuration mechanism that will support all phases of application development and deployment?

General Context

A project team needs an immediate solution to building configurable applications in the early stages of development and recognizes that the mechanism must be flexible enough to allow them to migrate toward more sophisticated configuration mechanisms in the future.

---

[2]The author originally wrote this chapter before Java hit the computing mainstream. As part of the first wave of evangelists, he was pleased to have further validated this system, as every pattern has been shown to be applicable in building application architectures for early adopters of the Java platform.

Specific Context

Our development team wants the ability to customize certain features of the application at runtime. They are familiar with .INI files, where key/value pairs are arranged in sections within a file, and would like to have a similar feature for their Java prototype. However, when the application is deployed, they would like to move these configuration values from the local file to an existing configuration database already in use within the company. The team requires that the transition from file-based to database-based configuration be as seamless as possible in order to reduce the need for additional coding and testing.

Forces

- Earlier iterations in development usually require much less sophisticated application configuration facilities than later iterations.

- Enterprise applications need a consistent configuration mechanism that supports applications of all sizes and that provides continued support throughout the application's stages of development.

- A configuration mechanism that grows and matures with the system should not necessarily grow in complexity.

- The applications should be insulated from both the mechanism for retrieving values and from the physical source that is ultimately used for configuration.

Solution

Create a configuration framework that separates the physical source of the configuration information from the mechanism used to access the data.

Structure

Figure 10.1 illustrates the UML diagram of the basic structure of the configuration framework.

Participants

ConfigFacility. Central manager class that provides a common interface to the underlying concrete ConfigSource.

ConfigSource. Abstract interface defining the operation that will be supported by all concrete ConfigSource implementations. Serves as the contract between the ConfigFacility and the various ConfigSource implementations.

FileConfigSource. An example concrete ConfigSource class that implements getValue() by reading from a file.

Other ConfigSources. Any other concrete implementation of the ConfigSource interface. Examples include LDAP servers, databases, and Windows Registry.

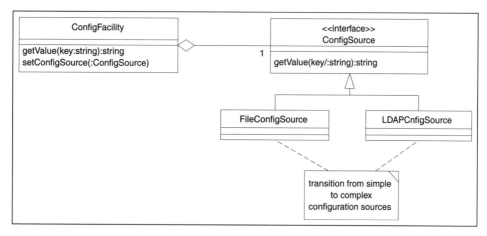

Figure 10.1   Configuration framework model.

Implementation

In its simplest form, the configuration framework requires only two cooperating classes. A very basic structure is presented in Figure 10.1, and the opportunity to enhance the model can be divided into two areas: beefing up the functionality of the ConfigFacility and enhancing the ConfigSource interface (and thus the resulting concrete classes).

With minimum effort, the ConfigFacility class can be extended to include additional accessor methods that return the various configuration values as types other than string. This may also be accomplished by using a separate wrapper class, a form of the Decorator pattern [Gamma 1995]. It might also include a method to refresh the pool of values in a more dynamic environment where configurations change frequently and where programs need to be able to react to those changes.

The ConfigSource interface certainly has room for improvement, although the simple interface shown in Figure 10.1 satisfies the general problem this pattern addresses and allows for a variety of configuration strategies. Some alternatives are to allow sets of configuration values to be treated as layered sections such that values from one set can override parent sets. This could be supported with new methods in the ConfigSource interface that support iterating over sections and keys within a section.

For our Java development team, we can create a straightforward FileConfigSource that allows them to use the familiar INI structure and then later provide another implementation that accesses the central database. Changing strategies in this case is a matter of updating the one place where the specific ConfigSource is plugged into the ConfigFacility. This is typically done once in a centralized initialization routine.

Related Patterns

In this implementation, ConfigFacility is associated with a concrete ConfigSource class at runtime. This can be considered an example of the Strategy pattern. Additionally, the ConfigFacility is typically implemented as a Singleton so that it can be accessed easily throughout the application [Gamma 1995].

10.2.2 Pattern 2: Message-Logging Framework

In this section, the message-logging framework pattern is explained.

Problem

How will multiple applications in a system employ a straightforward and consistent message-logging strategy?

General Context

Message logging is one example of a general application facility that is typically needed early on in development to help with capturing and displaying debugging and error-related output. If a formal solution is not provided in the initial phases, it becomes increasingly difficult to retrofit existing code with the common approach as the project progresses.

Specific Context

The Java development team working on the conference room scheduling application has decided that all message output should be divided into four categories: debugging, informational, warning, and fatal. They would like to redirect each of these categories to different destinations including dialogs, the shell prompt, persistent files, and databases. However, they do not want to learn multiple logging interfaces for interfacing with each of these output formats as is required with the core Java platform. They need a way to start coding immediately and worry about specific output strategies later.

Forces

- Most applications need a flexible message-logging mechanism that allows them to log messages to a variety of destinations (files, screens, dialogs, databases, and so on) using a set of standard message formats.

- All applications built on the same technology platform should share a single, common, established mechanism to avoid separate and/or conflicting message-logging implementations.

- Any formal logging mechanism should be easy to use, requiring little or no configuration.

- The mechanism should be straightforward to customize to allow for more complex logging features and functionality.

- Applications must be written such that they are insulated from the physical logging mechanism. It should be possible to describe the outbound message and its related format without directly specifying the mechanism used to deliver it.

Solution

Create a message-logging framework that separates the management and configuration of message logging from the objects that are responsible for physically logging the messages. This framework creates *logical destinations* that can be separately mapped to one or more physical destinations. The framework provides two important functions. First, it defines the operations that are used to configure logical destinations, allowing for the straightforward formatting of the outbound messages. Second, it provides a mapping strategy that connects logical categories to physical message loggers.

The framework should define two categories of classes: management object(s) and message loggers; additionally, it should describe how the objects from these two categories can be assembled or naturally extended to provide missing or advanced features.

In the first category, the logging facility is likely to be implemented as a single, central object that is used by all application objects to manage the setup and configuration of message loggers within an application. Configuration typically occurs in the application initialization routine (see Pattern 4: Common Programming Model). This Singleton object [Gamma 1995] should provide a default configuration that makes it straightforward to locate and use without any required setup.

The second category defines a class hierarchy of different message loggers, each of which can be plugged individually or in combinations into the management facility.

Structure

Figure 10.2 illustrates the UML diagram of two categories of classes that comprise the basic structure of the message-logging framework.

Participants

LogFacility

- Manages the creation and deletion of logical destinations through log categories

- Maintains the MsgLogger(s) associated with each category

- Provides level of indirection between application object and physical destination

MsgLogger. Provides straightforward interface for all concrete MsgLogger classes.

FileMsgLogger. An example concrete MsgLogger class that implements logMsg( ) by writing messages to a file.

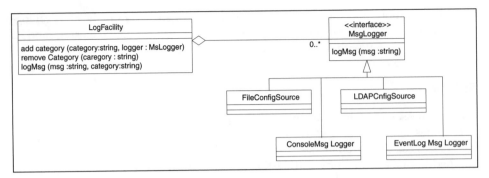

Figure 10.2 Message-logging framework model.

> **Other MsgLoggers.** Any other concrete implementation of the MsgLogger interface. Examples include standard out (screen), window status bars, and Windows NT Event Log.

Implementation

The basic operations of the LogFacility class allow the application objects to create new log categories identified by a name string and a concrete MsgLogger object, remove an existing category, and finally, log messages via those categories.

Implementation 1

Figure 10.2 shows a straightforward implementation that would maintain a single MsgLogger object per log category. Applications using this implementation would have the flexibility of changing the physical logger associated with a log category to dynamically redirect the output at runtime. An optional extension to this model allows log categories to be turned off or disabled temporarily. There are several ways to do this. One would be to create a NullMsgLogger that discards all outbound messages logged to that category, sending it to the bit bucket [Woolf 1997]. This would require reestablishing a new MsgLogger if the log category were ever to be reenabled.

Another technique would be to have a flag associated with each log category such that the connection to a MsgLogger could be maintained and reinstated very easily. Going any further down this path will likely lead to modeling the log category as a separate class.

Implementation 2

The LogFacility could be extended to allow one or more MsgLogger objects per log category. Applications using this enhanced LogFacility could have a single call to logMsg( ) result in the message being sent to many destinations.

The Java development team begins building the prototype using a simple MsgLogger implementation that writes all messages to the console. Over time, as new file-based and dialog-based MsgLogger implementations become available, they update the application in one place to plug in the new strategies without affecting the hundreds of lines of code where calls are made to logMsg( ).

Related Patterns

Like the ConfigFacility implementation, LogFacility is another example of the Strategy pattern [Gamma 1995]. In fact, the Strategy pattern and its variations provide the basic structure of many delegation-based frameworks [Pree 1996]. Additionally the LogFacility is typically implemented as a Singleton so that it can be accessed easily throughout the application [Gamma 1995].

10.2.3 Pattern 3: Application Is a Class

In this section, "an application is a class" pattern is explained.

Problem

How can an application itself be accurately represented in the various object models and benefit from the same advantages of inheritance, encapsulation, and polymorphism?

General Context

An organization is looking to design and build an overall application infrastructure that will be used to develop one or more major systems.

In the absence of third-party tools or frameworks, many organizations have a difficult time getting started with developing applications based on new technology platforms. Initial applications are often more like prototypes or modified demos and thus should not serve as the basis for later, more wide-scale development. A definite application structure is ultimately needed to introduce and ensure consistency among the different programs. Treating the application as another object in the model, however, is rarely considered during application design.

Specific Context

The development team has completed their formal Java training and with their Java reference manuals close by are comfortable with designing applets from scratch. Unfortunately, the scheduling application is not web-based and will not use applets. Instead, the application will consist of a stand-alone graphical client program and a nonvisual server program. As a result, they are somewhat confused about where to begin designing and implementing these nonapplet applications.

Forces

- Many popular object-oriented languages still use a procedure approach to implement the application. In other words, the top-level program logic lives in a static main( ) routine.

- A general, well-understood program structure provided for all applications simplifies both development and maintenance.

- Novice developers or those new to the project should not need to spend a great deal of time learning the application architecture.

- There needs to be a way to share common application logic between programs without cutting and pasting identical lines of code.

Solution

Create a single Application class or a deeper class hierarchy. If the programming language forces the program to start with a main() routine, use it to instantiate and turn control over to the Application object. All applications in the system are derived from this class, which creates opportunities for reuse and centralized facilities.

The Application class is often abstract and defines a strict interface that can be used to create implementation dependencies for all derived application classes (see Pattern 4: Common Programming Model). This increases the consistency among applications and forces them to comply with architecture standards.

Structure

Figure 10.3 shows the UML diagram of an example Application base class and how new application subclasses will be created through inheritance.

Participants

Application. Base class for all applications in the system. Used to introduce common structure through abstract interface.

NewDerivedApp. Any new application is ultimately derived from this base class.

Implementation

As stated earlier, the Application class is typically abstract. The remaining patterns in the system focus on specific ways to use and extend the Application class to create a flexible, robust application architecture.

Some may consider this pattern too trivial to include in any formal pattern system. These critics either picked up this pattern early on in their careers or have found other

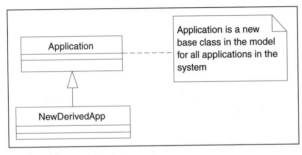

Figure 10.3 Application model.

techniques for achieving the same results. The author has had the misfortune of joining many large projects that were already in progress where the absence of a formal application class created a maintenance catastrophe. In these situations, each development team invented its own idea of what shape their application would take and, as a result, there was no consistency among the various approaches. This made introducing new services common to all applications (see Patterns 1 and 2) next to impossible and required new developers to learn the individual semantics of each group's approach. Of all the patterns in this system, this is perhaps the most critical and yet is perhaps the easiest to implement.

The Java development team determines that they require two application classes: UIApplication, which is used to build visual programs and which closely follows the Applet model, and Application, which is used for nonvisual programs. These classes are quickly adopted by the organization and placed in a common repository for use on all Java projects.

10.2.4 Pattern 4: Common Programming Model

In this section, the common programming model pattern is explained.

Problem

How do you provide and enforce a common programming model for large systems comprising tens or hundreds of applications?

General Context

Large enterprise systems desperately require a common, shared, and well-understood programming model to simplify development and ease long-term maintenance.

Specific Context

Since they have decided not to use applets, the Java development team is suddenly without any guidance on how to build both visual and nonvisual Java programs. The Applet's programming model of init( ) (called once), start( ) and stop( ) (called repeatedly over the life cycle of the applet), and destroy( ) (called once) seemed straightforward and universally accepted. With applets, it is intuitive where initialization logic and the main routine would be implemented. Would the same model work for other visual applications? What about for nonvisual applications?

Forces

- Most programming languages do not provide general program execution models.
- Developers left to their own devices will often invent and implement their own unique versions of an execution model in each program they write. These will

almost certainly differ between developers and even between programs written by the same developer.

- The programming model should be flexible to allow for many different types of applications.

- A programming model should be simple to learn and adhere to by all developers. That is, the model should be embedded in the application architecture such that each program written to work in the architecture inherently follows the same model.

Solution

Using the Application class introduced in the previous pattern (see Pattern 3: Application Is a Class), create an interface that defines the set of fundamental execution stages for any program. These stages should include, at a minimum, initialization, main body, and shutdown.

Structure

Figure 10.4 illustrates how the Application class can be used to prescribe a general programming model through the introduction of three methods.

Participants

Application. Common base class or interface for all applications with prescriptive programming model.

NewDerivedApp. All applications in the system are derived from and inherit the programming model imposed by the common base class.

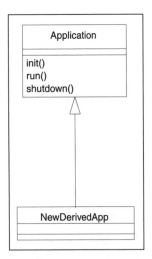

Figure 10.4 Programming model with three sequential stages.

Implementation

A common programming model immediately simplifies overall development. For example, every program written using the resulting architecture may be constructed and explained in a very generic fashion as shown in the following:

```
// Application pseudo-code leveraging common programming model
main()
    Application app = new NewDerivedApp(…)
    // the following logic is the same for any derived application!
    if ( app.init() == true ) {
        app.run()
    }
    app.shutdown()
```

Since application architectures are designed to provide the set of common or standard services for all programs, it is likely that only the initialization and shutdown logic would ever be implemented in the architecture itself. These methods may therefore provide default implementations in the base class(es) to further simplify application development. The run() method, however, which is typically used to define the main body of logic for the given program, is almost always left to the derived classes to implement.

In most object languages there are mechanisms that allow one to enforce a given strategy or model on all derived classes. For example, in C++ the use of pure virtual methods and in Java the use of (purely abstract) interfaces assist in supporting this technique. In most application architectures, the Application class will use such techniques to create a programming model that is purposely incomplete, thereby forcing derived application classes to implement the interface to create a valid program.

Armed with this pattern, the Java development team fleshes out the existing UIApplication class to use the Applet model of init(), start(), stop(), and destroy(). They also build a suitable server-side model into the Application class using init(), run(), and shutdown() methods. From that point on, their programs and all subsequently created applications built on the architecture share the same structure, reducing learning curves for new team members and simplifying the overall maintenance of the entire system.

Known Uses

As previously discussed, the Java Applet class uses this pattern in describing a model for all applets. The init(), start(), stop(), and destroy() methods create a common programming model for each class derived from the common java.applet.Applet base class.

Related Patterns

This pattern is tightly coupled with Pattern 3: Application Is a Class since the programming model is usually implemented as abstract methods in the common Application base class. The pattern describes a basic structure that can be expanded in powerful ways using other patterns like Pattern 6: Initialization Chains.

10.2.5 Pattern 5: Placeholder

In this section, the placeholder pattern is explained.

Problem

How do the architects build flexibility into the application architecture so that they can globally introduce anticipated improvements and/or new requirements in later iterations?

General Context

A project team is in the early iterations of developing the application technical architecture. The team has enough experience to recognize the need for ensuring flexibility in the unfolding design.

Specific Context

There are a number of features the Java development team expects to add to the scheduling application in the future. Some of these will likely benefit other applications that will be built in the future. The team is looking for a way to simplify the addition of these features without upsetting the overall architecture.

Forces

- Later iterations typically reveal new requirements.
- The ease of introducing new changes or features into an architecture is inversely proportional to the number of applications already implemented and/or deployed using the architecture.
- Future enhancements or modifications to the architecture should impact as few programs as possible. In other words, the architecture should incorporate release valves that prevent project combustion when the inevitable strikes.

Solution

In one of the early iterations of the architecture design, insert a placeholder class high up in the application class hierarchy that can be utilized in subsequent iterations to plug in additional functionality.

It should be noted that this solution conflicts with a well-known tenet of software design, the Open Closed Principle [Martin 1996]. The Open Closed Principle offers that good designs are generally open to extension (through inheritance, for example) and closed to modification. Since the Placeholder class introduced in this pattern is explicitly intended to be a centralized place for introducing changes to all applications in later design iterations, it might be considered harmful. The author would argue that the Placeholder solution is certainly preferred over the alternatives that have been shown to occur quite frequently on large projects. These include (1) introducing changes by force-fitting new classes in the middle of an existing application hierarchy, (2) having to repeat the same change in multiple places because there is no central place from which all applications derive, and (3) avoiding the introduction of a change at all because of the complications hinted at in the previous scenarios.

Structure

Figure 10.5 illustrates the definition and correct position of the Placeholder class in the application hierarchy.

Participants

Application. Base class for all applications in the system.

CommonApplication. The Placeholder where new functionality will be placed when necessary.

NewDerivedApp. All concrete applications are derived from CommonApplication and thus automatically inherit the new attributes and behaviors introduced there.

Implementation

The addition of a CommonApplication class in the application hierarchy provides the appropriate place to expand the architecture in ways that benefit all applications. This class should not be considered a dumping ground where miscellaneous behavior is

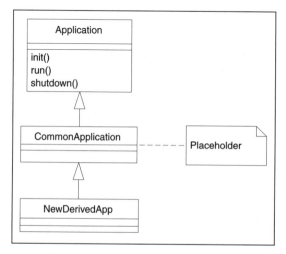

Figure 10.5   Placeholder model.

introduced simply because it is convenient. The development team should take great care in evaluating the functionality that is initially placed here as well as the ongoing additions that affect the entire architecture.

The following list includes some typical examples of globally applicable requirements that may benefit all applications but that tend to be introduced late in the development process. These can be easily incorporated into the CommonApplication class, which justifies its place in this pattern system.

Application access control. Simple or straightforward security checks such as "Can this user start this version of the application on this machine at this time?"

Verifying licensing keys. "Is the licensing agreement for this application still valid?"

Welcome banners. Fancy start-up images or greetings that precede or follow the normal execution of the application. Such information might relay the correct version, author, and copyright information about the application or provide channels for user feedback.

Application registration. Distributed applications may need to register with a central naming service to announce their arrival. Publisher and subscriber applications might share similar logic to register with an event broker to begin their respective processing.

Execution strategy selection. Applications may be constructed such that they can run with one of several execution strategies that would be defined and selected within a common application base class. Example strategies might include starting in recovery mode or debug mode versus normal mode.

Transport selection. Distributed applications can be built to rely on one of several underlying transport implementations. Selection of the appropriate transport (database, sockets, CORBA, and so on) would be performed in the common application base class.

Application coordination. Threaded applications need a common place to share and respond to error or exception information. The CommonApplication class provides that common and convenient location to coordinate these activities.

Like other patterns in this system, this particular solution may not be considered altogether revolutionary. The real power of this and the related patterns, however, is the enormous savings they provide in the design and implementation stages. These patterns create distinct points or hooks in the resulting architecture where changes can and should be made to incorporate new or changing functionality. It thus becomes very clear and obvious where changes must be made to incorporate new requirements or features. These hooks are as valuable to the overall system as the business rules and domain model. They warrant the use of these patterns and encourage us to look for other, similar structures and designs.

The Java development team reverts the UIApplication and Application classes to pure interfaces and adds Placeholder classes to both class hierarchies called CommonFrame (derives from java.awt.Frame) and CommonApplication, respectively. These new classes implement their respective application interfaces and delegate shared behavior to a third-party implementation class to further simplify global changes in the future.

Related Patterns

Placeholder is not a substitute for Application Is a Class and the preceding Structure section shows their relationship. Placeholder nestles in between the root Application base class and paves the way for upcoming patterns in this system, including Pattern 6: Initialization Chains.

10.2.6 Pattern 6: Initialization Chains

In this section, the initialization chains pattern is explained.

Problem

Within an application class hierarchy, how can derived application classes at all levels participate in the initialization and shutdown behavior?

General Context

A development project has implemented some or all of the patterns in this system and is looking for mechanisms to enhance the flexibility of the resulting application architecture.

Specific Context

Now that the visual and nonvisual programming models have been incorporated, the Java development team wants to leverage the functionality that is typically reserved only for constructors where derived classes participate in method call chains that span the entire class hierarchy. Specifically, the initialization routine that is called after construction is an ideal place to insert class-specific configuration logic such that every class in the hierarchy gets a chance to participate in a call in a predictable, orderly fashion. It is not clear to the inexperienced team how to set up such a chaining structure to implement this type of behavior.

Forces

- While a majority of the initialization and shutdown logic can be handled by the one or more levels of application base classes, there will be cases where the most derived application classes will need to perform additional logic exclusively at their own level.

- The need to perform custom initialization or shutdown logic should be optional. More generally, any such enhancement to an architecture should not create additional programming burdens for the application developer.

- The mechanism for introducing such flexibility should work within rather than alter or upset the overall application architecture.

Solution

Use a template method [Gamma 1995] along with well-structured hook method logic [Pree 1996] to create specific initialization and/or shutdown call chains that provide flexibility in the application architecture. The introduction of new virtual (template) methods in a common base class, for example, must be accompanied by and supported by rigid programming practices in the hook methods to achieve and maintain a consistent model (see *Implementation*).

Structure

Figure 10.6 illustrates the basic structure of the initialization chain. The exact technique could also be used to create a shutdown chain.

Participants

Application. Base interface for all applications in the system. Defines common programming model including initialization and shutdown methods.

CommonApplication

- A common base class where the initialization chains naturally fit.
- init( ) method becomes template method.
- Default implementations of the pre- and posthook methods are provided here as well.

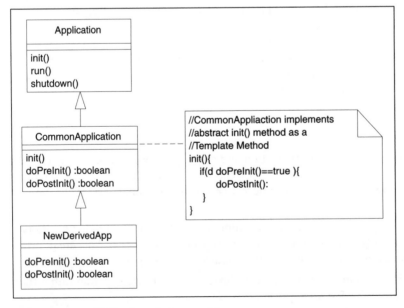

Figure 10.6   Initialization chains model.

NewDerivedApp. All concrete applications are derived from CommonApplication and override either or both of the optional chaining methods to perform local initialization logic.

Implementation

As stated in the Solution section, Initialization Chains requires more than the mere introduction of a template method and supporting pre- and posthook methods. There needs to be a rigid set of programming practices to create the chaining effect, where each class in the application hierarchy can participate in the initialization and shutdown logic flow.

The UML diagram in Figure 10.7 shows how derived application classes take special care to wrap local logic inside of calls to corresponding parent class methods in the order to achieve the chaining. This practice, if followed consistently, provides a flexible and scalable solution, where any class may safely participate in the standard programming model.

After a brief tutorial on how to establish and continue the chain logic outlined in this solution, the Java development team identifies appropriate classes in the application hierarchy to insert class-specific initialization logic. They use the doPreInit( ) method in

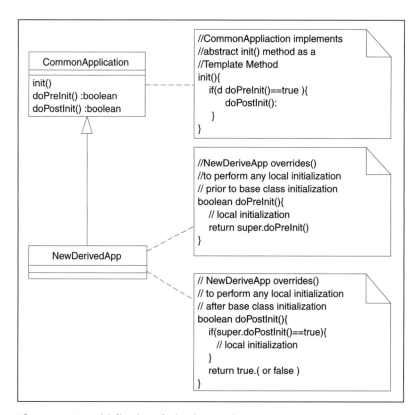

Figure 10.7 Initialization chains in practice.

a derived class to prime Java's system Properties object such that the base class can find suitable values for its configuration (using a PropertiesConfigSource in the Config-Facility framework). Similarly, the team uses the doPostInit( ) method in a derived class to register its server object(s) with the Object Request Broker (ORB) after the ORB has been initialized in the base class.

Related Patterns

As shown in the Implementation section, this pattern naturally fits within the CommonApplication class that implements the Placeholder pattern. The init( ) method in this pattern is an example of a template method; the doPreInit( ) and doPostInit( ) methods are hook methods. The use of template and hook methods is a common inheritance-based approach for building frameworks [Gamma 1995; Pree 1996].

10.2.7 Pattern 7: Application Types

In this section, the application types pattern is explained.

Problem

How does a development team properly segregate the different kinds of applications in the system and capture the unique information and behavior associated with each?

General Context

Client-server, event-based (that is, publish/subscribe), and other computing paradigms can create different categories of applications in the resulting systems. These differences are usually great enough to warrant distinction in the architectural models and in the application implementation.

Specific Context

The Java development team has suggested that its server program be generalized to simplify the development of other, similar applications. However, another unrelated project team is planning to build a batch-style program on the same architecture and doesn't see how a generalized server-specific architecture would assist them in their efforts. The architecture team is looking for a good way to segregate the various types of applications that will be built on the emerging infrastructure.

Forces

- Applications in a given system tend to conform to one of several basic types. These types can be interrelated as in client and server, publisher and subscriber; or unrelated as in batch versus On-Line Transaction Processing (OLTP), background daemon versus graphical user interface window.

- Applications that operate on different tiers typically take on different structures and exhibit distinct behaviors.

- Different application models will require different sets of supporting functionality from the application architecture.

- Development teams should be able to quickly learn and identify the different classifications of applications in the system being built.

Solution

Create one or more levels of application subclasses to capture the attributes and behavior associated with each type of program in the system. For example, in a three-tier model, a project might define a ClientApplication that runs on the desktop and a ServerApplication that lives at the middle or third tier. Certainly these classes will share some common behavior such as configuration and message logging, but their underlying architectures will be fundamentally different. Yet it is clear that any and all functionality that is relevant to client applications will be placed in the ClientApplication common base class and corresponding server behavior in the ServerApplication. This obvious separation and subsequent placement of functionality illustrates the true power of this pattern.

Structure

Figure 10.8 illustrates one example of Application partitioning via specific subclassing.

Participants

Application. Common base class for all applications.

ProducerApp. Captures all functionality common to producer applications in a publish/subscribe architecture.

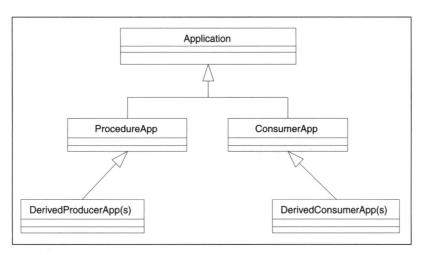

Figure 10.8   Application types model.

ConsumerApp. Captures all functionality common to consumer applications in a publish/subscribe architecture.

DerivedProducerApp(s)/DerivedConsumerApp(s). Remaining applications in the system are derived from one of two common base classes.

Implementation

It is beyond the scope of this pattern to describe all the potential implementation scenarios since the implementation of each level of base classes depends entirely on the proposed application architecture. For example, a system that intends to utilize both batch and OLTP processing would certainly create two corresponding subclasses. Because batch programs do not typically rely on direct user input, the BatchApplication subclass would have very little in common with the OLTP subclass that might require a graphical user interface model. It is often surprising how a simple decision such as this can lead to elegant designs and extendible, maintainable systems.

The Java development team proceeds with producing a ServerApplication class that suits their immediate needs and that is also useful for other teams building similar applications. The architects, prompted by other development efforts, create a BatchApplication sibling class to make an explicit distinction between the two application types.

Known Uses

This pattern is so common that good architects rarely even acknowledge it. It is likely to have been used (knowingly or unknowingly) in any large, successfully implemented system. Certainly the current Interactive Development Environments (IDEs) employ this pattern upon creation of a new program. The user/developer using these tools is typically faced with a dialog in the early stages of defining the project about whether he or she wants to create an application, applet, menu application, standalone application, library, component, and so on.

Related Patterns

The Application Types pattern works very well with the Application Is a Class pattern described earlier in this system, since each level of application subclasses ultimately derives from a common base class. It also works with the Placeholder pattern.

10.2.8 The Framework Recipe

In this section, the framework recipe is explained.

Problem

How does an architect apply the patterns in this system to create an application framework?

Context

An architect or architecture team is planning on using some or all of the patterns in this system to create an application architecture from scratch for some new technology.

Forces

- Most recipes include diagrams or pictures of the finished product, which prove to be extremely valuable for the novice or first-time user.

- Optional ingredients or procedures—ones that can be safely omitted—should be clearly marked or indicated.

- Recipes must have directions that are simple to follow. They should have a clear starting point and one or more clearly defined ending points. Recipes should also identify potential variations on the process where they exist.

- Recipes often identify tasks that can be performed in parallel. Any opportunity for parallel development during implementation should be highlighted and discussed.

Solution

The architecture team should implement the framework patterns in the exact order in which they are presented here. The system is arranged such that dependencies from any given pattern are only on previously implemented components. The first two patterns in the system describe the *optional* components of the application framework, while the remaining patterns specify how to construct a robust application hierarchy to support large-scale development. The following Implementation section provides a detailed set of directions for the entire process.

Picture (Structure)

Many of the diagrams presented in the system showed multiple patterns working together. Figure 10.9 illustrates the complete framework model that incorporates all the components. Note the clear indication of optional framework components as well as the points in the application hierarchy where subsequent application development begins. Additional detail is provided in the Implementation section that follows.

Ingredients (Participants)

- Configuration Framework pattern
- Message-Logging Framework pattern
- Application Is a Class pattern
- Common Programming Model pattern
- Placeholder pattern

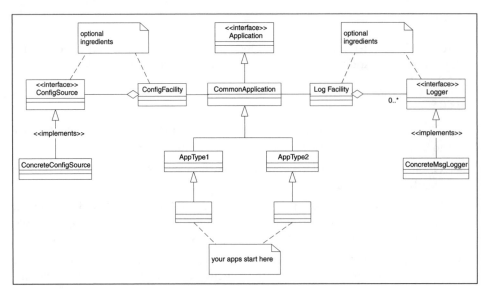

Figure 10.9 Application framework model.

- Initialization Chains pattern
- Application Types pattern

Steps (Implementation)

If the patterns presented in this system represent the ingredients, then the following set of steps form the directions for the Framework Recipe.

Step 1

Begin by building the optional configuration and message-logging frameworks, which can be implemented and tested independently of the application hierarchy in the framework. Since there are no interdependencies between these two components, these efforts are able to proceed in parallel. Each resulting framework can be set aside and will be folded into the application hierarchy in a later step. Figure 10.10 shows the UML diagram of the current state of the architecture after this step.

Step 2

Combine the patterns Application Is a Class and Common Programming Model into a new abstract class or interface. The result is the single common base class for all applications in the system. This base class is completely generic and reusable across projects. Figure 10.11 shows the UML diagram of the current state of the application hierarchy in the framework after this step. The remaining steps in this recipe build upon this.

Step 3

Create the Placeholder class and add it into the application hierarchy by having it implement the Application interface. Once this class is in place, the team can imple-

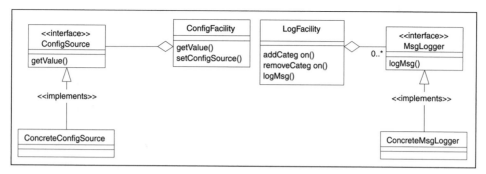

Figure 10.10   Step 1 of the recipe.

ment the Initialization Chains pattern to create powerful initialization and shutdown procedures. Figure 10.12 shows the UML diagram of the current state of the application hierarchy in the framework after this step.

Step 4

This optional step is where the configuration and message-logging frameworks built in the first step can be added to the framework batter via the Placeholder class. Either or both frameworks can be included, to taste. Figure 10.13 shows the UML diagram of the current state of the application hierarchy in the framework after this step.

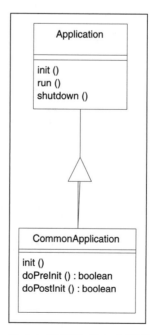

Figure 10.11   Step 2 of the recipe.   **Figure 10.12**   Step 3 of the recipe.

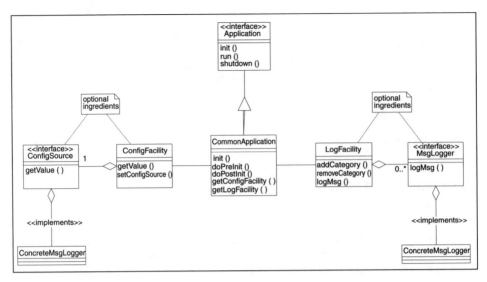

Figure 10.13   Step 4 of the recipe.

Step 5

Where it is necessary, the last step in this recipe explains how new derived application classes can be added to the framework to represent the different application types in the system. This step may take time to fully implement as a system. It is often delivered in increments and the full set of required application classes might not be known up front. This is the last step in this version of the recipe. The resulting framework should be sufficient to begin large-scale application development. Figure 10.14 shows the UML diagram of the current state of the application hierarchy in the framework after this step.

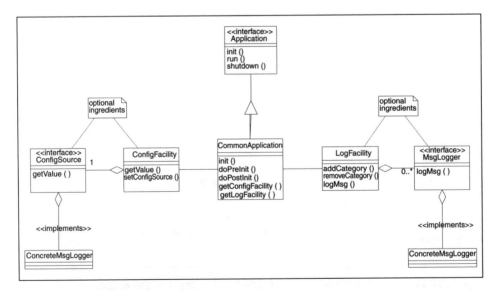

Figure 10.14   Step 5 of the recipe.

Known Uses

There are at least four application frameworks implemented in C++ and Java that incorporate each of these and other framework patterns. Athens Architectural Components, a set of packages for building robust Java application frameworks, is one implementation that is available from ISA Services, Inc. Athens expands on the patterns presented here and offers a much more complete implementation of the overall application framework. More information is available from ISA Services at info@isaserv.com.

Related Patterns

Each of the participants or ingredients in this recipe is presented as individual patterns in this system.

10.3 Summary

This chapter introduces a system of seven patterns that apply to the design and development of application architectures. A pattern system refers to a collection of related patterns that naturally fit together to accomplish a larger goal. Although the patterns in such a system can be, and often are, used independently (for example, Configuration Framework or Message-Logging Framework), the intentional grouping indicates that the patterns provide a much more robust solution when combined. For this system, that assumption holds true. The use of the recipe metaphor here represents an attempt to better organize the material and make the application of these patterns more straightforward. It is expected that the structure and order suggested by the Framework Recipe will help to simplify expansion of this system as it grows to include other application framework patterns.

The resulting application framework that is created by implementing these patterns is intended to help software development teams better prepare for the adoption of new technologies that will ultimately be used to support an organization's business. Along with these patterns, the author encourages the use of formal analysis and design methods, coupled with a defined and repeatable process to ensure success. In addition, the seven patterns here represent a small percentage of the available resources on this subject.

10.4 References

[Buschmann 1996] Buschmann, F., R. Meunier, H. Rohnert, and M. Stal. *Pattern Oriented Software Architecture: A System of Patterns*. New York: John Wiley & Sons, 1996.

[Fayad-Laitinen 1998] Fayad, M.E., and M. Laitinen. *Transition to Object-Oriented Software Development*. New York: John Wiley & Sons, 1998.

[Gamma 1995] Gamma, E., R. Help, R. Johnson, and J. Vlissides. *Design Patterns: Elements of Reusable Object-Oriented Software*. Reading, MA: Addison-Wesley, 1995.

[Martin 1996] Martin, R. The Open Closed Principle. *C++ Report,* January 1996.

[Pree 1996] Pree, W. *Framework Patterns*. (SIGS Management Briefing Series). New York: SIGS Books and Multimedia, 1996.

[Roberts-Johnson 1997] Roberts, D., and R. Johnson. Evolving frameworks: A pattern language for developing object-oriented frameworks. In *Pattern Languages of Program Design 3*. (Software Patterns Series). Reading, MA: Addison-Wesley, 1997.

[Shaw-Garlan 1996] Shaw, M., and D. Garlan. *Software Architecture—Perspectives on an Emerging Discipline*. Upper Saddle River, NJ: Prentice Hall, 1996.

[Woolf 1997] Woolf, B. Null object. In *Pattern Languages of Program Design 3*. (Software Patterns Series). Reading, MA: Addison-Wesley, 1997.

10.5 Review Questions

1. What is design pattern?

2. What is application architecture?

3. Would you name similar patterns to the following patterns:
   - Message-Logging Framework
   - Common Programming Model
   - Initialization Chains

4. Define briefly the problem, the solution, and the consequences of the following patterns:
   - Configuration Framework
   - Message-Logging Framework
   - Common Programming Model
   - Placeholder

10.6 Problem Set

1. Implement the following patterns:
   - Configuration Framework
   - Message-Logging Framework
   - Common Programming Model
   - Placeholder

2. Share with your class your experiences of implementing the preceding four patterns.

3. Create behavior models using state-transition diagrams (STDs) for three of the patterns in this chapter.

4. Use object-interaction diagrams to model how the participants communicate for any of the patterns in this chapter.

CHAPTER 11

Capturing Hypermedia Functionality

Hypermedia technology has been growing fast in some areas such as distributed repositories (like, for example, the World Wide Web) and collaborative work [Balasubramanian-Turoff 1994]. Furthermore, hypermedia features are being recognized as helpful and necessary, even though the user may not be fully aware of their presence [Bieber 1995]. For example, help systems in commercial applications, such as Microsoft's Windows standard Help System, give the user the chance of exploring an information base, while Microcosm [Davis 1992] allows the definition of links between different third-party applications. Key features that characterize hypermedia applications are forward and backward navigation, annotation, map browsing, history maintenance, access structures to a navigational subspace as indexes or guided tours, context-sensitive access, bookmark facilities, and so on [Bieber 1995]. The inclusion of these characteristics in information systems has been called the *hypermedia functionality approach* [Oinas-Kukkonen 1995].

As pointed out in [Bieber 1995]: "What benefit do users gain from hypertext support in computational applications? Managing the myriad of interrelationships in a computational application's knowledge (data and calculated information) is difficult for a user. . . . Augmenting an application with hypertext support results in new ways to view and manage the application's knowledge, by navigating among items of interest and annotating them with comments and relationships (links)."

The hypertext paradigm has become popular since the emergence of the WWW, and many people expect that web viewers will host most of the cooperative applications in the near future (even those running in an intranet) [Yourdon 1996]. However, adding hypertext features to computational applications is not so easy. Development environments for web information systems do not encourage the construction of navigational structures, as they treat navigation as just another application behavior; furthermore, current object-oriented software design methods do not take into account the navigational dimension of this type of applications.

This chapter reports our experience while building an application framework that provides a substrate for extending software systems with hypertext capabilities. Our work is focused on enhancing object-oriented information systems, improving the access to their information resources by adding a navigational front end, and seamlessly integrating this navigation functionality with the proper application's computations. We were interested in retrofitting existing object-oriented applications in a transparent way, or at least requiring only minor modifications to their base classes. As an additional result, we wanted to improve a systematic design method for building applications that combine the outstanding features of the hypertext paradigm with other types of software behavior.

An OO framework named OO-Navigator has been developed for this purpose. It models the hypermedia functionality concepts in components that are interleaved between an application's objects and their interface. This conforms to a three-layered architecture where the layers are application, hypermedia, and interface. The resulting interface is then enhanced with anchoring facilities, navigation, annotation, history maintenance, and other features that we have already mentioned.

The structure of this chapter is as follows: We start off our work with an example; next, we outline the framework's architecture and give some details about the process of building applications using our framework; we then present the framework's design in terms of a set of design patterns that generate its architecture; finally, we discuss some further work with the framework.

11.1 An Example

Hypertext has proved to be useful to enhance Computer-Aided Software Engineering (CASE) environments [Cybulski 1992]. Usual facilities in these information systems, such as graphic editors customized to a given methodology, code generators, or consistency checkers, can be empowered by allowing the designer to create meaningful relations among design artifacts that can be navigated later. For example, we can select a hotword in the specification and navigate to an analysis document related to that requirement; we can link code back to design documents or forward to test cases; we can build guided tours with selected documents, thus allowing the designer to show managers how business rules were mapped to running examples. Many of these relationships may be directly derived from the corresponding methodology metamodel (see later discussion), while others may be built opportunistically by the CASE user.

We have extended a CASE tool supporting Jacobson's OOSE methodology [Jacobson 1992] with hypermedia and animation facilities using OO-Navigator [Alvarez 1995]. In Figure 11.1 we show a subset of the tool's design model (which follows closely the OOSE metamodel); for the sake of simplicity, we have omitted classes representing browsers and editors and we have considered only the use case and analysis model. The user of this CASE tool will instantiate the classes in Figure 11.1 while developing a project.

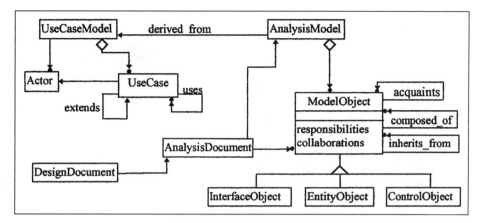

Figure 11.1   The CASE tool design model.

We improved the CASE functionality by allowing its users to create links among documents, annotate a design document with their comments, define collections of documents that may be traversed sequentially, and so on.

In this example, we can see why it is difficult to combine the specific application's behavior with navigation facilities without polluting the object model. Although the CASE designer could define new collaborations among its classes to support navigation, some relationships would be difficult to predict, such as those defined opportunistically by the CASE user. Another possibility might have been improving the interface, giving it a hypertext flavor; however, if the interface is task-oriented we would end up linking tools instead of design artifacts and it is not clear what the meaning of a link between two browsers is, how we would keep each browser's state, and so on.

In both cases we would find ourselves struggling to implement forward and backward navigation mixed with the CASE functionality due to the fact that we would be dealing with different concerns. Moreover, the hypertext functionality would not be reusable and we would have to implement it again for each application that needed it. We decided to decouple hypertext functionality and implement it as part of an application framework providing classes that implement navigation, history management, and so on.

We next present an overview of the architecture underlying OO-Navigator.

11.2 The OO-Navigator Architecture

The architecture of an application using OO-Navigator contains three main components: the object model, the hypermedia view, and the interface. The object model comprises the application objects, the hypermedia view is implemented by framework classes, and the interface level may display either application objects enriched with hypertext-aware widgets or the interface of framework objects.

In Figure 11.2 we can see a simplified sketch of the kind of object interactions that we will find in an application using the framework. For each object that we intend to

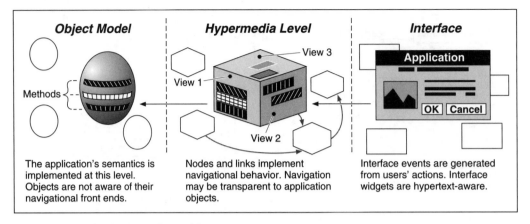

Object Model

Methods

The application's semantics is implemented at this level. Objects are not aware of their navigational front ends.

Hypermedia Level

View 3

View 1

View 2

Nodes and links implement navigational behavior. Navigation may be transparent to application objects.

Interface

Application

OK Cancel

Interface events are generated from users' actions. Interface widgets are hypertext-aware.

Figure 11.2 The framework's architecture.

explore with a hypertext-like style, we may associate one or more nodes. Each node in turn may have different views, one for each possible user profile or need (we can see a node as a prism, such that each face shows a particular view—see Figure 11.3). As we will explain later in this chapter, nodes act as objects' observers allowing perception of some of the objects' attributes and providing access to some of their methods.

For each relationship in the object model that we pretend to navigate, we will create links connecting the corresponding nodes. We may also define indexes and other access structures [Garzotto 1993], providing access to related nodes. Nodes, links, and indexes are created by instantiating corresponding classes in the framework; once instantiated, these objects represent the navigational front end of our application, allowing both navigation across objects and the ability to trigger the underlying application behavior.

For each node view we will create one or more interface objects. These objects implement interface controls that will allow either the activation of link anchors in the node

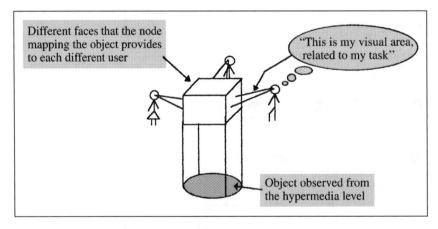

Different faces that the node mapping the object provides to each different user

"This is my visual area, related to my task"

Object observed from the hypermedia level

Figure 11.3 Node views over an object.

or the triggering of methods in one or more objects associated with that node. When an application object already has a user interface, we may wrap it with a special type of node that will intercept users' actions and delegate them accordingly.

Once an application with this architecture begins, its behavior is mainly interface-driven. There will be some interface objects that, depending on the application style, will be either simple node interfaces, the representation of an index, or even complex browsers. When the user generates an interface event—for example, pressing a button or selecting a menu option—some node will receive a message that, in turn, will require sending another one either to the associated object or to another hypermedia object (a link, for example). Each time a link is traversed, a new interface object is opened (the one corresponding to the node at the end of the link).

By decoupling the three layers in the application's architecture, we achieve a high degree of modularity. In this way, classes in the framework can evolve independently of any application and we can add new hypermedia components to existing applications without affecting their structure.

11.3 Using the Framework

The instantiation of OO-Navigator consists of several steps, involving both hypermedia and interface components.

Designing a good-quality hyperdocument, either as a stand-alone application or as part of a more complex system (as it happens when using OO-Navigator), is not an easy task. There are many design issues to be considered regarding the navigational and interface structures [Nielsen 1995]. We use the Object-Oriented Hypermedia Design Method (OOHDM) [Schwabe 1996] as the underlying methodology for instantiating the framework. For the sake of conciseness, we will only discuss which steps should be followed to create a running application using OO-Navigator; design and methodological guidelines can be found in [Schwabe 1996].

11.3.1 Creation of Hypermedia Components

In order to extend an object-oriented application with hypermedia components, we need to create different objects from classes provided by the framework:

- A hypermedia object that stands for the network of nodes connected by links and keeps track of the navigation history

- User profiles for each different actor in the system for which a particular interface will be provided

- Node classes as sets of similar nodes and unclassified nodes

- Node views for each user profile and each view's representations or interfaces

- Link classes as sets of similar links and unclassified links

- Access structures such as indexes and guided tours

As we show in this chapter, OO-Navigator comprises a set of classes allowing the creation of the aforementioned hypermedia components, plus the collaboration model among hypermedia objects and application ones. We next refine the activities in defining each component.

Create an Instance of the Class Hypermedia

This object is responsible for maintaining the graph of nodes and links and for building dynamic navigation histories.

Define a Point of View for Each Different User Profile and the Transitions Permitted between Points of View

Definitions of user profiles may be based on the same idea of *actors* as in the OOSE methodology (Jacobson et al. 1992). The CASE tool may, for example, have a view for the client and each different developer role: analyst, designer, programmer, tester. Permitted transitions may be defined accordingly, when the same user may play different roles.

Define Node Classes and Unclassified Nodes

A *node class* defines common properties of a group of nodes that contain the same attributes, look alike, and are related to other nodes in the same way. When extending an OO application, node classes are derived from application classes that are chosen to participate in the hypermedia web. This is to say that application classes, instances of which will be provided with a navigational interface, are mapped to node classes. When a node class is defined in this way, nodes are automatically created for each instance of that application class. This type of node stands for navigational views of an application's objects; moreover, they are *observers* of those objects.

The concept of a node class is implemented by the class NodeClass. NodeClass is further specialized into AtomicNodeClass and CompositeNodeClass. Instances of AtomicNodeClass are derived from one or a few strongly associated application classes, while instances of CompositeNodeClass derive from a composition hierarchy of classes. For example, both application classes UseCase and Actor may derive in one instance of AtomicNodeClass. This means that the same node interface will display an instance of UseCase together with the corresponding actor that interacts with that Use-Case. On the other hand, the application class UseCaseModel that aggregates UseCase should be derived from an instance of CompositeNodeClass. In this way the navigational interface of a UseCaseModel will automatically provide an access structure to its parts, the UseCases. A complete list of node classes for our example can be found in the appendix to this chapter.

It is not only possible to derive nodes from an application's objects, we can also define *unclassified nodes*, those that appear at the hypermedia level, to enhance the hypermedia functionality.

Figure 11.7, later in this chapter, shows the complete hierarchy of nodes defined in the OO-Navigator framework. ObjectNodes are those instantiated automatically by node classes, but the user may also define the following:

HyperNodes, to add information related to the hypermedia view as presentation information, as multimedia data, or to provide access points (for example, CASE tool presentation page, help information nodes).

CollectionNodes, grouping nodes by way of different strategies, organizing the navigation space in a meaningful way (for example, *collaboration* nodes, grouping nodes that represent interacting objects in the model of the application being designed with the CASE tool; *analysis documents* nodes; *pattern x* nodes, relating nodes that represent objects in a certain design pattern).

Navigators, to add navigation capabilities to graphical interfaces already provided by the application (for example, a *class browser* node, providing anchors over the programmer's class browser; a *method browser* node).

Specify Node Views for Each User Profile and Representations for Each Node View

The concept of a node view allows a node to show a different subset of its attributes and of its anchors for links, depending on the reader. This is also known as a *context-sensitive interface,* which is frequently utilized in learning systems. OO-Navigator implements this concept with the class NodeView, which models the face that a node will show for a particular point of view (see Figure 11.3).

It is in this activity that the contents of nodes are defined. During this activity, it is necessary to associate every aspect of the object that returns data or performs some action with a *slot* in a NodeView. The node will use that aspect as a message to the object whenever it needs to get or set the information or delegate actions that the node does not understand as the activation of a link.

Moreover, different *representations* can be defined inside each NodeView in order to change the appearance or the media of the same piece of information. This means that each NodeView defines the set of data to be displayed under a given point of view, and each representation inside the view will define how to display that data.

Define Link Classes and Unclassified Links

Links represent the association between two or more nodes. They activate navigation through their origin anchors contained in a node's interfaces. Instances of the class LinkClass allow the automatic creation of all links departing from each node of a Node-Class. LinkClasses are derived from relationships in the underlying application model.

An instance of LinkClass is configured with its origin NodeClass, destination (another NodeClass, or a particular node), cardinality of the destination (single or multiple), the way the destination is obtained (statically defined, computed dynamically, or created on a link's activation), and, optionally, a meaning (a name for the link) and a block of postconditions to be executed at link activation. An example of a link post-condition is to start an animation in the destination node. A LinkClass defined in this way automatically creates instances of ClassifiedLink, a subclass of Link, between the correspondent origin and destination. It is worth noting that the origin of a link is fixed at initialization time, but the destination may be defined to be computed, as what will occur at each link activation.

Some LinkClasses in our example would be: Uses-LC, between the node class UseCase-NC and itself, with multiple cardinality of the destination, and computed dynamically to the UseCases used by the original one, and Implementation-LC, between the node class DesignDocument-NC and the navigator node Class Browser. A complete listing of link classes can be found in the appendix to this chapter.

A link may also be derived from an associative object; in this case it will contain a reference to that object, from which it can also extract its name and postconditions. Links derived from associative objects are called ObjectLinks (see Figure 11.6).

Unclassified links are the counterpart of unclassified nodes and are created without being derived from relations in the application. These are instances of the class UnclassifiedLink and are configured by the origin and destination nodes, meaning, and postconditions. They are used to connect single nodes in an opportunistic way.

Figure 11.4 shows a simplified picture of the hypermedia model for the CASE tool. We use the OOHDM notation of [Schwabe 1996], in which rectangles are Nodes or NodeClasses and arrows represent Links. CompositeNodeClasses are represented by divided rectangles, where the CompositeNodeClass is shown above the dotted line and parts are shown below. Indexes are not drawn, but by default they automatically appear each time a 1:*N* cardinality link is activated, allowing the desired destination to be selected.

Define Access Structures

Hypermedia applications usually provide indexes and guided tours. Indexes provide direct access to a group of topics, and guided tours are used by hypermedia authors to help the reader in learning a topic. The framework provides both possibilities by the classes Index and GuidedTour, in the AccessStructure hierarchy. A

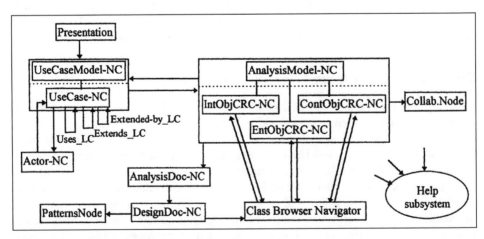

Figure 11.4 Hypermedia model for our CASE tool.

CollectionNode must be created first, defining the set of nodes to be accessed. Then, the desired access structure is created over the collection, thus allowing multiple ways of accessing the same collection.

11.3.2 Interface Design

The user interface for each node must be defined. More precisely, as each node may have many representations, each of them must be implemented. We extended the Visual-Works canvas with hypermedia-aware widgets to define the nodes' interfaces. Anchors for the activation of links may be defined in separate buttons or as hotwords inside the widgets' content.

Finally, it is worth saying that a visual tool was constructed to help during the whole framework instantiation process. Consequently, the user does not need to write any code except for filters and postconditions blocks, which, so far, have to be written using Smalltalk syntax. We derived the whole hypertext view for the CASE tool by using this visual tool.

11.4 Describing the Architecture with Patterns

While designing the framework, we used several well-known design patterns that shaped our main architectural decisions concerning the relationships among application and framework components. We next discuss the most outstanding ones: Observer, Composite, Typed Object, and Decorator. Variations to the Strategy and Observer patterns for the hypermedia domain were also discovered while constructing the framework. They can be found in [Rossi 1996].

11.4.1 Design of the Relationships among Objects, Nodes, and Interfaces: The Observer Pattern

This section describes the design of relationships among objects, nodes, and interfaces using observer pattern [Gamma 1995]. The observer pattern is discussed as a problem-solution pair, accompanied by the context of usage. Discussion of consequences of using this pattern and related patterns are included.

Context of Usage

OO-Navigator aims at retrofitting existing applications, enhancing them with hypermedia functionality, and integrating navigation with their behavior. Nodes are considered as intermediate interfaces to objects; they add anchors for links to provide a way to explore objects' relationships. Nodes may have different views and each view may have different interfaces (representations).

Problem

How do we map data and behavior encapsulated in objects of the application to hypermedia components and ensure that they remain consistent with each other?

Many factors need to be considered with this problem:

- Nodes need to be updated each time the associated object changes. In the same way, graphical interfaces for nodes need to be updated each time the node changes.

- Links need to be created and deleted with the creation or deletion of relationships between objects, to maintain links consistent with underlying relationships.

- Objects of the underlying application should not be aware of nodes; in this way the application may still be used without hypermedia functionality or it may be extended and maintained separately.

- Similarly, nodes should not care about their interfaces.

- Finally, nodes that do not map an application's objects and links that are not derived from the objects' relationships may also be defined.

Solution

We use the Observer pattern [Gamma 1995], outlined in the following considerations.

The last factor in the preceding list indicates that we should define different subclasses of Node to represent those that observe an application's objects and those that do not; they are called ObjectNode and HyperNode, respectively. In the same way, links mapping relations of the underlying model are instances of ClassifiedLink, and links added by hand in the hypermedia level are instances of UnclassifiedLink, both of which are subclasses of Link.

ObjectNodes are aggregations of NodeViews and know the object(s) they observe; each NodeView defines a data or action slot for each aspect mapped from an object. ObjectNodes are thus dependents of the associated objects by way of their data slots. These slots are, in fact, implemented as Aspect Adapters [Woolf 1995], with the addition of anchors. Anchors are then shown as *sensible areas* included in the graphical interface.

ObjectNodes may observe more than one object at a time—for example, consider the object standing for a UseCase. This object collaborates with its Actor. Even if we define UseCase and Actor nodes, we may want the UseCase node to contain information from both objects, for example, the actor's name; this effect is achieved by letting ObjectNodes observe many related objects.

HyperNodes are also aggregations of NodeViews, but they are not associated with an application's objects. The data they display is stored in Value Holders [Woolf 1995] or Proxies [Gamma 1995] in the case of multimedia data that is stored in a file. Examples of HyperNodes are a presentation page, nodes with animations of UseCases, and any one created by the user of the tool that is not supported by the tool's model.

Links may map associative objects, that is, objects that express relationships among others. These are called ObjectLinks and they become dependents of those objects. ObjectLink is a subclass of ClassifiedLink.

The graphical interface becomes a dependent (in the sense of Observer) of a particular representation of a Node.

The hierarchies obtained appear as in Figures 11.5 and 11.6. The Node hierarchy will be extended by the next pattern.

Consequences

- The use of the Observer design pattern dictates the main architectural structure of an application using OO-Navigator.

- We can easily combine navigational behavior (as traversing hypermedia links) with more conventional computational behavior. Data panes display information and allow link activation through sensitive areas (as hotwords). Buttons can dispatch a message to be sent to an application object or they can also be anchors.

- Nodes are more than Observers in the sense of [Gamma 1995]; they not only provide different dimensions to display objects, but they also add navigational information (for example, anchors for links). In effect, they can also be viewed as *navigation wrappers*.

Related Patterns

The whole structure of the hypermedia network should reflect the underlying application model; that is, the relationships among nodes should mimic those among corresponding objects, as shown, for example, with the use of the Composite pattern.

11.4.2 Design of the Aggregation of Nodes: The Composite Pattern

This section describes the design of aggregation of nodes using composite pattern [Gamma 1995]. The composite pattern is discussed as a problem-solution pair, accompanied by the context of usage. Discussion of consequences of using this pattern and related patterns are included.

Context of Usage

When building hypermedia applications, it is useful to group complex nodes in aggregation hierarchies to capture *part-of* semantics. Besides, most hypermedia design methodologies provide formal methods for dealing with composite nodes.

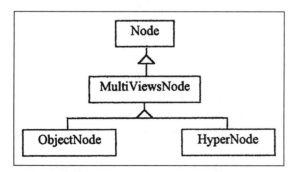

Figure 11.5   Preliminary Node hierarchy.

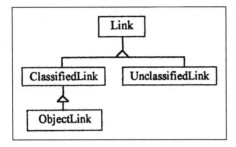

Figure 11.6 Link hierarchy.

Problem

How can we make use of composition relationships defined in the underlying application for better organization of the hypermedia space? On the other hand, how should nodes related in different ways be grouped in order to provide better access to them?

The factors involved in this problem are as follows:

- Objects of the underlying application may already be defined as composites, and nodes mapping those objects should reflect that structure. Just using links between composite and components to map the conceptual relationship does not reflect a hierarchy of composition.

- Nodes not mapping application objects, that is, HyperNodes, may be linked in the usual way, but should not reflect a hierarchy structure. It is better to reserve that organization for ObjectNodes, because artificial hierarchies of composition (those not present in the underlying model) could confuse the reader.

- The aggregation of nodes in collections should be allowed, in order to provide a navigational subspace, tailoring the reader navigation.

Solution

The Composite pattern [Gamma 1995] was used twice in the Node hierarchy.

ObjectNodes may be aggregated such that they reflect the underlying application's structure. Thus, ObjectNode is subclassified in AtomicNode and CompositeNode, the last being an aggregation of ObjectNodes.

Any kind of Node should be able to be aggregated in a Collection with set-based semantics. Individual nodes may look different depending on the current user context, but a collection will look the same regardless of the point of view. Consequently, CollectionNodes have a single view.

The resulting hierarchy of Node is shown in Figure 11.7.

Consequences

- The same consequences that are defined for the Composite pattern.

- CompositeNodes are used when structuring is needed beyond pure link-based navigation, reflecting a component hierarchy that was defined in the underlying model.

- CollectionNodes are created when a subset of related nodes is to be defined, as a way to organize the navigational subspace.

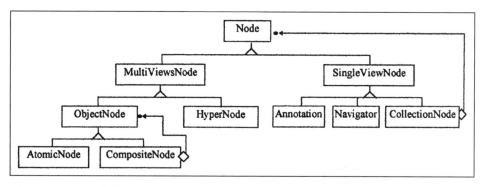

Figure 11.7   Node hierarchy.

- CollectionNode may be used to implement Navigational Contexts [Schwabe 1996].

Related Patterns

As the next section explains, the subclassification of ObjectNode induced a subclassification of NodeClass.

CollectionNode does not define the way its elements will be accessed. The means of accessing a CollectionNode is defined by an AccessStructure (Index or GuidedTour) that is annexed to the collection. This also allows more than one access structure to be defined for a collection conjunctively or disjunctively.

A CollectionNode may be created in different ways (selecting from a NodeClass those nodes that fulfill some predicate, or selecting the destination NodeClass of a LinkClass, manually joining or intersecting other CollectionNodes, and so on) [Garzotto 1994]. The Strategy pattern [Gamma 1995] was used in a separate hierarchy called CollectionStrategy, with one subclass for each creation alternative. A particular strategy is attached to the CollectionNode at creation time, and, when the CollectionNode is to be opened, it interacts with its strategy in order to obtain its elements.

11.4.3 Design of the Classification of Nodes and Node Views: The Type Object Pattern

This section describes the design of the classification of nodes and node views using the type object pattern [Johnson-Woolf 1997]. The type object pattern is discussed as a problem-solution pair, accompanied by the context of usage. Discussion of consequences of using this pattern and related patterns are included.

Context of Usage

The navigational model must be defined following the underlying application model of classes and relationships among classes; when nodes and links reflect the application (and domain) model, users find navigation more intuitive [Garzotto 1993].

Problem

How should the framework capture the relationships between nodes that map objects of the same application class?

The considerations involved in this problem are as follows:

- Defining a different subclass of ObjectNode for each set of nodes mapping instances of the same application class would result in a class explosion that will be just a mirror of the base application model.

- The class ObjectNode is subclassified by other criteria, independently of the underlying application, as we will soon see.

- It is known to be preferable to instantiate existing classes of a framework instead of creating new classes each time it is used.

- Each node may have different views or faces to show itself, depending on the current point of view. Thus, each node is an aggregation of node views.

This problem and the related considerations (except the last one) also appear with respect to links.

Solution

The Type ObjectPattern [Johnson-Woolf 1997] was used to solve this problem. The class NodeClass was defined, with subclasses AtomicNodeClass and CompositeNodeClass. Instances of AtomicNodeClass act as classes for instances of AtomicNode, and instances of CompositeNodeClass act as classes for instances of CompositeNode.

Being that a Node is an aggregation of NodeViews, we applied the same pattern for creating instances NodeView; each NodeClass is an aggregation of instances of NodeViewClass, which are used as prototypes to create NodeViews for each node (see Figure 11.8).

Instances of subclasses of NodeClass are defined as dependents of the corresponding application class, so each time a new application object is created a corresponding node is also instantiated and connected with that object.

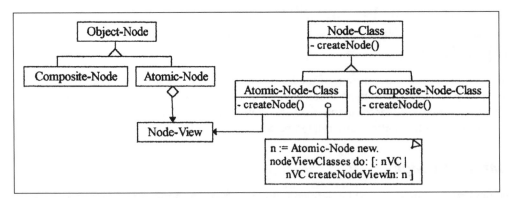

Figure 11.8   Relationship between ObjectNode and NodeClass.

LinkClass was defined in a similar way; its instances act as classes for Classified-Links.

Consequences

- We obtained all the advantages reported for Type Object [Johnson-Woolf 1997].
- Nodes and their views are created automatically with the definition of their NodeClasses.
- The framework's architecture looks more compact, more like a blackbox, because the user does not need to know it in detail, as would be required to be able to subclassify its components (for example, Nodes and Links).

Related Patterns

The further classification of NodeClass into subclasses that behave as factories of instances of the corresponding ObjectNode subclass follows the same purpose and structure proposed by the Abstract Factory pattern [Gamma 1995].

11.4.4 Extending an Existing Interface with Hypermedia Functionality: The Decorator Pattern

This section describes extending existing interface with hypermedia functionality using decorator pattern [Gamma 1995]. The decorator pattern is discussed as a problem-solution pair, accompanied by the context of usage. Discussion of consequences of using this pattern and related patterns are included.

Context of Usage

Not only should we capture the model of the application but also its interface if it exists and its results are useful for the user. Those interfaces must somehow be incorporated into the hypermedia space.

Problem

How can we enrich a graphical interface of the application with navigation capabilities, without modifying it?

The interacting considerations are as follows:

- When an existing application is extended, it usually provides a graphical interface allowing user interaction; we would like to include it in the hypermedia space by adding anchors for links to and from it.
- The interface provided may not be modifiable in order to replace normal widgets with hypermedia-aware widgets (those that allow anchors to be defined, displayed, and activated). Even if it is possible to modify that interface, it may not be the correct solution if we want to maintain the application untouched and so still be able to execute it outside the hypermedia space.

■ It is not reasonable to use inheritance, because it would imply redefining all responsibilities of Node in each subclass of an interface class.

Solution

We have used the Decorator pattern [Gamma 1995] in defining the Navigator class in the Node hierarchy. For instance, Navigator acts as a *transparent* over the node, with anchors for links shown on demand only when the user explicitly wants to navigate. The designer may define the anchors over items of a list (which will become an access structure of demand) or over a piece of text (hotword) or other kind of media. The user will also be able to create annotations dynamically, just selecting and defining the anchor to link it.

The way in which Navigators are defined implies that they should have a single view. It follows, then, that Navigator is a subclass of SingleViewNode, as we can see in the Node hierarchy (see Figure 11.7).

As an implementation note, using the Navigator class does not require any change of the existing graphical interfaces, nor does it require a subclassification of their classes. This was possible thanks to the way in which VisualWorks saves the specification of a graphical interface as a literal array that can later be parsed.

Consequences

It is possible to extend existing applications even when an interface is provided with them.

11.5 Summary

We have briefly described some of the object-oriented patterns that we use in the design and implementation of a framework for adding hypermedia functionality to object-oriented applications. The use of patterns helped us during the design process by providing a common vocabulary for communicating our ideas. We used patterns in order to check out our design decisions and many times we found simple and elegant designs of micro-architectures by comparing our ideas with those in [Gamma 1995]. Even when the instantiation of a pattern required major implementation decisions, we could always recast the conceptual pattern intent to the original one.

We have also discovered some new patterns such as Navigation Strategy and Navigation Observer [Rossi 1996] as variations of their counterparts in [Gamma 1995] for the hypermedia field. The use of patterns has also helped us to make the framework evolve from a whitebox to a blackbox [Roberts-Johnson 1997].

11.6 References

[Alvarez 1995] Alvarez, X., G. Dombiak, A. Garrido, M. Prieto, and G. Rossi. Objects on stage: Animating and visualising object-oriented architectures in a CASE environment. *Proceedings of the International Workshop on Next Generation of CASE Tools, NGCT 1995, Jyväskylä, Finland, June 12–13.* Paris: Université de Paris Press, 1995.

[Balasubramanian-Turoff 1994] Balasubramanian, V., and M. Turoff. Incorporating hypertext functionality into software systems. *Workshop on Incorporating Hypertext Functionality into Software Systems I,* New Jersey Institute of Technology, Edinburgh, Scotland, September 1994. Institute for Integrated Systems Research Technical Report #95-10, 1994.

[Bieber 1995] Bieber, M. On integrating hypermedia into decision support and other information systems. *Decision Support Systems* 14(1995):251267.

[Cybulski 1992] Cybulski J., and K. Reed. A hypertext based software engineering environment, *IEEE Software,* March 1992, pp. 62–68.

[Davis 1992] Davis, H., W. Hall, I. Heath, G. Hill, and R. Wilkins. Towards an integrated environment with open hypermedia systems. *Proceedings of the ACM Conference on Hypertext, ECHT 1992,* pp. 181–190, Milan, Italy, December 1992.

[Gamma 1995] Gamma, E., R. Helm, R. Johnson, and J. Vlissides. *Design Patterns: Elements of Reusable Object-oriented Software.* Reading, MA: Addison Wesley, 1995.

[Garzotto 1993] Garzotto, F., P. Paolini, and D. Schwabe. HDM: A model-based approach to hypermedia application design. *ACM Trans. Info. Syst.* 11(1), January 1993:1–26.

[Garzotto 1994] Garzotto, F., L. Mainetti, and P. Paolini. Adding multimedia collections to the Dexter model. *Proceedings of the European Conference on Hypermedia Technology, ECHT 1994,* pp. 70–80, Edinburgh, Scotland, September 1994.

[Jacobson 1992] Jacobson, I., M. Christerson, P. Johsson, and G. Overgaard. *Object-Oriented Software Engineering.* Reading, MA: Addison-Wesley, 1992.

[Johnson-Woolf 1997] Johnson, R. and B. Woolf. Type object pattern. In *Pattern Languages of Program Design 3,* Robert Martin, Dirk Riehle, and Frank Buschmann, Editors. Reading, MA: Addison-Wesley, 1997.

[Nielsen 1995] Nielsen, J. *Multimedia and Hypertext: The Internet and Beyond.* Academic Press Inc., 1995.

[Oinas-Kukkonen 1995] Oinas-Kukkonen, H. Developing hypermedia systems: The hypertext functionality approach. *Proceedings of the Basque International Workshop on Information Technology, BIWIT 1995,* San Sebastian, Spain, July 1995, pp. 2–8. Los Alamitos, NC: IEEE Society Press, 1995.

[Roberts-Johnson 1997] Roberts, D., and R. Johnson. Patterns for evolving frameworks. In *Pattern Languages of Program Design 3,* pp. 471–486, Robert Martin, Dirk Riehle, and Frank Buschmann, editors. Reading, MA: Addison-Wesley, 1997.

[Rossi 1996] Rossi, G., A. Garrido, and S. Carvalho. Design patterns for object-oriented hypermedia applications. In *Pattern Languages of Program Design 2,* pp. 177–191, John Vlissides, James Coplien, and Norm Kerth, editors. Reading, MA: Addison-Wesley, 1996.

[Schwabe 1996] Schwabe, D., G. Rossi, and S. Barbosa. Systematic hypermedia design with OOHDM. *Proceedings of the Seventh ACM International Conference on Hypertext, Hypertext 1996,* Washington, DC, March 1996.

[Woolf 1995] Woolf, B. Understanding and using the ValueModel framework in VisualWorks Smalltalk. In *Pattern Languages of Program Design,* pp. 467–494, James O. Coplien and Douglas Schmidt, editors. Reading, MA: Addison-Wesley, 1995.

[Yourdon 1996] Yourdon, E. Java, the web and software development. *IEEE Computer,* August 1996, pp. 25–30.

11.7 Review Questions

1. Why should you define a framework to encapsulate hypertext functionality?

2. What is the key difference between navigation and other computations?

3. Compare the relationships among nodes and objects with the one existing in the Observer design pattern. What are the differences?

4. Why do you think it is important to separate nodes from their interfaces?

5. What is the advantage of using the Type Object pattern instead of defining Node Classes as "first-class citizens"?

6. In which cases is it wiser to use Decorator instead of Observers in our framework?

11.8 Problem Set

1. Suppose you have to build a web information system for an electronic bookstore (like Amazon.com). In this application you will have both transactional processing and navigation. (Explore Amazon to understand this problem.)

   a. Define the object (conceptual) model of the application.

   b. Define at least three different user profiles and specify the differences among these profiles.

   c. Study how to define different node structures for each user profile.

   d. Write a use scenario for each important usage of the system.

   e. Document when you have navigation and when you have conventional computations.

2. Implement in Smalltalk (or Java) the abstract class Node. Analyze how to plug it into different application classes. Implement Links and explore how to navigate from node to node.

3. Design and implement a similar kind of interface decoration as shown in this chapter. When would you use it?

11.9 Projects

Project 1: Design and implement a framework to build electronic bookstores. The framework should include facilities for navigating among products and for ordering and paying for them. To simplify the project, implement only a custom interface (not a web-based one). Use the ideas in this chapter to separate different concerns in the framework.

11.10 CASE Tool Appendix

Table 11.1   Atomic Node Classes

ATOMICNODECLASSES	DEFINITION
UseCase-NC	Derived from classes UseCase and Actor.
Actor-NC	Derived from Actor.
InterfaceObjectCRC-NC	Derived from InterfaceObject.
EntityObjectCRC-NC	Derived from EntityObject.
ControlObjectCRC-NC	Derived from ControlObject.
AnalysisDocument-NC	Derived from AnalysisDocument.
DesignDocument-NC	Derived from DesignDocument.

Table 11.2   Composite Node Classes

COMPOSITENODECLASSES	DEFINITION
UseCaseModel-NC	Derived from composite class UseCaseModel, aggregating nodes of UseCase-NC as parts.
AnalysisModel-NC	Derived from composite class AnalysisModel, aggregating nodes of InterfaceObjectCRC-NC, EntityObjectCRC-NC and ControlObjectCRC-NC as parts.

Table 11.3   Hyper Nodes

HYPERNODES	DEFINITION
Presentation	Presentation of the CASE tool.
All nodes for the help subsystem	

Table 11.4   Collection Nodes

COLLECTIONNODES	DEFINITION
PatternNodes	Each PatternNode joins a selection of CRC nodes that represent objects interacting in the same pattern.
CollaborationNodes	Each CollaborationNode joins a selection of CRC nodes representing collaborators of an object.

Table 11.5   Navigator Nodes

NAVIGATORNODES	DEFINITION
Class Browser Navigator	Defined over the graphical interface for the VisualWorks ClassBrowser.

Table 11.6   Link Classes

LINKCLASSES	DEFINITION
Uses_LC	Between UseCase_NC and itself, with multiple cardinality of the destination, and computed dynamically to the UseCase_NCs used by the origin one.
Extends_LC and Extended-by_LC	Note that: Extended-by was a relation not present in the model, but we can add it by defining the inverse relation.
Acquaints_LC, Composed-of_LC and Inherits-from_LC	Between CRC_NCs.
Triggers-LC	Between Actor_NC and UseCase_NC, multiple destination, and computed dynamically to the UseClass_NCs that are triggered by the origin Actor_NC.
To Analysis_LC	Between UseCaseModel_NC and AnalysisModel_NC, single destination and computed dynamically to the AnalysisModel_NC that corresponds to the origin UseCaseModel_NC.
To UseCaseModel_LC	Between AnalysisModel_NC and UseCaseModel_NC, single destination, and computed dynamically to the UseCaseModel_NC that corresponds to the origin AnalysisModel_NC.
To AnalysisDocument_LC	Between AnalysisModel_NC and AnalysisDocument_NC, single destination, and computed dynamically as it corresponds.
To DesignDocument_LC	Between AnalysisDocument_NC and DesignDocument_NC, single destination, and computed dynamically as it corresponds.
To Implementation_LC	Between DesignDocument-NC and the Class Browser Navigator.
To Class Implementation_LC	Between node classes representing CRCs and Class Browser Navigator, single and fixed destination, with the postcondition of opening the browser in the correspondent class.

Table 11.7   Unclassified Links

UNCLASSIFIEDLINKS	DEFINITION
To the UseCase Model	Between the HyperNode Presentation and the NodeClass UseCaseModel_NC; with multiple cardinality of the destination.
To CRC	Between Class Browser Navigator and the node classes representing CRCs, single destination, and dynamically computed to the CRC node of the class that is currently displayed in the browser.

Tables 11.1 through 11.7 provide some of the components of the CASE tool example, shown in Figure 11.4.

Understanding Frameworks

Frameworks [Johnson 1988, Sparks 1996] promise to dramatically reduce the time and effort needed to develop complete applications. When designing a framework, the designer identifies certain key methods of certain key classes as virtual or pure virtual functions (in C++ [Stroustrup 1991] terminology; for concreteness we use C++ terminology and notation but our approach is not in any way C++ specific; note also that we use the terms *function* and *method* interchangeably). Although these methods will be provided definitions by the application developer, the framework designer usually has some ideas on what kinds of behaviors these methods should exhibit, such as which methods should be invoked at what points. This flow of control is what the framework designer implements in the (nonvirtual) methods of the framework and is one of the main contributions that the framework makes to the various applications that might be built using it.

The main task of a developer who wishes to build an application using the framework is to provide definitions for the virtual methods of the framework. The application builder must have a good understanding of what the designer of the framework expects of these methods and at what points they might be invoked. Unless the behaviors of the methods in the derived classes as implemented by the application builder are consistent with the expectations of the framework designer, the application is unlikely to function properly. The framework designer typically tries to express these expectations by choosing appropriate names for the methods and classes in question, as well as informally explaining them in the framework documentation. Such informal expressions often provide adequate guidance to the application builder, especially in the case of modest-size frameworks for standard application domains. But as the sizes of frameworks grow, and as frameworks for a variety of areas are developed, it is necessary to use more reliable methods for understanding the flow-of-control behavior implemented by the framework, for expressing the framework designer's expectations of the code in the concrete derived classes defined by the application builder, and for combining the framework behavior with appropriate information about the methods implemented in these concrete derived classes, to obtain a useful specification of the entire application. Our goal in this chapter is to develop such methods.

There are four related problems we must address in order to develop such methods. First, we must develop a precise notation that can be used to specify the framework, including its flow-of-control behavior. This will tell us at what points the virtual functions might be invoked. Second, we need a procedure for combining this specification with appropriate information about the code provided by the application builder. We need to obtain the specification of the complete application; the ultimate users will be interested only in this final specification since as users they are mainly concerned with how the entire application will behave, not the fact that it was built on the framework, nor questions about which part of the behavior exhibited by the application comes from the framework and which part from the code supplied by the application builder, and so on. Third, we need a procedure that the framework designer can use to check that the framework does indeed meet its specification. And, fourth, application builders need a similar procedure to check that the codes they have provided meet their specifications. We address each of these problems in *Section 12.2*, after introducing a somewhat simple model of frameworks in the next section. Our focus in this chapter, and in particular in *Section 12.2*, will be on the first two problems: developing ways to specify the framework and to obtain the specification of the complete application.

The key idea underlying our approach to specifying the behavior of frameworks is to use traces—sequences of function calls and returns—to capture the control flow implemented by the framework. As we said before, this flow-of-control behavior is one of the key contributions that the framework makes. When trying to specify the framework, we cannot expect to do so in terms of the precise functional effect of this sequence of calls since the methods being called are virtual; indeed, the whole point of the framework is that different applications built on it will typically provide quite different bodies for these methods, with very different corresponding (functional) effects. What we need to do instead is to provide an abstract specification of how control flows among the various virtual methods, and that, as we will see, is exactly what our trace-based approach allows us to do. Each element of the trace of a framework will represent a call to and the corresponding return from a virtual function; the details of what information is recorded in these elements we will postpone to *Section 12.2*.

The framework will, in general, also provide functional behavior that should be common to all applications built on this framework. We will use standard pre- and postconditions to specify this aspect of the framework's behavior. Even virtual methods may be defined in the framework, and its specification will include their behaviors. Many languages, including C++, have the notion of a pure virtual function that does not have any definition associated with it in the base class. Although we will not consider such functions in the current chapter, it would be easy to extend our approach to include such functions. The behaviors associated with such functions in the framework's specification should then be considered as constraints that application designers must satisfy when they provide actual definitions for them.

One further point should be noted: We will be working mostly with what are called *concrete* specifications; see, for example, [Soundarajan 1997]. In other words our specifications of functions are in terms of their effects on the data members of the classes we are dealing with. When trying to understand the behavior of the framework and the application in terms of how they are built, naturally we have to work with such specifications since the behavior they exhibit is realized in terms of these components. Once we have an understanding of the concrete behavior of the entire application, we can use standard ways [Liskov 1994] to convert it into an abstract specification in terms of a conceptual model.

The problems of using OO have been remarked on by many authors; see, for example, [Fayad-Schmidt 1997] and Chapters 1 and 3. One important issue is that of documentation and it is particularly critical for frameworks, as has been noted by a number of authors [Bosch 1998; Campbell 1993; Johnson 1997]. Most of these authors focus on informal documentation rather than precise specifications of the kind we are interested in. We believe both informal documentation, perhaps using examples as suggested by some authors, as well as precise specifications are useful and should be considered as complementing each other. Helm et al. [Helm 1990] use their formal notion of contracts to describe many relations between objects, but their goal seems more toward using contracts for mechanical execution rather than for documentation. We will return to the relation between the approach we propose and that of other authors in the final section of this chapter, but one point is worth noting here: Approaches such as those of [Dhara 1995; Liskov 1994; Meyer 1988] that are used for specifying the behavior of normal OO programs are not well suited for dealing with frameworks. The problem is that these approaches tend to downplay the contribution of virtual functions to overall system behavior. More precisely, suppose f is a virtual method in a class B; the usual approaches require us to provide a sufficiently general characterization of f such that definitions of f in the various derived classes of B all satisfy this characterization. Further, and this is what makes these approaches unsuitable for use with frameworks, the only knowledge that clients have regarding f is whatever is provided by this general characterization; the differences between the definitions of f in different derived classes of B are abstracted away. For frameworks this would mean that all applications built on a given framework would be equivalent to each other since the only differences between them is in how they define the virtual functions of the framework! Clearly, we need a different approach to the specification of framework behavior, one that will allow us to distinguish between these applications.

The rest of this chapter is organized as follows: The next section presents a simple model of frameworks that we will use throughout the chapter. Although not every framework will fit this model, it is general enough to illustrate the main issues that must be dealt with in documenting the behavior of frameworks. In the third section we consider how an application developer refines a framework F by providing appropriate definitions for the various virtual functions of F, and we contrast this type of behavioral refinement with the standard notion of procedural refinement. Next, we introduce our notation for specifying the behavior of the framework, using traces for capturing the flow-of-control behavior. We then consider the question of how an application developer can combine the behavior of the framework specified in this manner with the behaviors exhibited by the developer's definitions of the virtual functions to arrive at the behavior of the framework. In *Section 12.3* we briefly consider how our approach may be applied to a (simplified version of a) diagram editor framework; this is a fairly typical framework and is based on a framework developed in Horstmann's textbook [Horstmann 1995]. In the final section we summarize our approach, briefly relate it to other approaches, and reiterate the importance of both formal and informal documentation in understanding frameworks.

12.1 A Simple Model of Frameworks

We will say that a class A is abstract if at least one of its methods is virtual. A class, all of whose methods are nonvirtual, is a concrete class. A framework F will consist of the following classes:

- A concrete class C, which we will also call the Controller class of F. C will have a distinguished method named run. As the name suggests, it is this method that primarily decides how control flows among the various methods of the various classes of F.

- Zero or more other concrete classes C1, ..., Cm.

- One or more abstract classes A1, ..., An.

In addition to the run function, many frameworks also include a mechanism for initialization in order to allow some information about the actual application to be passed to the framework. Different frameworks use different ways to achieve this initialization. (Thus, in the diagram framework of [Horstmann 1995], each of the various classes of nodes and edges defined by the application code must be *registered* with the framework before the run function is invoked; the diagram framework uses two functions, registerNode and registerEdge, for this purpose.) In order to have a simple and uniform model, we will assume that the controller class C provides a single initialize function that will handle these tasks. To use the application built on F we—that is, the *main program*—must first call the initialize function; when that finishes, we invoke the run function and start using the application.

An application A developed using F will have, corresponding to each abstract class Aj of F, one or more derived classes CA[j,k], each of which will provide definitions for some or all of the virtual functions of Aj. If definitions are provided in each of the derived classes in each of CA[j,k] for all the virtual functions of the corresponding base classes of F, the application will be a complete application; otherwise, it will still be a framework, although a more concrete one than F. Generally, we will assume that definitions for all the virtual functions of F are being provided. For simplicity, we will also assume that no new classes (that is, classes that do not inherit from Aj) are introduced by the application builder.

The main program using the application will only have an object, let us call it d, of type C. d will be initialized first, followed by a call to:

```
run:    d.run();
```

In the example of *Section 12.3*, we consider a framework for dealing with a collection of figures. The only concrete class is the controller class; the single abstract class is called F, for figure. The term *abstract class* is commonly used to denote a class that has at least one pure virtual function. But we will not take special note of pure virtual functions, focusing instead on virtual functions that have a definition in the base class, to be overridden by the definition that the application developer will provide. Thus we use the term *abstract class* to distinguish it from a concrete class that has no virtual functions, pure or otherwise. In the application we consider, we will provide two concrete classes called C (for Circle) and T (for Triangle), respectively, as derived classes of F. In the main program, we declare a CF object d, initialize it, and then run the application by calling run, as previously shown.

Returning now to the general case, objects of type C, such as d, will have components of type C1, ..., Cm as well as A1, ..., An (or, rather, CA[1,1],...); the main program itself will not have any objects of these types. Inside the run function we will call the functions defined in C1, ..., Cm and A1, ..., An (some of which will be virtual, and hence will call the corresponding functions defined in the appropriate concrete classes defined in CA[j,k]) to act upon these components of the main object d. In the example of *Section 12.3*, d will have two figure objects of (possibly) different types. In the run function, we will manipulate these components by invoking the various functions defined in the figure class F, which will result, if the function we invoked was virtual, in the execution of the corresponding function body defined in the appropriate concrete figure class C (Circle) or T (Triangle), respectively. (Note that for simplicity we follow the C++ convention that the number and types of the parameters of the virtual functions in the base class must match exactly the [number and] types of the parameters of the corresponding functions in the derived classes; other more general requirements such as contravariance or covariance are also possible [Abadi 1995], but we won't consider them in this chapter.) In the patterns literature (see [Gamma 1995]) this situation is called "a *template* method (run) calling a *hook* method (the virtual function)." Before concluding this section, we should note a couple of points regarding our model. First, as we said before and has been noted by several authors, perhaps the most important contribution that the framework makes is relieving the application developer from having to worry about how control should flow among the various methods of the various classes. In our model, this is highlighted by the run function. Second, many existing frameworks such as those for simulation of various phenomena, and frameworks for GUIs, fit reasonably well within our model, at least in a conceptual sense (although there may be syntactic mismatches; the control function may not be called run, for instance). Moreover, we believe that the main ideas underlying our approach to specifying and understanding frameworks, which are really the focus of this chapter, will also be applicable to frameworks that don't strictly follow our model, so there is no harm in using the simple model.

12.2 Behavioral Refinement: From Frameworks to Applications

The run function of F provides a *behavioral skeleton* for the entire application with the virtual functions being empty shells in a sense. Suppose f is such a virtual function and it is a member of the abstract class A. The application builder will define the body of f when defining the concrete class or, as happens in the example in the next section, if there is more than one concrete class corresponding to A, then the body of f corresponding to each concrete class that inherits from A. Thus, the designer refines the behavioral shell corresponding to f. But in doing so, the designer must not violate the constraints imposed on these functions by the framework designer; in other words, the redefined body of the virtual function must satisfy its specification as given in the specification of F. In addition—and this, of course, is the point of using virtual functions—when defining the body of f, the application developer will build in additional functionality, usually in terms of its effect on new member variables introduced in the concrete class.

A simple, if artificial, example will make the point clear. Suppose an abstract class in F has an integer member variable x. Suppose there is a virtual function changeX in this class. The framework designer may impose a constraint that says that corresponding to a call d.changeX(), the final value of the member x of d when changeX finishes execution must be greater than its value when changeX started execution, and the other members of d must have the same values as they did before the call. This can be expressed quite easily using standard pre- and postconditions for changeX(). Thus, using the notation #x to denote the value of x before the call under consideration, the postcondition of changeX() will be as follows:

$$\text{post} \cong (x > \#x) \tag{1}$$

What if the framework designer imposed a more severe constraint, something like this:

$$\text{post} \cong (x = \#x + 1) \tag{2}$$

Doesn't this specify the effect of the function body precisely? Indeed, assuming that x is the only member variable of the class in question, it defines exactly the effect of changeX. Frameworks that impose constraints such as specification (2), leaving as they do little or no freedom to the application developer, would hardly seem to deserve being called frameworks. But such is not the case; the point is that the added behavior that the application developer is usually interested in providing is in terms of the effect that the virtual function has on new member variables in the derived class(es), and the framework, of course, imposes no constraints on what changeX may or may not do to these new components. Thus, the precise effects of the function bodies defined by the application builder, including the effects on any new member variables introduced by the application code, will only be captured in the specification of that code. This information will then be combined with the specification of F to obtain the behavior of the entire application, in particular, of the run function.

We should note that, while behavioral refinement bears some resemblance to the standard notion of procedural refinement, there is an important difference: As in procedural refinement, we must ensure that the definition that an application developer provides for a virtual method f meets its constraints, that is, satisfies its specification in the framework. But, unlike in procedural refinement, we are very interested in the additional behavior provided by this f and, what is more, this additional behavior leads to additional behavior being exhibited by the run function and we are interested in arriving at a corresponding richer specification for run. In other words, we are not just trying to verify that the particular refinement of f that the application developer has provided meets the constraints contained in the specification of the framework; we are also trying to arrive at a specification corresponding to the richer behavior of the entire application, given the particular refinement that the application builder has implemented.

12.2.1 Specifying the Framework

In this subsection we will consider how a framework F may be specified. In order to simplify the presentation, we will assume that we have only two classes in F, a concrete class C and an abstract class A. C will contain only the run function, which is nonvirtual. C will contain a single member variable x of type A; it may also contain other member variables of predefined types (such as integers). The class A will contain a nonvirtual function f and a virtual function g. Note that f will not call g; allowing this would make it a template method calling a hook method like run and this would complicate the discussion, because in specifying f we would have to use an approach similar to the one described later for specifying run. The function run will call g and may call f; the call to g will be of the form x.g(…). Allowing for more classes, more functions, and more member variables would not introduce any major conceptual complexities in the formalism, but we would have to introduce appropriate notational mechanisms for distinguishing between them, and these would add considerable complexity to the presentation. (As noted in *Section 12.1*, one important function that the controller class C would include in most frameworks is an initialize function. One important task of this function is to assign the appropriate actual type, that is, the identity of the particular derived class of A that x is an instance of. How this is achieved is somewhat language specific and we do not wish to go into these details here. In the example in the next section, we will just assume that by the time the main program invokes the run function, the actual types of all the member variables such as x have indeed been initialized.)

In order to specify F, we must specify the behaviors of each of f, g, and run. The specification of f is perhaps the easiest. We just use standard pre- and postconditions specifying, respectively, the conditions that the state—that is, the values of the member variables—of A must satisfy when f is called, and the condition that the state will satisfy when it finishes execution. In our experience, the postcondition is best expressed as an assertion over the state at the time of the call to f and the state when f finishes, rather than just the latter, and we will use the # notation for this purpose. Thus if y is a member variable of A, then #y in the postcondition of f refers to the value of y at the time of the call to f, and y refers to its value when f finishes. Since f is nonvirtual, it cannot be redefined by the application developer; thus, the specification of f in the final application is the same as in F.

The specification of g is similar. The application developer, when defining a derived class corresponding to A, will provide a new definition for g. We require that this new definition continue to satisfy the specification of g given as part of the specification of F. This is required since, in reasoning about run in F, we will make use of this specification of g. In a sense, this specification of g expresses the constraints that the framework designer imposes upon the application developer. That developer may redefine g as he or she chooses, so long as the behavior specified as part of F continues to be satisfied.

The most interesting function is, of course, run. Here again we use pre- and post-conditions, but the postcondition will involve not just the state of the member variables (including x) of C when run finishes, but also the trace of calls to g that run goes through during its execution. Given such a specification, the application developer will be able, as we will see in *Section 12.2.2*, to combine this with the specification of g, as redefined in the application (that is, in the derived classes of A) to arrive at the specification of run appropriate to his or her particular application.

Let us consider another simple, but again artificial, example. Suppose C contains only the single member variable x of type A. Suppose A has a single member variable v of type integer, and a single member function g, which is virtual, receives no parameters and only increases the value of v by 1. The specification of g in F will be as follows:

```
pre.g   ≅   true                                                    (3)
post.g ≅   (v = #v+ 1)                                              (4)
```

Suppose next that the body of run is as follows:

```
x.g(); x.g();
```

(In C++ we would have to use pointers explicitly in order to ensure that the g that is invoked is the one defined in the derived class; we ignore this language detail.)

In the specification of run, we will use τ to denote the trace of calls it makes to the virtual function g; note that only calls to virtual functions are recorded in τ. Each element of τ corresponds to a single call to, and the corresponding return from, a virtual function. The element specifies the identity—that is, the name of the function called, the object on which the function was applied, the state of the object at the time of the call and at the time of the return, as well as the values of any parameters to the function and any results returned by the function. In an actual specification we may include as much or as little of this information as we (as framework designers) choose. This is no different from writing specifications that omit information that is not of interest to the specifier about the function being specified. The specification of run for this example is as follows:

```
pre.run   ≅   true                                                  (5)
post.run ≅   [ (x.v = #x.v + 2)
              ∧ (|τ| = 2 ∧ τ.o[1] = τ.o[2] = x
                 ∧ τ.f[1] = τ.f[2] = g) ]                          (6)
```

The $\wedge$ symbol denotes logical *and*. The first clause in the postcondition asserts that when run finishes, the value of x.v will be 2 greater than at the start; the second clause asserts that during execution, run will call virtual functions twice ($|\tau|$ is the length of τ), and in each call the function that is called is g and the object on which the function is applied is x. Note that we cannot conclude, from this specification, that the value of x.v when g is called the first time is the same as at the start of run, nor that its value is one greater when g is called the second time. That is indeed the case, given the body of run that we previously wrote down, but this information has not been included in this specification. For all we can tell from this specification, run might add 100 to x.v prior to each call to g and then subtract 100 from it after the return from g! Or, alternately, it may be the case that run saves the initial value of x.v in some local variable and sets x.v to some completely arbitrary value before calling g twice in a row, and after the return from the second call resets x.v to its original value and then adds 2 to it.

But we could, if we chose to do so, provide a stronger specification of run that would rule out these possibilities. All we would have to do is add to the specification the fact that the state of x.v at the time of the first call to g is the same as at the start of run and that the state of x.v at the time of the second call to g is the same as at the return from the first call. Would such added information be useful? Suppose the application developer decides to add a new member variable—call it w—in the derived class D of A. Suppose also that the body the developer provides for g copies the value of v into w before incrementing v by 1 and then returning. (Note that incrementing v by 1 is required by the specification of g given earlier as part of the specification of the framework; the code supplied by the application developer for g is necessary to satisfy this requirement.) Then, given the preceding specification of run, we would not be able to conclude that following a call to run the value of x.w is 1 greater than the value of x.v at the start of the call. With a stronger specification, we would indeed be able to arrive at this conclusion.

In general, if in the specification of the framework, especially in the specification of the trace of the run function, we leave out any information about which virtual functions are invoked, on what objects they are invoked, or what the states of these objects are at the time of the invocations, an application designer may not be able to establish the complete behavior of the run function, specifically its effects on new member variables introduced in the derived classes he or she defines, for this particular application. The flip side is that including all of this information makes the specification relatively more complex. Thus, the framework designer must, to an extent, anticipate what sorts of information are likely to be useful for the application developer and include all of that in the specification.

Two final points are worth noting. First, if run were a nonterminating function (as in most real frameworks), we would use invariants rather than postconditions for specifying its behavior, but the basic ideas remain applicable. Second, while the idea of recording in a trace the calls made by the run function to virtual functions is fairly straightforward and even natural, the resulting specifications can be quite complex even for simple run functions. In particular, if run had a variety of possible sequences of actions that it would choose from and if these choices depended upon values returned by the calls to the virtual functions, it would be impractical to explicitly list all possible values of the trace τ. We believe, however, that using appropriate formal notations, such as regular expressions, can considerably simplify these specifications; and we intend to pursue these possibilities in future work.

12.2.2 Specifying the Application

Let us now turn to application. The application builder will define derived classes corresponding to the abstract classes of F and provide definitions, in these derived classes, for all the virtual functions of corresponding base classes. Thus, in our model this developer will provide one or more derived classes corresponding to A; in each of these classes the developer can introduce new member variables and must provide definitions for g. In order to simplify the presentation in this section, we will assume that only one derived class corresponding to A is introduced and we will name this class D. The definition of f will be inherited unchanged from A, since f is not a virtual function.

The specification of f is also inherited unchanged. Or, rather, it is strengthened slightly: We can be sure that the values of the new member variables introduced in D will be the same at the end of each call to f as at the start, since these variables did not even exist when the body of f was written (as part of the base class A). For instance, if u were such a variable, the corresponding clause added to the postcondition of f would be (u = #u).

The specification of g will also be stronger, but for a different reason. The application developer has provided a new body for g and its new specification will correspond to this new body. But the new body of g must continue to meet the specification given for it by the framework designer. This is important since, in reasoning about run, that designer has most likely relied upon this specification of g. If the new body of g did not satisfy this specification, that reasoning would no longer be valid. Many OO languages, including C++, allow the derived class definition of g to invoke the base class definition, so if the application developer wanted the effect of the new g on the variables of A to be the same as in the base class, he or she would only have to supply the code for manipulating the new member variables introduced in D. However g is implemented, the new specification for it will reflect the behavior of the new g and will be a strengthening of its original specification.

The most interesting function is, of course, run. Because it calls g, and g has been redefined in the application to exhibit richer behavior, the behavior of run in the application will also be correspondingly richer. One possibility would be to just use the specification provided by the framework for run; this specification would still be valid (since g continues to satisfy the specification on which this specification of run is based). But this is not a satisfactory alternative, since the power of frameworks derives from the richer behavior exhibited by run and, in order for us to be able to reliably exploit this richer behavior, it must be captured in a specification. A second possibility would be to arrive at a new specification corresponding to the richer behavior by reanalyzing the body of run, using information from the new specification of g when reasoning about the effect of calls in run to g during this reanalysis. This is also not a good alternative, since it would be inconsistent with the basic philosophy of frameworks that you have to design, and by implication analyze, a framework only once, not once for each new application. In our approach we do not have to settle for either of these alternatives. We can instead use the trace-based specification of run as provided by the framework designer, plug in the behavior of g corresponding to the calls to g recorded on the trace, and arrive at an enriched specification of run.

Consider again the example from *Section 12.2.1*. Suppose in the derived class D we introduce a new variable w and the redefined g increments this variable by 1 (in addition to incrementing v by 1, since it would not otherwise meet its original specification). Thus the new postcondition of g would be as follows:

$$\text{post.g} \cong [(v = \#v + 1) \land (w = \#w + 1)] \tag{7}$$

Given this, and given specification (6), we can arrive at the following postcondition for run:

$$\text{post.run} \cong [(x.v = \#x.v + 2) \land (x.w = \#x.w + 2)] \tag{8}$$

This is admittedly an artificially simple example, but the idea should be clear. Since the original specification of run includes information about which virtual functions are called, and in what order, we can, when we redefine these functions in the applications, combine that information contained with information about the behavior of the redefined functions to see what richer behavior run will exhibit—in particular, what effect it will have on the new member variables. In this particular application, what the redefined g did to the new member variable w did not depend upon the value of v. So the fact that the original specification of run did not specify the relation between the value of x.v at the start of run and at the time of either call to g did not prevent us from arriving at specification (8). In practice, as framework designers, we should make sure that the specification in the framework of run includes all information that potential application developers might need.

So far, we have focused attention on specifications. The enriched specification of run was obtained by using the information contained in specification (6), the framework specification of run, and combining it with the stronger postcondition specification (7) of g. This is a verification step and has to be formally justified. Similarly, when verifying that the body of run as defined in the framework meets its specification, we will need appropriate rules; specifically, these rules must account for the effect of a virtual function call on the trace, of appending an element recording the identity of the function being called, the object to which the function is being applied, the state of the object at the time of the call and at the time of the return, and the values of any parameters passed to and results received from the function. We will omit the formal details of these rules; in [Soundarajan 1998] we deal with a related problem and the rules presented there can be tailored to deal with the current situation. One point that is worth noting here is the similarity of this situation with that in reasoning about the behavior of distributed programs. Trace-based approaches are commonly used [Misra 1981; Soundarajan 1984] for dealing with such programs, a trace being associated with each process of such a program to record its communications with other processes of the program. The axioms for dealing with such communication commands in this setting are similar to the axioms we need for dealing with virtual function calls in the current setting. Similarly, the rules in the distributed program setting that allows us to combine the specifications of individual processes of a program to arrive at a specification of the complete program are similar to the rules we need for arriving at a strengthened specification of run, given its (trace-based) specification in the framework and given the stronger specification for the virtual functions in the application.

12.3 Case Study: A Simple Diagram Editor Framework

We will briefly see how our approach may be applied to a simple framework. The framework we consider is based on one presented by Horstmann [Horstmann 1995]; Horstmann's framework is for dealing with a collection of figures made up of nodes and edges, for moving the figures around, for drawing and erasing them, and so on. To keep the discussion simple, and to avoid getting into graphics issues, we will consider a highly stripped-down version of that framework.

Our framework will consist of a concrete controller class CF and an abstract class F (for figure). Let us first consider F. The details of what a figure actually is will, of course, not be specified in the framework—that is, what the application developer will do when he or she designs the derived classes of F, based on the needs of the particular application. In F, we provide some basic features that all kinds of figures will have. Let us start with the (protected) member variables of F, as follows:

```
int x, y; // coordinates of 'anchor point'
int ic; // is figure currently 'iconified'?
```

Every figure has an *anchor* point; for a circle, this might, for instance, be the center. If the value of ic is 1, that indicates that the figure is currently iconified.

Next, consider the functions of F, all of which are virtual:

```
virtual void iconify(){ ic := 1; }
virtual void deIconify(){ ic := 0; }
virtual void move( int dx, int dy ){ x := x+dx; y := y+dy; }
virtual void blowUp( int f ){ ; }
virtual void blowDown( int f ){ ; }
virtual int isIn( int u, int v ){ return 0; }
```

iconify and deIconify are intended to do what their names suggest. In the class F, all these can do is to set ic to the appropriate value. The application developer must provide appropriate redefinitions for them in the derived class(es) so that they behave as desired for the particular type of figure in question. That is why these functions are virtual. Move() will move the figure by dx,dy. But, of course, it is not enough to just move the coordinates of the anchor point. The figure (or its iconified version) must be *redisplayed* at its new location; that is why this function is virtual so the application developer can provide appropriate definition(s) for it.

blowUp and blowDown (shrink might have been a more conventional name for the latter function, but blowDown was too tempting in its contrast with blowUp!) expand and contract the figure by the specified factor. In F, there is really nothing for these functions to do (since they should not change the coordinates of the anchor point or whether the figure is currently iconified or not), so they have empty bodies. isIn checks whether the point with the specified coordinates u,v is inside the figure. This function is also virtual because the way to carry out this check very much depends upon the geometry of the particular figure, and so the function must be defined by the application developer.

Let us consider the specification of F. As we saw in the last section, we need to provide pre- and postcondition specifications for each of these functions. The preconditions for all of them are true. In the postconditions, we often need to assert that several of the member variables are unchanged by the function in question; we will use the ! notation for this purpose; thus, the clause !(x,y) (read as "Don't touch x,y!") in the specification of iconify says that this function will not change the values of x,y.

```
post.iconify   ≅  [!(x,y) ∧ (ic = 1)]
post.deIconify ≅  [!(x,y) ∧ (ic = 0)]
post.move(dx,dy) ≅ [!(ic) ∧ (x = #x+ dx) ∧ (y = #y+ dy)]
```

```
post.blowUp(f) ≡ [!(x,y,ic)]
post.blowDown(f) ≡ [!(x,y,ic)]
post.isIn(u,v) ≡ [!(x,y,ic) ∧ (result ∈ {0,1})]          (9)
```

All of these specifications are straightforward. For instance, the specifications of iconify and deIconify say that they do not change the values of x,y and have the appropriate effect on ic. When the application developer redefines them in the derived class(es), he or she must ensure that the redefinitions continue to satisfy these specifications. So, for instance, deIconify may not change the values of x,y and must set the value of ic to 0.

Similarly, the application developer is at liberty to redefine move as he or she chooses, so long as it makes the changes previously specified to the values of x,y and leaves the value of ic unchanged. blowUp and blowDown may be defined as we choose, but they cannot change the values of any of x,y or ic.

The specification of isIn is worth remarking upon. Note first the special symbol, result; this is used (borrowing a convention from [Meyer 1998]) to denote the value returned by this function. This specification says that the value returned by isIn is either 0 or 1. Given that the body of isIn as defined in the preceding code actually returns 0, why this weak specification? Because if we strengthened it to, say, (result = 0), the application developer, when redefining isIn, will be forced to return this same value! In fact, in the class F, we have no way to decide whether the given point (u,v) is within the figure in question. So the value 0 being returned here is arbitrary; it is meant to be overridden by the appropriate value in the derived class. That is what the specification of isIn reflects. (It might perhaps be better to define isIn as a pure virtual function and not provide it any body in F. The application developer will then be forced to provide definitions for it in each derived class of F. Even if we do this, though, it is important for the framework designer to provide a specification for isIn, in particular, the part !(x,y,ic), since, otherwise, the application developer may not realize that isIn is not supposed to mess up the coordinates of the anchor point or whether a figure is iconified or not.) In one respect, this specification of isIn is weak; there is nothing to prevent the derived class designer from defining a body for isIn that returns 0 when the specified point is actually in the given figure and 1 when it is not, or even return 0 and 1 at random. But there is no way to include in the formal specification of F anything that represents our intuition that this function should check whether the given point lies within the figure or outside the figure and return 1 or 0 accordingly. That is why formal specifications such as ours should not be considered as replacing informal documentations, but rather as complementing them.

Next, consider the controller class CF. CF has two member variables f1,f2, both of type F. These are the figures that this framework will let us work with. In a more realistic framework, such as the one in [Horstmann 1995], the user of the application would be able to create as many figures as he or she wanted and would not be stuck with two. But this would require us to handle language-dependent issues such as creation of new objects, and we prefer to avoid these questions by assuming a fixed number of figures. The run function will input a sequence of edit requests and carry out each one. An edit request will contain the following information: the coordinates of a point m, the identity of the edit operation to be performed—one of iconify, deIconify, move, blowUp, or blowDown—and, in case the operation is either blowUp or blow-

Down, the factor by which the figure should be expanded or contracted, or if the operation is move, the amount that the figure should be moved by. The point m may be thought of as the current mouse location. In other words, an edit request gives us the current mouse location, as well as the desired operation, and, in response, run will carry out that operation on the figure at that location; if there is no figure at the given location, no action will be taken.

The code in run( ) for processing an edit request is fairly simple. Let us assume that the components of the request are mx,my, the coordinates of the mouse position; op, a character string (one of Iconify, DeIconify, and so on) that identifies the operation; fac, the factor if the operation is blowUp or blowDown; and dx,dy, the distance by which to move the figure if the operation is move. All we need to do is check if the given mouse position is within either of the figures f1,f2 and if it is, invoke the appropriate operation on that particular figure. If it is within both figures, we apply the operation on f1; if it is within neither, we do nothing.

```
if ( f1.isIn( mx, my ) == 1 ) {
    if ( op == "Iconify" ) { f1.iconify( ); }
    else if ( op == "DeIconify" ) { f1.deIconify( ); }
    else if ( op == ". . . " ) { f1...( ); } . . .
        }
else if ( f2.isIn( mx, my ) == 1 ) {
    if ( op == "Iconify" ) { f2.iconify( ); }
    else if ( op == "DeIconify" ) { f2.deIconify( ); }
    else if ( op == ". . . " ) { f2....( ); } . . .
}
```

The complete run function is just repeated execution of this code for each edit request. Note the importance of the virtual functions in this code. In the framework, we do not have a complete implementation of isIn, since that function depends on the type of figure we are dealing with. Nevertheless—and, indeed, this is the power of the framework approach—we are able to design the framework code to make use of this function and call other functions based on the results returned by this function.

How do we specify run? We will just consider a single edit request; dealing with a sequence of requests would simply mean repeating what we do when dealing with a single request. This seems to be a common feature of most interactive applications, including those built on frameworks; this was the reason for our earlier suggestion that it may be useful to develop specially tailored notations that borrow ideas from regular expressions and other similar formalisms to simplify the specification of such systems.

The particular request we consider corresponds to the Iconify operation; others are handled in a similar manner:

$$
\begin{aligned}
&\texttt{post.run(mx, my, "Iconify")} \cong \\
&\quad [\ !(\texttt{f1.x, f1.y, f2.x, f2.y}) \\
&\quad \land \ ((|\tau| = 2 \lor |\tau| = 3) \land (\tau.o[1] = f1) \land (\tau.f[1] = \texttt{isIn(mx,my)}) \\
&\qquad \land ((\tau.res[1] = 1) \Rightarrow \\
&\qquad\quad ((|\tau| = 2) \land (\tau.o[2] = f1) \land (\tau.f[2] = \texttt{iconify}) \\
&\qquad\qquad \land (f1.ic = 1) \land (!(f2.ic)))) \\
&\qquad \land ((\tau.res[1] = 0) \Rightarrow
\end{aligned}
$$

$$((\tau.o[2] = f2) \wedge (\tau.f[2] = isIn(mx,my))$$
$$\wedge((\tau.res[2] = 1) \Rightarrow$$
$$(((|\tau| = 3) \wedge (\tau.o[3] = f2) \wedge (\tau.f[3] = iconify)$$
$$\wedge(f2.ic= 1) \wedge (!(f1.ic))))$$
$$\wedge((\tau.res[2] = 0) \Rightarrow$$
$$(((|\tau| = 2) \wedge (!(f1.ic, f2.ic))))))))] \qquad (10)$$

This asserts that the coordinates of the anchor points of f1,f2 are not affected by carrying out this request; that run, in carrying out this request, makes either two or three virtual function calls; that the first call is to isIn, with the object being f1, and the argument being the point, with the coordinates, (mx,my), which was part of the original request; if the result of this call (t.res[1]) is 1, there is one more call to a virtual function, this one being iconify, the object being again f1. If the result of the first call to isIn is 0, there is another call to isIn, the object this time being f2; here again, the argument is the point (mx,my); if the result of this call is 0, there are no more virtual function calls, and the ic components of both f1 and f2 remain unchanged; if the result is 1—from the specification of isIn in the framework, we know that the only possible results of this call are 0 and 1—there is one final call, this time to iconify, the object being f2.

Consider now an application built using this framework. We will have two concrete derived classes of F, the class C for Circles, and the class R for Rectangles. C will have two extra members:

```
int rad; // radius of circle
int count; // number of times iconified: to be explained shortly
```

R will have three extra member variables:

```
int length, width; // length and width of rectangle.
int color; // has value 1, 2, or 3 : to be explained shortly
```

The isIn function for C is easy to define; we compare the distance of the given point from the center—that is, the anchor point—of the circle and if it is less than or equal to rad, the point is in the circle. But this is true only if the circle is not currently iconified. We will assume that an iconified circle will be displayed as a small circle of radius 0.5 cm. Hence:

```
virtual int isIn( int u, int v ) {
    if ( (ic==0) && (dist(x,y,u,v) ≤ rad) ) return 1;
    if ( (ic==1) && (dist(x,y,u,v) ≤ .5) ) return 1;
    return 0; }
```

The function dist (x,y,u,v) returns the distance between the point (x,y) and the point (u,v). The code for isIn for the R class is similar and we will omit it.

Now consider the functions iconify and deIconify. In practice, both of these will change the state of the screen; since we do not want to get involved with graphics details regarding the screen, we will associate a different (and somewhat arbitrary) behavior with these functions in each of C and R. (One thing we cannot change is what these functions do to the variable ic, since that is dictated by the specification of the framework. Nor can we define these functions to modify x,y, since that too is forbidden by the specification of the framework.) Suppose it is difficult to draw circles, so the designer of the circle class wishes to keep a count of the number of times a circle is being iconified and deiconified. The following definition of iconify serves this purpose, assuming that count is initialized by the constructor function to 0; note also that if the circle is already iconified, we do not increment count:

```
virtual void iconify( ) {
      if ( ic==1 ) return; ic := 1;
      count++;
}
```

Similarly, suppose the designer of R wishes to change the color of the rectangle each time it is iconified/deiconified, and that there are three colors to choose from, represented by the value of the color variable. Here is the code for iconify in the C (circle) class:

```
virtual void iconify( ) { if ( ic==1 ) return; ic := 1;
      color := (color + 1) mod 3;
}
```

These functions are easily specified. Thus, the specification for iconify for the C class is as follows:

```
post.iconify ≡ [ (!(x,y)
              ∧ [ ((#ic = 0) ∧ count = #count+ 1))
                  ∨((#ic = 1) ∧ (count = #count) ∧ (ic = 1))]
              ]
```

The specification of isIn for the circle class is a bit longer but not much more complex:

```
post.isIn(u,v) ≡
    [ (!(x,y,ic,count)
    ∧ ((ic = 0 ∧ distance((x,y),(u,v)) ≤ rad ∧ result = 1) ∨
       (ic = 0 ∧ distance((x,y),(u,v)) > rad ∧ result = 0) ∨
       (ic = 1 ∧ distance((x,y),(u,v)) ≤ .5cm ∧ result = 1) ∨
       (ic = 1 ∧ distance((x,y),(u,v)) > .5cm ∧ result = 0) ))) ]
```

where distance is the standard function for computing the distance between two points. We will the leave the similar specifications for the rectangle class to the reader.

The next step is to plug these stronger specifications into specification (10) to obtain a stronger specification of run appropriate to this particular application. But first we need to know, for each of f1 and f2, whether it is an instance of C or R. Once we have this information, we will be able to choose between the specification of, say, isIn from the class C or the class R when this function is applied to the object f1 or f2. In an actual framework, the initialize function of CF will allow the user to decide the class that each of these objects is an instance of. Here we will just assume that f1 is an instance of C and that f2 is an instance of R. This will allow us to strengthen, for instance, the clause

$$[(\tau.res[1] = 1) \Rightarrow ((|\tau| = 2) \land (\tau.o[2] = f1) \land (\tau.f[2] = iconify)$$
$$\land (f1.ic= 1) \land (!(f2.ic))))]$$

from the specification (10) of run by adding the following to the right side of the preceding implication:

$$[(\#f1.ic = 0) \land distance((f1.x,f1.y),(mx,my)) \le f1.rad] \Rightarrow$$
$$[(f1.ic = 1 \land f1.count = \#f1.count + 1) \land . . .]$$

This assures us that if f1 is currently not iconified, and if the mouse is within the distance rad of the center of f1, then following the call to iconify, f1 will indeed be iconified
(and count incremented). This is precisely the richer behavior that run acquires as a result
of the definitions in the class C, and we arrived at this without reanalyzing the framework, which was our goal. The most complex part of this task is working with the trace-
based specification of the run function. As we noted before, we hope the task will become
considerably simpler if we can develop appropriate special notations for dealing with
such specifications, and we intend to explore ways of doing this in future work.

12.4 Summary

OO frameworks can allow application developers to develop, with relatively little
effort, entire applications tailored to their particular needs. But this requires the application developers to have a good understanding of the framework; in particular, they
need to know the behavior that the functions they define in their derived classes are
required to exhibit. There are various means by which application developers can
acquire this knowledge. Thus, for instance, if the framework designer chooses the
names of the various methods carefully, that can convey a lot of information to the
application developer. Studying existing applications developed using the framework
in question is another important approach that developers can employ to encourage an
understanding of how the framework is meant to be used. We have proposed complementing these approaches by formally specifying the behavior of the framework.

Like most formal approaches, our specifications can be somewhat difficult to understand, especially in the beginning. But, again, as with most formal approaches, the payoff is that one gets a precise understanding of exactly what requirements the functions
defined by the application developer must meet. Consider again the example of the diagram editor framework. The name isIn conveys a lot of information about this function,
and one might question the need for a formal specification. But suppose an application
developer decided to define a new type of figure corresponding to doughnuts. Should
isIn return 0 or 1 if the given point is within the hole in the doughnut? We cannot
answer by looking at figures like circle and rectangle because such a situation doesn't
arise for these figures. Nor does the name of the function allow us to answer the question. But the specification of isIn that we wrote as part of the specification of the framework makes it clear that this decision is up to the application developer, since the only
conditions that the framework specification imposes on the behavior of this function are
that it not change the values of any of x,y,ic and that it return 0 or 1 as the result. But at
the same time, the specification does not convey the intuition—as does its name—that

this function is intended to tell us whether the given point is inside the figure in question. Thus, the formal specification *complements* other approaches, such as suitable choice of names and illustrative examples, rather than replacing them. The formal specification also makes it clear that should application developers choose to ignore the intuition conveyed by the name of the function, as well as the guidance of the example applications, they may do so, as long as the requirements imposed by the formal specification are satisfied. This is important because occasionally the developer may find ways to use the framework that were unintended by the framework designer or at least that are different from those suggested by such things as the names of the functions, as well as other applications that may have been developed using the framework.

While the approach we have proposed, including the use of traces to record the virtual function calls, is fairly natural, the resulting specifications are rather difficult to read and understand. This seems primarily due to the lack of suitable notations for expressing simple properties of traces, so that we had to resort to low-level primitives (such as considering each element of the trace individually). We plan to develop appropriate notations that will make the expression of common behaviors easier to write and to read. This, we believe, will substantially improve the usefulness of our specifications.

Another extension we need is to generalize our model of frameworks. The model we have used in this chapter, while it seems to be a reasonable fit for many simple frameworks, is not general enough. We intend to apply our approach to specifying an actual framework (for collecting and disseminating medical information of a particular type) developed by Mamrak et al. [Mamrak 1997]. We believe this exercise will allow us to generalize the model so that it will be suitable for realistic frameworks.

Finally, there is also the question of whether the programming language is too constraining. Thus, for instance, C++ requires that the number and types of parameters received by a virtual function like isIn in the derived class be the same as that in the base class. This certainly makes the language, as well our model and the resulting specification issues, simpler, but does it prevent us from building interesting frameworks? Isn't it conceivable that an application developer might want to develop a particular derived class for which the appropriate isIn function requires some additional parameters? How do we allow this (without, of course, abandoning type safety, and so on)? This is clearly a much more difficult question and we hope that attempting to generalize our specification technique to deal with such frameworks will shed some light on what needs to be done.

12.5 References

[Abadi 1995] Abadi, M., and L. Cardelli. On subtyping and matching. *Proceedings of ECOOP 1995*, Aarhus, Denmark, August 1995, pp. 145–167. Springer-Verlag, 1995.

[Bosch 1998] Bosch, J., M. Mattsson, and M.E. Fayad. Framework integration: Problems, causes, solutions. Accepted for publication to *Communications of the ACM*, 1999.

[Campbell 1993] Campbell, R.H., and N. Islam. A technique for documenting the framework of an object-oriented system. *Computing Systems* 6: 363–389.

[Dhara 1995] Dhara, K.K., and G.T. Leavens. Forcing behavioral subtyping through specification inheritance. In *ICSE-18*, pp. 27–51. Springer-Verlag, 1995.

[Fayad-Schmidt 1997] Fayad, M.E., and D.C. Schmidt. Object oriented application frameworks. *CACM* 40(10), October 1997.

[Gamma 1995] Gamma, E., R. Helm, R. Johnson, and J. Vlissides. *Design Patterns: Elements of Reusable OO Software*. Reading, MA: Addison-Wesley, 1995.

[Helm 1990] Helm, R., I. Holland, and D. Gangopadhyay. Contracts: Specifying behavioral compositions in object oriented systems. *OOPSLA-ECOOP*, pp. 169–180, October 1990, Printed as SIGPLAN Notices, 25 (10).

[Horstmann 1995] Horstmann, C. *Mastering Object-Oriented Design in C++*. New York: John Wiley & Sons, 1995.

[Johnson 1988] Johnson, R., and B. Foote. Designing reusable classes. *JOOP* 1:22–35.

[Johnson 1997] Johnson, R. Frameworks = components + patterns. *Communications of the ACM*, Theme Issue on Object-Oriented Application Frameworks, Mohamed E. Fayad and Douglas Schmidt, editors, 40(10), October 1997: 39–42.

[Liskov 1994] Liskov, B., and J. Wing. A behavioral notion of subtyping. *ACM TOPLAS* 16:1811–1841.

[Mamrak 1997] Mamrak, S., J. Boyd, and I. Ordonez. Building an information system for collaborative researchers. *Software Practice and Experience* 27(3):253–263.

[Meyer 1988] Meyer, B. *Object-Oriented Software Construction*. Englewood Cliffs, NJ: Prentice Hall, 1988.

[Misra 1981] Misra, J., and K. Chandy. Proofs of networks of processes. *IEEE TSE* 7:417–426.

[Soundarajan 1984] Soundarajan, N. Axiomatic semantics of CSP. *ACM TOPLAS* 6:647–662.

[Soundarajan 1997] Soundarajan, N., and S. Fridella. Inheriting and modifying behavior. *Proceedings of TOOLS 1997*, pp. 148–163, B. Meyer, R. Ege, Singh, editors. Los Alamitos, CA: IEEE Computer Society Press, 1997.

[Soundarajan 1998] Soundarajan, N., and S. Fridella. *Enriching Subclass Specifications*. Technical report, available at www.cis. ohio-state.edu/~neelam, 1998.

[Sparks 1996] Sparks, S., K. Benner, and C. Faris. Managing OO framework reuse. *Computer*, Theme Issue on Managing Object-Oriented Software Development, Mohamed E. Fayad and Marshall Cline, editors, 29(9), September 1996:52–62.

[Stroustrup 1991] Stroustrup, B. *The C++ Programming Language*. Reading, MA: Addison-Wesley, 1991.

12.6 Review Questions

1. What does *flow of control* mean in a framework?

2. Explain briefly what *traces* are. What information do they give us about a framework?

3. What are the key components of an application framework? Is it possible to have a framework that has no concrete classes? No abstract classes? Explain briefly.

4. What do the pre- and postconditions of a method tell us about the method? Why is it that the postcondition of a method involves two states, whereas the precondition involves only one?

5. What does the ! notation mean (in specifications)? Does it appear in the precondition or postcondition or both? Is it possible to have a method whose specification does not have the ! appear anywhere in it, or is it a necessary component of every method specification?

6. Suppose we have two methods in a class. Is it possible (or likely) that they have the same precondition? The same postcondition? The same precondition and the same postcondition? Explain.

7. Which methods' specifications would you expect to find the trace appear in? Why? Explain.

8. What does it mean to *plug* the behavior of a method defined by the application developer *into* the specification of a base class method?

12.7 Problem Set

1. Consider the example at the start of *Section 12.2*. Write the code for the method changeX() that satisfies the specification (1) given in that section. Does your method also satisfy specification (2)? If yes, explain whether this happened because of the details of the particular method you wrote or whether it will be true in general.

2. Consider the conditions given in specifications (3), (4), (5), and (6) of *Section 12.2.1*. Suppose the class C contains two variables x and y (rather than just x as in the discussion in the chapter), both x and y being of type A, and the body of the run() function is changed to be as follows:

x.g(); y.g()

3. What changes, if any, would you make to specifications (3), (4), (5), and (6)? Explain your changes.

4. Later in *Section 12.2.1* it says that if information about which virtual methods are invoked is omitted from the specification of run(), then an application designer may not be able to establish the complete behavior of run(). Can that happen in this example? In other words, would it be possible to rewrite specifications (5) and (6) of run() so that this problem manifests itself? If yes, show how you would do it; if not, explain why such a thing cannot happen in this example.

5. Consider the blowUp() and blowDown() methods of the diagram editor framework discussed in *Section 12.3*. These methods receive a parameter f (of type int). Why does this parameter not appear anywhere in specification (9) of these methods? Explain briefly.

12.8 Projects

Project 1: Find a simple application framework, and document it precisely using the approach suggested in this chapter. (This requires considerable background in formal specification and verification; it will require the student to have had a course in that subject.)

CHAPTER 13

Capturing Framework Requirements

The creation of a software product that is unlike any that a company, team, or individual has ever created before is a rare incident. Instead, the daily software development task usually involves the incremental creation of new features for existing products [Maguire 1994]. Even if a product is a totally new venture, chances are that elements with similar characteristics can be found within one of the company's existing products. In short, most development efforts contain commonality at a variety of different levels. Distilling these characteristics and developing them once instead of reinventing them may save design and development time, provide an extensible product architecture, and decrease maintenance costs.

Several techniques have been advanced for capturing and reusing this commonality. The class concept is fundamentally a technique for reusing object definitions. Idioms, design patterns, and frameworks have all been used with success at differing levels of granularity. A framework can capture the commonality within and across several applications.

Recently, a new approach to framework development has been offered that requires no investment in implementation [Taligent 1995]. This approach calls for framework development through the analysis of a problem domain. However, the framework design team has no way of systematically capturing this knowledge in the context of user requirements. The Taligent approach is an a priori approach to building frameworks but lacks an explicit process for accumulating this domain knowledge.

This chapter presents a new technique, called *use-case assortment*, that supports the capture of domain information during use-case modeling, which is then used for a framework development effort. Use-case assortment is a step that occurs between requirements analysis (where use cases are created) and analysis modeling. The assortment or grouping of use cases with common properties provides a mechanism for identifying frameworks without investing a substantial amount of resources for implementation. Once the business need for a framework is identified, a use-case abstraction process allows framework requirements to be distilled in the form of abstract use cases. These abstract use cases are transformed through analysis and design modeling techniques to create framework designs. This technique is based partially on research [Major 1997] and partially on our experience in several companies with framework development projects that span multiple domains and companies.

The technique also takes advantage of change cases [Ecklund 1996] to ensure that the resulting framework is extensible. A change case represents a potential, rather than a current, requirement. By considering future requirements in the analysis, our technique produces frameworks that are more robust with regard to future change.

13.1 Background

The creation and refinement of this framework requirements gathering, capturing, and tracing technique is the result of several years of evolution in our framework development processes. Over the course of this time, the authors have created frameworks for a broad spectrum of domains. These domains have ranged from the very low level (design), such as a framework for persistence, to a high-level (business) framework for order entry. Our first framework experience, a communications framework [Bitterer 1995], was small enough so that its identification and creation was the result of a desire to reuse and refactor the existing code.[1]

As our framework experience grew, we began to recognize conditions favorable to framework opportunities before and during the development of the application. We found that through framework opportunity recognition, we could produce viable frameworks by using the refactoring approach. The next logical step was to find a formal method for soliciting, capturing, and tracing framework requirements [Jacobson 1995]. Initially, we used a use-case approach [Meszaros 1994] to create framework requirements and augmented it by prototyping [Bowser 1995] these requirements. Creating such a requirements process was necessary due to the multisite development effort and the large number of developers involved.[2]

Convinced that use cases and domain analysis were the keys to specifying accurate framework requirements for existing domain knowledge, we continued to build use-case expertise and refine the process of developing frameworks. In the course of time, we found that domain expertise, the ability to think abstractly, and a solid framework development process were the keys to successful framework development. Furthermore, a straightforward and repeatable framework requirements gathering process provides the first step in the process to create your successful framework.

---

[1]The techniques used to build this framework were developed by Ralph Johnson [Johnson-Foote 1988].

[2]A large-scale framework was developed in Canada and used by developers in the United States.

13.2 Framework Requirements

As we stated earlier, a framework may be identified and extracted from a series of related implementations or it may be abstracted from an analysis of the domain in which the framework will reside. The *refactoring approach* uses existing implementations of the stand-alone versions of the common elements to create a common set of general and supporting classes. This approach is the one commonly used in the industry today. The *a priori approach*, on the other hand, identifies these classes prior to any implementation of the common elements through requirements analysis and domain expertise.

For an a priori approach to framework development to be successful, all four of Reenskaug's conditions must be addressed in advance of framework development [Reenskaug 1996]. These conditions are listed in Figure 13.1. Since all but one focus on framework requirements,[3] this is the logical place to begin. Satisfying these requirements must be a natural part of our framework development process.

13.2.1 Requirement Levels

Not all requirements are created equally. There is a hierarchical classification that includes business, application, and design requirements. Moving down the hierarchy leads to an increasingly narrow focus. An individual business requirement specifies functionality that affects a larger set of use cases than does a typical application requirement.

Business processes may be implemented via multiple cooperating applications. This type of requirement is generally captured in business-level use cases [Jacobson 1992]. For example, the business requirements for a system that implements the operating process for an airline could result in an application that performs airline scheduling and an application that performs route acquisition.

At the next level, application requirements may be satisfied by multiple design components. The requirement of loaning books in a library may be performed by an application with requirements to check out books, check in books, and scan a mem-

---

[3]All of the conditions except the business justification.

There must be multiple elements with common characteristics.

Requirement for the framework must be well understood.

Sufficient business justification must exist for the framework.

Patterns must be abstracted.

Figure 13.1 Reenskaug' s generalized framework conditions.

bership card. These requirements may be captured in application-level use cases [Jacobson 1992].

Finally, there are requirements that can be satisfied by the selection of the appropriate design. For example, an application may have to communicate in different network environments and thus support multiple communication protocols. Another example is the need to be able to handle dates beyond the year 2000. These requirements eliminate certain design choices and thus fall into the design requirement category. One technique for capturing these requirements is in the form of software contracts [Lajoie 1995], which serve as design-level use cases.

The requirements for a framework can be divided into the same three levels, but they are more abstract, more general. If the business systems, the applications, and the design characteristics are thought of as the ensembles, then the abstracted characteristics of each of these elements form a corresponding set of frameworks. In other words, if there is an isomorphism between use cases at each of the requirement levels and some ensemble implementation, there is also an isomorphism between the abstractions at each level and the corresponding framework.

There are three levels of frameworks: enterprise, application, and design, which correspond to these three levels of requirements, as shown in Table 13.1. As use cases provide a uniform, multilevel approach to requirements gathering, frameworks provide a uniform, multilevel approach to architecture. Although there are multiple levels of use cases and multiple corresponding levels of frameworks, there is a single process for gathering the requirements for these frameworks (Reenskaug's condition 2) and abstracting patterns (Reenskaug's condition 4).

13.2.2 Use-Case Assortment

Use-case assortment is an a priori technique for developing requirements for a framework. The technique combines a set of modeling heuristics with an analysis technique that identifies abstractions. The result of applying use-case assortment is a use-case model that provides the framework developer with the same type of guidance that the application use-case model provides the application developer.

A form of abstract use case is the key to capturing requirements for a priori framework development. Detecting the patterns that lead to these abstract use cases requires some simple heuristics. When the patterns are detected, use cases exhibiting the same pattern are grouped together. This process partitions the use cases into sets, where all of the use cases in a set follow a common pattern. We call this *use-case assortment*. Once the use cases are grouped, the pattern is distilled and isolated into an abstract use case.

Table 13.1   Corresponding Levels of Requirements: Use Cases and Frameworks

REQUIREMENTS LEVEL	USE-CASE LEVEL	FRAMEWORK LEVEL
Business	Business use case	Enterprise framework
Application	Application use case	Application framework
Design	Software contract	Design framework

This abstract use case represents all of the characteristics common to the use cases in the group.

Use-Case Modeling Heuristics

In this section we present a set of four heuristics that support the analysis technique described in the next section. The heuristics guide the identification of abstractions that are added to the use-case model.

Frameworks always have two distinct clients. This implies two relations that should be reflected isomorphically in our use-case model. The first is the user of the framework, that is, the person or system (depending on the level of framework) that receives value from the framework. This relationship is reflected in the use-case model as a common actor shared between the two use cases of the ensemble, as shown in Figure 13.2.

> **Heuristic 1:** Use cases that represent common behavior, but that do not share a primary actor (the actor to whom the use case yields measurable value), may be grouped by creating an abstract actor.

To illustrate the usefulness of a common primary actor, consider a call-processing example in which POTS and ISDN are both supported. These use cases consider the initiation of a phone call from a telephone switch point of view. In the two use cases, Originate POTS Basic Call and Originate ISDN Basic Call, there are different primary actors (POTS Telephone and ISDN Terminal, respectively), as shown in Figure 13.3. Creating a framework that services both actors is difficult due to their differing needs.

To group the use cases in this example requires an abstract actor, Customer Premise Equipment, to be inserted into the use-case model. Abstract actors allow abstract use cases to be created when they do not share a primary actor. However, the implementation of a framework based upon abstract actors requires an abstract interface for the framework and ensemble client.

The second type of client is the ensemble that requires the context of the framework within which to operate. Since the ensemble represents a concrete use case and the framework represents an abstract use case in the use-case model, this relationship is reflected by the *uses* relationship between use cases.

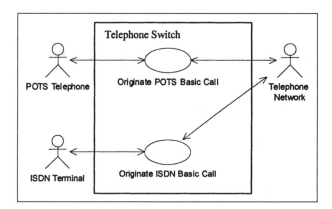

Figure 13.2 Two call processing use cases.

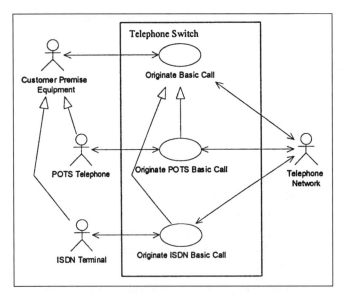

Figure 13.3   Refactored call-processing use-case model.

Heuristic 2: Each ensemble use case must follow all of the behavior defined in the framework use case, although the ensemble use case may determine how it will follow that behavior.

This is a fairly natural rule for abstract use cases for object-oriented software systems, but it leads to an interesting observation. A framework generally compartmentalizes its ensembles. In this way the framework allows the ensembles to add their own application logic for various phases of execution. These are actual states within the framework itself called *hot spots* [Pree 1995]. What happens within these states is up to the ensemble. For example, a communications framework might have four such phases: connection establishment, sending, receiving, and disconnection. The ensemble use case or software contract for TCP/IP describes different behavior for each of these states than does its APPC ensemble use-case counterpart.

The layers of use cases in the initial model can be used to guide the abstraction process.

Heuristic 3: When two use cases have an extends relationship with the same higher-level use case, their primary actors should be specializations of the abstract primary actor associated with the higher-level use case.

The extends relationship between the two use cases is an acknowledgment of some degree of commonality. The two actors associated with two related use cases also have commonality in the sense that they both require the same service from the system. The abstract actor covers a more general scope than a primary actor. However, the abstract actor will not represent the entire set of services required by either of the primary actors. This refactoring results in a new abstract actor plus two primary actors that now inherit from the abstract actor.

The domain model will also be structured and that structure should be paralleled in the framework's use-case model.

Heuristic 4: Use cases that describe action on a common domain object should be grouped under a common actor.

An object encapsulates more than just a set of methods and variables. It encapsulates a concept. When two or more use cases interact with the same domain object, they will be describing conceptually related tasks. Domain objects that form frameworks work in concert to perform services for their ensembles. Grouping[4] use cases that include framework domain objects together will identify a higher-level behavior that should be represented in the requirements for the framework.

For example, suppose two abstract use cases, Originate Basic Call and Originate Feature[5] use the same domain object, DigitCollector. Each of these use cases may be refactored to use (through the uses relationship) a new Collect Digits use case (by heuristic 4). The Collect Digits use case shares the common actor of the two use cases (or a common abstract actor by heuristic 1). Digit collection then becomes a requirement for a service for a call-processing framework.

The Analysis Technique

This technique utilizes a refactoring of the basic use-case model to arrive at a set of requirements for the framework. The refactoring is guided by the set of modeling heuristics and the results of the domain analysis. This technique fits within a comprehensive framework development strategy; however, we will continue to focus only on the requirements specification phase of the development process. In this section we will summarize the analysis technique.

The fundamental activity of the use-case assortment technique is the grouping of use cases with similar behavior under a common abstract actor. This results in a model in which the use-case model is decomposed into sets of use cases, each associated with an abstract use case. The analysis technique is iteratively applied to the use-case model until no further useful abstract actors or use cases can be identified. There are three phases to use-case assortment, each is similar to a corresponding step in use-case modeling.

The first phase is the identification of abstract actors. Abstract actors allow a wider range of use-case groups in the search for commonalties. These actors are created by relating the roles that the various actors play in the system. Heuristic 3 can be used as one means of identifying potential patterns in which the concrete actors are updated in the use-case model to inherit from the abstract actor. For example, a doctor and a nurse may perform slightly different roles but exhibit common behavior with respect to a patient status application. These actors may inherit from the abstract actor creatively.

The second phase is the definition of abstract use cases by refactoring the initial use-case model. The refactoring process proceeds in similar fashion to the process for refactoring class hierarchies. Common behavior among a set of use cases is identified; that behavior is generalized and described in a new use case. The preexisting use cases are rewritten to reference the new use case via the appropriate relation. Use-case modeling heuristics 1, 2, and 4 are applied to the application use-case model.

---

[4]In some cases, the use case must be refactored to accomplish this.

[5]A feature is a service provided in addition to normal call processing such as call forwarding and must be activated through a sequence of digits (such as *55), a feature key, or provisioning.

The domain analysis model can assist in identifying commonality, as stated in heuristic 4. Use cases will refer to concepts in their algorithm descriptions. By locating those use cases that reference common domain objects, use cases can be grouped and abstracted. This partially addresses what Opdyke and Johnson identify as the most difficult part of refactoring: determining whether two behaviors are the same [Opdyke 1995]. In this case, the commonality is action on a single object.

The refactored use-case model contains relationships similar to those in an object model. The model includes abstract actors, generalized use cases as well as sub–use cases that are aggregated within multiple use cases. This process is shown in Figure 13.4.

The third phase is the complete description of each abstract use case. In the creation of abstract use cases, the elements from domain analysis often aid in the abstraction process. It is sometimes difficult to create the appropriate level of abstraction simply from the prose found in a set of use cases. Creating abstract superclasses for the domain elements found in the grouped use cases can be instrumental in the description of the abstract use cases. The abstract superclasses should be completely described in an updated domain model and form the core of the framework analysis model.

The link between abstract and concrete use cases is made via *extension points* [UML 1997]. Extension points are section names in the prose of the use case that are common to the abstract and concrete use cases. In the abstract use case, these sections describe a superset of the behavior expected in the ensembles. The concrete use case describes the expected behavior from the individual ensemble. Message sequence diagrams, state charts, and use-case maps [Buhr 1996] may be useful in refining the extension points and the information contained in these sections. The goal of extension points in the abstract use cases is to allow the framework to remain flexible to handle future ensembles. Extension points map directly to a framework's hot spots.

These three steps can be repeatedly applied to the revised models. The process creates new abstract use cases, actors, and domain classes. The process terminates when no additional commonality can be identified or when the concrete use cases and domain classes are atomic[6] [Major 1997].

Although use-case assortment follows a similar, albeit more abstract, process to use-case modeling, these two activities should generally remain separate. The reason that use-case assortment is separated from use-case modeling (requirements gathering) is that the technique is most successful when there is a comprehensive use-case model

---

[6]*Atomic* means that the class cannot be further subdivided and remain a model of a concept.

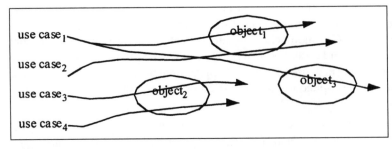

Figure 13.4   Tracing the use cases into the domain model.

Table 13.2 Comparison of Approaches

PHASE	USE-CASE MODELING	USE-CASE ASSORTMENT
1	Find actors	Find abstract actors
2	Find use cases	Identify abstract use cases through grouping
3	Describe use cases	Describe abstract use cases

from which to work. There are, however, projects where the commonality is obvious very early in the development process. In these situations, use-case assortment may be applied concurrently with use-case modeling. Each use-case assortment phase should follow the completion of the corresponding use-case modeling phase. See Table 13.2.

In most cases, the commonality is not readily apparent.[7] Using the comprehensive use-case model and the domain model allows maximum effectiveness in the search for patterns. This a priori approach is more successful as the size of the use-case model increases, since there is a more comprehensive set of constructs upon which to draw.

13.2.3 Creating a Business Case

The last element required for framework development is the business case. A business case may be made on a variety of levels and the use-case model may assist in determining the appropriate level. Techniques continue to evolve to improve the prediction of the amount of effort required to develop applications based upon use cases. With a well-defined requirements basis (use-case model) to work from, the creation of such a business case for a priori frameworks is much easier than under the refactoring approach and can be completed much earlier in the project life cycle. The case can also be evaluated prior to a large investment in code.

Under certain circumstances, a business case is not really necessary. In the communications example, there may be a need not only to provide a range of communication protocols but also to support several delivery platforms. Using the criticality and frequency measures in the use cases, the decision might be to create a TCP/IP framework capable of supporting multiple platforms as the logical first step in creating the more general communications platform. This incremental approach minimizes up-front risk and provides for succeeding increments to build on the proven strengths of the earlier increments.

13.2.4 Large Use-Case Models

Frameworks can be created for entire systems or subsystems and they can be created for systems large or small. Much of our experience comes from the large models required for telecommunication systems. The size of these models and projects presents special challenges but also presents significant opportunities for identification of commonality. Even systems that begin as moderate-size systems grow over time. New

[7]This is illustrated by the popularity of the refactoring approach to framework development.

versions of the system must usually provide all of the functionality of the past versions in addition to their new functions. Here we consider the implications of our technique on the size of the model.

The result of an increase in functionality can be larger amounts of code, larger design models, larger analysis models, and larger use-case models. The largest increase in the use-case model usually comes from the use cases themselves. As the number of use cases in a single domain model increases, common elements start to emerge. Since the use cases document the requirements for the development effort, commonality in the product will be reflected in the use cases. Commonality will be factored by the analysis technique into additional abstract use cases and into concrete (sub–) use cases that are defined by *extending* existing use cases and by *using* use-case fragments, which represent small, common sequences of behavior. This results in a larger number of individual use cases, but the model is easier to understand and less redundant.

Change cases, use cases that reflect anticipated system changes, add to the scope (and size) of the use-case model. Change cases also aid in the business justification of frameworks, as they allow a better determination of the multiplicity of ensembles. By grouping these change cases under the same abstract use cases as existing requirements, the analysis technique provides a context within which the impact of a change can be realistically estimated.

Excessive use-case modeling can lead to *use-case explosion,* in which a project becomes bogged down in the requirements gathering phase. This problem is caused by one of two possible factors. The first cause is that too much detail may be placed in a use case or its sub–use cases. The appropriate decomposition using the uses and extends relationships will reduce some of the redundancy and reduce the complexity of the model; however, this results in an increase in the absolute number of use cases. The second cause is that an excessive number of change cases may be written. Change cases beyond what is expected in the foreseeable future should be included only if they are broadly stated or part of a definitive plan.

Use-case assortment partitions the use cases in the model and groups them under three types of abstract use cases. This makes it easier to locate specific use cases in a large model. By starting with the abstract use case that covers the area of interest, the path along extends relationships leads to the required use case. The analysis technique will also identify commonality among actors that are, on the surface, very dissimilar—for example, human operators and software systems—but are very similar with respect to uses of the software under development. This often leads to substantial reduction in the size of the model by combining use cases for actors that share the same abstract actor. The analysis technique will also result in a model that is more maintainable. By decomposing the use cases, they are more modular. The uses relationship reduces the scope of changes and thus reduces the impact of change on the model. This is particularly important for an a priori technique that will rely on iteration to arrive at a robust model.

13.3 Related Work

Capturing framework requirements and related issues have been studied by others, such as Gause and Weinberg (*Section 13.3.1*), Taligent (*Section 13.3.2*), Jacobson, Griss, and Jonsson (*Section 13.3.3*), and Koskimies and Mossenbock (*Section 13.3.4*).

13.3.1 Gause and Weinberg

Gause and Weinberg [Gause 1989] provide a general method for grouping requirement attributes. Their method lists the attributes and the details of these attributes in the following form:

```
Attribute = (list of attribute details)
```

For example, when designing an application with a requirement to support multiple communication platforms, this grouping would be organized in the following way:

```
Communication Platform = (TCP, NetBIOS, APPC, SPX)
```

Their approach gathers common characteristics of an application[8] but has no way to translate these requirements into reusable software elements.

13.3.2 Taligent

The Taligent [Taligent 1995] approach views domain expertise as the pivotal element necessary to create frameworks. This experience is leveraged to provide the basis for an a priori framework development approach. What is missing from their approach is an overall process for collecting this knowledge and translating it into a framework. This approach is restricted implicitly to application and design frameworks, as their experience has been in the areas of operating systems design.

13.3.3 Jacobson, Griss, and Jonsson

Jacobson, Griss, and Jonsson [Jacobson 1997] approach the idea of framework development from another direction. Their approach is also an a priori approach. They utilize use cases to identify component systems using feedback from application engineers. This requires the application engineers to create their own application expertise (similar to the Taligent approach) to be captured in use cases. These component system use cases then provide the basis for component engineering in a manner similar to application development. In fact, they view these components as products.

We believe framework use cases to be a special case of the component system use case. However, component system use cases described by Jacobson, Griss, and Jonsson have no relationship to those use cases being developed for an application or business except that the components created by them should be usable by multiple applications described by the application use cases at the design level. This guarantee is provided by the domain expertise.

Jacobson, Griss, and Jonsson also define two types of frameworks: business and technical. These frameworks are similar to our respective business and design frameworks. They do not explain the relationship between these frameworks and the use cases, except in terms of component systems.

---

[8]Although their requirements process does not strictly apply to software.

13.3.4 Koskimies and Mossenbock

Koskimies and Mossenbock [Koskimies 1995] created a two-phase a priori framework development technique. The first phase involves stepwise generalization of the problem to provide a framework description for implementation. The second phase involves implementation of that framework, starting at the most generalized description.

Use-case assortment provides a similar approach to their first phase. However, we utilize use cases as a method for capturing the description and provide heuristics on how to generalize the use-case model. They focus mainly on the second phase of their technique and provide little information on how to capture the generalized framework requirements.

13.4 Summary

We have introduced a new technique for framework requirements gathering, capturing, and tracing called use-case assortment. This technique creates an isomorphism between the three known levels of abstract use cases (business, application, and design) and the comparable levels of frameworks. This isomorphism concept follows through to the actors and use-case relationships that structure these abstract use cases. We have additionally provided a process to determine these abstract use cases and abstract the pattern for the framework. These requirements can be used as part of an a priori or refactoring framework development process, as shown in Figure 13.5.

We therefore are able to satisfy three of Reenskaug's four framework conditions in advance of implementation. We are able to determine through grouping when there are multiple elements with common characteristics. The partitioned use-case model

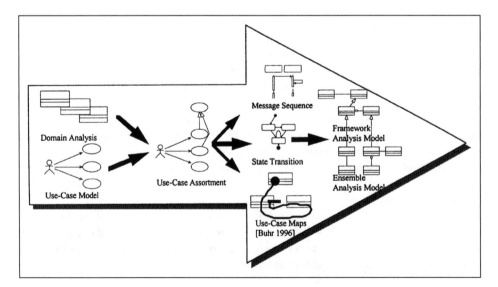

Figure 13.5 Use-case assortment in the context of the software engineering process.

that results from use-case assortment creates well-understood requirements for the elements of the framework. The pattern for the framework has been abstracted through use-case assortment. Satisfaction of the fourth framework condition is partially supported by this approach. The complete understanding of the creation of business cases for framework development is an area for future research.

13.5 References

[Bitterer 1995] Bitterer, Andreas, Michel Brassard, William Nadal, and Chris Wong. *VisualAge and Transaction Processing in a Client/Server Environment.* Upper Saddle River, NJ: Prentice Hall, 1995.

[Bowser 1995] Bowser, John, Granville Miller, and Thomas Pangborn. Building quality into switching software. *International Switching Software (ISS)*: 173–179.

[Buhr 1996] Buhr, R.J.A., and R.S. Casselman. *Use Case Maps for Object-Oriented Systems.* Upper Saddle River, NJ: Prentice Hall, 1996.

[Ecklund 1996] Ecklund, Earl F., Jr., Lois M.L. Delcambre, and Michael J. Freiling. Change cases: Use cases that identify future requirements. *Conference on Object-Oriented Programming Systems, Languages, and Applications (OOPSLA)*, pp. 342–358. New York: ACM Press, 1996.

[Gause 1989] Gause, Donald C., and Gerald M. Weinburg. *Exploring Requirements: Quality Before Design*, p. 164. New York: Dorset House Publishing, 1989.

[Jacobson 1992] Jacobson, Ivar. *Object-Oriented Software Engineering: A Use Case Driven Approach.* Reading, MA: Addison-Wesley, 1992.

[Jacobson 1995] Jacobson, Ivar. Formalizing use-case modeling. *Journal of Object-Oriented Programming* 8 (June 1995):10–14.

[Jacobson 1997] Jacobson, Ivar, Martin Griss, and Patrik Jonsson. *Software Reuse.* New York: ACM Press, 1997.

[Johnson-Foote 1988] Johnson, Ralph, and Brian Foote. Designing reusable classes. *Journal of Object-Oriented Programming* 1 (June/July 1988):22–35.

[Koskimies 1995] Koskimies, Kai, and Hanspeter Mossenbock. Designing a framework by stepwise generalization. *5th European Software Engineering Conference (ESEC 1995)*, pp. 479–498, Wilhelm Schafer and Pere Botella, editors. New York: Springer-Verlag, 1995.

[Lajoie 1995] Lajoie, Richard, and Rudolph K. Keller. Design and reuse in object-oriented frameworks: Patterns, contracts, and motifs in concert. In *Object-Oriented Technology for Database and Software Systems*, pp. 295–312, V.S. Alagar and R. Missaoui, editors. Singapore: World Scientific Publishing, 1995.

[Maguire 1994] Maguire, Steve. *Debugging the Development Process*, pp. xv. Redmond, WA: Microsoft Press, 1994.

[Major 1997] Major, Melissa L., and John D. McGregor. *A Qualitative Analysis of Two Requirements Capturing Techniques for Estimating the Size of Object-Oriented Software Projects.* Technical report, Clemson University, 1997.

[Meszaros 1994] Meszaros, Gerard, and associates. Experiences building large OO frameworks at BNR. *Oops Messenger* 5 (October 1994): 14–18.

[Opdyke 1995] Opdyke, William F., and Ralph E. Johnson. Creating abstract superclasses by refactoring. Unpublished work, 1995.

[Pree 1995] Pree, Wolfgang. *Design Patterns for Object-Oriented Software Development.* Reading, MA: Addison-Wesley, 1995.

[Reenskaug 1996] Reenskaug, Trygve, Per Wold, and Odd Arild Lehne. *Working with Objects,* p. 156., Greenwich, CT: Manning Publications, 1996.

[Taligent 1995] Taligent Inc. *The Power of Frameworks.* Reading, MA: Addison-Wesley, 1995.

[UML 1997] *UML Notation Guide version 1.1.* Available at www.Rational.com, 1997.

13.6 Review Questions

1. Why is it important to conduct domain analysis (Figure 13.5) in parallel with use-case modeling?

2. What is the relationship between use cases and the domain model?

3. An order entry business process and application suite contain the following use cases: Find Order, Marshall Order, and Store Order in Database. Which requirement level (business, application, and design) is each use case likely to be and why?

4. A use case provides measurable value to an actor. Who gets measurable value from the framework use cases (use cases refactored out of the use-case model for the purpose of creating frameworks)?

5. Why is an abstract interface necessary when an abstract actor is created as in heuristic 1? Hint: Consider an example of a framework that encapsulates multiple network communication protocols such as TCP/IP sockets and NetBIOS. What are the drawbacks of such an interface?

6. Consider the use of state charts in the implementation of a framework and its ensembles. What is the relationship between the state charts of each of the ensembles and the framework? Hint: Consider heuristic 2.

7. How can the use of *uses* (soon to be called *includes*) and *extends* in heuristic 3 lead to a natural refactoring of a use-case model where there is a high degree of commonality between use cases? Consider that the uses relationship is like delegation and the extends relationship is like inheritance in object-oriented design and programming.

8. Why should you group use cases that describe actions on a common domain object under a common actor (heuristic 4)?

13.7 Problem Set

1. Consider a business organization embarking on the development of a large project with several potential frameworks in it. What are the issues that they may face with respect to framework development? Consider Reenskaug's generalized framework conditions as a starting point.

2. How are framework use cases related to component use cases [Jacobson 1997]?

Develop a methodology for a large company with a separate reuse (framework) organization to use a hybrid approach (use-case assortment and component engineering) to develop a framework to meet the needs of a given development group. (This problem requires information from *Software Reuse* [Jacobson 1997]).

3. Create extension points for the framework use case Originate Basic Call in Figure 13.3. If you do not know anything about ISDN basic call, develop these from the logical states entered as you originate a Plain Old Telephone Service basic call.

4. You are an ATM machine vendor who has a successful cash machine that many banks are using. However, the Internet/web has changed the rules of commerce and the banks are asking for digicash machines that they can deploy on the web for e-commerce. You wish to enter this market and realize that you can reuse much of your software infrastructure from your ATM machine in your web servers. Create a use-case model of your existing ATM machine and your new digicash server (use your imagination but remember that it must be similar in some ways to your old system for banks to trust it). Refactor the commonality out in the form of framework use cases. Remember to conduct domain analysis. Extra credit: Build an analysis model for the two systems and the framework(s).

CHAPTER 14

Managing
Class Dependencies

A framework provides an abstract architecture that all application programs reuse [Johnson 1997; Johnson-Foote 1988; Nelson 1994; Pree 1995; Pree 1996; Schmid 1997]. The places inside a framework that vary from application program to application program are called the framework's hot spots [Johnson-Roberts 1997; Pree 1995; Pree 1996; Schmid 1997]. Hot spots encapsulate possible variations. They are said to represent axes of variability [Demeyer 1997].

Class dependencies occur when different hot spots aren't independent of each other, but represent the same axis of variability. When the framework is instantiated, choosing one class may imply that another class has to be chosen as well or that another class must not be chosen. Let's take a look at the following examples:

A framework supports application programs running on different platforms. The framework therefore provides different platform-specific implementations for several abstract classes. However, each individual application program is supposed to run on one specific platform; hence, each individual application program must only use concrete classes for this specific platform.

A framework supplies different user interfaces to its functionality. The different user interfaces consist of several classes, each of which must be used consistently in the application programs. Classes from different user interfaces must not be mixed.

The consistent use of concrete classes is the major requirement as far as managing this kind of dependencies is concerned. We say that an application program is consistent if it meets all consistency requirements. We say that a framework is consistent if it supports the consistency of all application programs derived from it.

But what does that mean? At least, the framework should allow us to statically check whether the classes of an application program fit together. An application program's inconsistency should be detected at compile time at the latest. This way, we get rid of unwanted effects during the application program's execution.

However, the advantages of building consistent frameworks aren't restricted to statically checking whether an application program consists of an appropriate combination of classes. As we will see, building consistent frameworks results in designs that increase the coupling between dependent classes, and reduce the coupling between independent classes. Building consistent frameworks therefore also contributes to the flexibility of a framework's architecture.

A straightforward idea to solve the class dependency problem is of course to introduce only one hot spot for each axis of variability and to have different hot spots represent orthogonal axes. Still, this is not always possible. For instance, in a framework that offers numerous platform-dependent implementations to several classes, each abstract superclass has to be considered a hot spot with respect to the platform choice. The decision of choosing a platform is included redundantly in each superclass.

As we will see, class dependencies are not uncommon and sometimes cannot be avoided. We therefore have to manage them.

There are different techniques to manage class dependencies. Reports on existing frameworks [Lewis 1995] show that some are commonly used in framework development. The techniques fall into the following categories:

Closely coupled classes. Sometimes dependencies between classes indicate that certain classes can only be used together. In this case, close coupling between those classes is appropriate. This means that one class holds, in its definition, a reference to another. While close coupling is normally considered undesirable, it is useful here since the dependent classes can take care of their dependencies themselves.

Consistent object creation. A special class can be introduced, which is assigned the task to create instances of those classes that underlie class dependencies. Instances of the special class are often called *factories*. A factory knows the consistency requirements placed on the classes it instantiates and makes sure that only valid combinations of objects are created.

Data-driven classes. Sometimes class dependencies can be avoided by making classes data-dependent. Different variations of a number of classes are not represented by several classes each. Rather, information that is used to parameterize a set of classes is extracted into persistent data. Because all these classes share the data, redundancy is avoided. When the persistent data is changed, the instances of all classes accessing the data change their behavior consistently.

Metalevel configuration. Class dependencies can be dealt with at a metalevel. Application programs can be thought of as different configurations of one generic program. Due to class dependencies, only certain configurations are valid, while others would lead to inconsistent application programs. Choosing a valid configuration on the metalevel yields a valid application program.

Within each category, there are several techniques that do vary in the underlying programming, but differ little in their overall intent. We will take a closer look at different techniques of each category and analyze their pros and cons later.

14.1 Case Study

Before we go into the more technical details, let's take a look at a small case study. This case study is a framework for interactive and animated presentations on the web.[1]

Figure 14.1 presents a screen shot of a presentation that was developed using this framework. This presentation consists of a sequence of slides and an interactive controller. The controller allows for navigation through the sequence of slides while the presentation goes on. The left side of the window is used by the current slide, while the controller is placed on the right side of the window.

The framework provides a number of classes that all presentations have in common. Furthermore, users can choose from a number of concrete classes for their presentations and have to add their own classes for whatever is specific to their individual presentations—for instance, specific animations.

The framework consists of 46 Java classes, 16 of which are abstract and describe the overall architecture. Of the 30 concrete classes, some are used in every presentation, while others are made available only to presentation developers. Furthermore, the framework makes extensive use of the Java Abstract Window Toolkit (AWT libraries) [Flanagan 1997].

In the following, we trace back parts of the development process and point out where and how class dependencies had to be managed. We cannot demonstrate all

[1]This framework was developed at Forschungszentrum Informatik (FZI), Karlsruhe.

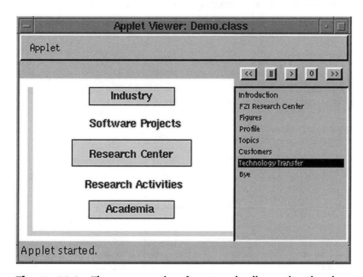

Figure 14.1 The presentation framework allows the development of interactive and animated presentations on the web.

techniques for managing class dependencies with this case study; however, the example gives a good overview of the problems and possible solutions.

The requirements for our framework are as follows:

- Each presentation consists of a sequence of slides.
- Each sequence of slides can allow a controller to interactively modify the order in which the slides are shown.
- Each slide consists of a set of different graphical elements or text elements that can be grouped recursively.
- Animations can be assigned to an element.
- Text elements allow switching between different languages.
- Presentations can be viewed from the World Wide Web in a platform-independent way.
- The framework is supposed to be extensible. In particular, it should be possible to add new types of graphical elements and new types of animations.

A first design includes the class Presentation as well as different containers for presentation elements, represented by the abstract class Tile. A tile can be a single slide or a sequence of slides or a controller. Each presentation consists of a set of tiles.

Using the Java AWT classes, we make Presentation a subclass of Applet. Being an applet, a presentation can be included on a web page [Flanagan 1997]. A class diagram of the design so far, but excluding the Java AWT classes, is presented in Figure 14.2.[2]

Next, we look for possible hot spots in our design:

Since our framework is supposed to run on different platforms, it has to offer different platform-specific variations for all objects that appear on the screen. This concerns the classes Slide and Controller, which contain the actual presentation elements, while a sequence consists of several slides but will not itself contain presentation elements.

---

[2]In our class diagrams we apply the OMT notation [Rumbaugh 1991], enriched by the use of dotted lines to represent class instantiation (object creation). If a class instantiation relationship points to an abstract class, this means that the source instantiates the destination's possible concrete subclasses. In addition, we use round-cornered boxes to represent data files.

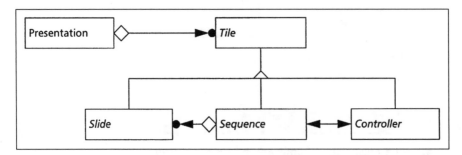

Figure 14.2   A first design includes the major classes of the presentation framework.

Our framework should allow for different types of controllers as far as function-ality is concerned. A standard controller allows the user only to move forward and backward through all slides, while a more sophisticated controller might allow programming, defining a duration time for each slide, superimposition, and so on. This variation concerns both the class Controller and the class Sequence, since the methods that a sequence offers must be sufficient for a con-troller to implement the algorithms it offers.

We have identified two variations concerning two different classes each. Class dependencies are going to occur between future subclasses of the classes involved. We have to deal with these class dependencies now.

Moreover, the class Controller is involved in two different variations, with respect to its functionality as well as to its platform-specific implementation. We therefore divide the class in two: the new class Controller provides the mere functionality, while the additional class Panel represents the controller's user interface. The reorganized class diagram is described in Figure 14.3.

There are two occurrences of class dependencies that we have to manage somehow:

- Whatever concrete subclasses are substituted for the abstract classes Sequence and Controller, they have to assume the same controller functionality.

- Whatever concrete graphical elements the instances of Slide and Panel use, they should work for the same platform.

Since a sequence of slides and a controller have to hold references to each other any-way, close coupling doesn't have to be a bad design. We therefore make the concrete subclasses of Sequence and Controller closely coupled classes. We can have specialized sequences create the controllers they need. In fact, we use a factory method, following the Factory Method pattern [Gamma 1995]. We introduce an abstract method in Sequence that defines an interface to instantiate Controller, which is overridden in the subclasses to let a standard sequence create a standard controller and let a sophisti-cated sequence create a sophisticated controller.

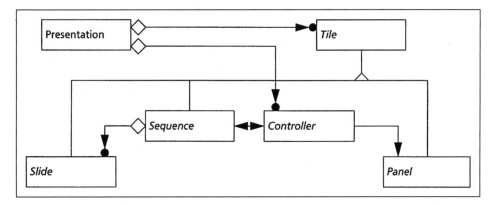

Figure 14.3 Assigning hot spots to variations makes a small reorganization necessary.

Because the classes Slide and Panel are independent of each other, we cannot use close coupling to ensure the consistent use of graphical elements. However, we can employ consistent object creation. We introduce a new class and let it consistently create the graphical elements that are used in Slide and Panel. We therefore introduce an abstract class GraphicalFactory that defines an interface for the creation of graphical elements. This class is called an *abstract factory,* according to the Abstract Factory pattern [Gamma 1995]. Its concrete subclasses create different sets of graphical elements for different platforms, which are used consistently by both slides and panels. Exactly one concrete factory object is created according to the actual platform.

As a consequence of closely coupling Sequence and Controller and introducing a factory for creating graphical elements to be used in Slide and Panel, we obtain the class hierarchy presented in Figure 14.4.[3]

Next, we consider slides and their contents in more detail.

Each slide contains several graphical elements. We distinguish between standard elements and animated elements. The Java AWT libraries provide the standard elements, represented by the classes SimpleElement and CompositeElement. Applying the Composite pattern [Gamma 1995], composite elements are recursively broken down into smaller graphical elements, which allows us to group graphical elements. Unanimated graphical elements can be added to our framework as concrete subclasses of SimpleElement.

For the animation of graphical elements, we introduce the classes AnimatedElement and Animation. Animated elements are part of the structure that recursively nests graphical elements. An animation can be assigned to an animated element. Examples of animations are a typewriter effect, which allows a text to appear on the screen letter by letter, and a coloring effect, which fills a circle or a rectangle with color after it appears on the screen.

To this end, another class dependency occurs. Not all graphical elements may be combined with all types of animation. A typewriter effect only makes sense for a text, while only a circle or rectangle can be filled with a color.

Since the classes AnimatedElement and Animation and their subclasses have to collaborate closely anyway, we can use close coupling to ensure the consistent use of animated elements and animations. We apply the Factory Method pattern [Gamma 1995] again and let concrete subclasses of AnimatedElement create those animations they can deal with. A class diagram is presented in Figure 14.5.

Finally, our case study also contains an example of data-driven classes. We must be able to switch between different languages easily. However, the text used in a presentation is distributed over several classes. There are unanimated and animated text elements, as well as other classes that use text. If we included text into these classes directly, switching from one language to another would not be easy. Furthermore, we

---

[3]The abstract factory class as well as several concrete subclasses that create sets of graphical objects for different platforms are part of the Java AWT library (Java's GUI Library which is know as the Abstract Windowing Toolkit (AWT) [Flanagan 1997]. We had to rename some of the classes, though, for the sake of terminology in the context of this case study. For instance, GraphicalFactory is called Toolkit in java.awt. We include these classes in our case study since we have used them in our framework and they are necessary to explain our design. However, to keep class diagrams reasonably small, the class diagrams do not include the classes that represent the different concrete graphical elements.

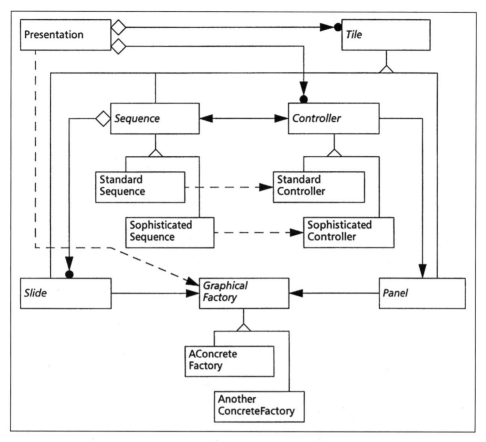

Figure 14.4 Sequence and Controller are being closely coupled, and a factory is introduced for the creation of graphical elements.

could end up with an inconsistent presentation mixing different languages. To meet our requirement, we extract all plaintext into a text file, which is accessed from wherever any text is needed and which can easily be replaced by a text file featuring a different language.

This is, in fact, a very simple example of data-driven classes, but it demonstrates how the extraction of commonly used parts into shared persistent data works in principle. We will learn about more sophisticated data-driven classes later. Moreover, our case study doesn't use metalevel configuration, but we will see examples of metalevel configuration later as well.

To summarize, our case study shows the following:

- Even in a framework as small as this, dependencies between classes occur.

- There are useful techniques to successfully manage these class dependencies.

- Applying these techniques might make some reorganization necessary.

The last point doesn't mean that reorganization is necessary for the purpose of managing class dependencies alone. Rather, what we can see is that looking for class

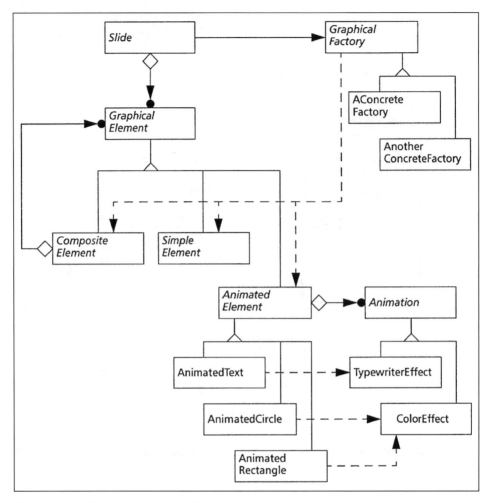

Figure 14.5 Elements and animations are being closely coupled.

dependencies and applying techniques to manage them can give valuable hints as to which class reorganizations might be necessary to obtain a good framework design.

14.2 Classification

Techniques for managing class dependencies can be classified using the following categories: closely coupled classes, consistent object creation, data-driven classes, and metalevel configuration. In the following, we take a look at different techniques from each category. We discuss the techniques' applicability, as well as their advantages and disadvantages. We use our case study to explain the techniques if possible and provide different examples otherwise.

14.2.1 Closely Coupled Classes

Classes are closely coupled if their instances use each other in such a way that the classes cannot be used separately. Several techniques use close coupling to solve the dependency problem.

Factory Methods

Factory methods [Gamma 1995] allow subclasses of an abstract class to decide which objects they create. Figure 14.6 presents an example from our case study.

The method createAnimation is overridden in the subclasses of AnimatedElement to make sure that a typewriter effect is applied only to a text, and a color effect is applied only to a circle.

Factory methods are frequently used in frameworks described in the literature. As an example, HotDraw [Johnson 1992] is a framework for graphical editors that allows figures to be manipulated using the figure's handles. Since all concrete figures create their own handles, each figure can make sure that its handles' effects are valid for the figure. Further examples of factory methods are presented in the Design Pattern Catalog [Gamma 1995].

Constrained Generic Parameters

A similar result can be obtained with constrained generic parameters, provided the programming language used offers constrained genericity, like Eiffel [Meyer 1992] does. A constrained generic parameter defines which classes may be used as actual generic parameters when the generic class is instantiated. Figure 14.7 gives an example.

In this example, Animation or a subclass of Animation has to be used as an actual generic parameter when AnimatedElement is instantiated. However, the generic pa-

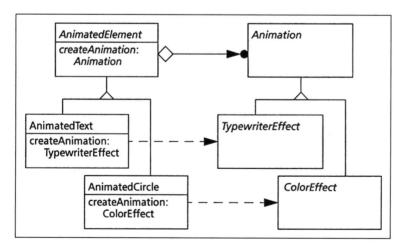

Figure 14.6 Factory methods allow subclasses of an abstract class to decide which objects they create.

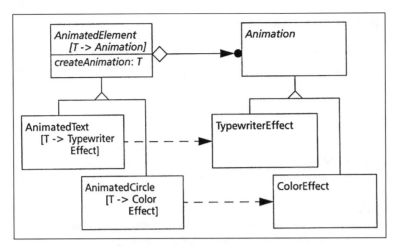

Figure 14.7 Constrained genericity can be employed to specify which classes an object can instantiate.

rameter is constrained further in the subclasses of AnimatedElement, ensuring that AnimatedText is only instantiated with TypewriterEffect or a subclass, and Animated-Circle is only instantiated with ColorEffect or a subclass as actual generic parameters. In contrast to factory methods, the method createAnimation need not be overridden in the subclasses of AnimatedElement to hardwire the corresponding classes.

The mechanism of close coupling literally hardwires dependent classes; these classes contain textual references to each other and cannot be used separately. Therefore, closely coupling classes for the purpose of ensuring their consistent use is reasonable only if the classes involved have to collaborate closely anyway.

As a consequence, dependent classes are grouped together so that they can be reused together. Hence, closely coupling dependent classes can lead to designs with reusable subsystems.

Close coupling allows consistency requirements placed on single instances to be ensured. While many of the other techniques for managing class dependencies focus on the consistent use of classes across an entire application program, close coupling focuses on the consistent use of collaborating class instances. For instance, a presentation may include text, graphics, typewriter effects, and coloring effects all together. However, we have ensured that these objects collaborate only in consistent ways.

14.2.2 Consistent Object Creation

The task of creating consistent sets of objects with respect to certain class dependencies can be assigned to a special class. Instances of such a class are often called factories. We distinguish between different types of factories.

Abstract Factory

An abstract factory [Gamma 1995] provides an interface for the creation of consistent sets of objects. Its concrete subclasses decide on a specific set of objects to create.

Clients don't create these objects themselves but direct a request for creation to the factory object. Figure 14.8 presents an example from our case study.

Different concrete factories create graphical elements for different platforms. Only one concrete factory object is created; hence, only consistent sets of graphical elements exist.

Using an abstract factory to create platform-specific objects is fairly typical; another typical scenario is to have an abstract factory provide an interface for the creation of graphical objects for different look-and-feel variations.

The preceding example is included in the Java AWT libraries [Flanagan 1997] that we have used for our case study. Many examples of abstract factories can be found in existing frameworks such as ET++ [Weinand-Gamma 1995]; other examples are documented in the Design Pattern Catalog [Gamma 1995].

State-Driven Factory

It is not always necessary to introduce different concrete factory subclasses. Sometimes it suffices to have one concrete factory class whose instances can instantiate different consistent sets of objects. The decision on which set of objects is instantiated merely depends on the factory object's actual state. Figure 14.9 shows how a state-driven factory would look in the preceding example.

State-driven factories are able to achieve consistency just as abstract factories are. However, state-driven factory classes tend to include lengthy case statements. They are useful only when there is just a small number of different sets of objects to instantiate.

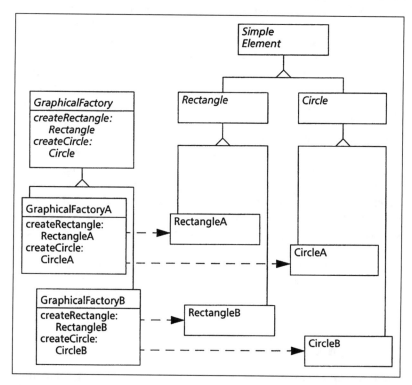

Figure 14.8 An abstract factory provides an interface for the creation of consistent sets of objects.

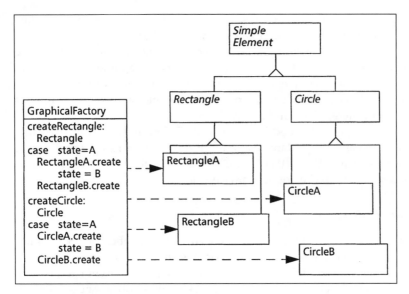

Figure 14.9 A state-driven factory creates consistent sets of objects depending on its internal state.

However, if a programming language such as Smalltalk [Goldberg 1983] is used, which allows classes to be treated as objects, the case statement can be avoided, since an object can simply store the class that has to be instantiated [Alpert 1998].

Introducing a factory causes an additional level of indirection as far as object creation is concerned, since clients must not instantiate objects directly, but have to direct a request for object creation to the factory. Normally, the loss of efficiency caused by this indirection can be ignored. However, it should be taken into account, for instance, when designing a distributed system with, maybe, clients and factory running on different machines.

Factories are immensely useful for managing class dependencies concerning the use of classes across an entire application program. Often, factories are employed to ensure the consistent use of objects that are unrelated except for the fact that corresponding variations have to be used. For instance, in the example, Rectangle and Circle are unrelated classes (which therefore must not be closely coupled), although over the entire presentation only corresponding variations of rectangles and circles may be used.

Factories also offer the advantage that they allow an application program to be reconfigured at runtime. By changing the state of a state-driven factory or by replacing one concrete factory by another, and by updating the objects already created, an application program can be dynamically customized. For instance, an application program that uses a factory to create screen objects for different look-and-feel variations can switch from one look and feel to another at runtime.

14.2.3 Data-Driven Classes

Unlike the techniques from the previous categories, data-driven classes don't assume that variations of a class are represented by several subclasses. All variations of a class are represented by the class itself. However, the class shows a parameterized behavior depending on persistent data stored in a file. Different degrees of flexibility can be achieved by data-driven classes.

Table-Driven Classes

In our case study, we have extracted text from all over a presentation into tables. A table is introduced for each language, as shown in Figure 14.10.

There are many examples of information that is typically used by several classes and can easily be extracted into a commonly shared data structure. For instance, platform-specific information can sometimes be extracted into a configuration file.

Runtime Interpretation

Extracting information into commonly used data structures isn't restricted to mere tables. For a more ambitious example of data-driven classes, we take a look at a framework for warehouse management systems in the pharmaceutical industry.[4]

Application programs derived from this framework are used in various pharmaceutical companies. These application programs differ in many details. For instance, there are different algorithms for storing and retrieving products, depending on the type of warehouse, its temperature, humidity, and so on. These algorithms vary from company to company and, therefore, from application program to application program.

Consistency requirements state, of course, that only consistent sets of storage and retrieval algorithms may be used.

Moreover, it must be easy to adapt application programs to the specific needs of a pharmaceutical company. Therefore, only the stable parts of the framework are implemented in a compiled programming language, in this case C++ [Stroustrup 1991]. This includes the classes Warehouse and Product, as well as the classes Storage and Retrieval that represent the stable parts of the algorithms for storage and retrieval, following the Strategy pattern [Gamma 1995].

The framework's hot spots include the variable parts of the algorithms for storage and retrieval. These are extracted into files that can be accessed from all classes inside the framework. The files contain program fragments for storage and retrieval written

---

[4]This framework was developed in a collaboration between Forschungszentrum Informatik (FZI), Karlsruhe, and a software company located in Karlsruhe.

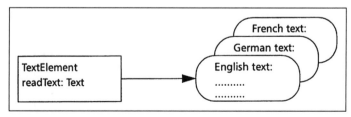

Figure 14.10 Table-driven classes use simple data stored in a table consistently.

in an interpreted programming language, in this case Tcl/Tk [Ousterhout 1994]. The program fragments are interpreted by the Tcl interpreter, which is called from the classes Storage and Retrieval.

To allow the Tcl/Tk programs to access C++ objects—in particular, instances of Warehouse—a wrapper class for Warehouse has to be introduced. A WarehouseWrapper object receives a string-valued parameter, extracts from it the name of the method to call as well as its parameters, and performs the method call on the Warehouse object, as shown in Figure 14.11.

The framework is indeed very flexible; the algorithms for storage and retrieval can be adapted to the special requirements of different companies without recompilation.

The framework's consistency is guaranteed, since the flexible parts of the algorithms for storage and retrieval are not represented by subclasses. Changing the Tcl/Tk programs causes a consistent change in the parameterized behavior of Storage and Retrieval.

Because variations aren't represented by several classes but by one class with a parameterized behavior, all variations share the same class interface. If this is too restrictive, data-driven classes cannot be applied to ensure consistency. However, as we have seen, even program fragments can be extracted into data files. Therefore, the flexibility achieved through data-driven classes shouldn't be underestimated.

However, the more powerful the parameterization of framework classes through extracted data is, the more effort has to be taken to process the data files. If the data files include programs that need interpretation, an interface becomes necessary, such as the interface represented by the interpreter and the wrapper class in our example, which may lead to a loss of efficiency.

Data-driven classes allow an application program to be reconfigured at runtime. For instance, in application programs derived from the warehouse management frame-

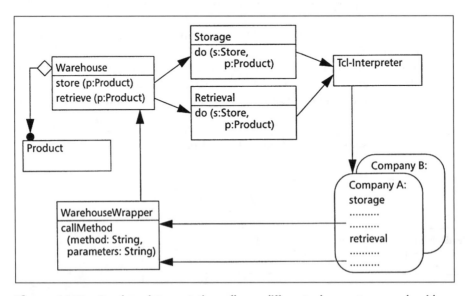

Figure 14.11   Runtime interpretation allows different classes to use algorithms consistently.

work, the algorithms for storage and retrieval can be changed while the application program is running.

14.2.4 Metalevel Configuration

Dependencies between classes can be managed from a metalevel. This way, we restrict the ways in which application programs are put together from the components a framework offers.

Configuration Management

A configuration management system can store information about which combinations of framework classes form valid application programs. When the framework is instantiated, the configuration management system ensures that the instantiation process yields a valid application program.

General guidelines concerning the partitioning of code into components stored in a configuration management system [Woolf 1996] can be extended to solve the dependency problem. For instance, let us consider the warehouse management system example. Suppose the different algorithms for storage and retrieval have to be implemented through different subclasses of Storage and Retrieval for efficiency reasons. Figure 14.12 shows the consistent configurations that a configuration management system can define.

Both configurations A and B represent consistent combinations of framework

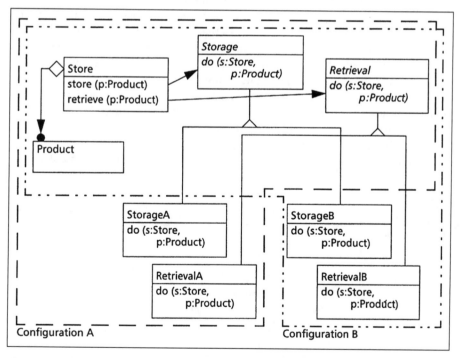

Figure 14.12 A configuration management system can describe sets of classes that can be used together consistently.

classes. A configuration management system can guarantee consistent application programs if it defines exactly these configurations to be valid.

Configuration management systems are commonly used to support multiple platforms or multiple look-and-feel styles.

As far as multiple look-and-feel styles are concerned, similar results can be obtained by generating consistent configurations of graphical elements. Some frameworks for graphical user interfaces include a GUI builder that allows for generating consistent sets of widgets only. Consistency requirements on widgets can be expressed as constraints on the combination of widgets. Tools that use constraints to support multiple styles when building user interfaces have long been available [Borning-Duisberg 1986].

Broker

The configuration of an application program can be delayed until runtime. Request broker architectures such as Common Object Request Broker Architecture (CORBA) [Mowbray 1995; Siegel 1996] can be employed to implement this idea, provided that the broker supports the trading service.

A trader stores metalevel information that allows objects to learn dynamically about the services that other objects provide. Once an object has registered with the trader, the trader can inform clients about this object's services and their properties. The literature often compares the trading service to the yellow pages of a telephone book [Mowbray 1995; Siegel 1996].

As an example, let us consider how the presentation framework from our case study can be implemented using the trading service. Animation objects register with the trader and inform the trader of the properties of their animations. Elements can request from the trader a list of animations that match their properties. Because the trader returns references to only those animations that can be applied to the element, consistency is ensured. A diagram is presented in Figure 14.13.

Broker technology isn't common as far as managing class dependencies in frameworks is concerned, although some examples have been documented [Mowbray 1995; Mowbray-Malveau 1997]. However, broker technology is, of course, the state of the art in the area of distributed systems. This suggests that using brokers to guarantee consistency can be particularly useful in frameworks in distributed environments. Any-

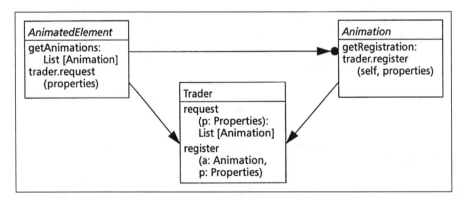

Figure 14.13   Broker technology allows objects to find out the other objects with which they may collaborate.

way, while combining broker and framework technology does seem promising given the background of managing class dependencies, some effort is still needed for this idea to mature.

14.2.5 Classification Summary

Table 14.1 summarizes the classification of the techniques discussed. All techniques contribute to the overall goal of designing consistent frameworks. We list the techniques that we have introduced and review their major characteristics.

14.3 Related Work

Reducing the number of class dependencies, and managing those class dependencies that cannot be avoided, is one aspect of the construction of flexible frameworks. Not surprisingly, managing class dependencies in frameworks shows parallels to various design ideas that can increase a framework's flexibility.

First, the hot-spot approach aims to encapsulate variability inside a well-defined set of places within a framework. Various strategies aimed at the identification of hot spots have been described [Johnson-Roberts 1997; Pree 1995; Pree 1996; Schmid 1997]. Hot spots are identified with the intention of separating what is likely to change from what is probably stable. The encapsulation of the nonstable parts reduces the number of class dependencies and so increases a framework's flexibility.

Table 14.1 The Techniques from Each Category Have Several Characteristics in Common

CATEGORY	TECHNIQUES	CHARACTERISTICS
Closely coupled classes	Factory methods Constrained generic parameters	Groups relate classes for later reuse Hardwires these classes Ensures consistency requirements placed on single instances
Consistent object creation	Abstract factory State-driven factory	Ensures consistency requirements placed on objects that are otherwise unrelated Makes a factory object responsible for the creation of these objects Allows for the reconfiguration of an application program at runtime
Data-driven classes	Table-driven classes Runtime interpretation	Represents different variations by one class with parameterized behavior Possible only when different variations don't require different interfaces Allows for the reconfiguration of an application program at runtime
Metalevel configuration	Configuration management Broker	Ensures consistency from a metalevel Requires additional tools or technology

Next, object-oriented design patterns are mature design fragments for object-oriented software. Design patterns are particularly important for framework construction [Johnson 1997]. Specifically, several creational patterns from the Design Pattern Catalog [Gamma 1995] can be used to manage class dependencies, and underlie several of the techniques presented in this chapter. While the focus of these patterns is on increasing a framework's flexibility in the first place, their side effect is to ensure that application programs consist of components that fit together.

Finally, managing class dependencies from a metalevel bears a resemblance to the design of reflective architectures. Reflective architectures are particularly useful for evolving software systems [Buschmann 1996; Foote-Yoder 1996]. Reflection can be employed to add functionality and to manage unforeseen requirements and constraints. Class dependencies are one example of such constraints, and a framework's metalevel configuration is an example of how flexibility can be achieved through the software's ability of reflection.

14.4 Summary

To conclude, let us review the major insights we have gained into the design of frameworks in the presence of possible dependencies between the framework's classes.

- We have seen that during the design of a framework, and even during the design of a relatively small framework, requirements can occur concerning the consistent use of the framework's classes in the application programs.

- Consistency requirements can occur wherever a framework is designed to be flexible. Therefore, we have to look out for hot spots and identify the axes of variability they represent. We have to check whether there are other hot spots in our frameworks that represent the same or similar axes of variability. In this case, dependencies are likely between the classes involved in the different hot spots.

- We have identified a number of techniques for managing dependencies between classes. Which technique we are going to use depends upon the actual design scenario and how it matches the techniques' applicability. Of course, we have to consider the pros and cons of the different techniques.

- Applying the techniques is relatively straightforward when the classes involved are closely related in the framework. There's not much of a problem when the classes collaborate directly or when at least they are located in the same subsystem. However, if we have identified dependencies between classes that, so far, are hardly connected inside the framework, a reorganization of the class structure becomes necessary. It is impossible to say in general how this reorganization looks; it depends heavily on the actual design scenario.

- Once we have applied techniques to manage all class dependencies in a framework, we obtain a consistent framework design. This allows us to statically check whether an application program is consistent.

Because the techniques presented increase the coupling between dependent classes and reduce the coupling between independent classes, they support a framework design process that results in flexible and reusable designs.

14.5 References

[Alpert 1998] Alpert, S., K. Brown, and B. Woolf. *The Design Patterns Smalltalk Companion.* Reading, MA: Addison-Wesley, 1998.

[Borning-Duisberg 1986] Borning, A., and R. Duisberg. Constraint-based tools for building user interfaces. *ACM Transactions on Graphics* 5(4), April 1986.

[Buschmann 1996] Buschmann, F., R. Meunier, H. Rohnert, P. Sommerlad, and M. Stal. *Pattern-Oriented Software Architecture: A System of Patterns.* New York: John Wiley & Sons, 1996.

[Demeyer 1997] Demeyer, S., D.T. Meijler, O. Nierstrasz, and P. Steyaert. Design guidelines for tailorable frameworks. *Communications of the ACM,* Theme Issue on Object-Oriented Application Frameworks, Mohamed E. Fayad and Douglas Schmidt, editors, 40(10), October 1997.

[Flanagan 1997] Flanagan, David. *Java in a Nutshell,* 2nd ed. Sebastopol, CA: O'Reilly & Associates, 1997.

[Foote-Yoder 1996] Foote, B., and J. Yoder. Evolution, architecture and metamorphosis. In *Pattern Languages of Program Design,* vol. 2, J. Vlissides, J. Coplien, N. Kerth, editors. Reading, MA: Addison-Wesley, 1996.

[Gamma 1995] Gamma, E., R. Helm, R. Johnson, and J. Vlissides. *Design Patterns: Elements of Reusable Object-Oriented Software.* Reading, MA: Addison-Wesley, 1995.

[Goldberg 1983] Goldberg, A., and D. Robson. *Smalltalk-80: The Language and Its Implementation.* Reading, MA: Addison-Wesley, 1983.

[Johnson 1992] Johnson, R. Documenting frameworks using patterns. *Proceedings of OOPSLA 1992—Object-Oriented Programming Systems, Languages, and Applications.* Sigplan Notices 27(10). ACM Press, 1992.

[Johnson 1997] Johnson, R. Frameworks = (Components + Patterns). *Communications of the ACM,* Theme Issue on Object-Oriented Application Frameworks, Mohamed E. Fayad and Douglas Schmidt, editors, 40(10), October 1997.

[Johnson-Foote 1988] Johnson, R., and B. Foote. Designing reusable classes. *Journal of Object-Oriented Programming* 1(2). SIGS Publications, 1988.

[Johnson-Roberts 1997] Johnson, J., and D. Roberts. Evolving frameworks. In *Pattern Languages of Program Design,* vol. 3, R. Martin, D.Riehle, and F. Buschmann, editors. Reading, MA: Addison-Wesley, 1997.

[Lewis 1995] Lewis, T., ed. *Object Oriented Application Frameworks.* Greenwich, CT: Manning Publications, 1995.

[Meyer 1992] Meyer, B. *Eiffel: The Language.* Englewood Cliffs, NJ: Prentice Hall, 1992.

[Mowbray 1995] Mowbray, T. *The Essential CORBA: Systems Integration Using Distributed Objects.* New York: John Wiley & Sons, 1995.

[Mowbray-Malveau 1997] Mowbray, T., and R. Malveau. *CORBA Design Patterns.* New York: John Wiley & Sons, 1997.

[Nelson 1994] Nelson, C. Frameworks—A forum for fitting the task. *IEEE Computer* 27(3), March 1994.

[Ousterhout 1994] Ousterhout, J. *Tcl and the Tk Toolkit.* Reading, MA: Addison-Wesley, 1994.

[Pree 1995] Pree, W. *Design Patterns for Object-Oriented Software Development.* Reading, MA: Addison-Wesley, 1995.

[Pree 1996] Pree, W. *Framework Patterns.* New York, NY: SIGS Books, 1996.

[Rumbaugh 1991] Rumbaugh, J., M. Blaha, W. Premerlani, F. Eddy, and W. Lorensen. *Object-Oriented Modeling and Design.* Englewood Cliffs, NJ: Prentice Hall, 1991.

[Schmid 1997] Schmid, H.A. Systematic frameworks design by generalization. *Communications of the ACM,* Theme Issue on Object-Oriented Application Frameworks, Mohamed E. Fayad and Douglas Schmidt, editors, 40(10), October 1997.

[Siegel 1996] Siegel, J. *CORBA Fundamentals and Programming.* New York: John Wiley & Sons, 1996.

[Stroustrup 1991] Stroustrup, B. *The C++ Programming Language*, 2nd ed. Reading, MA: Addison-Wesley, 1996.

[Weinand-Gamma 1995] Weinand, A., and E. Gamma. ET++—A portable, homogenous class library and application framework. In *Object Oriented Application Frameworks,* T. Lewis, editor. Greenwich, CT: Manning Publications, 1995.

[Woolf 1996] Woolf, B. Partitioning Smalltalk code into ENVY/Developer components. In *Pattern Languages of Program Design,* vol. 2, J. Vlissides, J. Coplien, and N. Kerth, editors. Reading, MA: Addison-Wesley, 1996.

14.6 Review Questions

1. What is the definition of a consistent framework?

2. Which are typical consistency requirements?

3. Under which conditions is close coupling considered useful for managing class dependencies?

4. What are the main advantages of using factory classes for managing class dependencies?

5. Which techniques ensure consistency requirements placed on classes, and which ensure consistency requirements placed on single instances?

6. Which techniques allow application programs to be dynamically reconfigured at runtime?

7. Which techniques can be used to manage dependencies between algorithms?

8. Which techniques are affected by the choice of the programming language, since they require special features?

14.7 Problem Set

1. Design a small presentation for your organization or your university using the presentation framework. Set up a class diagram including both the framework classes and the presentation-specific classes. Explain how instances of these classes will be created and how the instances will interact.

2. Extend the presentation framework so that it supports the superimposition of slides when a sequence of slides is shown. Different kinds of superimposition should be possible. If additional class dependencies occur during the framework extension, apply appropriate techniques to manage them.

Designing the architecture of frameworks is a mission with many potential traps and pitfalls. Especially subjects like distribution and heterogeneous components introduce additional complexity to framework architectures, which easily outweighs their advantages, such as reusability and additional reliability. Since frameworks serve as generic software systems, the design of which can be reused as the basis for many applications, the architecture's importance should not be underestimated. Thus, formal specification becomes essential already at the design stage.

In this contribution we emphasize the necessity of formal architecture design for application frameworks. We propose our approach, which serves as a basis to formulate the semantics of frameworks—especially the interaction between constituent parts. Further, we briefly discuss how that evaluation of a framework's performance-related properties has direct impact on the architecture design. Finally, a distributed object-oriented application framework can be generated from the formally specified design architecture.

Related research with respect to development of application frameworks is done in many places. We concentrate here on related approaches that emphasize formal architecture design and the usage of architecture description languages (ADLs). A prominent example is Regis Orb Implementation (ROI [Crane-Dulay 1997]), an integration of the ADL REGIS/DARWIN [Magee 1994] with IONA Technologies' CORBA implementation ORBIX. UniCon (Language for Universal Connector Support [Shaw 1995]) investigates the idea that within an architecture description, distribution information is attached to connectors between distributed software components. In contrast to Regis/Darwin, our approach provides a richer language for describing semantic properties in interfaces and also comprises constructs for including performance-related properties. In addition, our concept for evaluating the architecture's nonfunctional properties is more flexible with respect to verification of temporal requirements as the UniCon approach, which also does not provide support for generating a distributed implementation.

In *SB4.1* we will first motivate the necessity for formal design of application frameworks and present our approach based on an architecture description language. Then in *SB4.2* we will discuss how performance-related properties influence the design.

SB4.1 Formal Architecture Design

Since a framework's main contribution to an application is the architecture it defines, the quality of an application framework depends directly on its design. Without a proper description of an application framework's design architecture, structured changes may not be possible. A rigorous description of the various framework subcomponents' interfaces and their interconnections becomes essential. This is true especially for maintaining actual applications where the generic framework parts and actualized hot spots are interwoven.

Often, design patterns are proposed for supporting the design of frameworks. While design patterns and application frameworks are highly synergistic concepts, design patterns are problem/solution pairs that are more abstract than frameworks and are

Continues

programming language independent. Patterns are smaller architectural elements than frameworks; frameworks typically embody lots of patterns. However, patterns only represent semiformal design support. They do not allow description of the semantics of distributed and object-oriented architectures with complex client-server relationships at a formal level. Thus, they also do not provide the benefits of formal architecture specification—automated implementation generation or performance evaluation for example. Especially in the discipline of developing application frameworks, these advantages of formal specification become essential. As automated correctness checking of functional and nonfunctional system properties leads to less error-prone and more reliable application frameworks, their reuse also does not lead to errors and produces more likely correct applications. Further, the unambiguous semantics of the application framework's hot spots facilitates a rigorous decision about how a framework has to be customized.

Our approach for formal specification of an object-oriented application framework's design architecture—including its functional as well as its nonfunctional properties such as performance-related or distribution-related information—is the ADL Π [Goedicke-Meyer1998]. It is based on the notion of reusable distributed software components. Its main advantage over other architecture description languages is the integration of many properties of software systems into one language for describing software components.

In Π, each component is described by four sections. The export section gives an abstract image of the component's realization, while the body section describes the realization of a component. According to the concept of formal import, only requirements to imported abstract data types are specified in the import section. At a different point in time of the architecture development, the import section has to be actualized with export sections of potential server components via use relations. Finally, in the common parameters section, abstract data types are stated, which are imported and exported unchanged.

Views can be seen as overlapping partial specifications of the component. Each section is specified by four views. The type view describes the component's invariant properties according to execution of operations by means of algebraic specification techniques. The imperative view defines imperative operation signatures and algorithms, and the concurrency view specifies possible orderings of operation executions. Finally, the interaction view encapsulates information related to distribution properties of components.

Exactly the formal import of a component formalizes an application framework's hot spots. These are parts of an architecture design that cannot be anticipated by the general application framework, but have to be generic and customizable with domain-specific knowledge. This adaptation of the application framework's hot spots is done by actualizing the formal import of the corresponding component with actual exports of some potential server components within use relations.

A distributed application framework can now be described as a configuration of potentially distributed components that communicate via local or remote use relations. For each remote use relation between two distributed components, a communication protocol and functional as well as nonfunctional attributes for this protocol can be specified. Further, in a component's interaction view, nonfunctional requirements regarding remote use relations and the performance of potential server components can be stated.

Tool support is provided by the web-based Π development environment PIES [Goedicke-Meyer 1998], which allows development of local as well as distributed application frameworks (based on C++, Java, and OMG's standard CORBA).

SB4.2 Performance Evaluation

In addition to functional correctness, quantitative aspects in terms of performance and reliability are of central importance within the design of object-oriented and distributed application frameworks. While in the preceding section we discussed that a modular and component-oriented design of application frameworks is essential, nonfunctional requirements of components as well as their interconnections have direct impact on the architecture design. Especially in the distributed case, performance properties of component interconnections may alter the components' design structure—for example, insertion of a proxy component in order to enhance the quality of a remote component connection. Thus, it is important to analyze the design model quantitatively in order to gain information about the distributed system's functional and nonfunctional behavior. This information may either justify design decisions or lead to changes in the design architecture.

Nonfunctional requirements (response time, throughput, and so on) have impact on framework design a priori; that is, the analysis and assessment of a component's performance should be possible while the entire design architecture is still unfinished. Such requirements should also have an a posteriori impact; that is, measuring the efficiency of the components' implementations. Using the Π language, the functional behavior of distributed components and their connections can be described, as well as performance-related attributes of this architecture. For functional as well as performance-related evaluation, we use the Queuing Specification and Description Language QSDL [Diefenbruch 1996].

The transformation of a QSDL specification to an executable program for simulation and validation of the specified system is performed automatically by the tool QUEST [Diefenbruch 1996]. In [Diefenbruch-Meyer 1996] we have identified interfaces between the component model in Π and the system specification in QSDL using ViewPoints, a method engineering and integration framework [Finkelstein 1992]. Thus, performance requirements of a software system identified in its component model can be evaluated in its corresponding QSDL system. Finally, the simulation results can also be transferred back to the Π world by means of the ViewPoints framework.

SB4.3 Summary

In this contribution we have presented a general overview of our approach as an example for developing and evaluating application frameworks based on a formal architecture

Continues

SIDEBAR 4
FORMAL DESIGN AND PERFORMANCE EVALUATION *(Continued)*

description language. More information with respect to our approach and tool support can be found at www.cs.uni-essen.de/Fachgebiete/SoftTech and www.cs.uni-essen.de/Fachgebiete/SysMod.

SB4.4 References

[Crane-Dulay 1997] Crane, J.S., and N. Dulay. A configurable protocol architecture for CORBA environments. *Proceedings of ISADS 1997,* Berlin, Germany, April 1997.

[Diefenbruch 1996] Diefenbruch, M., J. Hintelmann, and B. Mueller-Clostermann. The QUEST-Approach for the performance evaluation of SDL-Systems. *Proceedings of IFIP TC6/6.1 Int. Conference on Formal Description Techniques IX,* Kaiserslautern, Germany, October 1996.

[Diefenbruch-Meyer 1996] Diefenbruch, M., and T. Meyer. On formal modeling and verifying performance requirements of distributed systems. *Proceedings of the Second World Conference on Integrated Design and Process Technology,* Austin, Texas, December 1996.

[Finkelstein 1992] Finkelstein, A., J. Kramer, B. Nuseibeh, L. Finkelstein, and M. Goedicke. Viewpoints: A framework for integrating multiple perspectives in system development. *International Journal of Software Engineering and Knowledge Engineering* 2(1992):31–57.

[Goedicke-Meyer 1998] Goedicke, M., and T. Meyer. Formal design and performance evaluation of parallel and distributed software systems. *Proceedings International Symposium on Software Engineering for Parallel and Distributed Systems,* in conjunction with 20th International Conference on Software Engineering, Kyoto, Japan, April 1998.

[Magee 1994] Magee, J., N. Dulay, and J. Kramer. Regis: A constructive development environment for distributed programs. *IEE/IOP/BCS Distributed Systems Engineering Journal* 1(5), May1994:304–312.

[Shaw 1995] Shaw, M., R. DeLine, D.V. Klein, T.L. Ross, D.M. Young, and G. Zelesnik. Abstractions for software architecture and tools to support them. *IEEE Transactions on Software Engineering* 21(4), April 1995.

Framework Development Approaches

Part Five consists of five chapters and two sidebars. Part Five discusses framework development approaches, such as systematic generalization, hot-spot-driven development, framework layering, framelets, understanding macroscopic behavior patterns in use-case maps and composing modeling frameworks in Catalysis, and enduring business themes (EBTs).

Chapter 15 discusses framework design by systematic generalization, which overcomes the inherent complexity of framework design by clearly separating the design of a class model for a fixed application from the framework domain from the introduction of variability in generalization steps, and by separating the analysis and specification of a hot spot from the high-level design of a hot-spot subsystem and its implementation by a generalizing transformation.

A generalization cycle analyzes and specifies the characteristics of a variable aspect in a hot-spot specification, determines the high-level design of the hot-spot subsystem, which usually follows a design pattern that provides the specific kind of variability and flexibility required, and transforms the class model by introducing the hot-spot subsystem.

Chapter 16 describes hot-spot-driven framework development. Most excellent object-oriented frameworks are still the product of a more or less chaotic development process, typically carried out in the realm of research-like settings. Overall, flexibility has to be injected into a framework in appropriate doses. Framework adaptation takes place at points of predefined refinement that are called *hot spots*. As the quality of a framework depends directly on the appropriateness of hot spots, hot-spot identification has to become an explicit activity in the framework development process. Means for documenting and communicating hot spots between domain experts and software engineers become crucial.

This contribution first discusses the few essential framework construction principles, that is, how to keep object-oriented architectures flexible for adaptations. The chapter introduces hot-spot cards as means to capture flexibility requirements and illustrates how to apply them in combination with the essential framework construction principles. The presented heuristics form a hot-spot-driven framework design process, which leads to a more systematic framework construction with fewer (re)design iterations.

Chapter 17 introduces concepts and techniques for structuring large application frameworks. Frameworks are a key asset in large-scale object-oriented software development. They promise increased productivity, shorter development times, and higher quality of applications. To achieve this, frameworks should be designed such that they can evolve and be easily reused, adapted, and configured. Drawing on experience in large-scale industrial banking projects, this chapter describes concepts and techniques for domain partitioning, framework layering, and framework construction. In particular, this chapter discusses how domain aspects relate to framework structure, how frameworks are layered to accommodate domain needs, and how the resulting framework layers are integrated without tight coupling.

Sidebar 5 introduces the notion of framelets, which are essentially small frameworks. Thus, framelets can be easily understood and modified. As framelets are not aimed at complex application domains, they can also be assembled without the problems associated with the combination of large frameworks. Our first experiences with framelets demonstrate that these architectural building blocks allow the integration of framework technology into legacy applications. Furthermore, framelets might form a suitable means for structuring software architectures.

Chapter 18 describes how to understand macroscopic behavior patterns with use-case maps. Object-oriented frameworks provide a powerful construction technique for software, but understanding the behavior of applications constructed from them is well known to be difficult, for a number of reasons: (1) The first-class representation of the framework in code centers around construction; system structure and behavior are visible only in a second-class way, in widely scattered details. (2) The desired system view is not a concrete thing, but an abstraction. (3) The use of design patterns, a common practice in frameworks, may obscure the system view by making intercomponent interactions more indirect than they would otherwise be. (4) The use of combinations of design patterns obscures the system view because pattern combination is not yet a well-defined subject. (5) Both the desired system view and design patterns are abstractions, so gaining system understanding requires combining multiple abstractions, for frameworks that make serious use of design patterns. (6) Although framework class organizations are fixed, systems constructed from frameworks are self-modifying while they are running, and self-modifying software is notoriously difficult to understand. (7) Specific applications are visible only in framework customization details. This chapter illustrates by example how a general technique called *use-case maps*—invented by the author for describing complex systems of any kind—can help to alleviate these difficulties. To indicate the range of applicability, the examples are drawn from frameworks in very different application domains: HotDraw for GUIs and ACE for communications. The objective is to raise the visibility in the framework community of the UCM approach to alleviating these problems, not to prove UCMs solve them or to provide a cookbook for solving them.

Chapter 19 discusses how the Catalysis method generalizes the concept of frameworks to object modeling and specification activities, permitting construction of specification and design models by composition. This work enables specification and modeling activities to be much more *constructive*, where models are generated from appropriate generic specification models based on particular aspects of the problem at hand.

Sidebar 6 briefly presents insights for software development strategy selection and some of the highlights of a relatively new approach called *enduring business themes* (EBTs) that works well for systems that must be highly change-centric. The EBT approach leads to software systems that can accommodate unexpected change with a minimal ripple effect. It avoids the use of successive refinement, so there is an abrupt discontinuity between requirements and the ensuing models. The approach also accommodates different developer skill levels more effectively than most traditional solutions.

CHAPTER 15

Framework Design by Systematic Generalization

A framework is a generic application that allows different applications to be created from a family of applications. All applications from the family form a subdomain of an application domain, such as interactive commercial applications or part-processing manufacturing cells. We call this subdomain the *framework domain.* A variable aspect of a framework domain is called a *hot spot,* whereas a fixed aspect is called a *frozen spot* [Pree 1995; Schmid 1996a]. Different applications from a domain differ from one another with regard to at least one of the hot spots.

Because a framework incorporates flexibility and variability, framework design was considered some years ago as a complicated art requiring "a great deal of experience and experimentation" [Johnson-Foote 1988] and is certainly much more complex than the design of a single application. Design patterns [Gamma 1995] provide great assistance and support in framework design. Even still, there remains sufficient complexity, as expressed in [Beck-Johnson 1994]: "The design starts as a fuzzy cloud representing the system to be realized. . . . As patterns are applied to the cloud, parts of it come into focus. . . . The sequence in which patterns are considered is one of the most important skills possessed by experts." In particular, the complexity stems from the difficulty of overseeing and understanding many different, variable aspects at a time.

Framework design is made easier by clearly separating different issues. The most important point is that you should not start to design a framework by trying to model its variability and flexibility at once. Instead, you should design a fixed application from the framework domain and generalize it only when you understand the fixed case. Second, you should not work on different, variable aspects at one time, but separate one clearly from the other. Third, you should capture and specify exactly the degree of variability and flexibility that are required before you design a solution for how to provide them. This principle of software engineering, proven in application development that is simpler than framework development, should be applied to framework design and development.

Based on practical experience with several frameworks (for example, see [Schmid 1995, 1996a]), we have developed an approach to framework design that follows these rules and separates different issues clearly. Considering framework design as a generalization problem, we start from a fixed class structure, which models a fixed application from the framework domain, and transform it by a sequence of generalizing transformations. Each of them introduces a hot spot into the class structure. For a hot spot, we show how to construct from its analysis and specification the high-level design of a hot-spot subsystem and how to construct from the high-level design the implementation of the hot-spot subsystem in the framework class structure.

In this way, framework design, which was an intuitive process based on experience, becomes a constructive process based on guidelines that put intuition into action in a structured way.

In the sequel, we describe the underlying concepts and the activities into which we partition framework design. An overview of the different activities is given before describing them in detail. As a running example we will use an editor framework derived from the Lexi example in [Gamma 1995], to allow for a comparison between a more intuitive and this structured approach. Before the concluding section, a complete sequence of generalizing transformations, resulting in an editor framework, is described.

15.1 Framework Design Activities

As shown in Figure 15.1, the construction of a framework consists of four activities:

- The application modeling activity
- The hot-spot analysis and specification, which is subdivided into the hot-spot high-level analysis and the hot-spot detail analysis and specification

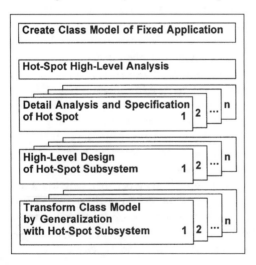

Figure 15.1 Framework design activities.

- The hot-spot high-level design
- The generalization transformation

The modeling activity develops, by object-oriented analysis, a fixed class model from the framework domain. The hot-spot analysis and specification is subdivided into the hot-spot high-level analysis and the hot-spot detail analysis and specification. The hot-spot high-level analysis collects all hot spots and describes them briefly. The hot-spot detail analysis and specification activity is done for each hot spot; it analyzes the variability and flexibility requirements in detail and describes, following a given list, the hot-spot characteristics. The hot-spot subsystem high-level design activity derives the classes and structure of a hot-spot subsystem from the hot-spot character-istics. The generalization transformation activity generalizes the class model by replac-ing a fixed aspect with the hot-spot subsystem that results from the high-level design activities.

Figure 15.1 presents these activities in a causal relationship from top to bottom. This means an activity can be done only when the corresponding activities above it are accomplished. For example, the high-level design of hot-spot subsystem 2 can be done only after the detail analysis and specification of hot-spot 2 are finished. *Section 15.9* will discuss the relation of design activities to development cycles.

15.2 Application Modeling Activity

The application modeling activity develops a class model of a fixed application from the framework domain. The class model contains fixed instances of the concepts and entities of the framework domain, and the fixed relationships among them. It is created by an object-oriented analysis. Since it plays no role in which an object-oriented analy-sis method is used, no detailed description of this activity is given. In this chapter, we use Coad-Yourdon diagrams [Coad-Yourdon 1991] for analysis and design. For their description, see Figure 15.2.

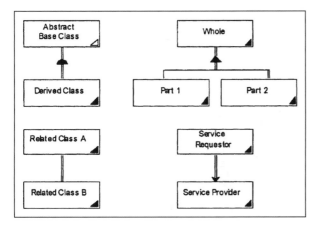

Figure 15.2 Coad-Yourdon notation.

We will use an editor that will be generalized to an editor framework as a running example. A simple, nonflexible editor allows editing of character sequences in an application window of a fixed appearance. The editor formats a character sequence, after input, following an algorithm that cannot be changed. It runs on a window system with a given look-and-feel standard.

The class model, presented in Figure 15.3, is the result of an object-oriented analysis. The class Composition models character sequences and their formatting. It has the following responsibilities:

- To insert and delete characters with a given position into or, respectively, from a character sequence

- To process the character sequence, in particular, to format it

- To display the character sequence in the application window

The Macintosh window system provides an Application Window. It is, like Dialog Window, a subclass of Window. Edit receives by Dialog Window the input of the end user (not represented in Figure 15.3), which may require that the character sequence be modified or processed. Edit analyzes this input and calls the corresponding methods of Composition.

15.3 Hot Spots and Hot-Spot Specification

A framework, as a generic application, embodies both an abstract design that is common to all applications from the framework domain and hot spots that allow the framework to be customized to application-specific requirements. Each hot spot incorporates a specific variable aspect as, for example, a set with different representations. When creating an application from the framework, you bind a hot spot to one or several of the different instances of its variability. You would bind the set hot spot to one of its implementation alternatives, such as a linked list, a balanced binary tree, or a hash table data structure. The case in which you bind a hot spot to several instances of its variability is less frequent. For example, you might bind a window to a chain of dec-

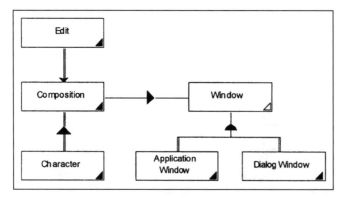

Figure 15.3 Class structure of a simple, nonflexible editor.

orations like a border and a scroller, or you might bind a hierarchy of directory and file objects to a hot spot in a tree structure.

Note that different kinds of variability and flexibility may be associated with a hot spot. An interface with different representations is a kind of variability that differs from a window with different decorations or from a flexible directory and file hierarchy.

The binding time characterizes the point of time at which an alternative is selected and bound to the hot spot. This may be done by an application developer at the time when an application is created from the framework, or by an end user at runtime of an application created from the framework. At runtime, the binding may be done either once or multiple times. For example, you must decide if decorations should be bound to a window when an application is created, or if an end user may bind the decorations once when he or she starts the application, or even repeatedly during use of the application.

As described, a hot spot lets you plug in an application-specific class or set of classes when you customize a framework to build an application. But you cannot plug in every class; you can plug in only a class that fits into the hot spot. There are two sides—or, more formally speaking, two interfaces—that make a class fit into a hot spot. The services that a class must provide to the framework (the called interface) are described by a responsibility, named R in Figure 15.4. This common responsibility generalizes from different alternatives. Thus, it defines a generalized, abstract concept that describes the commonalities of the variable aspect.

However, the services that one of the alternative classes may request from the framework (the interface to be called) are usually not described in a similar, clear way. In a blackbox framework, this is no problem, since it supplies a set of prefabricated-to-fit classes with the framework (see Figure 15.4 [left]). An application developer selects from these alternatives one or more that model the application and possibly also parameterize them. Whenever a suitable parameterization can express the variability of a hot spot or of a part of it, you should use a parameterized class instead of providing alternative classes, since this is simpler. In a whitebox framework, an alternative is developed and programmed as required (see Figure 15.4 [right]). This is difficult when a description of the interface to be called is missing. It may result in a long learning time until an application developer is familiar with the framework and can develop hot-spot alternatives.

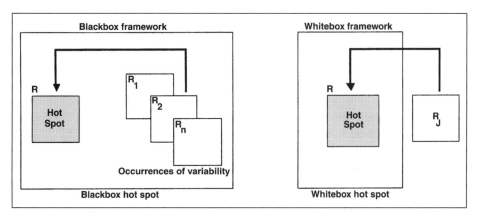

Figure 15.4 Hot spots in a blackbox and in a whitebox framework.

Another characteristic of a hot spot is its granularity. A hot spot is called *elementary* if it covers only one elementary variable aspect. A variable aspect is called elementary if it cannot be decomposed into a combination of smaller, mostly orthogonal variable aspects. Two variable aspects are orthogonal if the alternatives of one aspect may be exchanged independently of the other aspect. For example, consider a graph with a set of nodes and a set of arcs. Suppose there is a graph problem and four different algorithms to solve it; as discussed, there are different ways to represent a set. If the solution to the graph problem is considered as one hot spot, it is not elementary and there are 12 alternative solutions. When we split up this hot spot into the two elementary hot spots, variability of the graph algorithm and variability of the set implementation, there are 4 and 3, equaling 7, alternatives.

In a blackbox framework, hot spots must be elementary. Otherwise, the number of alternatives to be provided, being the product of the number of alternatives of each elementary variable aspect, becomes too large [Schmid 1996a]. Nonelementary hot-spot alternatives are called *component libraries;* frameworks with elementary hot spots are called *blackbox frameworks* by [Roberts-Johnson 1997]. In a whitebox framework, elementary hot spots are beneficial but not required, since an application developer chooses and implements only the one or few alternatives that are part of the specific application and is not interested in the other alternatives. However, with nonelementary hot spots, the chance for reuse of already developed, nonorthogonalized alternatives is much smaller. For an example, see [Brant-Johnson 1994]. Apart from the fine granularity, there is no strict distinction between blackbox and whitebox frameworks. A framework may provide more frequently used alternatives for a hot spot in blackbox mode and less frequently used or new alternatives in whitebox mode.

A hot-spot specification describes the following characteristics for each hot spot. In *Section 15.7,* we will show that we may derive the hot-spot implementation from these characteristics.

- Hot-spot name.

- Short description.

- The common responsibility R.

- Some concrete examples of alternative realizations of the variable aspect.

- The kind of variability required.

- Whether some (or all) of the variability may be covered by parameterization.

- Granularity of the hot spot. (If a hot spot is nonelementary, describe the elementary variable aspects and the reasons, why the hot spot was not decomposed.)

- Multiplicity characteristic, which gives the number (either one or n) and structuring (for n alternatives: either chain-structured or tree-structured) of the alternatives that may be bound to a hot spot. The multiplicity characteristic is directly related to the kind of variability.

- Binding time (application creation; runtime, once, or multiple times).

Suppose, for example, we require a hot spot with a collection class Set (hot-spot name), implemented with different data structures in different applications (short description). The common responsibility R are the set operations such as insert element, is element, and so on. They are identical for all implementations. Alternative Set representations are a linked list, a balanced binary tree, and a hash table data structure. The kind of variability required is the exchange of the implementation without having to change the client code; it cannot be covered by parameterization. The hot spot is elementary, since the different implementations are unrelated. The multiplicity is one, since, for a Set, there are one representation and implementation, which are—supposedly—selected and bound at application creation time to an application.

15.4 Hot-Spot Analysis

The hot-spot analysis collects and describes all variable aspects from the framework domain. It is an extension of the requirements analysis phase from application development and consists of two kinds of activities: the hot-spot high-level analysis, which collects all hot spots, and the hot-spot detail analysis, which creates the hot-spot specification for each hot spot. We will demonstrate the hot-spot analysis activity at the example of the editor, introduced in *Section 15.2*.

15.4.1 Hot-Spot High-Level Analysis

The hot-spot high-level analysis activity identifies and collects all hot spots from the domain and describes them briefly. You start with collecting hot spots since you should get an overview of all required variability and flexibility before going into details. Very often, it may be appropriate to proceed from a specialized application and ask which of its fixed aspects should be made flexible.

For the editor, we proceed from the class model described in *Section 15.2* and collect its aspects for which flexibility and variability would be required. With regard to the central editor functionality, the following are desirable:

- To have not only characters as basic elements of a document, but also to allow for other kinds of basic elements, such as graphics (hot spot 1)

- To allow for other composition facilities, in addition to the sequencing of basic elements (hot spot 2)

- To provide not only one, but different, formatting algorithms (hot spot 3)

With regard to the platforms supported, the following might be desirable:

- To make the editor portable on different window systems (hot spot 4)

With regard to the user interface, it might be desirable to provide the following:

- Variable application window embellishments, such as a border and a drawer (hot spot 5)

- Different look-and-feel standards (hot spot 6)

The hot spots are presented in Figure 15.5, ordered according to the level of abstraction and the anticipated use relation. The window system, used by all other aspects for their implementation, forms the lowest level. There are three separate abstraction hierarchies on this basis: one formed by the basic document element hot spot, aggregation

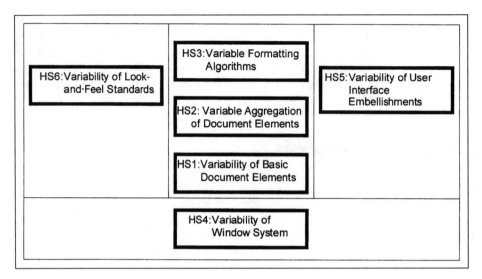

Figure 15.5   Hot spots in the editor domain.

hot spot, and formatting hot spot; another one by the look-and-feel hot spot; and the third by the user interface embellishments hot spot.

15.4.2 Hot-Spot Detail Analysis and Specification

The hot-spot detail analysis and specification activity is done separately for each hot spot. You analyze a hot spot and describe its characteristics, based on domain knowledge and application prototypes. If the result of a hot-spot analysis is that the number of alternatives is (too) large, you should try to partition the hot spot into orthogonal, elementary hot spots.

For example, consider three hot spots from the editor domain for a specification of their characteristics:

Hot spot 1: Variability of basic document elements

- Description: We want to have not only characters as basic document elements, but also graphics, raster pictures, and others when necessary. There are multiple instances of the hot spot, since there are many document elements in a document.

- The common responsibilities of basic document elements are that an element can print itself at a position of a graphic context; it can give its width, height, and so on.

- Character, graphics, and raster picture are different alternatives that may be supplied as a basic document element.

- The kind of variability required is that all basic document elements have a common interface but different implementations.

- No parameterization is possible.

- The granularity is elementary.
- The multiplicity is one, since one character (or one graphic, and so on) is supplied as a basic document element.
- The hot spot is bound at runtime, since an end user selects basic document elements at the runtime of an editor generated from the framework.

Hot spot 2: Variable aggregation of document elements

- Description: To allow for more facilities to compose a document than only the sequencing of basic elements.
- The common responsibilities of an aggregation are the same as for basic document elements and, in addition, include aggregation-related responsibilities.
- Row, column, and so on, are different alternative aggregations of document elements.
- The kind of variability required is that a document may be structured in a variable hierarchy of aggregations.
- No parameterization is possible.
- The granularity is elementary.
- The multiplicity is n, tree-structured, since we build a tree of aggregations.
- The hot spot is bound at runtime, multiple times, since an end user builds the aggregation hierarchy of a document at the runtime of an editor generated from the framework.

Hot spot 3: Variability of formatting algorithms

- Description: To provide not only one, but different formatting algorithms.
- The common responsibility is to format a document on a service request.
- Different alternatives are a simple and fast algorithm or a text formatting algorithm.
- The kind of variability required is that different algorithms can be used to format the document.
- No parameterization is possible.
- The granularity is elementary.
- The multiplicity is one, since one formatting algorithm is used at a time.
- The hot spot is bound at runtime, multiple times, since an end user selects a formatting algorithm repeatedly at the runtime of an editor generated from the framework.

For the other hot spots of the editor domain, we represent the result of the hot-spot detail analysis and specification in a tabular and abbreviated form. In particular, we omit the characteristics common responsibility, different alternatives, parameterization, and granularity.

Hot spot 4: Variability of a window system

- Description: To make the editor portable on different window systems.
- The variability required is a variable implementation of the window hierarchy.

- The multiplicity is one; binding: creation time.

Hot spot 5: Variability of user interface embellishments

- Description: Variable application window embellishments, such as a border and a drawer.

- The variability required is to attach different decorations to an object.

- The multiplicity is *n*, chain-structured; binding: creation time.

Hot spot 6: Variability of look-and-feel standards

- Description: Different look-and-feel standards of the user interface.

- The variability required is to create objects from different classes, such as buttons and dialog windows, from the same category, such as pm look and feel or Mac look and feel.

- The multiplicity is one; binding: creation time.

15.5 Hot-Spot Subsystem

A hot spot is implemented by a hot-spot subsystem [Schmid 1996a]. A hot-spot subsystem contains a base class (typically, abstract), concrete derived classes (see Figures 15.6 and 15.7), and possibly additional classes and relationships (see Figure 15.7). In all cases, the abstract base class defines the common responsibilities R for all hot-spot alternatives. A concrete derived class represents one of the instances of the variable aspect.

The detail structure of a hot-spot subsystem without additional classes and relationships, as presented in Figure 15.6, is either the well-known mechanism for interface inheritance or the implementation of the Template or Factory Method pattern, or a similar design pattern. When a subsystem contains additional classes and relationships, as presented in Figure 15.7, its detail structure implements more complex design patterns—for example, the Strategy pattern.

A hot-spot subsystem introduces variability that is transparent outside the subsystem, either by inheritance or by composition. With inheritance, there are, typically, no other classes except the base class and subclasses (see Figure 15.6); whereas, with composition, there is an additional class (see Figure 15.7). The variability is achieved by the dynamic binding of the caller (called the template method) of an abstract base class operation (called the hook method [Pree 1995]), via a polymorphic reference typed with the base class, to the subclass method executed. With inheritance, the polymorphic reference is attached to the hot-spot subsystem (for example, in Figure 15.6, in the Client); with composition, the reference is contained in it (for example, in Figure 15.7, in the Additional Class). There are also cases with a polymorphic reference both attached to and inside of the hot-spot subsystem (see the upcoming discussion of recursive subsystems).

Setting the reference(s) to a subclass object (which is called "configuring the hot-spot subsystem") lets you bind the hot spot. The effects of calling a hook method are generic: They depend on the way a hot-spot subsystem has been configured at binding time. When a hot spot is parameterized you usually set the parameter values when

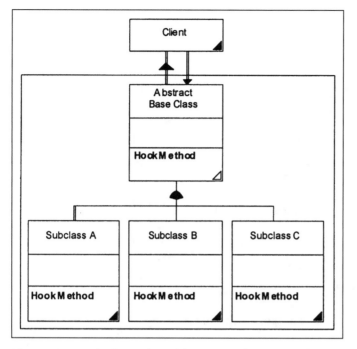

Figure 15.6 Inheritance-based hot-spot subsystem with polymorphic reference attached.

you configure the hot-spot subsystem, by constructor parameters, by special operations, or by reading data from configuration files.

We classify hot-spot subsystems into three categories according to the number and structure of subclass objects that may participate in providing a service requested from the hot-spot subsystem. A hot-spot subsystem is called:

- *Nonrecursive* if a service is provided from one subclass object

- *1:1 (chain-structured) recursive* if a requested service may be provided by *n* subclass objects, which are structured in a chain

- *1:n (tree-structured) recursive* if a requested service may be provided by a tree of *n* subclass objects

Recursive hot-spot subsystems (see Figure 15.8) contain a *has-a* relationship from a subclass (or the base class itself) to an object of base class type. This relationship is represented by a polymorphic reference. A 1:1 recursive subsystem contains a 1:1 relationship (that is, a reference); a 1:*n* recursive subsystem contains a 1:*n* relationship (that is, a set of references). When a caller, usually outside of the hot-spot subsystem, requests a service, the hook method of a base class or a subclass object may, if the hot-spot subsystem is recursive, act as a template method. It recursively requests a service from the hook method of another subclass object, to which it is connected by the has-a relationship. This proceeds along a chain or a tree structure until a leaf node or an empty reference is reached.

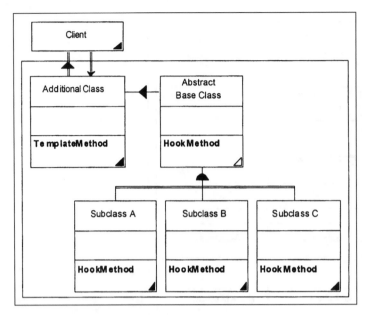

Figure 15.7 Composition-based hot-spot subsystem containing a polymorphic reference.

Design patterns, which describe typical, common, and frequently observed relationships among classes, help you determine the detail structure of a hot-spot subsystem. Nearly all of the design patterns from [Gamma 1995] (except Singleton, Facade, Flyweight, and Memento) provide a different kind of variability and flexibility. Each of them is centered around a base class and subclasses; some contain additional classes and/or relationships. Thus, each of these design patterns may be considered a hot-spot subsystem. The participant classes of the pattern and their cooperation describe the subsystem structure in more detail.

Most design patterns belong to the category of nonrecursive hot-spot subsystems, except for Chain of Responsibility and Decorator, which fall into the chain-structured category, and Composite and Interpreter, which fall into tree-structured recursive hot-

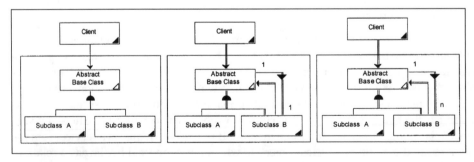

Figure 15.8 A nonrecursive, a chain-structured recursive, and a tree-structured recursive hot-spot subsystem.

Nonrecursive hot-spot subsystem design patterns:
      Interface Inheritance, Abstract Factory, Builder, Factory Method, Prototype,
      Adapter, Bridge, Proxy, Command, Iterator, Mediator, Observer, State,
      Strategy, Template Method, Visitor
1:1 recursive hot-spot subsystem design patterns:
      Chain of Responsibility, Decorator
1:n recursive hot-spot subsystem design patterns:
      Composite, Interpreter

Figure 15.9 Hot-spot subsystem categories with corresponding design patterns.

spot subsystems (see Figure 15.9). In Figure 15.9, we add interface inheritance as a pattern to the first category. Generally, it holds that each design pattern with participant classes that are structured like a hot-spot subsystem is suitable to provide variability and flexibility in a framework.

Binding of hot spots at runtime (either by interaction with an end user or by a lookup in tables or a plan [Schmid 1995, 1996a] requires a supporting class structure. In contrast, binding them at the time of application creation does not require this, since it is a kind of meta-activity from the application programmer side.

Let us return to the example of the Set collection hot spot (see *Section 15.3*) and consider the hot-spot subsystem that implements it. Its abstract base class Set defines the set operations. Each subclass—Linked List Set, and so on—contains a different data structure representation and implements the Set operations on it. The Set (with multiplicity of one) is implemented by a nonrecursive hot-spot subsystem, which is structured following the (nonrecursive) pattern interface inheritance. The Set is bound at application creation time by configuring a polymorphic reference to the desired set implementation subclass. Therefore, no additional classes for the support of configuration are required.

15.6 Hot-Spot Subsystem High-Level Design: Mapping Characteristics to the Subsystem Structure

The hot-spot subsystem high-level design activity derives the high-level design of a hot-spot subsystem from the characteristics of the hot-spot specification. This may be done in isolation from the rest of the framework class structure.

From the characteristics, Hot-Spot Subsystem Structure includes a description of the variable aspect, multiplicity, kind of variability, and flexibility required. The multiplicity characteristic allows a direct selection of the appropriate hot-spot subsystem category. A multiplicity of one is realized by a nonrecursive hot-spot subsystem, whereas a chain-structured multiplicity of n is realized by a 1:1, and a tree-structured multiplicity of n by a 1:n recursive hot-spot subsystem. The third characteristic, the kind of variability and flexibility required, allows a more detailed subsystem structure to be derived.

For example, the multiplicity characteristic—*n*, tree-structured—of the hot spot with a hierarchy of directories and files tells us that the hot spot is implemented by a 1:*n* recursive hot-spot subsystem. Within this category, there are two design patterns listed (see Figure 15.9), Interpreter and Composite. It is easy to see that the latter provides the required kind of flexibility. Thus, the more detailed structure of the 1:*n* recursive hot-spot subsystem is given by the Composite design pattern [Gamma 1995], which we implement instead of designing more details ourselves.

Generally, we select the design pattern that provides the required kind of variability and flexibility, instead of designing more details to the hot-spot subsystem of the selected category. When searching the appropriate design pattern, we restrict the search space according to the multiplicity characteristic of the hot spot, which divides the search space into three categories (see Figure 15.9).

Structuring a hot-spot subsystem following a design pattern has advantages, in addition to those obtained generally: the introduction of a more abstract description level, the saving of development effort, and improved communication and documentation. It provides a more understandable and more uniform structure of the hot spots as central points of a framework, with better documentation, both for application developers and the maintenance of a framework. Good documentation of hot spots and the design patterns applied is, obviously, very important, since it facilitates the understanding of a framework. Moreover, it obliterates the necessity for the exploration of a framework and for the search of the design patterns applied [Gangopadhyay 1995; Lange-Nakamura 1995].

When no design pattern with the required variability and flexibility can be found, the hot-spot subsystem category has the principal subsystem structure. Based on it, a detailed structure is designed.

Domain-related details about the hot-spot subsystem base class and subclasses follow from the characteristics: hot-spot name, description, common responsibility, alternatives, and parameterization. Certainly, with good domain knowledge, you can derive from them the interface of the base class and the implementation of the subclasses of the hot-spot subsystem. The base class interface defines the common responsibilities R and the pattern-related responsibility, whereas a derived class implements one of the different alternatives of the variable aspect and the pattern-related responsibility.

The binding time indicates whether a class structure in support of binding is to be added.

For example, consider hot spots 1, 2, and 3 of the editor. For hot spot 1, we derive from the multiplicity characteristic equaling 1 that the hot spot is implemented by a nonrecursive hot-spot subsystem. From the kind of variability characteristic—common interface with different implementations—we derive that the subsystem is structured according to the interface inheritance pattern. Similarly, we derive that the subsystem base class, called Glyph, defines the interface of a document element and that subclasses like Character implement it.

For hot spot 2, we derive from the multiplicity characteristic equaling *n*, tree-structured, that the hot spot is implemented by a 1:*n* recursive hot-spot subsystem. From the kind of variability characteristic—flexible hierarchical aggregation—we derive that the subsystem is structured according to the Composite pattern. Similarly, we derive that the subsystem base class defines the interface of a document element and the aggregation-related operations. There are leaf subclasses such as Glyph and aggregate-subclasses such as Line.

For hot spot 3, we derive from the multiplicity characteristic equaling 1 that the hot spot is implemented by a nonrecursive hot-spot subsystem. From the kind of variability characteristic—different formatting algorithms—we derive that the subsystem is structured according to the Strategy pattern. Similarly, we derive that the subsystem base class defines the service for formatting the document. The subclasses implement the different formatting algorithms.

15.7 Generalization Transformation

A generalization activity transforms the framework class structure and generalizes it with regard to one aspect. Before the generalization, the class structure usually contains this aspect as a frozen spot in the form of a specialized class or of a specialized responsibility as a part of a class, which has direct and fixed relationships to other classes. In some cases, an aspect is missing before the transformation. After the transformation, the class structure contains a hot-spot subsystem that represents this aspect.

A generalization transformation [Schmid 1996a] introduces the variability and flexibility of a hot spot into the class structure. You replace a fixed, specialized class, and possibly also directly related classes, with the hot-spot subsystem resulting from the high-level hot-spot subsystem design., When introducing an inheritance-based hot-spot subsystem like that presented in Figure 15.6, you replace the direct relationship between a client and a specialized class with a polymorphic relationship. When introducing a composition-based hot-spot subsystem like that presented in Figure 15.7, there remains a direct relationship between a client and the hot-spot subsystem, specifically set to the additional class that contains the polymorphic relationship. In both cases, the polymorphic reference is set at the hot-spot binding time to one of the hot-spot subsystem subclasses.

In addition to the polymorphic relationship, other relationships between the specialized class and other framework classes may exist in the original class structure before the transformation. You have to decide for each of them which class of the hot-spot subsystem should participate in the relationship after the transformation. A rule of thumb may help in the decision: If a class that is replaced by the hot-spot subsystem plays the active role in the relationship (for example, the role that *has-a* or *requests a service*), the relationship is connected after the transformation to this, possibly modified, class in the hot-spot subsystem. Otherwise, the relationship is connected to the base class or the additional class, as previously described.

Another consideration is whether the base class of the hot-spot subsystem is introduced as a new class into the transformed class structure, or whether the responsibility of an existing class is extended by the responsibility of the base class. In the first case, we speak of an *expanding* transformation, since we have expanded the original class structure by a new class. In the second case, we speak of an *extending* transformation, since we have extended an original class by new responsibilities.

Let us show an expanding transformation with regard to hot spot 1 (see Figure 15.10). We replace the class Character (Figure 15.10 [left]) with the hot-spot subsystem (Figure

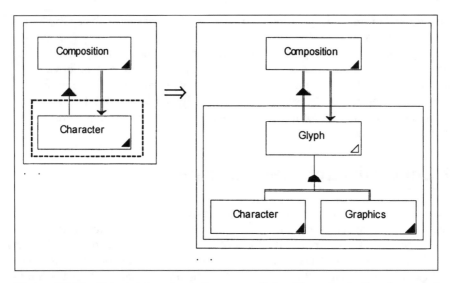

Figure 15.10   Hot-spot transformation generalizing Character to the document element Glyph.

15.10 [right]) designed in *Section 15.6*. This subsystem implements the interface inheritance design pattern. It has a new base class modeling the generalized document element, Glyph. The existing classes Character, Graphic, and so on, are subclasses. The methods of Glyph are hook methods that are called from template methods in Composition. The *has-as-part* relationship relating Composition to Character (where Character plays a passive role) is replaced by one relating Composition to the base class Glyph.

An extending transformation with regard to hot spot 2 (see Figure 15.11) generalizes one of the responsibilities of a Composition (to contain a sequence of Glyphs) by introducing the Composite-structured hot-spot subsystem designed in *Section 15.6*. We replace the classes Composition and Glyph (Figure 15.11 [left]) with a hot-spot subsystem with the base class Component and the subclasses Glyph and Composite. Instead of introducing a new subsystem base class Component, we extend the responsibilities of the original class Glyph by the Component responsibility from the Composite pattern. Thus, Glyph represents a generalized and aggregated document element (Figure 15.11 [right]). This transformation identifies the existing class Glyph with the new subsystem base class Component, and thus combines two hot-spot subsystems. The result is a flat class structure. The new base class Glyph has as subclasses both the subclasses of the newly introduced Composite hot-spot subsystem, such as Composite, and the subclasses of the original hot-spot subsystem, such as Character.

An expanding transformation with regard to hot spot 4 (see Figure 15.12) introduces the variability of supported window systems. We replace the class MacWindow (Figure 15.12 [left]) by the Bridge structured hot-spot subsystem (Figure 15.12 [right]). The subsystem contains the additional class Window and the base class WindowImp (Window Implementation) with different subclasses, such as MacWindowImp. From the original class MacWindow, the window implementation has been split off to the newly introduced class WindowImp, and the window interface has been generalized to class

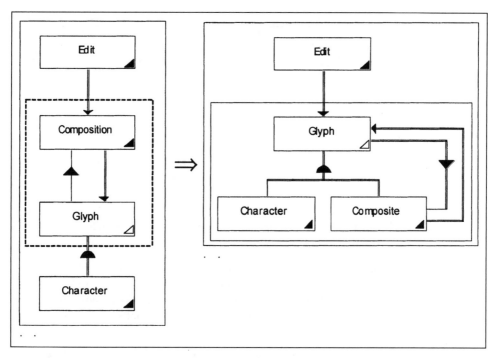

Figure 15.11   Hot-spot transformation generalizing the aggregation of Glyph.

Window. Window calls the WindowImp services that implement the window functionality. The relationships from outside classes such as Glyph to MacWindow remain connected to Window—that is, the modified class MacWindow—in the hot-spot subsystem.

15.8 Transformations Generalizing the Editor

After the illustration of some aspects of particular interest, we present the complete transformation sequence generalizing the simple editor (introduced in *Section 15.2*) to an editor framework. The starting point is the editor class structure presented in Figure 15.3.

We start by introducing hot spot 4, which generalizes the window system (see Figure 15.13). Details regarding this transformation were discussed in *Section 15.7*. When we split off the window implementation from the interface definition, the generalized window interface will differ from the interface of a specific window system like MacWindow. Therefore, we do this transformation before the transformation with hot spot 1, which introduces the class Glyph that requests services from Window. Otherwise, when we would do the transformation regarding hot spot 1 first, Glyph would request services from a specific window implementation, which would be modified with the next transformation.

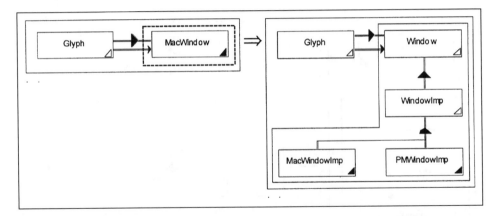

Figure 15.12 Hot-spot transformation generalizing the window implementation.

The next transformation introduces hot spot 1, the generalized document element. Details regarding this transformation (see Figure 15.14) were discussed in *Section 15.7*.

In the following transformation steps, we generalize the document aggregation structure (hot spot 2) and provide window embellishments (hot spot 5). This may be done in two ways:

- In extending transformations that extend Glyph by the responsibilities of the new hot-spot subsystem base classes

- In expanding transformations that introduce, with each hot-spot subsystem, a new base class

We will illustrate both design choices.

We start by presenting the extending transformations and introduce hot spot 2, generalize document structure, following the Composite pattern (see Figure 15.15). The responsibility of Glyph is extended by the pattern-related Component responsibility; only one Composite class, Line, is presented. Details were discussed in *Section 15.7*.

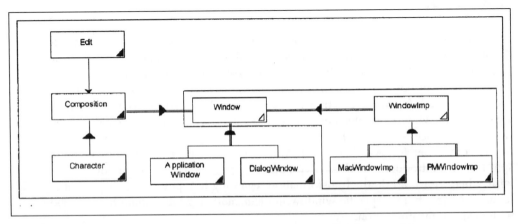

Figure 15.13 Simple editor with generalized window system implementation.

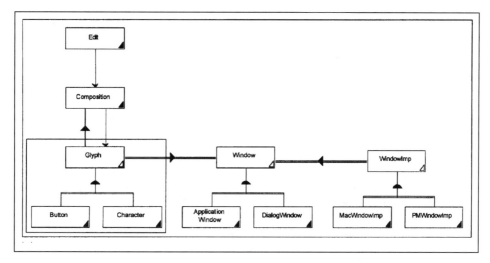

Figure 15.14   Editor with generalized document element Glyph.

Together with this transformation, we generalize the formatting in the regard that not only a whole document, but any subparts of it, may be formatted. This is done by an extending transformation, making Composition a subclass of Glyph embellishing it (1:1 recursive hot-spot subsystem).

In the third extending transformation, with regard to hot spot 5, we add variable window embellishments such as Border or Scroller. This is a new aspect that is not represented in a fixed form in the class structure shown in Figure 15.15. For this reason, the transformation (see Figure 15.16) does not replace an existing class. It introduces a hot-spot subsystem that implements the Decorator pattern. It has the base class Component and a derived abstract class MonoGlyph (the Decorator participant), from which concrete decorators like Border and Scroller are derived. The responsibility of Glyph is extended by that of the base class Component. Thus, we do not introduce a new base class.

The flat structure, which is the result of extending transformations, is shown in Figure 15.16. Glyph has, in addition to the document element responsibilities, the Composite class responsibility (from the Composite pattern), the Decorator class responsibility (from the Decorator pattern), and the Composition responsibility. This is a considerable number of responsibilities collected in one class! Another consequence of the flat structure is that there is, in the class structure, no control about the sequence in which the additional Glyph responsibilities are applied. We may build a tree of objects of type Glyph that contains any mixture of embellishments, formatters, and aggregations. For example, a document might contain a Line that formats, as a Composition, the aggregation of two Character objects that are embellished by a Border and a Drawer. It might be debatable whether this makes sense.

Alternatively, we may do three expanding transformations (see Figure 15.17). These are done in a similar way as those described; the only difference is that new hot-spot subsystem base classes ComposedGlyph, FormattedGlyph, and EmbellishedGlyph are introduced, and the existing base class is made, each time, a subclass of the new one.

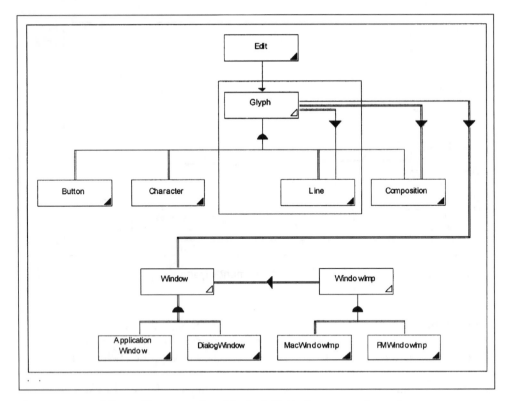

Figure 15.15   Editor with aggregation (Line) of Glyph document elements.

These transformations result in a layered structure with the new concepts ComposedGlyph, FormattedGlyph, and EmbellishedGlyph as subsystem base classes.

The layered class structure has the consequence that new responsibilities may be applied only in the following strict sequence: aggregation, embellishment, and formatting. This means Glyph objects may be composed by an aggregation hierarchy (ComposedGlyph). The completed aggregation—that is, the document—may be formatted (FormattedGlyph), and a formatted document may be decorated (EmbellishedGlyph).

We may leave the question open (since this chapter is not about how to structure editors) of whether a flat editor structure or a layered editor structure is more adequate. On first glance it seems that a combination of both structures would be the best solution. It combines, in a flat structure, Glyph and the aggregation facilities into a hotspot subsystem base class; and it puts EmbellishedGlyph into a separate layer. The reason is that it doesn't make much sense to embellish parts of a document. It may depend on the concrete requirements whether the formatting facilities are better layered out or included into Glyph. The point is that the systematic generalization process brought the question of flat or layered structure to light, which is not addressed with the Lexi example [Gamma 1995].

Eventually, we generalize the flat class structure presented in Figure 15.15 with hot spots 6 and 3. The transformation with regard to hot spot 6, look-and-feel generalization, implements the Abstract Factory pattern (see Figure 15.18). This transformation

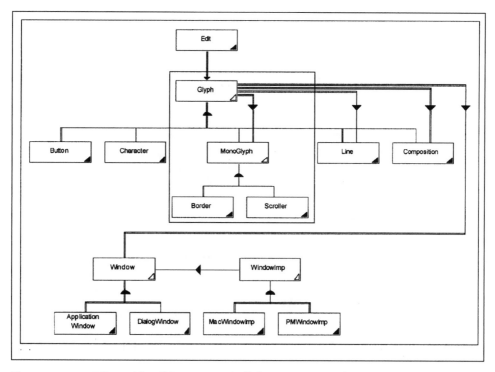

Figure 15.16 Editor with editing area embellishments (MonoGlyph, Border, and Scroller).

introduces not only one hot-spot subsystem, but *n* hot-spot subsystems. One subsystem, which does not replace an existing class, has the base class GUIFactory with a subclass for each look and feel, such as MacFactory and PMFactory. There is one subsystem for each GUI element—which replaces an existing class like Button with a base class like AbstractButton—defining the Button interface, and subclasses MacButton and PMButton for each look and feel. All hot-spot subsystem class hierarchies parallel each other.

The transformation with regard to hot spot 3, generalization of the formatting algorithms, follows the Strategy pattern to provide different formatting algorithms. It replaces the original Composition class with a Strategy-structured hot-spot subsystem. This contains, as an additional class, the new, modified Composition class, from which the formatting strategy, called Compositor, is split off. Subclasses of the Composition class, such as SimpleCompositor or TeXCompositor, implement the different formatting strategies. Figure 15.19 shows the result of the presented generalizing transformations, the editor framework class structure.

15.9 Summary

We have partitioned the introduction of a hot spot into three phases: hot-spot specification, hot-spot subsystem high-level design, and transformation of the framework

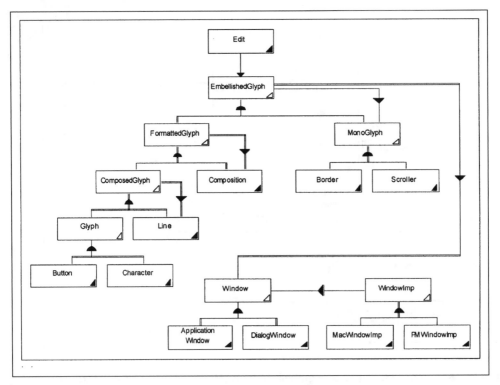

Figure 15.17   Editor with layered structure of embellishments, formatting, and aggregation.

class structure. Further, we have shown that there are rules for mapping a hot-spot specification to the hot-spot subsystem structure and a class structure with a fixed aspect to a generalized transformed class structure, where this aspect is variable. The generalization process transforms a class structure by a sequence of generalization transformations, each one per hot spot, based on these rules.

In conclusion, let us relate the presented design activities to the framework development process. Framework development is usually done in cycles. A framework development cycle adds either fixed functionality or variability to the framework class structure. Variability is added either in a systematic preplanned way, as described in this work, or in an unplanned way by organically growing functionality. The latter, which is not addressed in this chapter, requires restructuring cycles (see [Foote-Opdyke 1995]) to obtain a clear framework structure with hot-spot subsystems as described. The result of a development cycle is either a prototype or a new version of the framework.

The described framework design activities may be directly mapped to a spiral development cycle. A systematic generalization cycle is a specialization of the spiral development cycle. A spiral development cycle consists of the four phases: requirements analysis, high-level design, detailed design/implementation, and test/evaluation. A systematic generalization cycle consists of the four specialized phases: hot-spot analysis, high-level hot-spot subsystem design, detailed hot-spot subsystem design/implementation, and test/evaluation.

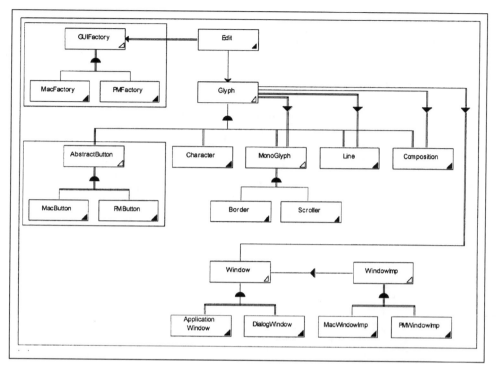

Figure 15.18 Editor with look-and-feel generalization (Button and GUIFactory with sub-classes).

You may perform the cycles, adding functionality or variability in different sequences. However, we contend that you should preplan the introduction of variability as much as possible and do it with systematic generalization cycles (instead of organically growing functionality). In the first development cycle, you should develop a fixed application from the domain or, as a prototype, central parts of it, in order to get a detailed understanding of a fixed slice of the domain. If the domain understanding is not good enough, similar cycles may follow. But, if at all possible, we recommend that you do the hot-spot high-level analysis in the next cycle in order to get an overview of the required variability as early as possible. This is followed by a sequence of cycles that add variability and also, if required, more functionality. For the cycles that add variability, you have to determine whether to include only one hot spot or several hot spots in a cycle.

For example, let us look at the development of the manufacturing framework OSEFA [Schmid 1995, 1996b]. In the first two small cycles, we developed for each a small but central part of an application from the framework domain, a Device Numerically-Controlled (DNC) coupling of a lathe Computerized Numerically-Controlled machine (CNC machine), and Robot-Control (RC coupling of a robot to a cell computer). Both couplings had an API such that they could be attached to a graphical user interface (GUI) and be used interactively for manual remote control of the machine and robot in a manufacturing cell. Thus, we achieved two objectives: We delivered the first product

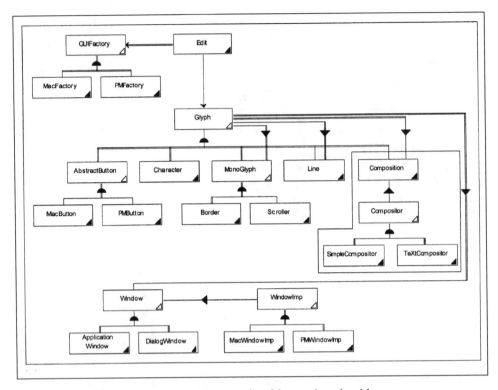

Figure 15.19   Editor framework with generalized formatting algorithms.

to our customer, and we validated our understanding of the core of the domain by a technical prototype. The third cycle both generalized previously developed functionality and added fixed functionality. We analyzed the variability of DNC and RC couplings and generalized it to an elementary, parameterized hot spot, and we added the fixed functionality of the cell control software that controls the working of a manufacturing cell. As a result, we had a running application for our manufacturing cell with a limited amount of variability. In the fourth cycle, we analyzed the variability required from the cell control software and generalized it with a number of hot spots, thus producing the final blackbox framework.

This framework development process differs in its emphasis from the framework evolution patterns described in [Roberts-Johnson 1997]. These react, rather, a posteriori, after organically grown functionality to generalization requirements. We emphasize that we should preplan evolution and generalize as much as possible a priori. For example, we recommend that you provide elementary, parameterized hot spots, whenever possible, from the beginning. The evolution patterns describe how to go from whitebox hot spots over nonelementary blackbox hot spots to elementary blackbox hot spots, which are eventually parameterized.

Certainly, not everything can be preplanned, and surprises will always happen to a framework developer. However, it is our experience that with the current knowledge, we are, by and large, able to carry out a systematic generalization process, even though we may fail with regard to a few items. Thus, we reduce effort and time to market compared to the organic evolution of frameworks in the past.

15.10 References

[Beck-Johnson 1994] Beck, K., and R. Johnson. Patterns generate architectures. *Proceedings ECOOP*. Berlin: Springer Lecture Notes in Computer Science, 1994.

[Brant-Johnson 1994] Brant, J., and R.E. Johnson. Creating tools in HotDraw by composition. In *Technology of Object-Oriented Languages and Systems TOOLS 13*, pp. 445–454, B. Magnusson, et al., editors. Englewood Cliffs, NJ: Prentice Hall, 1994.

[Coad-Yourdon 1991] Coad, P., and E. Yourdon. *Object Oriented Analysis.* Englewood Cliffs, NJ: Prentice Hall, 1991.

[Foote-Opdyke 1995] Foote, B., and W. Opdyke. Life cycle and refactoring patterns that support evolution and reuse. In *Pattern Languages of Program Design,* J. Coplien and D. Schmidt, editors. Reading, MA: Addison-Wesley, 1995.

[Gamma 1995] Gamma, E., R. Helm, R. Johnson, and J. Vlissides. *Design Patterns: Elements of Reusable Object-Oriented Software.* Reading, MA: Addison-Wesley, 1995.

[Gangopadhyay 1995] Gangopadhyay, D., and S. Mitra. *Design by Framework Completion.* IBM Santa Teresa Lab technical report STL TR 03.364, October 1995.

[Johnson-Foote 1988] Johnson, R.E., and Foote, B. Designing reusable classes. *Journal of Object-Oriented Programming* 2 (June 1988):22–35.

[Lange-Nakamura 1995] Lange, D., and Y. Nakamura. Interactive visualization of design patterns can help in framework understanding. *Proceedings OOPSLA 1995,* ACM SIGPLAN Notices 30(10), October 1995:342–357.

[Pree 1995] Pree, W. *Design Patterns for Object-Oriented Software Development.* Reading, MA: Addison-Wesley, 1995.

[Roberts-Johnson 1997] Roberts, D., and R. Johnson. Evolve frameworks into domain-specific languages. In *Pattern Languages of Program Design 3.* Reading, MA: Addison-Wesley, 1997.

[Schmid 1995] Schmid, H.A. Creating the architecture of a manufacturing framework by design patterns. *Proceedings OOPSLA 1995*, ACM SIGPLAN Notices 30(10), October 1995:370–384.

[Schmid 1996a] Schmid, H.A. Design patterns for constructing the hot spots of a manufacturing framework. *Journal of Object-Oriented Programming* 9(3), June 1996:25–37.

[Schmid 1996b] Schmid, H.A. Creating applications from components: A manufacturing framework design. *IEEE Software* 13(6), November 1996:67–75.

15.11 Review Questions

1. Which issues should you treat separately when designing a framework?

2. How do you obtain a framework class structure by generalization?

3. What is a hot spot of a framework?

4. By which characteristics can you specify the requirements of a hot spot?

5. What is a hot-spot subsystem?

6. How are hot-spot subsystems related to design patterns?

7. How is a hot-spot subsystem related to the hot-spot specification?

8. How can you generalize a given class structure?

9. What is a generalization transformation?

10. What is a systematic generalization cycle in framework development?

15.12 Problem Set

1. Take an existing framework and determine its hot spots and frozen spots. For each of the hot spots, try to give a hot-spot specification.

2. Take two (or more) similar applications from a domain that you know. Analyze what they have in common and what is different. Determine whether you could build a framework that embodied the common aspects. Determine the frozen spots and the hot spots of the framework, give each hot-spot specification, and design the hot-spot subsystem. Generalize the class structure of one of the applications to a framework class structure.

3. Consider three applications. One makes an offer for a life insurance policy, the second for a car insurance policy, and that third for a health insurance policy. Analyze what they have in common and what is different. Determine whether you could build a framework that embodied the common assets.

4. Determine the frozen spots and the hot spots of the framework in question 3, give each hot-spot specification, and design the hot-spot subsystem. Generalize the class structure of one of the applications to a framework class structure.

5. Consider the Java input/output framework for stream and file I/O. Which hot spots does it contain, which are the hot-spot subsystems implementing these hot spots, and according to which design patterns are they structured?

6. Consider the Java Abstract Windowing Toolkit (or Swing; it is a framework even though it is named differently!). Which hot spots does it contain, which are the hot-spot subsystems implementing these hot spots, and according to which design patterns are they structured?

Hot-Spot-Driven
Development

16.1 Hot Spots in Whitebox and Blackbox Frameworks

Frameworks are well suited for domains where numerous similar applications are built from scratch again and again. A framework defines a *high-level language* with which applications within a domain are created through *specialization* (in other words, adaptation). Specialization takes place at points of predefined refinement that we call *hot spots* [Pree 1995, 1996, 1997]. Specialization is accomplished through (blackbox) composition or (whitebox) inheritance, as explained subsequently. We consider a framework to have the quality attribute *well designed* if it provides adequate hot spots for adaptations. For example, [Lewis 1995], as well as many contributions in this book, presents various high-quality frameworks.

16.1.1 Hot Spots Based on Inheritance or Interfaces

The framework attributes whitebox and blackbox categorize its hot spots. A framework is neither pure blackbox nor pure whitebox. The term *whitebox framework* is used synonymously with *whitebox aspect of a framework*. A whitebox framework comprises incomplete classes, that is, classes that contain methods without meaningful default implementations. Class A in the sample framework class hierarchy depicted in Figure 16.1 illustrates

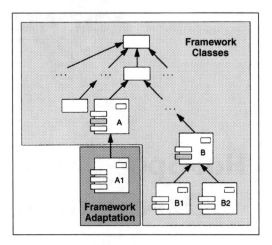

Figure 16.1   Sample framework class hierarchy
(from [Pree 1996]).

this characteristic of a whitebox framework. The abstract method of class A that has to
be overridden in a subclass is drawn in gray. The abstract method forms the hot spot in
this case.

Programmers modify the behavior of whitebox frameworks by applying inheritance
to override methods in subclasses of framework classes. The necessity to override
methods implies that programmers have to understand the framework's design and
implementation, at least to a certain degree of detail.

Java interfaces represent pure abstract classes consisting only of abstract methods.
Interfaces allow the separation of class and type hierarchies. In the sample class hierarchy in Figure 16.1, the abstract class A could be defined as an interface. In the original design, only instances of subclasses of A were type-compatible with A. In the case
of defining an interface A, an instance of any class in the class hierarchy that implements the interface is of type A. Of course, the whitebox characteristic of a framework
does not change in the case of using interfaces. If no classes implement an interface in
an adequate way, the programmer who adapts the framework also has to understand
partially the framework's design and implementation.

16.1.2 Hot Spots Based on Composition

Blackbox frameworks offer ready-made components for adaptations. Modifications
are done by simple *composition*, not by tedious inheritance. Programming software
component hot spots also correspond to the overridden method(s), though the one
who adapts the framework only deals with the components as a whole.

In the framework class hierarchy in Figure 16.1, class B already has two subclasses,
B1 and B2, that provide default implementations of B's abstract method. Let us assume
that the framework components interact as depicted in Figure 16.2(a). (The lines in Figure 16.2 schematically represent the interactions between the components.) A programmer adapts this framework, for example, by instantiating classes A1 and B2 and

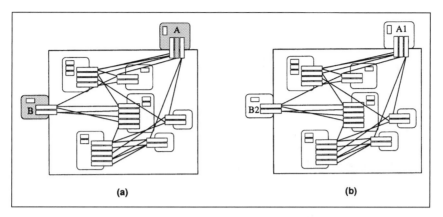

Figure 16.2 Framework (a) before and (b) after specialization.

plugging in the corresponding objects, as shown in Figure 16.2(b). In the case of class B, the framework provides ready-to-use subclasses; in the case of class A, the programmer has to subclass A first.

Remember that available frameworks are neither pure whitebox nor pure blackbox. If the framework is heavily reused, numerous specializations will suggest which blackbox defaults could be offered instead of just providing a whitebox interface. So frameworks will evolve more and more into blackbox frameworks when they mature.

16.2 Hook Methods as Elementary Building Blocks of Hot Spots

This section discusses the essential framework construction patterns that form the basis of the hot-spot-driven framework design process (see *Section 16.3*).

Methods in a class can be categorized into so-called hook and template methods: Hook methods can be viewed as placeholders or flexible hot spots that are invoked by more complex methods. These complex methods are usually termed *template methods* [Gamma 1995; Pree 1995; Wirfs-Brock 1990]. Note that template methods must not be confused with the C++ template construct, which has a completely different meaning. Template methods define abstract behavior or generic flow of control or the interaction between objects. The basic idea of hook methods is that overriding hooks through inheritance allows changes of an object's behavior without having to touch the source code of the corresponding class. Figure 16.3 exemplifies this concept, which is tightly coupled to constructs in common object-oriented languages. Method t( ) of class A is the template method that invokes a hook method h( ), as shown in Figure 16.3(a). The hook method is an abstract one and provides an empty default implementation. In Figure 16.3(b) the hook method is overridden in a subclass A1.

Let us define the class that contains the hook method under consideration as *hook class* H and the class that contains the template method as *template class* T. A hook class quasi-parameterizes the template class. Note that this is a context-dependent distinction, regardless of the complexity of these two kinds of classes. As a consequence, the

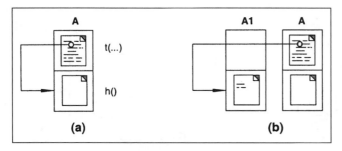

Figure 16.3 (a) Template and hook methods and (b) hook overriding.

essential set of flexibility construction principles can be derived from considering all possible combinations between these two kinds of classes. As template and hook classes can have any complexity, the construction principles subsequently discussed scale up. So the domain-specific semantics of template and hook classes fades out to show the clear picture of how to achieve flexibility in frameworks.

16.2.1 Unification versus Separation Patterns

If the template and hook classes are unified in one class, called TH in Figure 16.4(a), adaptations can be done only by inheritance. Thus, adaptations require an application restart *patterns unification* and *patterns separation*.

Separating template and hook classes is equal to (abstractly) coupling objects of these classes so that the behavior of a T object can be modified by composition, that is, by plugging in specific H objects.

The directed association between T and H expresses that a T object refers to an H object. Such an association becomes necessary, as a T object has to send messages to the associated H object(s) in order to invoke the hook methods. Usually an instance variable in T maintains such a relation. Other possibilities are global variables or temporary relations by passing object references via method parameters. As the actual coupling between T and H objects is an irrelevant implementation detail, this issue is not discussed in further detail. The same is true for the semantics expressed by an association. For example, whether the object association indicates a *uses* or *is part of* relation depends on the specific context and need not be distinguished in the realm of these core construction principles. Also note that T and H just represent types. So H, for example, could be a Java interface as well.

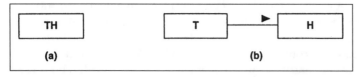

Figure 16.4 (a) Unification and (b) separation of template and hook classes.

A separation of template and hook classes forms the precondition of *runtime adaptations;* that is, subclasses of H are defined, instantiated, and plugged into T objects while an application is running. [Gamma 1995; Pree 1996] discuss various useful examples.

16.2.2 Recursive Combination Patterns

The template class can also be a descendant of the hook class, as seen in Figure 16.5(a). In the degenerated version, template and hook classes are unified, as seen in Figure 16.5(b). T as a subtype of H can manage another T instance. Thus, these patterns are termed *recursive compositions.* The recursive compositions have in common that they allow building up of directed graphs of interconnected objects. Furthermore, a certain structure of the template methods, which is typical for these compositions, guarantees the forwarding of messages in the object graphs.

The difference between the simple separation of template and hook classes and the more sophisticated recursive separation is that the playground of adaptations through composition is enlarged. Instead of simply plugging two objects together in a straightforward manner as in the Separation pattern, whole directed graphs of objects can be composed. The characteristics and implications are discussed in detail in [Pree 1995, 1996, 1997].

16.2.3 Hooks as Name Designators of GoF Pattern Catalog Entries

In this section we assume that the reader is familiar with the patterns in the pioneering Gang-of-Four pattern catalog [Gamma 1995]. Numerous entries in the GoF catalog represent small frameworks, that is, frameworks consisting of a few classes, which apply the few essential construction patterns in various more or less domain-independent situations. So these catalog entries are helpful when designing frameworks, as they illustrate typical hook semantics. In general, the names of the catalog entries are closely related to the semantic aspects that are kept flexible by hooks.

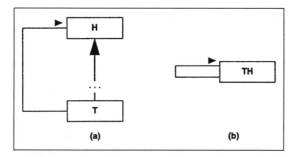

Figure 16.5 Recursive combinations of template and hook classes.

Patterns Based on Template-Hook Separation

Many of the framework-centered catalog entries rely on a separation of template and hook classes, as illustrated in Figure 16.4(b). Two catalog patterns, Template Method and Bridge, describe the Unification and Separation construction principle. The following catalog patterns rely on the Separation pattern: Abstract Factory, Builder, Command, Interpreter, Observer, Prototype, State, and Strategy. Note that the names of these catalog patterns correspond to the semantic aspect that is kept flexible in a particular pattern. This semantic aspect again is reflected in the name of the particular hook method or class. For example, in the Command pattern, "when and how a request is fulfilled" [Gamma 1995] represents the hot-spot semantics. The names of the hook method (Execute( )) and hook class (Command) reflect this and determine the name of the overall pattern catalog entry.

Patterns Based on Recursive Compositions

The catalog entries Composite, as illustrated in Figure 16.5(a) with a 1:many relationship between T and H, Decorator, as illustrated in Figure 16.5(a) with a 1:1 relationship between T and H, and Chain-of-Responsibility, as illustrated in Figure 16.5(b), correspond to the recursive template-hook combinations.

16.3 Hot-Spot-Driven Development Process

The pain of designing a framework is already described by [Wirfs-Brock-Johnson 1990]: "Good frameworks are usually the result of many design iterations and a lot of hard work." So don't expect a panacea. No framework will be ideal from the beginning. More realistically, there should be means to reduce the number of design iterations. Thus the term *framework development* expresses both the initial design and the evolution of a framework.

As the quality of a framework is directly related to the flexibility required in a domain, explicit identification of domain-specific hot spots can indeed help. Figure 16.6 gives an overview of the hot-spot-driven framework development process, which encompasses such a hot-spot identification activity. *Section 16.3.1* presents hot-spot cards, which have proved to be a simple yet effective means for documenting and communicating hot spots. The following outlines the core activities in the framework development process and their relationships.

Definition of a Specific Object Model

State-of-the-art object-oriented analysis and design (OOAD) methodologies support the initial identification of objects/classes and thus a modularization of the overall software system. For example, the Unified Method [UML 1997] picks out the best of Booch, Jacobson, and Rumbaugh [Booch 1994; Jacobson 1992, 1995, 1997; Rumbaugh 1991]. Class-Responsibility-Collaboration (CRC) cards [Beck 1989] help in the initial

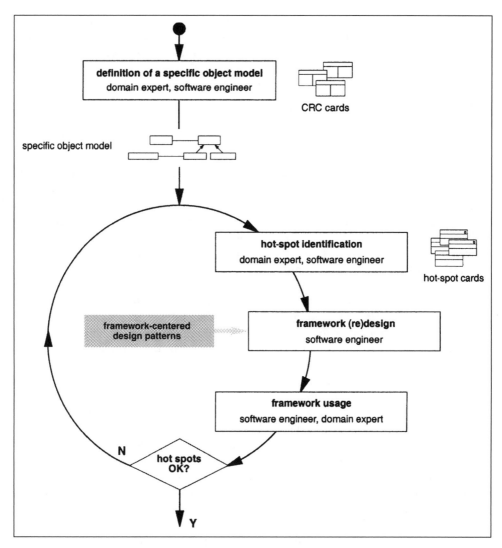

Figure 16.6 Hot-spot-driven development process (adapted from [Pree 1995]).

identification of objects and their associations. [Wilkinson 1996] discusses the usage of CRC cards in detail. Overall, object modeling is as challenging as any software development. Methodologies can only provide guidelines.

Object modeling requires primarily domain-specific knowledge. Software engineers assist domain experts in this activity. The distinction between domain expert and software engineer is a rather hypothetical one. It should just express the kind of knowledge needed. Of course, software engineers also have more or less deep domain knowledge.

Modeling a specific solution is already a complex and iterative activity, where object models have to be refined until they meet the domain-specific requirements. This comprises object/class identification and probably the complete development of a specific software system.

Before starting the framework development cycle, it would, of course, help considerably to already have two or more object models of similar applications at hand; identifying commonalities would be a lot easier. Unfortunately, this is typically not the case.

Note that the actual framework development process must build on top of a specific yet mature object model.

Hot-Spot Identification

Hot-spot identification in the early phases (for example, in the realm of requirements analysis) should become an explicit activity in the development process. There are two reasons for this: Design patterns, presented in a catalog-like form, mix construction principles and domain-specific semantics, as sketched in *Section 16.2.3*. Of course, it does not help much to just split the semantics out of the design patterns and leave framework designers alone with bare-bone construction principles. Instead, these construction principles have to be combined with the semantics of the domain for which a framework must be developed. Hot-spot identification provides this information. The synergy effect of essential construction principles paired with domain-specific hot spots is design patterns tailored to the particular domain (see *Section 16.3.1*).

The principal problem of this activity is that you cannot expect to get right answers if you do not ask the right questions. Often domain experts do not understand concepts such as classes, objects, and inheritance, not to mention design patterns and frameworks. As a consequence, the communication between domain experts and software engineers has to be reduced to a common denominator. Hot-spot cards (see *Section 16.3.1*) are such a communication vehicle, inspired by the few essential construction principles of frameworks outlined in *Section 16.2*.

One reason that explicit hot-spot identification helps can be derived from the following observations of influencing factors in real-world framework development: One seldom has two or more similar systems at hand that can be studied regarding their commonalities. Typically, one too-specific system forms the basis of framework development. Furthermore, commonalities should by far outweigh the flexible aspects of a framework. If there are not significantly more standardized (that is, frozen) spots than hot spots in a framework, the core benefit of framework technology—that is, having a widely standardized architecture—diminishes. As a consequence, focusing on hot spots is less work than trying to find commonalities.

Framework (Re)Design

After domain experts have initially identified and documented the hot spots, software engineers have to modify the object model in order to gain the desired hot-spot flexibility. Beginning with this activity, framework construction patterns, as presented in [Pree 1996] assist the software engineer. In other words, patterns describing how to achieve more flexibility in a framework do not imply satisfactory frameworks if software engineers do not know where flexibility is actually required. Hot-spot identification meets the precondition to exploit the full potential of framework construction patterns.

Framework Usage

A framework needs to be specialized several times, if not infinitely, in order to detect its weaknesses—that is, inappropriate or missing hot spots. The cycle in Figure 16.6 expresses the framework evolution process. Explicit hot-spot identification by means of hot-spot cards and framework construction patterns can contribute to a significant reduction of the number of iteration cycles.

16.3.1 Hot-Spot Cards as Means for Capturing Flexibility Requirements

Domain experts can easily think in terms of *software functionality*, and they know how software functions can support, for example, various business processes. As a consequence, software engineers should try to obtain answers to the following questions from domain experts:

- Which aspects differ from application to application in this domain? A list of hot spots should be the result of this analysis.

- What is the desired degree of flexibility of these hot spots; that is, must the flexible behavior be changeable at runtime and/or by end users?

As asking these questions directly fails in most cases, software engineers have to abstract from particular scenarios and look for commonalities and hot-spot requirements. So software engineers will produce hot-spot cards interactively with domain experts. *Section 16.3.2* discusses some useful hints regarding hot-spot identification. Figure 16.7 illustrates the layout of a hot-spot card.

A hot-spot card first provides the hot-spot name, a concise term describing the functionality that should be kept flexible, and specifies the desired degree of flexibility. Domain experts have to know that requesting runtime flexibility (adaptation without restarting) and/or the possibility of adaptation by the end user do not come for free. So this choice has to be made deliberately. Nevertheless, domain experts are tempted to demand maximum flexibility. Again, software engineers need to elaborate this aspect together with domain experts. The next section on the card summarizes the functionality.

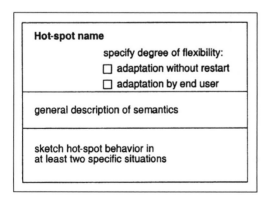

Figure 16.7   Layout of a hot-spot card.

This section should abstract from details. Finally, the functionality has to be described in at least two specific situations so that software engineers can better grasp the differences.

For example, if a framework for rental software systems is to be developed that can easily be customized for hotels, car rental companies, and so on, a domain expert would identify the rate calculation as a typical function hot spot in this domain. Rate calculation in the realm of a hotel has to include the room rate, telephone calls, and other extra services. In a car rental system, different aspects are relevant for rate calculation. Figure 16.8 shows a corresponding hot-spot card.

Hot-Spot Cards and Essential Construction Patterns

Based on flexibility requirements specified as a stack of hot-spot cards, software engineers must transform the object model. In this step, framework-centered construction patterns, as presented in *Section 16.3*, assist the software engineer. The following discusses the relationship between the information captured on hot-spot cards and framework construction patterns.

Function hot spots closely correspond to hook methods and hook classes. A hot-spot card contains information about the hot-spot semantics and the desired degree of flexibility, but not about which class/subsystem the hot-spot belongs to. Nevertheless, the integration of function hot spots into the object model turns out to be quite straightforward. The precondition of a smooth integration is the appropriate granularity of a function hot spot. Function hot spots should correspond to methods or responsibilities. For example, a useless hot-spot description expresses that database access should be flexible regarding a specific database.

In essence, a function hot spot with the right granularity implies that a hook method or a group of hook methods has to be added—either unified with the class where its template method resides or separated from it. Recall that a separation of template and hook classes forms the precondition of runtime adaptations. Table 16.1 summarizes

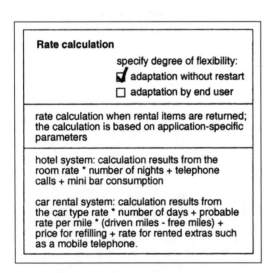

Figure 16.8 Sample hot-spot card.

Table 16.1 Transformation Rules for a Hot-Spot Card

ADAPTATION . . .	ADAPTATION BY END USER	OBJECT MODEL TRANSFORMATION
With restart	No	Additional hook method
Without restart	No	Additional hook method in separate hook class
With restart	Yes	Additional hook method + configuration tool
Without restart	Yes	Additional hook method in separate hook class + configuration tool

how to transform the object model according to the flexibility information on a hot-spot card object model transformation.

If none of the two check boxes (adaptation without restart, adaptation by end user) is marked, an extra hook method has to be introduced in an appropriate class. The hot-spot semantics usually suffices for finding the class and its template method for integrating the hook. Let us take the rate calculation hot-spot card as an example (see Figure 16.8), but assuming that none of the boxes is checked. We also assume that an abstract class RentalItem was added to the object model. We transform the object model according to the hot-spot card by simply adding a calcRate ( ) method to Rental-Item. The corresponding template methods, such as printInvoice ( ) and printOffer ( ), are in the same class (see Figure 16.9).

If adaptations of the calculation engine should be possible without application restart, the additional hook method has to be put into a separate class. Figure 16.10 illustrates the object model transformation. Thus, the rate calculation behavior of rental items can be changed by plugging in specific rate calculators.

How rate calculator objects are changed determines whether an end user should be able to accomplish this adaptation. One possibility would be to store the information regarding the calculation engine configuration in a resource file in plaintext. Reserva-

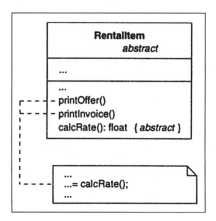

Figure 16.9 Hook method calcRate() resulting from a function hot spot.

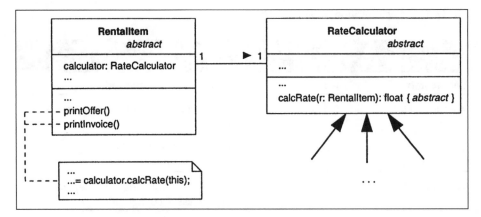

Figure 16.10   Hook class RateCalculator resulting from a function hot spot.

tion systems built with the framework read this resource file on start-up and when an end user requests this action explicitly. If the configuration file can be edited only by means of a text editor, many end users might refuse to effect such changes. On the other hand, end users could configure this system aspect if the resource file is edited interactively in a GUI editor.

Some hot-spot cards might require no additional hook methods or classes at all. Resources and adequate editors might allow the achieving of the same flexibility as an object model transformation. For example, if only different prices influence the rate calculation algorithm, an elegant solution just stores this information in a resource file or database table.

Note that "adaptation by end user" does not necessarily mean that no programming effort is required. For example, if several rate calculators exist, chances are high that an end user will find an adequate one. Otherwise, a specific rate calculator would have to be implemented first.

Recursive Template-Hook Combinations

So far, hot-spot cards correspond to the unification/separation of template and hook methods. The alert reader will observe the lack of hot-spot cards that reflect the recursive construction principles.

The design aspects covered by recursive template-hook combinations cannot be expressed in the reduced vocabulary of hot-spot cards. This vocabulary deliberately focuses on functionality and excludes concepts such as class interface definition and inheritance. So it is up to the software engineer to apply recursive construction principles in order to produce a more elegant and flexible architecture.

Nevertheless, we can likely recognize many construction principles by analyzing the object model at hand. Relationships labeled *part-of, consists of, manages, owns,* and the like indicate the GoF's Composite pattern. If an abstract class becomes overloaded, software engineers could opt for behavior composition through object chains. Some of the behavior is put into separate classes so that this behavior can then be added by object composition.

Having the characteristics of object hierarchies and collaborating objects in mind, software engineers can intuitively detect situations where they can apply these recursive construction principles.

16.3.2 Hints for Hot-Spot Mining

The assumption is rather naive that you have perfect domain experts at hand, that is, those who produce numerous helpful hot-spot cards just by handing out empty hot-spot cards to them. In practice, most domain experts are absolutely not accustomed to answering questions regarding a generic solution. The following outlines ways to overcome this obstacle.

Examine Maintenance

Most software systems do not break new ground. Many software producers even develop software exclusively in a particular domain. The cause for major development efforts that start from scratch comes from the current system, which has become hopelessly outdated. In most cases the current system is a legacy system, or, as [Goldberg 1995] expresses it, a *millstone*: You want to throw it away, but you cannot, as you cannot live without.

As a consequence, companies try the development of a new system in parallel to coping with the legacy system. This offers the chance to learn from the legacy system. If you ask domain experts and/or the software maintenance crew where most of the effort was put into maintaining the old system, you'll get a lot of useful flexibility requirements. These aspects should become hot spots in the system under development. Often, a brief look at software projects where costs became outrageous in the past is a good starting point for such a hot-spot identification activity. Of course, those parts where flexibility is provided in an adequate way have to be transferred from the old system to the new one.

Investigate Scenarios/Use Cases

Use cases [Jacobson 1995, 1997], also called *scenarios,* turned out to be an excellent communication vehicle between domain experts and software engineers in the realm of object-oriented software development. They can also become a source of hot spots: Take the functions incorporated in use cases one by one and ask domain experts about the flexibility requirements. If you have numerous use cases, you'll probably detect commonalities. Describe the differences between these use cases in terms of hot spots.

Ask the Right People

This last advice might sound too trivial. Nevertheless, try the following: Judge people regarding their abstraction capabilities. Many people get lost in a sea of details. Only a few are gifted with the ability to see the big picture and abstract from irrelevant details. This capability emerges in many real-life situations. Just watch and pick out these people. Such abstraction-oriented people can help enormously in hot-spot identification and thus in the process of defining generic software architectures. So take at least some developers of the current system who have abstraction capabilities on board the team that develops the new system.

16.4 Summary

The foregoing discussed technical aspects of framework development by presenting the essential framework design patterns and the resulting hot-spot-driven development process. But organizational measures are at least equally important to success, as framework development requires a radical departure from today's project culture. [Goldberg-Rubin 1995] present these aspects in detail.

Overall framework development does not result in a short-term profit. On the contrary, frameworks represent an investment that pays off in the long term. But we view frameworks as the long-term players toward reaching the goal of developing software with a building-block approach. Though the state of the art still needs profound refinement, many currently existing frameworks corroborate that frameworks will be the enabling technology in many areas of software development.

A word of advice for those who have not worked with frameworks so far: No methodology or design technique will help avoid this painful learning process. Toy around with some of the available large-scale frameworks and get a better understanding of the technology by first reusing frameworks intensively before jumping into framework development.

16.5 References

[Beck 1989] Beck, K., and W. Cunningham. A laboratory for object-oriented thinking. *Proceedings of OOPSLA 1989*, New Orleans, LA, October 1989.

[Booch 1994] Booch, G. *Object-Oriented Analysis and Design with Applications*. Redwood City, CA: Benjamin/Cummings, 1994.

[Gamma 1995] Gamma, E., R. Helm, R. Johnson, and J. Vlissides. *Design Patterns: Elements of Reusable Object-Oriented Software*. Reading, MA: Addison-Wesley, 1995.

[Goldberg 1995] Goldberg, A. What should we learn? What should we teach? *OOPSLA 1995*, Austin, TX; videotape by University Video Communications, http://www.uvc.com, Stanford, CA, 1995.

[Goldberg-Rubin 1995] Goldberg, A., and K. Rubin. *Succeeding with Objects: Decision Frameworks for Project Management*. Reading, MA: Addison-Wesley, 1995.

[Jacobson 1992] Jacobson, I., M. Christerson, P. Jonsson, and G. Övergaard. *Object-Oriented Software Engineering: A Use Case Driven Approach*. New York: Addison-Wesley/ACM Press, 1992.

[Jacobson 1995] Jacobson, I., M. Ericsson, and A. Jacobson. *The Object Advantage*. New York: Addison-Wesley/ACM Press, 1995.

[Jacobson 1997] Jacobson, I., M. Griss, and P. Jonsson. *Software Reuse: Architecture, Process, and Organization for Business Success*. New York: Addison-Wesley/ACM Press, 1997.

[Lewis 1995] Lewis, T. *Object-Oriented Application Frameworks*. Greenwich, CT: Manning Publications/Prentice Hall, 1995.

[Pree 1995] Pree, W. *Design Patterns for Object-Oriented Software Development*. Reading, MA: Addison-Wesley/ACM Press, 1995.

[Pree 1996] Pree, W. *Framework Patterns*. New York: SIGS Books, 1996.

[Pree 1997] Pree, W. *Komponentenbasierte Softwareentwicklung mit Frameworks*. Heidelberg, Germany: dpunkt, 1997.

[Rumbaugh 1991] Rumbaugh, J., M. Blaha, W. Premerlani, F. Eddy, and W. Lorensen. *Object-Oriented Modeling and Design*. Englewood Cliffs, NJ: Prentice Hall, 1991.

[UML 1997] *Unified Method*. Documentation set, Santa Clara, CA: Rational Software Corporation, 1997.

[Wilkinson 1996] Wilkinson, N. *Using CRC Cards: An Informal Approach to Object-Oriented Development*. Englewood Cliffs, NJ: Prentice Hall, 1996.

[Wirfs-Brock-Johnson 1990] Wirfs-Brock, R., and R. Johnson Surveying current research in object-oriented design. *Communications of the ACM* 33(9), September 1990.

16.6 Review Questions

1. What is the difference between blackbox and whitebox frameworks?

2. Hook methods correspond to a language feature of conventional languages. Which one is this? Explain the concept.

3. What is the relationship between abstract coupling and the Separation pattern?

4. Discuss the layout of hot-spot cards.

5. Why should hot-spot identification be placed in front of framework (re)design?

6. Discuss the transformation rules associated with hot-spot cards.

16.7 Problem Set

1. Choose a domain area and specify the flexibility requirements by means of hot-spot cards.

2. Choose a project where the GoF patterns were applied. Relate these spots to the essential framework construction patterns.

3. One value of hot-spot identification lies in its ability to shape consciousness: to introduce flexibility not for the flexibility's sake, but guided by domain requirements. Try to identify software systems where designers tried to maximize the system's flexibility. What are the consequences of this attitude?

4. Redesign an existing system by applying hot-spot cards and the corresponding transformation rules. What are the limits of hot-spot cards?

17

Structuring Large Application Frameworks[1]

Today, many businesses such as hospitals, banks, and insurance companies focus on the needs of the individual customer and organize their services accordingly. The customer needs become the center of attention and the service is adapted as required. The more specific the clientele's requirements, the more specialized the software solutions need to be. To achieve this flexibility, computer support is indispensable.

Over the past few years, we have designed and implemented such software solutions in various application domains. Employing object-oriented technology, frameworks have now been created that strongly support the development of new applications. However, frameworks alone aren't the answer to every problem. Both the construction and use of frameworks are so highly complex that software developers are confronted with almost insurmountable problems. In this chapter, we describe the problems we encountered, and the concepts and techniques we used to overcome them.

This chapter is based on a series of object-oriented software projects conducted at the RWG[2] [Bäumer 1996; Bürkle 1995], a company providing software and computing services to a heterogeneous group of approximately 450 banks in southern Germany. The projects have resulted in a family of applications covering virtually the whole area of banking—teller service, loans, stocks, and investment departments as well as self-service facilities. Developed over the past five years, the entire Gebos System[3]

[1]This chapter is an enhanced and revised version of [Bäumer 1997b].

[2]RWG stands for Rechenzentrale Württembergischer Genossenschaften (Württemberg Cooperative Bank Computing Center).

[3]Gebos stands for Genossenschaftliches Büro, Kommunikations, und Organisations system ("Banking Cooperative Office, Communication and Organization System).

comprises several frameworks and applications and includes 2500 C++ classes. Analysis of the Gebos System enables us to draw conclusions as to how frameworks can be further developed, reused, and adapted. The presented solution could be transferred to any kind of graphic workplace system embedded in the context of human work. The Gebos System was developed by following an evolutionary approach to software development (see sidebar titled *Getting the Tools and Materials Approach to Work*).

In the second section, we look at the main problems encountered during the design of large software systems. A large software system correlates the various tasks found in a business enterprise. It should be possible to adapt and configure such a system to the requirements of different workplaces in several enterprises. This can be achieved only by employing framework technology. For this reason, we now go on to describe and discuss the framework layers of the Gebos System. The following section describes layering techniques and divides frameworks into a concept and an implementation part. These parts are combined to form concept and implementation libraries. Finally, we present the Role-Object design pattern, which is used to make an object play different roles in different departments but stays well integrated.

17.1 Framework Layering in Large Systems

A framework models a specific relevant domain aspect using classes and objects. Abstract classes define the model and the interaction of their instances. Concrete classes provide default behavior and implementations of the abstract classes. The abstract classes specify the flow of execution and can be customized to specialized implementations by subclassing.

We describe an object-oriented software architecture using framework layers. The integration of different frameworks and their customization makes up the resulting system. Frameworks and framework layering must be rooted in the application domain in order to meet business needs. We therefore discuss first how we relate application domains to frameworks, before describing our layering concepts.

17.1.1 Application Domain Concepts

The services offered by an enterprise such as a bank can be divided into different areas of responsibility. Traditionally, banks organize their departments along these lines. Each department comprises specialists whose expertise is confined to their own specific field. We refer to these areas as *business sections* (for example, teller service, loans, investments; see Figure 17.2). Today, the traditional division into different departments is often supplemented by so-called service centers offering customers all-in-one service. Clerks working in a service center can perform most of the common tasks of the various business sections. These organizational alternatives have resulted in different types of workplaces. Concrete organization of work is referred to as the *workplace context* (see Figure 17.2). Examples of workplace contexts in the banking sector are:

GETTING THE TOOLS AND MATERIALS APPROACH TO WORK[4]

Leitmotif, design metaphors, document types, and prototyping are different tools to support software developers in understanding the users' tasks and the concepts of the application domain. To initiate and maintain the learning and communication process between developers and expert users, we are using an evolutionary concept of fast design and feedback cycles (see Figure 17.1). With these evolutionary cycles, we explicitly turn away from the traditional life-cycle strategies.

The evolutionary cycle is based on documents combined with prototypes.

We have successfully used a set of application-oriented document types that are well-known under various names in the literature [Bürkle 1995].

Scenarios describe the current work situation, the everyday tasks, and the objects and means of work. Scenarios are written by developers based on interviews with users and the various other groups involved.

Glossaries define and reconstruct the terminology of the professional language in the application domain. The entries in a glossary offer the first hints for relevant materials used in the application domain.

System visions anticipate future work situations. They are frequently supported by prototypes. They describe the developers' ideas of how tools, materials, automatons, process patterns, and folders for the future system will be arranged in the work environment and could be handled by users.

Prototypes are tangible objects for anticipating future situations from both use-related and technical perspectives. They are built out of components that match the design metaphors, allowing the users and developers to discuss delimitable parts of the system.

Instead of following the predefined work steps of a waterfall model with its sequence of milestone documents, we have identified three complementary and highly intertwined activities that developers carry out during the software development process: analyzing, designing, and evaluating. By *analyzing* the users' tasks, the developers gain an initial understanding of the concepts of the application area. This understanding is recorded in documents and prototypes (based on object-oriented classes and frameworks) within the activity of *designing*. To make sure that the understanding of these tasks and concepts is shared by the domain experts, the third activity of *evaluating* the documents and prototypes is performed.

For example, developers interview users at their workplaces (analyzing) and prepare scenarios (analyzing/designing) that are discussed with the interviewees and other users (evaluating). For the development of the new system on the basis of these scenarios, system visions are written (analyzing/designing) by developers and respective prototypes are realized (designing). These prototypes are afterward evaluated in workshops or hands-on sessions by users.

It is important to note that during the feedback cycles any problems that occur should direct us to the appropriate documents that need modification (see Figure 17.1). There is no predefined sequence of working with documents; in principle, all are available at any point. If some misunderstanding surfaces while evaluating a prototype, the developers

[4]This sidebar is an excerpt from [Lilienthal 1997].

Continues

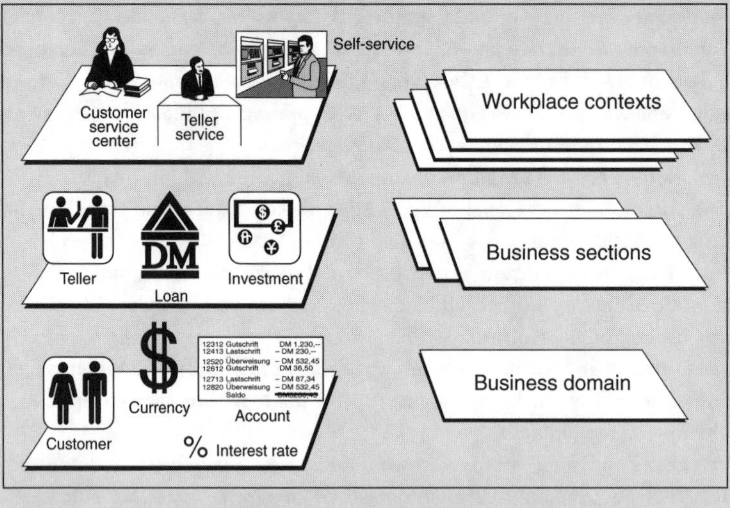

Figure 17.1 Evolutionary process with feedback cycles.

may decide that they need to write or rewrite more scenarios, glossaries, and system visions. Then they should be free to stop working on prototypes and start a new analyzing-designing-evaluating cycle with scenarios.

Customer service center. A customer receives advice on loans, bonds, or investments.

Teller service. Customers should receive swift and competent service for frequent and standard requests. Here, a clerk has to deal with deposits, withdrawals, transfers, and foreign currency.

Automatic teller machines and home banking. Bank services are made directly available to customers.

For every workplace context, there are potentially several *application systems*, depending on the specific domain requirements. For a workplace in a customer service center (see preceding list), we need an application system providing a proper blend of services from the different business sections. The customer consultant must have access to both the loan and the investment sections when conferring with a customer. At the same time, the system must allow simple transfers of money.

Although each application system is tailored to the needs of a particular workplace context, all of them should be built on the same basic platform. To illustrate this, let us consider the following situation. A customer profile exists in every department of a bank. In the loan department, sureties are an essential part of the customer profile. A surety serves to minimize the bank's losses in case of a customer's inability to pay. In other sections—for example, investments—the savings accounts form part of the customer profile. In both departments, though, the customer's name, address, and date of birth are an integral part of the profile. To develop software support for different workplace contexts, these differences and similarities need to be taken into consideration.

Our approach is to identify the core or common parts of the concepts and terms essential to running a business as a whole. We refer to these concepts and terms as the *business domain* (see Figure 17.2). Cooperation within an organization is possible only through the existence of these core elements in the business domain. In a bank, *account, customer,* and *interest rate* are examples of overlapping business domain concepts.

Modeling of the business domain can be done only where at least two business sections are already supported by software systems. Although the business domain forms the basis of the entire business, it is not available on its own. There is no one place in a bank where the account or the customer can actually be seen. From the different business sections, we need to reconstruct the core concepts behind the business domain, thereby ensuring a single integrated system.

Developing applications that not only suit a specific workplace but also incorporate these core concepts means that the frameworks must be organized along business domain, business section, and workplace context lines. To avoid unnecessary duplication, frameworks should be designed to encourage—or actually enforce—reuse of the business domain in the various sections. The reused framework components then become the basis for uniform and coherent application systems. In the following, we

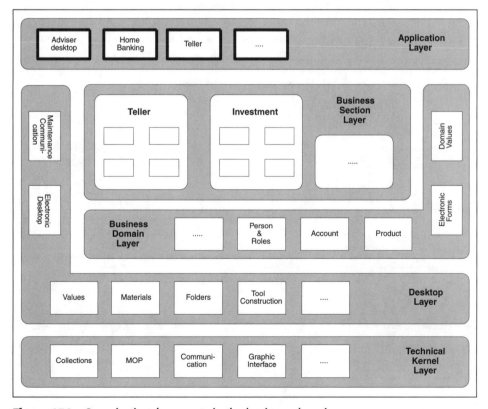

Figure 17.2 Organizational concepts in the business domain.

describe the close correlation between application domain concepts and framework architecture.

17.1.2 Layers of the Gebos System

The layers of the Gebos System are cut so as to take into account the distinction between the business section, the business domain, and the workplace context. Various application systems can be based on different business sections, and several business sections can be based on the same business domain. Two further framework layers make up the Gebos System and offer general software support (see Figure 17.3).

Application layers. Provide the software support for the different workplace contexts.

Business section layers. Consist of frameworks with specific classes for each business section.

Business domain layer. Contains the core concepts for the entire business.

Desktop layer. Comprises frameworks specifying the common behavior and general characteristics of applications.

Technical kernel layer. Offers middleware functionality and includes specific object-oriented concepts.

The framework layers in Figure 17.3 are not arranged vertically with the application layers at the top end and the technical kernel layer at the bottom. Instead, we have chosen a U shape consisting of the technical kernel layer, the business domain layer, and

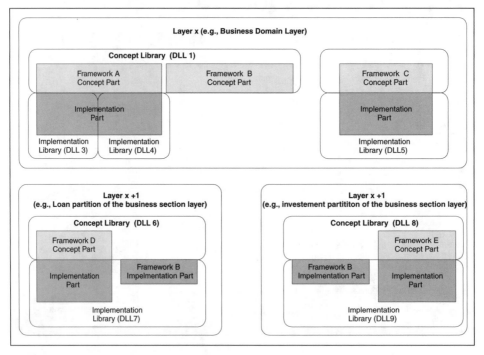

Figure 17.3 Layers and frameworks of the Gebos System.

the desktop layer. The U shape indicates that these three layers form the frame for the business section and application layers. Forcing the integration of the business section and application layers into the U-shaped frame means that further development can take place only within these boundaries. This constitutes the basis for the swift and efficient implementation of new application systems. Using the Gebos System, it is possible to configure and adapt new application systems for a hitherto unknown bank in a comparatively short time. We present the basic functionality of each layer and the relations between them in the following sections.

The Technical Kernel Layer

The technical kernel layer merely offers services to other layers and is used by the other framework layers—similar to a class library with an application programming interface (API) interface. In the Gebos System, this layer encapsulates and thus stabilizes middleware functionality. It consists of blackbox frameworks (see [Fayad-Schmidt 1997]). The frameworks in the technical kernel layer can be classified as:

Wrapper frameworks. Include frameworks that interact with the underlying operating system, the window system, client-server middleware, and data stores (such as relational databases, CD-ROM drives, or host-run databases).

Basic frameworks. Comprise specific object-oriented concepts such as a meta-object protocol, late creation, garbage collection including trace-tool support, and a container library.

The main issue is reusing the functionality encapsulated by the classes of the technical kernel layer. These frameworks are used by all other layers, especially the desktop layer. They can be reused across different business domains, as they do not incorporate any domain-specific knowledge.

The Desktop Layer

The desktop layer comprises frameworks that specify the common behavior of applications. The classes in the desktop layer characterize support for interactive workplaces. Framework examples of this layer are (see Figure 17.3):

The Tool-Construction Framework. Describes the general architecture of tools as well as their integration into an electronic workplace (see [Riehle 1995] and the *Design Metaphors within a Leitmotif* sidebar). This part of the layer can be compared with the MVC framework (see [Reenskaug 1996]).

The Folder Framework. Offers classes such as File, Folder, and Tray. Following the desktop metaphor, the Folder Framework provides the well-known look of modern applications, influenced by the Macintosh system.

The Value Framework. Consists of new value types. Programming languages (for example, C++) usually offer only a predefined set of value types, for example Integer, Char, and Boolean. The Value Framework enriches the standard types by providing classes that contain the basic mechanism for value types, which can be used only with value semantics.

In the desktop layer, the basic architecture and the look and feel of interactive application systems are defined. This design decision was made in order to ensure uniform behavior in the application systems, as well as technical consistency. The desktop layer frameworks are thus used like whitebox frameworks (see [Fayad-Schmidt 1997]) by subclassing and implementing abstract methods (see *The Business Section Layers* section). Frameworks in this layer can be reused in any kind of office-like business domain with graphic workplace systems.

DESIGN METAPHORS WITHIN A LEITMOTIF

When developing software, it is useful to have design metaphors that can guide this process and help to establish a vision of the future system. We have chosen *tools* and *materials* as the predominant metaphors of our approach [Bürkle 1995]. The motivation for this comes from observing everyday work. In many work situations people make an intuitive distinction between those objects that are *worked on*—that is, materials—and those that are *means of work—that is,* tools.

A tool supports recurring work procedures or activities. It is useful for various tasks and aims. A tool is always handled by its user, who decides when to take it up and what to do with it.

Materials are the objects of work that finally become the result or outcome of tasks. They incorporate pure application domain functionality. A material is worked on by tools according to professional needs. A material should be characterized by its potential behavior, not its internal structure.

In the banking project, the metaphor of an *automaton* was added. An automaton is characterized by (1) its being active over a long period in the background, and (2) running automatically with (adjustable) parameters based on a predefined algorithm. Automata are necessary to connect object-oriented systems to traditional environments, for example, IBM mainframes. They are equally useful for automating tasks in the application domain that do not rely on user interaction.

In addition to the design metaphors, we apply an overall guideline or *leitmotif,* which expresses our perspective on software development and use. Our leitmotif is the well-equipped workplace for office work; that is, we provide support for expert users in order to get things done. The leitmotif serves as an embedding context for the design metaphors.

A leitmotif and its design metaphors give a principal orientation for developers and users in the development process. It also determines how these parties interact in a software project. Following our leitmotif, the developers of software systems provide a service that is assessed by domain experts according to its suitability for their everyday work.

The Business Domain Layer

The business domain defines and implements the business's core concepts as a set of frameworks based on the desktop and kernel layer. The business domain layer thus forms the basis of every application system in the domain. It is crucial to make a proper distinction between the part of a core concept belonging to the business domain and the parts belonging to the business sections. If the chosen core concept in the business domain is too small, the missing parts have to be duplicated in each business section, and consistency has to be checked. If a core concept in the business domain becomes overloaded, the object that is to be transported between the various applications becomes cumbersome.

This layer consists of core-concept classes such as Account, Customer, Product, and various domain-specific value types. Although some implementations exist in the frameworks of this layer, most are whitebox frameworks and are rather thin. The final implementation is left for the business section layers.

The Business Section Layers

The business section layers are actually composed of a separate vertical partition for each business section. The frameworks in these partitions are based on the business domain layer, the technical kernel layer, and the desktop layer. The framework classes are implemented by subclassing the business domain and desktop layer classes. Usually, each subclass only implements the abstract methods predefined in its accompanying superclass. In this layer, the following classes can be found: borrower, investor, guarantor, loan, savings, loan account, savings account, and tools for performing business-section-specific tasks.

The business section frameworks may change more frequently than business domain frameworks. A business domain framework should not therefore incorporate any aspects of a core concept from a business section, unless it is relevant to most business sections. It should, however, provide hooks that can be easily extended and customized for applications using one or more business sections. To relate the core concepts of the business domain section to their extensions in the business section layers, the Role-Object pattern has been developed (see *Section 17.2.2*).

The Application Layers

The separation of the application layers from the business section layers is motivated by the need to configure application systems corresponding to different workplace contexts (see *Section 17.1.1*). The banks using the Gebos System range from small banks with only a few branches to large ones with over a hundred. Applications configured to meet the workplace context requirements of an individual bank can be found in this layer.

17.2 Framework Construction for Large Systems

We now look at the internal structure of frameworks and layers and the relations between them. First, the internal structure has to be chosen so as to minimize the coupling between different frameworks and application systems. Reopening of the frameworks during application system development should also be avoided. Second, the design and implementation of business domain frameworks should be independent of any business section framework. We have employed various patterns in the Gebos System, but the Role-Object pattern is particularly suitable for integrating business domain and business sections. The Role-Object pattern is therefore described in detail.

17.2.1 The Structuring of Frameworks into Library Layers

Based on the framework definition (see *Section 17.1*), we group class hierarchies together to form frameworks. A framework in the Gebos System does not correspond to a class hierarchy, but contains parts of different class hierarchies. This is in contrast to the more traditional way in which class hierarchies and frameworks correspond to one another (see Figure 17.7).

Each framework in the Gebos System is divided into a concept part and one or more implementation parts (see Figure 17.4). The concept part is modeled and implemented according to the concepts found in the application domain. The implementation part subclasses the corresponding classes of the concept part. The implementation part is developed, taking into account technical aspects. Without this separation, it is impossible to discuss the various dependencies between classes with an explicit focus on either the technical or the conceptual part.

After dividing each framework into a concept and *n* implementation parts, we physically package concept parts into concept libraries and implementation parts into implementation libraries. The structure of the concept libraries need not correspond to that of the implementation libraries. In our example, Framework A is divided into two implementation parts, each forming a separate implementation library. The concept parts of Frameworks A and B are packaged into one concept library.

The framework parts themselves are organized in layers, according to application domain concepts (see *Section 17.1*). Concept and implementation parts of the same framework do not, then, necessarily belong to the same layer (see Figure 17.4, Framework B). This organization enables us to describe a concept in the business domain layer and have different implementations according to specific business sections. For example, the frameworks in the business domain layer in Figure 17.3 consist only of concept parts for the core concepts. The implementation parts are located in the frameworks of the business section layers.

The use of classes belonging to other layers is restricted to concept classes of a framework. Changes in the implementation part of frameworks can then take place

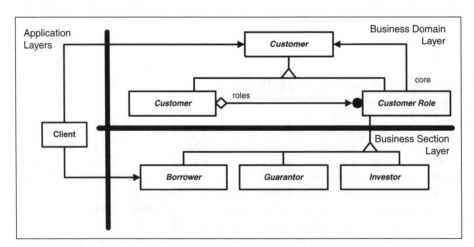

Figure 17.4   Dividing frameworks into concept and implementation parts.

without affecting those classes that use the concept part. To avoid cyclic dependencies, a framework should be used only by classes contained in frameworks of higher layers.

Providing libraries that include either several concept or implementation parts of frameworks per layer facilitates the configuration of different application systems. Each application system consists of only those libraries that are required for its functioning. The different frameworks are provided in DLLs to ensure that framework classes cannot be changed at will by application developers. All application systems are, then, built according to the same schema, and function in the same way. This is extremely important for classes that predefine and partially implement the flow of control for an application system (see discussion of the desktop layer).

To realize the decoupling of concept and implementation parts, clients should use a creational pattern—for example, Factory Method or Prototype [Gamma 1995]—to hide the selection of a particular implementation of a concept class. A pattern that has proved to be particularly effective in decoupling framework layers is the Product Trader pattern [Bäumer 1997a].

A prerequisite for the development of an integrated system (see *Section 17.1*) in a business domain is the division of frameworks. This division into concept and implementation parts allows us to provide a concept part in the business domain layer and several implementation parts in the business section layers. In the following section, we describe how to connect the classes of the concept part with those of the various implementation parts.

17.2.2 The Role-Object Pattern

A simple solution for connecting concept and implementation parts is to subclass a class from the business domain layer. However, subclassing has the effect that two instances of different subclasses are not identical. If they are meant to be conceptually identical, it becomes hard to keep them integrated as one logical object. We use the Role-Object pattern [Bäumer 1997c] to make one logical object span one or more layers. The core object, which resides in the business domain layer, is extended by role objects, which reside in the business section layers.

A role is a client-specific view on an object playing that role. An object may play several roles, and the same role may be played by different objects. An instance of a core concept belonging to the business domain may play several roles in different business sections. For example, in the loans business section, the customer could play the role of borrower or guarantor. In the investments business section, the customer could play the role of investor. These three roles could also be played by the same customer, both in real life and in the system model (see Figure 17.5).

We use a combination of design patterns, collectively called the Role-Object pattern, to let business sections attach roles to core-concept objects. Figure 17.5 shows the design of the customer example. Using the Decorator pattern, a core concept such as *customer* is defined as an abstract Customer superclass, without any implementation state. This is a pure interface. The class CustomerRole is a subclass of Customer and decorates a Customer object at runtime. The CustomerCore class implements the core of the Customer abstraction. We use Product Trader to create and manage role objects at runtime [Bäumer 1997a].

At runtime, instances of CustomerRole forward calls to the decorated Customer object (see Figure 17.6). This refers to a CustomerCore instance. Clients work either

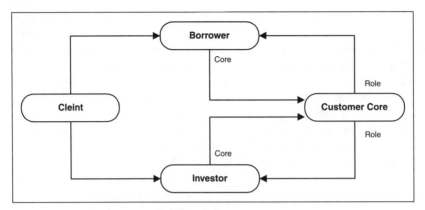

Figure 17.5 Role-Object pattern example.

with objects of the CustomerCore class, using the interface class Customer, or with instances of CustomerRole subclasses. By asking the CustomerCore object for a specific role, a client can obtain the respective role object.

The Role-Object pattern allows us to handle a complex logical object spanning several layers as one coherent, integrated object. Role objects from different business sections (for example, borrower, guarantor, or investor) share the same CustomerCore object. Business section–specific role objects can be created on demand, so that only those objects are created that are actually needed.

We view roles and classes as domain-modeling constructs. Other methodologies have chosen to reduce classes to pure implementation constructs, most notably [Reenskaug 1996]. For us, a class defines a domain abstraction, which includes the roles that class instances can play. A role defines a context-specific view of an object. On this level, we have to distinguish between technical and conceptual identities. The whole logical object has an identity of its own, even though its role objects maintain their own technical identity.

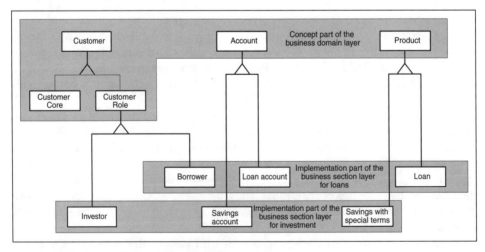

Figure 17.6 Role Object pattern at runtime.

17.2.3 Combining Roles and Frameworks

Using the Role-Object pattern frequently results in the concept part and its implementation parts being located in different layers (see Figure 17.4). The concept framework of the business domain layer consists of the Customer, CustomerCore, and CustomerRole classes, as well as other core concepts such as Account and Product. Their implementation can be found in implementation frameworks of different business section layers.

This organization of frameworks in concept and implementation parts (see Figure 17.7) ensures that extensions to any business domain concepts can be made without reopening the concept part of a framework. If a new business section has to be supported (for example, housing loans or foreign currency), a new layer with different implementation parts for the concept part of a framework is added to the system. Based on the added business section layer, new applications and extensions of existing applications can be implemented without affecting other layers.

Changes to one business section concern only the classes in the corresponding business section layer. If a new type of savings account is to be added to the investment layer, the implementation frameworks have to be extended by a new product and a new savings account. None of the other business section layers will have to be changed.

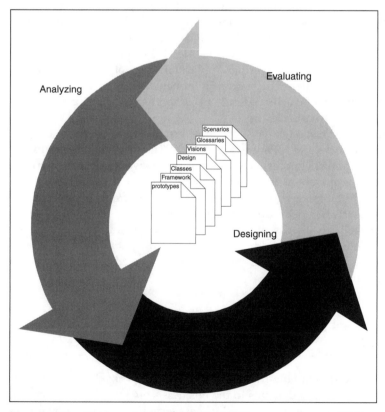

Figure 17.7 Classes of the Role-Object pattern spread over different frameworks.

Changes to the core concepts in the business domain layer are the only ones that affect all other layers. A change in the class Customer, Account, or Product will change all other layers (see Figure 17.7). Changes to a stable and well-designed business domain layer do not occur very often, though. Such changes can be caused only by a major reorientation of a company's overall business strategies and services. Figure 17.7 shows, in simplified form, the Gebos System layers and frameworks. The business domain layer does not consist of just one framework, but contains several frameworks (see Figure 17.3).

17.3 Related Work

Perhaps the best-known project concerned with large-scale object-oriented software development based on frameworks was that conducted by Taligent, Inc. A large set of frameworks is outlined in [Lewis 1995; Taligent 1995] and several other publications. Taligent groups sorted frameworks into categories, so that a hierarchy of categories emerges. Frameworks constituting abstract and incomplete solutions are complemented by *ensembles* of classes that introduce specific domain expertise by means of inheritance.

[Lewis 1995] presents several application frameworks of varying scale. The presentation of ET++ [Weinand 1995] shows a layering of frameworks in which applications are built on top of domain-specific frameworks, which are in turn built on top of general frameworks. The discussion of Unidraw [Vlissides 1995] shows that framework layering is different from traditional layering: Applications are not isolated from general frameworks by means of intermediate domain frameworks, but rather depend on both. Traditional layering can be achieved only by confining oneself to use relationships—using inheritance breaks the layers.

[Garlan 1995] discusses *architectural mismatch*, the term used to denote the integration problems of frameworks and software components. The discussion is conducted on a technical level. Identifiable problems result from a framework's implicit assumption about its context of operation, and they frequently conflict with one another. A well-known example is the integration of the main event loop from different frameworks, which is frequently handled in very different ways.

This related work fails to discuss the relationship between frameworks and the domains they are modeling, or to address framework integration problems on a domain level. We believe this chapter provides some remedy, addressing this neglected—though crucial—issue.

17.4 Summary

In this chapter, we have shown how frameworks can be categorized and layered in order to match their application domains to the business's organizational structures. We defined the categories of business domain, business section, and application framework. Based on these distinctions, we showed how frameworks can be layered in order to manage their dependencies and to reduce their coupling. We have shown how to split a framework into a concept part and several implementation parts, and how to support this split by the use of design patterns.

A particularly pertinent issue is building and maintaining logical objects that span several layers. We use the Role-Object pattern to adapt a core concept from the business domain to different business sections. Using role objects allows us to extend a core concept without having to change it, and therefore without having to touch the business domain frameworks.

The presented approach supports the development of frameworks and systems that are stable and at the same time can evolve gracefully and at different speeds.

17.5 References

[Bäumer 1996] Bäumer, D., R. Knoll, G. Gryczan, and H. Züllighoven. Large scale object-oriented software-development in a banking environment—An experience report. *ECOOP 1996—Object-Oriented Programming, 10th European Conference,* Pierre Cointe, editor. Linz, Austria: Springer Verlag, 1996, pp. 73–90.

[Bäumer 1997a] Bäumer, D., and D. Riehle. Product trader. In *Pattern Languages of Program Design 3,* Chapter 3. Reading, MA: Addison-Wesley, 1997.

[Bäumer 1997b] Bäumer, D., D. Riehle, W. Siberski, and M. Wulf. Role object. *Proceedings of the 1997 Conference on Pattern Languages of Programs* (PLoP 1997). Technical Report WUCS-97-34. Washington University Department of Computer Science, Paper 2.1, 1997.

[Bäumer 1997c] Bäumer, D., G. Gryczan, R. Knoll, C. Lilienthal, D. Riehle, and H. Züllighoven. Framework development for large systems. *Communications of the ACM* Theme Issue on Object-Oriented Application Frameworks, Mohamed E. Fayad and Douglas Schmidt, editors, 40(10), October 1997:52–59.

[Bürkle 1995] Bürkle, U., G. Gryczan, and H. Züllighoven. Object-oriented system development in a banking project: Methodology, experience, and conclusions. In *Human-Computer Interaction,* Special Issue: Empirical Studies of Object-Oriented Design 10(2, 3):293–336. New Jersey, Hillsdale: Lawrence Erlbaum Associates, 1995.

[Fayad-Schmidt 1997] Fayad, M.E., and D. Schmidt. Object-Oriented Application Frameworks. *Communications of the ACM,* 40 (10), October 1997.

[Gamma 1995] Gamma, E., R. Helm, R.E. Johnson, and J. Vlissides. *Design Patterns: Elements of Reusable Object-Oriented Software.* Reading, MA: Addison-Wesley, 1995.

[Garlan 1995] Garlan, D., R. Allen, and J. Ockerbloom. Architectural mismatch: Why reuse is so hard. *IEEE Software* 12(6), November 1995:17–26.

[Lewis 1995] Lewis, T. *Object-Oriented Application Frameworks.* New York: Prentice Hall, 1995.

[Lilienthal 1997] Lilienthal, Carola, and Heinz Züllighoven. Application-oriented usage quality, the tools and materials approach. Submitted for publication to *Interactions Magazine,* CACM, October 1997.

[Reenskaug 1996] Reenskaug, T., P. Wold, and O.A. Lehne. *Working with Objects: The OOram Software Engineering Method*. Greenwich, CT: Manning Publications, 1996.

[Riehle 1995] Riehle, D., and H. Züllighoven. A pattern language for tool construction and integration. In *Pattern Languages of Program Design*, Chapter 2. Reading, MA: Addison-Wesley, 1995.

[Taligent 1995] Taligent, Inc. *The Power of Frameworks*. Reading, MA: Addison-Wesley, 1995.

[Vlissides 1995] Vlissides, J. Unidraw: A framework for building domain-specific graphical editors. In *Object-Oriented Application Frameworks*, pp. 239–290, T. Lewis, editor. Greenwich, CT: Manning, 1995.

[Weinand 1995] Weinand, A., and E. Gamma. ET++: A portable homogeneous class library and framework. In *Object-Oriented Application Frameworks*, pp. 154–194, T. Lewis, editor. Greenwich, CT: Manning, 1995.

17.6 Review Questions

1. What is a framework within the concept of this chapter? Which kinds of frameworks are distinguished?

2. What is the relation between the concepts of *layer, framework,* and *pattern*?

3. Which patterns frequently occur in a layered architecture? What are their primary purposes?

4. What is a design metaphor? Name and explain the major design metaphors of this chapter.

5. Name and explain the most important document types of this chapter. What are they good for?

17.7 Problem Set

1. Explain the reasoning behind the distinction between business domain, business sections, and workplace context.

2. Name and explain the reasons behind the layers of an architecture according to the approach of this chapter.

3. Explain the approach of a Concept and Implementation Library. What are the benefits?

4. What is the Role pattern and why is it necessary?

5. Given the domain GUI-Construction, how would you distribute typical classes of a GUI-Framework (such as ET++) over the technical kernel, desktop, and business domain layers?

SIDEBAR 5
FRAMELETS—SMALL IS BEAUTIFUL

This sidebar introduces the notion of framelets. They are essentially small frameworks. Thus, framelets can be easily understood and modified. As framelets are not aimed at complex application domains, they can also be assembled without the problems associated with the combination of large frameworks. Our first experiences with framelets demonstrate that these architectural building blocks allow the integration of framework technology into legacy applications. Furthermore, framelets might form a suitable means for structuring software architectures.

SB5.1 Frameworks and Legacy Applications

Conventional wisdom implies that legacy applications and framework technology do not match well. Framework experts usually advise the development of a domain-specific architecture for the domain at hand. The legacy application would have to be replaced by the adapted framework. Most companies are not willing to pursue such a radical approach, which renders the investments into legacy applications worthless. Furthermore, the development of a complex framework from scratch represents a formidable risk. The brilliant architects who would be able to design domain-specific frameworks are often not available.

This situation forms the starting point of our considerations—that is, how framework technology can be harnessed in the realm of legacy applications. The legacy system at hand is a client-server application for a bank. Our approach is straightforward: Taking a look at the overall conventional system architecture and then at the underlying source code reveals that some quite small aspects of the system are implemented numerous times in a similar way.

For example, the legacy application relies on remote procedure calls (RPCs) implemented in C. The code associated with a particular RPC implies tedious programming work, in particular, handling the parameter value transfer for each RPC. For example, the return parameter types are C-style arrays, which have to be properly processed. The RPCs are too diverse to come up with a simple reusable procedure or function. Instead, we found that a small framework is the solution in order to automate the calling of remote procedures. The hot spot of the RPC framelet is the processing of parameters.

Another example of reimplemented code can be found at the client side of the legacy system. Most dialogs provide one or more list boxes (a.k.a. grid controls) together with buttons to add items to the list box, and to modify and remove them. Thus, these GUI elements and their interactions have to be implemented again and again. The associated programming task is another typical example of a piece of programming work that can easily be packaged into a small, self-contained framework. The hot spot of the so-called list box framelet is the dialog, which displays an item. Figure SB5.1 shows a sample specialization of the list box framework. The dialog on the left-hand side consists only of the framework's GUI and the button labeled Close. The arrows in Figure SB5.1 indicate the interactions between the framework components.

Continues

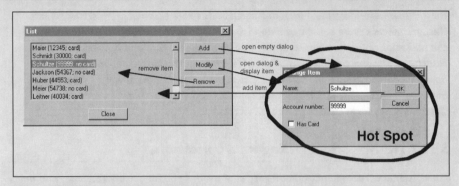

Figure SB5.1 A sample specialization of the list box framework.

Besides the RPC framework and the list box framework, we found a few other aspects that could be packaged as small frameworks. All these frameworks are implemented in Java and deployed as JavaBeans. As the legacy application is steadily extended (new dialogs) and changed, application developers already reuse these assets. Other parts of the legacy application are simplified by replacing source code fragments with calls to these frameworks. This reduces significantly the source code size and thus the maintenance costs in the long term. The next section will introduce the concept of a small framework, a *framelet*, and discuss its relationships with other architectural concepts.

SB5.2 Framelets as Architectural Units

The conventional idea of an application framework as an application skeleton has well-known drawbacks: A framework easily becomes a large and tightly coupled collection of classes that breaks sound modularization principles and is difficult to combine with other similar frameworks. Complex, implicit specialization interfaces are hard to manage by application programmers. For a discussion of problems in application frameworks, see, for example, Chapter 3, and [Casais 1995; Fayad-Schmidt 1997; Lewis 1995; Sparks 1996]. Our thesis is that only small software units should be whiteboxes.

These considerations and our experiences with reorganizing legacy systems led us to the concept of the framelet, a small framework. In contrast to a conventional application framework, a framelet:

- Is small in size (less than 10 classes)
- Does not assume main control of an application
- Has a clearly defined simple interface

Otherwise, a framelet follows the general principles of frameworks, in particular the Hollywood principle. Essentially, a framelet is thus a component that defines two interfaces: one for calling its services and another to be implemented by the specializer. This notion is particularly suitable for reorganizing legacy code: If one removes a part of a legacy system that represents some logically related services, usually that part will then contain dangling calls to other services provided by the rest of the legacy system. The latter calls correspond to the specialization interface: An implementation of the called routines must be provided in order to make the removed part functional. If the removed part is intended to become a reusable unit, the implementation of these routines can be given in different ways by different reusers. A natural way to implement such a unit is a small framework, that is, a framelet.

The relationships between framelets, layered architectures, components, and application frameworks can be explained as follows. Assume that a system has been organized as a layered architecture, and that you wish to make different layers reusable in other systems. First, consider the uppermost layer. If this layer is disconnected from the system, there will be a set of services that are called but not implemented in the layer. On the other hand, the only interface through which its own services can be accessed is the user interface (UI). This corresponds, therefore, to an application framework: The layer is a semifinished application.

Consider next the lowest layer, or a part of it. When disconnected, such a unit provides an interface for the services it implements, but it needs no specialization. This corresponds to a conventional blackbox component.

Finally, consider a middle layer. If the middle layer is disconnected as a separate unit, there will be both an interface defining the services provided by the unit itself and another interface specifying the methods that have to be implemented by a lower layer to make the unit functional. Such a unit could be implemented as a single framework with large service and specialization interfaces, but this kind of unstructured framework would be very hard to understand and use. The idea of a framelet is to split this framework into smaller parts corresponding to slices of a middle layer, with independent service and specialization interfaces. Hence, framelets can be viewed as a means to bring structure to reusable software.

SB5.3 References

[Casais 1995] Casais, E. An experiment in framework development. *Theory and Practice of Object Systems* 1(4):269–280.

[Fayad-Schmidt 1997] Fayad, M.E., and D. Schmidt. Object-oriented application frameworks. *Communications of the ACM* 40(10), October 1997.

[Lewis 1995] Lewis T., L. Rosenstein, W. Pree, A. Weinand, E. Gamma, P. Calder, G. Andert, J. Vlissides, and K. Schmucker. *Object-Oriented Application Frameworks*. Greenwich, CT: Manning Publications/Prentice Hall, 1995.

[Sparks 1996] Sparks S., K. Benner, and C. Faris. Managing object-oriented framework reuse. *IEEE Computer Theme Issue on Managing Object-Oriented Software Development,* M.E. Fayad and M. Cline, editors, 29(9), September 1996.

CHAPTER 18

Understanding Macroscopic Behavior Patterns with Use-Case Maps

This chapter contributes to methods to help humans understand and describe macroscopic behavior patterns[1] in software systems constructed from object-oriented frameworks. The behavior patterns we seek to understand are *system* properties exhibited by the running software. A system is a set of components that collaborate to achieve some overall purpose. Examples of components of software systems are objects; threads; processes; groups of these, often called *modules;* and groups of modules, often called *subsystems.* Our interest is in the runtime behavior of systems of such components constructed from object-oriented frameworks.

18.1 Understanding Macroscopic Behavior Patterns

The difficulty of understanding macroscopic behavior patterns exists to some degree for all software, but is particularly troublesome for software constructed from object-oriented frameworks, for the following reasons:

---

[1]The term *pattern* is used in this paper in two ways: a narrow technical one, as in *design pattern* and a broader one that reflects common English usage, as in *behavior pattern,* or *visual pattern.* The two meanings may sometimes converge. This overloading of the term is unfortunate, but seems unavoidable when a term with its own useful meaning in common usage is co-opted for a narrower technical purpose.

The first-class representation of the framework in code centers around component construction; system structure and behavior are visible only in a second-class way, in widely scattered details. The system structure (how components are organized into collaborating groups) may look quite different from the class organization that is explicit in textual object-oriented programming languages such as such as Smalltalk, C++, or Java. For example, multiple instances of a single class may be scattered throughout an executing program, playing different roles in different places in the runtime program, or an instance of a single class may play different roles at different times in different places in the runtime program. Understanding the system requires understanding how the instances come to play these roles over time and how the roles are played in the context in which the instances find themselves at a particular time. In other words, it requires an understanding of the system structure and how it evolves over time. However, source code written in textual object-oriented programming languages does not describe the system structure and behavior in a first-class way, but leaves them to emerge from widely scattered details in the code.

The system view we seek is not a concrete thing, but an abstraction. Because the system structure and behavior are not explicit in a first-class way in the source code of textual object-oriented programming languages, any view of it is an abstraction relative to code. Object-oriented frameworks implemented with textual object-oriented programming languages do not include such abstractions explicitly. So there is extra work required to understand systems constructed from such frameworks beyond that required to understand the framework itself.

The use of design patterns, a common practice in frameworks, may obscure the system view by making intercomponent interactions more indirect than they would otherwise be. This is not a criticism of design patterns, but simply a neutral observation of a fact. The frameworks we will study in this chapter, namely HotDraw [Buhr 1996b] and ACE, embody a number of design patterns that do this [Gamma 1995; Schmidt 1994, 1995]. On one hand, design patterns help program understanding by enabling humans to assume that details follow standard patterns. On the other hand, design patterns that introduce extra levels of indirection into interactions make the system view that is already buried in detail (point 1) even harder to understand. Experts will form intuitive understandings but nonexperts approaching a framework cold will have difficulty. For example, we found it quite difficult to abstract the system view from the code and documentation of the frameworks used as examples later in this chapter.

The use of combinations of design patterns obscures the system view because pattern combination is not yet a well-defined subject. Even relatively small-scale frameworks, such as the ones used as examples later in this chapter, use combinations of design patterns. Design patterns are typically described as independent entities, leaving it to the user to understand how to combine them. Pattern combination is not yet a well-developed subject, so combinations must be understood informally. Experts will develop an intuitive understanding but nonexperts must construct an understanding by painstakingly combining independent descriptions. Even very smart, experienced people may find the problem difficult when approaching a new framework embodying design patterns with which they are not familiar.

Both the system view we seek and design patterns are abstractions, so understanding requires combining multiple abstractions for frameworks that make serious use of design patterns. In general, abstractions are beneficial for understanding. However, practical frameworks leave it to the user to develop an understanding of this combination of abstractions. This is difficult for the following reasons. First, the system view is not explicit (points 1 and 2) and extracting it can be difficult (point 3). Second, combining design patterns is itself difficult (point 4). Thus, difficulty is piled upon difficulty. When the description technique for the abstractions is one such as UML [UML 1997] or ROOM [Selic 1994], we may be overwhelmed with detail for large, complex systems. Used for system description, techniques such as UML or ROOM are very detail-rich. This is because they center around specifying how behavior will be made to emerge at runtime (through the interchange of messages between components, driven by internal state transitions of components). Even when we stand back from *how* to use these techniques to describe *what* (in terms of example scenarios expressed as message interchange sequences), the result for large, complex systems will be many diagrams containing much detail. Experts can amortize the work of understanding this detail over many applications of the same framework, but even experts have need of more compact description techniques.

Although framework class organizations are fixed, systems constructed from a framework are self-modifying while they are running, and self-modifying software is notoriously difficult to understand. In self-modifying systems, the system structure evolves over time due to actions of its components; in other words, the system modifies itself. This increases the difficulty of understanding macroscopic system behavior. Descriptions must include not only intercomponent messages for ordinary behavior but also messages to change the system structure—namely, to create new components, destroy old ones, make components visible in new places and invisible in old ones, and move mobile components from place to place. Understanding macroscopic behavior patterns in systems with fixed structure is difficult enough in terms of detail-rich descriptions such as the ones mentioned in point 5. Adding self-modification exacerbates the problem.

Specific applications are visible only in framework customization details. Frameworks are for constructing a range of similar applications. This should mean that a basic system view exists that is common to all applications, only requiring embellishment for particular applications. However, we have seen that, in practical frameworks, no such view is directly available, but must be inferred by the user from code and multiple detail-rich design descriptions. Experts will understand it intuitively, but others may find it difficult.

18.1.1 Use-Case Maps

To alleviate the understanding problem, we offer use-case maps (UCMs) [Bordeleau-Buhr 1997; Buhr 1996a, 1997a, 1997b, 1998, 1999; Buhr-Casselman 1996]. UCMs are characterized in [Buhr 1998, 1996a, 1997a, 1997b, 1999] as a simple, visual notation for understanding and architecting the emergent behavior of large, complex, self-modifying systems. UCMs are said to be for *architecting behavior* to emphasize that they give *form* to macroscopic behavior patterns without specifying how the actual behavior will emerge at runtime. In common usage, the term *architecting* implies giving form to macroscopic structure. Here the term is extended to include macroscopic behavior in a way that is consistent with this usage. This chapter focuses on only the *understanding* purpose of UCMs. There are two reasons for this: (1) The examples are from existing frameworks developed without the aid of UCMs. (2) There are as yet no public-domain examples of frameworks developed with the aid of UCMs (the architecting purpose of UCMs has been exercised in industry in at least one framework development project, but this work has not been written up in the public domain). However, the *architecting* purpose of UCMs should be kept in mind.

Explanation of UCMs is left to the examples of *Section 18.1* and *Section 18.2*. See *Section 18.3* for further discussion of the properties and uses of UCMs. Features of UCMs for dealing with layering and decomposition of large-scale systems are mostly mentioned only in passing in this chapter because the examples are relatively small scale (although this does not mean they are simple); see [Buhr 1998, 1999] for a thorough treatment of these features.

The examples are not large scale enough to exhibit in any strong way the problem of detail-rich conventional descriptions swamping the reader in details. A reader can gain insight into this problem from the examples only by exercising some imagination. When looking at the non-UCM diagrams presented as examples here, imagine scaling up the system such that inch-thick stacks of such diagrams are required to describe the system. Then it is not difficult to imagine how UCMs can be useful as a way of condensing the essence of the system into many fewer diagrams.

18.1.2 Use-Case Maps and Frameworks

This chapter will lead us, step by step, to the conceptual model of frameworks indicated by Figure 18.1, in which UCMs provide a *system* view, high-level class relationships (methodless and messageless) provide a *construction* view, and all else is pushed down to the next lower level of abstraction, to be described by techniques such as those offered by UML and ROOM.

The words *system* and *construction* are easily overloaded with different meanings

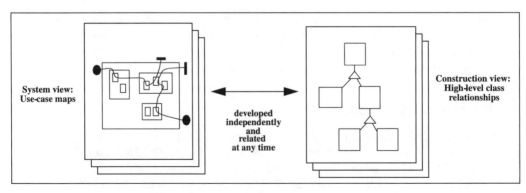

Figure 18.1 High-level view of frameworks.

and some readers may find that the meanings intended by Figure 18.1 conflict with their favorite ones. Finding precisely the right terms to describe these ideas is difficult, so we ask such readers to try to understand the meanings intended here, even if they disagree with the terms. The term *system view* means a description of a collaborating set of components as seen at runtime. The term *construction view* means a set of specifications from which system components may be constructed at runtime. These two views overlap in source code, but are distinct at this level of abstraction, as follows. On one hand, the system view provided by UCMs includes self-modification of system structure, so this is not part of the construction view. On the other hand, in programs, the code that implements the classes of the construction view provides not only the details that produce emergent system behavior at runtime, but also the constructors and destructors needed to achieve system self-modification. These aspects are separated at this level of abstraction as follows. The details that produce emergent behavior are deferred to a *lower level of abstraction*. The constructors and destructors implicitly form part of a *layer* underneath UCMs that provides a component factory.[2] Special UCM notations *imply* usage of this factory, without showing explicitly either its existence or how it will be used. The result is, at this level of abstraction, that only the system view describes runtime structure and behavior, including self-modifying behavior.

A key property of this way of looking at things is the distinction it makes between the *components* of the system view and the *classes* of the construction view. From a system perspective, at this level of abstraction, classes are specifications that may be used to construct operational components; they are not operational components themselves. Keeping the system and construction views distinct helps to keep design concerns distinct. This is important, because there are often trade-offs to be made between properties of systems, such as end-to-end response time along paths, and construction properties, such as extensibility.

The general form of this model is relatively independent of whether a framework is whitebox or blackbox. In either case, some concrete class in the construction view provides the starting point for constructing a system component. From this perspective, a blackbox framework is simply one that offers specifications for system components in more consolidated form.

This model provides a dramatic reduction in the number of diagrams required to understand the large-scale organization and behavior of systems constructed from object-oriented frameworks.

This model can also help to provide traceability down to details and up to requirements, where *down* and *up* indicate directions of decreasing and increasing abstraction. Upward traceability can be from UCMs to use cases. Downward traceability can be from UCMs to the use of design patterns to implement them (at the level of [Gamma 1995; Schmidt 1994, 1995]).

Developing this model for existing frameworks is simple on the construction side, because the model is represented in a first-class fashion in the code. However, on the system side, we need to find our way through widely scattered details and abstract from them. How to do this, as well as the nature of the results, is the subject of the rest of this chapter.

---

[2]Note the different implied meanings of the terms *level of abstraction* and *layer*: The former pertains to description techniques, the latter to the large-scale organization of systems (see [Buhr 1998] for more on how UCMs deal with the latter subject).

18.2 HotDraw

Although this section draws on a case study of HotDraw reported in [Buhr 1996b], the design model presented here is actually of an idealized version of HotDraw that was developed in [Buhr 1996b] as part of a reengineering exercise. The presentation here also comes at the model from a very different angle than previous presentations in [Buhr 1996b], which presented use-case maps first. Here we approach the framework first from a conventional perspective, with the objective of illustrating the complexity that can result, and then show the simplification that use-case maps produce.

18.2.1 Classes

From a code perspective, HotDraw is a set of Smalltalk classes that extends the standard Smalltalk class library to support a specific style of graphical user interface (GUI). The nature of the HotDraw class hierarchy is shown in Figure 18.2, leaving out methods and leaving out the classes of the standard Smalltalk class library used by HotDraw. In this diagram (as elsewhere in this chapter), we avoid elaborate class relationship notations, simply to avoid clutter; such notations are useful for detailed design, but we do not need them for the purposes of this chapter (labeled arrows suffice). In this particular diagram, boxes with thick lines identify classes used as examples in Figure 18.4, later in this chapter.

Some classes have inheritance relationships between them (shown as *isa* arrows). There may be many runtime relationships among the classes, of which this diagram shows only one example (a *contains* relationship). The runtime relationships are hidden in the details of the classes. In particular, behavior is generated through message-sending relationships not shown in this diagram. We could try to add more information about runtime relationships to this diagram to try to get insight into behavior, but such insight is better obtained by going to a more system-oriented view. From a system perspective, the classes are specifications that may be used to construct system components; they are not system components themselves.

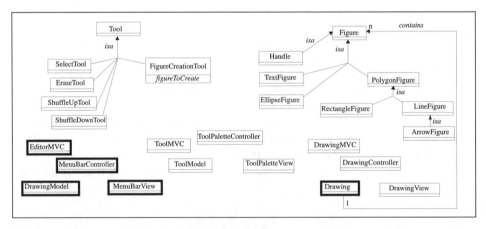

Figure 18.2   Nature of the HotDraw class hierarchy.

18.2.2 System Components

From a system perspective, the essence of HotDraw is a set of MVC components to control the different areas of the screen (Figure 18.3). MVC stands for Model/View/Controller, a well-known system structure in which the M part (the model) maintains data, the V part (the view) display data, and the C part (the controller) manages interactions with the human user for different views.

In the multi-MVC system, each MVC group is a system component that contains nested M, V, and C components, which in turn may contain other nested components. Figure 18.4 shows, on the left, one of HotDraw's MVC components (the Editor MVC) and, on the right, the relationships of its subcomponents to the classes that were highlighted in Figure 18.2. In this diagram, ME, VE, and CE identify the Model, View, and Controller components, respectively, of the Editor MVC (later, MT, VT, and CT, and MD, VD, and CD will identify elements of the ToolPalette and Drawing MVCs, respectively). Such MVC components are peers at the system level; the M, V, and C components are peers within each MVC component; and so on. The diagram illustrates the style of showing system structures in use-case maps: Sets of peer and nested components, without identification of interface elements, are arranged in fixed relative positions so that the arrangement can be recognized as a visual pattern.

This diagram uses a neutral component notation that is not entirely adequate for the purposes of use-case maps, but that will do for now—the use-case map of Figure 18.11 uses a more general notation that will be explained when we come to that diagram.

Showing the cross-references from classes to system components as arrows does not constitute a recommendation to document such cross-references this way (a textual list of name cross-references would suffice for that); what we are striving for here is a diagram to anchor in the mind's eye the difference between system components and classes.

This leads us to Figure 18.5, showing a *component context diagram* of the entire MVC system. The system is self-modifying because some of these components come into existence only when needed, and different ones may be needed at different times. It is the behavior of this set of components as a system in which we are interested. However, although Figure 18.5 shows a system, seeing it as an artifact is difficult because its structure is not explicit in the only declared structures in the code—class hierarchies—and its

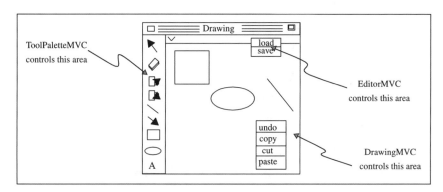

Figure 18.3   MVC components control HotDraw screens.

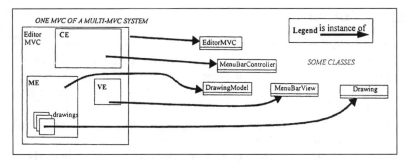

Figure 18.4 System components and classes.

behavior is not observable directly with our own eyes, but only through interactions with physical devices such as a screen, a keyboard, and a mouse. The physical devices are part of the system as whole, but seeing how the software affects them does not help us to understand how the software works internally as a system. We want to be able to see behavior patterns in such systems at a high level of abstraction, but this is difficult by conventional means without becoming swamped in details, as will now be shown.

18.2.3 Design Patterns and Messages

We will now study the message sequences required for one particular example of behavior: the selection of drawing in the Editor MVC to be displayed by the Drawing MVC, at a time when no drawing is currently displayed.

This example contains two interesting features:

It uses a design pattern, the Observer pattern from [Gamma 1995], to arrange the sending of the required messages. Actually the Smalltalk dependency mechanism is used—this is a design pattern, built into the standard Smalltalk class hierarchy, that provided a model for the Observer pattern. Use of this pattern makes inter-component message sequences hard to trace in the code, because they are indirect.

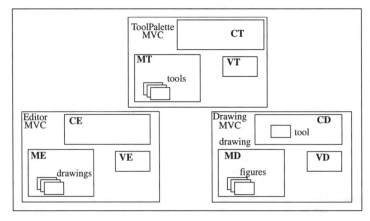

Figure 18.5 Component context diagram of the MVC system.

It illustrates system self-modification through the requirement for a selected drawing containing a new set of figures to move from being data in the Editor MVC to being executable code in the Drawing MVC. When no drawing is currently displayed, there is no drawing component in this position beforehand, so the effect is to put a new component in this position (Figure 18.6). The fact that only an identifier moves, not the whole component, is an implementation detail. The system effect is analogous to a Java applet moving from being data in one web site to being executable code in another.

Figure 18.7 displays the message sequences in HotDraw needed to accomplish the purpose of Figure 18.6 (the Observer pattern has more to it than message sequences, but those are all we are interested in for purposes of understanding behavior). The message sequences in Figure 18.7(a) are for ME as Subject1, and the ones in Figure 18.7(b) are for MD as Subject2. Notice that VD is an observer of both subjects and that there can be no Subject2 (no MD) until the message sequence of Figure 18.7(a) is completed. The movement of the drawing as data from the Editor MVC to become the model MD in the Drawing MVC in Figure 18.6 is accomplished at the end of the message sequence of Figure 18.7(a), upon VD's return from the getData( ) message to ME. This enables VD to register itself as an observer of MD, at the top of Figure 18.7(b), and thereafter to receive notifications of changes to drawing data. At the code level, we see changing visibility (of a drawing object by VD); at the system level, we see this as a component movement (of the drawing object into the MD slot).

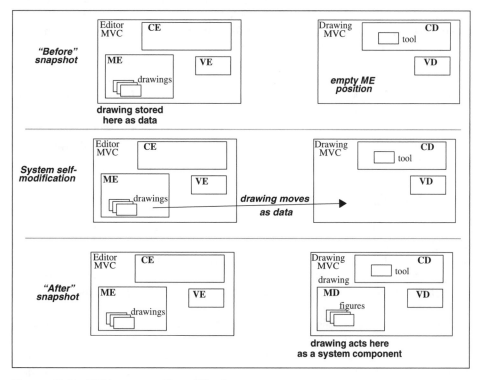

Figure 18.6 MVC system self-modification.

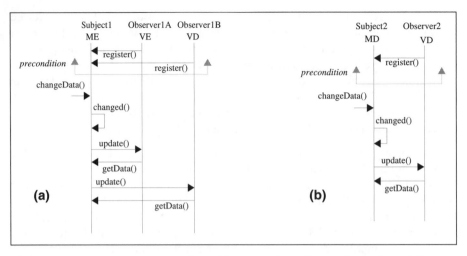

Figure 18.7   Message sequences in and between the Editor and Drawing MVCs.

This is a small-scale example, but complexity blows up when there are many components and many messages between them. Complexity factors are as follows: One is the sheer number of messages, and the detailed commitments they require, for a system of any size or complexity. Another is the difficulty of keeping the message sequences and the system structure associated in the mind's eye when there are many diagrams of message sequences. Another is the hiding of collaborations behind indirections resulting from the use of design patterns (for example, the changed-update sequences). Another is the lack of differentiation between messages that cause system self-modification—such as getData( ) at the end of the sequence in Figure 18.7(a)—from other types of messages, making the existence of self-modification very difficult to separate out as a system issue.

The result is that system meanings are buried under detail. Humans must mentally compose the pieces of the puzzle. In large systems, many diagrams may be required. If the details are known (as with existing frameworks), we get lost in them. If the details are not known (as is the case during forward engineering), there is nothing between requirements prose and the details to help discover the details.

18.2.4 Use-Case Maps

Use-case maps collapse message sequences into cause-effect sequences (see Figure 18.8).

In Figure 18.8, a cause-effect sequence is represented by a filled circle at the start, a bar at the end, and a path of any shape in between. This notation hides all the complexity factors associated with messages, enabling one to get a higher-level perspective. All that remains is a causal link, without any indication of how it is to be implemented. Cause-effect sequences are at a level of abstraction above messages, message directions, multiple back-and-forth messages, and message interchanges required to establish preconditions.

When we want to see the big picture, we simply concatenate cause-effect sequences to form paths (see Figure 18.9), along which *responsibilities* identify intermediate effect/cause points. Result: use-case maps.

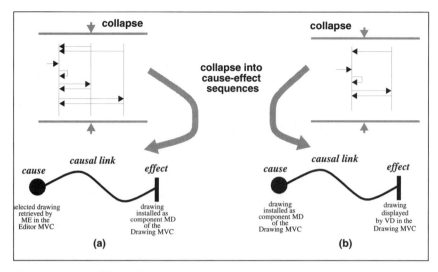

Figure 18.8   Collapsing message sequences into cause-effect sequences.

The term *use-case map* has its origins in the term *use case* [Jacobson 1992]. A *use case* is a prose description of system behavior that may embody a set of related scenarios of system operation. The word *use* does not necessarily imply human users or users outside the system. In general, a use-case map may embody scenarios involving many systems, subsystems, or components that are users of each other. In relation to use-case maps, scenarios are just the progression of cause-effect sequences along paths (in general, many such sequences may be in progress concurrently in a map at any time, or even along a single path, constrained only by preconditions). A use-case map presents this view as a requirement or explanation; there is no implication that the causal sequence has a first-class representation in the software.

Figure 18.10 (a segment of a path in the use-case map for HotDraw shown in Figure 18.11) consolidates the ideas in Figures 18.8 and 18.9 and also introduces some new notation.

The component notation illustrated by Figure 18.10 is generalized from the neutral one of Figure 18.5 as follows. It identifies primitive *objects* as boxes with rounded corners. Boxes with sharp corners are known as *teams*. These are concepts for systems, not programs, indicating that, *at the scale of the diagram*, teams are operational groupings (shown nested), and objects are primitive data or procedure abstractions. Here, all are instances of program classes, but, in general, they do not all have to be. The general-

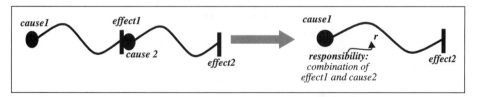

Figure 18.9   Use-case maps are formed by concatenating cause-effect sequences.

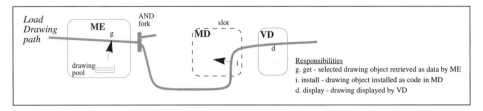

Figure 18.10 A fragment of a HotDraw use-case map.

ized component notation also explicitly indicates the dual nature of dynamic components of self-modifying systems, as data (in pools, shown by a special symbol) or code (in slots, shown as ordinary boxes with dashed outlines).

Figure 18.10 has three responsibilities along the path segment, named *get*, *install*, and *display*; these have been abstracted from Figure 18.8, using the technique of Figure 18.9. The convention illustrated here of showing shorthand labels along the paths, and listing the actual responsibilities to the side, is a standard one for reducing visual clutter in use-case maps.

The path notation in Figure 18.10 uses small *move* arrows between pools or slots, and paths, to indicate component movement: The arrow at *get* indicates movement of a drawing object, as data, out of a pool in ME; the arrow at *install* indicates movement of the same object into the MD slot to become an operational object there. *Get* and *install* are responsibilities shown with a special notation to highlight system self-modification. The third responsibility along the path, *display*, means that VD displays the new drawing on the screen.

The map notation also provides for path forks and joins. The fork with the bar after ME is called an AND-fork and means that the paths are, in principle, concurrent after the fork (all this means for HotDraw is that we don't care about the relative order of sequences along the two paths). A mirror-image notation for AND-joins is available but not needed by this example. All other forks and joins in maps, such as those in Figures 18.11 and 18.18, are OR-forks or OR-joins that result from path superposition (different paths are combined into one map and some paths follow the same route, without any implication of synchronization between them).

Observe how much detail this map fragment omits relative to message sequence diagrams like Figure 18.7, while at the same time giving the essence of behavior, including both ordinary behavior and self-modification. The complicated business of making the drawing object visible to VD through the multiple registration, notification, and retrieval messages associated with the Observer pattern is hidden, but the effect is expressed directly in a simple and easy-to-understand fashion. We can use diagrams like this as traceability tools for identifying where design patterns such the Observer pattern are used at a more detailed level, by simply providing traceability pointers in the map documentation.

Figure 18.11 presents a use-case map for three connected use cases for the multi-MVC system of HotDraw: (1) Load Drawing, (2) Select Tool, and (3) Select Figure. These paths could be concatenated to show one large causal sequence, but this is not necessary to get a good system view. All we need to know to understand the larger

1-2-3 sequence is that a precondition of 2 is completion of 1 and a precondition of 3 is completion of 2 (preconditions and postconditions are part of the textual documentation of use-case maps). Responsibilities are omitted in this figure because we do not need them to understand its general nature (however, they are implied).

Let us now trace the LoadDrawing path in Figure 18.11. At CE, a user interaction would be decoded as a request to load a drawing. At ME, the requested drawing would be moved from a pool. At VE, the drawing name would be displayed in the editor area of the screen. At MD, the drawing would enter the slot. At VD, the figures of the drawing would be displayed in the drawing area of the screen. This should be enough information to understand the general nature of the map as a whole.

The use-case map of Figure 18.11 has an elegant regularity about it. The version of HotDraw we studied had more irregular paths. However, this irregularity was easy to see only after the paths had been drawn. When we saw it, we found we could make the paths regular with relatively minor coding changes. It seemed that the irregularity was due to shortcuts taken by coders. The changes made the code immediately more understandable. Regularity seems a desirable property, because it aids understanding, reuse, maintenance, and evolution, but its presence or absence is difficult to see when immersed in details. This suggests that use-case maps are useful, not just for understanding frameworks, but also for designing them.

Not only do use-case maps eliminate the complexity problems of understanding systems in terms of messages, they also have other advantages, as illustrated by Figure 18.11: They enable us to show behavior patterns as recognizable visual patterns superimposed on structure, in a way that allows us to combine many behavior patterns into

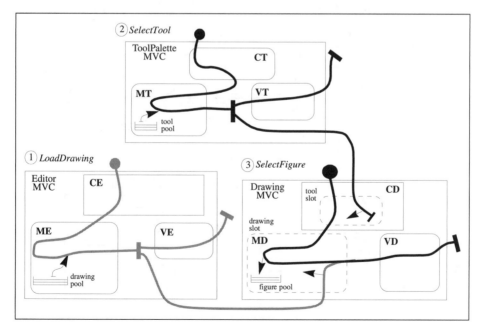

Figure 18.11   A use-case map for an idealized version of HotDraw.

one diagram. They represent behavior patterns that could equally well be regarded as design patterns of a rather high-level kind (this viewpoint is presented in [Buhr 1996b]).

18.3 ACE

ACE is a public-domain C++ framework for communications applications. It comes with some canned applications, one of which, called the *gateway,* we will use as an example here (see Figure 18.12). The gateway application enables peer workstations in a network to interact through a gateway workstation. Some of the peers act as input peers that generate messages, and others act as output peers that consume messages. Messages are sent from any one input peer to the gateway workstation, which then routes the messages to one or more output peers. (The term *message* means two things in this section, depending on context. Here it means textual data sent between work-stations. Later it will also refer to intercomponent interactions in the gateway's system of software components. The meaning will be clear from the context.)

ACE manifests the same complexity factors as HotDraw, but in a more complex application domain, making it even harder to understand. Therefore, in the limited space here, we can only give a few highlights.

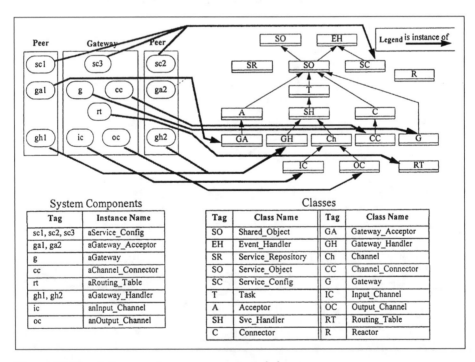

Figure 18.12   Gateway system components and classes.

System Components

Tag	Instance Name
sc1, sc2, sc3	aService_Config
ga1, ga2	aGateway_Acceptor
g	aGateway
cc	aChannel_Connector
rt	aRouting_Table
gh1, gh2	aGateway_Handler
ic	anInput_Channel
oc	anOutput_Channel

Classes

Tag	Class Name	Tag	Class Name
SO	Shared_Object	GA	Gateway_Acceptor
EH	Event_Handler	GH	Gateway_Handler
SR	Service_Repository	Ch	Channel
SO	Service_Object	CC	Channel_Connector
SC	Service_Config	G	Gateway
T	Task	IC	Input_Channel
A	Acceptor	OC	Output_Channel
SH	Svc_Handler	RT	Routing_Table
C	Connector	R	Reactor

18.3.1 Classes and System Components

Figure 18.12 gives an overview, in condensed form, of the main system components and classes in the gateway application and the relationships between them.

18.3.2 Design Patterns and Messages

The main ACE patterns we are concerned with here are the Reactor, Acceptor, and Connector. Another important ACE pattern, the Service Configurator, must be left out for lack of space. It supports creation and management of service objects. It is used in both the gateway and the peers to provide a generic initialization mechanism. We show only its effects in the use-case maps.

The Reactor pattern (see Figure 18.13) is used extensively in both gateway and peers as the underlying communication mechanism driving them. It supports event demultiplexing by providing a means of registering event handlers so that when an event occurs the correct event handler is notified. Events include communications events, timers, and Unix signals. Our use-case maps do not make explicit reference to this pattern, but assume it is supported by an underlying layer.

The Connector pattern (see Figure 18.14) and the Acceptor pattern (the partner of the connector, not illustrated because the nature of both patterns is sufficiently well illustrated by one of them) are used to establish interworkstation soft connections (for example, Unix sockets). The Connector pattern is used by the gateway and the Acceptor pattern by the peers. The Connector pattern supports the making of connect requests to particular network addresses. The Acceptor pattern supports listening for connect requests on a particular network address. Figure 18.14 shows the Connector pattern integrated into ACE, not in isolation.

Figure 18.15 shows some message scenarios that occur in the gateway node in relation to establishing a connection. These will not be explained further here; interested readers will no doubt be able to figure them out, but the point of presenting them here is to give a sense of the kind of detail that is required to describe behavior at the message level. A person has to hold the class and system pictures in the mind's eye while studying different message sequences and to relate the different diagrams to each other by mentally associating textual names of elements in them. This is a relatively

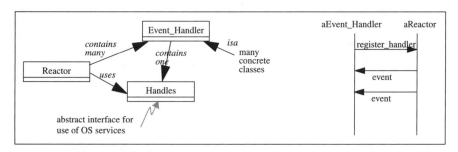

Figure 18.13 Some elements of the Reactor pattern.

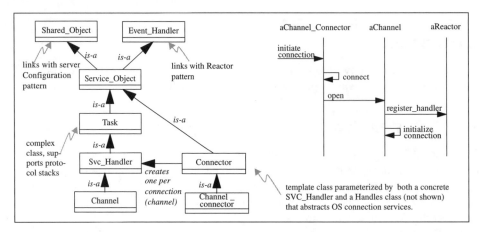

Figure 18.14   An overview of the Connector pattern in ACE.

small-scale system and these sequences show only part of its operation (for example, they do not show the self-modification that occurs during a configuration phase). Therefore, the amount of detail in this figure is not yet overwhelming. However, it is not hard to visualize how the amount of detail in sets of such figures can easily become overwhelming for large-scale systems.

18.3.3 Use-Case Maps

The way in which message sequences are collapsed into causal sequences in use-case maps was explained in the HotDraw example, so here we go directly to use-case maps.

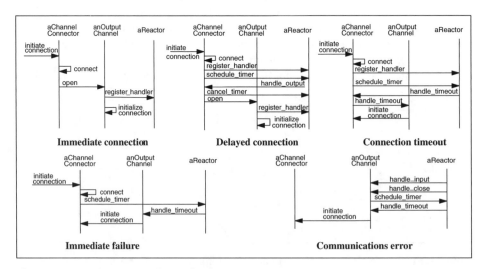

Figure 18.15   Some message sequences.

Figure 18.16 gives an overview of the normal operation of the gateway system after connections have been established, including termination behavior. The slots are populated during initialization and channel connection (see Figures 18.17 and 18.18). The lightning-strike symbol means abort all activity in progress along all paths to which it points. Figure 18.16 also illustrates a recommended style of documenting preconditions, postconditions, and responsibilities.

Figure 18.17 gives an incomplete, high-level view of initialization, just to indicate what is accomplished by the Configurator pattern (without explaining the pattern); postconditions are that service slots are populated.

Figure 18.18 gives, in one diagram, a relatively complete view of the behavior patterns involved in connecting and error handling. It covers all of the message sequences of Figure 18.15 in one set of paths superimposed directly on the system components. GSI and PSI continue from the end points GT and PT in Figure 18.17 (GSI also provides an internal start point in the gateway service for multiple connect scenarios for multiple peers). Figure 18.18 also adds the error path EI, which is traversed if a peer that was previously initialized as a receiver mistakenly tries to act as a sender.

The only new notational elements are timers and the synchronization bar between the gateway and the peer. Activity along a path entering a timer waits for a timeout period unless some action along another path clears the timer. The 2:2 synchronization bar indicates 2-in-2-out synchronization between the paths, meaning that two incoming scenarios, one along each path, result in two outgoing scenarios, one along each path. The incoming scenarios are synchronized at the bar. Although the reactor pattern

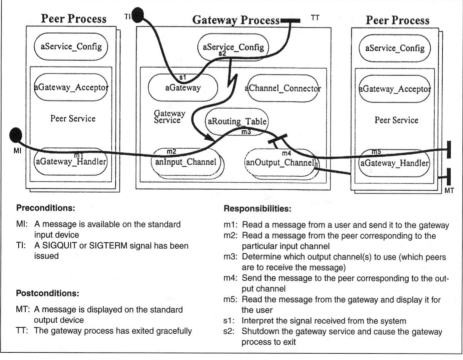

Preconditions:

MI: A message is available on the standard
     input device
TI: A SIGQUIT or SIGTERM signal has been
     issued

Postconditions:

MT: A message is displayed on the standard
     output device
TT: The gateway process has exited gracefully

Responsibilities:

m1: Read a message from a user and send it to the gateway
m2: Read a message from the peer corresponding to the
     particular input channel
m3: Determine which output channel(s) to use (which peers
     are to receive the message)
m4: Send the message to the peer corresponding to the out-
     put channel
m5: Read the message from the gateway and display it for
     the user
s1: Interpret the signal received from the system
s2: Shutdown the gateway service and cause the gateway
     process to exit

Figure 18.16   Basic gateway operation including termination.

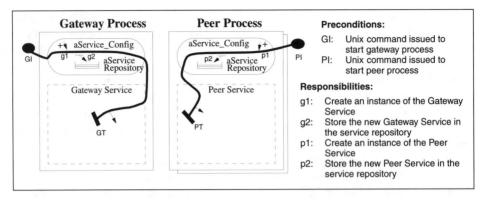

Figure 18.17 High-level initialization of gateway and peer processes.

is used for much of the messaging that implements this map, it does not appear explicitly in the map, because it is regarded as part of a support layer.

This map is different from the HotDraw one because its preconditions allow concurrent scenarios. Here is how to understand this map. Approach it with a collection of tokens (for example, different-colored beads) to put on the map to represent scenarios. Put a token on each start point from which a scenario may start concurrently, for example, at GSI, and at PSI for each peer. On the peer side, you will need many tokens for many peers, because each peer follows the PSI path independently in its own local context.

Then move each token along its path. The relative start times and rates of progression are undefined, so you may try different combinations to experiment with possible race conditions. When, along the GSI path, a token arrives at aChannel_Connector, it must

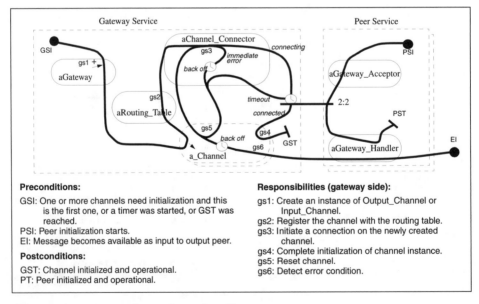

Figure 18.18 Connection and error handling patterns.

follow one of two possible outgoing routes (indicated by an OR-fork). Let us assume it follows the *connecting* route. Choosing this route assumes that aChannel_Connector has discovered, at gs3, that there are no conditions making the connection attempt with the selected peer impossible, such as an invalid network address. Meanwhile, other tokens continue moving along the PSI path at independent rates of speed.

Now we have many tokens converging on the synchronization bar. What happens depends on the order in which the tokens arrive there. If the GSI token arrives after the PSI token for the selected peer, synchronization will take place immediately for that peer, without starting the timer. This means you can move the GSI token along the path to GST and then return it to the start point to connect another peer. You can also move the PSI token for the now-connected peer to PST, and then remove the token from map.

Otherwise, the timer will be started and the GSI token must stop moving until the timer is cleared or runs out. While this token waits, you may start another token down the GSI path to connect another peer.

When the timer is eventually cleared or runs out, you must also continue moving the token that stopped. Now two tokens are tracing independent GSI scenarios. Eventually, many tokens may be moving or stopped at various points along the routes from GSI.

This is enough to give the idea. Many different possibilities exist for routes to be traced through this map, all of which represent possible system behaviors (in some maps routes may be constrained—for example, some combinations of incoming and outgoing routes through an OR-join-fork combination might be forbidden—but not in this example). Thus, the map can be used to understand different possible system behaviors, including pathological behaviors such as critical races or feature interactions.

The use-case map view of this application shows a number of objects that the reader might imagine should be threads, for example, the objects that occupy a_Channel slots. ACE supports making such objects either threads or passive objects, but the gateway software does not exercise the thread option. Instead, the Unix process handles the multiple channels directly. However, the existing paths in the use-case map do not have to be changed (a clarification of the precondition is helpful, to indicate that the controlling Unix process can start a new scenario when it has handed over the current one to a thread). In one case, the timeout context and associated matters must be sorted out by the Unix process; in the other, this sorting out is accomplished automatically by thread support services.

Figure 18.19 makes the connection back to the message sequences of Figure 18.15. The highlighted route through the map fragment shown on the left is implemented with the connection-timeout message sequence on the right. Other routes can similarly be related to message sequences. Thus, a map can be used as a context for understanding (and documenting) detailed behavior patterns.

18.4 Discussion

Because this chapter is about understanding and documenting existing frameworks, the focus has been on reverse engineering (constructing the view of Figure 18.1 by studying code). However, we hope that the reader will find it as obvious as we do that any technique that provides helpful system descriptions as a result of reverse engi-

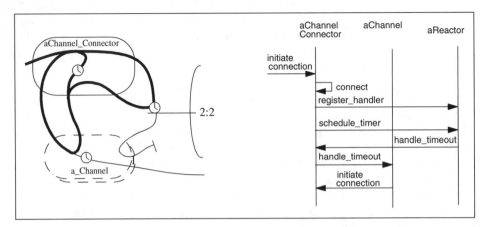

Figure 18.19 An example of traceability: connection timeout.

neering is likely also to be helpful for describing systems before the details are decided during forward engineering.

By means of two examples from very different application domains, we have given examples of steps in developing the system side of Figure 18.1:

- Develop a component context diagram of the system and document the relationships of its components to classes. This may require piecing the system picture together from a study of class relationships, design patterns, and code. Human judgment is required in deciding the level of granularity (for example, all code objects are not necessarily represented as system components at the scale of the particular diagram).

- Identify important use cases that will be used to understand the system.

- Develop an understanding of the use cases in terms of message sequences, by studying the details of the framework (all the examples in this chapter did this by documenting the message sequences in diagrams, but actual drawing of such diagrams may not be necessary if the sequences follow standard design patterns).

- Collapse the message sequences into causal sequences and concatenate causal sequences to form use-case paths. This is not a mechanical process; human judgment is required, for example, to decide when to collapse details into responsibilities or when to indicate cyclic behavior by preconditions instead of path loops. We used preconditions instead of a path loop to indicate repetitive behavior starting at GSI in Figure 18.16, to keep the map as simple as possible, without really sacrificing any insight into overall behavior. The objective is human-understandable paths, committed as little as possible to implementation details, that will give overall insight.

- Document the path preconditions, postconditions, and responsibilities.

- Combine use-case paths, as appropriate, into use-case maps.

- The result will be a high-level model along the lines of Figure 18.1.

- For traceability back down to details, provide pointers from this model to details required to implement it.

The following lists some desirable properties of any conceptual design model for understanding the operational nature of systems. Each list item is followed by a brief comment contrasting the ability of UCMs and conventional software design models to provide these properties (the comments in this list are restricted to well-known software methods and CASE tools, and do not cover formal methods, such as Petri nets, which are discussed later). Conceptual design models:

1. **Have the primary objective of aiding human reasoning at a high level of abstraction, as opposed to entering details into a computer tool.** UCMs are the only diagramming technique known to the author that was shaped solely by the need for this property. Others, such as [Jacobson 1992; Regnell 1996; Selic 1994; UML 1997], are shaped primarily by the need for machine executability of design models and/or machine translatability into code, thus forcing a commitment to details at the level of methods, functions, messages, interprocess communication, interfaces, internal state machines of components, and so forth, that get in the way of reasoning at a high level of abstraction.

2. **Are first class at the macroscopic level, meaning not dependent on details of components or code.** To the author's knowledge, there is only one other system-oriented notation that has this property, the *high-level message sequence charts* under development by the Z120 community (this reference covers only detailed message sequence charts, but examples of proposed high-level ones are given in [Regnell 1996]). However, this notation does not possess Property 3 and it clouds the mind's eye with boxes in the separate behavior diagrams that look like components but are not, exacerbating the problem of mentally superimposing behavior on structure.

3. **Combine system behavior and system structure into a single coherent diagram.** To the author's knowledge, only use-case maps possess this property at a high level of abstraction. Other diagramming techniques [Jacobson 1992; Regnell 1996; UML 1997] require mental combination of information in multiple diagrams.

4. **Express system self-modification in a compact, lightweight fashion that is easily combined with ordinary behavior but is also visually separable from it.** To the author's knowledge, only use-case maps possess this property strongly.

5. **Have diagrams that are easily grasped as visual patterns for a system as a whole.** Use-case maps can combine many behavior patterns in a single diagram in a way that enables the mind's eye to sort them out. Recognizing behavior patterns in superimposed sequence numbers or separate detailed message sequence charts is much more difficult, particularly because many diagrams must be viewed. These visual patterns have been argued elsewhere to be a new kind of design pattern [Buhr 1996b], but this is still a controversial view in the object-oriented community.

6. **Provide a macroscopic system view for forward engineering, reverse engineering, maintenance, evolution, and reengineering.** Only use-case maps and high-level message sequence charts provide reference views that are independent of details and so can be used to guide decisions about details. Use-case maps do it more compactly and simply (Properties 2–5).

7. **Encourage design experimentation.** The lightweight nature and ease of use in back-of-the-envelope style fosters a design process that satisfies requirements by proposing and evaluating design alternatives. This is difficult with techniques that require strong commitment to many details.

8. **Scale up.** The big picture remains lightweight because it is not composed from details, and the techniques of factoring, stubbing, and layering provide decomposition techniques that enable large systems to be described.

9. **Provide a high-level supplement for any detailed model/method.** The concepts are general and insensitive to the details of particular detailed design models/methods.

10. **Suggest a new concept of *architecting* behavior.** A design model along the lines of Figure 18.1, in which the operational side employs UCMs to achieve the aforementioned properties, is a new, useful, and practical form of architectural description. UCMs may be viewed as a technique for architecting the behavior of such systems, in the sense of attributing behavior to system structure [Buhr 1996b, 1996a]. There is no other technique known to the author that can do this in such a compact and human-understandable fashion.

11. **Can be saved for documentation and maintained without unreasonable effort.** The lightweight and compact nature of UCMs contributes to this property. However, tool support is desirable (a UCM editor is currently being developed for this purpose).

It is important to understand that use-case maps do not replace the other techniques referred to here, but supplement them to give a higher-level view. Work is proceeding on linking use-case maps to standard methods and tools in the object-oriented and real-time system domains (for example, [Bordeleau-Buhr 1997] links them to the ROOM methodology and toolset [Selic 1994], and future work is planned on linking them to UML [UML 1997]).

A common remark by skeptics is that anything that can be done with UCMs can also be done with some other technique. For example, causal sequences and self-modification can be represented by message sequence charts or Petri nets. This is like saying anything that can be done with higher-level programming languages can also be done with assembly language. In the author's opinion, such comments miss the point, which is finding better ways of aiding human understanding in the face of looming complexity brick walls.

Petri nets, in particular, seem to be a favorite of skeptics, who often suggest they are sufficient to do the job of UCMs. It is true that UCMs can be given execution semantics with formalisms such as Petri nets (students and collaborators have used both Petri nets and LOTOS for this purpose) and that sometimes UCMs can look a bit like Petri nets to the uninitiated. However, there are big differences. UCMs prescribe scenario paths and interpath relationships as first-class entities, but not how the scenarios or relationships will emerge at runtime; they are a declarative technique (which is why the term *architecting behavior* is appropriate, rather than *specifying behavior*). Petri nets are a technique for specifying behavior. They prescribe how scenarios will be generated but do not identify paths as first-class entities; their strength (executability) is a weakness from a UCM perspective (they force the user to become preoccupied with specifying execution details). Petri nets are better viewed as one of several useful techniques for implementing UCMs in a high-level way when executability is desired, not as replacements for UCMs.

Industrial experience with use-case maps may be summarized as follows: The approach always seems to skeptics to be too simple to offer anything new, until the skeptics hit a complexity brick wall. Then the approach appears to be welcomed by experts, novices, managers, and customers alike. Use-case maps reflect a common style of thinking among experts that can be easily communicated to others—a style that has been largely ignored by writers of method textbooks and vendors of CASE tools and, up to now, has lacked a first-class notational representation. Experience is proving the power of the approach in telephony systems, agent systems [Bordeleau-Buhr 1997], and banking systems, to name but a few types of systems. Personal communications to the author from users in industry, including students, collaborators, and readers of UCM publications, as well as the author's own experiences working with industry, all tend to support this conclusion.

18.5 Summary

We have identified a number of problems that arise in understanding the behavior of software constructed from frameworks and offered use-case maps to help alleviate the problems. The proposed approach makes coordinated use of use-case maps and high-level (methodless, messageless), but otherwise conventional, object-oriented descriptions, to provide a model of how the software works and is constructed as a whole. The chapter has illustrated, by example, a step-by-step process for developing such a model. A result of using the approach is a dramatic reduction in the number of details required for understanding the software as a whole. The model then can serve to provide traceability down to details and up to requirements, where *down* and *up* indicate directions of decreasing and increasing abstraction.

18.6 References

[Bordeleau-Buhr 1997] Bordeleau, F., and R.J.A. Buhr. The UCM-ROOM design method: from use case maps to communicating state machines. Submitted to the *Conference on the Engineering of Computer-Based Systems,* Monterey, CA March 1997, www.sce.carleton.ca/ftp/pub/UseCaseMaps/UCM-ROOM.ps.

[Buhr 1996a] Buhr, R.J.A. Use case maps for attributing behavior to architecture. *Fourth International Workshop on Parallel and Distributed Real Time Systems (WPDRTS),* Honolulu, Hawaii, April 15–16, 1996, www.sce.carleton.ca/ftp/pub/UseCaseMaps/attributing.ps.

[Buhr 1996b] Buhr, R.J.A. Design patterns at different scales. *Pattern Languages of Program Design (PLoP96)*, Allerton Park, Illinois, September 1996.

[Buhr 1997a] Buhr, R.J.A., and A. Hubbard. Use case maps for engineering real time and distributed computer systems: A case study of an ACE-framework application. *Hawaii International Conference on System Sciences (HICSS)*, Walaei, HI, January 7–10, 1997, www.sce.carleton.ca/ftp/pub/UseCaseMaps/hicss.ps.

[Buhr 1997b] Buhr, R.J.A., M. Elammari, T. Gray, S. Mankovski, and D. Pinard. Understanding and defining the behaviour of systems of agents, with use case maps. *Conference on Practical Application of Agents and Multi-Agent Technology (PAAM)*, London, England, April 1997, www.sce.carleton.ca/ftp/pub/UseCaseMaps/4paam97.ps.

[Buhr 1998a] Buhr, R.J.A. *Use Case Maps (UCMs) Updated: A Simple Visual Notation for Understanding and Architecting the Behavior of Large, Complex, Self Modifying Systems.* Carleton report (excerpt of a chapter to appear in a forthcoming ACM book on object-oriented methods), www.sce.carleton.ca/UseCaseMaps/ucmUpdate.ps, 1998.

[Buhr 1998b] Buhr, R.J.A., D. Amyot, D. Quesnel, T. Gray, and S. Mankovski. High level, multi-agent prototypes from a scenario-path notation: A feature interaction example. *Proceedings of the International Conference on the Practical Application of Agents and Multi-Agent Technology (PAAM)*, London, England, April 1998, www.sce.carleton.ca/ftp/pub/UseCaseMaps/4paam98.pdf.

[Buhr 1999] Buhr, R.J.A. Use case maps as architectural entities for complex systems. *IEEE Transactions on Software Engineering*, Special Issue on Scenario Management, December 1999.

[Buhr-Casselman 1996] Buhr, R.J.A., and R.S. Casselman. *Use Case Maps for Object-Oriented Systems.* Upper Saddle River, NJ: Prentice Hall, 1996.

[Gamma 1995] Gamma, E., R. Helm, R. Johnson, and J. Vlissades. *Design Patterns: Elements of Reusable Object-Oriented Software.* Reading, MA: Addison-Wesley, 1995.

[Jacobson 1992] Jacobson, I., M. Christerson, P. Jonsson, and G. Övergaard. *Object-Oriented Software Engineering (A Use Case Driven Approach).* Reading, MA:ACM Press, Addison-Wesley, 1992.

[Regnell 1996] Regnell, B., M. Andersson, and J. Bergstrand. A hierarchical use case model with graphical representation. Proceedings *ECBS96, IEEE Second International Symposium and Workshop on Engineering of Computer Based Systems*, March 1996.

[Schmidt 1994] Schmidt, D.C. ACE: An object-oriented framework for developing distributed applications. *Proceedings of the 6th USENIX C++ Technical Conference*, Cambridge, MA, USENIX Association, April 1994.

[Schmidt 1995] Schmidt, D.C. Reactor: An object behavioral pattern for concurrent event demultiplexing and event handler dispatching. In *Pattern Languages of Program Design*, J. O. Coplien and D.C. Schmidt, editors. Reading, MA: Addison-Wesley, 1995.

[Selic 1994] Selic, B., G. Gullickson, and P.T. Ward. *Real-time Object-Oriented Modeling.* New York: John Wiley & Sons, 1994.

[Shaw-Garlan 1994] Shaw, M., and D. Garlan. *Software Architecture: Perspectives on an Emerging Discipline.* Upper Saddle River, NJ: Prentice Hall, 1996.

[UML 1997] *Unified Modeling Language (UML) Notation Guide*, version 1.1 alpha 6 (1.1 c), 21 July 1997, ftp://ftp.omg.org/pub/docs/ad/97-07-08.ps.

18.7 Review Questions

1. Define with examples: use-case maps, HotDraw's classes, HotDraw's components, architecting behavior.
2. What do we mean by *system self-modification*?
3. What are the differences between use-case maps and Petri nets?

18.8 Problem Set

1. Explain the following statements with illustrated examples:
   - The system view we seek is not a concrete thing, but an abstraction.
   - The use of combinations of design patterns obscures the system view because pattern combination is not yet a well-defined subject.
   - Specific applications are visible only in framework customization details.
2. Show how use-case maps have been used in HotDraw.
3. Show how use-case maps have been used in ACE.
4. What are the pros and cons of use-case maps?

18.9 Projects

Project 1: Use the documentation approaches in Chapter 21 and provide examples of documentation for a HotDraw framework using examples and use-case maps. Compare the two approaches.

Project 2: Use the documentation approaches in Chapter 21 and provide examples of documentation for an ACE framework using contracts, cookbooks, and use-case maps. Compare the three approaches.

Project 3: Select a framework and, using the documentation approaches in Chapter 21, provide examples of documentation of the selected framework using examples, contracts, cookbooks, and use-case maps. Compare the four approaches.

Composing Modeling Frameworks in Catalysis

Reuse has been a long-sought-after goal in software development. In object-oriented design and programming, the concept of a *framework* has proven to be a very useful way to reuse skeletal implementations of architectural designs, while permitting customization to different contexts. However, pieces of code are by no means the only useful reusable artifacts; recurrent patterns occur in models, specifications, interactions, and refinements. Moreover, the basic object-oriented programming (OOP) unit of encapsulation—a *class*—is not the most interesting unit of describing designs; it is the collaborations and relationships between elements that constitute the essence of any design.

In this chapter we describe how the concept of frameworks has been generalized in the Catalysis method [D'Souza-Wills 1998] to object modeling and specification activities, permitting construction of specification and design models by composition. Catalysis is a UML- and OMG-compliant methodology for component- and framework-based development; some underlying concepts from this approach have been contributed by the authors to the definition of the Unified Modeling Language (UML) 1.0, as submitted to the Object Management Group (OMG) in January 1997, and the basic modeling framework ideas were described in [Wills 1995].

19.1 Frameworks—Beyond OOP

In this section we set up our goal for generalizing the concept of framework and illustrate it with an example.

19.1.1 OOP Frameworks

An object-oriented framework is often characterized as a set of abstract and concrete classes that collaborate to provide the skeleton of an implementation for an application. A common aspect of such frameworks is that they are adaptable—in other words, the framework itself provides some mechanisms by which it can be extended, such as by composing selected subclasses together in custom ways or defining new subclasses and implementing methods that either plug into or override methods on the superclasses.

There are some fundamental differences between the framework style and more traditional styles of reuse, as illustrated by the following example.

Design and implement a program for manipulating different shapes. Shapes are displayed differently. When a shape is displayed, show a rendering of its outline and a textual printout of its current location in the largest font that will fit within that shape.

Class-Library with Traditional Reuse

A *traditional* approach to reuse might factor the design as follows. Since the display of different shapes varies across the kinds of shapes, we design a shape hierarchy. The *display* method is abstract on the superclass—since shapes display themselves differently—and each subclass provides its own implementation. There are some common pieces to the display method, for example, computing the font size appropriate for a particular shape given its inner bounding box and printing out the location in the computed font. Hence, we implement a computeFont and printLocation method on the superclass. A typical subclass would now look like this:

```
class Oval extends Shape {
    private ovalData;
    private BoundingBox innerBox();
    public void display (GraphicsContext surface) {
        surface.drawOval (ovalData);
        box = innerBox();
        font = super.computeFont (box);
        super.printLocation (surface, font);
    }
}
```

Framework-Style Reuse

With a *framework* approach to reuse, our factoring looks quite different. We start off with the position that all shapes fundamentally do the same thing when they are displayed: render, compute a font for their inner bounding box, and print their location in that font. Thus, we implement at the level of the *superclass*:

```
class Shape {
    public void display (GraphicsContext surface) {
        renderShape (surface); // plug-point: deferred to subclass
```

```
        box = innerBox(); // plug-point: deferred to subclass
        font = computeFont (box);
        surface.printLocation (font);
    }
}
```

The actual rendering and computation of the inner box must be deferred to the sub-classes. However, *if* a subclass provided the appropriate bits for rendering and for the inner box, it could inherit and use the same implementation of display. Thus, we are imposing a consistent skeletal behavior on all subclasses, but permitting each one to flesh out that skeleton in its own ways.

Although this example focuses on a single class hierarchy, it extends to the set of collaborating abstract classes that are characteristic of frameworks. The Shape hierarchy, for example, requires certain services from the GraphicsContext object to display themselves. It is this partitioning of responsibility—between different shape classes, and between shapes and the GraphicsContext—that gives the design its flexibility. Thus, any packaging of a class as a reusable unit *must* also include some description of the behaviors expected of other objects—that is, their *types*.

Contrast

Note the contrast between the traditional and framework design approaches (Table 19.1 and Figure 19.1), in terms of factoring of code, degree of reuse, and consistency of resulting designs.

Table 19.1 Traditional versus Framework Design

TRADITIONAL	FRAMEWORK
Begin with the mind-set that the display methods would be *different*, and then seek the *common pieces* that could be *shared* between them.	Assert that the display methods are really the *same*, and then identify the *essential differences* between them to *defer* to the subclasses.
Focus on sharing the *lower-level* operations like computeFont and print-Location. The higher-level application logic is duplicated, and each one calls the shared lower-level bits. complete the	Share the *entire skeleton* of the application logic itself. Each application plugs into the skeleton where the pieces (like render, innerBox, particular Graphics-Contexts) are required to skeleton.
Most calls go from the application to the shared base.	Most (many) calls go from the frame-work skeleton to the individual applications; in fact, one of the hallmarks of a framework is *"don't call me—I'll call you."*
Define an interface that the applications can use to call the reusable parts	Define an interface representing demands that the reusable skeleton framework makes on the applications—the plug points for extension.

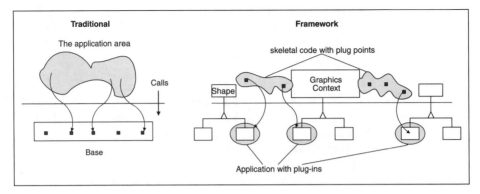

Figure 19.1   Traditional versus framework-style designs.

A significant part of framework design is factoring the *plug points* that are provided for adaptation or customization. This example requires that a subclass provide the missing behaviors. Other frequently recommended design styles for frameworks are based on composition; by composing an instance of a framework class with an instance of a customized other class, we adapt the behavior of the framework.

19.1.2 Our Goal

Our goal is to apply framework-like techniques to the modeling, specification, and implementation of systems in a methodical way. We want to construct domain models and requirements specifications and models from parts that themselves define skeletal and customizable models. The specifications for a particular problem should be constructed by applying the generic requirements and plugging in details for the problem at hand. On the implementation side, an implementation for the generic specification should be correspondingly customizable for the specialized problem specification (Figure 19.2).

A framework implementation thus provides a customizable solution to an abstract problem [Koskimes 1995]. If done right, the points of variability in the problem specifications—plug points on the specification side—will have corresponding plug points on the implementation side as well. Subclassing and overriding are just two of many techniques to specialize a framework implementation. Other implementation architectures also permit framework-style specialization and composition.

Our focus in this chapter is on the modeling and specification side.

19.1.3 An Example

Consider an example of a service company that delivers seminars. The operations of this company (hence, the requirements for any software system that supports its operations) can be decomposed into relatively orthogonal aspects—allocation of instructors and facilities to a seminar, on-time production of seminar materials for delivery, targeted marketing of seminars, invoicing and accounts receivable, and so on.

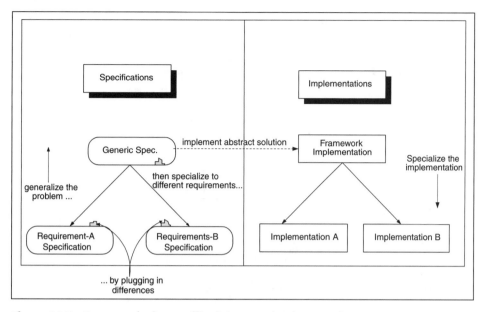

Figure 19.2   Frameworks for specification versus implementation.

One can readily conceive abstract specifications of each problem aspect, in isolation from the specifics of seminar delivery. This would result in a library of reusable abstract specification components, such as resource allocation, on-time production, marketing trends and events, and accounts receivable.

Resource Allocation

A simple, generic resource allocation framework can be defined as follows:

Assign a resource to a job if the resource type meets the requirements of the job.

This framework uses abstract types such as Job, Requirement, and Resource, and abstract relationships such as *meets* and *provides*. These will map to, for example, a car rental application in very different ways than they will to assigning instructors to seminars (see Figure 19.3).

Each box represents a typed role, the lines represent associations, attributes represent queries, and the model includes invariants (inv) and actions specifications (action), typically described using pre- and postconditions on the available queries. < . . . . > denotes a type that is a *placeholder*—in other words, specifically intended for substitution when applied to a particular problem.

If we wish to build an application for scheduling courses by assigning instructors and rooms to the course sessions, we apply ResourceAllocation twice, with different substitutions in each case: first, to assign rooms of particular room types to course offerings of specific courses; second, to assign instructors with particular skills to the courses. Thus, the application to instructors maps resource to instructor, resource type

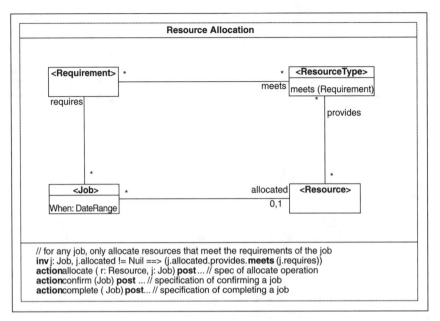

Figure 19.3   A generic specification framework and model for resource allocation.

to instructor skill, job to course offering, and job requirement to course title. The definition of *meets* will be correspondingly specialized as well.

The resulting model is then extended with information such as the certifications that determine the skill set of an instructor, the nature of room facilities (overhead projectors, computers, white-boards, and so on), and the queries that determine matching between provided facilities and course requirements (see Figure 19.4).

Material Production

Production might be modeled by a simple framework with Products, Items, and a Producer, where an order is placed to the producer whenever the stock level drops below some threshold. There are some invariants here to govern this placement of orders, and the relevant actions are use, reorder, and so on. This framework will be applied to Course Titles to order copies of Course Notes as needed (see Figure 19.5).

This framework includes a *generalized* action, labeled <reduce>. This states that any action that causes the inventory to drop below the threshold must also cause a new order to be placed for that product.

Marketing Trends

The marketing view might be interested in generic customers, products, and some trends indicated between customers and products, based on different indications from various indicators (purchases made, inquiries received, questionnaires, and so on). This framework might be applied to course customers scheduling courses. We have not expanded this framework with its invariants and actions (Figure 19.6).

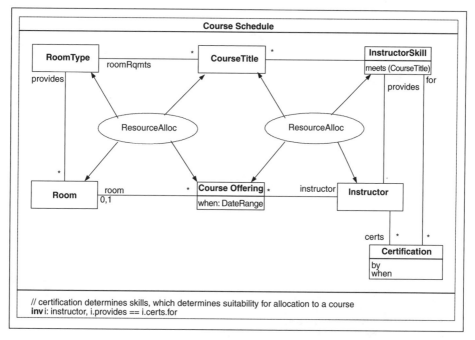

Figure 19.4 Applying a generic framework for allocating rooms and instructors.

Composing Generic Specifications and Models

Clearly, many generic requirements related to resource allocation, materials production, and market trends can be specified within the generic frameworks previously outlined. We would like to simply adapt, apply, and compose these frameworks to define the requirements for our specific application. Of course, these frameworks must now be related to our problem domain and to each other.

For seminar scheduling and delivery, certain aspects of resource allocation affect production as well as marketing and invoicing. Thus, we would want to treat rooms and instructors as resources to be allocated to course offerings, based on the facilities available in those rooms, and the skills and qualifications of instructors relative to the course title. In particular, we would like instructors to be matched based on certification exams they pass. We would want copies of the course title material to be produced whenever course offerings were confirmed (corresponding to confirm in the resource allocation framework). We would want purchase indications to accumulate when a customer scheduled a particular course title (for use in the marketing framework). Thus, our frameworks interact with each other. Each framework application contains the appropriate mappings from generic framework terms to the problem at hand (see Figure 19.7).

The full details of the resulting specification can be generated automatically from this set of framework applications.

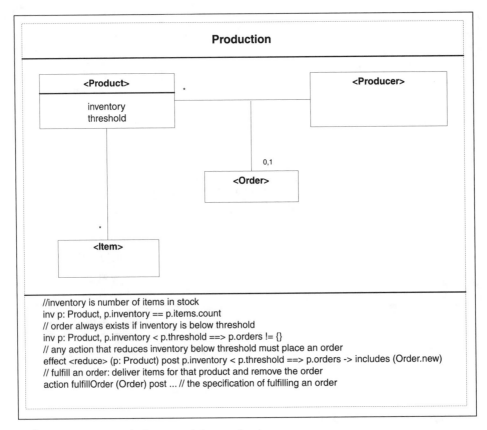

Figure 19.5 A generic framework for production.

19.1.4 Problems to Be Solved

There are several problems we must address before we are able to build requirement models by composing. These include the following:

Framework descriptions must be abstract, since they need to map to widely diverse situations—for example, assigning instructors with particular skills to teach courses, assigning cars to renters, or assigning video copies to club members. We should *not* interpret the generic models as specifications of implementation classes, with attributes representing stored instance variables and associations representing pointers between objects. Moreover, when we apply a framework, we substitute domain terms into the generic concepts provided by the framework. This is *not* a process of subclassing, or even of subtyping—for example, you could not assign a CourseOffering to a CarReservation! Instead, a family of mutually related types is being specialized by substituting new terms into the framework.

We can relate this to the traditional concept of subclassing and overriding or plugging-in. When you subclass, you inherit all the features of the superclass except the methods you override. This can be described as a *substitution* of certain methods for the superclass methods, with all other features used as is. With

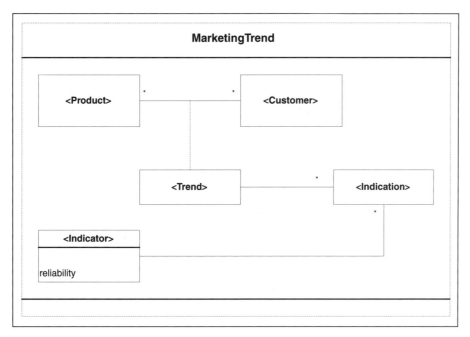

Figure 19.6   A generic specification framework for marketing trends.

our modeling frameworks, you specialize an entire family of related types and substitute for any of the types (and any of their features), while conforming to the rules imposed by the framework.

Although abstract, the generic models must be precise, to permit meaningful manipulation when composed. The generic resource allocation framework does not specify the details of the meet relation, by which a resource type meets the requirements of a particular job. However, the relationship can still be specified precisely and used in the rules that apply to (any adaptation of) that framework— for example, assign a resource only if its type meets the job requirements.

There must be ways to hook the frameworks together in a particular composition. For example, in describing the Production framework we do not know what other frameworks it will be composed with and what (unknown) actions may cause the inventory levels to decrease. If we composed this framework with others that dealt with customer consumption as well as with thievery and spoilage, then any one of several actions could cause new orders to be placed. This framework must impose constraints on actions that are completely unknown to it, in terms of their abstract effects.

Any framework or its composition could be described at many different levels of detail. For example, the Production framework could be described with very abstract actions such as reStock, or at a more detailed level with placeOrder, deliver, invoice, and so on. We must support framework descriptions at different levels of refinement and permit more abstract frameworks to be applied and composed before choosing which one of their available refinements to use in further design.

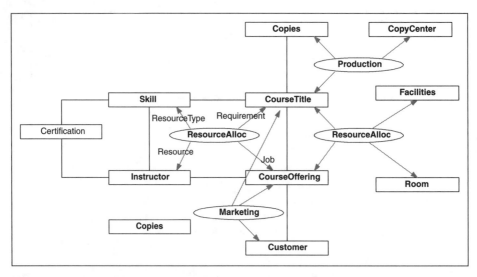

Figure 19.7 A problem specification model built by adapting and composing frameworks.

19.2 Frameworks Build on Types, Refinements, and Collaborations

These problems are addressed in Catalysis using four important concepts:

Types. Abstracting behavior using type models.

Refinement. Explicit mappings between levels of abstraction.

Collaborations. Abstracting joint behaviors and dialog.

Frameworks. A foundation for design composition and reuse.

19.2.1 Types and Classes

A type is an external view of (some interesting aspects of) the visible behavior of some set of objects. Any object that provides that behavior is a member of that type, regardless of its implementation, and is usable as such by a client that expected that type. A type is not the same as a class.

If a type does not specify an implementation, how do we accurately describe the behaviors required of objects of that type? The solution is to define a *type model*—an abstraction of the state of any possible implementation of that type—and specify the effects of the operations in terms of that model.

Figure 19.8 illustrates a CashRegister type[1] supporting startSale, addItem, delete-LastItem. When we write down the behavior specifications of these operations, we realize that we must discuss many new terms:

---

[1]Either the real kind, or one in cyberspace, used by some Java agent or a human.

- A set of available products, *products*—so we can say what happens when you enter a known versus an unknown product

- The price of every known product, *priceOfProduct(Product)*—so we can accumulate totals

- The quantity of each item within a sale, *quantity(Item)*—so we can describe the cost of that line item

- The sequence in which the items were rung up within this sale—so we can define the effect of deleteLastItem, and so on

These may be formalized as a set of queries as shown subsequently. Of course, there is no implication that these represent stored data or even any internal private methods. Rather, we require only that any correct implementation should exhibit the operations listed at the bottom of the type box and that a client's expectations of their behavior, as understood from this model, must not be disappointed. This in turn means that there must be a clear mapping to the model's queries from the variables or fields of any particular implementation (see Figure 19.8).

```
CashRegister::closeSale     ()              // a sample operation
specification
        post      currentSale == (allSales.last)@pre
```

The model may also be depicted visually as shown in Figure 19.9. We can depict any of the queries visually as UML associations: Notice the correspondence to Figure 19.8. Each association defines a pair of model queries. The choice between attribute and pictorial presentation of a query is a stylistic one (see Figure 19.9).

For example, in a language like Java we might have the following:

<<type>> CashRegister

products: Set<Product>
priceOfProduct (Product): money
itemsOfProduct (Product): Set<Item>
quantity (Item): integer
cost(Item): Money
itemsOfSale (Sale): Seq <item>...
currentSale: Sale
allSales: Seq<Sale>
inv currentSale Œ allSales

---

startSale ( ) -- a new Sale has been made the *currentSale*
addItem (Product, quantity)
deleteLastItem ( ) -- the last *item* of the *currentSale* has been deleted
closeSale ( ) -- *currentSale* has become the last *Sale* in *allSales*; paid
listSaleHistory ( )

Figure 19.8   A CashRegister type with its type model shown as textual queries.

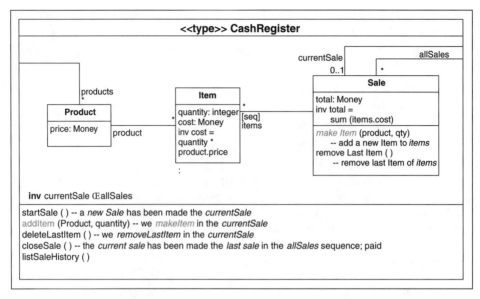

Figure 19.9   A CashRegister type with its type model shown as visual associations.

```
interface ICashRegister {
    Set<Products> products();
    Money priceOf (Product);
    startSale (); // specification: .....
    addItem (Product, quantity); // specification: ...
}
class CashRegisterA implements ICashRegister {
    Vector<Product> products;
    HashTable <Product, Money> prices;
    startSale () { ..... }
    addItem (Product, quantity) { .... }
}
```

Refinement: Class Implements Type

As already shown, a type specification uses a type model in order to express behavior guarantees. A class that implements that type makes its own implementation decisions. There should be a mapping from the concrete choices made in the class to the abstract queries and behavior guarantees made by the corresponding type. This mapping is called a *retrieval*.

Figure 19.10 shows a type called *SelectionList*, which might be used in the implementation of user selections for our CashRegister. It allows items to be added, deleted, selected, and deselected. The type model for specifying these operations includes a concept of count, which item is at which position, and which items are selected. There is also a convenience effect called *movedUp*, which could be defined completely in terms of the other queries.

We also have a class named ListBoxA and the retrieval to the type. While the representations are different, all terms used as queries in the type can be defined precisely based on the data representation selected (instance variables) in the class. As you can see, the retrieval is a property of the implements relation between class and type. In general, it is a property of any refines relationship, establishing the mapping between two type-models (the queries and their corresponding types) and the corresponding sets of actions (see Figure 19.10).

This approach to mapping from concrete to abstract is highly flexible. It permits the abstract descriptions to be precise (which we will need for meaningful composition of frameworks), yet does not unduly constrain the implementations of that type. For example, in our resource allocation framework, we could have many refinements of the meets relation, determined by instructor skills for courses, or room facilities for a course, or vehicle features for a car rental. Refinements also apply to collaborations, permitting us to describe decisions that affect the mutual interactions of multiple parties.

Actions, Roles, and Collaborations

The most interesting aspects of design and architecture involve partial descriptions of groups of objects and their interactions relative to each other. A collaboration defines a set of actions between typed objects playing certain roles with respect to other objects in that collaboration.[2] A collaboration provides an abstraction of multiparty interactions and of detailed dialogs between participants. It provides a unit of scoping—that is, constraints and rules that apply within, versus outside, the group of collaborators—and of conformance—that is, more detailed realizations of joint behavior.

[2]A collaboration spec makes precise the notion of a *role model* used in OORAM [Reenskaug 1996], with some differences in the treatment of object and role identity.

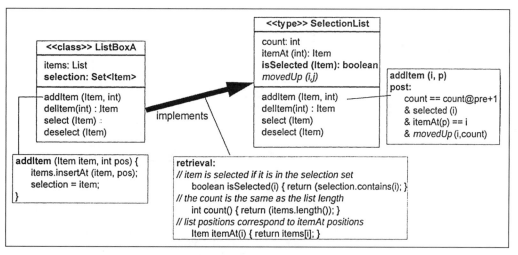

Figure 19.10 A class refines a type with a retrieval from concrete to abstract items.

A collaboration may be refined by a more detailed set of actions, either joint or localized. Many useful forms of refinement do not result in subtypes, but rather represent a refinement of the collaboration itself; in other words, all involved parties are affected. The following example illustrates this for multiple levels of abstraction in a buyer-seller interaction, from an abstract action sell(Set<Item>), to a more specific dialog of first pickup(Set<Item>), followed by pay(Sale), to the detailed level of startSale( ), addItem( ), . . . endSale( ) (see Figure 19.11). This refinement affects all participants, and a user manual for the cash register documents the retrieval.

What we are doing here is refining the entire collaboration—not the individual types—with an accompanying mapping (including a retrieval of type models) to justify the conformance claim. Note that Seller-2-Step is not a subtype of Seller-1-Step. A person (or software agent) expecting Seller-1-Step would not work successfully with its counterpart Seller-2-Step, which supports a different set of actions.

Once again, a design review would focus attention on the refinement. A collaboration refinement usually entails two different aspects:

The finer actions must be related to the more abstract ones: What sequences of finer actions induce each abstract one? State charts are good for specifying the sets of action sequences that correspond to each abstract one, and interaction diagrams (sequence or graph form) to illustrate specific scenarios. The pre- and post-specs of permitted sequences of finer operations should combine to fulfill those of the abstract actions.

At a finer level of detail, more detailed type models of each participant are needed. For example, when some sale items are picked up first, the seller must know the amount of the sale due (and possibly the selections) on the subsequent payment. Hence, the refined type model needs extra attributes for this, in addition to the more abstract level that just dealt with stocks and money (see Figure 19.12).

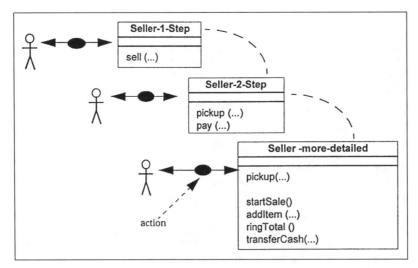

Figure 19.11   Multiple level of abstractions.

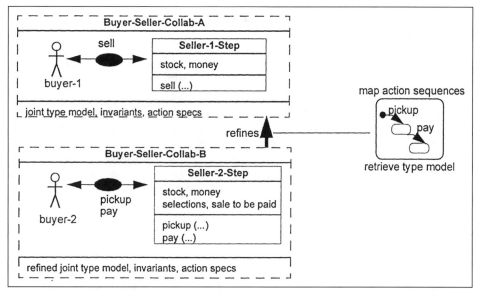

Figure 19.12   A collaboration refinement with the mapping from concrete to abstract.

Every object plays multiple roles in many collaborations; hence, it exhibits many different types. This is how we compose both specifications and implementations of frameworks, where each collaboration partially defines the joint behaviors of some sets of objects (see Figure 19.13).

19.3 Frameworks with Placeholders

This section defines a framework as a collaboration in which certain types have been designated as placeholder types and know as hooks (see Chapter 9) and hotspots (see Chapters 15 and 16).

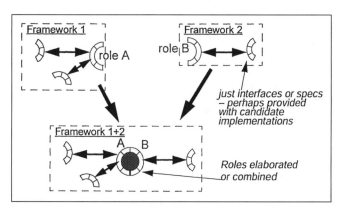

Figure 19.13   An object plays many roles.

19.3.1 Frameworks with Actions and Effects

Specifications, models, and designs all show recurring patterns of abstract structures and behaviors. The key to such patterns is the relationships between elements, as opposed to individual types or classes. An application of such a pattern specializes all the elements in parallel and mutually compatible ways, as opposed to an individual specialization of each element. A framework defines patterns in generic terms by utilizing placeholders for elements. It can be applied to a family of related types with appropriate substitutions to generate different models and designs. A framework may be a model or group of models for a collaboration, or a static relationship between objects, or a single type, or a class, or a package of related classes.

For the purposes of this chapter, a framework is a collaboration in which certain types have been designated as placeholder types—in other words, they are expected to be substituted when that framework is applied to a particular problem. Along with that substitution we will also map the queries, associations, and actions of that type to their counterparts in the problem at hand.

A typical example is the Subject-Observer pattern. This framework has two main sections, after its name: the internal collaboration (middle) and the external view (lower). The principal difference is that, from an external point of view, the objects always meet the invariant given at the bottom, whereas the internal collaboration is private—the actions between them are not intended for anyone else to send or receive (see Figure 19.14).

In this example, the external invariant ("Observer:: . . .") asserts what is essential about the subject-observer relationship: that the state of the observer is some function

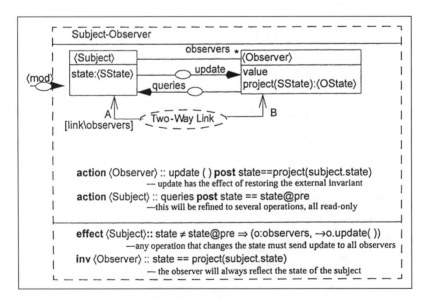

Figure 19.14 Subject-Observer pattern.

project of the state of the subject. The precise nature of the main types, the two state attributes, and the project function are different in each specialization of the framework, and its users will substitute their own.

For example, the framework could be applied to a computer-assisted design (CAD) system: The subject is a three-dimensional engine design, and the observer's different two-dimensional views or projections. As the end user develops the design, the views all keep up to date.

The internal collaboration shows the scheme by which the external invariant is preserved. There is a one-to-many link observer between the two participants, and this is governed by another framework, Two-Way-Link. Let's assume that this says everything we need about how a new observer registers with the subject.

The effect keyword signals that *every* other action must include this assertion as part of its postcondition. The problem domain types to which the framework is applied will have their own operations (such as rotate, move, and so on), and whoever designs them will have to observe the effect as an additional part of their specification.

The update action is specified as achieving the external invariant.

This framework may be applied to a pair of types—in this case, a Call Queue and a ThermometerIcon in a telephony application. In addition, the abstract queries, state and value, are mapped to the length of the call queue and the reading of the thermometer icon, respectively. The full detailed model can now be generated automatically (see Figure 19.15).

19.3.2 What Happens with Framework Composition?

From our partial framework application in Figure 19.4, a tool could automatically generate the resulting model, including all invariants and behaviors, as shown partially in Figure 19.13. This illustrates the value of abstracting problems into generic frameworks, from the point of view of improved reusability and easier understanding of complex models (see Figure 19.16).

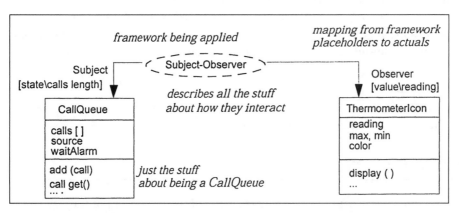

Figure 19.15 A framework application with substitutions for types and queries.

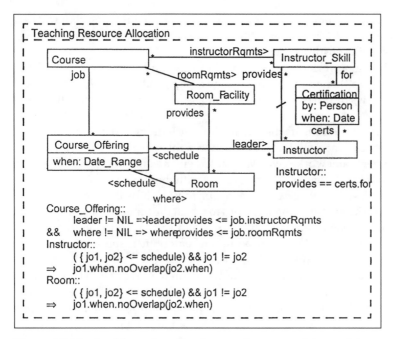

Figure 19.16   Applying a framework generates a complete model.

19.4 Examples of Frameworks

Frameworks are ubiquitous in Catalysis, applied from the level of business models, through many common design patterns [Gamma 1995], to very fundamental definitions. We briefly mention some examples here:

Barter. An exchange of two dissimilar kinds of items between two parties, based on some concept of equivalent value of those items. There are many possible refinements of the dialogs for a barter.

Trader. An object that establishes and consummates a barter between two other parties, with some payment (that can be modeled as secondary barters) for its services.

Subject-Observer. A framework in which some observers of a subject that has some abstract value attribute are kept in sync with any changes in that value.

Two-Way-Link. A pair of inverse pointers between two objects, representing an association.

TotalOrder. A framework that can be applied to any type that has an appropriate (transitive, and so on) "<" operator defined.

19.5 Summary

We have shown how the Catalysis method generalizes the concept of frameworks to object modeling and specification activities, permitting construction of specification and design models by composition. This work enables specification and modeling activities to be much more constructive, where models are generated from appropriate generic specification models based on particular aspects of the problem at hand.

19.6 References

[D'Souza-Wills 1998] D'Souza, D., and A.C. Wills, *Catalysis: Component and Framework-Based Development.* Reading, MA: Addison-Wesley, 1998.

[Gamma 1995] Gamma, E., Richard Helm, Ralph Johnson, and John Vlissides. *Design Patterns: Elements of Reusable Object-Oriented Software* Reading, MA: Addison-Wesley, 1995.

[Koskimes 1995] Koskimes, K., and H. Mössenback. Designing a framework by stepwise generalization. *5th European Software Engineering Conference*, Barcelona, Spain. *Lecture Notes in Computer Science 989*, pp. 479–497. New York: Springer-Verlag, 1995.

[Reenskaug 1996] Reenskaug, Trygve. *Working with Objects: The OORam Software Engineering Method.* Greenwich, CT: Manning, 1996.

[Wills 1995] Wills, A.C. Frameworks. *Proceedings of Object-Oriented Information Systems, December 1995,* Sun, Patel, and Sun. New York: Springer-Verlag, 1995.

19.7 Review Questions

1. What are the differences between traditional and framework reuse?

2. Debate with examples:

   - Single classes cannot be packaged effectively.

   - Frameworks provide plug points as interfaces for customization.

   - A framework implementation provides a customizable solution to an abstract problem.

   - A type needs a model.

   - Class implements a type.

3. Define and provide examples for the following: types, refinement, and collaborations.

19.8 Problem Set

1. What are the problems related to framework modeling by composition?

2. What are the differences between types and classes?

19.9 Projects

Project 1: Use the Catalysis method on any of your framework projects for analysis.

- Describe the pros and cons of the catalysis.

- Show how to transition from analysis to design.

SIDEBAR 6
ENDURING BUSINESS THEMES

All object-oriented analysis and design methods anticipate future change to some extent, but it has been our experience that systems that must support dramatic changes, in terms of both frequency as well as extent, require somewhat different techniques. The purpose of this sidebar is to briefly present insights for development strategy selection and some of the highlights of a relatively new approach called Enduring Business Themes (EBTs) that works well for systems that must be highly change-centric.

Most methods are based on successive refinement in that each model is an elaboration of the model from a previous step. For many applications, this works well, partially because there are clear traces between models. But for some applications that must allow a high degree of change, elaboration has an undesirable ripple effect whereby a small change in requirements cascades into a large change in the code. To be sure, there are occasions when the changes can be predicted in advance, and an experienced designer can avoid downstream ripple effects, but our experience has been that these occasions occur more often in textbooks than in practice. Therefore, we developed the EBT approach, which does not rely on successive refinement.

The EBT approach has several curious features, such as an abrupt discontinuity between requirements and the ensuing models. But it also seems to be more effective in that it accommodates varying skill levels more effectively. This is a frequently overlooked aspect of practical software development that has led to a number of project failures. [Cline-Girou 1998] discuss EBTs in some detail and this sidebar explores some of the implications and lessons learned from applying EBTs. Many of these lessons are probably inherent in approaches that are not based on successive refinement—in other words, approaches that are oriented toward developing systems with a high level of unpredictable change.

However, the nature and importance of change is not always clear in the beginning. Thus, we have evolved techniques for requirements capture and development strategy selection that gather the information needed to make intelligent decisions without making an early commitment to any particular method.

SB6.1 Requirements Definition

The following principles are frequently overlooked, but should be an essential part of defining requirements:

- Ask the right people the right questions.
- Focus on the stable parts, not the parts that change.
- Technology belongs in the business model.
- Assess the capabilities of the people.

Interviewing operations personnel is probably the worst way to understand the need for change. They are the best source for questions such as, "How are things done today?," particularly from a bureaucratic standpoint, but their vision is limited by the necessarily narrow focus of their role. To some extent, all internal personnel suffer from this same defect, and we believe that the best way to find out what business an organization is in is to interview its customers. Customers, who ultimately determine an organization's fate, view the organization for what it does for them and do not get lost in concerns about forms and organizational charts. Within an organization, the people responsible for strategy can offer the best advice as to what the future needs might be. Industry analysts should always be consulted for their insights, and it has become increasingly important to anticipate the impact new technology will have on the organization, so technologists should be consulted as well.

The experienced analyst will wonder, "What parts of this system might change?" but it is just as important to ask, "What part of this system will not change?" Sometimes this second question is easier to answer. By focusing on change, rather than stability, the tendency is to spend too much money designing the places in the system that might change, and too little money on the stable portion, which is the only true asset. We have found that many people fail to consider the stable aspects of the system as deeply as they should, and the result is less ability to accommodate change, not more.

Like most OO practitioners, we believed that technological considerations had no place in the requirements model or business model, and should be introduced rather late in the life cycle. Experience suggests that this notion is sometimes better in theory than in practice. Technology, and its technical implications, has an increasing impact on the way business is conducted, and the evolution of e-commerce is an example of technological change driving business change. So it frequently makes sense not to distinguish between pure business and technology, and to reflect this blurring throughout the life cycle. This makes it much easier to detect future requirements for change early in the process.

Finally, and most important, too many systems have been designed without regard to the skills of the development and maintenance teams. Theoretical purity may be important in some settings, but for most organizations the emphasis is on building a system that works over time. Why take approaches that the development team can't build or the maintenance team can't maintain? So, it is necessary to realistically assess the capabilities of the organization, even if the answer is unpopular, and choose the technical approach accordingly.

Once the requirements have been properly defined, there are four development strategies that should be considered (remember, the goal is to build systems that work, not to prove a theoretical point):

- Use the traditional structured approach using parameter files.

- Develop an OO application.

- Build an OO framework, which is extended with an OO programming language.

- Build an engine that processes the requirements specification as input.

Each of these approaches has a place, particularly if the technical capabilities of the organization are taken into account. In fact, the capability assessment may well render the strategy question meaningless. However, if the organization is capable of taking any

Continues

of these approaches, then the question becomes a trade-off between the degree of change needed and long-term versus short-term cost and benefits. It is important to recognize that, in the past, cost was the controlling factor. However, the need for rapid change requires a different approach that gives full weight to the revenue gains possible with the ability to quickly respond to changing business requirements.

We will now consider the fourth strategy, which attacks the problem of developing highly change-centric systems.

SB6.2 The Enduring Business Theme Alternative

Traditionally, change is anticipated by the abstractions of the concrete words in the requirements definition rather than the concrete words themselves. For example, a requirements specification that refers to a 1957 Chevrolet may result in a class called Automobile or even Vehicle. However, there are some applications, typically rule-driven, where the usual abstractions will not survive as time goes on, and nothing that appears in the requirements specification seems to be change-invariant. One solution in such situations is to look for an enduring business theme that underlies all of the requirements. For example, rule-driven call-center requirements specification may be viewed as the metaphor "follow these rules and procedures" with a list of textual rules and procedures that fill in the specifics of the metaphor. The fundamental ideas of EBTs are:

- Identify the enduring theme, such as "select and act" or "follow this recipe"—this theme is the part of the application that will not change over time and usually does not appear explicitly in the requirements specification.

- Build a framework that implements that theme and the supporting infrastructure.

The details of the requirements model are addressed late in the development cycle and do not receive an extensive treatment. Frequently, the specific text rules are handled as statements in an extensible "language of the business" that are read in at runtime, causing the appropriate objects, and in some cases even classes, to be created on the fly.

This is easier said than done. It can be very difficult to find or express the enduring theme, and [Cline-Girou 1998, Fayad-Altman 1999] explain some of the processes and difficulties. It is also a technical challenge to build a framework that supports an extensible language of the business as well as efficiently implements some of the difficult runtime operations that arise naturally.

It is important that the details of the requirements not invade the framework and that they be implemented closer to the leaves of the project's PERT (Program Evaluation and Review Technique) chart or dependency graph than to the root. This ensures that they are treated as throwaway elements rather than the backbone of the system. The exact way in which they are implemented is a significant policy decision that varies from one organization to another, but we have found that a domain-specific scripting language can be an effective way to implement the requirements specification, both the textual description of the business operation as well as the screen layouts. Such a language is much more than a 4GL, because it is based on words, phrases, and sentence structures that come from the problem domain rather than a predefined programming context. Therefore, the language can be used by nonprogramming business analysts to handle changes in the future without involving the development staff. Be warned that some development staffs will resist this benefit because it intrudes on what they view as their power base.

One of the benefits of the EBT approach is that it decomposes the organizational skills rather nicely. The assumption, often implicit, that each developer is somewhat of a problem domain expert as well as a developer is not realistic and usually does not make it easy to partition the part of the development that requires an expert from the part that can be done by those with more-modest talents. With EBTs, the development of the framework requires expert development skills of the first order; the development of the statements in the scripting language can be done by problem domain specialists without development skills, and the average developer can concentrate on building the bridges between the scripting language and the framework. We do not know which is more important, keeping average developers away from tasks that they can't handle or freeing experts to work only on the difficult tasks.

SB6.3 References

[Cline-Girou 1998] Cline, M., and M. Girou. Enduring Business Themes. Submitted for publication to *Communications of the ACM*, 1998.

[Fayad-Altman 1999] Fayad, M.E. and A. Altman. Accomplishing Software Stability. UNR-0025-99, UNR Technical Report, March 1999.

Framework Testing and Integration

Part Six is made up of one chapter and a sidebar. Part Six discusses issues related to framework testing and integration.

Chapter 20 discusses framework integration problems, causes, and solutions. Reuse of software has been one of the main goals of software engineering for decades. With the emergence of the object-oriented paradigm, an important enabling technology for reuse of larger components became available and resulted in the definition of object-oriented frameworks. Experiences with frameworks have shown that frameworks indeed provide considerable reuse in framework-based application development. However, whereas framework-based application development initially included a single framework, increasingly often multiple frameworks are used in application development. This chapter provides a significant collection of common framework composition problems encountered in application development together with an analytical discussion of the underlying causes for the problems. Based on the composition problems and the identified primary causes, this chapter describes and analyzes existing solution approaches and their limitations.

The composition problems discussed are (1) composition of framework control, (2) composition with legacy components, (3) framework gap, (4) overlap of framework entities, and (5) composition of entity functionality. The primary causes for these composition problems are related to (1) the cohesion between classes inside each framework, (2) the domain coverage of the frameworks, (3) the design intentions of the framework designers, and (4) the potential lack of access to the source code of the frameworks. The identified problems and their causes are, to some extent, addressed by existing solutions, such as the adapter design pattern, wrapping, or mediating software, but these solutions generally have limitations and either do not solve the problem completely or require considerable implementation efforts.

Sidebar 7 describes a method to incorporate the reusable Built-In-Tests (BITs) into object-oriented application frameworks (OOAFs). The reuse approaches to the BITs in OOAF development have been analyzed. The BIT method has extended the reusability of OOAFs from code to tests. By the BIT approach, highly testable and test reusable OOAFs can be developed on the same platform of the conventional OO software. The BIT method is a natural advance and supplementary to conventional OO technology for OOAF development. A wide range of applications of the BIT method has been found in OOAF development, testing, maintenance, and reengineering.

CHAPTER 20

Composition Problems, Causes, and Solutions

Reuse of software has been one of the main goals of software engineering for decades. From the early age of computer science on, the approach of constructing a system by putting together reusable components was a clear goal of software engineers. However, the early approaches—for example, function and procedure libraries—only provided reuse of small, building-block components. With the emergence of the object-oriented paradigm, an important enabling technology for reuse of larger components became available and resulted in the definition of object-oriented frameworks. An object-oriented framework can be defined as a set of classes that embodies an abstract design for solutions to a family of related problems [Johnson 1988]. In other words, a framework is an abstract design and implementation for an application in a given problem domain.

The presence of a framework influences the development process for the application. In [Mattsson 1996], we define the following phases in framework-centered software development:

The framework development phase. Normally the most effort-consuming phase, the framework development phase is aimed at producing a reusable design and related implementation in a domain. Major results of this phase are the domain analysis model and the object-oriented framework.

The framework usage phase. This phase is sometimes also referred to as the framework instantiation phase, framework customization phase, or application development phase. The result of this phase is an application developed reusing a framework. Here the software engineer has to adapt the existing framework. In the case of a whitebox framework, the software engineer makes changes and extensions to framework internals using mechanisms such as redefinition and polymorphic substitution. If the existing framework is a blackbox framework (that is, the user does not have to know about the framework internals), the customization is achieved through modification of the configuration interface using mechanisms such as predefined options (for example, objects) and switching mechanisms. For those parts of the application design not covered by reusable classes, new classes need to be developed to fulfill the application's requirements.

The framework evolution and maintenance phase. The framework, like all software, will be subject to change. Causes for these changes can be errors reported from shipped applications, identification of new abstractions due to changes in the problem domain, and so on.

The advantage of framework-based development is the high level of reuse in the application development. Although this advantage has been claimed by proponents of the technology, recently scientific evidence supporting this claim has also started to appear, for example, [Moser 1996]. Although the development of an object-oriented framework requires considerable effort, the corresponding benefits during application development generally justify the initial effort.

Traditional framework-based application development assumes that the application is based on a single framework that is extended with application-specific code. Recently, however, we have identified development in which software engineers make use of multiple frameworks that are composed to fulfill the application requirements. Experiences from the composition of two or more frameworks clearly show that frameworks generally are developed for reuse by extension with newly written application-specific code and not for composition with other software components. This focus on reuse through extension causes a number of problems when software engineers try to compose frameworks.

In this chapter, we study the problems that the software engineer may experience while composing frameworks. The identified problems are based on our experiences from developing frameworks for, among others, fire alarm systems [Molin 1996], measurement systems [Bosch 1998c], gateway billing systems [Lundberg 1996b], resource allocation and process operation [Betlem 1995], as well as existing literature about frameworks, for example, [Bosch 1998b; Mattsson 1996; Sparks 1996]. The composition problems that we identified are related to the composition of framework control, composition with legacy components, framework gap, overlap of framework entities, and composition of entity functionality. Our investigations into these problems have led us to the conclusion that the main causes for the problems are due to the cohesion between the classes in the framework, the domain coverage of the framework, the design intention of the framework designer, and the potential lack of access to the source code of the framework. In addition, we discuss the available solution approaches for addressing the identified problems and their causes, and the limitations of these solutions.

We believe the contribution of this chapter to be the following. First, it provides software engineers employing object-oriented frameworks with an understanding of the problems they may experience during application development, as well as an understanding of the primary causes and solution approaches. Second, it provides topics to researchers in object-oriented software engineering that need to be addressed by future research.

The remainder of this chapter is organized as follows. In the next section, four example frameworks are introduced that are used to illustrate the problems later in the chapter. Then, the framework composition problems that we identified are described. The subsequent section discusses the primary causes underlying the identified composition problems. Next, the various solution approaches for the identified problems are discussed, as well as their limitations, and the chapter is concluded in the succeeding section.

20.1 Object-Oriented Framework Examples

In this section, we discuss four frameworks that, in the remainder of the chapter, are used to exemplify and illustrate the discussion. These frameworks have been selected for their illustrative ability rather than for their industrial relevance. During the discussion, we assume that it is the intention to reuse two or more frameworks in one application, requiring the frameworks to be composed. The frameworks are a measurement systems framework, a graphical user interface (GUI) framework, a fire alarm framework, and a framework for statistical analysis. The following describes the involved frameworks. However, since most readers are familiar with GUI frameworks, this framework is not described.

In cooperation with EC-Gruppen AB, we have been involved in the design of a framework for measurement systems (see Figure 20.1). Measurement systems are systems that are located at the beginning or end of production lines to measure some selected features of production items. The hardware of a measurement system consists of a trigger, one or more sensors, and one or more actuators. The framework for the software has software representations for these parts, the measurement item, and an abstract factory for generating new measurement item objects. A typical measurement cycle for a product starts with the trigger detecting the item and notifying the abstract factory [Gamma 1995]. In response, the abstract factory creates a measurement item and activates it. The measurement item contains a measurement strategy and an actuation strategy and uses them to first read the relevant data from the sensors. After that the measurement item compares this data with the ideal values and subsequently activates the actuators when necessary to remove or mark the product if it did not fulfill the requirements. Refer to [Bosch 1998c] for a more detailed description of the framework.

The statistical analysis framework, in this context, will be used for the statistical analysis of the data gathered by the measurement system. Although measurement systems generally measure every production item, it is often beneficial to be able to collect measurement data and analyze it statistically to condense the amount of data and to increase the information value. Examples of statistical analysis on measurement item data are the correlation between measurements on items and the equipment that manufactured the items, and the distribution of measured items in various quality categories. The results of the analysis may be used online to adjust the settings for manufacturing equipment. In the remainder of this chapter, we will discuss two versions of the framework, one version providing only the core functionality for statistical analysis and a second version containing, in addition to the core function-

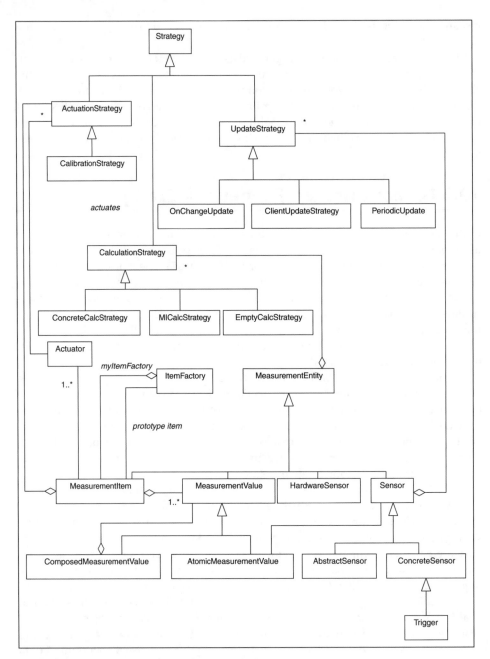

Figure 20.1   Measurement system framework.

ality, functionality for the graphical representation of statistical data, for example, histograms.

TeleLarm AB, a Swedish security company, develops and markets a family of fire alarm systems ranging from small office systems to large distributed systems for multi-building plants. An object-oriented framework was designed as a part of a major architectural redesign effort. The framework provides abstract classes for devices and communication drivers as well as application abstractions such as input points and output points representing sensors and actuators. System status is represented by a set of deviations that are available on all nodes in the distributed system. The notion of periodic objects is introduced, giving the system large-grain concurrency without the problems associated with asynchronous fine-grain concurrency. Two production instantiations from the framework have been released so far. The fire alarm framework has been described as a pattern language; see [Molin 1996] for more information. Figure 20.2 presents a schematic system view of the framework.

20.2 Framework Composition Problems

Several of the companies that we cooperate with are moving away from the traditional single framework–based application development to application development based on multiple frameworks that need to be composed with each other, with class libraries, and with existing legacy components. In this section, five composition problems are described that may occur when composing a framework with another software artifact. Although software engineers may encounter additional problems, we believe this list will cover the primary problems.

20.2.1 Composition of Framework Control

One of the most distinguishing features of a framework is its ability to make extensive use of dynamic binding. In traditional class or procedure libraries, the application code invokes routines in the library and it is the application code that is in control. For object-oriented frameworks, the situation is inverted and it is often the framework code that has the thread of control and calls the application code when appropriate.

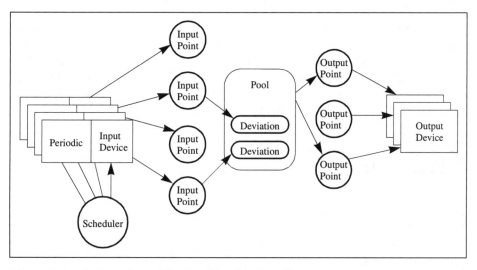

Figure 20.2   System view of the fire alarm framework.

This inversion of control is often referred to as the *Hollywood principle:* "Don't call us— we'll call you." Figure 20.3 illustrates this inversion.

In [Sparks 1996], a distinction is made between *calling* and *called* frameworks. Calling frameworks are the active entities in an application, controlling and invoking the other parts, whereas called frameworks are passive entities that can be called by other parts of the application—in other words, they are more like class libraries. One of the problems when composing two calling frameworks is that both frameworks expect to be the controlling entity in the application and in control of the main event loop.

An example is the composition of the measurement system framework and the GUI framework, as shown in Figure 20.4. The measurement system framework has, from the moment a trigger enters the system, a well-defined control loop that has to be performed in real time and that creates a measurement item, reads sensors, computes, activates actuators, and stores the necessary historical data. The GUI framework has a similar thread of control, though not in real time, that updates the screen whenever a value in the system changes—for example, that of a sensor—or performs some action when the user invokes a command. These two control loops can easily collide with each other, potentially causing the measurement part to miss its real-time deadlines and causing the GUI to present incorrect data due to race conditions between the activities.

Solving this problem is considerably easier if the frameworks are supplied with source code that makes it possible to adapt the framework to handle this problem. However, the control loop in the framework may not be localized in a single entity. Often it is distributed over the framework code, which causes changes to the control to affect considerable parts of the framework.

20.2.2 Composition with Legacy Components

A framework presents a design for an application in a particular domain. Based on this design, the software engineer may construct a concrete application through extension of the framework, for example, subclassing the framework classes. When the framework class only contains behavior for internal framework functionality but not the domain-specific behavior required for the application, the software engineer may want to include existing, legacy, classes in the application that need to be integrated with the framework. It is, however, far from trivial to integrate the legacy class in the application, since frameworks often rely heavily on the subclassing mechanism. Since the legacy component will not be a subclass of the framework class, developers may run into typing conflicts. We refer to [Lundberg 1996a] for a more extensive discussion.

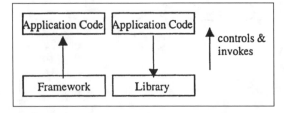

Figure 20.3   The inversion of control.

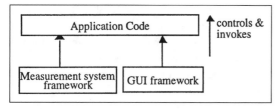

Figure 20.4 The problem of framework control composition.

The measurement system framework is used as an example to illustrate the problem. The framework handles the measurement cycle and provides for attaching a sensor, a measurement algorithm, and an actuator by specifying the interface classes Sensor, CalculationStrategy, and Actuator. The main classes in the framework are shown in Figure 20.5.

Assume that we have a library of legacy components with different types of sensors, actuators, and strategies for measurement and calculation, and that we have found suitable classes that we want to use in the three places in the framework's interface. Our library sensor class is called TempSensor, and it happens to be a subclass of the class Sensor, which is an abstract class, defined in our library. However, since the framework also defines a class Sensor, the usage of the library class will lead to conflicts. Even if the class name for the library superclass matches with that of the framework interface class, the class TempSensor cannot be used, because these names do not designate the same class. An alternative approach, which is used in Figure 20.3, is to make use of the Adapter design pattern [Gamma 1995] for class adaptation. This approach normally solves the problem, and identifies name clashes between class names in the framework and the legacy components. However, as we identified in [Bosch1998a], the Adapter design pattern has some disadvantages associated with it. One disadvantage is that for every element of the interface that needs to be adapted, the software engineer has to define a method that forwards the call to the corresponding method in the legacy class. Moreover, in the case of object adaptation, those requests that otherwise would not have required adaptation have to be forwarded as

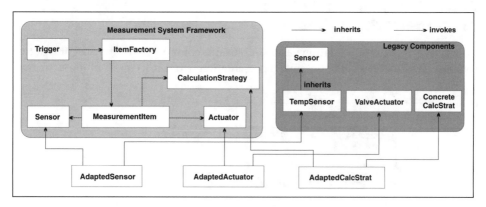

Figure 20.5 The measurement system framework and associated legacy classes.

well, due to the intermediate adapter object. This leads to considerable implementation overhead for the software engineer. In addition, the pattern suffers from the self problem and lacks expressiveness. Finally, since behavior of the Adapter pattern is mixed with the domain-related behavior of the class, traceability is reduced.

The problems related to integration of legacy components in framework-based applications are studied in more detail in [Lundberg 1996a].

20.2.3 Framework Gap

Often, when thinking about composition problems of components, the first thing that comes to mind is different kinds of overlap between the components, but there may also exist problems due to nonoverlap between the components. This occurs when two frameworks are composed and the resulting structure still does not cover the application's requirements. This problem is generally referred to as *framework gap* (see, for example, [Sparks 1996]).

If the framework is a called framework, the framework gap problem may be solved with an additional framework interface, including both the existing and the additionally required functionality. Figure 20.6 illustrates such a *wrapping* approach.

In the case where a calling framework lacks functionality, mediating software is needed to alleviate the problem. Consider two calling frameworks, A and B, and that we have a framework gap. The mediating software must provide functionality for informing framework A about the actions that had happened in framework B. This information must be presented for framework A in terms understandable to A. The mediating software may also need to cut out parts of the functionality offered by the frameworks. The functionality has to be replaced by the mediating software together with application-specific code that composes the functionality from frameworks A and B and the functionality required for the framework gap. The situation will now be that the two frameworks have to call the mediating software, which then calls the application-specific functionality. An additional problem is that the mediating software becomes dependent on the current framework versions, which may lead to rather complex maintenance problems for the application when new versions of the framework must be used.

20.2.4 Composition Overlap of Framework Entities

When developing an application based on reusable components, it may occur that two (or more) frameworks both contain a representation—that is, a class—of the same real-

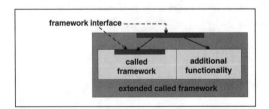

Figure 20.6 Called framework extended to fill the framework gap.

world entity, but modeled from their respective perspectives. When composing the two frameworks, the two different representations should be integrated or composed since they both represent the same real-world entity. If the represented properties are mutually exclusive and do not influence each other, then the integration can be solved by multiple inheritance. However, very often these preconditions do not hold and there exist shared or depending properties between the representations, causing the composition of the representations to be more complex. We can identify at least three cases where alternative composition techniques are necessary.

First, consider the situation where both framework classes represent a state property of the real-world entity, but the entity is represented in different ways. For example, a sensor in the fire alarm framework has a simple presentation which has a Boolean state for its value, while the same sensor in the measurement framework has more complex representations such as temperature and pressure. When these two representations of a sensor are composed into an integrated sensor, this requires every state update in one framework sensor class to be extended with the conversion and update code for the state in the other framework sensor class.

In the second case, assume that both framework classes represent a property p of the real-world entity, but one framework class represents p as a state and the other framework class represents p as a method. The value of the particular property p is indirectly computed by the method. For instance, an actuator is available both in the fire alarm and the measurement system frameworks. In an application, the software engineer may want to compose both actuator representations into a single entity. One actuator class may store as a state whether it is currently active or not, whereas the other class may indirectly deduce this from its other state variables. In the application representation, the property representation has to be solved in such a way that reused behavior from both classes can deal with it.

In the third case, the execution of an operation in one framework class requires state changes in the other framework class. Using the example of the actuator mentioned earlier, an activate message to one actuator implementation may require that the active state of the other actuator class needs to be updated accordingly. When the software engineer combines the actuator classes from the two frameworks, this aspect of the composition has to be explicitly implemented in the glue code.

20.2.5 Composition of Entity Functionality

Sometimes a real-world entity's functionality has to be modeled through composition with parts of functionality from different frameworks. Consider the case of a typical software structure with three layers, each represented by a framework: at the top is a user interface layer, in the middle an application domain–specific layer, and at the bottom a persistence layer. Our real-world entity is now represented in the application domain–specific framework, but some aspects of the entity have to be presented in the user interface layer, and the entity also has to be made persistent for some kinds of transactions, and so on. Just composing the respective classes from the three frameworks or using multiple inheritance will not result in the desired behavior. For example, changes of the state caused by messages to the application domain–specific part of the resulting object will not automatically affect the user interface and persistence functionality of the objects.

Thus, the software engineer is required to extend the application domain class with behavior for notifying the user interface and database classes, for example, using the Observer design pattern [Gamma 1995]. One could argue that the application domain class should have been extended with such behavior during design, but, as mentioned earlier, most frameworks are not designed to be composed with other frameworks but to be extended with application-specific code written specifically for the application at hand.

This problem occurred in the fire alarm framework, where several entities had to be persistent and were stored in nonvolatile memory, that is, an EEPROM. To deal with this, two objects—one application object and one persistence object—implemented each entity. These two objects were obviously tightly coupled and had frequent interactions, due to the fact that they both represented parts of one real-world entity.

20.3 Underlying Causes

The framework composition problems identified in the previous section can be related to a number of causes that underlie these problems. In this section, we discuss what we believe to be the four primary causes of these problems: framework cohesion, domain coverage of the framework, the design intention of the framework designer, and lack of access to the source code. In the following, each cause will be described.

20.3.1 Framework Cohesion

The main issue in the framework usage phase is to develop an application through reusing an existing framework. The existing framework has to be extended or composed with some other software artifact to realize the requirements of the application under development. Three different software artifacts that can be used for the adaptation and composition are new application-specific source code, class libraries, and other frameworks.

Virtually every application that is developed based on a framework will require application-specific code to be developed and, since this code is designed to be composed with the framework, composition problems rarely occur. However, as described earlier, if a class library or a framework has to be composed with our framework, several composition problems may occur. But why is it so hard to compose these software artifacts with our framework? One of the answers to this question is *framework cohesion*. The functionality of a class in the framework can be divided into various types. The two types relevant for the discussion here are the domain-specific behavior corresponding to the real-world entity that the class represents and the interaction behavior to communicate to other framework entities for mutual updating. The latter type of functionality we refer to as *cohesive behavior:* It establishes the cohesion between the entities in the framework. So, for a class from a class library or another framework to replace a class in the framework, this class not only has to represent the appropriate domain behavior but also correct cohesive behavior. Since the cohesive behavior is very specific for the framework, it is rather unlikely that a separately developed class will fulfill these requirements.

20.3.2 Domain Coverage

An object-oriented framework provides an abstract design for an application in some problem domain. However, the framework need not cover the complete domain but may contain classes for only a subset of the relevant entities in the domain. To determine whether a framework covers the complete domain is a rather subjective activity since application domains are not defined very precisely. For instance, we considered the measurement system framework that we developed to cover a complete application domain. During discussions with other software engineers, we found that they considered the framework to provide partial domain coverage since it provided only discrete measurement of items and did not incorporate continuous measurement required for, among other things, production of fluid products.

When composing a framework with another framework, a developer may experience no domain overlap, little overlap, or considerable overlap. No overlap between the frameworks will obviously not cause problems with respect to composition of overlapping entities, but it may be the source of a framework gap problem. Little domain overlap is often relatively easy to deal with since it only requires the adaptation of a few classes in both frameworks. Considerable overlap, however, may cause the reuse of one of the frameworks to be more effort consuming than writing the code from scratch. This problem is especially problematic for long-lived applications, since the frameworks on which an application is based often evolve over time, just like the application itself. Considerable redesign of a framework is then required to be repeated for every consecutive version of the application, if the application is to benefit from the improvements of later framework versions.

The solution for this problem is primarily a matter of standards. If an accepted definition of application domains and the boundaries between the domains would exist, framework designers could take these definitions into account, and composition of frameworks would probably require less effort since most gaps and overlaps could be avoided. However, defining a generally accepted classification of domains is far from trivial. For instance, the statistical analysis framework described in *Section 20.1* provides user interface functionality specifically for statistical representations, such as histograms and normal distributions. A general-purpose GUI framework will most likely not have support for these representations, but the statistical graphical representations may be very hard to integrate with the GUI framework. When defining standard application boundaries, the developer has to decide where such boundary functionality should be assigned, which is a nontrivial task.

20.3.3 Design Intention

Several authors have identified that a reusable software artifact has to be designed for reuse by adaptation and composition. Since class libraries generally have relatively low cohesion between the classes, it is often feasible to compose class library elements with existing software. Object-oriented frameworks, on the other hand, are generally designed for reuse through extension of the framework or through composition of framework components. Due to the high cohesion inside the framework, the composition with other frameworks or other existing software is generally hard.

We can identify two variants of framework composition: horizontal and vertical. Horizontal integration is the situation where the two frameworks that are to be composed can be found on the same layer in a software system. Vertical integration indicates the situation where one framework depends on the services of another framework, that is, a so-called layered system. For example, the measurement system framework and the statistical analysis framework are composed horizontally, whereas these two frameworks are composed vertically with the user interface framework. Independent of whether vertical and horizontal composition is used, an additional issue is whether there is one-way or two-way communication between the composed frameworks. Two-way communication often complicates the composition of the frameworks considerably.

In conclusion, the design intentions for the framework should be defined explicitly to make it easier for the software engineer to decide on the composability of a framework for the application at hand. It should be made clear whether the framework can be reused by extension only or that provisions for composition are available. In addition, it should be made clear whether the framework is intended for two-way communication or one-way communication. Since the design intention for most existing frameworks, generally implicitly, is for reuse by extension and one-way communication from the framework to the newly written application-specific code, it is a cause of the framework composition problems that we have identified.

20.3.4 Access to Source Code

Another, seemingly trivial, cause for framework composition problems is the lack of access to the source code of the framework. This lack of access can be a practical limitation where the framework has been delivered to the reusing software engineer in the form of a library of compiled code in combination with a set of header files. It may also be a conceptual lack of source code access due to the complexity of the code of the framework. The internal workings of the framework often are so complex that it will require considerable effort from the software engineer before he or she is able to make the changes necessary for composition purposes. Since research in software reuse has identified that the perceived effort required for reusing a component should be less than the perceived effort of developing the component from scratch, the conceptual lack of access to the source code may also constitute an important obstacle for framework reuse.

Access to the source code is important since framework composition, as identified earlier in this chapter, may require editing of the framework code to add behavior necessary for other frameworks. If no access to the source code is available, the only way to achieve the additional behavior required from the framework is through wrappers encapsulating the framework. However, as identified by [Hölzle 1993], wrapper solutions may cause problems such as significant amounts of additional code and serious performance problems. In addition, wrappers are unable to extend behavior in response to intraframework communication. For example, one framework object invoking another object in the framework may require an object in another part of the application to be notified. However, since the wrapper is unable to intercept this communication, it is not possible to achieve this.

20.4 From Problems to Causes to Solutions

In the previous sections, several framework composition problems and their primary causes have been identified. In this section, we start by relating the causes to the identified problems. Subsequently, the existing solution approaches for each problem are discussed and their limitations are identified.

It is important to note that some of the solutions will cause changes to the framework and thus result in a new version of the framework. This is not a problem for the actual application under development but may cause problems for previously developed applications using the framework. This problem of maintaining previously developed applications is often referred to as *backward compatibility.* The issue of backward compatibility will arise in other situations as well, for example, fault recognition in a previously developed application or incomplete domain understanding. A more extensive discussion of backward compatibility for frameworks and the selection of an appropriate maintenance strategy can be found in [Bosch 1998b].

Table 20.1 relates the framework composition problems to the identified causes. Each cell describes whether the cause is the primary source of the problem or complicates the solution of the problem, that is, whether it is a secondary cause. In the section following, these relations are explained in more detail and the available solution approaches are described.

20.4.1 Composition of Framework Control

The context for this problem is a situation where two frameworks are to be composed such that both assume ownership of the main event loop of the application. When composing two such frameworks, the threads of control of both frameworks have to be composed in some way. The main cause for this problem is that both frameworks are intentionally designed for adaptation and not for composition, which makes neither of the frameworks able to give up the control. Since the control loop often is deeply embedded in the source code of the framework, lack of access to the source code of the frameworks considerably complicates resolving the problem. Some changes to the control loop may even be impossible to achieve without changing the actual source code. For instance, events internal to the framework that are required externally in the application at hand, such as the notification of another framework, cannot be intercepted by framework wrappers or adapters but require actually changing the framework code. An additional factor complicating the composition of calling frameworks is the *cohesive behavior* inside the framework. The cohesive behavior, since it indicates the behavior of framework classes for updating the other framework classes, mixes the event behavior with the domain behavior of the classes. Since the event loop becomes implicit through the cohesive behavior, making changes to the event loop is more difficult due to the—potentially many—locations where code changes are required.

Table 20.1 Framework Composition Problems and Their Causes

	COMPOSITION OF FRAMEWORK CONTROL	COMPOSITION WITH LEGACY COMPONENT	FRAMEWORK GAP	OVERLAP OF ENTITIES	COMPOSITION OF ENTITY FUNCTIONALITY
Cohesive Behavior	Complicating factor	Primary cause	–	Complicating factor	Complicating factor
Domain Coverage	–	–	Primary cause	Primary cause	–
Design Intention	Primary cause	Complicating factor	–	Complicating factor	Primary cause
No Source Code Access	Complicating factor	Complicating factor	Complicating factor	Complicating factor	Complicating factor

Integrating the framework control from the composed frameworks requires changes to the event loops in the involved frameworks. This can be achieved by three solutions, as discussed in the following points.

Concurrency. One possible solution is to give each framework its own thread of control rather than merging the control loops. This solution approach can be used only when there is no need for the frameworks or the application code to be notified about events from the other frameworks. A disadvantage of this approach is that the application-specific objects that potentially are accessed by more than one framework need to be extended with synchronization code. An advantage is that no access to the source code is required.

Wrapping. A second solution is to encapsulate each framework by a wrapper intercepting all messages sent to and by the framework. The wrapper, upon receipt of relevant messages, can notify interested entities in the framework. This allows some level of integration of event handling in the framework-based application, but only based on events external to the framework. Internal framework events are not intercepted and can consequently not be dealt with.

Remove and rewrite. If external notification of internal framework events is necessary in the application, a solution is to remove the relevant parts of the control loops from the frameworks and to write an application-specific control loop that satisfies the needs from the involved frameworks and the application. This requires access to the source code. This may be difficult since the control loop often is not centralized to one framework entity but spread out in the framework; in other words, the cohesive behavior of the framework complicates the solution. This solution generally is a more effort-consuming approach than the previously indicated approaches.

20.4.2 Composition with Legacy Components

The software engineer may want to use legacy components in combination with the framework when a framework class does not contain the correct application-specific domain behavior for the actual application. In addition, a legacy library of classes with the required application-specific behavior is available that fulfills the application's requirements. The integration between a framework and legacy components is not as easy as one might expect due to the cohesive behavior of the framework, which makes it difficult to replace a framework class with a legacy class, and due to potential typing conflicts in the programming language. A complicating factor in solving the composition problem is that the framework is designed for adaptation and extension and not for composition. One approach is to design the framework for composition by means of the role concept. Obviously, access to the source code of the framework simplifies the composition, since one can change the framework to refer to the legacy class rather than a framework class. Some solutions to the problem of composing legacy components with a framework are discussed in the following sections.

Adapter design pattern. Composing a legacy component with a framework is almost a schoolbook example of a situation for which the Adapter design pattern has been designed. Provided that no name clashes occur, this solution is very suitable, but it results in some implementation overhead, as for each operation in the class interface that has to be adapted there must be methods that forward the request to the equivalent method in the legacy class. Additional drawbacks are that the Adapter pattern suffers from the self problem and traceability is reduced since pattern-specific behavior is mixed with domain-specific behavior for the class [Bosch 1998a].

Change framework. Provided the software engineer has access to the framework's source code, one possible solution is to change those parts of the framework that refer to the framework class that should be replaced by the legacy class.

Roles. As described in [Lundberg 1996a], a solution dealing with the problem once and for all is to represent the framework's reuse interface as a set of roles. A framework role is a description of the required behavior of the object that is taking the place in the reuse interface. By specifying the reuse interface as roles instead of as superclasses, we focus on the required services instead of the entire object. Using this solution, it is possible to fill the roles either with classes related to the framework or existing legacy classes, provided that the class fulfills the requirements. This, however, requires the framework to be designed based on this approach.

20.4.3 Framework Gap

The framework gap problem occurs when two (or more) frameworks have to be composed to satisfy the application's requirements, but the composition does not cover the requirements completely. Thus, we have a gap of missing functionality. The main cause for this problem is that the frameworks do not cover their respective domains sufficiently. As described earlier in the chapter, the definition of an application domain is still rather ad hoc, and this may lead to domain overlap or domain gaps when composing frameworks. Also for this problem, the lack of access to source code may complicate the solution to a framework considerably. In either case, one can identify a number of solution approaches for closing the framework gap.

Wrapping. As described earlier in this chapter (see, for example, Figure 20.4), one can extend the framework interface of a called framework with the missing functionality through an additional Application Program Interface (API). The wrapping entity, in this case, aggregates the original framework and the extension for closing the gap, but provides a uniform interface so that clients are unaware of the internal structure.

Mediating software. For a calling framework, the software engineer has to develop some kind of mediating software that manages the interactions between the two frameworks. The mediating software not only manages the interaction, but also contains the functionality required for closing the framework gap. Potential disadvantages are that it has proven to be rather difficult to develop mediating components and that the software becomes vulnerable to future changes of framework versions and thus is expensive to maintain.

Redesign and extend. If a developer has access to the source code of the framework and also intends to reuse the framework in future applications, the most fruitful approach may be to redesign the framework and extend the source code to achieve better domain coverage, thus bridging the gap.

20.4.4 Composition Overlap of Framework Entities

When two frameworks represent the same real-world entity, from their respective perspectives and with their own representations, and these frameworks need to be composed, the two representations of the real-world entity have to be composed as well. This constitutes the problem of overlap of framework entities. The main cause for this problem is that both frameworks cover part of the application domain, since the real-world entity has been modeled from different perspectives. The composition of the two framework classes is often complicated due to the cohesive behavior of the classes since, after the composition, actions in one class may need to notify the other framework class. We present four solution approaches to the problem:

Multiple inheritance. An obvious solution to this problem is to use multiple inheritance, but this requires that the properties of the classes not affect each other and are mutually exclusive, which is seldom the case. The main issue is to provide a solution that takes care of necessary updates and conversions between different representations provided by the two frameworks.

Aggregation. An alternative solution is to use aggregation instead of inheritance, which will result in an aggregate class that has each framework representation as parts. The aggregate class is the application's representation of the real-world entity. However, this approach requires that the source code be available for the frameworks, since the involved frameworks have to be changed so that every location in the framework that references the framework-specific representation of the real-world entity is replaced by a reference to the aggregate class. In addition, it is necessary that the interface of the aggregate class contain the framework class interface for both frameworks and the necessary conversion and update operations. The implementation of the aggregate class must, in appropriate methods and places, include the necessary conversion and update behavior. The major drawback of this solution is that both frameworks have to be changed and that a considerable amount of implementation overhead is required.

Subclassing and aggregation. Another solution that does not require changes in the frameworks is to subclass each framework class that represents the real-world entity. Both subclasses are involved in a bidirectional association relationship to enable update and conversion behavior. In addition, each subclass has to override the operations in the superclass. In the subclass implementation of relevant operations, there are calls to the corresponding subclass for conversion and updates and, in addition, the operations call the overridden operations in the superclass. A limitation of this solution is that the application's representation of the real-world entity is partitioned over two classes. To overcome this limitation, we may introduce an additional aggregate class that has the two subclasses as parts. The aggregate class solution also implies that the application-specific part of the code has to work with the aggregate class (to reach the part objects) and that there will be communication between the two subclass objects that will not pass the aggregate object.

Subject orientation. A fourth solution is provided by the subject-oriented programming approach [Ossher 1996]. Subject orientation supports composition of subjects—that is, an object-oriented program or program fragment such as a framework that models a domain in its own subjective way. Subjects can be composed, either as source code or as binary code. Since frameworks can be subjects, the subject-oriented approach may alleviate the problem of overlapping framework entities. However, although useful in theory, the lack of widespread tool support may make subject composition less appropriate in practice.

20.4.5 Composition of Entity Functionality

This problem occurs when a real-world entity has to be modeled through composition of parts of functionality from different frameworks, for example, composing application domain–specific functionality with persistence functionality. This means that the real-world entity is represented in an application domain–specific framework and has to be composed with functionality from a persistence framework. The cause for this composition problem of functionality is that the frameworks are designed for extension and thus it is not easy to add functionality. The cohesive behavior of a framework complicates the composition of functionality since it makes it difficult to break up the existing collaborations inside the framework and add the necessary functionality. Aggregation and multiple inheritance and the use of the Observer design pattern are discussed as possible solutions in the following text. A third solution may be the use of the subject-oriented programming approach [Ossher 1996], as described in the preceding section.

Aggregation or multiple inheritance. The simplest solution to this problem is to use multiple inheritance or aggregation to compose the framework classes with the required functionality into a single class. The problem with these solutions is that state changes caused by messages to the application domain–specific part of the composed object will not automatically influence the persistence functionality part of the object. One way to solve this is to add update behavior in appropriate places in the frameworks and the composed class, but this is a rather complex action to perform.

Observer design pattern. To overcome the problem with the previous solution, the application domain–specific class can be extended with notification behavior, for example, through applying the Observer design pattern [Gamma 1995]. This may seem an obvious solution; thus, it should have been included in the application domain–specific framework from the beginning. But, as often is the case, the framework is originally designed for extension and not for composition.

20.5 Summary

Object-oriented frameworks provide an important step forward in software reuse, since frameworks allow reuse of large components instead of the traditional small, building block–like components. Initially, frameworks were primarily used as the only reused entity in application development, and the application was constructed by extending the framework with application-specific behavior. During recent years—among other reasons, due to the increased availability of frameworks for various domains—there is a movement toward the use of multiple frameworks in application development. These frameworks have to be composed to fulfill the application's requirements, which may lead to composition problems.

In this chapter, we have studied the framework composition problems that may occur during application development, their main causes, the solutions available to the software engineer, and the limitations of these solutions. The composition problems that we identified are related to the composition of framework control, the composition of the framework with legacy components, the framework gap, the composition overlap of framework entities, and the composition of entity functionality. These problems are primarily caused by the cohesion of involved frameworks, the accuracy of the domain coverage of frameworks, the design intentions of the framework developer, and the lack of access to the source code of the framework. The identified problems and their causes are, to some extent, addressed by existing solutions, such as the Adapter design pattern, wrapping, or mediating software, but these solutions generally have limitations and either do not solve the problem completely or require considerable implementation effort.

To the best of our knowledge, no work exists that covers framework composition problems as a primary topic of study, but several authors have identified some composition problems. For instance, [Pyarali 1996] suggests not to assume ownership of the event loop during framework design and to stress flexibility of the design. [Yellin 1994] proposes the use of software adapters as a means to overcome the problem of type-incompatible interfaces between components. This problem is similar to that of the composition of framework control. A software adapter uses protocols, which defines the allowed sequences of message exchanges between the components, and it compensates for differences between the component interfaces. The software adapter also allows message exchanges to be initiated from either of components. [Sparks 1996] identified the framework gap problem and suggests ways of dealing with it. Also, [Garlan 1995] discusses the notion of architectural mismatch, which, although not specific to object-oriented frameworks, may also affect framework composition. Finally, [Hölzle 1993] discusses the problems of using wrappers to adapt components for use in applications.

The contribution of this chapter, we believe, is twofold. It provides software engineers using object-oriented frameworks for application development with an understanding of the problems they may experience during framework-based application development, as well as an understanding of the primary causes and solution approaches. Second, it provides researchers in object-oriented software engineering with topics that need to be addressed by future research.

20.6 References

[Betlem 1995] Betlem, B.H.L., R.M. van Aggele, J. Bosch, and J.E. Rijnsdorp. *An Object-Oriented Framework for Process Operation.* Technical report, Department of Chemical Technology, University of Twente, 1995.

[Bosch 1998a] Bosch, J. Design patterns as language constructs. *Journal of Object-Oriented Programming* 11(2), May 1988:18–32.

[Bosch 1998b] Bosch, J., P. Molin, M. Mattsson, P.O. Bengtsson, and M. Fayad. Object-oriented frameworks—Problems and experiences. In *Object-Oriented Application Frameworks*, M. Fayad, D. Schmidt, and R. E. Johnson, editors. New York: John Wiley & Sons, 1998.

[Bosch 1998c] Bosch, J. Design of an object-oriented framework for measurement systems. *Object-Oriented Application Frameworks*, M. Fayad, D. Schmidt, and R.E. Johnson, editors. New York: John Wiley & Sons, 1998.

[Gamma 1995] Gamma, E., R. Helm, R. Johnson, and J.O. Vlissides. *Design Patterns: Elements of Reusable Object-Oriented Software*. Reading, MA: Addison-Wesley, 1995.

[Garlan 1995] Garlan, D., R. Allen, and J. Ockerbloom. Architectural mismatch or why it's hard to build systems out of existing parts. *Proceedings of the Seventeenth International Conference on Software Engineering*, pp.179–185, Seattle, WA, April 1995.

[Hölzle 1993] Hölzle, U. Integrating independently-developed components in object-oriented languages. *Proceedings of ECOOP 1993*, Kaiserslautern, Germany, July 1993, pp. 36–56, O. Nierstrasz, editor, LNCS 707. New York: Springer-Verlag, 1993.

[Johnson 1988] Johnson, R.E., and B. Foote. Designing reusable classes. *Journal of Object-Oriented Programming* 1(2), June 1988:22–35.

[Lundberg 1996a] Lundberg, C., and M. Mattsson. On using legacy software components with object-oriented frameworks. *Proceedings of Systemarkitekturer 1996*, Borås, Sweden, 1996.

[Lundberg 1996b] Lundberg, L. Multiprocessor performance evaluation of billing gateway systems for telecommunication applications. *Proceedings of the ICSA Conference on Parallel and Distributed Computing Systems*, pp. 225–237, September 1996.

[Mattsson 1996] Mattsson, M. Object-oriented frameworks—A survey of methodological issues. Licentiate thesis, Lund University, Department of Computer Science, 1996.

[Molin 1996] Molin, P., and L. Ohlsson. Points & Deviations—A pattern language for fire alarm systems. *Proceedings of the 3rd International Conference on Pattern Languages for Programming*, Paper 6.6, Monticello IL, September 1996.

[Moser 1996] Moser, S., and O. Nierstrasz. The effect of object-oriented frameworks on developer productivity. *IEEE Computer*, Theme Issue on Managing Object-Oriented Software Development, Mohamed E. Fayad and Marshall Cline, editors, 29(9)September 1996:45–51.

[Ossher 1996] Ossher, H., M. Kaplan, A. Katz, W. Harrison, and V. Kruskal. Specifying subject-oriented composition. *Theory and Practice of Objects Systems* 2(3):179–202.

[Pyarali 1996] Pyarali, P., T.H. Harrison, and D. Schmidt. Design and performance of an object-oriented framework for high-speed electronic medical imaging. *Computing Systems Journal*, USENIX, 9(4), November/December 1996:331–375.

[Sparks 1996] Sparks, S., K. Benner, and C. Faris. Managing object-oriented framework reuse. *IEEE Computer*, Theme Issue on Managing Object-Oriented Software Development, Mohamed E. Fayad and Marshall Cline, editors, 29(9), September 1996:53–61.

[Yellin 1994] Yellin, D.M., and R.E. Strom. Interfaces, protocols, and the semi-automatic construction of software adapters. *Proceedings of the Ninth Annual Conference on Object-Oriented Programming Systems, Languages, and Applications (OOPSLA 1994)*, pp. 176–190, Portland, OR, October 23–27, 1994.

20.7 Review Questions

1. Explain the difference between calling and called frameworks.

2. Which are the underlying causes for the composition of framework control problem? Propose framework design guidelines that will alleviate or avoid the framework control problem.

3. What is meant by framework cohesion? What problem is caused primarily by framework cohesion?

4. What composition problems can be solved or alleviated using wrapping techniques? Name the primary disadvantages using wrapping techniques?

5. What possible solutions do there exist for the framework gap problem?

6. Give an example of a framework composition problem not mentioned in the chapter. Identify the causes and possible solutions with advantages and disadvantages.

SIDEBAR 7
BUILT-IN TEST REUSE

Object-oriented application frameworks (OOAFs) have extended reusability of software from code modules to architectural and domain information. This sidebar further extends software reusability from code and frameworks to built-in tests (BITs) in OOAF development. Methods for embedding BITs at object and OOAF levels are addressed. Behaviors of objects and OOAFs with the BITs in the normal and test modes are analyzed. Reuse methods of BITs in OOAF development are demonstrated. The most interesting development discussed in this sidebar is that the BITs in OOAFs can be inherited and reused like those of code. Therefore, both quality and productivity in test-built-in OOAF development can be improved by the BIT approach. The BIT method is also useful in reengineering of existing application frameworks.

This sidebar investigates the BIT method and reuse approach of BITs in OOAF development. Conventional testing of software is generally application-specific and hardly reusable, especially for a purchased software module or package. Even within a software development organization, software and tests are developed by different teams and are described in separate documents. These make test reuse particularly difficult [Binder 1994; Freedman 1991; Voas-Miller 1995].

The general concept of the BIT was introduced in [Binder 1994; Wang 1997] and the idea for inheriting and reusing conventional tests in OO software was reported in [Harrold 1992; Wang 1997]. This sidebar develops a practical method to incorporate both BIT and test reuse techniques. Applications and impacts of the reusable BITs in OOAF development are explored systematically.

SB7.1 Built-In Tests

BITs are a new kind of software test that are explicitly described in the source code of software as member functions (methods). Testing of conventional OO software focuses on generation of tests for existing objects and frameworks; the testable OOAF design method draws attention to building testability into objects and frameworks, so that the succeeding testing processes can be simplified and reusable. The most interesting feature of the BIT techniques is that tests can be inherited and reused in the same way as those of code in conventional OOAFs.

SB7.1.1 Built-In Tests at Object Level

By embedding test declarations in the interface and test cases in the implementation of a conventional object structure, a prototype BIT object can be designed, as shown in Figure SB7.1. The BITs can be a standard component in a test-built-in object structure. The BITs have the same syntactical functions as those of the standard constructor and destructor in an object. Therefore, the BITs can be inherited and reused in the same way as functions within the object.

A BIT object has the same behaviors as conventional objects when the normal functions are called. But if the BITs are called like member functions in the test mode—for example, *TestableObject :: TestCase1*, *TestableObject :: TestCase2*, . . . , and *TestableObject :: TestCaseN*—the object will be automatically tested and corresponding results are reported.

```
Class class-name {
                // interface
                Data declaration;
                Constructor declaration;
                Destructor declaration;
                Function declarations'
                Test declarations;          // Built-in test declarations

                // implementation
                Constructor;
                Destructor;
                Functions;
                TestCases;                  // Built-in test cases as new-
                                            // member functions (methods)

        } TestableObject;
```

Figure SB7.1   An object with built-in tests.

SB7.1.2 Built-In Tests at OOAF Level

The same test-built-in method described in Section SB7.1 can be extended naturally to the OOAF level. An OOAF with a BIT subsystem and BIT classes is shown in Figure SB7.2, where modules 1.n, 3.k, and 2.m are the BIT class clusters for the fully testable, partially testable, and application-specific subsystems, respectively. Subsystem 4 is a global BIT subsystem for testing the entire framework by predesigned event-driven threads and scenarios. The BIT classes and subsystems may introduce additional coupling for testing between classes. By limiting the coupling to be active in the test mode only, the BIT approach will not increase the complexity of an OOAF.

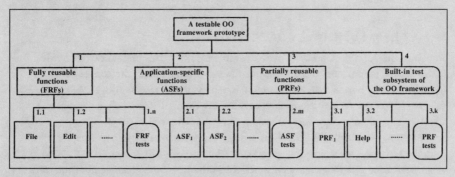

Figure SB7.2   A prototype of a test-built-in OOAF.

Continues

It is noteworthy, for the end users of a BIT framework, that the BITs for the Fully Reusable Functions (FRFs) and partially for the Partially Reusable Functions (PRFs) and the global BIT subsystem have already existed and are reusable. Therefore, new BITs, which an applied OOAF needs to concentrate on, are only in the Application Specific Functions (ASFs) and part of the PRFs and global subsystems. In this way, an ideal OOAF, which is testable, test–inheritable, and reusable at object, class cluster, and framework levels, is implemented. The test-built-in framework also possesses the feature of easy maintenance because it is self-contained for code, structure, as well as tests within a single source file. Thus, maintenance team and end users of the BIT OOAFs will no longer need to redesign and reanalyze the code, class structure, and tests during testing and maintenance.

SB7.2 Reuse of Built-in Tests

Corresponding to the deployment of BITs in an OOAF, reuse of the BITs can be implemented at object, class cluster, and OOAF levels for improving OOAF design quality and development productivity.

SB7.2.1 Reuse of BITs at Object Level

Functions of a BIT object can be categorized into normal and test modes. The former is applied for code reuse and the latter for test reuse. In the normal mode, a BIT object has the same functions as conventional objects. The static and dynamic behaviors are the same as those of the conventional ones. The application-specific member functions can be called by *ObjectName::FunctionName*; and the BITs are stand-by and without any effect on the runtime efficiency of the object.

In the test mode, the BITs in a test-built-in object can be activated by calling the test cases as member functions: *ObjectName::TestCaseI*. Each *TestCaseI* consists of a BIT driver and test cases for the specific object. Test results can be automatically reported by the BIT driver.

SB7.2.2 Reuse of BITs at OOAF Level

Similar to the BIT object, an OOAF with reusable BITs has the normal and test modes. In the normal mode, a BIT OOAF performs the same functions as the conventional frameworks. The normal FRF, PRF, and ASF functions in the test-built-in OOAF can be called by *ObjectName::FunctionName*; and the BIT class clusters and subsystem are stand-by and without any effect on the runtime efficiency of the OOAF.

A BIT OOAF has testing mechanisms ready at system, class cluster, and object levels from the top down, as shown in Figure SB7.2. The end users of an applied BIT OOAF can evoke and reuse all BITs as member functions in the test mode. Framework users can also build in additional BITs in the application-specific subsystem and classes of a framework.

SB7.3 Summary

This sidebar has developed a method to incorporate the reusable BITs into OOAFs. The reuse approaches to the BITs in OOAF development have been analyzed. The BIT method has extended the reusability of OOAFs from code to tests. With the BIT approach, highly testable and test-reusable OOAFs can be developed on the same platform of the conventional OO software. The BIT method is a natural advance and supplementary to conventional OO technology for OOAF development. A wide range of applications of the BIT method has been found in OOAF development, testing, maintenance, and reengineering.

SB7.4 References

[Binder 1994] Binder, R.V. Design for testability in object-oriented systems. *Communications of the ACM* 37(9), September 1994:87–101.

[Freedman 1991] Freedman, R.S. Testability of software components. *IEEE Transactions on Software Engineering* 17(6), June 1991:553–564.

[Harrold 1992] Harrold, M.J., J.D. McGregor, and K.J. Fitzpatrick. Incremental testing of object-oriented class structures. *Proceedings of the 14th International Conference on Software Engineering*, Melbourne, Australia, May 1992.

[Voas-Miller 1995] Voas, J.M., and K.M. Miller. Software testability: The new verification. *IEEE Software* 12(3), May 1995: 17–28.

[Wang 1997] Wang, Y., I. Court, M. Ross, G. Staples, and G. King. On testable object-oriented programming. *ACM Software Engineering Notes* 22(4), July 1997:84–90.

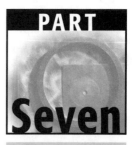

PART Seven

Framework Documentation

Accurate and comprehensible framework documentation is crucial to the success of medium- and large-scale application frameworks. The right framework documentation plays an essential role in understanding and extending the application frameworks to their highest potentials. Part Seven contains three chapters and a sidebar and covers several topics related to framework documentation.

Chapter 21 focuses on the documentation of frameworks rather than on framework development. This chapter shows that many approaches to documenting frameworks have been tried, and among these are several that have proven effective in reducing the learning curve. This chapter also presents guidelines for documenting a framework in order to facilitate the reuse of the framework by application developers.

Chapter 22 describes a set of guidelines for how to train new users unfamiliar with a framework's architecture, so they are able to understand the underlying concepts, and use and adapt the framework. This chapter describes an effective approach for training on the application frameworks.

Chapter 23 shows how to develop a representation of frameworks that satisfies the following goals: (1) a description of interobject behavior that supports both formal verification and understanding, (2) abstraction and generalization, (3) language independence, (4) an easy extraction of the descriptions from actual code, and, most important, (5) support for reuse-related tasks such as searchability, description of usage, incremental extension, and operationalization/realization. The main contributions of this work are a model that attempts to address these often conflicting goals and a set of tools to support the reuse of the life cycle of frameworks, from specification to integration.

Sidebar 8 describes the process of creating new solitaire games using the framework that consists of implementing a predictable collection of classes as subclasses of appropriate framework classes. Frameworks are amenable to documentation by examples. This sidebar shows how to design and document a Solitaire framework, from which many diverse games can be quickly built.

Documenting Frameworks

A framework is a collection of abstract classes that provides an infrastructure common to a family of applications. The design of the framework fixes certain roles and responsibilities among the classes, as well as standard protocols for their collaboration. The variability within the family of applications is factored into *hot spots* [Pree 1995], and the framework provides simple mechanisms to customize each hot spot (see Chapters 15 and 16). Customizing is typically done by subclassing an existing class of the framework and overriding a small number of methods. Sometimes, however, the framework insists that the customization preserve a protocol of collaboration between several subclasses, so customization requires the parallel development of these subclasses and certain of their methods.

A framework exists to support the development of a family of applications. Reuse involves an application developer, or team of application developers, customizing the framework to construct one concrete application. Typically, a framework is developed by expert designers who have a deep knowledge of the application domain and long experience of software design. On the other hand, a typical application developer who reuses the framework is less experienced and less knowledgeable about the domain. This is the situation desired by organizations, since they wish to leverage the expertise of their core software designers. However, a framework is not an easy thing to understand at first use: The design is very abstract, to factor out commonality; the design is incomplete, requiring additional subclasses to create an application; the design provides flexibility for several hot spots, not all of which are needed in the application at hand; and the collaborations and the resulting dependencies between classes can be indirect and obscure.

The large learning curve faced by the first-time user of a framework is a serious impediment to successfully reaping the benefits of reuse. How can an organization address this problem?

Clearly, the development process for frameworks is one area where answers might be found. One quality criterion for a framework is that it should be as simple as possible to understand and customize.

In this chapter, we wish to focus on another area—the documentation of frameworks—and not on framework development. Many approaches to documenting frameworks have been tried, and among these are several that have proven effective in reducing the learning curve. We discuss the previous work and present guidelines for documenting a framework in order to facilitate the reuse of the framework by application developers.

The reader is advised that our focus is on documentation that assists reuse of the framework by an *application developer*. First we discuss the various kinds of reusers of a framework and how their needs for documentation differ. Then we present the approaches that have been tried for documenting frameworks. We summarize these approaches as a set of guidelines on how to provide effective documentation for application developers.

We have relied on several books [Ackermann 1996; Cotter 1995; Lewis 1995; Pree 1995] and articles describing frameworks, as well as those papers dealing specifically with documentation of frameworks. Of particular note are the discussion in Chapter 3 of Pree's book [Pree 1995]; the synthesis of contracts, patterns, and motifs by [Lajoie-Keller 1995]; and our attempts to reuse the ET++ [Lewis 1995] and MET++ [Ackermann 1996] frameworks, where the documentation consists of examples, *man* pages for classes, and a cookbook accessible as hypertext.

21.1 Kinds of Framework Reuse

It is important to realize that the styles of documentation for frameworks discussed in the literature really address different audiences, or sometimes a combination of audiences. This web of conflicting aims needs to be unraveled, so here we look at the different kinds of people who reuse a framework.

Reuse by an application developer. An application developer wants to know how to customize the framework to produce the desired application. This is a very goal-directed activity, where the main priority is to know how to do something, rather than to understand why it is done that way. The application developer needs to know the relevant hot spots and how to customize them—that is, which classes to subclass, which methods to override, and whether combinations of classes and methods need to be specialized in unison to maintain a protocol of collaboration among the classes.

- The need is for prescriptive documentation.

- The application developer may not be a domain expert or an experienced software developer.

Reuse by a framework maintainer. A developer responsible for the maintenance and evolution of a framework must understand the design of the framework. The internal framework design and the design rationale must be known, as well as the application domain and the required flexibility of the framework.

There are many aspects of the framework that need to be grasped: the application domain; the overall architecture and its rationale; the reasoning behind the selection of the hot spots; which design pattern provides flexibility at each hot spot; and why each design pattern was selected. Furthermore, there are the usual requirements to understand the responsibility of each class, their interface contracts, and the shared responsibility (or collaboration) of classes. Information is needed at both a high level of abstraction and at a concrete level of detail.

- The documentation must be descriptive; it cannot be prescriptive, since the original designers can rarely predict how a framework might be extended through additional flexibility at hot spots, or additional hot spots.

- The developers are both domain experts and software experts.

Reuse by a developer of another framework. Framework developers seek ideas from existing frameworks, even if the framework is for another domain. Of particular interest are the design patterns that provide flexibility at hot spots. The developers require information primarily at a high level of abstraction, though the kinds of information needed are similar to those needed for framework maintainers.

The developers are expert software designers but not necessarily domain experts for the framework they are reusing.

Reuse by a verifier. Some application developers and framework developers may be concerned with the rigor of their system. They may have a need to verify certain properties of the system in order to satisfy stringent customer requirements. This requires formal methods of specification and verification.

Specification for reuse is generally more descriptive than prescriptive: The reuser is left to figure out the implications of the specification in terms of the desired customization. The main concerns are to clearly specify the obligations on a subclass and its methods that a developer may write, to specify any protocols that the developer can customize, and to specify the collaborations that must be supported by the developers' new subclasses.

Summary. The majority of framework reusers are application developers, and verifiers run a distant last.

What conclusions can we draw from this perspective of the many kinds of reusers? Different audiences require different information: different in the kind of information, different in the level of abstraction or detail, and different at the level of focus, either global or local. Our concern in this chapter is *documentation for application developers*.

21.2 Types of Documentation

A growing body of work has been done on documenting, specifying, and reasoning about frameworks. The frameworks under consideration are often chosen from toolkits for user interfaces and drawing programs. The emphasis is on documentation rather than specification, and, with the exception of the Contracts paper [Helm 1990], there is no concern for verification of correctness. Unfortunately, there is often little, or only anecdotal, evidence of the impact of the style of documentation on actual reuse of the framework.

In this section we discuss the various styles of documentation used.

Examples. The source code of *example applications* that have been constructed using the framework is often the first and only documentation provided to application developers. This documentation comes for free, since the example applications are created during the development process of the framework—a framework design may begin as an application that evolves into a framework, and then other applications are developed to confirm the reusability of the framework before the framework is rolled out for general use. Such examples, however, are complete applications often selected for their elaborate use of features and functionality. [Sparks 1996, page 60] found that, by themselves, these examples are too difficult for novice application developers, and that the introduction to framework hot spots needs to be more incremental, gradually going from the simplest forms of reuse to more advanced forms.

Documentation requires a graded set of training examples. Each should illustrate a single new hot spot, starting with the simplest and most common form of reuse for that hot spot, and eventually providing complete coverage. [Linn-Clancy 1992] offer valuable advice on designing and using examples. The ET++ framework comes with an extensive set of example applications. Most cookbooks (see the next section) revolve around a small number of simple example applications.

Recipes and cookbooks. A *recipe* describes how to perform a typical example of reuse during application development. The information is presented in informal natural language, perhaps with some pictures, and usually with sample source code. Although informal, a recipe often follows a structure, such as sections on purpose, steps of the recipe, cross-references to other recipes, and source code examples.

A *cookbook* is a collection of recipes. A guide to the contents of the recipes is generally provided, either as a table of contents or by the first recipe acting as an overview for the cookbook.

Patterns provide a *format* for each recipe and an *organization*. The organization follows a spiral approach, where recipes for the most frequent forms of reuse are presented early, and concepts and details are delayed as long as possible. The first recipe is an overview of the framework concepts and the other recipes. [Johnson 1992] introduced an informal *pattern language* that can be used for documenting a framework in a natural language. The documentation of a framework consists of a set of patterns, where each pattern describes a problem that occurs repeatedly in the problem domain of the framework and also describes how to solve that problem. Each pattern possesses the same format. The elements of a pattern are description of its purposes, explanation of how to use it, description of its design, and some examples.

[Lajoie-Keller 1995] introduce the term *motif* for Johnson's patterns in order to avoid confusion with design patterns. They use a template for a motif description that has a name and intent, a description of the reuse situation, the steps involved in customization, and cross-references to motifs, design patterns, and contracts. The design patterns provide information about the internal architecture, and the contracts provide more rigorous description of the collaborations relevant to the motif.

Active cookbooks [Schappert 1995] support the developer by combining the cookbook recipes with a visual design and development environment.

Cookbooks have been used with several frameworks, such as MVC (Model/View/Controller), MacApp [Lewis 1995], HotDraw [Johnson 1992], ET++, MET++, and Taligent's CommonPoint framework [Cotter 1995]. Many application developers have successfully learned a framework from a cookbook and the framework source code. [Johnson 1992, page 97] states that his cookbook is "the only documentation for a version of HotDraw that has been distributed since early 1992, and users say they are satisfied with it."

Contracts. A *contract* is a specification of obligations and collaborations. While the traditional *interface contract* [Meyer 1992] of a class provides a specification of the class interface and class invariants in isolation, an *interaction contract* [Helm 1990; Holland 1992] deals with the cooperative behavior of several participants that interact to achieve a joint goal. A contract specifies a set of communicating participants and their contractual obligations: the type constraints given by the signature of a method, the interface semantics of the method, and constraints on behavior that capture the behavioral dependencies between objects. A contract specifies preconditions on participants required to establish the contract, and the invariant to be maintained by these participants.

Originally, framework contracts were viewed as a mechanism to compose behavioral descriptions given by subcontracts. Contracts can be refined by either specializing the type of a participant, extending its actions, or deriving a new invariant that implies the old. Consequently, the refinement of a contract specifies a more specialized behavioral composition.

The role of contracts in Lajoie and Keller's [Lajoie-Keller 1995] documentation of ET++ is much more pragmatic than the original intent of [Helm 1990]. A contract supports a cookbook recipe with additional rigor in case a developer needs to consult a specification of collaborative behavior of classes.

Design patterns. A *design pattern* presents a solution to a design problem that might arise in a given context [Gamma 1995]. A design pattern provides an abstraction above the level of classes and objects. Design patterns capture design experience at the micro-architecture level, by specifying the relationship between classes and objects involved in a particular design problem. A design pattern is meta-knowledge about how to incorporate flexibility into a framework.

The description of a design pattern explains the problem and its context, the solution, and a discussion of the consequences of adopting the solution. The problem might be illustrated by a concrete example. The solution describes the objects and classes that participate in the design, and their responsibilities and collaborations. A collaboration diagram may be used to represent the same information. Examples of the solution being applied in concrete situations may be provided. The analysis of the benefits and trade-offs of applying the pattern is an important part of the design pattern description.

[Beck-Johnson 1994] illustrate the use of design patterns in developing the architecture for HotDraw, a framework for drawing editors. Design patterns are good at describing architectures, but a close look at the patterns used by Beck and Johnson for HotDraw show that they are of little use to an application developer, since they deal with the internal structure of the framework.

[Lajoie-Keller 1995] relegate design patterns to a support role for recipes. A design pattern illustrates relevant architectural issues, in case the application developer needs a deeper understanding of a recipe.

Framework overview. Setting the context of a framework is a first step in helping an application developer reuse a framework. The jargon of the domain can be defined and the scope of the framework delineated: just what is covered by the framework and what is not, as well as what is fixed and what is flexible in the framework. A simple application can be reviewed, and an overview of the documentation can be presented.

Such an overview is often the first recipe in a cookbook, though in the case of a framework developed in-house, a live presentation by the framework developers offers an opportunity to field questions from the application developers.

Reference manual. A *reference manual* for an object-oriented system consists of a description of each class, together with descriptions of global variables, constants, and types. Typically, a class description presents the purpose or responsibility of the class, the role of each data member, and some information about each method. A method description presents the functionality of the method, its pre- and postcondition, and an indication of which data members it affects or uses. The description of a class may be organized as a Unix *man* page.

For framework documentation, the descriptions can include additional material concerning the role of a class or method in providing flexibility for a hot spot, particularly whether a class is intended to be subclassed or a method to be overridden.

Traditional techniques for modules, such as the Larch family of interface languages, can be used for describing class interfaces and extended to include the obligations on subclasses as in Larch/C++. The Eiffel language supports design-by-contract [Meyer 1992] through the declaration of assertions, preconditions, and postconditions.

Reference manuals by themselves are not a very useful way to learn a framework.

Design notebooks. A *design notebook* collects information related to the design of hardware. The information will include background theory, analyses of situations, and a discussion of engineering trade-offs. While not specifically intended for frameworks, Schlumberger [Arango 1993] has adopted this approach with issue-driven design to capture the design rationale of software systems, as well as hardware systems and combined hardware/software systems. They call them *technology books* and *product books*. The information includes requirements, specifications, architecture, components, design, code, history, and the relationships among these various types of information. Background theory or domain information and analyses of trade-offs are crucial information. A hypermedia system supports access and navigation of the books.

Other. Recipes describe how to adapt the functionality of the framework. As such, they may refer to, or be documented in terms of, *use cases* or *scenarios* [Jacobson 1992] that describe the intended functionality. Similarly, a *time thread* [Buhr-Casselman 1992] for a scenario can depict when and where the scenario involves the framework and when and where it involves the customized code.

21.3 Guidelines

Let us summarize the past experience into guidelines on how to document a framework to assist application developers. The main point is to remember the audience: application developers, who may be somewhat inexperienced as developers or who may be in object-oriented technology and may be somewhat ignorant of the application domain. The next point is to accept that it requires effort to create the documentation: It will not be a free by-product of the development of the framework.

First, the application developers will need a context for the framework, so an *overview of the framework* should be prepared, both as a live presentation and as the first recipe in the cookbook.

Second, *a set of example applications* that have been specifically designed as documentation tools is required. The examples should be graded from simple through advanced, and should incrementally introduce one hot spot at a time. A hot spot that is very flexible may need several examples to illustrate its range of variability, from straightforward customization through elaborate customization with all the bells and whistles.

One of the simpler example applications should be used in the overview presentation. The cookbook recipes will use sample source code from the example applications.

Third, a *cookbook* of recipes should be written, and it should be organized along the lines of Johnson's pattern language. The recipes should use the example applications to make their discussion concrete. There will be cross-references between recipes, and between recipes and source code. There may also be cross-references to any other available documentation (such as a reference manual, contracts, or design patterns).

A good cookbook can use just pen and paper; however, a hypertext browser will help navigate cross-references [Meusel 1997].

That is all that is necessary for an application developer: overview, examples, and recipes.

21.4 Summary

It requires a large effort to understand any new software system, and application developers using a framework for the first time may find the framework particularly difficult to understand. If documentation is to alleviate this situation, it must be targeted to the needs of the application developer: How does the developer customize one or more hot spots of the framework in order to create an application?

These guidelines emphasize:

■ Prescriptive (how-to) information—since this is what application developers need

- Concrete examples—to counter the abstractness of a framework design
- Graded, or spiral, organization of information—to minimize the amount of information needed
- Focus on the task at hand

Access to more information, such as contracts, design patterns, or architecture, might also be available for consultation at rare times. Application developers should not need to regularly consult this information in order to do their job, but, on occasion, it might comfort the developer by dispelling the mystique of the inner workings of the framework or by clarifying some detail through additional rigor.

Simple, easy-to-use, effective documentation may be viewed as the acid test for the "goodness" of a framework design. It is hard to imagine that someone could possibly create good documentation when there is a poor design for the framework. So good design is a necessary, but not sufficient, prerequisite for good documentation.

Is this the final word? Certainly not, since we have focused on only one kind of framework reuser: application developers. They form the majority of reusers, but the concerns of framework developers and maintainers also need to be addressed. Reusable designs result from evolution and iteration, so both framework developers and maintainers deal with the evolution of a design. An important problem is, therefore, how to describe (and specify) the evolution of a design and the differences between two versions of the design of a framework.

21.5 References

[Ackermann 1996] Ackermann, P. *Developing Object-Oriented Multimedia Software*. Heidelberg, German: dpunkt Publishing, 1996.

[Arango 1993] Arango, G., E. Schoen, and R. Pettengill. A process for consolidating and reusing design knowledge. *Proceedings of 15th International Conference on Software Engineering*, pp. 231–242. Los Alamitos, CA: IEEE Computer Press, 1993..

[Beck-Johnson 1994] Beck, K., and R. Johnson. Patterns generate architectures. In *Object-Oriented Programming*, M. Tokoro and R. Pareschi, editors, LNCS 821, pp. 139–149. Berlin: Springer-Verlag, 1994.

[Buhr-Casselman 1992] Buhr, R.J.A., and R.S. Casselman. Architectures with pictures. *Proceedings of OOPSLA 1992*, pp. 466–483. New York: ACM/SIGPLAN, 1992.

[Cotter 1995] Cotter, S., and M. Potel. *Inside Taligent Technology*. Reading, MA: Addison-Wesley, 1995.

[Gamma 1995] Gamma, E., R. Helm, R. Johnson, and J. Vlissides. *Design Patterns: Elements of Reusable Object-Oriented Software*. Reading, MA: Addison-Wesley, 1995.

[Helm 1990] Helm, R., I.M. Holland, and D. Gangopadhyay. Contracts: Specifying behavioral compositions in object-oriented systems. *Proceedings of OOPSLA 1990*, pp. 169–180. New York: ACM/SIGPLAN, 1990.

[Holland 1992] Holland, I.M. Specifying reusable components with contracts. *ECOOP 1992*, pp. 287–308, LCNS 615. Berlin: Springer-Verlag, 1992.

[Jacobson 1992] Jacobson, I., M. Christorson, P. Jonsson, and G. Overgaard. *Object-Oriented Software Engineering: A Use Case Driven Approach*. Reading, MA: Addison-Wesley, 1992.

[Johnson 1992] Johnson, R. Documenting frameworks using patterns. *Proceedings of OOPSLA 1992*, pp. 63–76. New York: ACM/SIGPLAN, 1992.

[Lajoie-Keller 1995] Lajoie, R., and R.K. Keller. Design and reuse in object-oriented frameworks: Patterns, contracts, and motifs in concert. In *Object-Oriented Technology for Database and Software Systems*, pp. 295–312, V.S. Alagar and R. Missaoui, editors. Singapore: World Scientific Publishing, 1995.

[Lewis 1995] Lewis, T. *Object-Oriented Application Frameworks*. Greenwich, CT: Manning Publications, 1995.

[Linn-Clancy 1992] Linn, M.C., and M.J. Clancy. The case for case studies in programming problems. *Communications of the ACM* 35(3), March 1992:121–132.

[Meusel 1997] Meusel, M., K. Czarnecki, and W. Kopf. A model for structuring user documentation of object-oriented frameworks using patterns and hypertext. *Proceedings of ECOOP 1997*, pp. 496–510, LCNS 1241. Berlin: Springer-Verlag, 1997.

[Meyer 1992] Meyer, B. Applying design by contract. *IEEE Computer* 25(10), October 1992:40–51.

[Pree 1995] Pree, W. *Design Patterns for Object-Oriented Software Development*. Reading, MA: Addison-Wesley, 1995.

[Schappert 1995] Schappert, A., P. Sommerlad, and W. Pree. Automated framework development. *Symposium on Software Reusability* (SSR 1995), pp. 123–127, ACM Software Engineering Notes, August 1995.

[Sparks 1996] Sparks, S., K. Benner, and C. Faris. Managing object-oriented framework reuse. *IEEE Computer*, Theme Issue on Managing Object-Oriented Software Development, Mohamed E. Fayad and Marshall Cline, editors, 29(9), September 1996:52–61.

21.6 Review Questions

1. By categorizing the people using the application frameworks, describe the types of framework reuse.

2. Define with examples the following documentation approaches:

   - Examples
   - Cookbooks and recipes
   - Contracts
   - Design patterns
   - Framework overview

3. Describe how to document a framework to assist application developers.

CHAPTER

22

Empowering Framework Users

Often, people using a framework aren't the framework's authors. In addition, frameworks are almost always rather complex, and grasping the framework's underlying concepts is generally a major challenge and barrier to their effective application. Trainers need a set of guidelines for how to train new users unfamiliar with frameworks' architecture, so they are able to understand the underlying concepts and are able to use and adapt the framework. The goal of this chapter is to show how different techniques emphasize different aspects of the architectural design of a framework, and how these techniques can be combined into a general framework instruction method.

22.1 The Aim of Empowerment

The process of training and educating people in object-oriented design frameworks is a task with many unsolved problems. While many ideas are presented at OO conferences and published in journals each year about framework design, relatively little attention has been paid to effective techniques for educating people in using frameworks. It's hard for developers to understand an idea that somebody else had in his or her mind. Often, frameworks are bought from an outside vendor, in which case the knowledge simply isn't available. Current approaches to educating developers in frameworks fall into one of the following general categories:

Self-education. This is obviously the worst choice, because it's time consuming, and frequently the most important parts of the underlying architecture are very difficult to reverse-engineer. Documentation is rarely sufficient to support self-education, and as experience has shown, it's all too easy to get lost in details without the help of a global map of the architecture. The state of framework documentation is simply way below where it needs to be for self-instruction.

Mentoring. This approach is frequently implemented by hiring consultants from the framework vendor into the project and using them as mentors, or at the very least an expert to "look over their shoulders" and to understand what they're doing and why. This mentoring approach is the most frequently used of the three we list here. But this approach has a built-in conflict: Given consultants' rates, over time managers tend to expect the consultants to be directly productive, even when they were originally hired primarily to train the developers.

Training. This is the third option and the main focus of this chapter. The trainer, especially for frameworks, should also be an experienced consultant in the framework. Education in frameworks via training is not very common so far, perhaps largely because, to date, the framework industry has been more focused on consulting than on training.

The questions we address in the rest of this chapter are as follows:

- How can we effectively teach frameworks?
- Is there a general way in teaching frameworks, like there is in teaching programming languages, or is every framework so specific that there are few useful generalities in teaching?

All frameworks possess the following characteristics:

- Frameworks are built for reuse.
- Frameworks are *blackboxes*—parts of the framework can be used out of the box.
- Frameworks are *whiteboxes*—parts of the framework have to be adapted to meet the specific task.

We focus on these characteristics to help find a general method for empowering the use of frameworks. The framework instructor typically has a strong technical background and weak pedagogical training. Effectively training instructors, therefore, entails less focus on the subject matter and more focus on the pedagogical and didactical aspects of how things are best taught. There exist different practices in explaining object-oriented concepts to students; some work better than others and some may also work for different educators. Educating trainers has the additional challenge of evaluating the efficiency of the pedagogical approach. Such an evaluation may help us determine if the approach is transferable to other educators and also to another context.

22.2 Teaching Techniques

This chapter will show how different techniques emphasize different aspects of the inherent design of a framework. The key points are the applicability of these techniques as well as the combination of the methods for making the hidden concepts of the framework more understandable. In relation to the framework characteristics, the teaching techniques are also differentiated into blackbox and whitebox teaching.

The techniques introduced here have been widely used to teach both technical and business frameworks to engineers in industry.

22.2.1 Blackbox Teaching

Blackbox teaching is strongly related to requirements analysis in object-oriented analysis and design (OOAD). It helps to clarify the scope and boundary of a framework. At its heart, a blackbox is a high-level description of what the system will do, who will use it, and what it won't do. This phase of teaching takes into account which constraints are involved and which development approach will be considered. The blackbox approach initially focuses on *why* a specific architecture was developed. Educators often teach students solutions for problems the students never had. By first explaining the problem with an example derived from the student's world, they understand that there is a need for this framework. The students are more motivated and curious about how this specific problem is solved. This leads to a positive learning environment, which is the best learning motivation you can get: fascination.

When teaching frameworks, it is best when the instructor is conversant in the client company's domain. Often, it is easier for students to learn a business framework, because this framework solves a certain task problem from their business domain, so the students are familiar with the problem and alternative solutions. Teaching a system framework is correspondingly more challenging and time-consuming, since the students generally have less familiarity with the problem the framework purports to solve. When the students understand the purpose of the framework, it is much easier for them to understand the concepts. This is called *learning by judiciousness.* A key advantage of this teaching technique is that it obviates the need for time-consuming exercises and drills. To summarize, explain the problem first before explaining the solution.

The duration of blackbox teaching depends on the subject area in which the framework is used. If it is a business framework, it's quite short. The teaching duration gets longer when the framework is related to the development environment itself because the problem is probably too abstract and too far away from the students' everyday work.

22.2.2 Whitebox Teaching

The whitebox teaching approach regards the framework architecture from different perspectives. The difference lies in the concentration on either the design patterns that build the architecture or on the available hot spots. The goal of *pattern-oriented teaching* is to reduce the complexity of a framework by fragmenting it into smaller, easily understandable units—into design patterns, whereas the *hot-spot-driven teaching approach* shows the freedom and flexibility of the framework by discovering the dynamic and configurable points it provides.

Pattern-Oriented Teaching

Often, students' initial impression of a framework's architecture is that it's very complicated, but this impression quickly gives way to understanding when the architecture is broken down into smaller pieces. The smallest fragments should be known patterns, so the students are already familiar with or are able to learn about them in various books or articles. When the students aren't already familiar with the patterns, they can be effectively introduced to them via role playing, in which object roles are assigned to the students, so the students directly experience the operation of the patterns from the inside out. Every student plays one part of the concept for getting a deeper knowledge about the theory of the architecture. Students see how the different parts of the concepts work together and solve a bigger problem, and how several patterns are used to build the whole framework. To ensure that each student gets a broad understanding of the pattern, it is best if each student assumes different roles over several plays. This is a good approach to teach different message protocols, as well as structural patterns.

One technique simulates sending messages by throwing a softball between the students assuming various object roles. Games are typically most effective when closely simulating real systems. Conversely, actions that prolong a game and have already been clarified should be minimized.

The goals of such role playing are:

- All students should understand the overall functionality of the framework.

- Students should know all messages that are sent to keep the framework going.

- Students should recognize all methods that have to be implemented by specialized objects.

It is important to discuss and work these points out at the end of the role play, so everybody understands the framework as a whole, as well as understanding the patterns inside it. Students of role playing often find that when they get stuck doing coding exercises, it is helpful to give them a hint out of the role play, like: "Do you remember what your reaction was after catching the ball?" It is a good idea to exchange the roles the students are playing, so everybody gets a feeling for the framework. With changing roles, all the students have a chance to participate. If the group is bigger, they should split up into smaller groups, but it is good to put more people than there are roles in one group; the students not role playing should instead monitor that all messages are sent and implemented correctly.

The role play has a significant beneficial side effect: By using this kind of *active learning*, because they are really involved, the students don't get as bored, nor do they tire as quickly.

Hot-Spot-Driven Teaching

Following [Pree 1996], *hot spots* are points of predefined refinement where a framework can be adapted. By focusing on these flexible points, the students learn how to configure the framework in such a way that it fulfills a specific task. In hot-spot-driven teaching, students discover the reaction of the framework when changing the hot spots by completing a prepared exercise on the machine. This promotes *learning through reflection*, in which the task is presented by the instructor, and the students' job is to figure out the solution by drawing on their own experience [Anderson 1992]. Beyond examining the framework, students should be given the task of observing and reporting any differences in what they have learned compared with pattern-oriented teaching. It is important that they come to the same conclusion that they did during the earlier phase. To evaluate this, they have to ask themselves the following questions:

- What parts of the framework can be used out of the box?
- Which messages have to be sent to drive the framework's operation?
- Which methods have to be implemented to make the framework completely operational?

If there are differences, the educator is required to clear up misunderstandings. The hot-spot-driven teaching could be implemented incrementally, which means that this session progresses from simpler exercises to more complicated ones. Whereas in the first round the students can more or less watch the framework in operation, in the next round the students have to customize the framework for themselves in order to bring it to life.

22.3 Combining the Teaching Techniques

The combination of the different teaching techniques allows the training process to progressively dive into the framework. The basic idea of this "progressively diving into" is the *incremental teaching approach,* which explains a complex framework by using smaller and simpler frameworks and patterns to imprint the basic architecture. This approach leads one from one or more small frameworks to several medium frameworks to the large target framework. With each part they learn, the students become progressively more familiar with the context of the framework and the possibilities the framework offers them. The students should recognize the overall picture and comprehend how the objects are related and which messages are sent. It is important to point out what could be used out of the box and what has to be customized. In the first increment it is not necessary that the students understand it all in depth, because the architecture will be repeated several times in various ways.

As noted by Adele Goldberg [Goldberg-Rubin 1995], frameworks being taught are getting more and more complicated over time, requiring that frameworks be incrementally taught. It is even better if there are several small and medium-size frameworks from which to teach, so the students are getting a good understanding about layering of frameworks. The students can grasp the complex structure, because the difficult architecture of the target framework is introduced in different ways by repetition through smaller and simpler frameworks. This way the knowledge is strengthened by repetition.

The dotted arrow in Figure 22.1 shows how the combination of the techniques could lead to the next increment, for supporting incremental teaching. It is important that the instructor lead the discussion in the hot-spot phase toward the next requirements for the next, more complex layer of the problem. Students often discover the architecture themselves when working with the framework. It is essential that the educator recognize these requirements and use them in the next round in the blackbox teaching phase.

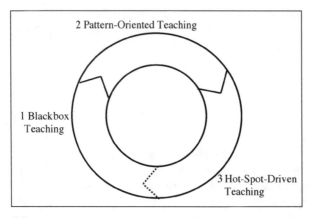

Figure 22.1   Pattern-oriented teaching.

22.3.1 Sample Setting

The sample setting we will use is from the Smalltalk world. It considers the implementation of AspectAdaptors in VisualWorks as an example framework. To illustrate how the incremental approach may be implemented, we will use various user interface frameworks implemented in VisualWorks. The first and smallest framework used is Model/View/Controller (MVC), which leads to the next two medium-size frameworks, the concept of ValueModels and AspectAdaptors, and concludes with the final target framework, which is the architecture of AspectAdaptors using subjectChannels.

Blackbox Teaching

A sample problem statement of the example framework could be outlined in the following manner: The students should imagine that they want to develop a user interface application. They need to define some business objects, which have to be presented in various user interfaces for different users—for example, in a bar chart, a pie, and a table. Every kind of view allows interaction, such as filling out the table, growing a bar with the mouse, and so on. Every change in the view should change the model, and every change of the model should be reflected in every view. As a consequence, there is a need for a mechanism responsible for this behavior.

Beginning with the second increment, the problem statement should be formulated by the students. For example, when discussing how AspectAdaptors work, it often happens that one of the students finds out that this framework solves the problem only when a part of the subject is changing, but doesn't help when the subject itself is changed. A reflection like this supports the instructor in implementing the increment, because the next, more complex framework attacks exactly this case. It is important that the educator take care that all the attendees understand these requirements; otherwise, they do not understand the scope of the blackbox in the next increment. This is also a good point at which to evaluate the learning process of the students.

Whitebox Teaching

Taking the preceding example and staying in the first increment of the course, the classes that build the Model/View/Controller framework, as well as the dependency mechanism, should be explained. All messages critical to the framework's functioning are outlined. In our running example, this would be any variant of *self changed*. The methods that must be implemented are also defined at this point—here, any variant of *update:*. In other words, only those parts that need to be explained in this phase are clarified at this point,

---

SUMMARY OF THE STATIC LAYOUT OF THE SAMPLE FRAMEWORK

For a better understanding of the sample setting, a description of the target framework, which is related to [ParcPlace 1996], follows.

The PersonInterface shows an example implementation of the framework. The details of a person are displayed in the PersonInterface. The firstNameWidget shows the first name of the current person. For displaying the first name, the person object has to provide a means for getting (firstName) and setting (firstName:) its first name. The model of the widget is an AspectAdaptor, who then remembers the above accessing messages. Figure 22.2 shows the static layout of sample framework.

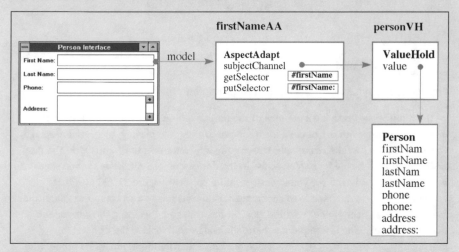

Figure 22.2   Static layout of sample framework.

The AspectAdaptor doesn't directly know the person object. This part has to be flexible, because the person object can change. The interface should provide the ability to display different persons and should not be fixed to one special person. Therefore, the AspectAdaptor has to figure out the receiver of the messages firstName and firstName: This is the reason that the AspectAdaptor uses the subjectChannel, which is a ValueHolder that knows the currently displayed person. At this point, the remaining objects of the framework are introduced: the widget that is told which model to use, the AspectAdaptor who knows about what to ask and whom to ask, the ValueHolder who knows whom to ask, and the domain object, which is the Person.

DYNAMIC INTERACTIONS IN THE SAMPLE FRAMEWORK

A key requirement for the MVC and related frameworks is that interfaces should present the current state of the current subject. This implies that any property change of the current subject or any change of the subject itself must update the interface.

The messages that are sent when a change occurs are shown in Figure 22.3.

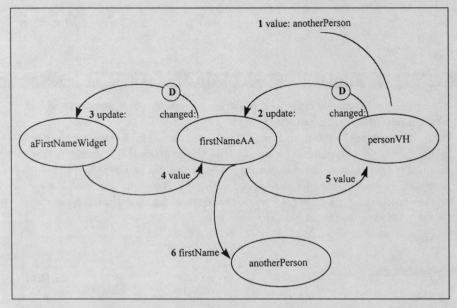

Figure 22.3   Dynamic interactions in the sample framework.

The numbers indicate the sequence of the message flow. Only the initial and final messages interact with the outside environment. During role playing, the initial message, value: (1), has to be called manually, starting the interactions in the framework. The final firstName (6) call has to be implemented in the domain object. All the other messages can be used out of the box, if the framework is set up correctly. Figure 22.3 shows that whenever the current person is to be changed, value: (1) has to be sent to the ValueHolder (personVH). This ValueHolder tells the world it has changed, triggering the dependency mechanism. Following the sequence chain, the widget will receive the update: (3) message, where the widget tries to display a new value. Therefore, it asks its model (the AspectAdaptor) for the value (4). As has been shown in the preceding static structure diagram, the AspectAdaptor (firstNameAA) knows whom and what to ask. So it is asking the personVH for the actual person (value (5)) and, later on, this current person for its firstName (6). The answer to this request is the result in which the widget was interested.

simplifying the discussion. In summary, *changed* is used out of the box, whereas *update:* has to be implemented. In the next round, the manner in which ValueHolders work will be explained along with information regarding what can be directly used and what has to be configured. These points are indicated when explaining AspectAdaptors in the next increment, then again when describing AspectAdaptors using subjectChannels.

Pattern-Oriented Teaching

Using role playing to teach MVC's Observer pattern, one student acts as the model, another plays the view, and a third plays the controller. Messages go back and forth by throwing a softball between the students.

It is important that the students thoroughly learn the role-playing rules up front, especially that the rules remain constant during the incremental procedure in the class. The basic rule is that the messages are passed by throwing the softball to the receiver object. The ball has to go back the same way, because every message returns a result. This means these rules for playing this example are more or less the same as for the AspectAdaptor example. When playing the AspectAdaptors using subjectChannels, the architecture can be simplified by using one student as the widget, one as the Aspect-Adaptor, and one as the model. But the model sits *on* a subjectChannel—here, on a chair—which is shown in the Figure 22.4.

The model is exchanged by placing a different student on the chair. Playing the framework in this way, the instructor starts the framework by tossing the ball to the first player. It is easier, especially in the beginning, to change just the firstName of the person sitting on the chair. So this person signifies that something has been changed by throwing the softball and saying *changed/update:* to the person playing the firstNameAA. This student passes the update: message on to the person playing the firstNameWidget. The widget has the easiest job: When receiving the update, it just returns the ball to the model by requesting the actual value. The person playing the firstNameAA always asks the one sitting on the chair for his or her firstName. It is important that the students understand that the framework still works, even if the subject is replaced by a different kind of object—as long as the new object implements the same protocol as the replaced object—here, as long as it understands firstName and firstName:.

Hot-Spot-Driven Teaching

It is a good idea to let the students take a look at a running framework by using the debugger and to allow them to experience what happens when changing parts of the framework, as well as understanding how messages flow in actual applications.

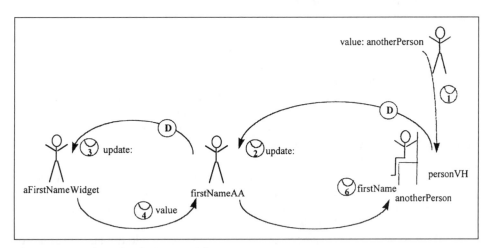

Figure 22.4 The role-playing model.

The next round in the exercise would be that the students have to customize the framework for themselves. The complexity of this depends on the framework. If possible, use an example problem from their domain, so they have a chance to reuse their solutions later on in the project. It is a good idea to use a more difficult example that gives the students the opportunity to develop a small application for themselves.

Incremental Framework Teaching

This is a good point for the class to reflect on what the students have learned. This helps cement in the students' minds where the boundaries of the framework are and leads naturally to identifying the requirements for the next, more complex framework. When first introduced to a new framework, especially when it is used to build a small initial application, students often express that the framework seems too complicated and amounts to overkill for developing small applications, or that a lot of code has to be reproduced for every application. A central focus of the training must therefore be for students to evolve their appreciation of the framework. By thoroughly understanding the problem space that the framework addresses, and especially how it would have to be implemented without the framework, most students quickly grasp why the framework's architecture is the way it is, and come to appreciate that it will, in fact, help students more quickly solve their work problems. So they are obtaining an understanding of how they can profit by using the framework.

22.3.2 Training Issues

Some training issues have to be considered when using this teaching approach. These issues are related to [Fayad-Cline 1996]:

- Teach the right thing.
- Teach the thing right.
- Support the next thing.

The first point, *teach the right thing*, means we should teach the thing the customer is able and willing to understand. Or in other words, we have to meet the students where they are. This is best accomplished by listening attentively to the students. Listening includes attending to nonverbal signs. It is important that the students are curious about the topic. This curiosity could best be established during blackbox teaching.

The second point, *teach the thing right*, is mainly based on communication. It is important to keep in mind the point first introduced in [Watzlawick 1968], that communication always takes place between a sender and a receiver, and that the effectiveness of a communication isn't measured by what the sender tells but what the receiver understands. If the communication does not work, the best approach won't help either party: In teaching, communication is everything! And different people pick up things differently, using different sensory modalities. Some learn most effectively by watching (visuals), some by listening (auditories), and some through action (kinesthetics). The role playing in pattern-oriented teaching is especially helpful for students of the third category to build their understanding.

The third point, *support the next thing*, means each topic should dovetail into and/or motivate the succeeding one. This way, the students are able to grasp the whole picture about the course contents as a seamless flow. This incremental characteristic is one of the key aspects of our approach. As previously explained, the discussion of the first increment (presenting the initial framework or pattern) should end in the problem statement of the next increment, creating an unbroken chain of motivation and understanding of the parts out of which the next level is constructed.

22.4 Summary

An approach for teaching frameworks has been presented that is intended to foster successful learning and not overwhelm the students with the complexity. The blackbox teaching approach indicates the *frame*, whereas the whitebox teaching approach illustrates how it *works*.

The students participate by acting as the objects involved in the framework and by examining what is going on in the framework while simulating it. This way, educators and students will have a much easier time teaching and learning frameworks. Early experience with this pedagogical approach suggests that it provides some powerful tools for both experienced and beginning framework instructors that will help them to be more successful (see the sidebar titled *A Sample Pedagogical Pattern*).

A SAMPLE PEDAGOGICAL PATTERN

Tell me and I'll forget;
show me and I may remember;
involve me and I'll understand.
—Chinese Proverb

Incremental Role Play

This pattern belongs to the category of pedagogical patterns. These reusable pedagogical design patterns provide an ability to communicate proven solutions to common problems in teaching.

Thumbnail

The complexity of object-oriented architectures is hard to understand with abstract explanations; therefore ask the students to behave as objects of the design and develop the design in several iterations.

Intent

How do you, as an instructor, trainer, or teacher, teach complex object-oriented architecture without losing the attention of your students (keep in mind that *students* include all of the people attending the course—both academics and within the industry)?

Continues

A SAMPLE PEDAGOGICAL PATTERN *(Continued)*

Indications

- The students already have an understanding of the object-oriented basics, such as sending and receiving messages.

- The students have to get familiar with a fairly complex architecture, like a framework.

Counter-indications

- You don't feel comfortable in performing role plays with this particular audience, possibly because the audience is made up of members of the board of directors.

- The audience size is smaller than 3 students.

- The audience size is larger than 20 people. The pattern is usable in a larger environment, but the audience will have to be divided into smaller groups.

- The course is set up in a distance learning environment.

Forces

- It's much easier for the students to understand a complex architecture when they understand the purpose of the concept. However, we often teach solutions for problems students have never experienced.

- Students understand complex concepts easier if you simplify them, but you cannot simplify some architectures without losing the idea.

- You'd like to provide a positive learning environment, but the difficulties in understanding complex concepts may frustrate students.

- Students understand new material better if they're involved because telling and showing is not the same as involving.

- Students often only believe in a technology when they have used it themselves, but it is time consuming to lead them through a whole project.

- Students can memorize new stuff better, if you repeat it several times, but it takes time to say the same things over and over again.

Solution

Invite your students to behave as the objects in a role play. Start with a simplified version of the concept and add further aspects as problems come up. See Figure 22.5.

The underlying concept of the pattern is its incremental structure. The architectures are getting more and more complicated over time. The pattern starts introducing a simple architecture, explains a more complex architecture in the next increment and concludes with teaching a large, really complicated architecture. The problems discovered in the Discussion Phase give raise to the next iteration. It helps if you find several small and medium-sized frameworks from which to teach, so the students are getting a good understanding about layering of architectures.

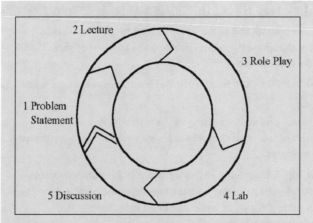

Figure 22.5 Students as objects in a role play.

Structure

Problem statement: Make students attentive to the problem the architecture solves.

Lecture: Explain the architecture, or rather the concept, so students get an understanding of how the problem is solved.

Role play: Every student plays one part of the concept to get a deeper understanding of the theory of the architecture. Students see how the different parts of the concepts all work together to solve a bigger problem. You can implement this part by using the Role Playing Pattern and/or the Physical Analogy Pattern (see the *Related Patterns* section for more information).

Lab: Students complete an exercise prepared by the instructor in order to figure out how the concept works. The instructions for the lab should be very detailed first with less detailed explanations while it's going on. The first step in the lab is more like an exercise in which the students fill in the gaps. In the next step it is more like a laboratory because the students explore the system themselves.

Discussion: This should be a student-centric discussion where students revisit what they learned during the lab phase. Lead the discussion toward the next problem (often the students come up with the problem themselves). In the discussion phase it's your responsibility to make this pattern really incremental.

Sample Setting

Problem statement: Show a problem out of the students' world. If you don't have any in mind just take one in which the problem idea is easily grasped. Imagine you want to develop a UI application, where you have to define some business objects and you want to view these business objects in different UIs for different users, such as a bar chart, a pie, and a table. You can interact with every kind of view, like filling in the

Continues

A SAMPLE PEDAGOGICAL PATTERN *(Continued)*

table, enlarging a bar with the mouse, and so on. Every change in the view should change the model, and every change of the model should be seen in every view. Therefore, we need something like a dependency mechanism.

Lecture: Explain which classes build the MVC framework and how the dependency mechanism works.

Role play: Here you'll need at least one student acting as the model, one playing the view, and one playing the part of the controller. Messages go back and forth by throwing a softball between the students.

Lab: Present the students first with a completed source example and let them examine the code with the debugger. Now they can see how the messages are sent and implemented in the real world. A more difficult example would be to let the students develop a small application for themselves.

Discussion: Staying with the MVC example, the students will probably state that MVC seems to be a rather complicated thing for developing just a small application, or students may comment that a lot of code has to be reproduced for every application. At this point, we you should explore the concept of ValueModels, which will start the next iteration of performing the pattern.

Discussion

This pattern shows students why somebody has introduced a particular software concept. Understanding the *purpose* of the concept motivates the students to know more about how this specific problem is solved. This leads to a positive learning environment, which is the best learning motivation you can get: *enthusiasm.*

The discussion phase should lead *incrementally* into the next problem statement, so it's easy to introduce the next, more complex concept. For the students it's easier to grasp the complex structure, not only because the simpler framework is often repeated by the more complex one. This way the knowledge is strengthened by repetition.

The students will obtain a better understanding of complex software concepts by giving them the chance to behave as the objects being involved in a role play. Teaching is certainly only successful if the new way of thinking is trained and exercised by *active learning.*

Experiences

You have to control the discussion so it leads to the next problem statement. For instance, in this example out of the Smalltalk world, exactly from the user interface framework, go from MVC—ValueModel, AspectAdaptor, to AspectAdaptor with subjectChannels.

You'll find it is a good practice to clarify the problem domain so that every student can identify the problem from his or her own experience. Do not try to discuss different solutions, since the goal is to introduce a specific concept like MVC and not wander into discussions of what else could have been developed. On the other hand, students will get frustrated very quickly if they see that their solution is not of much interest.

The lecture or theory itself should be as short as possible so you can start the role play as soon as possible.

Here are some suggestions for a successful role play:

- Ensure that students change roles at every increment.

- Play the game as close to reality as possible. Omit material which has already been clarified and therefore just prolongs the play. For example, explaining method lookup is not necessary. Don't be afraid of playing the game. My experience is that—especially in the industry—students are happy if they get a less abstract explanation, even in a really complex environment, like a bank.

- Make sure the lab develops step by step from more basic things in the concept to more complex ones.

Limitations

Keep in mind that there may be people in the audience with physical limitations that prevent their participation in an active role play as described in the sample setting. Instructors can make necessary changes to the sample setting in order to include all participants and their specific needs.

Resources Needed

Depending on audience size and setting, you'll need several softballs and a white board.

Example Instances of This Pattern

I have used this pattern to teach various aspects of Visual Works, such as MVC, ValueModels, AspectsAdaptors, and SubjectChannels. To teach the SubjectChannels I found it useful to simplify the architecture and use one student as the widget, one as the AspectAdaptor, and one as the model. But the model sits on a subjectChannel, on a chair. In this way I can change the model by placing a different student on the chair.

I have also trained other trainers to use the pattern and some have incorporated it into their repertoire. Joachim Schrader from BERATA GmbH, for instance, has used this pattern in the same context (that is, the user interface architecture in VisualWorks Smalltalk) as described here.

Richard Steiger from Ensemble Soft teaches the Java Foundation Classes with this pattern. He teaches how to build complex GUI applications with the help of a framework, called User Interaction Framework (UIF). He explains the architecture of the application by incrementally adding more and more features, picking a problem to solve at each stage.

Paul Dyson from Cumulus Systems Ltd. has used this pattern to teach the final-year Software Engineering course in the Electronic Systems Engineering degree at the University of Essex. He specifically used role play to describe the interactions of an MVC framework implemented in C++. What made it iterative was that they did one role-playing session before the students started on the project and one after it where they would demonstrate the interactions of their specific instantiation of the framework.

Continues

A SAMPLE PEDAGOGICAL PATTERN *(Continued)*

Related Patterns

Physical Analogy Pattern. This pattern, from Phil McLaughlin, is the basis of *Incremental Role Play*. The focus of this pattern is the fact that students new to object technology are frequently *told* about modeling objects in the real world. Physical analogy helps to demonstrate key concepts and presents a metaphor to students as a mental cross-reference for the topic. The students themselves form the analogies to the objects, so the experience is even more memorable. Unlike *Incremental Role Play*, *Physical Analogy* is not restricted to a certain audience size.

Concrete to Abstraction Pattern. This pattern, submitted by Ian Chai, may help you to find a path for your increments. This pattern has the focus on keeping students' interest when introducing them to their first patterns (or other abstractions). It starts with an example to which the students can relate. After the students are taken through the example, you can point out the aspects which can be applied in other instances, like general principles in the pattern, and then finally end up with describing the general pattern itself.

Three Bears Pattern. This pattern, from Kent Beck, can be combined with the Concrete to Abstraction Pattern to help students accept failure as a natural part of the design process. This pattern removes the fear of failure as a barrier to learning by making failure part of the goal.

Role Playing Pattern. This pattern, submitted by David Bellin, introduces a key technique used in CRC Card Analysis, after a team brainstorms and creates a list of candidate classes. This pattern is used in the *Incremental Role Play* in a different context.

References

The related patterns can be found at: *http://www-lifia.info.unlp.edu.ar/ppp/*.

22.5 References

[Anderson 1992] Anderson, Bruce. Task and reflection in learning to learn. In *Empowerment through Experiential Learning*. London: Kogan Page, 1992.

[Fayad-Cline 1996] Fayad, Mohamed, and Marshall P. Cline. Aspects of software adaptability. *Communications of the ACM* 39(10), October 1996.

[Goldberg-Rubin 1995] Goldberg, Adele, and Kenny Rubin. *Succeeding with Objects*. Reading, MA: Addison-Wesley, 1995.

[ParcPlace 1996] ParcPlace Systems. *Introduction to Smalltalk with VisualWorks*, course material, 1996.

[Pree 1996] Pree, Wolfgang. *Framework Patterns*. New York: SIGS Books, 1996.

[Watzlawick 1968] Watzlawick, Paul, et al. *Pragmatics of Human Communication: A study of Interactional Patterns, Pathologies, and Paradoxes*. London: Faber, 1968.

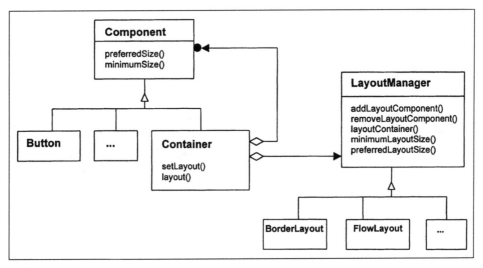

Figure 22.6   Part of the Java Abstract Window Toolkit (AWT).

22.6 Review Questions

1. What are the general characteristics of all frameworks?
2. What is the goal of blackbox teaching?
3. How could you support active learning?
4. What are hot spots?
5. In which teaching/learning approach do you focus on hot spots?
6. How do you implement the increment in the incremental teaching approach?

22.7 Problem Set

1. Discover the design patterns used in MVC.
2. Discover the hot spots in MVC.
3. Explain the *frame* (the scope and boundary) of CORBA.
4. Discover the design patterns of the following part of the Java Abstract Window Toolkit (AWT) as shown in Figure 22.6. Use the appropriate books to find out more about it.

Describing and Using Frameworks

Reusability is often cited as the major contribution of object orientation to the engineering of software. Since the late 1980s, it has become clear that classes as units of reuse are too small to realize the projected or promised benefits [Deutsch 1989]. This is due to two related factors. First, most classes tend to be rather small in size, and second, classes seldom perform useful behavior by themselves; they often *contribute* to a given function by interacting with other objects [Mili 1990]. This led researchers and practitioners alike to look into principles for designing and reusing collections of reusable interacting classes that, together, perform some useful functions (see, for example, [Deutsch 1989; Johnson-Foote 1988]). We refer to such collections of objects as *object frameworks*. Object frameworks can be of two kinds: *domain-specific frameworks*, which consist of a set of classes from a specific application (business) domain, and *design frameworks*, which consist of classes that implement a given *mechanism* or a *computer-related task*. We are interested in both kinds of frameworks, and in this chapter, we propose a representation and a search model that should accommodate both, and describe a preliminary Smalltalk prototype.

Developing and reusing object frameworks poses many challenges. From a development point of view, there are two competing goals. Before we invest in implementing a framework, we have to make sure that the design or domain it embodies is general enough that it will often be useful. At the same time, it must be precise enough to be programmable and to have a reasonable performance. This relies on a number of parameterization techniques that enable us to develop as much of a framework's generic functionality as possible, leaving only application- or usage-specific behavior to be developed. Such techniques include general object-oriented abstraction techniques such as abstract classes, which play the role of placeholders to be replaced by actual application classes or generic classes, which may be parameterized by such classes, or framework-specific techniques such as interface bridges (for example, the so-called pluggable adapters in Smalltalk's Model/View/Controller framework), or the broadcast-based management of interobject communication (for example, Smalltalk's dependents mechanism). From a reuse viewpoint, there are two challenges. First, we have to find a way of documenting frameworks succinctly, unambiguously, understandably, and in a way that can be matched against developers' needs and that can allow them to use it. These are conflicting needs and neither formal specifications (see, for example, [Hall-Weedon 1993; Helm 1990]) nor the so-called pattern languages (see, for example, [Gabriel 1994; Johnson 1994]) address all of them. Second, there is the problem of searching for relevant frameworks in the first place and, once one is found, searching for classes that support a given interface or ascertaining that a given class does. In this chapter, we propose a model for describing object frameworks that attempts to address these issues.

In *Section 23.1*, we provide a more thorough discussion of the challenges described earlier in the form of a set of requirements that our model must satisfy. In *Section 23.2*, we describe the model through a simple example involving two C++ frameworks dealing with event-based simulation systems and explore some framework relationships. *Section 23.3* describes the principles behind a preliminary Smalltalk implementation that integrates support for frameworks within a reusable components repository toolset. In particular, we describe a typical framework usage scenario, starting with need formulation through code integration. *Section 23.4* deals with the first two steps of such a scenario: search and realization. A framework packaging/ delivery mechanism is described in *Section 23.5*. We discuss related work in *Section 23.6*, and conclude in *Section 23.7*.

23.1 Requirements

In this section, we discuss the considerations that motivated us to choose the model described in *Section 23.2*. This concerns both the set of descriptive elements that our model must support, as well as the form that these elements must take.

23.1.1 Backward Applicability

Our purpose is as much to represent existing object frameworks in a way that makes them more useful and more usable as it is to propose a methodology for *building* an object framework, with a focus on detailed design and packaging issues. This means that we will be seeking a trade-off between a set of constructs that can be easily mapped to existing frameworks, despite their inadequate documentation or less than perfect packaging (from an abstraction point of view) and a set of constructs that represent all that we would ever want to know about an object framework and that rely on the use of novel abstraction techniques. We will see examples of these trade-offs throughout this section and the next.

23.1.2 Representing Interobject Behavior

A framework involves the collaboration of several objects. Understanding what a framework does and how it does it requires a description of the interactions between objects, or *interobject behavior*. Representing interobject behavior poses a number of challenges, including (1) choosing between representing the computational versus functional properties of the system and (2) choosing a trade-off between flexibility and abstraction, on the one hand, and ease of verification, on the other. We discuss the two sets of issues in the following paragraphs.

Computational versus functional aspects. The behavior of an object or system of objects may be described in terms of *computations* or in terms of *functions*.[1] The computational description tends to describe the behavior in terms of abstract, application-independent computational devices or application-independent transformations of data, regardless of their semantics. By contrast, a functional description describes interobject behavior in terms of application-meaningful and purposeful behavior. Computational (abstract) descriptions are useful for verification and validation purposes, and to ascertain the conformance of a given class or implementation to a desired behavior, provided that both are described computationally. However, they do not promote understandability and do not convey, in an application-meaningful way, the *purpose* of the behavior [Mili 1995] or relate it to developers and reusers' needs.

The distinction between functional and computational aspects becomes fuzzier with design patterns, and reusable designs in general, which are not distinguishable by what they do, but rather by optimizing different *design quality criteria.*

Flexibility versus ease of verification. One of the purposes of behavioral descriptions is to compare requirements on framework participants to actual specifications of candidate components. When choosing a behavior representation language, we have to make sure that it is abstract enough to support flexible matching between requirements and specifications that is independent of inessential implementation details. However, we also have to consider how to derive such specifications for existing frameworks or for frameworks yet to be designed. Practically, it would be helpful to have a simple relationship between such specifications and the actual code, so that the specifications can be extracted, in part or in full, from the source code.

In existing frameworks, interobject behavior is typically embodied in explicit cross-references (calls) between object methods. Using such cross-references as specification for interobject behavior has two inherent problems. First, it dictates one mode of interactions between methods, as opposed to another. For example, two processes or objects can communicate either through interruptions or through explicit calls; our choice for showing interobject linkage should be, to the extent that that is possible, mechanism-independent. Second, if we use explicit cross-references, we impose a nonessential *lexical coupling* between methods and objects, which makes the interchange of candidate

---

[1]The philosophy of science makes one such distinction between *behavior* (which we call computation) and *function*. Behavior is a simple input/output relationship, while function is behavior within the context of an englobing behavior [Darden-Rada 1988].

objects very difficult. This is as much a problem with the detailed design and implementation of the framework as it is a problem with describing it.

23.1.3 Describing Usage

Describing the usage for a framework, or any other reusable component, involves two issues. First, there is the issue of appropriateness of the framework to a given need or situation. Second, there is the issue of describing *how to use* the framework. The issue of appropriateness or *opportunity* is related to the description of interobject behavior mentioned earlier. With application-specific frameworks, both the framework and developers' needs will be expressed in the application domain language. With design patterns, we need a computational abstraction of what the pattern does *and* a description of which design criterion it maximizes. This is the approach followed by the design patterns community, where textual documentation, albeit informal, is carefully structured to reflect these distinctions (see, for example, [Gamma 1995; Johnson 1992]).

With regard to the *how to use* aspects, in addition to the traditional information that a reuser needs to know such as the acceptable types of parameters and any side effects, object frameworks have the distinction of requiring assembly. This may involve three things: (1) selecting participants, (2) preparing participants so that they can interact with the other components of the framework, for example, by adding bridge methods, and (3) instance creation and linkage. The selection is usually based on the role played by the participant. The preparation is often required because the *actual* participant that plays the right role may not have the proper interface.

23.1.4 Scalability and Extensibility

Scalability means that we should be able to build and describe complex frameworks by assembling simpler ones, or, equivalently, we should allow the participant of a framework to be another framework. Extensibility means that we should be able to incrementally augment or specialize the functionality of a framework. These requirements imply that a framework be packaged as a unit with its own external interface and its internal structure, similar to the way classes are packaged.

Finding the *external interface* of a set of interacting objects requires a *closure* operation on the set of messages that they exchange within each interaction sequence so that, from the outside, such a sequence may be assigned a method-like signature. This is difficult, both computationally and in terms of ascribing a useful meaning to the resulting signature—not a problem with class methods, which tend to be cohesive. Another difference between class packaging and framework packaging has to do with the information hiding that typically characterizes their respective boundaries (see, for example, [Wegner 1992]). While a class may be seen and reused as a blackbox, to use a framework, we need to have access to its participants. At best, a framework may be seen as a parameterized (generic) blackbox.

23.1.5 Searchability

We envision a two-stage search. In the first stage, a developer specifies a need, and we have to find the reusable component that best satisfies that need. Depending on the need and how it is expressed, the answer could be a method, a class, or an object framework. If the answer is an object framework, we then have to search for suitable participants or validate candidate ones.

The first stage of the search raises a number of issues related those of closure, unit packaging, and computational versus functional descriptions. First, a developer's need will typically be expressed in a synthetic fashion without referring to a specific architecture or to a distribution of responsibilities between interacting objects, compelling us to find a synthetic way of expressing the functionality of a framework that abstracts the specific participants. Second, a functional need will often be expressed in terms of application semantics, which has to be matched to whichever description is available for the functionality of the framework. Consider the query, "I need a way that allows me to represent dynamically the load of the CPU using a bar chart." If we had an application framework in the library that deals with processes, we may find a single class—say, ProcessMonitor—that does (encapsulates) just that. If not, we need to translate the query into application-independent, programmatic terms, such as, "I need a way that allows me to represent dynamically the <attribute> of <an object> using <a graphical object>." Such a query is aware of the distinction between a model object and a graphical object, and might retrieve the MVC framework, if it was available. Yet a more abstract formulation might say, "I need a mechanism for propagating state changes between related objects," which would retrieve Smalltalk's *dependents* mechanism, which is used, among other places, in the MVC. Developers need to express their needs in whichever language can be matched to available, or automatically derivable, descriptions for frameworks. Looking at the problem another way, these three formulations could also be successive translations by a search engine as it fails to find adequate matches. They can also describe nodes along a generalization or extension path of frameworks, moving from the {Process, ProcessMonitor} framework, to the {Model, View, Controller} framework, to the {Object, Dependent} framework.[2]

The second phase of the search involves interface matching between framework participants and concrete classes. Our major concern is that such a matching be workable on existing class libraries, without requiring extensive manual packaging.

23.2 Model

In this section, we describe our model for representing object frameworks and the prototype implementation that we are currently developing. Our presentation will focus on those aspects that are interdependent and that involve some of the trade-offs previously discussed. First, we explain the motivation behind the major constructs used to represent object frameworks through two examples. In *Section 23.2.2*, we summarize the representation model. In *Section 23.2.3*, we discuss our approach to the unit packaging of object frameworks. We conclude in *Section 23.2.4* with some implementation notes.

---

[2]The last should be {Object, Object}, but for readability purposes, and because framework participants would refer to interfaces rather than classes, we use this characterization.

23.2.1 Example

We take the example of two frameworks that are part of the OSE Library [Dumpleton 1994], which are aimed at building process simulation systems (OTC_Simulation_Systems) and event-based systems (OTC_Event_Based_Systems), respectively. The frameworks weren't referred to as such in [Dumpleton 1994], but the unusually high-quality documentation described the component classes together. We use these examples to discuss the descriptive elements of the framework and address some of the packaging issues raised in the introductory section.

Describing What a Framework Does

In process simulation systems, there is a queue of jobs to be executed. A dispatcher retrieves the first job from the queue and executes the code associated with it. The OTC_Simulation_Systems framework offers two generic classes, OTC_Job and OTC_Dispatcher. A potential instance of this framework must include one or more instances of possibly different subclasses of OTC_Job, and a single instance of a class that specializes OTC_Dispatcher. We call these potential instances the *participants* of the framework. Each of these participants has to satisfy a predefined interface. For example, a job must understand the messages execute( ), destroy( ), and so on. The following shows what the specification of the participants and their interfaces looks like. We will be using what amounts to a C++-like notation, with some syntactic sugaring, to describe framework specifications and actual implementations.

```
Framework OTC_Simulation_System
{
    Participants :
        Interface : Dispatcher {
            Attributes :
                        jobQueue Queue;
            Signatures :
                        void initialize();
                    void initialize(IN queue Queue);
                    void schedule(IN job Job);
                    Integer run();
                    Integer dispatch()
            ...
        }
        Interface : Job {
            Signatures :
                        void execute();
                    void destroy();
            ...
        }
        Interface : OTC_Queue {
            Attributes :
                        jobs List<Job>;
            Signatures :
                        void add( IN job Job);
```

```
                      Job next();

              ...
              }
        d Dispatcher;
        j* Job;
        q Queue
    ...

  }
```

Notice that both Dispatcher and Job are names of *interfaces*, which may or may not correspond to actual classes. In practice, however, interfaces are typically represented by *abstract classes* and, to make sure that candidate participant classes support such interfaces, we require that they be subclasses of the abstract class. The next example shows one such class, Count_Job. The class Count_Job provides implementations for the methods required in the interface and adds its own methods and instance variables.

```
Class Count_Job : public OTC_Job {
public:
        Count_Job()
        :runnable(OTCLIB_TRUE) {};
        void kill () { runnable = OTCLIB_FALSE;}
        void execute();
        void destroy();
private:
        static int count;
        OTC_Boolean runnable;
}
```

The interaction between the participants of the framework may be described using the following cycle:

1. The dispatcher receives the message run().

2. The dispatcher sends the message dispatch() to itself.

3. The dispatcher sends the message next() to the queue, which returns some job jb.

4. The dispatcher sends the message execute() to jb.

5. When the jb terminates, the dispatcher sends it the message destroy().

There are different ways of representing this interaction. A plausible C++ implementation might look like the following:

```
void Dispatcher::run() {
        Int result = 1;
        while (result > 0) result = dispatch();
        return result;
}
Int Dispatcher::dispatch() {
        Job * jb;
        jb = jobQueue -> next();
```

```
        if (jb == 0) return 0;
        jb -> execute();
        jb -> destroy();
        return 1;

}
```

In this implementation, the message dispatch() refers *explicitly* to the messages of the other participants that are involved in this sequence. Such a practice should be discouraged both for describing interobject behavior and for implementing it, as mentioned in *Section 23.1.2*. Our approach for representing this behavior is to use a generic message connection notation, which can be easily mapped to a variety of message connection mechanisms and control paradigms. For the time being, we use a single connector denoted by $\Rightarrow$. The symbol $\leftarrow$ is used for assignment.

$$d.run\,(\,) \Rightarrow d.dispatch\,(\,) \Rightarrow \begin{bmatrix} i\leftarrow q.next\,(\,) \\ i.execute\,(\,) \\ i.destroy\,(\,) \end{bmatrix}$$

The preceding message sequence corresponds to a unit of behavior that can be performed by the framework. For scalability purposes, we need to package this unit as a single message (see *Section 23.1*). This requires a closure operation on message sequences that assigns to a message sequence a single message that has the same *external* signature as the original sequence. Figure 23.1 shows a message flow graph where a boundary is drawn around the components of a framework.

Through closure, MF can be considered as a single message addressed to the framework as a whole, and whose inputs are INPUTS(MF) = $\{p_0, p_1\}$ and whose outputs are OUTPUTS(MF) = $\{p_5, p_6\}$. In general, we can define INPUTS(MF) as the minimal set of parameters that would enable the triggering of all the messages in the flow graph. In this case, these are the input flows that have not been produced by any other message. Similarly, we can take OUTPUT(MS) as the set of all outputs that were produced but not consumed by other messages. Other closure formulas are also possible.

A more useful characterization of message flow graphs takes into account the side effects of the messages being executed, in addition to inputs and outputs. The side effects include state changes for preexisting objects and the creation of new objects.

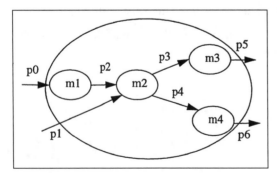

Figure 23.1   Message flow graph MF.

Both can be captured using preconditions and postconditions. Pre- and postconditions follow a somewhat similar pattern to the inputs and outputs, but expressed in logical terms.[3] Short of characterizing those side effects precisely and being able to reason about them analytically, we chose to extend the definition of message output to include the object being acted upon (and possibly modified) and the objects being created. In other words, we view the output of a message as a triplet <receiver, created objects, actual outputs>. Consider the following example:

```
void Dispatcher::initialize() {
        Queue* q;
        q = new Queue;
        initialize(q);
}
void Dispatcher::initialize(Queue* jq) {
        jobQueue = jq;
}
```

With our definition of message output limited to return values, the preceding sequence (flow) can be represented by the sequence MS = *d.initialize()* $\Rightarrow$ *d.initialize(q)* and INPUT(MS) = {q}, which is not accurate. With our new definition of output, INPUT(MS) = { }.

In addition to the closure on inputs, outputs, and side effects, we need to assign a single *name* to each message flow graph. This name, chosen by the framework '*packager*', is used to refer to the message flow graph when we embed a framework within another.

How to Use a Framework

As mentioned earlier, in the actual simulation framework, the interfaces Job, Queue, and Dispatcher are, in fact, abstract classes. As such, some of their methods are already fully implemented and some are pure virtual. In order to use the framework, we need to subclass these classes with the *option* of redefining existing methods and the *obligation* to define the pure virtual ones. This kind of information depends on the fact that interfaces are actual classes and on the semantics of C++. In fact, we consider this as two pieces of information. The first is the interface of the abstract class (without implementation), and the second is an implicit assertion that says that this abstract class provides a partial implementation for this interface. For this reason, we decided not to include information about which methods to redefine and which to implement in the formal description of the framework itself. For the time being, this kind of information is included in a textual attachment.

To create an actual instance of the framework, we need an *instantiation scenario*. The documentation typically shows code fragments of some "main()" program with a set of declarations, participant initializations, and *interparticipant connections*. The following code fragment shows an example instantiation scenario taken from [Dumpleton 1994]:

---

[3]This is special case of the identity wp($S_{1\Rightarrow} S_2$,R) = wp(S_1,wp(S_2,R)), where wp stands for *weakest pr-condition*, R stands for a desired result (postcondition), and S_1 and S_2 stand for two programs [Dijsktra 1976].

```
        . . .
    main() {
        static OTC_Job job;
        OTC_Dispatcher::initialize();
        OTC_Dispatcher::schedule(&job);
        . . .
}
```

Notice the declaration of job and the call to "schedule(&job)," which connects job to the job queue of the dispatcher.[4]

Typically, the documentation combines instantiation and example usage (in the form of a message sequence) in the same code fragment. We chose to isolate the creation and connection part and package it in a *function* whose parameters are initialization parameters for the various participants. If the framework were to be considered as a C++ class where the participants are data members, this would be a constructor. The difference between a typical constructor and a framework instantiation scenario is the way the various participants are scoped and interconnected. In a regular class, data members are referred to by name, live beyond the call that initialized them, and all have the same life span. In our case, instantiation scenarios must return one of the participants, and that participant must have explicit connections to the others. This is another example of binding between participants that should be avoided, both in specifications and in implementations.

For specification purposes, we choose to specify (code) instantiation scenarios like constructors, that is, refer to participants by name as if they were data members (see Figure 23.3). It is relatively easy to go from this kind of specification to actual C++ code that includes local declarations of the members, but the opposite is not true since we couldn't tell which local variables are participants and which are not.

When to Use the Framework

Given all the difficulties discussed in *Sections 23.1.3* and *23.1.5*, for the time being we focus on semistructured textual descriptions such as the ones used for design patterns. Gamma et al. used three descriptors called *Intent*, *Motivation*, and *Applicability* [Gamma 1995], which convey two pieces of information: (1) what the design pattern achieves in terms of attaining some design goal (for example, platform independence)—embodied in *Intent*, and (2) situations in which such a design goal is desirable (*Motivation*, which gives an example, and *Applicability*, which gives rules for recognizing such situations). Neither piece of information is derivable, even remotely, from the behavioral specification of a design pattern, and such information has to be entered manually. With application-specific object frameworks, the nature of the participants is indication enough of the opportunity for using a framework, and this becomes more of a search issue.

---

[4]For readers not familiar with C++, the syntax OTC_Dispatcher::initialize( ), where OTC_Dispatcher is the name of the class, suggests that the method initialize( ) is a *static member* of the class (equivalent to class method in Smalltalk) and that we assume that there is a single dispatcher per program run.

Extending the Framework

The simulation system (SS) framework is used to implement the event-based system (EBS) framework. The two frameworks have several relationships, including the following.

Addition of new classes of participants and/or specialization of existing ones. OTC_Dispatcher and OTC_job facilities are mainly extended by the classes OTC_Event (events) and OTC_EVAgent (agents). An event may be created and sent to an appropriate agent. The delivery of an event to an agent is made by creating and adding a job to the dispatcher queue with the queue method of the event. For an event e and an agent a, the message is "$e{\Rightarrow}$queue(a.id( ))." The created job is different from the others of the simulation system. For this purpose, the EBS framework derives a new class from OTC_ Job (OTC_EventJob) with some extra facilities to take into account the particularity of event jobs as shown in the following code.

```
class OTC_EventJob : public OTC_Job {
public:
        int target()const {return myTarget;};
        int event() const {return myEvent;};
        void execute();   // Delivers the event to the agent

private:
        int  myTarget; // the ID of the agent.
        OTC_Event* MyEvent; // the event
```

An event can also be sent without creating a delivery job; this is possible by using the deliver method of the event. In this case we don't need to use the dispatcher queue.

Extension of message flow graphs. The queued delivery of events to agents uses the simulation framework's basic run cycle (select, run, destroy). The created event job is scheduled like any other job type and is selected from the queue. The following code shows the method queue of OTC_Event:

```
void OTC_Event::queue(int theAgentId) {
        OTC_EventJob* theJob;
        theJob = new OTC_EventJob(theAgentId,this);
        OTC_Dispatcher::schedule(theJob);
}
```

Thus, whereas in the simulation systems framework we schedule a preexisting job j using the sequence MS_1 d.schedule(j) $\Rightarrow$ q.add(j), the event-based system framework enables us to schedule the delivery of an event e; that is, it supports the longer sequence MS_2 e.queue(id) $\Rightarrow$ d.schedule(j_{id}) $\Rightarrow$ q.add(j_{id}). In this case, a sequence of SS is a *suffix* of a sequence of EBS. In the more general case of message flow graphs (instead of linear sequences), we can have more complex relationships, based on graph inclusion. For example, the SS framework supports the following message *flow graph*,

MF_1, where the (round) bracket notation means that three piled messages are triggered by d.dispatch( ) and are executed in the sequence top to bottom:

$$d.run\ ( ) \Rightarrow d.dispatch\ ( ) \Rightarrow \begin{cases} i\leftarrow q.next\ ( ) \\ i.execute\ ( ) \\ i.destroy\ ( ) \end{cases}$$

The EBS framework, on the other hand, supports a different version of execute, which, in turn, triggers a sequence of two messages, yielding the following flow graph (MF_2):

$$d.run\ ( ) \Rightarrow d.dispatch\ ( ) \Rightarrow \begin{cases} & i\leftarrow q.next\ ( ) \\ i.execute\ ( ) \Rightarrow & e.deliver\ (id) \quad \Rightarrow a.handle\ (e) \\ & i.destroy\ ( ) \end{cases}$$

One of the differences between this extension and the previous one is that the trace of MS_1 was included in the trace of MS_2, while this is not the case for the pair MF_1,MF_2. We define message flow graph extension informally in the following; we first define message pair specialization:

Message pair specialization. A message pair x.f(...) $\Rightarrow$ y.g(...) specializes x'.f'(...) $\Rightarrow$ y'.g'(...) if:

- x' is identical to, or specializes x, and f' is identical to, or conformant to f.

- y' is identical to, or specializes y, and g' is identical to, or conformant to g.

Message flow graph extension. A message flow graph MF_1 extends a message flow graph MF_2 if:

- For all message pairs x.f(...) $\Rightarrow$ y.g(...) in MF_2, there exists a message pair x'.f'(...) $\Rightarrow$ y'.g'(...) in MF_1 that specializes it.

- For all message cascades x.f(...) $\Rightarrow y_1.g_1(...)\ (OP_i\ y_i.g_i(...))^*$ in MF_2, there exists a corresponding message cascade x'.f'(...) $\Rightarrow y'_1.g'_1(...)\ (OP_i\ y'_i.g'_i(...))^*$ in MF_1 such that for all i, x.f(...) $\Rightarrow y_i.g_i(...)$ specializes x'.f'(...) $\Rightarrow y'_i.g'_i(...)$.

The operator OP_i stands for explicit sequencing (corresponding to pile notation in the preceding examples) or parallelism.

The two basic relations between framework components support two kinds of relationships between frameworks: *generalization* and *aggregation*. Generalization is based on the substitutability principle: *A framework F_1 specializes a framework F_2 if, wherever F_2 is expected, F_1 can fulfill its role.* This means that F_1 has at least the same components as F_2 (or behaviorally conformant ones), and if the message sequences restricted then those common components are equivalent. Formally:

Framework generalization. A framework F_1 with participants $P_1,...,P_m$ and message flow graphs $MF_1,...,MF_o$ is a specialization of a framework F'_1 with participants $P'_1,...,P'_n$ and message flow graphs $MF'_1,...,MF'_p$ if:

- For all $1 = i = n$, there exists $1 = j = m$ such that P'_j is a specialization of (or identical to) P_i.

- For all $1 = r = p$, there exists $1 = s = o$ such that MF'_s extends MF_r.

Framework aggregation is defined in such a way that references to F_1's participants in F_2 be removed and replaced by a reference to a single participant whose interface is (a subset of) F_1's interface. Let $PART(F)$ be the set of participants in a framework, and $PART(MF)$ the set of participants. Semiformally:

Framework aggregation. A framework F_1 with participants $P_1,...,P_m$ and message flow graphs $MF_1,...,MF_o$ is a component of a framework F'_1 with participants $P'_1,...,P'_n$ and message flow graphs $MF'_1,...,MF'_p$ if:

- For all $1 = i = m$, there exists $1 = j = n$ such that P'_j is identical to P_i.

- For each MF'_s of F_2 such that $PART(MF'_s) \cap PART(F_1) \neq \varnothing$, there exists a message flow MF_j of F_1 such that $MF'_s = MF_j \oplus MF'_{s,j}$ and $PART(MF'_{s,j}) \cap PART(F_1) = \varnothing$.

In the preceding definition, $MF'_{s,j}$ is the message flow graph obtained by "gutting out" MF'_s of the message pairs or cascades found in MF_j.

We have just begun to explore the relationships between frameworks found in actual code libraries, and our experience has been that the relationship between any two frameworks is a complex combination of aggregation and generalization relationships between the frameworks themselves and/or common subcomponents or generalizations. One can imagine a frameworks browser that generates (virtual) common generalizations of frameworks, for example, for the purposes of navigation.

23.2.2 Basic Representation Model

The previous examples illustrated only some aspects of object frameworks. We introduce in this section the full notation and discuss those aspects not brought up earlier. This model corresponds to the one implemented in our prototype toolset. Aspects related to the representation of framework relationships, which were not implemented in the current version of our prototypes, will be discussed in *Section 23.2.3*.

The description of an object framework consists of five descriptive slots, as shown here:

```
Framework <name> {
        Variables:
                Var1 : Type1;
                ...
        Participants:
                Part1 : Interface1 ;
                ...
        Constraints:
                Rel1(Parti ,...,Partj,Varm,...,Varn);
                ...
        Tasks:
                Task1 (Inp1 : IN T1,...,Inpi: IN Ti,
```

```
                            Out₁    : OUT T'₁,...,Outₖ: OUT T'ₖ) {
                     Part₁.f(Inp₁) ⇒ Partⱼ.f(Inpⱼ) ...;
                        ...
                     }
                ...
    Instantiations:
            Scenario₁ (p₁: T₁,...,pᵢ: Tᵢ) {
                Part₁.initialize(p₁);
                   ...
                }
             ...
    }
```

The slot *variables* contains variables that are specific to the framework as a whole, but not related to any participant in particular. These could be state or *status* variables, or variables used to bind participants to each other. For a model/view framework where model changes are buffered, a state variable could indicate whether the model and the view are in sync. Another use of variables is illustrated later.

Constraints describe invariant relationships that must hold during the lifetime of the framework. An object framework may go through a transitory phase during which a constraint is not satisfied, but the idea is that if a transaction completes successfully, all constraints should be satisfied in the end. We distinguish between three kinds of constraints: (1) constraints between participants, (2) constraints between a participant and a variable, and (3) constraints between a participant and a constant. Constraints between participants take the form of a relationship between their attributes [Mili 1996]. In a model/view framework, we can constrain the value of an instance variable of the model to the height of the graphical bar (a view) representing the model in a bar chart (a composite view). Constraints between participants and variables may be used to represent dependencies between framework participants and the outside environment. If the variable represents a sensor, for example, this would be one way of relating sensed data to the participant responsible for handling it. Constraints between participants and variables may also be used to represent a many-to-many constraint between n participants (for example, $n \times (n + 1)/2$ connections) by n connections to a common variable.

Constraints and message flow graphs are tightly coupled. Message flow graphs that, transitorily, violate constraints will contain subsequent messages that reinforce them. Conversely, what would have been a single state-modifying message on a constrained participant becomes a trigger for an entire message flow graph whose sole purpose is to reestablish the constraint. In the model/view framework, the methods that change the state of model (m) variables that have a graphical rendering *have to* call the methods that update the view (v)'s corresponding parameter, and its graphical display, as in:[5]

```
m.set<an attribute name>(x) ⇒ v.update(<an attribute name>,x)
```

---

[5]In Smalltalk's Model/View/Controller framework, such connections are achieved as follows: (1) Views are made *dependents* of models, (2) whenever a model changes state, it broadcasts a message to its dependents, notifying them of the change, and (3) dependents decide whether to react to the change, depending on the nature of the change. This scheme relieves models from knowing specifically which view method to call in each case.

We can go one step further. If we represent a constraint such as:

```
m.volume  →  v.barHeight
```

where → means that whenever the left-hand side changes, the right-hand side has to follow suit, we can imagine a constraint parser that automatically adds a call to v.set-BarHeight(x) at the end of the method m.setVolume(x). Alternatively (and more easily), the constraint parser can add an after-method to the call to m.setVolume(x).

We believe that, given a catalog of such constraints and corresponding transformations, we can account for most of the cases of interparticipant constraints and message connections. This approach would have several advantages:

- Simplifying the specification of object frameworks: All we have to do is specify the constraints, and the message sequences/connections will be derived automatically.

- Ensure static connections between the participants without having to create named instance variables that point from one to another.

- Ensuring message connections between the participants implicitly, by avoiding the lexical binding between their methods.

Admittedly, the interconnections within an object framework involve more than propagating state variables. Further, a specification method has to accommodate existing frameworks and, possibly, support the extraction of such specifications from the code; if existing frameworks are not programmed according to this constraint style, it will not be possible to delineate such constraints and their enforcement sequences. Theoretically, however, we can represent and implement behavior and behavioral composition using logic and constraint-logic programming languages (see, for example, [Freeman-Benson 1989; Saraswat 1989; Wilk 1991]). Further, we have shown in [Mili 1996] that we can support behavioral composition within an imperative language using a combination of constraints and a properly tuned message-sending protocol.

For the time being, we will use the constraint notation for documentation purposes only. Further, we include message sequences in the description of a framework even if all the sequences can be inferred from the specified constraints. In the long run, we advocate a constraint-based interobject behavioral composition. We are currently developing a set of practical design guidelines based on the results in [Mili 1996] and intend to try them out to reengineer a number of existing frameworks, including the event-based simulation framework mentioned earlier.

23.2.3 Representing Framework Relationships

We described in *Section 23.2* relationships between frameworks that fall into two general categories, generalization and aggregation. Representing these relationships is important for the usual reasons, such as *abstraction* (representing different levels of detail), *economy of representation*, and *incremental definition* of frameworks. We choose to represent specialization and aggregation the usual way, that is:

Specialization. We describe a framework by only what distinguishes it from its generalizations.

Aggregation. We represent the fact that a framework A is included in a framework B by having one of the participants of B be an A, or an interface identical to A's closure.

Our definition of aggregation from *Section 23.2.1* corresponds to the way a tool would uncover the occurrence of one framework within a bigger framework; once that occurrence has been established, all of the participants of the component framework and their corresponding message sequences will be replaced by the component framework's closure interface. We will discuss in *Section 23.6* issues related to packaging a framework into a class and transforming code that refers to framework components.

An extension of the template of the previous section wouldn't need any new constructs to represent aggregation, but would simply allow for the specification of a framework that is being extended:

```
Framework <FM₁> extends <FM₂> {
        Variables:
            . . .
        Participants:
            Part'₁ renames Part₁;
            Part₂ : Interface'₂ specializes Interface₂;
            . . .
        Constraints:
            . . .
        Tasks:
            Task'₁ (I'₁ : IN T'ᵢ,₁,..., O₁: OUT T'ₒ,₁,...)
                overrides
                Task₁ (I₁ : IN Tᵢ,₁,...,O₁: OUT Tₒ,₁,...)
                {...}
            Task'₂ (...)
                {...}
            . . .
        Instantiations:
            Scenario'₁ (p'₁: T'₁,...,p'ⱼ: T'ⱼ) overrides
                Scenario₁ (p₁: T₁,...,pᵢ: Tᵢ)
                {...}
            Scenario'₂ (...)
                {...}
            . . .
}
```

We assume here that framework FM_2 has a participant named $Part_1$, which has been renamed in framework FM_1. We also assume that FM_2 has a participant named $Part_2$, whose interface has been specialized from $Interface_2$ to $Interface'_2$. We believe that it is important to support renaming because framework name participants usually indicate roles within a group of collaborating objects, and when an object is added to the collaboration, the roles might change slightly. $Task'_1$ *overrides* (or *masks*) the inherited $Task_1$, whereas $Task_2$ is a completely new task. Notice that $Task'_1$ has a different, and not necessarily conformant, interface from that of $Task_1$. For instance, our definition of message flow graph extension allows for new messages to be appended to various paths in the graph, and those messages might require additional inputs or produce additional outputs. Notwithstanding those additional inputs and outputs, we know that the signature of $Task'_1$ is type-conformant to that of $Task_1$ because the participants of FM_1 are specializations of the participants of FM_2. Explicitly specifying the task that is being overridden helps the compiler distinguish between a redefinition from an overloading in the case of ambiguity.[6]

This could be problematic, depending on what we want to do with the framework extension relationship. If we view *extension* as a development-time relationship, then there is no problem in having a task override an inherited one with a nonconformant signature. If we want extension to imply behavioral substitutability or subtyping, then we need a way of handling nonconformant redefinitions. Basically, the problem arises in the following case:

```
(1)  FM2 someObject;
     ...
(2)  someObject = someFunction(...);
(3)  someObject.Task1(i₁,...,o₁,...);
```

The issue here is what happens if someFunction returns an FM_1 instead of an FM_2. There are two potential solutions to this problem. The first is to disallow message flow graph extensions that require additional outside inputs (that is, inputs not produced by other messages within the graph) and produce external outputs (that is, outputs not consumed by other messages within the graph). The second solution is to use optional parameters to represent the additional inputs and outputs. The additional outputs are not a problem, as a program that does not make use of them will ignore them. However, the handling of the additional inputs presumes the existence of meaningful defaults for them.

We have not had enough practical experience with framework relationships to decide whether behavioral substitutability is really important and to figure out what the restrictions on the acceptable message flow graph extensions entail in practical terms. Our inclination is that frameworks are mostly expressions of design ideas, and, notwithstanding the practical gains accrued from packaging frameworks as classes (see *Section 23.5*), the biggest gain will come from *design reuse*.

23.3 Implementation

When we set out to develop a representation of frameworks, applicability to existing frameworks was a major concern. Another overriding concern was a noncommitment to an interaction/coordination mechanism between framework participants, hence the idea of message sequences to represent interobject behavior. When we set out to *implement* this representation, another major concern was to integrate support for frameworks within an ongoing, prototype, reusable components repository tool. In this section, we discuss these issues and give a high-level description of the implementation.

---

[6]The ambiguity would be greater here if we allowed redefinitions with a different number of parameters. The second is to say that $Task'_1$ *masks* $Task_1$, even though the signatures may be different.

23.3.1 Interfaces versus Classes

Our representation of frameworks must take into account two factors. First, whereas classes in class libraries constitute *concrete* reusable *code* components, frameworks embody *reusable designs* or *reusable configurations* of *abstract* components. Second, we wish to treat frameworks as single, class-like components thanks to closure operations.

In existing frameworks, the distinction between participant specifications (interfaces) and actual implementations is not very clear, as a *class* would often represent both. Further, language properties such as typing and early versus late binding, and programming style, may further confuse matters, making interfaces and implementations virtually inseparable. For example, in C++, participant interfaces are embodied in *abstract classes* from which actual participants *must* inherit. To complicate things even more, the *abstract classes* themselves may be partially implemented, and only a handful of methods may have to be defined in the derived subclasses. Moreover, the participants of a framework refer to each other, as in the case where the method of one participant uses another one as a parameter. In typed languages such as C++, where subclassing is used as the subtyping mechanism, we are forced to represent even the application-dependent classes by actual C++ *abstract classes,* from which the framework users have to derive the actual classes.[7] The Java language does make the distinction between *interfaces* and *classes*, which makes it easier to map our model to Java frameworks.

Our representation of frameworks must distinguish between interfaces and abstract classes, even when a single (physical) reusable component embodies both. It must also be aware of the *implicit* and *undocumented* programming language–level dependencies between participant interfaces and implementations, and between different participants.

23.3.2 Components Object Model

Our implementation of the representation of object frameworks was guided by three considerations:

- Integration into a (research) prototype class library tool
- Distinction between classes and interfaces
- Representation uniformity between interface descriptions and framework descriptions, and between method descriptions and message sequence descriptions (or instantiation scenarios)

The existing library tool manipulated classes, views, instance variables (and parameters), and methods. *Views*[8] were first introduced as *subsets* of the set of variables and methods of a class, and were later extended to handle renaming of variables and methods. When we introduced frameworks into our tool set, the need to separate interfaces from classes led to the model excerpted in Figure 23.2a, where views are henceforth represented by interfaces.

---

[7]In Smalltalk's Model/View/Controller framework, the class library contains an "abstract class" called Model, although developers need not subclass it for their application-specific classes.

[8]This concept is a generalization of C++'s three visibility interfaces: *private, public,* and *protected.* Each class can have several interfaces, which are made available to—possibly different—kinds of client programs.

Figure 23.2a shows that all entities support *behaviors*, be they frameworks, interfaces, or classes, but some support *abstract behaviors*—in this case, just signatures—while others support *concrete* behaviors—an implementation along with a specification.

Part of the behavior's hierarchy is shown in Figure 23.2b. The representation of classes is constructed by language parsers (both Smalltalk and C++ parsers), which

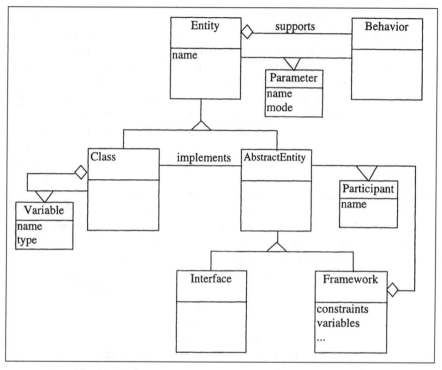

Figure 23.2a   Classes, interfaces, and frameworks.

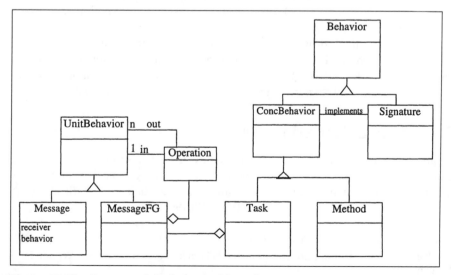

Figure 23.2b   Excerpts of the behavior hierarchy.

read in source file and extract class definitions (see, for example, [Mili 1997]). The model of Figure 23.2a is geared toward typed languages (typed instance variables and parameters), but can handle untyped language as well by leaving the type field empty.[9] For each class, an instance of Interface is created that represents the locally defined behaviors; inherited behaviors are computed on the fly when needed, for example, for comparison purposes (see framework search and realization in *Section 23.4*). Conversely, framework packaging, to be discussed in *Section 23.5*, generates a class implementation for a framework. Figure 23.2b shows excerpts from the behaviors hierarchy. Note that framework tasks are considered as concrete behaviors since tasks include more than signature (the closure of inputs and outputs), but show the actual sequence of messages. Further, not all behaviors supported by concrete classes are concrete behaviors: C++ virtual methods are abstract behaviors.[10] Tasks are shown to have a component that is a message flow graph. A message flow graph is an operation on a set of *units of behaviors,* which could be simple messages or other message flow graphs. The operation is an *n*-ary relation between an *input message* and the set of messages (or message flow graphs) triggered by that message (*output messages*). The output messages are done either serially or in parallel.

Figure 23.3a shows a prototype frameworks editing tool. The top section, with three lists, is self-explanatory. The middle section consists of the various participants, along with their interfaces. The currently selected participant, ej, is of interface Event_job (the star means that we have more than one participant of this interface). The lists, Operation signatures and Attributes, describe the interface Event_job. The Tasks section of the interface lists the signatures of the tasks and the corresponding message sequences. Message sequences are first entered in the text area and then *compiled.* The compiler prompts the developer for a name and a return variable (hence, type) and generates the rest of the signature using the default closure formula (see *Section 23.2.1* and *Section 23.2.2*). The developer has the option of adding or removing outputs from the signature. Figure 23.3b shows the graphical representation of an example of a message sequence. The root node represents the task and the other nodes represent the messages of the sequence corresponding to this task. Finally, an edge means that a method invoked in a message (source node) sends another message (target node). The Instantiation scenarios section in Figure 23.3 is similar in principle to the tasks section.

We have implemented additional tools for visualizing and editing textual documentation for the frameworks. Both tools can be invoked through action menu options within the Frameworks list. The tools used for searching and using frameworks are discussed briefly next, and then in some detail in *Section 23.4* and *Section 23.5*.

23.3.3 A Usage Scenario

Our representation and manipulation of frameworks is part of a toolset for managing reusable software components. Frameworks are but one kind of reusable components that developers can search for, browse, and integrate into their own applications. A typical reuse cycle will look something like this [Mili 1995]:

---

[9]For Smalltalk, we used the value Object, which is the root of the class hierarchy.

[10]In Smalltalk, the equivalent to pure virtual methods is methods that raise the exception SubclassResponsibility.

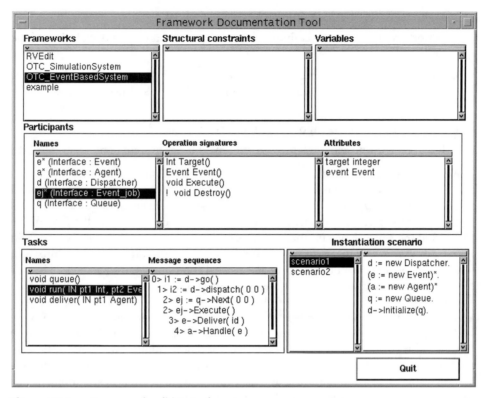

Figure 23.3a   Framework editing tool.

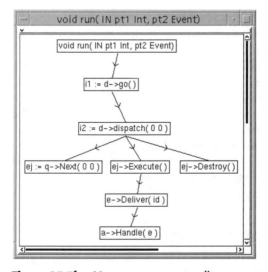

Figure 23.3b   Message sequence editor.

1. Formulate a description of the problem to be solved.

2. Perform a search on the component repository based on the description of the problem.

3. Assess the retrieved components for their reusability and quality. If one is of good enough quality, and close enough to the expressed need, proceed to the next step.

4. Adapt the retrieved component to the problem at hand.

5. Integrate the—possibly adapted—component in the system at hand, and test it.

We wish to stress the distinction between steps 1 and 2, and the fact that the search that is submitted to the component repository is based on the description of the need and not necessarily *that description* itself. The biggest problem encountered by the users of component libraries is the fact that developers don't always know the *form* of the solution to their problems and thus can't formulate queries very effectively (see [Mili 1997]). For example, if we use a procedural library, we search for sort procedures as a function, whereas with a library of object-oriented components, we will be looking for *classes* that implement sorted collections. The same applies to searching for classes versus searching for frameworks. If we know that what we are looking for has been addressed by a *single* class, then we can formulate a search query on a class. Otherwise, we have to find a way of searching on frameworks specifically, or find a way such that the same query can retrieve a class or a framework indifferently. We opted for the second solution. For instance, there are two ways of searching for components in our system. First, we perform a natural language search on the textual descriptions of our components, be they external textual documents, comments used within source files, or textual annotations on classification facets [Mili 1997]. These algorithms work equally well with classes and frameworks. The second search method consists of describing the needed component as an interface (see *Section 23.4.1*). Thanks to the closure operation on framework tasks and instantiation scenarios, the same query can match classes and frameworks.

What happens next depends on the kind of retrieved component. If the retrieved component is a class, the usual class reuse mechanism may take place—for example, using as is, extending through inheritance, or composing with other objects. If the retrieved component is a framework, then a lot remains to be done. Recall that a framework is a *design idea* or an *execution pattern* and not just an executable piece of code. Hence, once we have found a framework that satisfies some external behavior, we have to find a *realization* or *specific implementation* of the framework within the context of the application at hand. We call this step *framework realization*, because it involves realizing the generic design idea within the context of the application at hand. At the very least, this involves specifying the application-specific participants of the framework, in case the framework comes with fully concrete components, and those components will do the task at hand. More typically, framework realization involves, for each or for some participant(s), the following:

1. Finding a class that satisfies the behavioral requirements of the participant.

2. Finding the class that comes closest to satisfying those requirements, and then performing one or a combination of the following:

a. Subclass it to add the missing behavior or customize the existing one.

b. Compose it with other components to support the required behavior.

c. Wrap it within a component to adapt its interface to the required one.

3. Once this is done, we have to assemble the framework components and integrate them into the system.

We provide automated tools for supporting steps 1 to 3. Steps 1 and 2 are supported by a variant of signature matching (see *Section 23.4.2*). Step 3 is supported by the operation of *packaging* frameworks as classes. Packaging is not required, per se, to support the integration of the realization of a framework into an application. It has a number of other advantages, such as scalability and performance optimizations (see *Section 23.5*). However, by treating the realization of a framework as a single class with its own constructor/assembler and methods, we encapsulate and centralize the interactions with the components of the framework. We will also show in *Section 23.5* how framework packaging can help improve the maintainability of code that uses a framework and shield it from future evolutions of the framework.

23.4 Framework Search and Realization

Within the context of our reusable component repository, we had developed a set of search algorithms that used *extrinsic* information such as external textual documentation and a faceted classification. Such algorithms included string search algorithms and multifaceted component retrieval algorithms. User experiments with a class library showed that string-search algorithms performed better than multifaceted retrieval algorithms [Mili 1997] and were not explored any further in the context of frameworks. We will limit our discussion to search methods based on intrinsic information and, more specifically, signature matching algorithms. Query formulation and the actual signature matching are discussed in *Section 23.4.1*. Instantiating a framework for a particular application is discussed in *Section 23.4.2*. We conclude in *Section 23.4.3* with a discussion on the effectiveness of signature matching as a substitute for behavioral conformance and on ways to implement interobject behavior without creating code-level dependencies.

23.4.1 Formulating and Matching Interface Queries

Broadly speaking, a developer specifies an interface for which he or she wishes an *implementation,* and the system looks for reusable components that support the interface. Those components could be either single classes or frameworks whose message sequences and instantiation scenarios have been abstracted or *closed* into signatures. We will first describe query specification and then the actual matching.

Figure 23.4 shows the query interface tool. A developer specifies the query in the upper part of the window, and the results are shown in the bottom part. A query consists of a set of method signatures, expressed in terms of *interfaces* (and not *classes*),

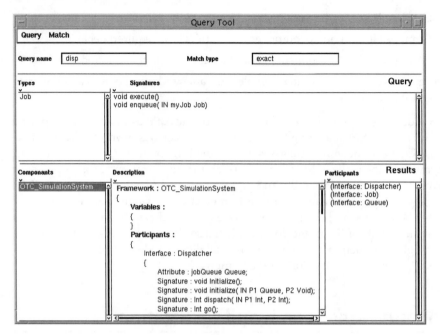

Figure 23.4   Interface matching query tool.

along with those interfaces (types) that are referenced in operation signatures and that have no known implementations in the library. For those types, the developer needs to specify a list of equivalent types/interfaces from the library so that matching can take place. In the preceding example, if the developer had *asserted* that Job was *equivalent* to any of OTCJob, OTCEventDelivery, or OTCProcess, then we would be looking for any component that supports a method with the following signature:

```
void execute()
```

and any *one of* the following signatures:

```
void enqueue (IN myJob OTCJob), or
void enqueue (IN myJob OTCEventDelivery), or
void enqueue (IN myJob OTCProcess)
```

Deciding on the equivalence of Job to OTCJob, OTCEventDelivery, and OTCProcess may itself be the result of an interface matching operation: Upon realizing that Job is not defined, a developer may choose to spawn another search window and specify the interface of the new type using method signatures. This potentially recursive process has to have a termination: Either the developer specifies an interface in terms of known types and the search tool is able to match it to existing components, or the developer asserts the equivalence of types explicitly.

The actual interface matching ignores method names and uses type matching. We support three variations of the matching algorithm: an *exact match*, which takes into account parameter types and positions; the *permuted match*, which does the matching, modulo parameter positions; and *conformance matching*, which takes into account parameter positions, but will match contravariant signatures. Matching can return either a single class interface or a framework interface. The Description subpane shows a textual representation of the interface. For the case of a framework, the textual representation is generated from a template using the structural representation of the framework. For the case of a class, the textual representation consists simply of the C++ header file. The Participants subpane lists the set of participants—the case of frameworks—or data members/instance variables, for the case of classes. The example of Figure 23.4 shows a framework interface.

23.4.2 Framework Realization

Once it is determined that a given framework fits the bill, we have to find implementations for the participants of the framework. A *complete* (*partial*) realization is one where we find an implementation for *each* (*some* of the) participants in the framework; the implementation of a participant may be found in the library of components or may have to be constructed. In general, the participants that play an application-independent role are provided in the library, while the ones that depend on the application at hand are to be constructed or otherwise provided by the framework user. For example, in Smalltalk's Model/View/Controller framework, only the model classes have to be provided by the framework user (developer); the Smalltalk class library contains classes that implement most of the common view and controller behaviors (modulo few parameterizations).

Symbolically, let $\{I_1, I_2,...,I_n\}$ be the set of participant interfaces to be matched and $Imp(I_i) = \{C_{i,1},...,C_{i,k}\}$ the set of classes that match the interface I_i. A realization of the framework consists of a tuple $<C_1,...,C_n>$ where $C_i \in Imp(I_i)$. Note that we could have $I_i = I_j$ for some $i \neq j$ because the framework can have more than one participant with the same interface. Further, for a given pair i,j such that $I_i = I_j$, we could have $C_i \neq C_j$ if we choose different implementations for two participants that have the same interface.

For the case of C++ frameworks, the interface of a framework participant—a non-concrete library component—may match the interface of a C++ abstract class C_a—a concrete library component according to the preceding definition. Clearly, such classes should be identified as such, and, given two classes that implement the same interface, the more completely defined class should be presented first. It will often be the case that such classes will be in a class-subclass relationship. Further, in existing C++ frameworks where participants are embodied in abstract classes, a realization of the framework often requires, for language typing reasons, that actual realizations use *subclasses* of those abstract classes. This is due to the fact that framework participants refer to each other by type. For example, the class Dispatcher (which implements the interface Dispatcher) refers to the *abstract* class Job in its source code. Thus, if we use the class Dispatcher in the simulation system framework, we have to—from a programming language point of view—use a subclass of the abstract class Job. The problem can be made worse if specializations/subclasses of Dispatcher need to refer to specializations of Job; this is one of the problems that give rise to the Factory Method or Factory Class pattern (see, for example, [Gamma 1995]). Consider a framework with two participants $I_1 = \{f(int,I_2)\}$ and $I_2 = \{g(int)\}$, and the class $C_1 = \{f(int,C_2)\}$. First, C_1 is a candidate realization participant only if C_2 matches I_2. Further, C_1 may be used *only* if we pick C_2 or a subclass thereof as an I_2 participant. In other words, if $\{I_1, I_2,...,I_n\}$ is the set of participant interfaces to be matched and $Imp(I_i)$ is the set of classes that match the interface I_i, the set of realizations $<C_1,...,C_n>$ of the framework, where $C_i \in Imp(I_i)$, is *not* the Cartesian product $Imp(I_1) \times ... \times Imp(I_n)$, but rather a *proper subset* thereof.

Generally speaking, framework realization is a constraint satisfaction problem whose solutions are tuples of mutually coherent participant implementations. Our current implementation of the prototype does not perform this global realization process, and the developer has to choose a realization one participant at a time. In the preceding example, we have to establish that C_2 implements I_2 before we can establish that C_1 implements I_1. We introduced the concept of *conditional matching*, whereby an implementation is presented as satisfying an interface *if* some <interface, implementation> pairs are shown to match. In this example, we have:

```
Match(I₁, C₁) ⇐ Match(I₂, C₂)
```

For each participant interface I and library class C, the expression Match(I,C) can have four possible values:

- *Unknown*, in case the pair has not been evaluated

- *(Probably/proven) false*, in case it has been evaluated and was found to be false, independently of everything else

- *Conditionally true*, in case it was evaluated, and was found to be true provided that Match(I′,C′), for some pairs <I′,C′> where I′ was referenced in I and C′ was referenced in C, was either unknown or found to be conditionally true

- *True*, if it was evaluated and was found to be true

When the value of an expression Match(I,C) is changed, from unknown to one of the other values, or from conditionally true to either true or false, that change is reflected on the conditionally true expressions Match(I′,C′) that depend on Match(I,C). In essence, we have a truth maintenance system/network that is updated through developer actions. Under this new version, the matcher still does not attempt to find a global solution on its own, but at least the developer will have, from the start, all the information he or she needs to find such a solution, one participant at a time, and will be guided by the dependencies through the process.

In the example shown in Figure 23.5, we were only able to assert that the class OTCDispatcherGI matches the interface Dispatcher because we had already established that OTCJobQueue (second line of the left-side signatures list) matched the interface Queue, and that OTCJob (tenth line of the same list) matched Job; if we hadn't, we wouldn't even have been able to suggest or suspect that OTCDispatcherGI is a candidate for the interface Dispatcher.

We could still run into a problem in case of a circular dependency. Consider the framework with participant interfaces $I_1 = \{f(int,I_2)\}$ and $I_2 = \{g(int, I_1)\}$, and the class $C_1 = \{f(int,C_2)\}$ and $C_2 = \{g(int, C_1)\}$. We have:

```
Match(I₁, C₁) ⇐ Match(I₂, C₂), and
Match(I₂, C₂) ⇐ Match(I₁, C₁)
```

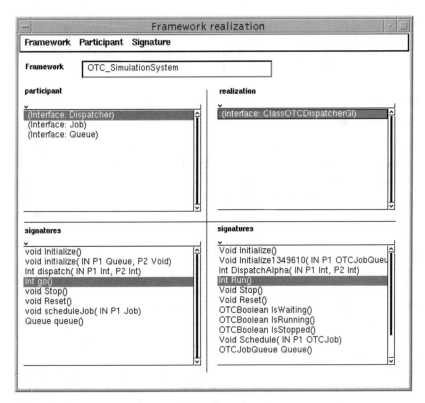

Figure 23.5   Framework realization interface.

In this case, a developer is stuck and will have to explicitly posit (state) either Match(I_1, C_1) or Match(I_2, C_2).

Finally, note that a given class C_i can match an interface I_i in several ways and have a different justification or precondition for each one. Consider the interface I_1 = {f(int,I_2), g(int, I_3)} and the class C_1 = {h(int,C_2)}. C_1 can match I_1 in one of two ways:

```
Match(I₁, C₁)  ⇐  Match(I₂, C₂),
```

or

```
Match(I₁, C₁)  ⇐  Match(I₃, C₂)
```

which correspond to mapping function f(.,.) to h(.,.) versus mapping g(.,.) to h(.,.). When we present a solution to the developer, we have to specify the exact mapping between types and implementations. In general, a single component realization may itself be seen as a set of pairs {<I_1,C_1>,...,<I_n,C_n>}, where Match(I,C) evaluates to true for some pairs and to conditionally true or unknown for the others. We are currently experimenting with variants of the rudimentary interface shown in Figure 23.5 to integrate the new information (specific type mappings for a given <I,C> pair and their status) and to offer the required functionalities to incrementally build and visualize the framework realization.

23.4.3 Discussion

This section provides detailed discussion on two major issues: (1) the effectiveness of signature matching and (2) the effect of object interaction style.

On the Effectiveness of Signature Matching

Notwithstanding the algorithmic difficulties inherent in signature matching, we are finding out, through simple tests with the ObjectStore Environment (OSE) library, that signature matching is weak in general when dealing with utility-like classes, as opposed to domain-specific ones. The problem is made worse in a loosely typed language like C++ where the basic types int, char, and void * (generic pointer) are heavily overloaded for genericity purposes (see, for example, [Mili 1994b]). The example of Figure 23.5 shows several functions with no input parameters and no return types, or a Boolean return type.[11] Our choice of signatures as a behavioral description mechanism was motivated by the fact that signatures can be extracted automatically from the source code. This description can be extended to include other information that can be extracted from the code. The simplest (and least analytical) way uses method *names* as well as their type signatures, for the purposes of matching, based on the assumptions that names reflect semantics, with known disadvantages (see, for example, [Mili 1995]). We are using name matches to *rank* rather than *filter* the candidates that match based on types alone. Name matching relies on some lexical processing to increase the possibility of matching (for example, reducing method names to word stems (see, [Mili 1997]).

A second alternative augments the description of the behavior of a method by the signatures of the methods *it* calls. Extracting such information for methods of classes is done by a C++ parser [Mili 1997]. Extracting it for methods of participant interfaces can be done by analyzing the message flow graphs of the framework: collecting, over the set of message flow graphs where a particular participant method appears, the set of messages immediately (as opposed to transitively) triggered by it. Implementing this matching alternative is a bit more involved, in part because of the circular dependencies, and has not been evaluated yet. Since both alternatives rely on the basic type-based signature matching, we will be offering developers with all three variants (vanilla-flavor type-based signature matching, type-based with names, and type-based with signature matching of *called* methods), with the last two helping to filter out spurious matches or breaking ties. Later versions may accommodate some variations in the signatures such as optional parameters and type conformance instead of type identity; only experimentation will tell if the heavier machinery is worth the trouble.

On the Effect of the Object Interaction Style

The traditional way of composing the behaviors of objects is through explicit references to the objects and to their methods. This creates dependencies between the objects, which precludes their independent reuse and limits the range of objects that can fill a

---

[11]OTCBoolean, which is essentially an int.

particular role. We have long advocated (see, for example, [Mili 1990, 1996]), along with others (see, for example, [Borning 1986; Freeman-Benson 1989; Wilk 1991]), a declarative interobject behavioral composition mechanism, as a way of building independently reusable objects and of providing greater possibilities for behavioral composition [Mili 1996]. Roughly speaking, objects respond to messages by executing methods and by notifying other interested parties (other objects or constraints) of any state changes that may have resulted. This notification will in turn trigger other objects to execute other methods, and so forth. What makes this mechanism effective is the fact that the notifier need not know explicitly the identity of the objects to be notified (their ids or even their classes), nor the specific actions (methods) to take in response to these notifications; this information resides in an external table[12] that can be updated programmatically, instead of being hardwired in the source code of the participants. This paradigm serves as the basis for many user interface frameworks (see, for example, [Barth 1986], Smalltalk's Model/View/Controller), but is rarely followed to the letter in industrial-strength frameworks, in part for efficiency reasons. Our structural model of frameworks provides for the representation of such dependencies (*constraints* and, to some extent, *variables*, see *Section 23.2.2*) and we can imagine either a framework compiler that would translate such constraints into explicit calls between framework participants, or a runtime dispatcher that would assure the coordination during execution.

Other behavioral composition paradigms could be considered. One such paradigm consists of coding framework participants as parameterized/generic types à la Ada's generic packages or C++'s templates (see, for example, [Tracz 1993]). For example, using C++'s templates, we could define the class Dispatcher as follows:

```
template<class Job> class Dispatcher {
        . . .
        void schedule()                    {
            if (_currentJob->getPriority() >...)
                . . .
        }
        . . .
private:
        Job* _currentJob;
        . . .
}
```

In this case, we can use any actual/concrete class in lieu of the type parameter Job *as long as it supports the methods invoked on it from Dispatcher's methods* (for example, the method getPriority() in the preceding example). This solution does not limit us to subclasses of some predefined abstract class, as was the case with the OSE simulation framework discussed earlier. However, the specific realization of Job has to provide methods with the appropriate signatures *and names*. Artifacts such as *pluggable adaptors* (for example, Smalltalk's MVC library) or *software connectors* (see, for example, [Yellin-Strom 1994]) have been proposed as a way of bridging nomenclature and other kinds of mismatches. They may be used to support any composition technology, but are most valuable for the ones that have to rely on source-level dependencies.

---

[12]Much like a dispatch or an interrupt table.

23.5 Framework Packaging

One of the goals of our representation model was scalability, or embeddability, whereby we try to package frameworks in such a way that they can be participants of other frameworks. In this section, we are concerned with the packaging of the source code itself of a framework realization into a single unit. We first look at the motivations behind the packaging, and then the problems it raises and the way we addressed them in the context of our current implementation. It should come as no surprise that we will package framework realizations as classes, and we will discuss the advantages of such a packaging by referring directly to class properties.

23.5.1 Motivations

Packaging framework realizations as classes is a good way of physically packaging framework-related source code. For instance, a framework may involve the creation and management of data entities other than the participants themselves (framework variables), which need to live and be accessible during the operation or lifetime of the framework. We need a construct to group these variables, and a class offers the right combination of visibility scoping and lifetime scoping. Further, such classes may be used to encapsulate framework-specific processing such as message sequences and instantiation scenarios. Packaging frameworks as classes is also good for reuse purposes, as it abstracts away the implementation details of the framework, making it easier to program with the framework, and shielding the resulting programs from any changes in the underlying structure of the framework. By programming directly into the framework's interface, we shield our programs from iterative refinements of the framework, which may lead to redistributions of functionalities among the participants—for example, by splitting the functionality of a participant into two new participants. Naturally, one might argue that by wrapping all the functionality into a monolithic class, we are defeating the benefits of building an event-based system as a collaboration of several classes, which are (1) the independent reuse of those classes and (2) the flexibility obtained by breaking down the functionality, providing a wider range of behaviors. We are *not* defeating those benefits because we envision framework packaging as a *delivery mechanism* and not as a *construction mechanism*: We still develop and maintain (and reuse) participants separately, and *combine them at will for framework realization*.

A second important motivation for framework packaging has to do with providing a *locally optimized* interobject behavioral composition mechanism, based on a generic and possibly inefficient one. This is important for framework developers who want their frameworks to be more widely reusable and with a wider range of components. It is also important for framework users who want to find a greater range of participants to choose from, but want an efficient implementation for object intercommunication. Assume that we use a notification-based mechanism to coordinate objects. This means that participants do not need to trigger each other explicitly. For example, Smalltalk supports a notification-based mechanism for object coordination, called a *dependency mechanism*, through which the environment maintains a list of dependents for each object, which are notified anonymously when that object wishes to inform the world about changes it underwent. While this mechanism is very flexible, it can be fairly inefficient because *all the dependents* of a particular object are notified whether the changes taking place in that object concern them or not. Packaging allows us to hard-code a specific dependency, but in a way that keeps both objects independent. For example, the task *schedule* for the simulation system is defined as follows:

```
void schedule (IN Job j){
        0> d->scheduleJob(j)
              1> q->add(j)
}
```

where d stands for the dispatcher and q for the queue, and says that the invocation of the message "scheduleJob( )" on the dispatcher triggers the invocation of the message "add" on the queue. If the framework developer had intended a notification-based mechanism between participants, a particular implementation of the Dispatcher interface would not need to know about the queue. However, when we assemble the components of a specific realization (an instantiation scenario), we will have to register the queue q as a dependent of d in the global dependents table. With packaging, we can generate a method as follows:

```
void OTCSimulationSystem::schedule (Job j){
        d->scheduleJob(j);
        q->add(j);
}
```

where OTCSimulationSystem is the class generated to represent the framework and schedule the method representing the task with the same name.

23.5.2 Packaging Procedure

We have developed a first version of a C++ framework packager which maps abstract framework descriptions and specific participant realizations into actual C++ code. The FPOTC_SimulationSystem example (see following) shows excerpts of the generated class definition for the framework simulation system. We first summarize the most important transformations from framework description to source code and then comment on specific constructs. Roughly speaking, the generation rules for the class declaration are as follows:

- Framework → class, where <class name> = "FP" .<framework name>
- Framework participants, variables → data members, where:
  - <member name> = <participant/variable name>
  - <member type> = pointer to the class matching <participant interface/variable type>

When the participant is a collection of objects (for example, j*, where * is the Kleene star), the member type is a container class capable of holding the type of the participant.

- Tasks → function members, where:
  - <function name> = <task name>

- <function signature> = <task signature>, where we substitute interfaces by realization classes, OUT (parameter passing mode) by reference passing (&)

- Instantiation scenarios → constructors, where:

  - <constructor signature> = <instantiation scenario signature>, where we substitute interfaces by realization classes

In case we have several instantiation scenarios with the same signature (the case of the following FPOTC_SimulationSystem example), we define a parameterless constructor, but several initialization functions with automatically generated names.

Note that the container class used for multivalued participants depends on the contents of the library. Our packager has options for defining default container classes—in this case, the template class OTC_Collection<T>. Other language-specific default options should be specified, such as the default mapping of built-in types/interfaces,[13] ways of handling OUT parameters (as "&" versus as pointers), and so on.

```
class FPOTC_SimulationSystem {
public:

        // constructors
        FPOTC_SimulationSystem() ;

        // initialization methods

        virtual void initialize_scenario1();
        virtual void initialize_scenario2();

        // access methods

        OTC_Dispatcher* getDispatcher();
        OTC_JobQueue* getQueue();
        ...

        // tasks

        virtual int runSimulation();
        virtual void schedule(OTC_Job* theJob);

private:
        // data members
        OTC_Dispatcher* dispatcher;
        OTC_JobQueue* queue;
        OTC_Collection<OTC_Job>* jobs;
}
```

The actual code generation involves additional rules, which may be divided into general rules, policy rules, and language-specific rules. General rules include the sub-

[13]We use the abstract type Integer in framework descriptions. It can be mapped to a C++ int, long, unsigned, and so on.

stitution of interface names by actual class names, and of message names by the corresponding realization class method names. Policy rules have to do with things such as the underlying message sequencing mechanism—for example, deciding whether each message invokes the immediately subsequent one(s), as is done here, versus using a notification-based mechanism. Language-specific rules are self-explanatory and deal with message-sending syntax, iteration constructs, and the like. The source code generated for the framework tasks and instantiation scenarios is inevitably incomplete because our notation for message flow graphs does not include all of the control information (alternation, loops) and should not be cluttered with low-level operations. Users of a framework package should derive from the generated class and redefine locally the methods whose generated code is incomplete, which explains why the function methods that correspond to tasks and instantiation scenarios are all declared virtual (see FPOTC_SimulationSystem example).

```
FPOTC_SimulationSystem::FPOTC_SimulationSystem()
        :jobs(new OTC_Collection<OTC_Job>)
        {}

void FPOTC_SimulationSystem::initialize_scenario2() {
        dispatcher = new OTC_Dispatcher;
        queue = new OTC_JobQueue;
        dispatcher->Initialize(queue);
}

...

int FPOTC_SimulationSystem::runSimulation(){
        return dispatcher->run();
}

void FPOTC_SimulationSystem::schedule(OTC_Job* theJob){
        dispatcher->schedule(theJob);
}
```

At the time of this writing, we have just completed our first version of the framework packager, and we don't yet have practical experience to evaluate the usefulness of the generated method bodies. The important issue, from a maintenance and a reuse point of view, is to figure out whether the manually written code in developers' derived classes is invalidated by a regeneration of the base class. Some of the work we are currently pursuing deals with identifying the simple cases of changes in the framework structure that would have no effect on the derived code and/or localizing, as narrowly as possible, the scope of those effects.

23.6 Related Work

There has been a lot of interest recently in object frameworks of various forms, including some of the work mentioned in *Section 23.1*. Work on the specification, development, and use of object frameworks can benefit from the following areas:

Representation of behavioral compositions. Interest in describing functional or *behavioral* compositions predates the object-oriented paradigm, and some of that work has carried over to the object-oriented domain. There is a wide spectrum of composition paradigms, depending on the level of abstraction of the language and its granularity. There is a range of *module interconnection languages* [Hall-Weedon 1993] from the fairly formal LIL (see, for example, [Goguen 1986]) and other descendants of OBJ, which focused on algebraic specification of parameterized data types, to the more practical languages or language extensions, which are concerned mostly with verifying that a set of collaborating modules satisfy each other's expectations in terms of supported interfaces (see, for example, ANNA [Tracz 1993], *contracts* [Helm 1990]). Researchers have shown that this requirement is not only needlessly strict (for example, [Yellin-Strom 1994]), but also insufficient, as a lot of the assumptions about the behavior of peer modules are not explicit in their interfaces (see, for example, [Garlan 1995]). On the more abstract level, we have a range of logic-based composition techniques embodied in constraint and logic programming languages (see, for example, [Saraswat 1989; Wilk 1991]). These languages have the advantage of supporting composition while obviating the need for cross-referencing (*lexical binding*) between components. However, they are too far removed from procedural (practical) languages and are of limited use in practice. Work on reactive and discrete-event systems benefits from a long tradition and a number of formal results on both the validation and verification aspects of compositions [Mili 1995], but is too cumbersome for more traditional applications. Our own approach to *constraints* combines the declarative and (composability) aspects of declarative-style compositions, with an imperative object-oriented programming style (see [Mili 1990, 1997]).

Search and realization issues. Software reuse research has traditionally focused on packaging and search issues for reusable components [Mili 1995]. The sharing of reusable component libraries over the Internet[14] will bring search issues back to the forefront as developers now have the option of choosing between components from numerous, heavily overlapping component libraries. Within the context of the two-phase search (see *Section 23.1.5*), we see two kinds of issues: (1) issues of *closure,* as we have to match individual behavioral specifications to compositions of such specifications, and (2) the issue of finding potential participants for a given framework. The first problem is a notoriously difficult one (see, for example, [Lam-Shankar 1992]), and we may have to settle for the verification of necessary but insufficient conditions or use heuristic techniques that rely on structured documentation. The second set of issues is an instance of the more general problem of matching class specifications to class implementations, which has been studied under various forms both theoretically (see, for example, [Chen 1993; Goguen 1986; Guttag 1985; Mili 1994a]) and practically (see, for example, [Zaremski-Wing 1993]). At issue are both the decidability of interface matching itself, as well as the usefulness of matches. Typically, the more information used in the matching process, the more significant the matching. However, the additional information often comes at a great expense or relies on unrealistic assumptions. We have been careful to limit our investigation to constructs that are readily available in existing frameworks code or to ones that can be easily extracted.

---

[14]The library from which the two example frameworks was retrieved via a rudimentary web keyword search.

Packaging issues. The problem of packaging a set of interacting objects/modules into a module arises quite often in OO work, be it at the modeling/analysis level (for example, [Mili 1990]) or at the code level with things such as module interconnection languages ([Hall-Weedon 1993]). Some of the issues include deciding on what to expose to the outside world and what to hide, as well as providing the same kind of flexibility through the encapsulation interface. Interestingly, much of the work on packaging frameworks seems to come from the practical arena, with the revival of code generators in general and user interface generators in particular. While much of the work on user interface frameworks during the 1980s focused on better delineation of user interface functionalities and separate packaging of those functionalities (for example, the MVC framework [Reenskaug 1995], Interviews [Linton 1989]), the newer generation of development tools and environments (see, for example, ParcPlace/.Digitalk's VisualWorks and Parts product lines, IBM's VisualAge/Smalltalk environment) focus on providing developers with the means to specify the external behavior and appearance of interfaces, but relieve them of the implementation details of the frameworks by generating automatically the glue code that ties the MVC pieces together.[15] In essence, this trend is moving frameworks from a paradigm for the *user* of reusable components, to a paradigm for the *developer* of such components. Issues of maintainability of frameworks and the interoperability of frameworks that share participants need to be addressed, and we have barely scratched the surface.

23.7 Summary

In this chapter, we described ongoing research at the University of Quebec to develop a representation for object frameworks that supports a number of often conflicting goals, not the least of which is our desire for solid theoretical underpinnings and immediate applicability. Our theoretical work progresses hand in hand with prototyping efforts that aim at making our ideas workable. Our research strategy has been to cover the entire life cycle of development with frameworks—albeit not at great depth—with the purposes of identifying the major issues that need to be addressed so that we can provide effective and robust support for programming with object frameworks.

From a theoretical standpoint, there are a number of outstanding issues. First, we are exploring the range of useful relationships that may exist between object frameworks and that support extensibility and scalability. We have seen in *Section 23.2.1* two examples of such relationships. Along with exploring the various kinds of relationships, we will explore design or style guidelines that would make such frameworks more separable. Second, there remain a number of outstanding issues with the packaging of message flow graphs as single messages through *interface closure*. For the time being, we have used default conservative closure rules. Notwithstanding the fact that such a closure may carry extraneous parameters, it ignores the interplay of pre- and postconditions between the messages in the flow graph and may lead to inconsistent or indeterminate parameter values. Further, our closure algorithm abstracts some aspects of object synchronization and creates atomic boundaries around essentially

---

[15]Which makes it even harder to teach good OO design practices with such tools and environments.

nonatomic operations. This means that the *interface* closure of a task may not always be a faithful abstraction of what happens within the task; additional *behavioral/dynamic* information may need to be included. This problem is not specific to frameworks; it arises with reusable software of all sorts [Garlan 1995; Kiczales-Lamping 1992]. Finally, we are also experimenting with the generation of message sequences from the specification of structural constraints (see *Section 23.2.2*). Key to this effort is the construction of a catalog of such constraints.

From a practical standpoint, we are developing tools for automating the extraction of framework specifications. Other aspects of our work required that we build a C++ parser that uses static type analysis to extract static cross-references between methods belonging to various classes. We are augmenting this parser to extract framework-specific message flow graphs by (1) limiting the call graphs to those that are initiated by methods that are part of the required interfaces of framework classes and (2) by performing some measure of data flow analysis to trace actual framework participants (as opposed to their types) through a call graph; tracing a variable through casting and polymorphic assignment is proving to be quite a challenge. We are also refining the tools already developed. First on our agenda is the interface matching tool in general and the framework realization tool in particular. We are currently working toward a realistic data set, so that our methods and tools can be validated experimentally.

23.8 References

[Barth 1986] Barth, Paul. An object-oriented approach to graphical interfaces. *ACM Transactions on Graphics* 5(2), April 1986:142–172.

[Borning 1986] Borning, Alan, and Robert Duisberg. Constraint-based tools for building user-interfaces. *ACM Transactions on Graphics* 5(4), October 1986:345–374.

[Chen 1993] Chen, Patrick S., Rolh Hennicker, and Matthias Jarke. On the retrieval of reusable components. In *Advances in Software Reuse,* selected papers from the *Second International Workshop on Software Reusability,* pp. 99–108, Lucca, Italy, March 24–26, 1993, IEEE Computer Society Press.

[Darden-Rada 1988] Darden, Lindley, and Roy Rada. Hypothesis formation using part-whole interrelations. In *Analogical Reasoning: Perspectives in Philosophy and Artificial Intelligence, D.* Helman, editor, Netherlands: Reidel, and Dordrecht Publishers, 1988.

[Deutsch 1989] Deutsch, Larry P. Design reuse and frameworks in the Smalltalk-80 programming system. In *Software Reusability,* vol. II, Ted J. Biggerstaff and Alan J. Perlis, editors. Reading, MA: Addison-Wesley/ACM Press, 1989.

[Dijkstra 1976] Dijkstra, E.W. *A Discipline of Programming.* Englewood Cliffs, NJ: Prentice-Hall, 1976.

[Dumpleton 1994] Dumpleton, Graham. *OSE: C++ Library User Guide.* Parramatta, Australia: Dumpleton Software Consulting Pty Ltd, 1994.

[Freeman-Benson 1989] Freeman-Benson, Bjorn N. Kaleidoscope: Mixing objects, constraints, and imperative programming. *Proceedings of OOPSLA 1989,* pp. 77–88, October 1989, ACM Press.

[Gabriel 1994] Gabriel, Richard P. The failure of pattern languages. *Journal of Object Oriented Programming,* February 1994, pp. 84–88.

[Gamma 1995] Gamma, Erich, Richard Helm, Ralph Johnson, and John Vlissides. *Design Patterns: Elements of Reusable Object-Oriented Software*. Reading, MA: Addison-Wesley, 1995.

[Garlan 1995] Garlan, David, Robert Allen, and John Ockerbloom. Architectural mismatch: Why reuse is so hard. *IEEE Software* 12(6), November 1995:17—26.

[Goguen 1986] Goguen, Joseph A. Reusing and interconnecting reusable components. *Computer*, February 1986, pp. 16–28.

[Guttag 1985] Guttag, John V., James J. Horning, and Jeannette Wing. An overview of the Larch family of specification languages. *IEEE Software* 2(5), September 1985:24–36.

[Hall-Weedon 1993] Hall, Pat, and Ray Weedon. Object-oriented module interconnection languages. In *Advances in Software Reuse,* selected papers from the *Second International Workshop on Software Reusability*, pp. 29–38, Lucca, Italy, March 24–26, 1993, IEEE Computer Society Press.

[Helm 1990] Helm, Richard, Ian Holland, and D. Gangopadhyay. Contracts: Specifying behavioral compositions in object-oriented systems. *Proceedings of OOPSLA 1990*, Ottawa, ON, October 22–25, 1990, ACM Press.

[Johnson 1992] Johnson, Ralph E. Documenting frameworks using patterns. *Proceedings of OOPSLA 1992*, pp. 63–76, Vancouver, BC, October 18–22, 1992, ACM Press.

[Johnson 1994] Johnson, Ralph. Why a conference on pattern languages. *Software Engineering Notes* 19(1), January 1994:50–52.

[Johnson-Foote 1988] Johnson, Ralph E., and Brian Foote. Designing reusable classes. *Journal of Object-Oriented Programming*, August/September 1988.

[Kiczales-Lamping 1992] Kiczales, Gregor, and John Lamping. Issues in the design and documentation of class libraries. *Proceedings of OOPSLA 1992*, pp. 435–451, October 1992, ACM SIGPLAN Notices, Vol. 27, No. 10.

[Lam-Shankar 1992] Lam, Simon S., and Udaya Shankar. Specifying modules to satisfy interfaces: A state transition approach. *Distributed Computing* 6:39–63.

[Linton 1989] Linton, Mark, John Vlissides, and Paul Calder. Composing user interfaces with interviews. *IEEE Computer*, February 1989, pp. 8–22.

[Mili 1990] Mili, Hafedh, Johen Sibert, and Yoav Intrator. An object-oriented model based on relations. *Journal of Systems and Software* 12, May 1990:139–155.

[Mili 1994a] Mili, Ali, Rym Mili, and Roland Mittermeir. Storing and retrieving software components: A refinement-based approach. *Proceedings of the Sixteenth International Conference on Software Engineering*, Sorrento, Italy, May 1994.

[Mili 1994b] Mili, Hafedh, Odile Marcotte, and Anas Kabbaj. Intelligent component retrieval for software reuse. *Proceedings of the Third Maghrebian Conference on AI and SE*, pp. 101–114, Rabat, Morocco, April 1994.

[Mili 1995] Mili, Hafedh, Fatma Mili, and Ali Mili. Reusing software: Issues and research directions. *IEEE Transactions on Software Engineering* 21(6), June 1995:528–562.

[Mili 1996] Mili, Hafedh. On behavioral descriptions in object-oriented programming. *Journal of Systems and Software*, August 1996.

[Mili 1997] Mili, Hafedh, Estelle Ah-Ki, Robert Godin, and Hamid Mcheick. Another nail to the coffin of multi-faceted component classification and retrieval. *Proceedings of 1997 Symposium on Software Reuse (SSR 1997)*, Boston, MA, May 1997.

[Reenskaug 1995] Reenskaug, Trygve. *Working with Objects*. Englewood Cliffs, NJ: Prentice Hall, 1995.

[Saraswat 1989] Saraswat, Vijay A. Concurrent constraint programming languages. Ph.D. thesis, Carnegie Mellon University, January 1989.

[Tracz 1993] Tracz, Will. LILEANNA: A parameterized programming language. In *Advances in Software Reuse,* selected papers from the *Second International Workshop on Software Reusability,* pp. 66–78, Lucca, Italy, March 24–26, 1993, IEEE Computer Society Press.

[Wegner 1992] Wegner, Peter. Dimensions of object-oriented modeling. *COMPUTER,* Special Issue on Object-Oriented Computing, 25(10), October 1992:12—20, IEEE CS Press.

[Wilk 1991] Wilk, Michael. Equate: An object-oriented constraint solver. *Proceedings of OOPSLA 1991,* pp. 286–298, Phoenix, AZ, October 6–11, 1991, ACM Press.

[Yellin-Strom 1994] Yellin, Daniel, and Robert Strom. Interfaces, protocols, and the semi-automatic construction of software adapters. *Proceedings of OOPSLA 1994,* pp. 176–190, Portland, OR, October 1994, ACM Press.

[Zaremski-Wing 1993] Zaremski, Amy M., and Jeannette M. Wing. Signature matching: A key to reuse. In *Software Engineering Notes* 18(5): 182–190, proceedings of the first *ACM SIGSOFT Symposium on the Foundations of Software Engineering,* 1993.

23.9 Review Questions

1. The representation of interobject behavior raises several dilemmas. Can you think of one and name the trade-offs involved?

2. Why is the scalability of frameworks important?

3. In existing C++ code frameworks, some of the participants may be described in terms of abstract classes where some methods refer to other participants *by name* in the source code. Actual instance uses of the framework will use specialization (or extensions) of the provided participants. Can you think of a way of ensuring that a specific instantiation uses mutually consistent participant specialization? Hint: Think in terms of design patterns.

4. This chapter proposes a method for collapsing message flow graphs into single signatures. In what way is the signature maximal?

5. Can you think of a way of capturing interactive inputs using the closure operation mentioned in this chapter?

6. What is the difference between *framework search* and *framework realization*?

7. C++ frameworks use abstract classes for three purposes: (1) to describe the obligations of the participants, (2) to ensure, through polymorphism, that participant realizations can interoperate, and (3) to provide some reusable code that actual participants may reuse. How would you handle this in Java?

23.10 Problem Set

For any of the following problems, the reader/student is encouraged to get in touch with the authors for feedback and/or (hopefully) lively exchanges. Please contact Hafedh.Mili@uqam.ca.

1. *Framework search:* Develop data structures and algorithms for performing itera- tive search expansion (*Section 23.1.5*), going from the most application-specific to the most generic framework fragment.

2. *Message flow graph extension:* The idea behind framework extension is that of behavioral substitutability. An extended version of a framework should do what the framework does, plus some other things that will not affect its basic behavior. Message flow graph extension is defined conservatively, whereby we can find one-to-one mapping between the messages pairs and control constructs (sequencing and parallelism) between message flow graphs that are in an exten- sion relationship.

   Define more flexible message flow graph extension relationships based on simple topological relationships between the message flow graphs—for exam- ple, adding terminal nodes to the acyclic graph or adding wrapper (before or after) code.

3. *Constraints:* Pick an application domain with which you are familiar. Develop a catalog (between 4 and 10) of constraints within the domain.

   Extract (constraint -> message flow graph) dependencies (*Section 23.1*).

   Record your impressions, and discuss the worth of the model of constraints.

4. *Framework documentation:* Take a framework with which you are familiar. Isolate the interactions of a handful (between two and five) classes, and document the framework using the model presented in this chapter. Please note those aspects with which you had the most difficulty (lack of clarity, rigidity, cumbersomeness, lack of precision, and so on).

5. *Framework realization:* Framework packaging is the process of packaging a partic- ular realization (instantiation) of a framework in a class-like unit.

   a. What are the advantages of framework packaging? Do you see other benefits than the ones mentioned by the authors?

   b. The authors mention the possibility of reverse-engineering/packaging exist- ing code that uses a framework's participants into code that uses only the new packaged unit's interface. For example, if we have a framework FM with par- ticipants P1, P2, and message flow graph

   > mfg1: p1.f(a) ->p2.g(b)-> ...

   we should replace references to p1.f( ) in client code by

   > fmPack.mfg1(a,b,...);

   where fmPack is the instance of the framework package that stands for p1, p2, and so on.

   Identify a set of rules for performing the required code transformations to go from code that refers to framework participants individually, to code that refers to the framework as a package. Pay particular attention to the meaning of *self* or *super* (in Java), or *this* and qualified method references in C++.

SIDEBAR 8
DOCUMENTING FRAMEWORKS: SOLITAIRE IS NOT ALONE

A framework is an object-oriented abstract design for a particular kind of application and usually consists of a number of classes, including an abstract class for each major component [Johnson-Foote 1988]. Documenting a framework consists of supplying information and instruction about the purpose, use, and architecture of the abstract design.

Most software documentation is by description or reference manuals. Frameworks are particularly suited to documentation by example. [Johnson 1992] suggests a method for documenting frameworks by using examples, introduces each major component of the framework, gives an example, and then summarizes the major component. Johnson documents the HotDraw graphical editing system in this manner. [Krasner-Pope 1988] document the Model/View/Controller framework in Smalltalk-80 by giving examples of its use. Examples make the problem domain clearer. They can be used to show how features of a design can be implemented. Each example describes how to solve that particular problem within the problem domain of the framework.

We have chosen to document a Solitaire framework by example. By studying the examples, program designers can learn to use the framework quickly and effectively. This work supports Johnson's contention that examples "make frameworks more concrete, make it easier to understand the flow of control and help the reader to understand the rest of the documentation" [Johnson 1992].

This sidebar presents only the barest of introductions to the Solitaire framework. For the full paper, source code of the framework, and source plus executables for a number of games built from the framework, please visit www.rh.edu/~dave.

SB8.1 Purpose of the Solitaire Framework

The solitaire framework is a set of classes that can be used to implement computer solitaire card games. The major classes in the framework are GAME, PILE, CARD, and DECK. These classes are abstractions that are used to create concrete objects that constitute the game. Cards are displayed on the screen either face up or face down and are grouped in stacks called *piles* according to a layout specification. Figure SB8.1 shows the layout for the Klondike game of solitaire. The Stack, Waste, Foundations, and Columns are all piles of cards. A game is played by selecting a card from one pile, the source, and then selecting a destination pile. The rules for both the source and destination piles are checked and the card is moved if the move is determined to be valid.

We supply a number of user interface classes with the framework, including a visual version of each of the logical classes previously mentioned. However, the logical classes have no knowledge of the visual classes. This means that if a Solitaire designer likes the look and feel of our visual classes, then he or she can get a potentially very big boost toward designing and implementing his or her own game. On the other hand, if the designer prefers a different appearance—say, a collection of buttons instead of a menu bar—he or she can still use all of our logical classes with no change.

Rules of the games are defined by creating subtypes of the Pile class and defining the methods that determine what cards are allowed to be selected from a pile and what

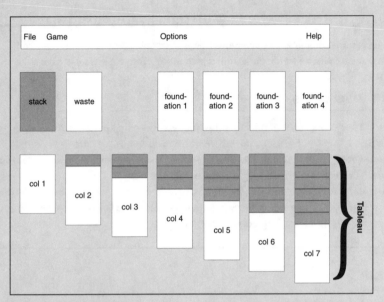

Figure SB8.1   Klondike.

cards are allowed to be added to a pile. The framework supplies basic types for Stack, Waste, and Foundation types of piles. Most of the work involved in building a new game consists of figuring out what kinds of piles the new game requires. These fall into three broad categories:

A Pile that is already implemented in the framework. For example, a number of games can use the Waste Pile from the framework as is.

Piles that are close to those implemented in the framework. For example, the framework has a class Foundation, a subclass of Pile that represents the places where, in many games, the cards should end up. How you add to a Foundation pile differs from game to game, but typically you can't remove cards from a Foundation. If a game has a Foundation pile, we can usually just inherit from the framework Foundation class and fill in one feature, the one about inserting into the Pile.

Piles that are really different. These usually inherit from Pile, but we may need to fill in quite a bit. We then do a bit of research to see if this new kind of pile is common enough to merit representation in the Framework.

Frameworks are seldom really finished—they evolve.

SB8.2 Summary

The process of creating new solitaire games using the framework consists of implementing a predictable collection of classes as subclasses of appropriate framework classes.

Continues

SIDEBAR 8
DOCUMENTING FRAMEWORKS: SOLITAIRE IS NOT ALONE *(Continued)*

Frameworks are amenable to documentation by examples. We have designed and documented a Solitaire framework from which many diverse games can be quickly built.

SB8.3 References

[Johnson 1992] Johnson, R.E. Documenting frameworks using patterns. *Proceedings of OOPSLA 1992,* October 1992, pp. 63–76. New York: ACM/SIGPLAN.

[Johnson-Foote 1988] Johnson, R.E., and B. Foote. Designing reusable classes. *Journal of Object-Oriented Programming,* 1(2), June/July 1988:22–35.

[Krasner-Pope 1988] Krasner, G.E., and S.T. Pope. A cookbook for using the model-view-controller user interface paradigm in Smalltalk-80. *Journal of Object-Oriented Programming* 1(3), August/September 1988: 26–49.

PART

Eight

Framework Management and Economics

Part Eight contains three chapters and one sidebar, and covers framework investment analysis, framework structural and functional stability evaluation, framework management, and the future research direction in the component-based framework technology.

Chapter 24 covers strategic analysis of application framework investments. The goal of this chapter is to assist managers in the strategic planning process for investments in application framework technology. The principal contribution of the chapter is the presentation of a value-based approach to investment planning that encourages the elaboration and evaluation of strategic options within a disciplined strategic and economic framework. Strategic options are elaborated with respect to their potential for improvement of the organization's competitive position and its ability to participate in economically profitable markets. Both the operational and strategic sources of value in organizational reuse capability are exploited through active management of technical and market risk. The innovations in this chapter include the introduction of concepts and techniques from option pricing theory and their application to the evaluation of strategic framework investment scenarios such as new market entry, market repositioning, and investment timing.

Chapter 25 describes a method that evaluates the structural and functional characteristics of framework architectures as they evolve with the development of new versions. Using this method, developers and managers can objectively assess the relative extent of changes in the framework architectural characteristics and, from this, make inferences about the framework's architecture stability. In this approach, the structural and functional characteristics of framework architectures are evaluated using a suite of object-oriented design metrics. The values of the metrics for successive versions of frameworks are computed and compared to determine the extent of change in architectural characteristics between versions. This method has been applied to all publicly released versions of the Microsoft Foundation Classes (MFC) and Borland Object Windows (OWL) application frameworks to evaluate changes in characteristics and compute the extent of change between versions. The evaluations show that the most significant causes of architectural changes between versions are the reworks in collaborations between classes, the assignment of responsibilities to classes, and the addition of new classes to enhance the features and capabilities of the framework systems. A key attribute of this method is that it can be easily modified to include different suites of architectural characteristics and metrics for evaluation, thus providing a practical framework for architecture stability assessment that is adaptable to different domains and environments.

Sidebar 9 describes the expectation mismatch between vendors and customers. Here are two major components of this mismatch: The views and the needs of the customer do not coincide with those of the vendors.

Chapter 26 discusses the future direction of research in component-based framework technology.

CHAPTER 24

Strategic Analysis of Application Framework Investments

The brief history of application frameworks has been focused primarily on technical issues. That is changing today, as more and more organizations are recognizing the potential of application framework investments to improve their strategic position in the markets they serve. But to realize this potential, an approach firmly grounded in the disciplines of business strategy is needed. *Value-Based Reuse Investment* (VBRI) integrates principles drawn from value-based management [McTaggart 1994]—which has been adopted by many of today's most successful companies—with concepts drawn from recent thinking on capturing information technology (IT) business value. The VBRI approach was developed for investments in reusable software in general, but is especially well-suited to investments in application frameworks, due to their role in the acquisition of *organizational reuse capability*.

An essential premise of VBRI is that the principal source of value of investment in organizational reuse capability is in the *strategic options* it generates. Through the introduction of principles drawn from the field of option pricing theory, these strategic options are linked to an established discipline of economic value. This explicit linkage between strategy and economic value supports an approach to strategic planning whereby management is actively involved in the continuous formulation, evaluation, and implementation of strategic options.

24.1 Software Reuse Economics and Organizational Reuse Capability

The Software Engineering Institute introduced the notion of organizational software development *capability* with its popular Capability Maturity Model. It has proven to be a useful approach to the analysis of how and when organizations transform technical capabilities into strategic capabilities. Several variants of the Capability Maturity Model have been proposed in the area of software reuse. For example, Bassett describes a model with five Reuse Maturity Levels (*ad hoc*, *latent*, *project*, *systemic*, and *cultural*) [Bassett 1996]. Another important model, the Reuse Capability Model developed at the Software Productivity Consortium [Davis 1993], foresees four levels:

Opportunistic. Reuse is practiced at the level of the individual project. Project staff bear primary responsibility for reuse-oriented activities. Reusable assets are acquired according to the technical needs of the project development teams.

Integrated. Project staff and management work together to define organization-wide reuse processes and assets that may be used over multiple projects. Assets are acquired according to the anticipated technical needs of the development teams.

Leveraged. A product-line reuse strategy is defined that takes into account sets of related products. Metrics are used to measure costs and benefits. Reusable assets are acquired according to current requirements of customers in the product markets.

Anticipating. Management creates new business opportunities by exploiting the organization's reuse capabilities. Future, anticipated market needs drive the acquisition of reusable assets. New technologies are seen as strategic drivers. The reuse infrastructure is flexible enough to adapt rapidly to market evolution.

The traditional kinds of reuse supported by heterogeneous component repositories are reflected in the opportunistic level of the Reuse Capability Model, whereas organizational policies such as reuse *best practice* initiatives are reflected in the integrated level. A large body of work has been carried out to develop metrics [Poulin 1997] and economic models [Lim 1996] to measure the cost reduction and various quality and productivity factors that are relevant to this type of reuse. These metrics and models are characterized generally by their project-level—even component-level—focus, and can be applied directly by project staff during project execution. Little work in strategic planning exists for these levels of the Reuse Capability Model, largely because it is not really necessary—reuse at these levels is usually aimed at the improvement of existing projects and processes.

Although application frameworks exhibit some characteristics of the lower levels of the Reuse Capability Model, they exhibit even more characteristics of the upper levels. Fayad and Schmidt observe that frameworks *leverage* domain knowledge to support the development of families of related applications, or *product lines* [Fayad-Schmidt 1997]. For example, Chapter 17 describes the framework-based development of a family of applications in the banking domain. Up until now there have been few metrics and economic models for the analysis of product-line approaches, but several projects are currently under way to fill that gap. For example, both the Software Engineering Institute and the European Software Institute have launched significant product-line initiatives.

More and more, however, application frameworks are seen to support the activities of the highest anticipated level of the Reuse Capability Model. Codenie, De Hondt, Steyaert, and Vercammen describe how framework technology plays a *strategic* role in their business of creating software for television stations [Codenie 1997]. They cite the adaptive nature of frameworks as a factor that enables flexible response to new and rapidly changing market opportunities, resulting in a competitive advantage [Codenie 1997]. Citing considerable experience with frameworks not only at the technical level but also at the *managerial* level (a key characteristic of the anticipating level of the Reuse Capability Model), they emphasize that their primary focus is market-oriented rather than technology-oriented. They go on to note, however, that ". . . the details of using a framework as a strategic weapon in attacking a vertical market are largely neglected in the literature." It is here that VBRI seeks to fill the gap.

The capital investment process always consists of two basic kinds of activities: *strategic planning* (the identification of lines of business to pursue) and *capital budgeting* (the financial analysis, allocation of resources, and monitoring of performance in projects in the chosen lines of business). In a sense, they are two ways of looking at the same problem—whereas strategic planning is top-down, capital budgeting is bottom-up. Indeed, Brealey and Myers characterize strategic planning as *capital budgeting on a grand scale* [Brealey-Myers 1996]. The activities of the lower levels of the Reuse Capability Model share the bottom-up characteristics of capital budgeting; those of the higher levels exhibit the top-down characteristics of strategic planning. Ideally, the two views will complement each other, providing an integrated view of the capital investment process, where the link between strategy and economic value is made explicit. The rest of the chapter is devoted to a discussion of the VBRI approach to strategic planning and financial analysis.

24.2 Strategy: A Value-Based Investment Framework

Strategy elevates us to the level of the business, and strategic decisions far overshadow capital budgeting decisions in their potential for value creation or destruction. In fact, a business strategy by its nature does not concern single projects, but a *bundle of projects*. For example, a strategy involving application framework technology will give rise to a number of individual projects, which may include technology investment, research and development, personnel training and deployment, and marketing activities. A manager developing such a strategy cannot even begin to foresee what all these projects *are*, much less calculate their individual economic values. This is, in its essence, what makes strategic planning so difficult—and what makes excessive stand-alone analysis of individual projects a futile exercise. But even if we concede that it is impossible to foresee all of the parameters, factors, and conditions that will affect the value of a strategy, we *can* arrive at an understanding of what creates business value and let this understanding inform our strategic planning process. The first step is the adoption of a single, coherent overall governing objective: the *maximization of economic value over time*.

Although this governing objective may seem self-evident, by no means do companies always pursue it in their actions. Application frameworks have been constructed for many different kinds of product markets and, therefore, are particularly susceptible to misuse in the indiscriminate pursuit of *product market* objectives, such as market share and customer satisfaction. Product market objectives, even when fully achieved, may or may not contribute to the maximization of value over time. A company that achieves a dominant share of its market will, in fact, destroy value if it does not earn over and above its cost of capital—on the contrary, *reduction* of market share (through appropriate focusing) would be the appropriate strategy in that case. Similarly, pursuit of enhanced customer satisfaction has been a successful strategy in many cases, but this strategy does not always *automatically* contribute to economic value maximization. Likewise, in today's fast-moving software industry, it is tempting to stress reduction of time to market on all product introductions; yet it is only one of many possibly conflicting considerations (as will be seen in the section on financial analysis).

In order to ensure that only those strategies are pursued that really have the potential to make a positive contribution to economic value, an investment framework is needed within which to reason about value creation. In VBRI we make use of the *Market Economics/Competitive Position* (MECP) framework [McTaggart 1994], illustrated in Figure 24.1. This framework supports a fundamental assertion: The primary determinants of economic value are the profitability of the markets in which a company participates and its competitive position within those markets. In consequence, the *only* criterion that determines the potential of a particular strategy to create value is whether it enables the firm to participate in economically attractive markets and/or improve its competitive position within those markets. Companies with a strong competitive position in attractive markets will nearly always create value, whereas those with a weak competitive position in unattractive markets will nearly always destroy value. In the other cases, the

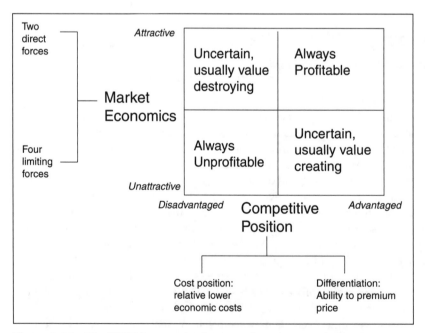

Figure 24.1   The MECP investment framework.

situation with respect to value creation is unclear, and the challenge to management is to try to change the company's position within the framework.

In VBRI, therefore, strategic planning becomes a process of developing strategic options and evaluating them against the MECP framework; this process gives a company a valuable focus for strategy development.

24.2.1 Competitive Position

The forces of competition are such that it is difficult to create and sustain economic value in any markets, particularly those with unattractive economics. But experience has shown that the competitive position of a company has the potential to dominate over market economics in its potential for value creation. This is partly true because a company that can establish a powerful and sustained competitive advantage can often influence directly the economics of the markets in which it participates.

However, a misunderstanding of the drivers of value creation often lead to strategies that ultimately have no effect at all on the competitive position of a company. The MECP framework tells us that there are two (and *only* two) fundamental possibilities for achieving competitive advantage:

- Product offering advantage
- Relative economic cost position advantage

A product offering advantage arises from successful *differentiation*, whereby an economic cost position advantage results from lower production costs. Strategic options have value only to the extent that over time they contribute to competitive advantage in one of these two ways, ultimately translating into higher margins and/or higher market share.

Economic Cost Position

Cost reduction capability through software reuse has been appreciated for many years, and little needs to be added to the discussion. Application frameworks provide even more cost reduction capabilities:

Reduced production cycle time. In competitive situations where reduced cycle time is critical, the many advantages of application frameworks have been documented in great detail and need not be elaborated further.

Lower production costs, higher productivity. Application frameworks are being designed to enable platform independence and increased modularity, allowing framework-based developers to lower their production costs by picking and choosing among the most cost-efficient alternatives available. In addition, labor costs may be lowered through the improved developer productivity that has been associated with framework-based development. Reduced maintenance costs have also been associated with application frameworks.

Product and process innovation. Application frameworks give rise to the promise that innovation can be encouraged not only in the design *process*, but in the very design of the *products* and services themselves. Previously used development processes (for example, the waterfall model) will be replaced with innovative new processes that can lower overall development costs significantly. In addition, this different perspective on software development and structure may encourage imaginative new product and service designs.

Process complexity reduction. Even in cases where the basic underlying development process remains essentially unchanged, its complexity could be reduced considerably through leveraging of application framework facilities that handle complex technical and business subprocesses (application distribution, financial accounting procedures, and so on).

Differentiation

Although the economics of a cost position strategy are straightforward, well-understood, and in successful use in many organizations, the economics of differentiation are much less well understood. Yet one of the primary competitive advantages foreseen for application frameworks is the possibility of differentiation of framework-based products or services, particularly through customization. Thus, it is important to understand clearly the economics of differentiation. A differentiation (or *offering*) advantage is obtained when customers perceive a product to be superior to its competitors in terms of quality, satisfaction, or performance. Being merely *different*, however, is not the same as being *differentiated*. In our experiences, managers tend to overestimate the uniqueness of their offerings. In the value-based approach, we use a precise, measurable definition: Differentiation occurs only when the *customer's* perception of superiority is sufficient that it is *possible for the offering to be priced at a premium* relative to competitive offerings. At this point, management has a strategic option that may be exploited in one of two ways:

- Raise prices as much as possible without losing market share.

- Hold prices even and exploit the differentiation advantage to gain market share.

Thus, it becomes possible to observe the extent to which differentiation has really occurred, by measuring explicitly either (1) the size of the price premium, (2) the increase in market share, or (3) a combination of both. These explicit value measures can deliver information about the level of differentiation that diverges significantly from what management believes is really happening. As an example, a few years ago Marakon Associates worked with a business unit in which the manager was a firm believer in differentiation as a competitive strategy and was confident that he had achieved technical superiority in all of his product lines. Yet by the differentiation measures previously described—price relative to competitors and market share—he had managed to achieve a superior combination of price and market share with only two of five product lines [McTaggart 1994]. Thus, in spite of the clear *difference* in his product lines to the competition, he had not achieved *differentiation* according to a value-based definition. On the contrary, research with the customers showed that in most of his product lines, he was actually at a significant differentiation disadvantage: The users had become sufficiently comfortable and skilled with the previous versions of his products that they were not willing to pay the premium to upgrade to his new versions—a phenomenon often seen in the software industry.

Similarly, the differentiation advantages obtained through framework technology can turn out to be a mirage if not planned and measured in an objective, disciplined manner. Consider, for example, framework technology for the construction of graphical user interfaces. They allow a software developer to construct an infinite number of different graphical interfaces, perhaps even customized for each individual end user. But will these *different* user interfaces result in *differentiation* of the underlying product, or will differentiation depend on some other characteristic, such as the core functionality delivered by the product?

Developing a Competitive Strategy

There is no single answer to the question of whether it is preferable to pursue an economic cost position or a differentiation strategy. In a commodity market, where competition is primarily price-based, a cost advantage can be essential to success. But in highly differentiated markets, where there is little price competition, a cost advantage may not contribute greatly to building consistent profitability over time. This highlights again the basic lesson of the governing objective of value maximization: Any single product market objective may or may not contribute to value creation, depending on the circumstances in which the company finds itself.

The investment of resources in framework development or acquisition should be directed to the characteristics that support the chosen competitive strategy—otherwise they are wasted, since they will not make a contribution to economic value creation. But management should be aware that there are choices to be made in this respect. [Demeyer 1997] indicates at length about the two conflicting technical characteristics of application frameworks that relate directly to this issue: *reusability* and *tailorability*. The reusability of frameworks in related applications contributes most directly to a cost reduction strategy. In contrast, the tailorability of frameworks makes a stronger contribution to a differentiation strategy. Since reusability and tailorability can be conflicting goals in an application framework, management may need to make choices about the relative priorities of each, in light of its overall business strategy. Consider, for example, the decision of whether to build or buy application frameworks, discussed by Fayad and Schmidt, together with their three-level classification scheme of *system infrastructure, middleware,* and *enterprise application frameworks* [Fayad-Schmidt 1997]. The first two kinds of frameworks are especially intended to support the cost-efficient production of software. A company in a line of business where price competition dominates may find it worthwhile to make major investments in these types of frameworks, including a decision to build rather than buy, in order to bring this kind of strategic competence in-house. As an example, imagine a company whose line of business consists solely of providing reliable data archival services to customers at the lowest prices possible. Infrastructure and middleware technology can help it take advantage of the best mix of platforms and distribution strategies to keep prices low while expanding market share. In contrast, imagine a company whose main line of business is to provide highly differentiated, customized services in a vertical market (such as telecommunications services) at premium prices. Here a highly tailorable enterprise application framework provides critical support. Middleware and infrastructure frameworks will have little strategic importance in this case and may be bought from third-party vendors as necessary for technical support.

24.2.2 Market Economics

Although in traditional markets competitive strategy is generally more critical than market economics, this is not necessarily true in the markets in which application framework technology is deployed. The information revolution is facilitating the emergence of new markets (and market niches) with vast possibilities for value creation for those who are able to take advantage of them. Application frameworks can support the creation of market opportunities at the highest level of the Reuse Capability Model. The *market economics* component of the MECP framework is concerned with *participation strategy*: the entry into profitable markets and exit from unprofitable markets, whereby markets and market segments may be defined in a number of meaningful ways (such as by country or end user). As Figure 24.1 shows, there are two direct forces and four limiting forces that affect the attractiveness of a market and tend to place a ceiling on the prices that can be obtained. The two direct forces are the *intensity of direct competition* and *customer pressures*. Some information technology markets are characterized by fiercely intense direct competition, such as the market for relational databases. Even more important can be the power of sophisticated customers to limit profitability. In Internet markets, customer pressures have succeeded in lowering prices to zero (literally) in many cases. In other markets, such as the enterprise resource planning market, customers are used to paying high premiums for services.

The four limiting forces on market profitability are:

Intensity of indirect competition. When substitutes for a company's product or service exist, it has the effect of placing a ceiling on the prices charged, to avoid switching to the substitute. The Internet is creating substitutes for the traditional distribution of many kinds of media, from books to music. In this light, it is not difficult to see the strategic utility of flexible multimedia application frameworks for tracking technology advances [Posnak 1997].

Threat of competitor entry. Markets with low barriers to entry have a ceiling on their profitability, because prices generally have to be kept low in order to protect market share and make it economically unfeasible for competitors to enter. Recent maneuvers in the World Wide Web browser market provide ample illustration of this situation. Application framework technology vendors would seem to be exempt from this kind of threat, but with the appearance of free middleware products, the commercial vendors will have some difficult pricing decisions to make.

Supplier pressures. Although this force would not seem to be relevant to the current discussion, consider that the development of application framework technology solutions generally requires highly skilled, expensive labor resources, which can drive up the cost of production dramatically and limit the firm's capacity to operate profitably. Hopefully, this downward pressure of labor costs on profitability will be mitigated by an increase in productivity as experience is gained with framework technology.

Regulatory pressures. Some markets, such as aerospace, defense, and the environmental industry, are subject to heavy regulations that limit profitability. Up until now, this has also been true in many segments of European industry (for example, telecommunications), although with the wave of privatization occurring in recent years this situation may change.

Since value creation is highly concentrated, the potential can exist for an enterprise to increase its value several times over in a relatively short time by entering profitable markets and by exiting unprofitable markets that produce large economic losses. [McTaggart 1994] notes that there are three basic guidelines to follow when considering market entry.

First, the market itself should be economically profitable and likely to remain so. Some markets, such as defense electronics, have declined significantly in profitability in recent years. Others, such as multimedia and certain segments of the Internet services market, have yet to show evidence that the average participant can consistently turn a profit. In addition, a high degree of uncertainty is often associated with market profitability forecasts in the high-technology arena; in the section on financial analysis we will discuss how to incorporate considerations of this type of uncertainty.

Second, there should be sufficient confidence in the company's ability to sustain a competitive advantage in the targeted market. This may involve leveraging framework technology to increase customer satisfaction through better, more rapid response to their particular needs, as discussed by [Codenie 1997]. Or it may involve a cost reduction strategy through acquisition of middleware frameworks.

Third, the barriers to market entry should not seem insurmountable. In mature markets with entrenched competition, entry can be nearly impossible—few would seriously consider entering the personal computer operating system market today. However, many new information technology markets (such as electronic commerce), with essentially no entrenched competition and no sophisticated customer base, offer great opportunities.

Developing a Participation Strategy

The essential question in a market participation strategy is: What capabilities and strategy can enable the company to enter attractive markets? Experience has shown that one of the most powerful entry strategies is to enter simultaneously in several closely related segments. Framework technology can support a strong offering in several related segments of a newly entered market through exploitation of commonalities in a product-line strategy. For example, Chapter 17 describes an analysis of several related segments in the banking domain, resulting in a layered framework architecture to support the combined offering. In the case of electronic commerce, an enterprise may identify several related segments, such as retailing, credit card transaction processing, telemarketing, secure cybercash transactions, publicity, and advertising. After a competitor analysis, the company's own offering is encapsulated in a suitable framework (or combination of several frameworks) in order to create and sustain a strong competitive advantage on entry. The economics of market entry will be examined in the section on financial analysis, along with another important strategic consideration in market entry: the *timing* of entry. On the one hand, if there are not yet strong competitors in the targeted market, it may be advantageous to make an early, preemptive entry with a strong offering. On the other hand, management often sees the considerable commitment of financial, organizational, and human resources implied by application framework technology as effectively *irreversible*, and understandably hesitates to make the commitment in an uncertain market environment. The choice of how to exploit the timing option can have significant effects on the value created by market entry.

Although the capture of new market opportunities is an important factor in a market participation strategy, an equally important factor in value creation is the *reduction of participation in unprofitable markets*, which should be considered as soon as a company's competitive position deteriorates to the point where economic losses are continually sustained. One type of exit strategy relevant to framework technology is the rationalization of unprofitable product lines. Many software service companies attempt to serve a variety of markets with often redundant capabilities. A framework-based approach to the creation of a meaningful strategy at the leveraged level of the Reuse Capability Model can lead to a streamlined product offering in those markets where the company can truly create a substantial competitive advantage. Domain analysis can help reveal which kind of product line can be sustained in a cost-effective way by the company.

A *combined* entry and exit strategy can be particularly attractive in today's rapidly evolving information technology environment. [McTaggart 1994] describes how Hewlett-Packard successfully pursued an entry/exit strategy in the electronic calculator market in the 1980s. Aiming only for the high-end segment of the market, they would introduce an innovative new offering at premium prices, reaping significant cash flows, until the mass-market competition began to catch up in functionality. The company would not attempt to lower prices and meet the competition head-on, but instead would plow revenues back into research and development. When revenues from the current product offering began to dry up, they would exit that segment, reposition themselves, and reenter at a higher level with a new, even more innovative offering.

Framework technology is ideal for the support of this kind of combined entry/exit strategy. Codenie et al. observe that ". . . a framework's objective is to consolidate the domain knowledge during earlier projects so that it can be reused in future projects to realize a product goal" [Codenie 1997]. A company can exit an unprofitable market segment supported by its framework technology, plow its revenue into framework enhancement, and reenter a new segment with a stronger competitive position. Bassett observes that in this way, organizations can "anticipate changing market conditions . . . they occupy market niches that have short half-lives; they quickly tailor products and services for their customers to a level of sophistication that their competitors cannot match" [Bassett 1996].

The role of framework technology in consolidating knowledge is central to the *conservation of business value* when exiting a market segment, so that it can be reused when entering a new market segment. (We will come back to this issue in the section on financial analysis.) Thus, the continuous enhancement of application frameworks to incorporate and conserve business value can become a key element of a company's market participation strategy. As Codenie et al. aptly note, ". . . as the business evolves, so must the framework" [Codenie 1997].

24.2.3 An Expanded View of Risk Management

Before leaving the section on strategy, a discussion is warranted on the role of risk management in strategic planning. The software development community has traditionally defined risk in pessimistic terms: Risk is something to be avoided, reduced, conquered, mitigated. This view of risk results from the myopic perspective associated with the lower levels of the Reuse Capability Model. At these levels, the technical risk associated with specific projects is the principal concern. In contrast, the upper levels of the Reuse Capability Model elevate us to the level of business strategy. Yet even at these levels, strategic thinking often tends to view only low-risk, stable environments as good candidates for framework technology, justifying the large up-front investments required [Codenie 1997]. But this view is mistaken, because it still only considers technical risk. In addition to project-level technical risk, there is *market* risk, which brings valuable opportunities with it as well as uncertainties.

In today's fast-changing, volatile software market, risk and opportunity go hand in hand, and the strategic investments characterized by many framework investments cannot afford to view risk in pessimistic terms. As Brealey and Myers say, the purpose of risk management should not be to reduce risk, but to *add value* [Brealey-Myers 1996]. Risk management should properly identify those risks that are worthwhile taking and those that are not—as Lister says, ". . . only stupid risks are bad." Indeed, markets that exhibit high risk and volatility often present the most valuable opportunities [Lister 1997]. A willingness to undertake well-chosen risks can prove a great source of value for the enterprise. In the next section, we will see how taking on increased market risk can actually *increase* rather than reduce the value of an investment.

At the lower levels of the Reuse Capability Model, we often speak of *management support* for reuse-related activities. This expression accurately reflects the fact that, at these levels, responsibility rests mainly in the hands of the technical project personnel. It also conveys an idea of business as usual, whereby management intervention is neither needed nor desired—the business-level strategic decisions have already been made. In contrast, the primary responsibility for risk management at the upper levels of the Reuse Capability Model migrates from the technical project personnel firmly into the hands of management. At these levels, the mere *support* of management is not sufficient—the active *involvement* of management is necessary for the creation of strategic options and then the evaluation not only of the risks associated with these options, but also of the value-adding market opportunities they present to the enterprise. The analysis of application framework investments cannot occur in a narrow project-level context of efficiency improvements, but rather in the broader context of strategic investment, where technical risk, market risk, and business opportunities are analyzed in an integrated fashion. In this section, we have presented the strategic elements of Value Based Reuse Investment. In the next section, we discuss how these elements are integrated with the financial indicators of value creation.

24.3 Finance: Linking Strategy to Value

In the previous section, we discussed many kinds of strategic options that may be formulated during the strategic planning process, ranging from operational cost reduction to combined market entry/exit scenarios. But formulation of strategic options is only half the story. [McTaggart 1994] observes that "strategic planning must be rigorous and objective. This means, among other things, that it will require managers to generate high-potential strategic options for comparison on the basis of their value creation potential for the company. It also means that good strategic planning cannot be done without numbers." This observation brings us back to the central tenet of VBRI: Strategic planning can be meaningful only when linked to the economic consequences of the strategies that are elaborated in the planning process.

Disciplined economic evaluation of information technology investments has never been an easy proposition [Clemons 1991]. An entire school of economists is currently engaged in a lively and vigorous debate about the best metrics and methods for capturing the full business value of investments in information technology. [Simmons 1996] discusses a number of different approaches. But there remains widespread agreement among those thinking seriously about the issue—and in the most successful companies—that even new approaches must start from the foundations upon which all modern thinking about economic value rests.

24.3.1 Discounted Cash Flow and Operational Value

In describing the *firm-foundation* theory of investment valuation, Malkiel discusses the concept of the *intrinsic value* of an investment. He credits John B. Williams with working out the basic theory of intrinsic value and its definition: the discounted value of all future cash flows resulting from the investment [Malkiel 1996]. The idea of intrinsic value corresponds to the more formal concept of *present value*: the value today of cash flows in the future. The technique of *discounted cash flow* (DCF) is widely used for the calculation of *present value* and is still the best way to capture sources of operational value in framework-based projects at the lower levels of the Reuse Capability Model—in particular, with respect to strategies for improving economic cost position in well-established lines of business.

If we assume that cash flows are net flows, in the sense that they represent the difference between costs and benefits in each period, then the *net present value* (NPV) of an investment can be expressed as follows:

$$\text{NPV} = \frac{C_0 + C_1}{(1 + r)} + \frac{C_2}{(1 + r)^2} + \ldots + \frac{C_n}{(1 + r)^n}$$

Here C_i is defined as the *net cash flow* in period I, and r is the *discount rate*. If the investment is risk-free then r is simply the risk-free *rate of return* such as that guaranteed by Treasury bills. If the investment carries associated risk (such as a stock or a real-world project), then r is generally higher, reflecting the higher uncertainty of returns. If a proposed investment has a net present value greater than zero, then it is considered worth undertaking. A very entertaining introduction to discounted cash flow concepts, particularly the relationship between discount rates and risk, can be found in [Malkiel 1996].

To illustrate the technique, consider a simplified generic scenario for the deployment of framework technology in a well-established line of business, illustrated in Table 24.1. We postulate three successive time periods of equal duration (for example, one year): an initial period of framework development, followed by a second period of application development, and a third period of operations and maintenance. Amounts are expressed in thousands of dollars. Negative amounts represent cash outflows; positive amounts represent cash inflows. Forecasts may be based upon estimates obtained from the application of the best available reuse metrics and cost models [Frakes-Terry 1996].

Table 24.1 Discounted Cash Flow Evaluation of Generic Framework Scenario

CASH FLOWS	FRAMEWORK DEVELOPMENT	APPLICATION DEVELOPMENT	OPERATIONS
Revenues	100	350	600
Programming labor	−600	−100	−25
Maintenance	−100	−50	−25
Net cash flows	−600	200	550

If we assume a discount rate of 15 percent, then for this scenario the net present value is −10, which would discourage the up-front investment. The relative sizes of the numbers reflect the observations of many authors about the economic characteristics of framework projects: an early period of heavy investment and scarce cash inflows, followed by later periods of cost savings and higher revenues. For example, in describing the large up-front costs associated with framework development, Doscher and Hodges note that "the initial cost of specification and implementation is further increased by costly framework skills, added education, validation and conformance testing" [Doscher-Hodges 1997].

This also illustrates why it can be so difficult to make the business case for application frameworks. The up-front costs and lead time before revenues begin to flow weigh heavily on a traditional discounted cash flow calculation. The distribution of labor and revenues in more traditional development projects generally produces more revenue earlier. Even the promise of future high revenues coupled with low maintenance costs is often not good enough. Many application framework projects have never been launched because the up-front costs simply could not be justified.

At the lower levels of the Reuse Capability Model, the decision not to invest under this generic scenario may well *be* the correct one. After all, in a well-established line of business with a well-defined operational scenario, the forecast of costs versus benefits and their comparison through a discounted cash flow calculation represent the best available measure of the economic worthiness of the investment. For a specific project, if this measure tells us that the costs of introducing framework technology are not outweighed by the foreseeable benefits over the life span of project operations, then the investment is unjustified.

However, this measure does not always tell the full story. The discounted cash flow approach to cost/benefit analysis of framework investments is predicated on a scenario of *business as usual*, with a foreseeable future and a stable operating strategy. It cannot be denied that frameworks can contribute to improvement of this kind of business scenario—in particular, through improvement of economic cost position and product offering. We have discussed in the section on strategy how each of these kinds of improvement can be measured, and they create value within the MECP framework by improving the company's competitive position. Yet the upper levels of the Reuse Capability Model introduce other considerations that are related to the market economics component of the MECP framework. These considerations are predicated on new business models, where new markets are opened up by the introduction of new ideas and technology, and active management reacts in response to rapidly changing market conditions with the value-adding exploitation of strategic organizational reuse capabilities. Is it impossible to estimate the value of these benefits, so often considered to be intangible?

24.3.2 Real Options and Strategic Value

We consider dangerous the way of thinking that insists that the strategic value of information technology must remain intangible and therefore incalculable. It is a step toward vagueness in concept and away from realistic, grounded financial estimates. We believe, along with many others, that the central notions associated with intrinsic value can be conserved so that the discipline brought by valuation can be preserved. The field of option pricing theory has proven to be a potent link between the analysis of traditional sources of value and the more intangible sources of value seen in information technology investments. It is no accident that this theory of economic value has a direct bearing on the concept of *strategic options* on which VBRI is predicated. Applied within the context of the MECP framework, it can help solidify the link between strategy and economic value at all levels of the Reuse Capability Model.

Financial options have been traded on general and specialized stock exchanges for decades. They are special forms of *derivative* securities—that is, their value depends on the value of an underlying asset. A *call option* gives the owner the right, but not the obligation, to buy an asset on a specified future expiration date, at a specified *strike* or *exercise* price. Similarly, a *put option* gives the owner the right (but not the obligation) to sell an asset for a specified price on an expiration date in the future. A *European* option can be exercised only on the expiration date, whereas an *American* option can be exercised at any time before the expiration date. The flexibility afforded by options has made them a popular instrument for investors on both ends of the spectrum: for aggressive investors exploiting the leverage of options for speculation and for conservative investors using options for hedging against possible future downturns. As we will see, there are useful parallels in framework-based investment strategies.

Option pricing theory seeks to understand the fair prices that investors should pay when they buy options, taking into account the relative parameters such as time to expiration, difference between current price and strike price, and so on. Black and Scholes developed a formula for the exact pricing of options that is regularly used in daily trading [Black-Scholes 1973]. The mathematics associated with the formula are beyond the scope of this discussion—we are more interested in the implications of the theory for the strategic planning and decision-making process. Fortunately, it is possible to make immediate use of the formula without dwelling unnecessarily on technical details. Many spreadsheet packages and special calculators exist to make the use of the formula a simple matter. Let us assume the availability of a spreadsheet function of the following form for calculating the value of a European call option:

CALL (V, E, T, RF, STDDEV)

The parameters involved in this function highlight the factors affecting the value of an option.

- V, the current market price (value) of the stock
- E, the exercise price of the call option

- T, the number of days to expiration of the option
- RF, the prevailing risk-free interest rate (for example, the Treasury bill rate)
- STDDEV, the instantaneous standard deviation of the stock's returns

The pricing of put options is essentially the mirror image and involves exactly the same parameters.

Discounted cash flow was developed for the valuation of financial instruments such as stocks and bonds, and then was mapped onto the real world of capital budgeting for projects, as we have seen in the preceding section. In a similar vein, the real world has borrowed again from the financial world in applying option pricing theory to the valuation of strategic options in capital investment projects. Over the past two decades, applications have been found in sectors as diverse as petroleum exploration and the insurance industry. Consider some real options that can be found in information technology investments:

Option to expand. Also known as a *growth option*, it concerns the creation of future product market opportunities through up-front, pioneering investment. An example would be the development of an application framework preparatory to entering the electronic banking services market.

Option to abandon. In a sense the opposite of a growth option, it concerns the ability to abandon a current investment scenario without losing part or all of the value of the investment. An example would be developing an accounting system around a commercial database that can be reused for another project if this project is abandoned (instead of developing it around a custom solution that would lose its value under abandonment).

Option to defer. This is the ability to defer an investment while waiting for better information. An example would be a decision not to buy a new version of a software product while waiting for a possibly superior version the following year.

Option to switch inputs or outputs. This option concerns the possibility to change either the process (inputs) or products (outputs) of a system. An example would be a component-based software process or customizable user interface building systems.

The introduction of option pricing theory allows us to account for two important characteristics of investments at the upper levels of the Reuse Capability Model:

The notion of active management. We discussed in the section on strategy that in strategic framework technology investment, management plays a key role in value creation by intervening to alter the course of a business strategy as events unfold. This notion is not present at the lower levels, where a project unfolds according to a known, foreseeable scenario, nor is it reflected anywhere in the DCF model of investment.

Explicit acknowledgment (and exploitation) of uncertain market conditions. We have discussed at length the futility of strategic planning and risk management without considering the business risks and opportunities associated with the market. Discounted cash flow analysis considers market factors only in an indirect, relatively one-dimensional fashion (in the discount rate).

This approach makes an important contribution to the managerial decision-making process by enforcing discipline in reasoning about the value of the strategic options made possible by application framework investments. Instead of departing from the solid foundation of value-based thinking and making vague statements about intangible benefits, we adopt the principle of trying to obtain an estimate of the intrinsic value of a strategic option in an *augmentation of,* rather than *departure from,* value-based thinking. By avoiding generalities and, instead, reasoning in a concrete fashion, decision makers are forced to focus their analyses and make grounded, realistic estimates. It is an important step toward the *integration* of the strategic planning and capital budgeting processes that we discussed earlier.

New Market Entry: The Growth Option

Let us now return to one of the most important strategic activities at the anticipating level of the Reuse Capability Model: the exploitation of organizational reuse capability to enter new markets with attractive market economics. New market entry is an example of a company's market *participation strategy*, and an important component of the MECP framework. As an example, let us now consider an emerging market that has been cited often in the context of application framework technology: electronic commerce. In a typical scenario for attacking this market, a company might consider a preliminary strategic investment, consisting of developing an application framework that contains the core business logic for many kinds of financial transactions and services. Company management feels that the electronic commerce market could boom, but there is still a high degree of uncertainty about whether this boom will actually occur. (For example, the market around Teletext never really developed as expected.) Management faces a difficult decision. The competition isn't sleeping—if the investment is not made now, it will not be possible at a later date to gain a foothold in the electronic commerce market if and when it does explode.

More concretely, suppose that in 1998 the company has the opportunity to carry out a pioneering three-year research and development project for electronic banking services for a large bank. The project itself generates some revenues, and it could be carried out within budget if the software were custom-built. But management is considering additional investment to build a full-blown framework within the project, because this should put the company in a strategic position to enter the larger market later. Framework-based application development with high-quality business components may be the only way to sustain a substantial competitive advantage in the expected highly competitive environment. How can management reason about the economic value of the essentially strategic option that framework technology investment would create to enter this new market? The first step is to separate clearly the pioneering framework development stage from the subsequent stage of full entry into the market:

Stage 1: Pioneering investment. In the year 1998, the company commits resources up front to a project that includes research and development of application framework technology for electronic banking services. (Normally this will consist not only of research and development, but also consolidation of domain knowledge and experience.) The required investment is $600,000. The present value in 1998 of all projected cash flows from the pioneering project over its lifetime, discounted at 20 percent, is estimated to be $550,000.

Stage 2: Market entry. Management believes that the decision about market entry must take place in 2001, when the company plans to commit resources to full entry into the electronic banking services market. The required investment will be $1,500,000—well over double the investment for the pioneering stage. The present value in 2001 (the year of market entry) of all future cash flows from operations in the market is projected (at a 20 percent discount rate) to be $1,400,000.

Unfortunately, a straightforward cost/benefit analysis of each of the ventures makes them both look like losers:

- NPV(pioneering investment project including framework construction) = 550 – 600 = (–50)

- NPV(electronic banking services venture) = 1400 – 1500 = (–100)

Yet clearly this analysis does not capture the strategic intention of the framework-building project: to create the opportunity to participate in a possibly burgeoning electronic banking services market. Viewed this way, the initial project can be seen as creating a growth option—an option to make a larger follow-on investment if the market develops favorably. This view also makes it possible to introduce market uncertainty directly as a parameter in the decision-making process. This is done by estimating the *volatility*, or standard deviation of annual returns of the electronic banking services venture. In practice, this might be done by considering the volatility of returns of ventures or stocks in similar market segments, or by forecasting several different market evolution scenarios, estimating the cash flows for each scenario and calculating the volatility across the cash flows for the individual scenarios [Damodaran 1996]. Let us suppose in this case that the uncertainty surrounding the future of the electronic banking services venture is such that a standard deviation of annual returns of 30 percent must be assumed. Suppose also that the prevailing risk-free (for example, Treasury bill) annual interest rate is 10 percent. We can determine the present value in 1998 of the expected cash flows of the electronic banking services venture by discounting back three years at 20 percent.

$$\text{PV (electronic banking services venture in 1998)} = \frac{1400}{(1.2)^3} = 810$$

We now interpret the initial framework construction project as a European call option on the expected returns of the electronic banking services project ($810 in the year 1998) for an exercise price of $1500 (the required investment) in three years. We would use our hypothetical spreadsheet function to calculate the Black-Scholes value of the call option [Black-Scholes 1973] as follows:

CALL (V = 810, E = 1500, T = 3 * 365, RF = 10%, STDDEV = 30%) = 81

Thus, the *expanded* net present value of the initial framework-building pioneering venture is not only its traditional NPV (the discounted value of net returns over its lifetime), but also the value of the growth option to enter the electronic banking services market.

NPV (pioneering venture) = DCF value + growth option = (–50) + 81 = 31

This is a *positive* outcome, when the full intention of the pioneering venture is taken into account, and triggers the up-front commitment of resources to the pioneering investment—even in the face of a negative NPV forecast. This seemingly counterintuitive result can be understood by recalling the nature of the pioneering framework technology investment as a strategic *option*. It gives management the option, *but not the obligation*, to make the larger follow-on investment in the electronic commerce venture if market conditions evolve as hoped. If the market does not evolve favorably, then management can change the investment scenario and cut its losses by choosing not to make the follow-on investment. This is why we speak of *active* management intervention with respect to strategic investment scenarios. Note also how we were able to incorporate strategic considerations while still remaining firmly within the discipline of determination of intrinsic value. The DCF component accounts for value creation at the lower levels of the Reuse Capability Model; whereas the growth option component accounts for value creation at the upper levels.

In order to highlight the insights that this approach can give us into the strategic decision-making process, let us carry out a *sensitivity analysis*. Sensitivity analysis helps to deepen our understanding of the effects of variations in key parameters. In discounted cash flow analysis, it is the estimated cash flows that are the primary parameters of the calculated value. In an options-oriented analysis, however, the palette of parameters that can be varied and studied is richer.

Table 24.2 illustrates the effects of variation in the gross value of the electronic banking services project on the value of the growth option. As the gross project value rises from the base case (810 in Scenario 1) all the way up to a maximum of 1300, the value of the growth option increases dramatically, as high as 352. This reflects the intuition that the bigger the prize, the more valuable the option that keeps the possibility open to obtain the prize.

Table 24.3 illustrates the sensitivity of the growth option to volatility in the returns of the electronic banking services project. Here we see a dramatic illustration of the principle discussed in the section on risk management: Higher market risk actually *increases* the value of an opportunity. In order to understand this seemingly counterintuitive insight, we appeal once again to the principle of active management: Management has the ability to exploit favorable market developments, while minimizing the negative effects of unfavorable developments. In a market evolution scenario with little variation (5 percent in Scenario 1,) there is little chance that the net present value of the electronic banking services venture will deviate from the dismal figure that was

Table 24.2 Sensitivity of Growth Option Value to Gross Project Value

SCENARIO	V	E	T (MONTHS)	RF	STDDEV	CALL
1	810	1500	36	10%	30%	80
2	1000	1500	36	10%	30%	165
3	1100	1500	36	10%	30%	221
4	1200	1500	36	10%	30%	284
5	1300	1500	36	10%	30%	352

Table 24.3   Sensitivity of Growth Option to Market Volatility

SCENARIO	V	E	T (MONTHS)	RF	STDDEV	CALL
1	810	1500	36	10%	5%	0
2	810	1500	36	10%	20%	32
3	810	1500	36	10%	40%	135
4	810	1500	36	10%	70%	300
5	810	1500	36	10%	100%	446

forecast by the discounted cash flow analysis. Thus, the option to undertake this surely losing venture is completely worthless. But in a booming market evolution scenario, where the value of the electronic banking services venture could rise as much as 100 percent above the forecast NPV (Scenario 5), the market positioning afforded by the pioneering venture is worth a great deal—over half the forecast value of the electronic banking services venture itself. This offers an important insight for managers: An enormous potential for value creation is presented by the new, highly volatile markets of today's information technology industry.

Table 24.4 illustrates the sensitivity of the growth option to variations in the time horizon between the pioneering venture and the electronic banking services venture. The base case is illustrated in Scenario 3. As the duration of the time horizon contracts to only one year in Scenario 1, the value of the growth option reduces to effectively zero. Intuitively, this happens because there is little time for favorable market evolution in such a short time horizon—which brings us back once again to the original (dismal) DCF forecast. As the time horizon increases up to five years in Scenario 5, so does the value of the growth option that is being kept open to take advantage of favorable market developments. But note that the value of the option is considerably more sensitive to the volatility of market returns than to the time horizon.

Conserving Business Value: The Option to Abandon

The growth option of the previous section represented a case of market *entry*. However, we saw in the section on strategy that a company's market participation strategy

Table 24.4   Sensitivity of Growth Option to Time Horizon

SCENARIO	V	E	T (MONTHS)	RF	STDDEV	CALL
1	810	1500	12	10%	30%	5
2	810	1500	24	10%	30%	36
3	810	1500	36	10%	30%	80
4	810	1500	48	10%	30%	129
5	810	1500	60	10%	30%	179

also includes market *exit* considerations. The governing objective of economic value maximization is also served by abandoning unprofitable, value-destroying lines of business. In today's constantly changing information technology environment, the danger of a market segment becoming suddenly unprofitable is especially high, due to technology advances, competitor entry, and customer pressures. But the cost of abandoning a market segment can be high, and it is reasonable for companies to look for ways to protect their considerable investments if the decision to abandon should be taken. In particular, the conservation of the value of existing business assets becomes important if the company is pursuing the kind of combined entry and exit participation strategy discussed earlier. At the same time that technology advances and business practices render entire market segments obsolete, they create entire new market segments. A company that is able to exit, reposition itself, and reenter at new levels of sophistication is in the possession of a considerable competitive advantage.

Suppose that a company is pursuing a line of business in the computer-aided educational services market. The slow, steady, and profitable growth of the market segment has permitted the company to establish itself at a satisfactory level of economic profitability over the past several years, with a well-known service product line (including CD-ROM-based instructional packages) and competent, experienced personnel. But management has noted the rapid advance of multimedia technology over the past few years and its probable impact on the market in which the company participates. In particular, the rise of the Internet has brought not only technological advances with it but also an increase in competition and a larger expected variety of competing services, including new services (for example, Web-based training) that did not exist previously. Increased direct and indirect competition is to be expected, through new entry and through substitute products and services.

Management is now planning its next generation of services and technological support. If the business continues as usual, it is certainly the best policy to continue with the same technological support infrastructure. However, management has identified another strategic option: to make additional investment and consolidate the knowledge obtained over the years into application framework technology that would allow it to adapt and defend its services in case of unforeseen (but feared) market developments. This additional investment may take place in the form of multimedia infrastructure frameworks such as that described by [Posnak 1997], which would help the company ensure its base technology against becoming obsolete through substitute technology. It may also include higher-level frameworks similar to that described by [Goldberg 1997] that would consolidate the logic of its curriculum offerings in a more formal, flexible manner and provide some insurance against radical changes in the nature of computer-assisted educational services. In both cases, the extra investment is significant in terms of technology, training, and realignment of business processes, and management would like to know the value of the strategic option that would be created by this investment. Essentially, it must compare the economics of two scenarios:

- Expanded NPV (Scenario 1) = NPV of business without framework technology

- Expanded NPV (Scenario 2) = NPV of business with framework technology + option to abandon

Management already understands that the NPV of the business with the extra framework technology investment is lower than the NPV of the business without framework technology if the current scenario continues as before, but it also understands that the extra insurance against a deterioration in its current business conditions has value. Cast in terms of option pricing theory, the growth option of the previous section was an example of a call option—it pays off in case of an upturn in market conditions. The option to abandon is an example of a put option—it pays off when the value of the underlying investment sinks below a certain level, providing insurance against a market downturn.

Suppose that management estimates that the gross value today of its educational services business is $100,000. It considers that the uncertainty of market evolution is such that the standard deviation associated with this estimate is 60 percent. The prevailing risk-free interest rate is assumed to be 3 percent. Management decides that it will operate for 18 months and make the decision whether to abandon the current business strategy at that point, depending on how the market has evolved. This corresponds to the characteristics of a European option. (Although it would possibly be more realistic to think in terms of an American option, which would permit the company to abandon the business strategy at any time, there are technical complexities in the evaluation of American options that would needlessly detract from our examination of the decision-making process here.) Finally, after consulting with the technical staff, management estimates that in case of abandonment of the current strategy, around 85 percent of the value of its investment in the business would be conserved if it was based upon framework technology—to a great extent because it would drastically reduce the effort required to regroup and redirect its strategy. Our spreadsheet function would evaluate this option as follows:

PUT (V = 100, E = 85, T = 1.5 * 365, RF = 3%, STDDEV = 60%) = 18

An estimated value of $18,000 gives management a more tangible basis on which to reason about the amount of strategic value added by the extra investment in framework technology. As before, sensitivity analysis can help management improve its grasp of the key parameters affecting its strategic scenarios. Intuitively, it would seem that the value of the abandonment option created by framework technology investment should depend on the amount of business value the technology is able to encapsulate and conserve. As Table 24.5 illustrates, this intuition is correct.

As the value conserved in abandonment rises from the base case shown in Scenario 4, the value of the option also rises, until in the rather idealistic case of Scenario 1, where all of the value of the business is conserved, the value of the option to abandon amounts to over 25 percent of the value of the business itself.

Table 24.5   Sensitivity of Abandonment Option to Abandonment Value

SCENARIO	V	E	T (MONTHS)	RF	STDDEV	PUT
1	100	100	18	3%	60%	25.9
2	100	95	18	3%	60%	23.0
3	100	90	18	3%	60%	20.2
4	100	85	18	3%	60%	17.6
5	100	80	18	3%	60%	15.1

Table 24.6 Sensitivity of Abandonment Option Value to Volatility of Returns

SCENARIO	V	E	T (MONTHS)	RF	STDDEV	PUT
1	100	80	18	3%	10%	0.1
2	100	80	18	3%	25%	2.8
3	100	80	18	3%	50%	11.4
4	100	80	18	3%	75%	20.7
5	100	80	18	3%	100%	29.6

As in the case of the growth option, however, it is the uncertainty associated with market evolution that gives the option its real value. Table 24.6 illustrates a set of scenarios where only 80 percent of the value of the business is conserved by the framework technology investment in conditions of market exit. In the stable market conditions of Scenario 1, reflected in a standard deviation of only 10 percent of returns, the extra investment in framework technology is wasted. But as market conditions become increasingly volatile, the value of the abandonment option rises rapidly, up to nearly 30 percent of the value of the business in the extreme case illustrated in Scenario 5. Not only does this illustrate the powerful influence of market volatility, it also reminds us of the key role of management in intervening *actively* to mitigate the effects of a market downturn on the business.

Managing Market Timing: The Option to Defer

In our discussion of growth options we saw that economic uncertainty can motivate early investment in framework development in order to create an option for large follow-on product market investments. Such early investments are important when the decision has been made to attempt entry into a market; the option requires time to build (certainly the case in framework development); and the expected market evolution is such that subsequent entry would be too expensive or too late when the time for the follow-on investment arrives.

Purchasers of application frameworks often have a different perspective. Their problem isn't necessarily *whether* to invest, but *when* to invest. For example, along with the high uncertainty associated with the market, there might also be uncertainty associated with the rate of maturation of framework technology. A company investing in a software development project for multimedia services in today's volatile economic and technical climate in that market sector may worry that in a year's time:

- The multimedia market has developed differently than expected.

- Multimedia framework technology has become available in the meantime that would have provided a much better technical solution than the ad hoc solution that had to be adopted only a year before.

Even mature framework technology can lead to a similar dilemma. The purchase of application framework technology is often seen as an effectively *irreversible* investment because of the large financial, technical, and organizational commitment it involves. (Purchasers of enterprise resource planning frameworks often complain that they become unwilling partners for life with the framework supplier, tied to the supplier's technology, training, and business processes.)

Astute managers sense instinctively that sometimes it is preferable to wait for better information than to undertake even a good investment immediately—for by doing so, they may enhance the value of the investment even further. Yet they are also aware of the opposing pressures of time to market, usually manifested in terms of lost revenues due to delayed market entry or the effects of competition. In simple terms, the risk of investing too soon must be balanced against the risk of waiting too long. In a strategic analysis of this situation, it is useful to think of the manager's latitude in the timing of his or her investments as an *option to defer investment*. Let us consider now how to value this type of strategic option and render it useful to managers in their decision-making process.

Consider an independent software vendor that would like to participate in the market for outsourcing of enterprise management software services (such as inventory and sales management). Entry into this market will involve becoming a business partner of one of the vendors of enterprise applications frameworks for these kinds of services. The investment will be significant, involving technology purchase, as well as training of personnel as certified applications development partners. The total investment required is $125,000. The market economics look attractive, and the gross value of the prospective business has been estimated to be $130,000. It is estimated that after it is launched, the business will produce an annual cash flow equal to 15 percent of the gross value of the project. Since the business under this scenario has a positive net present value of $5000, there seems to be no reason not to invest immediately and begin producing revenues.

But there is a problem. The market is still shaking out and management is not sure whether the enterprise application framework vendor it is considering as a business partner will emerge as the most popular vendor. If it does, then revenues are likely to soar; but if it does not, then the value of the business will diminish greatly. Once management has teamed up with its business partner, it will have taken an effectively irreversible step, and therefore it is considering waiting a year to see how the market evolves before placing its bets. But that will mean giving up the revenues that immediate investment would produce. How can management reason about the relative values of each strategic option?

As noted, the essential dilemma faced by management involves balancing the increased value of waiting to invest (because of active management's ability to exploit increased exposure to market uncertainty) against the drain of lost cash flows due to delayed investment. A similar dilemma is faced by the holder of an option on a stock that pays *dividends*. The holder of a stock is entitled to receive the dividends on the stock from the moment he or she acquires the stock. But the owner of an option is not entitled to receive dividends until the option is actually exercised. Thus, although we have seen in the section on growth options that the value of an option normally increases with its time to expiration, a dampening effect on its value arises from the lost dividend payouts.

Since we are more interested here in gaining insight into the decision-making process than in the details of option valuation, we make use of an extended Black-Scholes formula [Black-Scholes 1973], together with some simplifying assumptions.

Although modeling the timing decision as an American option that could be exercised at any time up to its expiration date would be more realistic (as in the case of the abandonment option), we will finesse the implementation problems associated with the evaluation of this type of option by modeling a *pseudo-American* option [Damodaran 1996] with a series of European options that can be exercised at a series of discrete dates (for example, at three-month intervals). Furthermore, we will assume that the prospective investment produces cash flows at a continuous rate at some percentage of its gross value, analogous to a *continuous dividend yield* on a stock. These assumptions will limit the precision of our analysis, but still convey a sense of how the value of the option is affected by the key parameters.

In our example, the $125,000 investment can be viewed as the exercise price of an option on the gross value of the business. If exercised immediately, the option is simply worth the value of the business minus the exercise price—its net present value. Its value after one year can be estimated by making further assumptions about the evolution of the gross value of the business. For example, suppose that management accounts for the uncertainty in the evolution of the market by estimating a standard deviation of annual returns on the prospective business of 20 percent. Assuming the current risk-free interest rate to be 5 percent, we make use of an extended Black-Scholes formula for the evaluation of *European call options with continuous dividend yield*, by adding the DIV parameter to represent the estimated annual cash flows as a percentage of the gross value of the business [Black-Scholes 1973]:

CALL (V = 130, E = 125, T = 365, RF = 5%, STDDEV = 20%, DIV = 15%) = 6.1

Thus, the NPV of the business if launched after one year would be increased by over $6000, despite the missed revenues from the first year's operations. In other words, it is better to wait.

Table 24.7 conveys a feeling for the value of the option to defer as the time to defer increases. Our base case (Scenario 3) of one year is not, in fact, the optimal length of time to wait. The value of the option increases from 6.0 at four months to a peak of 6.2 at nine months, before the missed revenues begin to drag down the value of the option as the time interval increases.

As Table 24.8 illustrates, the magnitude of the cash flows that are missed by waiting to invest has a significant effect. If the business produces cash flows at an annual rate of only 5 percent of its gross value (Scenario 1), then these lost cash flows do little to offset the value added by waiting out market developments. But when the lost revenues

Table 24.7   Sensitivity of Option to Defer to Time Interval

SCENARIO	V	E	T (MONTHS)	RF	STDEV	DIV	CALL
1	130	125	4	5%	20%	15%	6.0
2	130	125	9	5%	20%	15%	6.2
3	130	125	12	5%	20%	15%	6.1
4	130	125	18	5%	20%	15%	5.7
5	130	125	24	5%	20%	15%	5.2

Table 24.8 Sensitivity of Option to Defer to Rate of Cash Flow Generation

SCENARIO	V	E	T (MONTHS)	RF	STDEV	DIV	CALL
1	130	125	12	5%	20%	5%	12.2
2	130	125	12	5%	20%	10%	8.8
3	130	125	12	5%	20%	15%	6.1
4	130	125	12	5%	20%	20%	4.1
5	130	125	12	5%	20%	25%	2.6

amount to as much as 25 percent of the gross value of the business (Scenario 5), then even the value added by exploiting market volatility is effectively wiped out, and there is little incentive to wait.

Once again, however, Table 24.9 illustrates the dramatic effects of market volatility on the value of an option. In a stable scenario with essentially no forecast deviation from the estimated NPV (Scenario 1), there is no reason to wait—nothing is likely to change, and the revenues will be lost. But as market uncertainty rises, the value of the option to wait rises rapidly, up to a significant percentage of the project's value at a standard deviation of 50 percent (Scenario 5). This provides yet another confirmation of the importance of viewing risk management as a way of adding value not only by *reducing* risk when appropriate, but by *taking on* risk when appropriate.

The Value of Flexibility: The Option to Switch Use

Consider the hypothetical example of a company that pursues business interests providing information technology solutions in the financial management and human resource management sectors. One business strategy may be to create custom solutions for each of these different market sectors. Another may be to base the solution upon a shareable application framework that makes it possible to switch among business sectors as demand fluctuates. How can the value of the flexibility afforded by the framework-oriented solution be estimated?

This is an example of an *option to switch use*. The option to switch use underlies the rationale for *flexible manufacturing systems*, a paradigm that has been used by Bassett

Table 24.9 Sensitivity of Option to Defer to Volatility in Returns

SCENARIO	V	E	T (MONTHS)	RF	STDEV	DIV	CALL
1	130	125	12	5%	10%	15%	1.9
2	130	125	12	5%	20%	15%	6.1
3	130	125	12	5%	30%	15%	10.5
4	130	125	12	5%	40%	15%	15.0
5	130	125	12	5%	50%	15%	19.4

and others to describe framework-based software construction capability, as well as component-based software engineering capability [Bassett 1996]. The discrete valuation techniques that are generally used to analyze this type of option [Cox 1979] are beyond the scope of this treatment, but we expect to see more work in this area in the future.

24.4 Summary and Related Work

We have presented a value-based view of investment in which the objective of economic value maximization governs the strategic planning process. But in strategy development, as in software development, there are no silver bullets. Value-based strategic planning is one of the most difficult challenges faced by management, because no individual product market strategy is ever universally valid. As [McTaggart 1994] observes,

> Value based strategic planning upholds no particular orthodoxy of business strategy. For instance, if more market share, more customer service, more quality, or reengineering the manufacturing process to increase efficiency will create more value for the business, it is a good thing. If the effort does not create higher value, further investment in share, service, quality, or efficiency is unjustified. There is no a priori view on whether markets should be served globally or locally, large scale is better than small scale, a full product line is better than a focused product line, vertical integration is better than outsourcing, cost or differentiation should be the basis of competitive advantage, growth should be sacrificed for higher Return on Equity, or vice versa. The right answers to these questions will depend on a detailed understanding of the financial and strategic determinants of value for the business, and the options afforded by the strategic value drivers for a particular business.

VBRI thus views reuse investment planning as a continuous process of formulating strategic options and evaluating them with respect to their potential for value creation, either by improving the organization's competitive position or its market economics, or both. The MECP framework adopted by VBRI is presented in detail by [McTaggart 1994]. Many of the principles embodied in this strategic framework have their origins in the work of [Porter 1985]. Bassett also discusses at length the nature of strategic organizational reuse capabilities deriving from investments in framework technology [Bassett 1996].

Present value concepts in the valuation of capital investment projects are explained in many texts, both informally [Malkiel 1996] and formally [Brealey-Myers 1996]. Due to the importance of market considerations in large investments in organizational reuse capability, VBRI introduces concepts from the field commonly known as *competitive strategy under uncertainty* [Porter 1985]. Dixit and Pindyck provide a particularly extensive presentation of the notion of *irreversible investment* under uncertainty that we have highlighted with regard to application framework technology investments, and they relate it to the notion of options [Dixit-Pindyck 1994]. There are many good texts available on the mathematical elements of option pricing theory [Hull 1993]. The perspective on organizational information technology capabilities as real options is represented by several initiatives, such as the work at the Boston University School of Management [Kulatilaka 1996]. We caution that in emphasizing the contribution of an options perspective to value-based strategic planning we have glossed over many important conceptual and practical issues in the application of option pricing theory to capital investment projects. [Trigeorgis 1996] gives a thorough treatment of these issues.

Future work includes consideration of other techniques for strategic planning under uncertainty, such as scenario planning [Heijden 1996] and the incorporation of VBRI principles into the life-cycle process of developing strategic organizational reuse capabilities. Several authors recommend that application framework development should take place within an iterative, spiral life-cycle model, where risk management serves to mitigate technical risk from one iteration to another [Fayad-Schmidt 1997]. We have proposed that market risk considerations be incorporated into the risk management process in order that active management intervention may add value by redirecting strategy according to changing business conditions, possibly taking on *more* market risk when appropriate. [Sullivan 1997] has taken an options perspective on the spiral model of software development, suggesting that each stage of development may be viewed as an option on the activities of the next stage. They go on to propose an options perspective on the software design process itself, suggesting that it provides a more rigorous way of reasoning about a variety of well-accepted but informal design heuristics.

We have discussed the four levels of organizational capability that are identified in the Reuse Capability Model. Many organizations have already realized significant benefits from reuse investment at the lower levels of the model. Application framework technology investment promises even more significant benefits; but the potential of application framework technology for value creation can be realized only if it is exploited at *all* levels of the Reuse Capability Model. That is the goal of Value Based Reuse Investment.

24.5 References

[Bassett 1996] Bassett, P. *Framing Software Reuse: Lessons from the Real World*. Upper Saddle River, NJ: Yourdon Press, 1996.

[Black-Scholes 1973] Black, F., and M. Scholes. The pricing of options and corporate liabilities. *Journal of Political Economy* 81(May/June 1973): 637–659.

[Brealey-Myers 1996] Brealey, R., and S. Myers. *Principles of Corporate Finance*. New York: McGraw-Hill, 1996.

[Clemons 1991] Clemons, E.K. Evaluation of strategic investments in information technology. *Communications of the ACM* 34(1), January 1991: 22–36.

[Codenie 1997] Codenie, W., K. De Hondt, P. Steyaert, and A. Vercammen. From custom applications to domain-specific frameworks. *Communications of the ACM*, Theme Issue on Object-Oriented Application Frameworks, Mohamed E. Fayad and Douglas Schmidt, editors, 40(10), October 1997:71–77.

[Cox 1979] Cox, J., S. Ross, and M. Rubinstein. Option pricing: A simplified approach. *Journal of Financial Economics* 7(3), March 1979:229–263.

[Damodaran 1996] Damodaran, A. *Investment Valuation: Tools and Techniques for Determining the Value of Any Asset*. New York: John Wiley & Sons, 1996.

[Davis 1993] Davis, T. The reuse capability model: A basis for improving an organization's reuse capability. *Proceedings of the 2nd International Workshop on Software Reuse*, pp. 126–133, Lucca, Italy, March 1993.

[Demeyer 1997] Demeyer, S., T.D. Meijler, O. Nierztrasz, and P. Steyaert. Design guidelines for tailorable frameworks. *Communications of the ACM,* Theme Issue on Object-Oriented Application Frameworks, Mohamed E. Fayad and Douglas Schmidt, editors, 40(10), October 1997:71–77.

[Dixit-Pindyck 1994] Dixit, A., and R. Pindyck. *Investment under Uncertainty.* Princeton, NJ: Princeton University Press, 1994.

[Doscher-Hodges 1997] Doscher, D., and R. Hodges. SEMATECH's experiences with the CIM framework. *Communications of the ACM,* Theme Issue on Object-Oriented Application Frameworks, Mohamed E. Fayad and Douglas Schmidt, editors, 40(10), October 1997:82–87.

[Fayad-Schmidt 1997] Fayad, M.E., and D. Schmidt. Object-oriented application frameworks. *Communications of the ACM* 40(10), October 1997:32–38.

[Frakes-Terry 1996] Frakes, W., and C. Terry. Software reuse: Metrics and models. *ACM Computing Surveys* 28(2): 415–435.

[Goldberg 1997] Goldberg, A., S. Abell, and D. Leibs. The LearningWorks development and delivery frameworks. *Communications of the ACM,* Theme Issue on Object-Oriented Application Frameworks, Mohamed E. Fayad and Douglas Schmidt, editors, 40(10), October 1997:78–81.

[Heijden 1996] van der Heijden, K. *Scenarios: The Art of Strategic Conversation.* New York: John Wiley & Sons, 1996.

[Hull 1993] Hull, J. *Options, Futures, and Other Derivative Securities.* Englewood Cliffs, NJ: Prentice Hall, 1993.

[Kulatilaka 1996] Kulatilaka, N., P. Balasubramanian, and J. Storck. Managing information technology investments: A capability-based real options approach. Working paper 96-35, School of Management, Boston University, Boston, MA, 1996.

[Lim 1996] Lim, W. Reuse economics: A comparison of seventeen models and directions for future research. *Proceedings of the 4th International Conference on Software Reuse,* pp. 41–50, Orlando, FL, 1996.

[Lister 1997] Lister, T. Risk management is project management for adults. *IEEE Software* 14(3), May/June 1997:20–22.

[Malkiel 1996] Malkiel, B. *A Random Walk Down Wall Street.* New York: W.W. Norton & Co., 1996.

[McTaggart 1994] McTaggart, J., P. Kontes, and M. Mankins. *The Value Imperative.* New York: The Free Press, 1994.

[Porter 1985] Porter, M. *Competitive Advantage: Creating and Sustaining Superior Performance.* New York: The Free Press, 1985.

[Posnak 1997] Posnak, E., G. Lavender, and H. Vin. An adaptive framework for developing multimedia software components. *Communications of the ACM,* Theme Issue on Object-Oriented Application Frameworks, Mohamed E. Fayad and Douglas Schmidt, editors, 40(10), October 1997:43–47.

[Poulin 1997] Poulin, J. *Measuring Software Reuse: Principles, Practices, and Economic Models.* Reading, MA: Addison-Wesley, 1997.

[Simmons 1996] Simmons, P. Quality outcomes: Determining business value. *IEEE Software* 13(1), January 1996:25–32.

[Sullivan 1997] Sullivan, K., P. Chalasani, and S. Jha. Software design decisions as real options. Technical report 97-14, Department of Computer Science, University of Virginia, Charlottesville, VA, 1997.

[Trigeorgis 1996] Trigeorgis, L. *Real Options.* Cambridge, MA: The MIT Press, 1996.

24.6 Review Questions

1. What should be the governing objective of an enterprise?

2. What are the two basic kinds of activities involved in the capital investment process?

3. Name and explain the differences between the levels of reuse maturity in the Software Productivity Consortium's reuse capability model.

4. According to the MECP framework, what are the two determinants of value creation?

5. Explain how application frameworks can support a combined entry/exit market participation strategy.

6. What is the purpose of risk management?

7. How do the application framework characteristics of *reusability* and *tailorability* make different contributions to a competitive strategy?

8. What characteristic of application framework investments tends to discourage investment decisions based upon discounted cash flow valuation?

9. List four types of options that may arise in application framework investments.

10. What are the determinants of the value of an option?

11. Does high uncertainty increase or decrease the value of an option to invest?

24.7 Problem Set

1. A business is earning a return on capital above its cost of capital. What must be true about its market economics and competitive position?

2. Using the Market Economics/Competitive Position (MECP) framework, identify two ways in which a business that is earning a return on capital below its cost of capital can create value.

3. An approach to valuation commonly used by managers is *payback*: the time needed to recover the cost of an investment (whereby cash flows are usually not discounted). Consider two alternative projects: a framework-based project, in which an application framework is built in the early phases with high increasing returns expected in later phases, and a traditional development project, where early, more modest investment is limited to programmer training, producing earlier returns that diminish gradually. Suppose that the two projects have the following cash flow profiles over a six-year horizon:

	c_0	c_1	c_2	c_3	c_4	c_5
Traditional Approach	−800	−400	1200	1000	900	800
Framework Approach	−4500	−3500	500	2500	5000	9000

Calculate the payback year for each project. Then, assuming a discount rate (cost of capital) of 11 percent, calculate the net present value of each project.

Which project should be accepted based on payback time?

Which project should be accepted based on NPV?

If the two approaches yield contradictory results, state which approach is preferable, explaining your reasons.

4. In the discounted cash flow calculation, we have seen that the denominator is adjusted to account for risk by using a higher discount rate k instead of the risk-free rate r, where k > r. Equivalently, we could adjust the numerator, to obtain *certainty equivalent* cash flows—so-called because they represent the equivalent certain (risk-less) cash flows that would yield the same NPV as the risky cash flows. Develop a general procedure for transforming risky cash flows (discounted at a rate k) into risk-free cash flows (discounted at a rate r). Apply this procedure to the cash flows in the previous problem, using k = 11 percent and r = 5 percent. Verify that the net present values of the risky and risk-free cash flows are the same.

5. Shortly after its initial public offering, FramePower, a dynamic young application framework technology company, is trading at $50 per share. You have purchased 100 European call options with six months to expiration and an exercise price of $45. Suppose that at the end of those six months the share price of Frame-Power will either have risen to $75 (the rosy scenario) or dropped to $35 (the dismal scenario) with equal probability. What will be the total value of your 100 call options at expiration under each scenario?

Suppose that a friend of yours decides on a different investment strategy. He buys 75 shares of FramePower and finances part of his purchase with a bank loan of exactly $2549, which he must repay with interest at the prevailing rate of 3 percent on six-month bank loans. (He is permitted to round the interest payment to the nearest dollar.) Calculate the total value of his investment at the end of six months under each of the rosy and dismal scenarios. What was the total out-of-pocket cost to your friend for his investment? What price should *you* have paid for your 100 call options? Explain.

24.8 Projects

Project 1: With the dismantling of the national telephone monopolies all over the world, the open market suddenly presents enormous opportunities. The telecommunications enterprise where you work has given you a mandate to create a business unit that will compete in the market for rapid customized call service creation (private numbering plans, automatic call routing, and so on). The only way to achieve the flexibility and efficiency to participate in this quickly evolving market is to base your approach on object-oriented application framework technology.

Carry out an investigation of this market segment. Then create a competitive strategy for your business unit, in which you identify the market forces affecting it, the competitive threats, and how you plan to counter them. Explain how your chosen business strategy maximizes value using the Market Economics/Competitive Position framework.

Create an organizational structure for your business unit, explaining how you will produce and finance the framework and associated component technology. Develop alternative organizations, for example, centralized framework and component production as a centrally financed project versus centralized framework production, with components produced in separately financed projects. Explain the advantages and disadvantages of each type of organization. Develop a plan for smooth technological evolution of the business unit over time.

Project 2: Investigate option pricing theory and its relationship to real-world investments in IT infrastructure technology. Create a *sensitivity analysis workbench*, a program that calculates Black-Scholes option values, allows you to vary key parameters, and graphs the results in a variety of powerful visual ways (3D, overlaid charts, and so on). Use the workbench to explore other application framework investment scenarios that contain embedded real options. If time permits, incorporate discrete option pricing methods (for example, multiplicative binomial trees) into your workbench and explore their advantages and disadvantages with respect to the Black-Scholes method.

CHAPTER 25

Evaluating Structural and Functional Stability

Typically, object-oriented application frameworks are large and sophisticated systems that provide the structure and functionality for rapid development of applications within the framework's domain through design and code reuse (unlike class libraries, which only provide code reuse). Frameworks provide this significant improvement in design and code reuse through mechanisms and techniques that encapsulate and implement, by the use of abstraction, the most frequently used domain functionality in a context-independent architecture. The use of encapsulation and abstraction techniques also ensures that framework systems provide the necessary flexibility and extendability to develop different types of custom applications around the framework architecture.

Frameworks make their functionality available to application developers through an inversion-of-control mechanism, wherein the developer only provides the customization code needed to create a new application [Fayad-Schmidt 1997]. As a result, experienced framework developers can normally realize significant improvements in productivity with the use of domain frameworks for custom application development. However, this improvement in productivity can be realized only after an initial investment of time and resources in learning the framework. The effort required to learn and effectively use frameworks is influenced by numerous factors, including the framework's structural and functionality stability, complexity, and documentation.

The development of successful and highly reusable, easy-to-use, and extendable framework systems requires time, experienced technical expertise, and domain knowledge. To a great extent, the challenge in developing successful frameworks lies in identifying the requirements of a framework. This is because of the difficulty of foreseeing all the different ways in which custom applications will want to use a framework solution and the difficulty in identifying the essential concepts and functionality of a domain that needs to be supported by the framework solutions.

As a result, most popular and successful framework systems gradually evolve over a period of many years because of changes to incorporate new or modified requirements and fixes to problems detected in earlier versions. Typically, several versions of a framework are developed and released before a stable, reliable, and mature system is developed. While early versions of a framework often support only core domain functionality, later versions incorporate additional capabilities and features that are aimed toward making the frameworks complete, robust, flexible, and easy to use.

The focus of this chapter is on exploring and understanding the causes and nature of changes in object-oriented framework architectures as they evolve with the development of new versions. Both the structural and functional characteristics of framework architecture designs are explored and assessed through objective measurement techniques. Architectural characteristics that can change between versions are identified and evaluated using a suite of metrics. An extent-of-change measure is defined to evaluate net change between versions and is used as an indicator (index) of framework design (structural + functional) stability. The approach is illustrated by applying it to the assessment of several versions of the Microsoft Foundation Classes (MFC) and Borland Object Library (OWL), which are popular frameworks used for the rapid development of Windows applications.

25.1 Metrics and OOAF Characteristics Assessment

The switch to the object-oriented paradigm and framework applications has changed the elements that we use to assess software characteristics [Bansiya 1997a]. Traditional software product metrics that evaluate product characteristics such as size, complexity, performance, and quality must be changed to rely on some fundamentally different notions such as encapsulation, inheritance, and polymorphism, which are inherent in the object-oriented paradigm and characteristics of frameworks such as inversion of control, complexity, and reuse.

However, one of the significant benefits of using an object-oriented approach is that it naturally lends itself to an early assessment and evaluation. Object-oriented methodologies require significant effort early in the development cycle to identify objects and classes, attributes and operations, and relationships. Encapsulation, inheritance, and polymorphism require designers to carefully structure the design and consider the interaction between objects. The result of this early analysis and design process is a blueprint for implementation. The approach, therefore, provides the information needed to assess the architectural quality of a design's classes, structure, functionality, and relationships before they are committed to an implementation [Bansiya 1998].

Many new metrics [Bansiya 1997b; Basili 1996; Chidamber 1994; Fenton 1997; Li 1995; Lorenz 1994; Pfleeger 1997] have been defined to measure the characteristics of object-oriented design artifacts such as classes, hierarchies, and systems. The metrics can be applied in the early stages of object-oriented application framework (OOAF) development to ensure that the design and its architecture have favorable internal properties that will lead to the development of a quality end product. The metrics information gives developers an opportunity to fix problems, remove irregularities and nonconformance to standards, and eliminate unwanted complexity early in the development cycle. This can significantly help in reducing reworks during and after implementation, as well as designing effective test plans, and better project and resource planning.

In order to deliver a significant improvement to the process of building large and complex object-oriented application frameworks, one of the issues that needs to be addressed is that of internal architectural characteristics assessment and the relationship/impact of changes in characteristics on the stability and maturity of framework solutions. This means we must identify architectural characteristics to evaluate and develop metrics that can be applied early in the development process to give reliable measures. We must also develop some quantifiable ways to relate the measured framework internal characteristics to the overall architectural stability attribute. Finally, the process of measurement and evaluation needs to be such that it can be automated using tools.

25.2 Framework Stability

Stability is frequently used as an attribute in describing software systems. However, the issue of software system stability and its assessment has not been widely researched and addressed. To an extent this is because the concept of stability in the context of software systems is considered subjective, and because there is no consensus on what exactly stability means for software systems. This has several parallels with the issues of *quality* in software systems. Stability, like quality, means different things to different people, and like quality, it is easier to comment about the stability of a software system after you use it and see it.

Assessment of framework stability can benefit developers, managers, and customers in making informed decisions about the framework's development and use. Customers of a framework can use the information in evaluating and selecting a framework from several alternatives. This information can provide a degree of confidence in the framework's reliability and robustness for its users. Stable frameworks are likely to have fewer bugs and be more reliable and robust than evolving frameworks. Developers of a framework can use the stability information in assessing the impact of changes and decide when to release new versions of the system. Management can use the information in cost and effort estimations. Empirical information collected from the assessment of successful frameworks can be valuable in guiding the development of new frameworks and can be used to develop criteria for framework stability classification. For instance, a classification based on the *extent of change* in frameworks, with categories such as volatile, evolving, and mature, can be developed in order to characterize the stability of framework architectures.

This chapter focuses narrowly on the question of object-oriented application architecture stability and its relation to structural and functional characteristics. We define a *stable* version of a framework as one that provides maximum domain coverage and requires minimum effort to support development of custom applications within the domain. This definition of stability for framework systems is a measure of the stability of the framework's structure and functionality. This definition of framework architectural stability requires the availability of several framework versions and computation of extent of change between the versions.

25.3 Framework Architecture Assessment Method

The four steps that are key to this object-oriented framework architecture assessment approach are as follows:

1. Identifying the structural and functional characteristics that evaluate the architecture of frameworks.

2. Defining or selecting metric(s) to assess each of the characteristics.

3. Collecting metrics data for the characteristics from several versions of the frameworks.

4. Analyzing the changed architectural characteristics and computing the extent of change in the architecture between versions of the framework.

25.3.1 Identifying Characteristics for Framework Architecture Assessment

When implemented, object-oriented application framework systems are simply a collection of interacting objects/classes. The classes that implement objects use encapsulation and abstraction to create class hierarchies for internal design and code reuse and polymorphism for flexibility and extendability. The interaction between objects is defined by relationships identified during design and implemented in one of several ways, such as containment, aggregation, delegation, method invocation, or parameters to methods.

While several different causes, such as framework quality, capabilities, domain coverage, or technological changes, can cause frameworks to change, all changes, to varying degrees, will impact (change) the structure or the functionality of the framework solution. The changes in architectural characteristics of object-oriented frameworks can be primarily evaluated over the entire system or with respect to the design of individual classes, as shown in Figure 25.1. At system level, the overall architecture of the framework as represented by the collaborations (interactions) among classes and the structuring of classes in inheritance hierarchies is evaluated. While classes are the building blocks of the overall framework design, the classes themselves are used as blackboxes in the system-level architecture assessment.

In the class-level evaluations, the focus of assessment and changes is the structure, functionality, and collaboration (relationships) of individual classes between versions. Typically, the core structure of objects is detailed by the data declarations that are made in class specifications [Gamma 1995]. The functional characteristics of objects are specified by the method declarations that are also included in the class definitions. Data and method parameter declarations that use other user-defined objects also define the collaboration characteristics of a class with other classes in the system. Figure 25.1 shows the classification of framework characteristics that are evaluated and analyzed in this chapter.

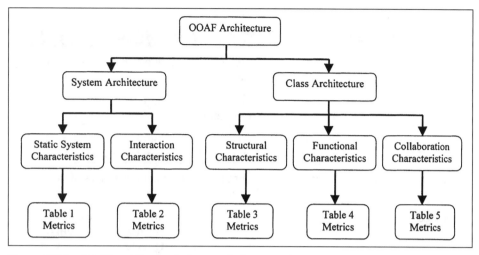

Figure 25.1   OOAF architectural characteristics to evaluate.

25.3.2 Design Metrics for Architectural Structure Assessment

There are two groups of characteristics (see Figure 25.1) that are used to evaluate the overall framework: design architecture and three groups of characteristics that are used to assess individual classes. Separate suites of metrics are used to evaluate the different groups of characteristics. The sets of characteristics selected and evaluated can be different from the ones used here for reasons such as the importance of a characteristic, the granularity of assessment needed, or the accuracy of evaluation.

The framework characteristics are evaluated using a group of static design structural characteristics and a group of interaction characteristics. The static system characteristics provide high-level structural information of the design. At the system level, we are interested in knowing the overall size/scope/extent of the design and learning about key architectural characteristics such as the structure of inheritance hierarchies (in other words, whether they are deep and narrow or shallow and wide) and the number of high-level concepts designed. The suite of metrics defined in Table 25.1 describes the structural characteristics of interest that are evaluated for framework architecture assessment. While the *number of classes* in the system is used as a measure for design size, the *number of class hierarchies*, the *number of single* and *multiple inheritances*, and the *average depth* and *width* of class inheritance hierarchies are used to evaluate the shape of framework design structures [Bansiya 1997b].

Object interaction (collaboration) structures result from various forms of dependencies between objects. Here we are interested in evaluating the extent of the dependencies and the nature of relationships between objects. While the actual interactions that take place can be determined only at program runtime, it is possible to estimate the extent of the permitted interactions from the class definitions, because the runtime interactions/collaborations are enabled by the data and method declarations that are specified in the classes. The services (public methods) that classes declare are used by objects and thus represent a service-level dependency. The presence of parent classes within inheritance hierarchies also represents an implicit dependency for child classes

Table 25.1 Metrics for Assessment of Framework Structural Characteristics

METRIC NAME	DESCRIPTION
Design size in classes	Count of the total number of classes in the system.
Number of hierarchies	Count of the number of class hierarchies in the system.
Number of single inheritances	Count of the number of classes (subclasses) that use inheritance in the system.
Number of multiple inheritances	Count of the number of instances of multiple inheritance in the system.
Average depth of inheritance	Average depth of inheritance of classes in the system. Computed by dividing the sum of maximum path lengths to all classes by the number of classes. Path length to a class is the number of edges from the root to the class in an inheritance hierarchy.
Average width of inheritance	Average number of children per class in the system. Computed by dividing the sum of the number of children over all classes by the number of classes in the system.

on parent classes. Classes can also be coupled via data declarations of user-defined objects. Table 25.2 describes a set of characteristics and a corresponding suite of metrics that evaluate the interaction structure of framework designs.

The three nonoverlapping groups of structural, functional, and interactional (see Figure 25.1) characteristics cover most of the important class architecture characteristics to evaluate. The core of every object is a data structure that complies with the data

Table 25.2 Suite of Metrics to Evaluate Interaction Characteristics of a Framework Design

METRIC NAME	DESCRIPTION
Number of services per class	Average of the number of public methods in all classes.
Average number of parents per class	Average number of distinct (parent) classes from which a class inherits information. This metric is different from the average depth of inheritance metric because it takes into account instances of multiple inheritances.
Direct class coupling	Average number of distinct classes with which a class may collaborate. This measure includes classes that are directly related by attribute declarations and parameter declarations in methods.

declaration made in the object's class definition. As classes evolve over several versions, the structures of objects may change because of new data declarations, changes to definitions of existing declarations, or complete deletion of existing declarations. As a result, there are several characteristics of class structures that can be assessed and evaluated for changes. Table 25.3 lists and defines four such important characteristics selected for assessment of structural changes to classes. An objective in selecting this suite of characteristics has been to keep the number of metrics small while evaluating the most important data declaration characteristics. The characteristics selected for assessment can have actual measures that may overlap, for instance, with the metrics *number of data members* (NOD) and *number of reference attributes* (NRA); data declarations that are *references* get counted twice. However, this overlap is not significant for the analysis presented here, because the analysis is based on relative differences between versions, and the same suite of metrics is used for evaluations of all versions. The issue of overlapped measures can be resolved by reducing the granularity of assessment. This would, however, require a larger suite of metrics to use in the evaluation process.

The functional characteristics of classes center on the definition and use of class methods (services). Because there are several types of qualifiers (such as virtual, inline, static in C++) and access controls (public, protected, private) that can be used to qualify method declarations, defining assessments that do not overlap will require a large number of metrics. Since the objective is to illustrate the method of framework evaluation, only a small number of important class functional characteristics (described in Table 25.4) are selected for the assessment. The class interaction characteristics evaluate the dependency of individual classes on other classes in the system. The class interaction characteristic measures described in Table 25.5 are also used to compute the interaction characteristics of the overall framework design (see Table 25.2).

Table 25.3 Metrics for Assessing Structural Characteristics of Individual Classes

METRIC	NAME	DESCRIPTION
NOD	Number of attributes	Count of the number of data declarations in a class.
NAD	Number of abstract data types	Count of the number of user-defined objects (ADTs) used as attributes in a class, which are therefore necessary to instantiate an object instance of the (aggregate) class.
NRA	Number of reference attributes	Count of the number of pointers and references used as attributes in a class.
CSB	Class size in bytes	Computes the size of the objects in bytes that will be created from a class declaration. Size is computed by summing the size of all attributes declared in a class.

Table 25.4   Metrics for Assessing Functional Characteristics of Individual Classes

METRIC	NAME	DESCRIPTION
NOM	Number of methods	Count of all the methods defined in a class.
NOP	Number of polymorphic methods	Count of the methods that can exhibit polymorphic behavior. Such methods in C++ are marked as *virtual* methods.
NPT	Number of unique parameter types	Count of the number of different parameter types used in the methods of a class.
NPM	Number of parameters per method	Average of the number of parameters per method in a class. This is computed by summing the parameters of all methods and dividing by the number of methods in a class.

25.3.3 Collecting Metrics Data for Framework Versions

The metrics data for the classes of a framework system is collected using an automated tool, QMOOD++ (Quality Metrics for Object-Oriented Designs) [Bansiya 1997b], that implements the metrics described in Tables 25.1 through 25.5. The class definitions (typically communicated using header files) of a framework contain all the information necessary for the metrics computation, since the metrics defined in Tables 25.1 through 25.5 are design metrics—that is, they can be computed from the information available in the detailed class specification of an object-oriented system.

The Microsoft MFC and Borland OWL frameworks are representatives of a class of several graphical user interface (GUI)–based application development frameworks currently used by developers in both Windows and other environments for rapid application development. These two frameworks were selected because several (five

Table 25.5   Metrics for Assessing Relational Characteristics of Individual Classes

METRIC	NAME	DESCRIPTION
NOA	Number of parents	Count of all classes from which a class inherits information.
NOC	Number of children	Count of the number of immediate children (subclasses) of a class.
DCC	Direct class coupling	Count of the different number of classes that a class is directly related to. Includes classes that are directly related by attribute declarations and message-passing (parameters) in methods.

MFC and four OWL) versions of the framework that have been developed are publicly available.

Analyzing Changes in Framework System Structure

Table 25.6 shows the data collected for the structural metrics described in Tables 25.1 and 25.2 for the five versions of MFC and four versions of OWL frameworks. The data collected leads to interesting architectural characterizations of the two frameworks. For instance, while MFC does not use multiple inheritance, the OWL frameworks depend significantly on the use of multiple inheritance; while the number of methods for MFC classes falls in an average range of 45 to 114, the number of methods for OWL classes ranges from 24 to 38 on the average; and MFC classes have significantly (approximately two times) higher class coupling than OWL classes. The metric values of the number of hierarchies and the average depth and width of inheritance hierarchies, which characterize the shape (structure) of class inheritance hierarchies, indicate that MFC has a narrow, deeply nested inheritance structure, whereas OWL has a wide and shallow inheritance structure.

Computing Extent of Change in Framework System Structures

To compute the extent of change in the framework system architectures between versions, the metric values for the framework versions are normalized with respect to the metric's values in the previous version of the frameworks. The relative values of metrics for the first versions of MFC and OWL frameworks are set to unity for reference. Table 25.7 shows the normalized metric values (computed by dividing the actual metric values of a version with the metric's value in the previous version) of the MFC and OWL frameworks. The normalized metric values of the framework versions are summed to compute an *aggregate-change* value (see Table 25.7). This aggregate-change

Table 25.6   Actual Architecture Assessment Metric Values of MFC and OWL Frameworks

DESIGN METRIC	MFC					OWL			
	V 1.0	V 2.0	V 3.0	V 4.0	V 5.0	V 4.0	V 4.5	V 5.0	V 5.2
Design size	72	92	132	206	233	82	142	357	356
Hierarchies	1	1	1	5	6	12	16	29	27
Single inheritances	66	84	117	174	194	34	56	202	198
Multiple inheritance	0	0	0	0	0	9	13	30	30
Depth of inheritance	1.68	2.11	2.45	2.33	2.3	0.78	0.81	1.42	1.41
Width of inheritance	0.92	0.91	0.89	0.85	0.83	0.52	0.49	0.65	0.64
Number of parents	1.68	2.11	2.45	2.33	2.30	1.00	0.97	1.56	1.55
Number of methods	44.6	75.6	95	114	109	27.7	24	37.2	36.8
Class coupling	6.03	7.59	9.02	9.33	8.94	1.87	2.26	4.73	4.71

Table 25.7 Normalized Architecture Assessment Metric Values of MFC and OWL Frameworks

DESIGN METRIC	MFC					OWL			
	V 1.0	V 2.0	V 3.0	V 4.0	V 5.0	V 4.0	V 4.5	V 5.0	V 5.2
Design size	1	1.28	1.43	1.56	1.13	1	1.73	2.51	1.00
Hierarchies	1	1	1	5	1.20	1	1.33	1.81	0.93
Single inheritances	1	1.27	1.39	1.49	1.11	1	1.65	3.61	0.98
Multiple inheritance	1	1.00	1.00	1.00	1.00	1	1.44	2.31	1.00
Depth of inheritance	1	1.26	1.16	0.95	0.99	1	1.04	1.75	0.99
Width of inheritance	1	0.99	0.98	0.96	0.98	1	0.94	1.33	0.98
Number of parents	1	1.26	1.16	0.95	0.99	1	0.97	1.61	0.99
Number of methods	1	1.70	1.26	1.20	0.96	1	0.87	1.55	0.99
Class coupling	1	1.26	1.19	1.03	0.96	1	1.21	2.09	1.00
Aggregate change (V_i)	9.0	11.01	10.57	14.14	9.31	9.0	11.18	18.57	8.86
Extent of change(V_i-V_1)	0.0	2.01	1.57	5.14	0.31	0.0	2.18	9.57	−0.14

value for the first versions of the framework (V_1) equals the number of metrics (nine) used in the system-level architecture assessment. The extent-of-change value for subsequent versions is computed by taking the difference of the aggregate change (V_i) of a version (i, with i > 0) with the aggregate-change (V_1) value of the first version.

The extent-of-change measure can be used as an indicator (index) of overall framework architecture stability. The value of the measure indicates the relative stability of the system architecture structure: While higher values of the measure are reflective of greater instability in the structure, values closer to zero indicate greater stability. MFC version 5.0 has a stability index of 0.31, which is significantly closer to zero than a stability index of 5.14 for MFC version 4.0 and therefore points to a higher stability for the MFC 5.0 architecture. Similarly, OWL version 5.2, with extent of change equal to 0.14 is also indicative of the significantly higher stability of the OWL 5.2 system architecture.

Analyzing Changes in Framework Class Architectures

The metrics defined in Tables 25.3 and 25.4 can be computed in two ways, depending upon whether the information defined within classes is the only information used in the metric computations or the information inherited from parent class(es) is also used for the metric computations. This latter interpretation requires analyzing a class and all its ancestors in the computation of the metrics for the classes. While the former definition of metric assessment is useful to compute and determine the actual number of changes made, the latter interpretation is meaningful to understand and compute the extent of effect of a change. Typically, changes made to the internal constituents of parent classes in a framework ripple the effects of the changes to all descendant classes of the parent class [Gamma 1995]. Because the focus of this chapter is on evaluating the number of changes and the overall effect of the changes made—that is, the *extent of effect*, the metrics in Tables 25.3 and 25.4 are computed based on the information defined locally within the classes and information that is inherited from parent classes. Finally, the values for metrics in Tables 25.3 through 25.5 are computed independently for all classes in each version of the frameworks in order to compute changes in class characteristics between versions.

Computing and Analyzing the Extent of Changes in Class Characteristics

There are 11 class characteristics (Tables 25.3 through 25.5) that are computed for each of the classes. Any of these characteristics of a class can change between successive versions of a framework. The metric values of classes in one version of the framework are compared with the metric values of the classes in the predecessor version of the framework. If the value of a particular metric changes from one version to the next, it is defined as *one unit of change*. The 11 metric values of each class are compared with the metric values of the class in its predecessor version to compute the total *number of units changed* for the classes. The extent of change for a framework version is the *sum of units changed* in all classes between a version and its predecessor.

When the metrics values between successive versions of classes are compared to determine the changed metrics of a class, it is possible that a class is present in only one of the two versions being compared (this will happen with new classes and existing classes that have been removed). In these cases, no change in the metrics value is considered for such classes and the extent of change is computed only for classes that are present in both of the compared versions.

The computation of changes is done between all successive versions, such as between MFC versions 1.0 and 2.0, 2.0 and 3.0, 3.0 and 4.0, and 4.0 and 5.0. Table 25.8 shows, for MFC and OWL framework versions, the number of classes whose metric values have changed between successive versions for each of the metrics defined in Tables 25.3 through 25.5. For instance, the *number-of-ancestors* (NOA) metric changed values for 18 classes between MFC versions 1.0 and 2.0. The cause for this large-scale change in the NOA metric values of classes was the restructuring of the MFC class hierarchy that resulted from the introduction of several new classes in the middle of the class hierarchy. The extent of the restructuring change decreases as expected from a value of 18 to 11 between MFC versions 2.0 and 3.0, to 5 between versions 3.0 and 4.0, and finally to 0 between versions 4.0 and 5.0, clearly indicating that a stable structure for class organization was reached by version 5.0. The sum of all number-of-ancestors (NOA) changes between the five versions of MFC is 34, as shown in the units-changed column of Table 25.8, along with the percentage of the total change that this metric represents.

The class characteristics that change the most frequently are related to methods (services) and method parameters, such as the *number of methods* (NOM) with a change close to 18 percent, the *number of polymorphic* functions (NOP) with 12 percent, the average *number of parameter types* (NPT) with 16 percent, and the average *number of parameters per method* (NPM) with 17 percent. Similar high-percentage changes in functional characteristic metrics are observed with the OWL versions. The values in the last row (totals) of Table 25.8 are the sums (along each column) of all the metric changes between successive versions. For instance, there was a total of 439 changes for MFC between version 1.0 and 2.0. This value increased to 546 between versions 2.0 and 3.0 and to 847 between versions 3.0 and 4.0, before dropping to 448 between versions 4.0 and 5.0.

Table 25.8 Changes in MFC and OWL Class Characteristics

METRICS	MFC					OWL			
	V1 ℰ V2	V2 ℰ V3	V3 ℰ V4	V4 ℰ V5	UNITS CHANGED(%)	V1 ℰ V2	V2 ℰ V3	V3 ℰ V4	UNITS CHANGED(%)
NOC	7	10	12	12	41 (1.8%)	7	12	4	23 (3.1%)
NOA	18	11	5	0	34 (1.5%)	4	1	0	5 (0.7%)
DCC	29	46	77	23	175 (7.7%)	8	28	10	46 (6.3%)
NOM	68	84	126	120	398 (17.5%)	16	62	75	153 (21%)
NOP	64	81	119	12	276 (12.1%)	0	20	36	56 (7.6%)
NPT	68	87	124	93	372 (16.3%)	10	37	87	134 (18%)
NPM	68	84	124	117	393 (17.2%)	15	64	90	169 (23%)
NOD	49	47	83	25	204 (8.9%)	1	48	11	60 (8.2%)
NAD	6	10	21	5	42 (1.8%)	1	17	2	20 (2.7%)
NRA	14	38	66	15	133 (5.8%)	1	5	6	12 (1.6%)
CSB	48	48	90	26	212 (9.3%)	2	39	17	58 (7.9%)
Total	439	546	847	448	2280	65	333	338	736

The number of changes increases between versions 1.0 and 2.0, 2.0 and 3.0, and 3.0 and 4.0 and then decreases between versions 4.0 and 5.0. The versions that are involved with the increasing values of changes can be characterized as evolving versions of a framework, and the versions that are associated with decreasing values of changes can be characterized as mature versions of a framework. According to this characterization, MFC versions 1.0 through 4.0 are evolving versions of the framework, and MFC 5.0 is the mature version of the framework solution. Using this characterization of the OWL framework assessment indicates that all evaluated versions represent evolving versions.

Computing and Analyzing the Number of Changes in Framework Classes

The changes in class metric values discussed so far are with respect to the extent of changes in the 11 metrics and the distribution of the changed characteristics with respect to metrics and versions. However, this analysis does not answer questions such as, What is the actual number of unit-changes per class?, What is the average number of units changed per class?, or What is the distribution of classes as a function of the number of changes?

Analyzing change data with respect to the number of units changed provides the answers to these questions. For this analysis, the number of changes for each class is determined independently. The number of changes ranges from zero for classes that have no changes to 11 for classes, all of whose evaluated characteristics are changed between versions. This distribution of the classes as a function of the number of changes is shown in Table 25.9 for all MFC and OWL framework versions. The table also shows the computed average number of units changed per class between versions.

The computed values of the average number of units changed per class in Table 25.9 provides an interesting measure for overall framework architecture stability. The average number of changes made to classes in the early evolving versions of MFC is 6.46, 6.13, and 6.72 between versions 1.0 and 2.0, versions 2.0 and 3.0, and version 3.0 and 4.0, respectively. This average number of changes drops to 3.4 between versions 4.0 and version 5.0. This significant change (drop of ~50 percent) in the average number-of-changes measure is important because it indicates that there were significantly fewer changes in the MFC 5.0 than in all its predecessors. Such a transition can be used as an indicator of architectural stability with respect to structural and functional changes.

25.4 Summary

The principal contribution of this chapter has been in the introduction of an objective technique for evaluation of object-oriented framework structures. A framework assessment method is presented for evaluating changing structural and functional characteristics of object-oriented application framework solutions between versions. The method is used to develop an extent-of-change measure between versions of frameworks that can be used as a measure for framework architectural stability. Evaluating framework characteristics and the resulting characteristic changes between versions can be of value to developers and managers to verify conformance to design goals and principles. The concept of changes can also be used for effort and cost estimation in the development

Table 25.9   Class Distribution as a Function of the Number of Changes

UNITS CHANGED	MFC				OWL		
	V1 Æ V2	V2 Æ V3	V3 Æ V4	V4 Æ V5	V1 Æ V2	V2 Æ V3	V3 Æ V4
0	4	3	6	74	57	64	247
1	0	2	1	7	5	6	10
2	0	1	0	18	8	8	18
3	3	2	3	76	2	9	35
4	14	27	22	12	3	19	25
5	2	10	17	5	4	4	9
6	15	8	3	4	1	15	2
7	13	4	12	2	0	8	2
8	10	17	53	6	0	4	2
9	7	14	12	2	0	0	0
10	4	4	3	0	0	1	0
11	0	0	0	0	0	0	0
Number of classes	72	92	132	206	80	138	350
Avg. no. of units changed	6.46	6.13	6.72	3.4	2.83	4.5	3.28

and maintenance of framework solutions. The results of assessing class and framework characteristics are also useful for critically assessing the causes and impact of the structural and functional architectural changes on quality attributes such as framework architecture understandability, maintainability, flexibility, and extendability.

The framework evaluation method presented in this chapter was illustrated by applying it to assess the characteristics of several versions of two large Windows application development frameworks, MFC and OWL. The results of the case studies showed interesting and promising results for framework architectural stability characterization. The framework evaluation method presented is flexible in that different characteristics can be selected for evaluation, and the suites of metrics used to assess the characteristics can be changed based on domain, organization goals, and development environment, thus providing a completely flexible approach for object-oriented application framework evaluation.

The work presented in this chapter with respect to framework evaluations is relatively new and therefore needs to be continued and validated on several fronts. The method and its application need to be applied to the evaluation of more framework solutions. Results from the evaluation of a large number of frameworks can help develop empirical characterization of the nature of framework development. Although this chapter focused primarily on the assessment of static system and class architectural characteristics that would be evaluated from framework class definitions, it would be valuable to identify and evaluate dynamic collaboration characteristics of objects along with the changes that occur in the collaboration patterns between versions.

25.5 References

[Bansiya 1997a] Bansiya, J. An object-oriented design quality assessment model. Ph.D. thesis. The University of Alabama in Huntsville, 1997.

[Bansiya 1997b] Bansiya, J., and C. Davis. Using automated metrics to track object-oriented development. *Dr. Dobb's Journal* 272 (December 1997).

[Bansiya 1998] Bansiya, J., and C. Davis. A quality assessment model for object-oriented designs. Submitted for publication to *IEEE Transactions on Software Engineering,* 1998.

[Basili 1996] Basili, B., L. Briand, and W.L. Melo. A validation of object-oriented metrics as quality indicators. *IEEE Transactions on Software Engineering* 22(10), October 1996:751–761.

[Chidamber 1994] Chidamber, S.R., and C.F. Kemerer. A metrics suite for object-oriented design. *IEEE Transactions on Software Engineering* 20(6), June 1994:476–493.

[Fayad-Schmidt 1997] Fayad, M.E., and D.C. Schmidt. Object-oriented application frameworks. *Communications of the ACM* 40(10), October 1997:32–38.

[Fenton 1997] Fenton, N.E., and S.L. Pfleeger. *Software Metrics: A Rigorous and Practical Approach.* PWS Publishing Company, 1997.

[Gamma 1995] Gamma, E., R. Helm, R. Johnson, and J. Vlissides. *Design Patterns: Reusable Elements of Object-Oriented Design.* Reading, MA: Addison-Wesley, 1995.

[Li 1995] Li, W., S. Henry, D. Kafury, and R. Schulman. Measuring object-oriented design. *Journal of Object-Oriented Programming,* July/August 1995, pp. 48–55.

[Lorenz 1994] Lorenz M., and J. Kid. *Object-Oriented Software Metrics: A Practical Guide.* Englewood Cliffs, NJ: Prentice Hall, 1984.

[Pfleeger 1997] Pfleeger, S.L., R. Jeffery, B. Curtis, and B. Kitchenham. Status report on software measurement. *IEEE Software* 14(2), March 1997.

25.6 Review Questions

1. What characteristics of framework systems can influence their understandability and usability?

2. What is the challenge that is referred to in this chapter that significantly influences the development of successful frameworks?

3. What concepts and characteristics of object-oriented systems and application frameworks make the use of traditional software metrics difficult in OOAF assessment?

4. Why are object-oriented designs considered more amenable to early assessment and evaluation than traditional designs?

5. What are the benefits of an early assessment of framework design architecture?

6. Why are automated tools that collect metrics data important for software measurement and evaluation?

7. What parallels are drawn between stability and quality in this chapter?

8. Why is the evaluation of framework architecture and stability useful and important?

9. What key characteristics of framework systems does the definition of stability used in this chapter depend on?

10. What are the four steps to the architecture stability assessment method presented in this chapter?

11. Framework systems are evaluated at two levels in the assessment method described in this chapter. What are these two levels?

12. Name two of the most common causes of changes in framework architectures?

13. Name the system characteristics that are assessed to evaluate framework architectures?

14. What are the main types of interaction (relationships) characteristics observed in framework solutions?

15. When using a suite of metrics in software evaluation, the definitions of the metrics must avoid overlap of information (data) used in their computation. Name two different ways by which this kind of overlap in information (data) used by different metrics can be avoided.

25.7 Problem Set

1. Only a small number of class characteristics (defined in Tables 25.3, 25.4, and 25.5) were used to illustrate the architecture assessment method in this chapter. What other class characteristics would be useful to evaluate and include in analyzing framework classes?

2. The definition of metrics (Tables 25.1 through 25.5) used in this chapter has been slanted to allow for evaluation of object-oriented framework designs represented in C++. Which of the metrics (in Tables 25.1 through 25.5) need to be changed to allow for assessment of object-oriented framework design represented in the Java programming language?

3. Provide new definitions for the design metrics that you have identified in question 2 and that need to be changed to allow for evaluations of OOAF's designs represented in the Java programming language.

4. The three metrics defined in Table 25.5 measure different forms of class coupling. Although coupling in general is not desirable, some forms of coupling are more acceptable than others. Explain which of the couplings defined in Table 25.5 are desirable/acceptable and which are not.

5. Framework systems have several key architectural structural and functional characteristics that make them significantly different from traditional software systems. What are some of these characteristics? Do the metrics defined in Tables 25.1 and 25.2 cover these characteristics? If the characteristics are not covered by the metrics in Tables 25.1 and 25.2, what are these characteristics? Define design metrics that can be used to evaluate these characteristics.

6. In the MFC and OWL framework evaluation studies presented, the versions of MFC were normalized with respect to other MFC versions and not OWL versions. Similarly, the OWL versions were also normalized with respect to other OWL versions and not MFC versions. Why do you think this was done? Would it be meaningful to normalize all versions of MFC and OWL frameworks with respect to each other?

25.8 Projects

Project 1: A new release of MFC is now available with C++ V6.0. Assessment of MFC versions 1.0 to 5.0 was done in this chapter. Now extend the assessment to include MFC version 6.0. Follow the method as illustrated in this chapter. The major steps that you need to carry out to include this version in the framework assessment study are as follows:

- Collect the design metric data for MFC 6.0 and include this data in Table 25.6.

- Normalize the new metric values collected in Table 25.7.

- Compute the extent of change in terms of units changed between MFC 5.0 and 6.0, and add a new column labeled "V5 -> V6" in Table 25.8. Also update the units-changed column of Table 25.8.

- Compute the number of changes in framework classes and update Table 25.9 to include the data for number of units changed between versions 5.0 and 6.0.

- Does the inclusion of version 6.0 in the MFC framework evaluation impact or change the trends in the results that were observed with MFC versions 1.0 to 5.0? If the new data and results change the trends that are observed (in Tables 25.8 and 25.9) within the earlier releases of the software, explain why the results are different. Explain any other unexpected or surprising behavior that you may observe with the inclusion of MFC 6.0 or any future versions of MFC or OWL frameworks.

- Use QMOOD++ or a similar automated tool to collect the system and class data for the new framework releases.

Project 2: One of the underlying goals in developing the framework architecture structural and functional stability method presented in this chapter was that the assessment should be possible before any part of the framework is implemented. Therefore it was required that all the information evaluated by the design metrics should only rely on information available in class declarations, which are defined well before the methods of the classes are implemented. While the benefit of using only class declarations in the assessment is that the entire evaluation process can be carried out well in advance of the framework implementation, the process leaves out assessment of several implementation characteristics. Now if we change the goals of our framework stability study to allow for a postdevelopment analysis, which therefore allows for inclusion of information from methods implementations, what changes would you make to the assessment approach presented in this chapter? Specifically, what implementation characteristics of a classes' methods would you want to evaluate? What existing or new metrics would you use in your assessment, and what results do you expect to observe from such an assessment? Explain in detail your implementation assessment approach and the observed results.

Future Trends

26.1 Future Research Areas

Over the next several years, we expect the following framework-related topics will receive considerable attention by researchers and developers:

Reducing framework development effort. Traditionally, reusable frameworks have been developed by generalizing from existing systems and applications. Unfortunately, this incremental process of organic development is often slow and unpredictable since core framework design principles and patterns must be discovered from the bottom up. However, since many good framework exemplars now exist, we expect that the next generation of developers will leverage this collective knowledge to conceive, design, and implement higher-quality frameworks more rapidly.

Greater focus on domain-specific enterprise frameworks. Existing frameworks have focused largely on system infrastructure and middleware integration domains (such as user interfaces [Gamma 1995; Pree 1994] and OS/communication systems [Campbell-Islam 1993; Hueni 1995; Schmidt 1997]). In contrast, there are relatively few widely documented exemplars of enterprise frameworks for key business domains such as manufacturing, banking, insurance, and medical systems [Fayad-Hamu 1999; alSafadi 1999]. As more experience is gained in developing frameworks for these business domains, however, we expect that the collective knowledge of frameworks will be expanded to cover an increasingly wide range of domain-specific topics, and an increasing number of enterprise application frameworks will be produced [Fayad-Hamu 1999]. As a result, benefits of frameworks will become more immediate to application programmers, as well as to infrastructure developers.

Blackbox frameworks. Many framework experts [Johnson-Foote 1988] favor blackbox frameworks over whitebox frameworks, since blackbox frameworks emphasize dynamic object relationships (via patterns like Bridge and Strategy [Gamma 1995]) rather than static class relationships. Thus, it is easier to extend and reconfigure blackbox frameworks dynamically. As developers become more familiar with techniques and patterns for factoring out common interfaces and components, we expect that an increasing percentage of blackbox frameworks will be produced.

Framework documentation. Accurate and comprehensible documentation is crucial to the success of large-scale frameworks. However, documenting frameworks is a costly activity and contemporary tools often focus on low-level method-oriented documentation, which fails to capture the strategic roles and collaborations among framework components. We expect that the advent of tools for reverse-engineering the structure of classes and objects in complex frameworks will help to improve the accuracy and utility of framework documentation. Likewise, we expect to see an increase in the current trend [Fayad-Hamu 1999; Hueni 1995; Schmidt 1997] of using design patterns to provide higher-level descriptions of frameworks.

Processes for managing framework development. Frameworks are inherently abstract, since they generalize from a solution to a particular application challenge to provide a family of solutions. This level of abstraction makes it difficult to engineer their quality and manage their production. Therefore, it is essential to capture and articulate development processes that can ensure the successful development and use of frameworks. We believe that extensive prototyping and phased introduction of framework technology into organizations is crucial to reducing risk and helping to ensure successful adoption [Fayad-Hamu 1999].

Framework economics. The economics of developing frameworks includes activities [Fayad-Hamu 1999; Hamu-Fayad 1998] such as the following:

- Determining effective framework cost metrics that measure the savings of reusing framework components versus building applications from scratch.

- Estimating cost for accurate forecasting of the cost of buying, building, or adapting a particular framework.

- Performing investment analysis and justification to determine the benefits of applying frameworks in terms of return on investment. Favaro surveyed all the reuse investment analysis approaches in [Favaro 1996].

Lim surveyed 17 reuse economic models in [Lim 1996]. We expect that the focus on framework economics will help to bridge the gap between the technical, managerial, and financial aspects of making, buying, or adapting frameworks [Fayad-Hamu 1999; Hamu-Fayad 1998].

Framework standards. In order to develop, document, integrate, and adapt long-lived application frameworks, standards are a must. As application frameworks become more complex and more widely accepted, standards become invaluable and increasingly essential. Standards ensure consistency and form a base from which to justify the framework cost and protect the investment. We believe that several standards will emerge, including framework development, framework adaptation, framework interoperability, and integration standards.

26.2 References

[alSafadi 1999] alSafadi, Yasser. Frameworks in the Healthcare Domain. *Domain-Specific Application Frameworks*, M.E. Fayad and R. Johnson, editors, New York: Wiley & Sons, 1999.

[Campbell-Islam 1993] Campbell, Roy H., and Nayeem Islam. A technique for documenting the framework of an object-oriented system. *Computing Systems* 6(4), Fall 1993.

[Favaro 1996] Favaro, John. A comparison of approaches for reuse investment analysis. *Proceedings of Fourth International Conference on Software Reuse,* Orlando, FL, April 1996.

[Fayad-Hamu 1999] Fayad, Mohamed E., and David S. Hamu. Object-oriented enterprise frameworks. Submitted for publication to *IEEE Computer,* 1999.

[Gamma 1995] Gamma, Erich, Richard Helm, Ralph Johnson, and John Vlissides. *Design Patterns: Elements of Reusable Software Architecture.* Reading, MA: Addison-Wesley, 1995.

[Hamu-Fayad 1998] Hamu, David S., and Mohamed E. Fayad. Achieve bottom-line improvements with enterprise frameworks. *Communications of the ACM,* August 1998.

[Hueni 1995] Hueni, Herman, Ralph Johnson, and Robert A. Engel. Framework for network protocol software. *Proceedings of OOPSLA,* Austin, TX, October 1995.

[Johnson-Foote 1988] Johnson, Ralph E., and Brian Foote. Designing reusable classes. *Journal of Object-Oriented Programming.* SIGS 1(5), June/July 1988:22–35.

[Lim 1996] Lim, Wayne C. Reuse economics: A comparison of seventeen models and directions for future research. *Proceedings of Fourth International Conference on Software Reuse,* Orlando, FL, April 1996.

[Pree 1994] Pree, Wolfgang. *Design Patterns for Object-Oriented Software Development.* Reading, MA: Addison-Wesley, 1994.

[Schmidt 1997] Schmidt, Douglas C. Applying design patterns and frameworks to develop object-oriented communication software. *Handbook of Programming Languages,* vol. I, Peter Salus, editor. Macmillan Computer Publishing, 1997.

26.3 Review Questions

1. Suggest five more areas of future research in application framework technology.

2. Debate the following positions:

   - Benefits of frameworks will become more immediate to application programmers, as well as to infrastructure developers.

   - Many framework experts [Johnson-Foote 1988] favor blackbox frameworks over whitebox frameworks.

   - Documenting frameworks is a costly activity and contemporary tools often focus on low-level method-oriented documentation, which fails to capture the strategic roles and collaborations among framework components.

SIDEBAR 9
FRAMEWORK MAINTENANCE: VENDOR VIEWPOINT

The advantages of frameworks, especially their potential for reducing costs through adaptability and reuse, have been discussed thoroughly. The challenges frameworks present have also been well covered. This sidebar addresses some of the support issues facing the smaller organization in supporting a framework. While the focus here is on vendors supplying system infrastructure and middleware frameworks [Fayad-Schmidt 1997; Fayad-Laitinen 1998] to multiple customers in different organizations, most of the ideas apply as well to in-house suppliers and to enterprise frameworks. The central idea is that the same characteristics that make frameworks reusable also place a serious support burden on the framework vendors, who must plan their technical and support strategy accordingly. The strategy must take account of the fact that the vendor has very limited control over the framework's use by the customer and cannot expect perfect communication or a perfect meshing of maintenance goals.

Internal and commercial frameworks measure success by the extent of their reuse. But any worthwhile software system evolves over time. New features are added, performance is enhanced, and new software environments and new hardware platforms are supported. In addition, framework architectures will evolve and whitebox components will migrate toward blackbox implementations. At the same time, new framework users will have new needs that are not met by the current version. This evolutionary process brings with it some problems that must be addressed by both the customer and the vendor. The vendor, in order to remain competitive, must remain involved in customer issues.

SB9.1 Vendor/Customer Expectation Mismatch

The challenge of *impedance mismatch* [Bosch-Mattsson-Fayad 1998; Fayad-Hamu 1998] between frameworks and applications has been documented, but the *expectation mismatch* between vendors and customers can be just as difficult to address. There are two major components of this mismatch: The views and the needs of the customer do not coincide with those of the vendor. Here are some examples of these differences.

A classic misreading of intent for framework vendors is to assume that their customers intrinsically care about the framework product. In fact, customers don't care nearly as much about the framework as the vendors do. Their application, not the framework, is their primary concern. One manifestation of this is the view vendors have that customers should be expected to master all facets of the framework. But customers, reasonably enough, master only the minimum they need to use the framework adequately. This means that customers may not even fully understand the high-level architecture of the framework and will not be highly motivated to put in more effort than necessary. This suboptimal usage may frustrate the vendor, but the customer may not be able to justify the greater investment in effort required to use the framework optimally.

Similarly, vendors are often more interested than customers in design quality and integrity, as measured by such metrics as orthogonality and appropriate usage. Customers are interested first in making their application work, and second in sustainable design.

This difference does not make vendors right and customers wrong, or vice versa. It is a difference in goals that should be understood.

Another classic misreading is that problems can be cleanly divided between vendor errors and customer misunderstandings. The reality is that all errors are vendor errors until shown otherwise. Then, even if the error is the customer's misuse of the system, the vendor must still help the customer find a suitable solution.

Examples of other areas where the vendor must provide extra help include dealing with incompatible classes and architectural changes. The customer may extend the functionality of a particular class according to the principles laid out by the framework vendor, but framework changes may make the extensions incompatible. As developers change their system, they may purposely or inadvertently modify the architecture of the system. Such changes can adversely affect the reliability and performance of the system. Again, the vendor must be prepared to help the customer assess and correct these problems.

The difficulty of debugging frameworks, with their inversion of control and possible inaccessibility of source code, requires the vendor to provide extra help in debugging. Once again, this is a usability issue. If the vendor supplies debugging guides and perhaps special hooks in the framework, then human support can be reduced. Note that some vendors worry about making their proprietary system too vulnerable to inspection and reverse engineering, thus compromising its value. This concern must be weighed against the equally valid concerns of the customer, who must be able to develop, debug, and maintain the application of which the framework is a part. Too much protection may make the system harder to work with and ultimately make the framework less competitive.

All these issues are related to the problems of documentation. Documentation is a critical, high-cost element because it is the only way the framework can be used. There are a number of promising methods for improving the technical documentation of a framework, such as describing patterns, documenting component contracts, and including detailed component resource usage and performance information. But even with these advances, documentation is not effective unless customers find it usable. This means that vendors won't know how good their documentation really is until they test it with customers. A subtle side effect is that without customer testing, the documentation may inadvertently guide customers toward unintended use of the framework.

Vendors may expect that customers will consult extensively in the use of the framework and will provide feedback on problem areas. Customers, however, have other priorities. While serious problems will certainly be identified, minor problems may not be. Weaknesses found by developers are likely to be dealt with locally and not reported back to the vendor because of time pressures, inexperience, or inattention. Worse, developers may install corrections that never get reported back. Since the problems do not get reported, the vendor never fixes them, and it becomes increasingly difficult to migrate to new versions of the framework.

In order to ameliorate such problems, the vendor must be very proactive in learning about the customer's experience with the framework. This means, if possible, talking directly to the application developers and designers rather than relying on satisfaction

Continues

surveys or reports from customer representatives who are not directly involved in using the framework. Even so, if the framework is too sensitive to suboptimal use, then maintenance costs will be high and customer satisfaction will be low. In short, customers cannot be compelled to use a framework in an ideal fashion, and thus vendors must be prepared to compensate.

SB9.2 Maintenance Is a Continuing Cost

Even very well written frameworks take effort to modify. The fact that a framework is well designed and well documented does not imply that making changes will be trivial. It only implies that changes can be made effectively. Modifications will still require the extensive participation of senior designers and developers. They must carefully weigh the effect of changes on the framework users and be sure that changes do not compromise the integrity of the framework, its resource usage, or its performance.

A shockingly common management error is the belief that relatively inexperienced people can do maintenance (both corrective and perfective). The smaller the development group, the more serious this error is. Developers who are doing maintenance are not developing new software. Unless the organizational strategy correctly assesses the need to involve senior people in maintenance, they will find themselves jeopardizing new development projects.

It's worth noting that trying to reduce maintenance by starting out with a blackbox framework is probably a bad idea. Until the vendor and customers have had enough experience with the framework in real situations, blocking access to the framework's inner workings will just make it harder to use and maintain. Customers are much more likely then to find the framework unsatisfactory.

SB9.3 Support: Revenue or Cost?

Support is a tricky issue for vendors. For large systems, a support contract is common practice and will be expected by the vendor and user. Support, then, can be a source of revenue to the vendor. The vendor can plan for certain support costs and hire support personnel accordingly. These support people can be trained to the system and take over from the vendor's development personnel, who will return to their primary functions.

For smaller organizations and smaller frameworks, the situation is quite different. Often, the cost of support must be bundled into the price of the framework, and support costs must be kept low in order to remain competitive. While it would be useful to hire support personnel in advance of sales to deal with customer issues, it might be difficult to justify economically. Unfortunately, it is often the developers who then take on initial support, thus preventing their assignment to future development. Such a diversion of development resources must be figured into the cost and schedule of development for the vendor.

A framework for multiple customers will require some changes not wanted by all. As mentioned in the next section, it may make some customers reluctant to upgrade to new framework versions. Likewise, the vendor cannot afford to add features that serve a particular customer but have little general applicability. This poses a problem for both the vendors and customers.

One possible solution is to provide special contracting. If the customer has some requirements that are too extensive to be handled by the designed-in customization mechanisms, it can contract to have the vendor, or developers who work closely with the vendor, make the modifications. This makes real sense if the changes fall largely in the domain of the framework vendor. These changes, however, may not be general enough to justify their incorporation into the standard framework product. Thus, they must be handled as a separate product version.

SB9.4 Why Customers May Not Want to Upgrade

Another factor complicates framework support: maintenance of older framework versions. Not only can customers not be compelled to upgrade their applications to new framework versions, they will often have good reasons not to upgrade. Consequently, only unsuccessful frameworks will be without multiple versions. Valid reasons for not upgrading include the following:

Stability concerns. The current version of the framework is functional and the new version has substantial changes that could affect the stability of their product. The customer might also be in the midst of development, where the introduction of an updated framework could adversely affect costs and schedules.

Undesired characteristics. The new version may have some undesirable characteristics for a particular customer, such as increased resource usage or reduced performance of some particular functionality.

Architectural differences. The new version may have architectural changes that require major changes in the customer's application.

Development environment. The new version may require new development tools, such as new compiler versions, new source code control systems, or even new hardware platforms.

Contractual issues. There may be contractual issues that keep the customer from upgrading. For example, the customer may be contractually obligated to a third party to keep a certain version of their software. Another question is who pays for acceptance testing?

Local changes. As previously mentioned, customers may not report every small problem they find with a framework but may just incorporate their own local changes. They may also have customizations that require extra effort to upgrade. As local changes accumulate, customers become less amenable to upgrading their application.

In these cases, attempting to force the customer to upgrade will be unsuccessful. Thus, some arrangement must be made to support older or different versions.

One possibility is to increase support fees after some period for older versions of frameworks. This will help cover the effort of maintaining multiple versions and will

Continues

SIDEBAR 9
FRAMEWORK MAINTENANCE: VENDOR VIEWPOINT (Continued)

provide at least a limited incentive for customers to make the change to a new version (if possible).

Thus, framework vendors must plan to support multiple versions of their products. In order to do this, a strong configuration management system must be in place, and changes must be carefully controlled. Note that the choice of configuration management systems may have a customer impact. Unless the framework is supplied only as binary objects, many source code control systems include configuration data in the source files themselves. Version updates may affect the customer's source code control efforts.

SB9.5 New Uses, New Problems

As new customers adopt the framework, another set of problems arises. First, a new application is likely to exercise the framework in new ways that were not anticipated. This may reveal resource or performance problems that were not evident in prior uses. In addition, errors may be revealed (especially in the processing of error cases). Even with rigorous testing by the framework vendor, it is very likely that installation in a new environment will uncover new problems. Second, there may be subtle differences in the architecture of the new application that cause equally subtle integration problems. As a result, the vendor must plan for the costs of extra testing and integration efforts for each new customer. This may well mean a higher initial price for the framework.

SB9.6 Summary

A framework is a serious investment for both vendor and customers, not only in direct financial cost but also in continued effort. Obviously, customers look for applicability, quality, and value in frameworks, but they evaluate the vendor's potential for long-term survival. Vendors who underestimate the cost of framework support have limited potential for survival. In order for framework vendors to be attractive to customers, and in order to achieve longevity, they must understand the continuing costs of maintaining frameworks and align their business and technical practices accordingly.

SB9.7 References

[Bosch-Mattsson-Fayad 1998] Bosch J., M. Mattsson, and M.E. Fayad. Frameworks integration problems, causes, and solutions. Submitted for publication to *Communications of the ACM,* 1998.

[Fayad-Hamu 1998] Fayad, M.E. and D. Hamu. Object-oriented enterprise frameworks. Submitted for publication to *IEEE Computer,* 1998.

[Fayad-Laitinen 1998] Fayad, M.E. and M. Laitinen. *Transition to Object-Oriented Software Development.* New York: John Wiley & Sons, 1998.

[Fayad-Schmidt 1997] Fayad, M.E., and D. Schmidt. Object-oriented application frameworks. *Communications of the ACM* 40(10), October 97:32–38.

Glossary

The definitions in this glossary are arranged in alphabetical order and were contributed by the authors of this book. A definition may be a single word, such as *component;* a phrase, such as *design pattern;* or an acronym, such as *UML.* Multiple definitions are also included, using enumeration.

The following cross-references are used to show relationships between definitions and to indicate their respective chapters:

See refers to a different entry for the definition of a synonym.

See also refers to similar and related definitions.

(#) indicates the chapter in which the term is discussed.

Abstract class. A class that is not instantiable and that standardizes the interface for subclasses *(16)*.

Abstract method. A method with a dummy implementation; abstract methods are typically part of abstract classes *(16)*.

Access structure. An element of a hypermedia application that provides a different organization of a set of nodes and/or links and therefore allows a different means of navigation. Usual access structures are indexes and guided tours *(11)*.[1]

Action. (1) An interaction between two or more objects, represented by an ellipse. Usually documented with a postcondition, which states the effect on some or all of the participants. An action in general can be broken down into smaller actions: It repre-

---

[1]Chapter 11 definitions are given in the context of hypertext and hypermedia.

sents a dialog or transaction between the participants *(19)*. (2) For visual builders, a method of a class that has been specially marked as accessible to (that is, callable by) visual builders *(5)*.

Active learning. Learning by doing. The students are actively involved in the learning process *(22)*.

Adaptability space. The amount of variation within a knowledge domain that is allowable without violating the semantic constraints of that domain *(6)*.

Alexandrian pattern. A pattern that is described in terms of a solution to a problem in a context *(2)*.

Anchor. An area indicating the presence of a link inside a node *(11)*.

Annotation. A piece of information that does not have meaning by itself, but explains or expands another piece of information *(11)*.

Application architecture. A software infrastructure that supports the development of well-behaved, robust applications through a set of common services (for example, frameworks, libraries, components) and that guides their overall design and construction by formalizing patterns and programming idioms *(10)*.

Application developer. Those who add application-specific functionality to and/or adapt an object-oriented framework to produce an application from the framework *(9)*.

Application generators. These are based on a high-level, domain-specific language that is compiled to a standard architecture. Designing a reusable class library is a lot like designing a programming language, except that the only concrete syntax is that of the language in which it is implemented *(1)*.

A priori framework development. An approach to framework development that identifies and designs frameworks prior to any existing implementation of common elements *(13)*.

Architectural abstraction. Architecture is one perspective on software, and in this perspective we form abstractions through which to understand the software. Such abstractions are termed *architectural abstractions*. An architectural abstraction has four characteristic aspects: structure, functionality, abstraction, and reusability. Design patterns, modeling patterns, metapatterns, and frameworks are all examples of architectural abstractions *(2)*.

Association. A relationship between two objects that may exist at any one moment in time. In Catalysis, equivalent to a pair of attributes *(19)*.

Attribute. (1) In analysis and high-level design (and, in particular, in Catalysis), something that can be asked about the state of an object. Not necessarily implemented as a variable in an object-oriented design *(19)*. (2) For visual builders, a property of a class that has been specially marked as accessible to visual builders. This may require standard accessors of the form getX and setX, where X is the name of the property *(5)*. *See also* **Action, Event, Part.**

Average depth of inheritance. The average depth of inheritance of the classes in a system. Computed by dividing the sum of the maximum path lengths to all classes by the number of classes. Path length to a class is the number of edges from the root to the class in an inheritance hierarchy *(25)*.

Average number of parents per class. The average number of distinct (parent) classes from which a class inherits information. This metric is different from the average depth of inheritance metric because it takes into account instances of multiple inheritances *(25)*.

Average width of inheritance. The average number of children per class in the system. Computed by dividing the sum of the number of children over all classes by the number of classes in the system *(25)*.

Behavioral refinement. The task performed by an application developer in providing specific definitions for the virtual methods of the abstract classes of the framework, resulting in the refinement of the behavior exhibited by the methods of the framework *(12)*.

Blackbox framework. A blackbox (or parameterized) framework is based on composition. The behavior of the framework is customized by using different combinations of classes. A parameterized framework requires deep understanding of the stable and flexible aspects of the domain. Due to its predefined flexibility, a blackbox framework is often more rigid in the domain it supports. In general, a framework has parts that can be parameterized and parts that need to be customized through subclassing *(3)*. *See also* **Whitebox framework.**

Blackbox teaching. Teaching a framework by describing the scope and boundaries of it. The focus is on the purpose and the frame of the framework *(22)*.

Calling and called framework. A calling framework is an active entity, proactively invoking other parts of the application, whereas a called framework is a passive entity that can be invoked by other parts of the application *(3)*. *See also* **Hollywood principle.**

Class size in bytes (CSB). Computes the size of the objects in bytes that will be created from a class declaration. Size is computed by summing the size of all attributes declared in a class *(25)*.

Clique. A group of classes that interact together and are used together to perform a given task within an application *(6)*.

Collaboration. A description of the interactions between two or more objects, described independently of the other roles the participating objects might play. A collaboration can be described with a model framework *(19)*.

Competitive strategy. The component of business strategy in which an organization determines how it will compete in its chosen product markets, either by pursuing an advantaged economic cost position or an advantaged product offering through differentiation *(24)*.

Composition-filters. An aspect-oriented programming technique whereby different aspects are expressed in terms of declarative and orthogonal message transformation specifications. Here, aspects are concepts, which affect the quality and/or semantics of software components. Composition filters can be attached to the objects programmed in different object-oriented languages *(6)*.

Constraints. A constraint (as a framework construct) is a mandatory relationship between the participants of the framework, including some internal variables to the framework. Constraints are behavioral invariants *(23)*.

Context-sensitive access. This allows a different set of links and/or information to be provided for different contexts *(11)*.

Deriving software from knowledge domains. This approach aims to realize a structure that preserves mapping from the abstractions of the knowledge domain of a problem into the abstractions of software components *(6)*.

Descendant. A class that inherits from another class, but not necessarily as a direct subclass *(16)*.

Design patterns. A means of capturing and communicating the design of object-oriented systems *(16)*.

Design size in classes. A count of the total number of classes in the system *(25)*.

Differentiation. The willingness of customers to pay a higher price for a product or service due to higher perceived value *(24)*.

Direct class coupling (DCC). The average number of distinct classes with which a class may collaborate. This measure includes classes that are directly related by attribute declarations and parameter declarations in methods *(25)*.

Direct class coupling (DCC). A count of the number of different classes to which a class is directly related. DCC includes classes that are directly related by attribute declarations and message passing (parameters) in methods *(25)*.

Economic cost position. The relative competitive position of a business in a particular product market with respect to total operating costs *(24)*.

Economic value maximization. The pursuit of superior economic returns over time as an organizational governing objective *(24)*.

Ensemble use case. A use case designed to represent part or all of the concrete functionality found in a framework's ensemble *(13)*.

Enterprise application frameworks. These frameworks address broad application domains (such as telecommunications, avionics, manufacturing, and financial engineering) and are the cornerstone of enterprise business activities. Relative to system infrastructure and middleware integration frameworks, enterprise frameworks are expensive to develop and/or purchase. However, enterprise frameworks can provide a substantial return on investment since they support the development of end-user applications and products directly. In contrast, system infrastructure and middleware integration frameworks focus largely on internal software development concerns. Although these frameworks are essential to rapidly create high-quality software, they typically do not generate substantial revenue for large enterprises. As a result, it is often more cost effective to buy system infrastructure and middleware integration frameworks rather than build them in-house *(1)*.

Event. For visual builders, a change to a part's state that causes a notification to be sent out informing any listeners (a.k.a. observers) that the state change has occurred *(5)*. *See also* **Action, Attribute, Part** [Gamma 1995].

Exemplars. Exemplars consist of a concrete implementation provided for all of the abstract classes in a framework, along with their interactions, to provide a means of understanding the design and behavior of the framework *(9)*.

Expectation mismatch. A difference in expectations caused by differing needs and views between vendors and customers. An example of expectation mismatch is the vendor's expectation that customers are intrinsically interested in the vendor's product, but in fact, the customers expect to learn no more than is necessary to use the vendor's offering *(Sidebar 9)*.

Flow-of-control behavior. The model of interactions, that is, how control flows between the various methods of various classes of the framework *(12)*.

Framework. (1) A framework is a reusable, semicomplete application that can be specialized to produce custom applications. In contrast to earlier object-oriented reuse techniques based on class libraries, frameworks are targeted for particular business units (such as data processing or cellular communications) and application domains (such as user interfaces or real-time avionics). Frameworks like MacApp, ET++,

Interviews, ACE, Microsoft's MFC and DCOM, JavaSoft's RMI, and implementations of the OMG's CORBA play an increasingly important role in contemporary software development *(1)*. (2) A framework describes the architecture of an object-oriented system, the kinds of objects in it, and how they interact. It describes how a particular kind of program, such as a user interface or network communication software, is decomposed into objects. It is represented by a set of classes (usually abstract), one for each kind of object, but the interaction patterns between objects are just as much a part of the framework as the classes *(1)*. (3) Frameworks are a component in the sense that vendors sell them as products, and an application might use several frameworks bought from various venders. But frameworks are much more customizable than most components. As a consequence, using a framework takes work even when you know it, and learning a new framework is hard. In return, frameworks are powerful; they can be used for just about any kind of application and a good framework can reduce the amount of effort required to develop customized applications by an order of magnitude *(1)*. (4) A framework provides a standard way for components to handle errors, to exchange data, and to invoke operations on each other. The so-called component systems such as OLE, OpenDoc, and Beans are really frameworks that solve standard problems that arise in building compound documents and other composite objects. But any kind of framework provides the standards that enable existing components to be reused *(1)*. (5) A framework is a collection of interacting objects defined essentially in terms of (a) the individual objects' obligations (interfaces), and (b) patterns of communication between the objects. A framework is a design idea plus, potentially, a set of components that can fulfill some of the participants' roles *(23)*.

Framework builder. The framework builder designs and implements a generic object-oriented framework and can also provide information concerning the purpose and the intended use of the framework in the form of additional documentation, including hooks *(9)*.

Framework cohesion. The functionality of a class can be divided into domain-specific behavior, corresponding to the real-world entity the class represents, and the interaction behavior, to communicate to other framework classes and objects. The latter type of functionality, which establishes the cohesion between the classes and objects in the framework, is referred to as *framework cohesion*. Framework cohesion is a major cause and complicating factor for a number of framework composition problems such as framework composition with legacy components and composition of framework control *(20)*.

Framework composition. The activity in which software engineers use two or more object-oriented frameworks in the development of an application. During composition, the software engineer may experience a number of composition problems—for example, framework gap or composition of framework control. Sometimes referred to as *framework integration (3)*. *See also* **Hollywood principle.**

Framework gap. A framework composition problem that may occur when a software engineer composes two frameworks whose functionality seems to solve the current application's needs. But, for some reason, the composed frameworks do not completely fulfill the needs and there is a gap of missing functionality. This gap of missing functionality is called the framework gap *(3)*.

Framework integration. *See* **Framework composition.**

Framework packaging. This is the process by which a framework realization is packaged as a single, class-like unit. The advantage of such packaging is to hide the internal structure that implements some outside behavior according to some design-level criterion *(23)*.

Framework realization. This is the process by which a given framework is instantiated to solve a particular problem. Realization includes (a) selecting the appropriate library components, (b) using them as is or extending them, and (c) defining application-specific components *(23)*.

Framework search. This is the process of searching for a framework based on some expression of what is needed. Frameworks may be described using extrinsic properties (documentation) or intrinsic properties (signature) *(23)*.

Framework use case. A use case designed to represent functionality found in a framework. Multiple framework use cases may be required to document all of the functionality required of the framework *(13)*.[2]

Frozen spot. An aspect of a framework that is not designed for adaptation *(16)*.

Harvesting design. The process of extracting reusable design and code elements from existing solution domains for the development of new application components or frameworks *(8)*.

Hollywood principle. In traditional class or procedure libraries, the application code invokes routines in the library and it is the application code that is in control. For object-oriented frameworks, the situation is inverted and it is often the framework code that has the thread of control and calls the application code when appropriate. This inversion of control is often referred to as the Hollywood principle, in other words, "Don't call us—we'll call you" *(3)*.

Hook(s). The points at which an object-oriented framework can be adapted by application developers. Using a structured template, each hook gives a specific requirement that it fulfills and then documents how to extend the framework to meet the requirement *(9)*.

Hook method. Corresponds to a hot spot in a framework *(16)*.

Hot spot. A place where framework adaptation takes place *(16)*. *See also* **Hook(s).**

Hot-spot-driven teaching. Teaching a framework by explaining the hot spots in it *(22)*.

Hot word. An anchor on a word *(11)*.

Hypermedia application. An application that provides the user with navigational access among the nodes that form the information base *(11)*.

Hypertext-aware widgets. Sensitive area of a graphical interface that is associated with one or more anchors for links and allows the activation of those anchors *(11)*.

Incremental teaching. Bottom-up framework teaching, by using several simpler, constituent frameworks to expose the overall architecture *(22)*.

Inheritance. A concept that allows sharing, extending, and/or modifying behavior offered by a class *(16)*.

Inversion of control. The runtime architecture of a framework is characterized by an inversion of control. This architecture enables canonical application processing steps to be customized by event handler objects that are invoked via the framework's reactive dispatching mechanism. When events occur, the framework's dis-

---

[2]Other interesting terms (not invented by the authors but used in our chapter): *hot spot* [Pree 1995], *extension point* [UML 1997], *abstract actor* [Jacobson 1997], *ensemble*.

patcher reacts by invoking hook methods on preregistered handler objects, which perform application-specific processing on the events. Inversion of control allows the framework (rather than each application) to determine which set of application-specific methods to invoke in response to external events (such as window messages arriving from end users or packets arriving on communication ports) *(1)*.

Iteration. A single pass through the development life cycle including the phases of analysis, design, construction, testing, and generalization. An iterative development process utilizes several complete passes through these phases to incorporate new or changing requirements as well as lessons learned during construction and testing *(10)*.

Knowledge graph. A graph in which nodes and relations correspond to the concepts of knowledge and their dependencies, respectively. Within the context of framework development, a knowledge graph that corresponds to the domain knowledge of a framework is called the *knowledge domain* of that framework *(6)*.

Learning by judiciousness. The task is explained in the whole conception *(22)*.

Learning through reflection. The students learn by reflecting the tasks through their own experience *(22)*.

Lightweight Directory Access Protocol (LDAP). A simplified, standard Application Programming Interface (API) for accessing naming and directory services endorsed and supported by a large majority of the software industry *(10)*.

Link. The representation of a relation between two or more nodes that allows navigation *(11)*.

Market economics. The level of profitability and growth of the average participant in a product market. In profitable markets, the average participant consistently earns returns above the cost of equity capital *(24)*.

Measurement systems. A class of systems used to measure the relevant values of a process or product. These systems are different from the better known process control systems in that the measured values are not directly—that is, as part of the same system—used to control the production process that creates the product or process that is measured. A measurement system is used for quality control on parts entering production or on those already produced that can then be used to separate acceptable from unacceptable items or to categorize the products in quality categories *(14)*.

Message. An alternative term for method invocation (the term *message* was introduced to stress the dynamic binding aspect of method calls) *(16)*.

Message flow graph. A graph whose nodes represent method invocations by objects in the framework, while links represent data/message dependencies. Message flow graphs combine functional dependencies and control information (for example, parallelism and sequentiality of method invocations) *(23)*.

Metapatterns. A means of capturing and communicating the design of frameworks and of actively supporting the design pattern approach *(16)*.

Middleware integration frameworks. These frameworks are commonly used to integrate distributed applications and components. Middleware integration frameworks are designed to enhance the ability of software developers to modularize, reuse, and extend their software infrastructure to work seamlessly in a distributed environment. There is a thriving market for middleware integration frameworks, which are rapidly becoming commodities. Common examples include ORB frameworks, message-oriented middleware, and transactional databases *(1)*.

Model framework. A template from which models can be instantiated. Captures the static and dynamic relationships between objects playing different roles *(19)*.

Navigation. The action of visiting hypermedia nodes by following links *(11)*.

Node. A unit of information in a hypermedia application *(11)*.

Number of abstract data types (NAD). A count of the number of user-defined objects (ADTs) used as attributes in a class, which are therefore necessary to instantiate an object instance of the (aggregate) class *(25)*.

Number of attributes (NOD). A count of the number of data declarations in a class *(25)*.

Number of children (NOC). A count of the number of immediate children (subclasses) of a class *(25)*.

Number of hierarchies. A count of the number of class hierarchies in the system *(25)*.

Number of methods (NOM). A count of all the methods defined in a class *(25)*.

Number of multiple inheritances. A count of the number of instances of multiple inheritance in the system *(25)*.

Number of parameters per method (NPM). The average of the number of parameters per method in a class. It is computed by summing the parameters of all methods and dividing by the number of methods in a class *(25)*.

Number of parents (NOA). A count of all classes from which a class inherits information *(25)*.

Number of polymorphic methods (NOP). A count of the methods that can exhibit polymorphic behavior. Such methods in C++ are marked as *virtual* methods *(25)*.

Number of reference attributes (NRA). A count of the number of pointers and references used as attributes in a class *(25)*.

Number of services per class. The average of the number of public methods in all classes *(25)*.

Number of single inheritances. A count of the number of classes (subclasses) that use inheritance in the system *(25)*.

Number of unique parameter types (NPT). A count of the number of different parameter types used in the methods of a class *(25)*.

Object request broker (ORB). Any technology that enables object programs to transparently communicate across process boundaries and optionally between languages using the same semantics used in local calls (within the same process space). Examples include the Object Management Group's CORBA architecture, Microsoft's DCOM, and Java's built-in RMI solution *(10)*.

Option pricing theory. A branch of financial theory that studies the determination of the fair market value of options *(23)*.

Organizational reuse capability. The potential of an organization to create business value through the exploitation of reuse-related technological and strategic abilities *(24)*.

Part. For visual builders, a class that has been specially enabled to allow access to some or all of its properties and methods, and that notifies listeners (observers) when certain of its states have changed *(5)*. *See also* **Action, Attribute, Event**.

Participation strategy. The component of business strategy in which an organization determines which product markets it will serve and how it will enter profitable markets and exit unprofitable markets *(24)*.

Part interface. Interface composed of three clearly defined programming interface features: attributes, actions, and events (JavaBeans uses the terms *properties, methods,* and *events*) *(5)*.

Passive learning. Learning by listening, mostly incorporated by lecture-style teaching *(22)*.

Pattern-oriented teaching. Teaching a framework by describing the design patterns that are used in it *(22)*.

Pedagogical patterns. Documentations of tried and tested approaches to object technology (OT) education that have evolved over time (defined by Sharp et al.) *(22)*.

Postcondition. A Boolean expression relating the states before and after an action or operation *(19)*.

Publish/subscribe. A programming model typically used in distributed systems whereby the various components are intentionally decoupled such that one or more listeners (that is, subscribers) are registered to receive messages asynchronously from one or more publishers. This decoupling, often achieved through the use of an intermediary (CORBA event channel, message queue, and so on) results in greater flexibility, as the publisher and subscriber do not need to be running at the same time to share information, and the introduction of new publishers and subscribers to the system at any time is relatively trivial *(10)*.

Real options. A branch of management science that applies concepts from option pricing theory to real-world capital investment projects *(24)*.

Reenskaug's generalized framework conditions. A set of four conditions that are necessary and sufficient for a successful framework development project. These conditions were introduced in a more specific form by Trygve Reenskaug, Per Wold, and Odd Arild Lehne *(13)*.

Refactoring approach to framework development. An approach to framework development that distills frameworks from existing implementations of common elements *(13)*.

Refinement. The relationship between a more abstract and a more detailed description (of a business, specification, or design); or the process of making a refinement *(19)*.

Software architecture. Several interacting software components *(16)*.

Specification of framework. Precisely specifying the functional behavior implemented by the methods of the framework, as well as the flow-of-control behavior provided by the framework *(12)*.

Specification of the application. The (functional) specification of the application, obtained by suitably combining the information in the specification of the framework with information about the behavior implemented by the methods supplied by the application developer *(12)*.

Strategic options. The specification of alternative choices in either competitive strategy or participation strategy that are different from those currently pursued by the organization *(24)*.

System infrastructure frameworks. These frameworks simplify the development of portable and efficient system infrastructures such as operating system and communication frameworks, and frameworks for user interfaces and language processing tools. System infrastructure frameworks are primarily used internally within a software organization and are not sold to customers directly *(1)*.

Template method. Corresponds to a frozen spot in a framework *(16)*.

Traces. A way of recording the interactions between the various (virtual) methods of the framework *(12)*.

Type. A description of the behavior expected of an object, independently of its implementation. A type lists a set of operations or actions and specifies each in terms of its effect on a set of attributes and associations *(19)*.

Unified Modeling Language (UML). The UML is an international standard for capturing analysis and design information for systems of varying complexity through a set of well-defined models and diagrams. UML represents the collaborative work of major object methodologists and incorporates, among other things, use cases, class and interaction diagrams, state and activity diagrams, as well as component and deployment diagrams *(10)*.

Use-case assortment. The process of partitioning use cases into sets where all of the use cases in the set follow a common pattern *(13)*.

Use-case explosion. The proliferation of use cases in such a way that the project becomes bogged down in the requirements-gathering phase *(13)*.

Whitebox framework. In a whitebox (or inheritance-based) framework, the framework user is supposed to customize the framework behavior through subclassing of framework classes. A framework often is inheritance-based in the beginning of its life cycle, since the application domain is not sufficiently well understood to make it possible to parameterize the behavior (in other words, become a blackbox framework). In general, a framework has parts that can be parameterized and parts that need to be customized through subclassing *(3)*.

Whitebox teaching. Teaching a framework from the inside out; the focus lies on how it works *(22)*.

Index of Authors

This author index is arranged in alphabetical order by last name and includes the following information for each author: last name, first name, affiliation, country, primary e-mail, URL, chapters contributed, and a brief biography.

Aksit, Mehmet, Ph.D. Department of Computer Science, University of Twente, the Netherlands, email: aksit@cs.utwente.nl, URL: www.cs.utwente.nl/~aksit, Chapter 7, pp. 169–198.

Mehmet Aksit is an associate professor at the University of Twente. He is the leader of the Twente Research and Education on Software Engineering (TRESE) project. He was the program cochair of the 1997 European Conference on Object-Oriented Programming (ECOOP '97). He has served as a program committee member for various international conferences, and he was the tutorial chair of the ECOOP '92 conference. He has been a user and developer of object-oriented systems since 1983. Together with the members of the TRESE project, he has introduced an aspect-oriented programming technique based on composition filters, atomic delegations, associative inheritance and delegation mechanisms, abstract communication types, fuzzy-logic-based object-oriented methods and design algebra. He has identified and defined a set of new problems related to object-oriented analysis and design.

Alencar, Paulo S.C., Ph.D. Department of Computer Science, University of Waterloo, Ontario, Canada, e-mail: alencar@csg.uwaterlo.ca, Sidebar 2, pp. 163–166.

Paulo S.C. Alencar is a research associate professor of computer science at the University of Waterloo (Canada). His current research, teaching, and consulting interests include software engineering and formal methods in software engineering. He is a member of the Institute of Electrical and Electronics Engineers (IEEE), the IEEE Computer Society, the Association for Computing (ACM), Canadian Information Processing Society (CIPS), and American Association for Artificial Intelligence (AAAI).

Bansiya, Jagdish, Ph.D. Computer Science Department, Southern Polytechnic State University, Marietta, Georgia, USA, e-mail: jbansiya@cs.uah.edu, URL: indus.cs.uah.edu, Chapter 25, pp. 599–616.

Jagdish Bansiya is an assistant professor in the Computer Science Department at the Southern Polytechnic State University in Marietta, Georgia. He received a B.S. in computer science and engineering from the University of Roorkee (India) in 1990 and an M.S. and a Ph.D. in computer science from the University of Alabama in Huntsville in 1992 and 1998, respectively. His research interests are in all aspects of object-oriented development and software engineering, particularly object-oriented frameworks, design metrics, design patterns, and distributed object computing. He is a member of the Institute of Electrical and Electronics Engineers (IEEE) and the Association for Computing (ACM).

Bäumer, Dirk. OTI Software Technology Center, Zurich, Switzerland, e-mail: dirk_baeumer@oti.com, URL: www.oti.com, Chapter 17, pp. 395–413.

Dirk Bäumer was the chief architect of the GEBOS system at RWG Stuttgart from 1991 to 1997. Then he was a research scientist at TakeFive Software AG in Zurich (Switzerland), the company that developed the SNiFF+ software development environment. He is currently working for OTI in Zurich. He received a master's degree in computer science from the University of Stuttgart (Germany) and a doctoral degree in computer science from the University of Hamburg (Germany).

Bengtsson, PerOlof. Department of Computer Science and Business Administration, University of Karlskrona/Ronneby, Sweden, e-mail: PerOlof.Bengtsson@ipd.hk-r.se, URL: www.ide.hk-r.se/~ARCS, Chapter 3, pp. 55–86.

PerOlof Bengtsson received his M.Sc degree in software engineering from the University of Karlskrona/Ronneby, Sweden, in 1997. From 1995 to 1997 he worked as a quality assurance and reuse consultant at the Ericsson subsidiary, Ericsson Software Technology AB, Sweden. He is currently a Ph.D. candidate at the University of Karlskrona/Ronneby. His research interests include software architecture design and evaluation, especially methods for predicting software qualities from software architecture.

Bergmans, Lodewijk, Ph.D. Ericsson Mobile Communications, Lund, Sweden, e-mail: lbergmans@acm.org, URL: www.cs.utwente.nl/~bergmans, Chapter 7, pp. 167–198.

Lodewijk Bergmans studied computer science at the Faculty of Computer Science, University of Twente, the Netherlands. He received a Ph.D. from the University of Twente. His dissertation, entitled "Composing Concurrent Objects," dealt with object-oriented concurrent systems, addressing the issues of reusable concurrency and synchronization in object-oriented programming languages and analysis and design methods, including graphical notations and implementation aspects. Currently he is working as a software architect for GSM phones with Ericsson Mobile Communications in Lund, Sweden.

Boone, Jean. IBM Corporation, Research Triangle Park, North Carolina, USA, e-mail: jpboone@us.ibm.com, Chapter 8, pp. 199–214.

Joan Boone is a software engineer in IBM's Software Solutions Division at Research Triangle Park, North Carolina, where she develops products and participates in customer engagements that use object technology. Her recent activities focus on the development of components that integrate products with IBM's application development tools. These include components that facilitate development of distributed applications with IBM's San Francisco business frameworks and components that enable applications for systems management. Prior to joining IBM, she worked on several large software development projects for NASA's space shuttle program and the Federal Aviation Administration's air traffic control system. She received an M.S. in computer science from the University of North Carolina at Chapel Hill and an M.S. in applied science from the College of William and Mary in Williamsburg, Virginia.

Bosch, Jan, Ph.D. Department of Computer Science and Business Administration, University of Karlskrona/Ronneby, Sweden, e-mail: Jan.Bosch@ide.hk-r.se, URL: www.ide.hk-r.se/~bosch, Chapter 3, pp. 58–86, and Chapter 20, pp. 467–491.

Jan Bosch received an M.Sc degree from the University of Twente, the Netherlands, in 1991 and a Ph.D. from Lund University, Sweden, in 1995. He currently acts as a professor of software engineering at the University of Karlskrona/Ronneby, where he heads the Architecture and Composition of Software (ARCS) research group. Research activities within ARCS include software architecture design methods, techniques for assessing quality requirements such as maintainability at the architectural level, product-line architectures, object-oriented frameworks, in particular framework design and composition and design patterns. He is the coeditor of the ECOOP '97 workshop reader published by Springer-Verlag in the Lecture Notes in Computer Science—LNCS series and the initiator and coordinator of SARIS, a Swedish network on software architecture involving both academia and industry.

Buhr, Ray J.A., Ph.D. Department of Systems and Computer Engineering, Carleton University, Ottawa, Canada, e-mail: buhr@sce.carleton.ca, Chapter 18, pp. 415–439.

Ray Buhr is a professor in the Department of Systems and Computer Engineering, Carleton University, Ottawa, Canada. He was educated at Queen's University, Kingston, Canada (B.Sc., engineering physics, Gold Medallist, 1959), University of Saskatchewan (M.Eng., electrical engineering, 1960), and Cambridge University, England (Ph.D., control engineering, 1966). He entered the software field through computer control and became fascinated by the contrast between the strength of techniques for representing control systems diagrammatically and the weakness of techniques for representing software systems diagrammatically. He has authored five books and many technical papers in his specialty, and has acted as a consultant and research collaborator to a wide variety of industries internationally.

Butler, Gregory, Ph.D. Department of Computer Science, Concordia University, Montreal, Canada, e-mail: gregb@cs.concordia.ca, URL: www.cs.concordia.ca/~faculty/gregb, Chapter 21, pp. 495–503.

Gregory Butler is an associate professor in computer science at Concordia University, Montreal, Canada. He obtained his Ph.D. from the University of Sydney in 1980 for work on computational group theory. He was on the faculty of the Department of Computer Science at the University of Sydney from 1981 to 1990. He has held visiting positions at the University of Delaware and Universitaet Bayreuth. He is a major contributor to the Cayley system for computational group theory, modern algebra, and discrete mathematics.

Carpenter, Susan G. IBM, Research Triangle Park, North Carolina, USA, e-mail: carpnter@us.ibm.com, Chapter 5, pp. 143–152.

Susan Carpenter is an information development team leader at IBM's Software Solutions Laboratory in Research Triangle Park, North Carolina. She has written on C++, Java, and Smalltalk topics for almost five years.

Cline, Marshall, Ph.D. MT Systems Company, Dallas, Texas, USA, e-mail: cline@parashift.com, Sidebar 6, pp. 460–463.

Marshall Cline is president of MT Systems Company, which develops object-oriented systems for large corporations. He received his Ph.D. in electrical and computer engineering from Clarkson University.

Cowan, Donald D., Ph.D. Department of Computer Science, University of Waterloo, Ontario, Canada, e-mail: dcowan@csg.uwaterlo.ca, Sidebar 2, pp. 163—166.

Donald D. Cowan is professor emeritus of computer science at the University of Waterloo (Canada) and director of the Computer Systems Group. His research interests include software engineering with particular emphasis on component-based approaches. Professor Cowan is the founding chairman of the Computer Science Department at Waterloo. He currently directs the Education Program for Software Professionals, a professional upgrading program for software specialists.

Denomméé, Pierre. Department of Computer Science, Concordia University, Montreal,Canada, e-mail: denomme@cs.concordia.ca, URL: www.cs.concordia.ca/ ~grad/denomme, Chapter 21, pp. 495–503.

Pierre Denomméé is a Ph.D. student in computer science at Concordia University in Montreal. He holds a master's degree in computer science from Concordia University, completed under the supervision of Gregory Butler; a bachelor of applied science degree in computer science, software development option, from the Université du Québec à Montréal. He also has a B.Sc. in physics from the Université de Montréal.

D'Souza, Desmond F. ICON Computing Lab, Austin, Texas, USA, e-mail: dsouza@ iconcomp.com, URL: www.catalysis.org, www.catalysis-europe.org, Chapter 19, pp. 441–463.

Desmond F. D'Souza is senior vice president of component-based development at Platinum Technology's ICON Computing Lab, working on tools and methods for effective software engineering. Since 1985 he has helped model and build systems in finance, systems management, computer-aided design (CAD), and telecommunications, and is a frequent speaker at conferences and companies worldwide.

Eckstein, Jutta. Consultant, Munich, Germany, e-mail: jeckstein@acm.org, URL: ourworld.compuserve.com/homepages/jutta_eckstein, Chapter 22, pp. 505–521.

Jutta Eckstein has been engaged in training and consulting in object technology and software system design since 1990. She is an independent trainer and consultant in the area of object-oriented application development. Before being self-employed, she worked for Integral Development and ParcPlace Systems (today ObjectShare) for many years as a trainer and consultant. Jutta is a member of the Association for Computing (ACM).

Favaro, John M. Intecs Sistemi S.p.A, Pisa, Italy, e-mail: favaro@pisa.intecs.it, Chapter 24, pp. 567–597.

John M. Favaro was born in Vallejo, California. He is currently a senior consultant at Intecs Sistemi in Pisa, Italy, where he heads the advanced software methodologies group. He is technical lead in an initiative with the Italian telecommunications authority for the development of techniques for domain analysis at the operational and business process levels. He is European cochair of the IEEE Subcommittee on Software Reuse. He received an M.S. in electrical engineering and computer science from the University of California at Berkeley, and a B.S. in computer science and mathematics from Yale University.

Favaro, Kenneth R. Marakon Associates, London, United Kingdom, Chapter 24, pp. 567–597.

Kenneth R. Favaro was born in Vallejo, California. He is a partner and head of European operations for Marakon Associates, a management consulting firm specializing in value-based management. He received an M.B.A. from the Stanford University Graduate School of Business, where he was an Arjay Miller scholar, and a B.S. in civil engineering from Stanford University, where he was Phi Beta Kappa.

Fayad, Mohamed E., Ph.D. Department of Computer Science and Engineering, University of Nebraska, Lincoln, Nebraska, USA, e-mail: fayadm@acm.org, URL: www.cse.unl.edu/~fayad, lead editor of this book, front matter (pp. xv–xxiii) and back matter (pp. 625–634, 635–651), book parts (pp. 1, 87, 167, 215, 349, 465, 493, 565), Chapter 1 (pp. 3–27), Chapter 3 (pp. 55–86), Chapter 26 (pp. 617–634), Sidebar 7 (pp. 169–198), and the book web site materials (www.wiley.com/compbooks).

Mohamed Fayad is an associate professor of computer science and Engineering at the University of Nebraska, Lincoln. He was an associate professor at the University of Nevada (1995–1999). He has more than 15 years of industrial experience. He has been actively involved in more than 60 object-oriented projects for several companies. He has been the guest editor of five theme issues: *CACM's OO Experiences* (October 1995), *IEEE Computer's Managing OO Software Development Projects* (September 1996), *CACM's Software Patterns* (October 1996), *CACM's OO Application Frameworks* (October 1997), and *ACM Computing Surveys—Application Frameworks* (June 1999). He has published articles in *IEEE Software, IEEE Computer, Journal of Object-Oriented Programming (JOOP), ACM Computing Surveys,* and *CACM.* He is a distinguished speaker and has given lectures, tutorials, and seminars at national and international conferences, universities, and companies. Dr. Fayad is a senior member of the Institute of Electrical and Electronics Engineers (IEEE), a senior member of the IEEE Computer Society, and a member of the Association for Computing (ACM), and he served on several conference program committees, such as TOOLS USA '96 and

Hong Kong QSD '96. In addition, he is an IEEE Distinguished Speaker; an associate editor, an editorial advisor, and a columnist for *Communications of the ACM IEEE Software, Al-Ahram* (the Egyptian newspaper); editor-in-chief of *IEEE Computer Society Press—Computer Science and Engineering Practice Press* (1995–1997); and an international advisor for several universities. He received an M.S. and a Ph.D. in computer science from the University of Minnesota at Minneapolis. His research topic was entitled, "Object-Oriented Software Engineering: Problems and Perspectives." He is the lead author of *Transition to OO Software Development* (John Wiley & Sons, 1998) and lead editor of this three-volume work on object-oriented application frameworks (John Wiley & Sons, 1999).

Fontoura, Marcus F. Departamento de Informatica, PUC-Rio, Brazil, Sidebar 2, pp. 163–166.

Marcus F. Fontoura is a Ph.D. candidate in the Departamento de Informatica at PUC-Rio (Brazil). His current research interests include software engineering in general and, in particular, web-based education systems and object-oriented analysis and design.

Froehlich, Garry. Department of Computing Science, University of Alberta, Canada, e-mail: garry@cs.ualberta.ca, Chapter 9, pp. 219–236.

Garry Froehlich is a Ph.D. candidate at the Department of Computing Science at the University of Alberta, where his research interests involve the study and use of object-oriented frameworks. Other research interests include distributed systems and electronic commerce. He received an M.Sc. at the University of Saskatchewan where he worked on automated support for process modeling and enactment.

Garrido, Alejandra. Department of Computer Science, University of Illinois at Urbana-Champaign, USA, e-mail: garrido@students.uiuc.edu, Chapter 11, pp. 267–287.

Alejandra Garrido is a licentiate in computer science from the Universidad Nacional de La Plata (University of La Plata), Argentina. She is at present a graduate student at the University of Illinois at Urbana-Champaign. Alejandra Garrido has been a member of the Laboratorio de Investigacion y Formacion en Infomatica Avanzada (Laboratory for Research and Training in Advanced Computer Science, or LIFIA), a research group at the Department of Computer Science at University of La Plata, Argentina, since 1993.

Girou, Mike, Ph.D. MT Systems Company, Dallas, Texas, USA, e-mail: girou@parashift.com, Sidebar 6, pp. 460–463.

Mike Girou is chairman of MT Systems Company. He received a Ph.D. in mathematics from the University of Missouri at Columbia.

Goedicke, Michael, Ph.D. Department of Mathematics and Computer Science, University of Essen, Germany, e-mail: goedicke@informatik.uni-essen.de, Sidebar 4, pp. 345–348.

Michael Goedicke is professor of computer science in the Department of Mathematics and Computer Science at the University of Essen, Germany. He studied computer science at the University of Dortmund and received his diploma degree (master's degree) in computer science there in 1980. He received his Ph.D. in 1985 and his habilitation in 1993 from the Department of Computer Science of the University of Dortmund as well. His special field of interest is specification of software systems and software engineering. He is principal investigator in various national and international research projects and is currently conducting research in formal methods and languages for designing parallel and distributed software systems based on the idea of software components and frameworks.

Gryczan, Guido. University of Hamburg, Germany, e-mail: gryczan@informatik .uni-hamburg.de, URL: swt-www.informatik.uni-hamburg.de, Chapter 17, pp. 395–413.

Guido Gryczan has been a senior researcher in the Software Engineering Group of the Informatics Department of Hamburg University since 1991. He received a master's degree in informatics from the Technical University of Berlin and a doctoral degree from the University of Hamburg.

Hamu, David S. TRW, Inc., Phoenix, AZ, USA, e-mail: dhamu@acm.org, Sidebar 1, pp. 83–86.

David Hamu is a manager of systems integration at TRW Integrated Supply Chain Solutions. He is currently working with clients who are implementing enterprise frameworks in high-technology manufacturing applications. He is a graduate of Arizona State University's College of Business with a master of science degree in information systems.

Hoover, H. James, Ph.D. Department of Computing Science, University of Alberta, Canada, e-mail: hoover@cs.ualberta.ca, Chapter 9, pp. 219–236.

Jim Hoover is an associate professor of computing science at the University of Alberta. He has an M.Sc. from the University of Toronto, worked for Bell-Northern Research, ran a consulting company, and obtained his Ph.D. in complexity theory from the University of Toronto in 1987. His current research has a software engineering focus. At the formal level, it involves the application of proof-theoretic techniques to the specification and construction of correct programs. At the engineering level, he is also interested in building application frameworks for constructing high-quality engineering tools.

Jacobsen, Eyðun Eli. The Maersk Mc-Kinney Moller Institute for Production Technology, University of Southern Denmark, Denmark, e-mail: jacobsen@mip.ou.dk, URL: www.mip.ou.dk/~jacobsen, Chapter 2, pp. 29–54.

Eyðun Eli Jacobsen is working toward a Ph.D. at the Maersk Mc-Kinney Moller Institute for Production Technology at the University of Southern Denmark, Denmark. His interests include software design, object-oriented programming, frameworks, and design patterns. He received his master's degree from the Department of Computer Science at Aalborg University, Denmark, in 1996.

Johnson, Ralph E., Ph.D. Department of Computer Science, University of Illinois at Urbana-Champaign, USA, e-mail: johnson@cs.uiuc.edu, URL: www.cs.uiuc.edu/ users/~johnson, coeditor of this book, Chapter 1, pp. 3–27.

Ralph E. Johnson is on the faculty of the Department of Computer Science at the University of Illinois. He is the leader of the UIUC patterns/Smalltalk group and the coordinator of the senior projects program for the department. His professional interests cover nearly all things object-oriented, especially frameworks, patterns, business objects, Smalltalk, the Common Object Model (COM), and refactoring. He has been to every Object-Oriented Programming, Systems, Languages, and Applications (OOPSLA). He received his Ph.D. and M.S. degrees from Cornell and his B.A. from Knox College. He is a member of the Association for Computing (ACM) and the IEEE Computer Society. He is a coauthor of *Design Patterns: Elements of Object-Oriented Software* (Addison-Wesley, 1996). He is also coeditor of this three volume work on object-oriented application frameworks (John Wiley & Sons, 1999).

Jolin, Art. TecTeam Consulting Group (Java and C++), IBM Corporation, Research Triangle Park, NC, USA, e-mail: jolin@raleigh.ibm.com, Chapter 5, pp. 143–152, and Chapter 6, pp. 153–166.

Art Jolin designs and writes frameworks and class libraries for IBM Corporation. He has been in software development for 21 years and in object-oriented architecture and framework development since 1990. He has previously worked in the areas of distributed computing, file systems, user interface design, and development tools. He is currently a consultant-for-hire through IBM's TecTeam for VisualAge Java and C++.

Jones, Steven R. ISA Services, Inc., Chicago, IL,USA, e-mail: srjones@isaservices .com, URL: www.isaservices.com, Chapter 10, pp. 237–266.

Steven Jones is a software architect with ISA Services, Inc., a Chicago-based systems integrator specializing in Java and Common Object Request Broker Architecture (CORBA) enterprise solutions. He has been working exclusively with distributed object technologies and has built robust application frameworks to support distributed object systems for a number of Fortune 500 companies. He is a vocal proponent of crafting large-scale, reusable software by applying patterns and frameworks in a disciplined design approach. He speaks on these topics regularly at various conferences, seminars, and user groups around the country.

King, Graham, Ph.D. Research Centre for Systems Engineering, Southampton Institute, Southampton, United Kingdom, e-mail: graham.king@solent.ac.uk, Sidebar 7, pp. 487–491.

Graham King's first degree profile is computing and electronics and in his early career he carried out research into aspects of data compression and pattern recognition. This work culminated in a master of philosophy award and he subsequently went on to be awarded a Ph.D. in advanced architectures for signal processing by Nottingham-Trent University, United Kingdom. He was appointed head of the Informatics Research Centre at Southampton Institute in 1993, and after acting as dean of the systems engineering faculty, he was appointed head of research and postgraduate study. In this role, he is responsible for a major research center that specializes in all aspects of software quality. He has been principal investigator for a number of Engineering and Physical Sciences Research Council projects as well as many industry-funded programs. He was reader in computer systems engineering from 1992 to 1994 before achieving full professorial title in 1995.

Knoll, Rolf. RWG GmbH, Stuttgart, Germany, e-mail: rolf_knoll@rwg.email.com, URL: www.rwg.de, Chapter 17, pp. 395–413.

Rolf Knoll is the team leader for technical architecture of client-server software at the RWG GmbH in Stuttgart, Germany. The RWG is responsible for developing and maintaining integrated software systems for banks (Volks und Raiffeisen-banken), as well as other enterprises, in southwestern Germany. He joined the RWG in 1993 as a software engineer. Before studying informatics in Stuttgart and Uppsala, Sweden, Rolf studied architecture.

Koskimies, Kai, Ph.D. Tampere University of Technology, Helsinki, Finland, e-mail: kk@cs.tut.fi, Sidebar 5, pp. 411–413.

Kai Koskimies is a professor at Software Systems Laboratory, Tampere University of Technology. He has led several research projects concerning language implementation tools, tools for dynamic modeling and visualization of object-oriented systems, tools for object-oriented framework development and specialization, and the telecom software design environment.

Laitinen, Mauri. Laitinen Consulting, Tahoe City, CA, USA, e-mail: laitinen@acm.org, Sidebar 9, pp. 620–624.

Mauri Laitinen, principal in Laitinen Consulting, has more than 25 years of experience in software development and software management. He was one of the founders of Autodesk, Inc., a world leader in the development of computer-aided design and modeling software. At Autodesk, he created and directed the Quality Assurance Department, which had responsibility for ensuring high standards for the development, production, and maintenance of software and documentation. As Director of Software Development at Autodesk, he managed the development of the AutoCAD and AutoSketch group of products. Previously, he held management positions at Control Data Corp. and Information Systems Design, Inc., and developed software for Bechtel, Computer Sciences Corporation, and Jet Propulsion Labs. He is a co-author with Mohamed E. Fayad *of Transition to Object-Oriented Software Development* (John Wiley & Sons, 1998). He is a member of the Institute of Electrical and Electronics Engineers (IEEE) and the Association for Computing (ACM).

Lavin, Dave. OTI, Raleigh, NC, USA, e-mail: Dave_Lavin@oti.com, Chapter 5, pp. 143–152.

Dave Lavin has developed software in C, Smalltalk, and C++ for over 15 years. He has worked for IBM Cape Kennedy, Florida, as well as RTP, North Carolina. He was part of the visual builder team for the IBM VisualAge C++ project, versions 1 through 3.5. He is currently working for the OTI (Object Technology International) subsidiary of IBM.

Lilienthal, Carola. University of Hamburg, Germany, e-mail: Carola.Lilienthal@ informatik.uni-hamburg.de, URL: swt-www.informatik.uni-hamburg.de, Chapter 17, pp. 395–413.

Carola Lilienthal has been a research assistant in the Software Engineering Group of the Informatics Department of Hamburg University since August 1995. Before studying computer science, Carola worked for two years at a German private bank.

Liu, Ling, Ph.D. Department of Computing Science, University of Alberta, Canada, e-mail: lingliu@cs.ualberta.ca, Chapter 9, pp. 219–236.

Ling Liu is an assistant professor in the Department of Computer Science and Engineering at Oregon Graduate Institute. She has been doing research on extending object technology for more than 10 years and has published more than 40 articles in international journals and conferences. Her research interests include object-oriented design, languages, and systems; distributed object management; object technology to various data-intensive applications and web applications; and design and development of adaptive software systems.

Lucena, Carlos J.P., Ph.D. Departamento de Informatica, PUC-Rio, Brazil, Sidebar 2, pp. 163–166.

Carlos J.P. Lucena is a full professor in the Departamento de Informatica at PUC-Rio (Brazil) since 1982. His current research interests include software design and formal methods in software engineering. He is a member of the IEEE Computer Society and various other scientific organizations. He is also a member of the Editorial Board of the *International Journal on Formal Aspects of Computing* (Springer-Verlag).

Magnusson, Boris, Ph.D. Department of Computer Science, Lund Institute of Technology, Sweden, e-mail: Boris@CS.LTH.se, URL: www.cs.lth.se/home/Boris_ Magnusson, Chapter 4, pp. 89–141.

Boris Magnusson is a professor in the Department of Computer Science at the Institute of Technology, Lund University. He has an M.Sc. in engineering physics (1976) and a Ph.D. in computer science (1984), both from Lund. He has been at the department since 1976 and was chairman from 1986 to 1993. He was one of the designers and implementers of the Simula system developed at Lund. He has been active in the object-oriented community since the beginning and has taken part in program committees and in organizing several conferences such as European Conference on Object-Oriented Programming (ECOOP), Technology of Object-Oriented Languages and Systems (TOOLS), and Object-Oriented Programming, Systems, Languages, and Applications (OOPSLA) in this field, as well as (ICSE) International Conference on Software Engineering, ESEC, and SCM in the field of software engineering. His current research interests include programming languages (concurrent and real-time programming), environments (compilers, garbage collection, embedded systems), and configuration management.

Major, Melissa L. Software Architects, USA, e-mail: major@software-architects .com, Chapter 13, pp. 309–323.

Melissa L. Major is a consultant and site manager for Software Architects. She has worked for Computer Aid, Broadway & Seymour, BNR/NORTEL, and as a contractor with Microsoft. She has a master's degree in computer science and has been a Ph.D. student at Clemson University. She has taught computer science courses for Clemson University and Limestone College. She has managed testing efforts and constructed software development processes including testing processes for companies such as Lucent Technologies.

Marcelloni, Francesco, Ph.D. Dipartimento di Ingegneria della Informazione, Elettronica, Informatica, Telecomunicazioni, Università degli Studi di Pisa, Italy, e-mail: france@iet.unipi.it, URL: www.iet.unipi.it/~france/~france.html, Chapter 7, pp. 167–198.

Francesco Marcelloni received his M.Sc. degree in electronic engineering and his Ph.D. degree in computer engineering from the University of Pisa in 1991 and 1996, respectively. His Ph.D. dissertation dealt with object-oriented models and fuzzy-logic-based methods in software development. From 1994 to 1995 and from June to December 1997 he was a visiting researcher at the University of Twente, where he joined the TRESE project. Currently he is an assistant professor at the Dipartimento di Ingegneria dell'Informazione of the University of Pisa.

Mattsson, Michael. Department of Computer Science and Business Administration, University of Karlskrona/Ronneby, Sweden, e-mail: Michael.Mattsson@ide .hk-r.se, URL: www.ide.hk-r.se/~michaelm, Chapter 3, pp. 55–86, and Chapter 20, pp. 467–491.

Michael Mattsson received his M.Sc. degree in mathematics from the University of Växjö, Sweden (1988) and the licentiate of engineering degree in computer science from Lund University, Sweden (1996). He is currently at the University of Karlskrona/Ronneby, where he lectures in the Master of Software Engineering program. He is a member of the Architecture and Composition of Software (ARCS) research group.

McGregor, John D., Ph.D. Department of Computer Science, Clemson University, Clemson, South Carolina, USA, e-mail: johnmc@cs.clemson.edu, Chapter 13, pp. 309–323.

John D. McGregor is an associate professor of computer science at Clemson University and a senior partner in Software Architects, a software design consulting firm specializing in object-oriented design techniques. He has conducted funded research for organizations such as the National Science Foundation, DARPA, IBM, and AT&T. He has developed testing techniques for object-oriented software and developed custom testing processes for a variety of companies. He is coauthor of *Object-Oriented Software Development: Engineering Software for Reuse* (Van Nostrand Reinhold) and also of *A Practical Guide to Testing Object-Oriented Software* (to be published by Addison-Wesley).

McKim, James C., Ph.D. Department of Computer Science, Rensselaer Polytechnic Institute, CT, USA, e-mail: mckim@rpi.edu, Sidebar 8, pp. 199–214.

James C. McKim, Jr., holds a Ph.D. in mathematics from the University of Iowa. He has taught mathematics and computer science for more than 25 years, the last 10 mainly to working professionals. He is the coauthor of two mathematics textbooks and the author of several articles in both computer science and mathematics.

Meyer, Torsten. Department of Mathematics and Computer Science, University of Essen, Germany, e-mail: tmeyer@informatik.uni-essen.de, Sidebar 4, pp. 345–348.

Torsten Meyer studied business computing at the University of Essen and received his diploma degree (master's degree) there. Since 1996 he has been research assistant in Michael Goedicke's group, Specification of Software Systems, within the Department of Mathematics and Computer Science at the University of Essen. His special fields of interest with respect to his Ph.D. work are software architecture, configurable distributed systems, Common Object Request Broker Architecture (CORBA), and graph transformation.

Mili, Hafedh, Ph.D. Département d'informatique, Université du Québec à Montréal, Canada, e-mail: mili@larc.info.uqam.ca, Chapter 23, pp. 523–564.

Hafedh Mili is an associate professor of computer science at the University of Quebec in Montreal. He holds an Engineering Diploma from the Ecole Centrale de Paris (1984), Paris, France, and a Ph.D. in computer science from George Washington University (1988), Washington, D.C. He has published close to 40 referenced conference (such as OOPSLA—Object-Oriented Programming, Systems, Languages, and Applications, TOOLS—Technology of Object-Oriented Languages and Systems) and journal papers (such as *IEEE Transactions on PAMI, SMC, SE*) in these areas. He recently founded INFORMILI Inc., a computer services company that specializes in training and consulting in object orientation and software reuse. Its first client is the Canadian Federal Government.

Miller, Granville G. Make Systems, Cary, NC, USA, e-mail: gmiller@makesys.com, Chapter 13, pp. 309–323.

Granville Miller has spent 13 years in the software industry working on object-oriented systems. He is a pioneer in the application of use cases in the development of advanced frameworks for software systems. At Make Systems, he is the manager of the frameworks and network visualization group, responsible for developing reusable components for network resource planning tools. At IBM, he was one of the original developers responsible for IBM's VisualAge product. Following that, he orchestrated a link between the business engineering group and an object center with a single use-case-driven software development process. For more than a decade, he has been driven to advance OO technology in the computer industry, including IBM, Nortel, BroadBand Technologies, and Make Systems.

Molin, Peter, Ph.D. Department of Computer Science and Business Administration, University of Karlskrona/Ronneby, Sweden, e-mail: Peter.Molin@ide.hk-r.se, URL: www.ide.hk-r.se/~ARCS, Chapter 3, pp. 55–86.

Peter Molin received a licentiate of technology in software engineering in 1997. Prior to that his experience was in Ada compiler development and the development of fire alarm systems. After a period working as an assistant professor at the University of Karlskrona/Ronneby, Sweden, his current position is manager of Mobile Applications Lab, a part of the Ericsson group.

Nelson, Torsten. Department of Computer Science, University of Waterloo, Ontario, Canada, e-mail: torsten@csg.uwaterlo.ca, Sidebar 2, pp. 163–166.

Torsten Nelson is a Ph.D. candidate in the Department of Computer Science at the University of Waterloo (Canada). His current research interests include software engineering, software analysis and design, and object-oriented software systems.

Nowack, Palle. The Maersk Mc-Kinney Moller Institute for Production Technology, University of Southern Denmark, Denmark, e-mail: nowack@mip.ou.dk, URL: www.mip.ou.dk/~nowack, Chapter 2, pp. 29–54.

Palle Nowack is currently a Ph.D. student at the Maersk Mc-Kinney Moller Institute for Production Technology at the University of Southern Denmark, Denmark. His professional interests include systems design, conceptual modeling, software architecture, and object-oriented software development. He received his master's degree from Aalborg University in 1996.

Predonzani, Paolo. DIST—Università di Genova, Italy, e-mail: predo@dist.unige.it, URL: sayuri.dist.unige.it, Sidebar 3, pp. 210–214.

Paolo Predonzani is currently a research associate at the Department of Electrical and Computer Engineering of the University of Calgary. He received the laurea degree in computer engineering in 1997 from University of Genova, Italy. His main interests are domain analysis and engineering, business process modeling and reengineering, activity-based costing, and management.

Pree, Wolfgang, Ph.D. Department of Computer Science, University of Constance, Germany, e-mail: pree@acm.org, URL: www.altissimo.com, Chapter 16, pp. 379–393, and Sidebar 5, pp. 411–413.

Wolfgang Pree is a professor of computer science at the University of Constance and head of the Software and Web Engineering Group. His research covers various areas of software engineering, in particular, object and component technology, software architectures, and human-computer interaction. He is the author of *Design Patterns for Object-Oriented Software Development* (Addison-Wesley, 1995). He presented numerous tutorials on that topic at conferences such as OOPSLA, TOOLS, and ECOOP. He was a visiting assistant professor at Washington University in St. Louis (1992–1993), and a guest scientist at Siemens AG Munich (1994–1996).

Raines, David C. Department of Computer Science, Rensselaer Polytechnic Institute, Willington, CT,USA, e-mail: dave@rh.edu, Sidebar 8, pp. 562–564.

David Raines recently completed his master's degree in computer science from Rensselaer Polytechnic Institute. He has been a software engineer and Unix system administrator for 14 years.

Riehle, Dirk. Ubilab UBS, Zürich, Switzerland, e-mail: Dirk.Riehle@ubs.com or riehle@acm.org, URL: www.ubs.com/ubilab or www.riehle.org, Chapter 17, pp. 395–413.

Dirk Riehle is a researcher at Ubilab, the IT innovation laboratory of UBS. He is interested in the software architecture of object and component systems and their use in the banking domain. His most recent work includes a metalevel architecture for distributed object systems and a design and integration methodology for object-oriented frameworks.

Rossi, Gustavo, Ph.D. LIFIA, Universidad Nacional de La Plata, Argentina, e-mail: rossi@sol.info.unlp.edu.ar, URL: www-lifia.info.unlp.edu.ar/~rossi, Chapter 11, pp. 267–287.

Gustavo Rossi has been a full professor at the University of La Plata, Argentina, since 1982. He is also head of Laboratorio de Investigacion y Formacion en Infomatica Avanzada (Laboratory for Research and Training in Advanced Computer Science, or LIFIA), a research group at the Department of Computer Science at the Universidad Nacional de La Plata (University of La Plata), Argentina. He completed his Ph.D. at Pontificia Universidade of Rio de Janeiro, Brazil. Gustavo has been teaching courses such as Programming Methodologies, Object-Oriented Programming, and Seminar of Hypertext and Hypermedia at the University of La Plata. He was also a speaker at several seminars on object-oriented software engineering, object-oriented programming, and hypermedia design.

Rüping, Andreas, Ph.D. sd&m software design & management GmbH & Co.KG, München, Germany, e-mail: rueping@acm.org, Chapter 14, pp. 325–348.

Andreas Rüping received a diploma (master of science) from the Faculty of Computer Science at the University of Dortmund and a Ph.D. from the Faculty of Computer Science at the University of Karlsruhe, Germany. From 1991 to 1996, he was a member of the research staff at Forschungszentrum Informatik (Research Center for Computer Science), Karlsruhe. Since 1997, he has been a senior software engineer at sd&m software design & management, Munich. Andreas Rüping has managed several projects in the areas of object technology, reengineering, Internet technology, and quality management.

Sahraoui, Houari, Ph.D. Centre de Recherche Informatique de Montréal, Canada, e-mail: houari.sahraoui@crim.ca, Chapter 23, pp. 523–564.

Houari A. Sahraoui is a senior researcher at the Research on Computer Science Center of Montreal (CRIM), adjunct professor at the University of Quebec in Montreal, and associate member of LIP6 (Computer Science Laboratory of Paris 6). He holds an engineering diploma from the National Institute of Computer Science (1990), Algiers, Algeria, and a Ph.D. in computer science from the Université Pierre & Marie Curie, Paris, France (1995).

Schmid, Hans Albrecht, Ph.D. Fachbereich Informatik, Fachhochschule Konstanz, Germany, e-mail: schmidha@fh-konstanz.de, Chapter 15, pp. 349–378.

Hans Albrecht Schmid has a diploma (M.Sc.)in electrical engineering from the University of Stuttgart, a diploma (M.Sc.) in computer science from the Institut Nationale Polytechnique de Grenoble, and a Ph.D. in computer science from the University of Karlsruhe (1973). He was visiting assistant professor in the Department of Computer Science at the University of Toronto. He was head of the research group on database management systems in the Department of Computer Science at the University of Stuttgart. From 1977 to 1987, he held different technical lead and management positions with the IBM development laboratory in Boeblingen. Since 1987, he has been professor of computer science at the University for Applied Research, Konstanz, Germany.

Schmidt, Douglas C., Ph.D. Department of Computer Science, Washington University, St. Louis, Missouri, USA, e-mail: schmidt@cs.wustl.edu, URL: www.cs.wustl.edu/~schmidt, coeditor of this book, Chapter 1, pp. 3–27.

Douglas Schmidt is an associate professor in the Department of Computer Science and in the Department of Radiology at Washington University in St. Louis, Missouri. His research focuses on design patterns, implementation, and experimental analysis of object-oriented techniques that facilitate the development of high-performance, real-time distributed object computing systems on parallel processing platforms running over high-speed ATM networks. He received B.S. and M.A. degrees in sociology from the College of William and Mary in Williamsburg, Virginia, and an M.S. and a Ph.D. in computer science from the University of California, Irvine (UCI), in 1984, 1986, 1990, and 1994, respectively. He is a member of the USENIX—The Advanced Computing Systems and Association, Institute of Electrical and Electronics Engineers (IEEE), and the Association of Computing (ACM). He is also coeditor of this three-volume work on object-oriented application frameworks (John Wiley & Sons, 1999).

Sorenson, Paul G., Ph.D. Department of Computing Science, University of Alberta, Canada, e-mail: sorenson@cs.ualberta.ca, Chapter 9, pp. 215–236.

Paul Sorenson is professor and chair of the Department of Computing Science at the University of Alberta. He was formerly head of Computational Science at the University of Saskatchewan. His current research interests are in object-oriented frameworks, software engineering environments, and software process and quality. He has coauthored texts in data structures and compiler construction that appear in the McGraw-Hill Computer Science Series. He was recently a member of the Canadian Natural Sciences and Engineering Research Council's Committee on Research Grants and Group Chair for Computing and Information Science and Electrical Engineering. He is currently board chairman of the newly formed WestMOST Consortium, a consortium of nine western Canadian universities, two software technology centers, and several industrial partners, which is developing an industry-oriented master's of software technology program.

Soundarajan, Neelam, Ph.D. Department of Computer and Information Science, Ohio State University, Columbus, Ohio, USA, e-mail: neelam@cis.ohio-state.edu, URL: www.cis.ohio-state.edu, Chapter 12, pp. 289–308.

Neelam Soundarajan is an associate professor in the Computer and Information Science Department at Ohio State University. His primary research interests are in object-oriented and distributed systems, in particular, in the specification and verification issues involved in dealing with these systems.

Succi, Giancarlo, Ph.D. Department of Electrical and Computer Engineering, University of Calgary, Canada, e-mail: Giancarlo.Succi@enel.ucalgary.ca, URL: www .enel.ucalgary.ca/People/Succi, Sidebar 3, pp. 210–214.

Giancarlo Succi is associate professor at the Department of Electrical and Computer Engineering of the University of Calgary. He received the laurea degree in electrical engineering in 1988 from the University of Genova, Italy. His main interests focus on software engineering and reuse, the software development process, accounting techniques, and legal issues. In addition, he is interested in the implementation of declarative languages on massively parallel architectures and distributed systems.

Tekinerdogan, Bedir. Department of Computer Science, University of Twente, the Netherlands, e-mail: bedir@cs.utwente.nl, URL: www.cs.utwente.nl/~bedir/, Chapter 7, pp. 169–198.

Bedir Tekinerdogan holds an M.Sc. in computer science from the University of Twente, the Netherlands. Currently, he is a Ph.D. candidate at the University of Twente. He has done work on atomic transactions and object-oriented analysis, design, and programming. He was coorganizer of several workshops including the ECOOP '96 workshop on adaptability in object-oriented software development, the ECOOP '97 and ECOOP '98 workshops on aspect-oriented programming, and the ECOOP '98 workshop on automating the object-oriented software development.

Valerio, Andrea. DIST—Università di Genova, Italy, e-mail: Andrea.Valerio@dist .unige.it, URL: sayuri.dist.unige.it, Sidebar 3, pp. 210–214.

Andrea Valerio is currently a Ph.D. student at the University of Genova, Italy. He received the laurea degree in electronic engineering in 1995 from the University of Padova, Italy. His main interests are software reuse, domain analysis and engineering, software process description, and software quality.

Vaucher, Jean, Ph.D. Université de Montréal, Département d'Informatique et RO, Canada, e-mail: vaucher@IRO.UMontreal.Canada, URL: www.iro.umontreal.ca/ ~vaucher, Chapter 4, pp. 89–141.

Jean Vaucher is full professor in the Department of Computer Science. He has been at the University of Montreal since 1970 and chaired the department from 1980 to 1983. He studied electrical engineering at the University of Ottawa, graduating in 1962. He obtained his Ph.D. in 1968 from the University of Manchester (United Kingdom). He has been active in many top-level committees including Natural Sciences and Engineering Research Council of Canada's (NSERC) Grants Selection Committee for Computing and Information Sciences. His main interests are software engineering, object-oriented programming, and operating systems.

Vernazza, Tullio, Ph.D. DIST—Università di Genova, Italy, e-mail: tullio@dist .unige.it, URL: sayuri.dist.unige.it, Sidebar 3, pp. 210–214.

Tullio Vernazza is associate professor at the Department of Communication, Computer, and System Sciences of the University of Genova. He is also the head of the Software Production Engineering Lab at the University of Genova. His main interests range from software engineering to electronics and computer architectures.

Wang, Yingxu, Ph.D. IVF Centre for Software Engineering, Gothenburg, Sweden, e-mail: yingxu.wang@acm.org, Sidebar 7, pp. 487–491.

Yingxu Wang received a Ph.D. in the United Kingdom and a B.Sc. in Shanghai. He is a senior research fellow with the IVF Centre for Software Engineering, Sweden, and a Ph.D. supervisor in the School of Computing, Information Systems, and Mathematics at South Bank University, London. He has been a professor of computer science at Lanzhou Tiedao University, China, since 1994, and was a visiting professor at Oxford University in 1995. He is a member of the Institute of Electrical and Electronics Engineers (IEEE), Technical Committee on Software Engineering/Software Engineering Standards Committee (TCSE/SESC), the Association for Computing (ACM), Boston Computing Society (BCS), and ISO/ICE JTC1/SC7. He is a principal investigator of EC SPRITE S2 projects PROBE, IPSSI, PULSE, ASSIT, ISO 15504 Part 5, as well as Swedish projects National Benchmark, Y2K, and PILOT. He has published 86 papers in software engineering research. He is a guest editor of the *Annals of Software Engineering* and a senior reviewer of *IEEE Computer*.

Wills, Alan Cameron, Ph.D. TriReme International Ltd., United Kingdom, e-mail: alan@trireme.com, URL: www.trireme.com, Chapter 19, pp. 441–463.

Alan Cameron Wills is technical director of TriReme International Ltd., consulting and training clients in many fields, including banking, telecommunications, and manufacturing. He has worked on methods and tools since 1982 and specializes in making frontline research practical and available for mainstream software engineering.

Young, Howard. IBM, USA, Sidebar 6, pp. 460–463.

Howard Young is an executive consultant for IBM, where he applies advanced technology to complex business problems. His technical interests include object-oriented and web-based applications.

Züllighoven, Heinz, Ph.D. University of Hamburg, Germany, e-mail: Heinz .Zuellighoven@informatik.uni-hamburg.de, URL: swt-www.informatik.uni-hamburg .de, Chapter 17, pp. 395–413.

Heinz Züllighoven has been a professor in the Software Engineering Group of the Informatics Department of Hamburg University since October 1991. He graduated in mathematics and German language and literature, and he holds a doctoral degree in computer science.

Index

A

Abandonment option, 585–588

Abstract actors, 313, 318

Abstract base class, of hot-spot subsystem, 362

Abstract behavior, 541–542
verifying, 66–67

Abstract classes, 4–5, 293, 529, 540
base class, 362
in development, 66
subclassing, 531, 547

Abstract domain model, 35

Abstract factories, 330, 334–335

Abstractions, 417
architectural, 29–32, 50–52
level of, 419

Abstract methods, 5

Abstract Window Toolkit (AWT), 4

Accessors, 156, 225–226, 228
use of, 229–231

ACE, 428–433
design patterns and messages, 429–430
use-case maps, 430–433

Action interface, 144

Activate statement, 104, 107

Adaptability space, 179–181, 196–197

Adapter design pattern, 481–482

Adopt and orphan convention, 158

Aggregation, 483, 484, 534, 535
representation of, 537–539

AlarmRoutine, 125

Alexandrian patterns, 30, 38. *See also* Design patterns

Algol, 60, 92

Algorithms, 171

Analysis patterns, 45

Analysis technique, 315–318

Andrew Toolkit, 7

Animations, 133–134

Applet programming model, 240

Application access control, 254

Application architecture, 237
pattern system for, 241–265

Application descriptor, 201, 205

Application developers, documentation for, 496

Application development phase, 59. *See also* Framework usage phase managing, 69

Application domains, and frameworks, 396–400

Application framework investments, 567
and reuse capabilities, 568–569

Application frameworks, 219. *See also* Frameworks; Size Engineering Application Framework (SEAF) project; Task management framework design

Application generators, 15–16

Application is a class pattern, 247–249

Application layers, 400, 403

Application modeling, 355–356

Application requirements, 311–312

Applications, 59
coordination of, 254
debugging, 71
framework applicability to, 69–70
parts of, 17
registration of, 254
segregating, 258–260
specifying, 297–299
testing, 63

Application shell, 201

ApplicationShellView class, 205–206

Application-specific increments (ASIs), 68

Application systems, 398

Application types pattern, 258–260
verifying, 71

A priori approach, 311, 319, 320. *See also* Use-case assortment
Architecting behavior, 417–418, 436
Architectural abstractions, 29–32
    abstraction, 51–52
    application of, 52
    development of, 52
    frameworks as, 50
    functionality, 51
    patterns as, 50–51
    reuse of, 52
    structure, 51
Architectural constraints, 184–185, 190
Architectural design, 62, 66. *See also* Design
Architectural mismatch, 72, 408
Architectural patterns, 39
Architecture, 213–214
    changes to, 621
    formal design of, 345–347
    reflective, 342
    upgrading and, 623
Architecture assessment method, 602–611
    characteristics for evaluation, 602
    design metrics for, 603–606
Architecture Description Languages (ADLs), 346
asAbc convention, 157
Athens Architectural Components, 265
Atomic node classes, 285
AttributeChangeEvent-to-action connection, 145
Attribute interface, 143–144
Attributes, visibility of, 93
Attribute-to-attribute connection, 145

B

Backward applicability, 524
Backward compatibility, 479
Barter framework, 458
BasicProcess Event, 123
Beans, 4
Beck, Kent, 520
Behavior:
    cohesive, 476, 479
    computational versus functional aspects of, 525

descriptions of, 550
    hierarchy of, 541–542
Behavior patterns:
    macroscopic, 415–419, 434–437
    use-case mapping of, 428, 433
Bellin, David, 520
Beta, 134
Billing gateway frameworks, 61, 72
Blackbox components, 200
Blackbox frameworks, 10, 17, 48, 58–59, 154, 169–170
    future research on, 618
    hot spots in, 357–358, 379–381
Blackbox teaching, 507, 510
Borland OWL framework:
    class architecture metrics, 608–611
    structural metrics for, 607–608
Bridge pattern, 182–183, 384
Brinch-Hansen, Per, 123
Broker architectures, 340–341
Bubble-Sort, 194–195
Built-in tests (BITs), 488–491
Business, velocity of, 83
Business case, 317
Business culture, transitioning for framework use, 65
Business domains, 399
    change in, 77–78, 407–408
    layers of, 400, 402–403
Business models, for framework development, 65
Business requirements, 311
Business section layers, 400, 403
Business sections, 396

C

C_P_System, 123
C++:
    argument type support, 148
    framework packager, 553–555
    versus Simula, 90
    templates, 551
Call-chaining mechanism, 24
Call/Detach primitives, 123
Called and calling frameworks, 58, 59, 74, 472
Call primitive, 96–97, 525

Capability Maturity Model, 568
Capital budgeting, 569
CardSort, 195
Catalysis, 441
    classes in, 450–452
    collaborations, 453–455
    framework examples in, 458
    refinement, 452–453
    types in, 450–452
Categories:
    of abstractions, 31–32
    frameworks, 33–37
Category library, 32
Chai, Ian, 520
Change, system support of, 460
Change cases, 310, 318
Class architecture, 214
Class dependencies, 325–327
    consistent object creation, 326, 330, 334–336
    management techniques, 332–341
    managing, 327–332
    metalevel management of, 326, 339–341
Classes, 406
    adding or extending, 533
    in architectural assessment, 602–604
    closely coupled, 326, 329, 333–334
    concrete, 5
    of construction view, 419
    data-driven, 326, 330–331, 336–339
    descriptions of, 500
    factories, 326, 330, 334–336
    framework packaging as, 552–555
    functional characteristics, 605
    versus interfaces, 540
    libraries, 4, 153–160
    metrics for assessing, 605–606, 608–611
    minimizing number, 153–154
    naming conventions for, 155–157
    notification in, 145
    number of changes in, 611
    versus parts, 145–147
    polymorphic relationships with clients, 367

reuse of, 523
Simula, 90, 92–93
structural characteristics, 605
subclassing, 405
table-driven, 337
use of, 155
visual builder standards for, 147–149
Class methods, 40–41
Class model, 355–356
Class Realtime, 122–123
Cliques, 154
Closure operations, 527, 530
Coad-Yourdon notation, 355
Code reuse, 14
Cohesive behavior, 476, 479
Collaborations, 453–455
Collection nodes, 273, 285
Common Object Model (COM), 4–5
Common Object Request Broker Architecture (CORBA), 340
CommonPoint, 57
Common programming model pattern, 249–252
Competition, intensity of, 574
Competitive position, 571–573
Competitive strategy, 573
Component context diagrams, 434
Component libraries, 7, 358, 544
Components, 4, 143–144, 213, 419
    context diagrams, 421
    versus frameworks, 15
    implementation inheritance of, 7
Component systems, 15
Composite node classes, 285
Composite pattern, 277–279, 384
Composition:
    communication between frameworks, 478
    descriptions of, 449
    horizontal and vertical, 478
    of hot spots, 380–381
    problems preceding, 448–449
    problems with, 72–75
    recursive, 383

of specifications and models, 447
Compositional rule of inference, 178
Composition overlap, 474–475
Composition problems, 468, 471–476
    causes of, 476–479
    solutions, 479–484
Composition techniques, research on, 190–191
Computer-Aided Software Engineering (CASE):
    atomic node classes, 285
    collection nodes, 285
    composite node classes, 285
    hyper nodes, 285
    hypertext for, 268
    link classes, 286–287
    navigator nodes, 286
    tools, 285–287
Concept libraries, 404
    and implementation parts, connecting, 405
Conceptual architecture, 67–68
Concrete behaviors, 541–542
Concrete classes, 292, 325–326
    derived, for hot-spot subsystem, 362
Concrete Data Types (CDTs), 12
Concrete specifications, 291
Concrete to Abstraction Pattern, 520
Concurrency, 481
Concurrent Pascal, 123
Conditional matching, 548
Conditional scheduling, 117–118
Configuration framework pattern, 241–244
Configuration management systems, 339–340
Connector pattern, 429
Consistent object creation, 326, 330, 334–336
Constrained generic patterns, 333–334
Constraints, 536–537, 551, 556
Construction view, 418–419
Constructors, call-chaining mechanism, 240
Contracts, 499
Control loop:
    changing, 479

removing and rewriting, 481
Controllers, 5, 146
    activation and deactivation of, 6
Cookbooks, 221, 498–499, 501
CORBA, 4–5
Core framework design, 58
Core implementation, 58
Coroutines, 90, 136
    scheduling, 136
    sequencing, 96–98
    Simula objects as, 96
CoStart/CoStop primitives, 123
Current function, 105, 107
Customization. *See* Framework usage phase
Cycle time, reduction of, 571

D

Dahl, O.-J., 91
Data abstraction, 5
Debugging, 12
    applications, 71
    vendor support for, 621
Decorator pattern, 281–282, 384
Default behaviors, 159
Delays, in SimIOProcess, 126
Delegation mechanism, 183, 190
DEMOS (Discrete Event Modeling on Simula), 131
DependencyManager class, 207, 208
Dependency mechanisms, 7
Design, 147, 163
    activities of, 354–355
    application modeling activity, 355–356
    complexity of, 353–354
    component-based, 163–165
    design intention, 477–478
    framework versus application, 21–22
    generalization transformation, 367–373
    harvesting, 199–209
    hot-spot analysis, 359–362
    hot-spot high-level design, 365–367
    hot-spot specification, 356–359

Design *(Continued)*:
hot-spot subsystem, 362–365
reuse, 14
traditional versus framework, 443–444
Design frameworks, 523
Design intentions, 477–478
Design metaphors, 402
Design models, properties of, 435–436
Design notebooks, 500
Design Patterns (Gamma), 16
Design patterns, 30, 32, 38–40, 221, 499–500
application of, 39–40
for class dependency management, 342
combinations of, 416
development of, 40
and framework design, 46–47
as hot-spot subsystems, 364–366
and metapatterns, 42–44
and modeling patterns, 45
Design processes, evolutionary approach, 397–398
Design requirements, 312
Desktop layers, 400–402
Detach primitive, 96–97
Developers, documentation for, 497
Development, 11, 21–22, 35–36
effort for, 70
hot-spot-driven, 379–392
improvements in, 571–572
managing, 69, 618
methods for, 65–66
multiple frameworks for, 468, 471
phases in, 467–468
problems and experiences with, 62–67
productivity measures, 70
reducing effort for, 617
strategies for, 461–462
Diagram editor framework, 299–305
Differentiation, advantages of, 572–573
DISCO, 130
Discounted cash flow (DCF) technique, 578–580

Dispatch filter, 183
Display method, 442
Distributed System Object Model (DSOM), 3–4
Documentation, 13, 18–19, 36, 63, 220–221, 495–502
audiences for, 496–497
on class interactions, 160
costs of, 65
for enterprise frameworks, 85–86
by example, 562–564
future research on, 618
guidelines, 501
of hooks, 222–223
instantiation scenarios and examples in, 531–532
methods for, 64
patterns for, 49
standards for, 65
task-based, 160
types of, 497–501
usability of, 621
Domain abstraction modeling, 167
Domain analysis, 21, 34–35, 62, 167
knowledge graph mapping, 181–189
knowledge modeling, 172–181
modeling patterns for, 47–48
pilot project descriptions, 170–172
Domain analysis and engineering (DA&E), 211–214
Domain architecture, 167
Domain context analysis, 167
Domain knowledge, 173
modeling, 189
Domain models, and frameworks, 211–214
Domains, 69
framework coverage of, 477
Domain scope, defining, 63–64
Domain-specific frameworks, 523, 617–618
Dynamic architecture, 214
Dynamic binding, 12, 471
in development, 66
Dyson, Paul, 519

E
EC-Gruppen AB, 60, 469
Economics, of framework investment, 618. *See also* Value-Based Reuse Investment (VBRI)
Editing tools, 542
Editor framework, 354, 356
detail hot-spot analysis, 360–362
generalization transformation of, 369–374
high-level hot-spot analysis, 359
Efficiency, of frameworks, 12
Eiffel language, 500
Empowerment of users, 505–521
Enduring business processes (ERPs), in enterprise frameworks, 84
Enduring Business Themes (EBTs), 66, 460–463
in enterprise frameworks, 84
Enterprise application frameworks, 10, 83–86
characteristics of, 84–86
Enterprise resource planning (ERP), 83
Entity functionality, 73–74
composition of, 484
composition problems and solutions, 475–476, 483–484
Entity overlap, 72–73
Ericsson Software Technology AB, 61
Error correction, 75, 76
ET++, 7, 57, 408
European Software Institute, 568
Event-based system (EBS) framework, extending, 533–535
Event interface, 144
Event list, 104
in Simulation, 107
Event loop, changing, 479, 481
Events, 103
Events sequencing. *See* Simulation
Event-to-action connections, 145

Event-to-script connection, 145

Evolutionary cycle, 397–398

Examples, 498, 501, 562

Execution strategies, 254

Exit strategies, 576, 585–588

Expectation mismatch, between vendors and customers, 620–622

Extends relationship, 314

Extensibility, 8, 533–535

Extension points, 316

F

Facilities, 109, 110, 112

Facility class, 110

Factories, 326, 336
  abstract, 330, 334–335
  state-driven, 335–336

Factory methods, 333

Features, 315
  adding, 224
  enabling, 223

Fire alarm framework, 60, 470–471
  composition overlap in, 475
  entity functionality composition problems, 476

Firm-foundation theory of investment valuation, 578

Flexibility, value of, 591–592

Flexible hot spots, 33

Flow control, 290

Folder framework, 401

Framelets, 411–413

Frames, 173

Framework adaptation, 35

Framework cohesion, 476–477

Framework control:
  composition problems with, 471–472
  event loop modification, 479, 481

Framework description language (FDL), 64

Framework design, 62. See also Design

Framework development phase, 59, 60, 467

Framework domain, 353. See also Domains

Framework evolution and maintenance phase, 59, 468

Framework gap, 474
  solutions for, 482–483

Framework implementation, 62

Framework layers, 396–403

Framework maintainers, documentation for, 497

Framework maintenance, 11–12, 620–624

Framework overviews, 500, 501

Framework packaging, 542

Framework realization, 544–545, 547–549
  packaging, 552–555, 557

Framework Recipe, 238, 241, 260–265
  implementation of, 262–264
  pattern system of, 241–265
  questions for, 239–240

Framework representation, 537–539
  components object model, 540–542
  implementation of, 539–545

Frameworks. See also Blackbox frameworks; Whitebox frameworks
  as abstraction category, 33–37, 50
  analysis reuse, 8
  application of, 7, 34–35, 69–70
  behavioral refinement of, 293–295
  benefits of, 8–9, 55–56
  built-in tests in, 489–491
  called versus calling, 58, 59, 74, 472
  challenges of, 11–12
  classification of, 9–10
  combining, 133–134
  composition-based, 170
  consistency of, 326
  construction of, 403–408
  cost reduction capabilities, 571–572
  defect removal, 12
  definition of, 3, 58, 467
  deriving from domain knowledge, 195–196
  descriptions of, 48, 449, 526, 528–532, 535–537
  design of. See Design

  development of. See Development
  documentation for, 36. See also Documentation
  domain features, 33
  and domain models, 211–214
  efficiency, 12
  evaluating, 19–20, 347, 600–611
  evolution of, 57, 75–78, 376, 387, 600
  examples of, 59–62
  extending, 533–535
  generalization and aggregation representation, 537–539
  history of, 57
  inheritance-based. See Whitebox frameworks
  integratability, 11
  investments in. See Value-Based Reuse Investment (VBRI)
  knowledge graph mapping to, 181–189
  layering, 396–403
  learning curve for, 11, 18–19
  maintenance, 11–12, 76–77, 620–624
  metapattern micro-architectural description of, 48
  model of, 292–293
  new uses for, 624
  OOP, 442–444
  overview of, 9
  parameterized. See Blackbox frameworks
  patterns in development of, 49
  with placeholders, 455–457
  problems and experiences with, 62–78
  release of, 67
  requirements, 309–320. See also Use-case assortment
  reusers of, 496–497
  versus reuse technology, 15–16
  specifying, 295–297
  stability of, 66, 601–602
  standards for, 12–13
  strengths and weaknesses of, 11–13

Frameworks (*Continued*):
structural characteristics, 33–34
testing, 63, 66–67
textual descriptions of, 532
understanding of, 70–71
usability guidelines, 153–160
use of, 17–18, 531–532
user interface type, 7
validation, 12
and viewpoints, 163–165
Framework usage phase, 59, 467–468
Frozen spots, 353, 367
Functional architecture, 214
Functional factoring, 31
Functionality, of abstractions, 31
Future research areas, 617–619
Fuzzy-logic reasoning framework, 171–172
constraints and adaptability space in, 180–181
dynamically changing implementations in, 182
implementation of, 188–189
knowledge domains in, 177–179
top-level knowledge graph in, 175–176

G

Gang-of-Four pattern (GoF) catalog, 383
Garbage collection, 90
and interactive systems, 120
Gateway application, 428–433
Gateway billing systems, 61, 72
Gause and Weinberg technique for grouping requirements, 319
Gebos System, 395–396
framework construction, 403–408
layers of, 400–403
Generalization, 534
representation of, 183–184, 537–539
Generalization transformation, 355, 367–374
expanding, 367–368, 371–372
extending, 368, 370, 371

Generalized modus ponens (GMP), 175
Genesis database system compiler, 7
get method, 117, 159
Glossaries, 397
Glue, 164–165
Gordon, G., 109
GPSS, 109
GPSSS, 109–113
example of, 112–113
implementation, 110, 112
Graphical user interfaces (GUIs):
OO programming for, 5
SimIOProcess for, 129
Graybox frameworks, 10
Growth option, 581–585
Guided tours, of hypermedia applications, 274–275
GUI framework, control problems with, 472
GUN C Compiler, 14

H

Hardware, design notebooks for, 500
Harvesting process, 200
candidate identification, 200–201
Head class, 100
Help systems, 267
Hoare, C.A.R., 91, 93
Hold procedure, 107
Hollywood principle, 74, 472
Hook classes, 40–41
Hook methods, 5, 8, 40–41, 219–221, 381–384
benefits of, 231–232
descriptions of, 222–223
grammar for, 235–236
level of support, 224
method of adaption, 223–224
in SEAF project, 225–232
HotDraw, 420–428
classes of, 420
design patterns and messages, 422–424
system components, 421–422
use-case maps, 424–428
Hot-spot cards, 386–391
function type, 388
Hot-spot-driven teaching, 508–509, 513–514

Hot spots, 58, 66, 325, 326, 353, 356
analysis of, 355, 359–362
binding, 356–357, 365
detail analysis, 360–362
development driven by, 379–392
granularity of, 358
high-level analysis, 359–360
high-level design, 355
hook methods for, 381–384
identifying, 328–329, 341, 386
mining, 391–392
multiplicity characteristic, 366–367
specification of, 358
subsystem of, 362–367
variability of, 357
Hot-spot subsystems, 362–365
high-level design activity, 365–367
1:*n* recursive, 363
1:1 recursive, 363
recursive, 363
Hypermedia applications, 267
architectural patterns, 275–282
indexes and guided tours of, 274–275
Hypermedia components, creation of, 271–275
Hypermedia functionality approach, 267
Hyper nodes, 273, 285

I

Ichbiah, Jean, 92
Idioms, 39
Image algebra, 174
Image processing framework, 171
constraints and adaptability space in, 180
dynamically changing implementations in, 182
implementation of, 188
knowledge domains in, 177
top-level knowledge graph in, 174–175
Implementation:
dynamically changing, 182–183

framework design techniques for, 444
increment, 58
Implementation libraries, 404
and concept parts, connecting, 405
Includes, multiple include protection for, 158
Incremental role play, 515–520
Increment implementation, 58
Indexes, for hypermedia applications, 274–275
Inference knowledge, 173
Inheritance, 5, 90
of built-in tests, 488
code, 131–133
mapping specializations to, 183–184
multiple, 483, 484
Simula support of, 94–95
Initialization chains pattern, 255–258
Initialize function, 292
Inner keyword, 94
Inner mechanism, 131–133
Innovation, encouraging, 571–572
Input/output handling, in SimIOProcess, 125–126
Inspect statement, in Simula, 96
Instantiation scenarios, 531–532
Integratability, of frameworks, 11
Interaction characteristics, metrics for, 603–604
Interaction contracts, 499
Interactive Development Environments (IDEs), 260
Interface contracts, 499
Interface design, 31
Interface objects, for node views, 270–271
Interfaces, 4–5
versus classes, 540
context-sensitive, 273
hypermedia extensions to, 281–282
matching operations, 545–547
and nodes and objects, relationships between, 275–277

representation of, 529, 557
user, 275
Internal increments, 58
application-specific, 59
Interobject behavior, 525–526
Interrupts, in SimIOProcess, 125
InterViews, 7, 57
Intrinsic value, of investments, 578
Invariants, for specifying run, 297
Inversion of control, 5, 8–9, 34, 98, 471–472
and code inheritance, 131
and debugging, 12
Investment valuation, 578–592
IO interrupts, 119
IOProcess class, 123
isAbc convention, 157
ISA Services, Inc., 265
Iteration, 21, 75, 78
and domain knowledge modeling, 189–190

J

Jacobson, Griss, and Jonsson technique for grouping requirements, 319
Java, 4–5
introspection ability, 148
versus Simula, 90, 134–136
Java Abstract Window Toolkit (AWT) classes, 327–332
Java Applets, 249, 251
Java Beans, 143
Java Foundation Classes (JFC), 4
Java frameworks, interfaces and abstract classes for, 5

K

KADS system, 173
KARL system, 173
Kindler, Evzen, 96
Knowledge domains, 176–179
framework derivation from, 195–196
inheritance semantics for, 190
Knowledge graphs, 172
knowledge domains, refining into, 176–179

mapping, 181–189, 197–198
top-level, 172–176, 196
Koskimies and Mossenbock technique for framework development, 320

L

Laboratory for Clinical and Experimental Image Processing, 171
Larch language, 500
Large application frameworks:
framework construction, 403–408
framework layering in, 396–403
Layers, 396–403, 419
Learning, methods, 68–69
Legacy applications, and frameworks, 411–412
Legacy components:
composing strategies, 481–482
composition problems with, 472–474
integrating, 75
Leitmotifs, design metaphors in, 402
Level of abstraction, 419
Lexical coupling, between methods and objects, 525–526
Libraries, debugging with, 71
Library layers, 404–405
Licensing keys, verifying, 254
Linkage superclass, 100
Links, 273
classes of, 100, 273–274, 286–287
unclassified, 274
LoadPCB instruction, 115

M

MacApp framework, 7, 57
learning time 68
Macintoshes, SimIOProcess application for, 129–130
Macroscopic behavior patterns, 415–419
Main object, 107
Maintenance, of frameworks, 11–12, 76–77, 620–624
Makila, K., 130
Management, active, 577, 581, 584

Man pages, 500
Manufacturing execution systems (MES), 83
Manufacturing framework, development of, 375–376
Market economics, 574–576
Market Economics/Competitive Position (MECP) framework, 570–571
competitive advantage options, 571
market economics, 574–576
risk management, 576–577
Market entry, 574, 575
growth option for, 582–585
Market exit strategies, 576, 585–588
Marketing modeling, 446
Market profitability, limiting forces, 574
Market timing, 588–591
Matching, interface, 545–549, 556
Materials, 402
McLaughlin, Phil, 520
Measurement systems framework, 60–61, 469
control problems with, 472
legacy component integration problems, 473
Mediating software, for framework gap, 474, 482
Mediator design pattern, 206
Mentoring, 68, 506
Message flow graphs, 530–531, 542
and constraints, 536
extending, 533–534
Message logging, 239, 244
Message-logging framework pattern, 244–247
Message pair specialization, 534
Message reflection, 188
Message sequence charts, 435
Metalevel configuration, and class dependencies, 326, 339–341
Metaobjects, 190
Metapatterns, 30, 32, 40–44, 221
application of, 41
and design patterns, 42–44
development of, 41–42
and framework structure, 48

recursive connection, 41
unification, 41
Methods:
access to, 95
asynchronous, 160
minimizing number, 153–155
naming conventions for, 155–157
overriding, 380
virtual, 93
Metrics, for framework evaluation, 600–601, 603–606
for class architectures, 608–611
collecting, 606–611
for structure characteristics, 607–608
MFCs (Microsoft Foundation Classes), 9
class architecture metrics, 608–611
learning time, 68
structural metrics for, 607–608
Middleware integration frameworks, 10
Modeless systems design, 159
Modeling, 5
framework design techniques for, 444
of generic specifications, 447
preciseness of, 449
Modeling patterns, 30, 32, 44–45
and design patterns, 45
for domain analysis, 47–48
Model/View/Controller (MVC), 5, 421, 423
file tool, 7
Modula, 123
Modularity, 8
Modules, 415
Monitors:
in GPSSS, 112
SimIOProcess, 128–129
Motifs, 498–499
Multiple views problem, 185
Multitasking, coroutines and, 96
MVCs, 5, 7, 421
self-modification, 423

N
Navigation, 202–204. *See also* Nodes

in hypermedia environments, 268–270
Navigator nodes, 273, 286
Nested classes, 95–96
90 percent/10 percent rule, 70
Node classes, 272, 285–287
Nodes:
aggregation of, 277–279
classification of, 279–281
and objects and interfaces, relationships between, 275–277
unclassified, 272–273
views of, 270
Node views, 273
classification of, 279–281
Notification, in classes, 145
Nygaard, Kristen, 91, 92

O
Object frameworks, 523. *See also* Frameworks
behavioral representation, 556
description of, 535–537
Module interconnection languages, 556
search and realization issues, 556
Object interaction, 5, 550–551
metrics for, 603–604
Object level, built-in tests at, 488–490
Object Linking and Embedding (OLE), 3
Object modeling, 384–386
modifying, 386, 388–389
Object-oriented (OO) application frameworks, 4–8. *See also* Frameworks
Object-oriented enterprise frameworks (OOEFs), 83–86. *See also* Frameworks
Object-Oriented Hypermedia Design Method (OOHDM), 271
Object request broker (ORB) frameworks, 9
Objects:
and nodes and interfaces, relationships between, 275–277
dependencies of, 552–553
interobject behavior, 525–526

reuse of, 550–551
Simula, 89, 92, 93, 96, 131
Observer pattern, 275–277, 422
   for entity composition, 484
   metapattern description of, 43–44
OO-Navigator, 268–269
   architectural patterns of, 275–282
   architecture of, 269–271
   instantiation of, 271–275
Open Closed principle, 252
OpenDoc, 3
OpenStep, 7
Operating systems, modeling, 114–119
Operator overrides, 157–158
Option pricing model, 580–582
Options, for frameworks, 224
   real, 581
Overriding, 444, 448

P

Package classes, 96
Packaging, 545, 552–555, 557
Palme, Jacob, 120
Parallel programming:
   levels of, 136
   and Simula, 90
Parallel systems, modeling, 103–104
Parameters:
   class, 93
   default values for, 159
Participants, 528
   and variables, constraints on, 536
   interactions between, 529–530
Participation strategy, 574–576
   growth option, 582–585
Part interfaces, 143–144
Parts, 143–144
   versus classes, 145–147
   connecting, 145
   visual builder standards for, 147–149
Pattern languages, 30, 38
Pattern-oriented teaching, 507–508, 513
Patterns, 16, 221. *See also*
   Design patterns; Meta-patterns
   analysis, 45

composite, 277–279
decorator, 281–282
in documentation, 498
for hypermedia applications, 275–282
for modeling, 44–45
object-oriented, 37–40, 50–52
observer, 275–277
options for, 224
type object, 279–281
unification and separation, 382
Pattern system, 241–265
Periodic objects, 60
Petri nets, 436–437
Physical Analogy Pattern, 520
Pilot projects:
   description of, 170–172
   domain knowledge modeling of, 172–181
   implementation of, 185, 187–189
   problems with, 181–186
Pioneering investments, 582–583
Placeholder pattern, 252–255
Placeholders, for frameworks, 455–457
Platform independence, 66
Pluggable adaptors, 551
Plug points, 444
Polymorphism, 5, 90, 158
Portability, 66
Postconditions and preconditions, 66, 81, 531
   for specifying framework, 295–296
PREDE pointer, 100
pred function, 100
Preemptive scheduling, in SimIOProcess, 128
Prefixing, 94
   conventions for, 156
Presentation framework, 327–332
prev function, 100
Priority scheduling, round-robin, 123
Procedures:
   code inheritance between, 131–132
   prefixed, 132
Process class, 103
Process Control Block (PCB) objects, 115

Processes, 90, 136
ProcessManager class, 123
Process operation frameworks, 61–62
Process scheduling, 134–136
Product books, 500
Product data management (PDM), 83
Production costs, lowering, 571
Production modeling, 446
Productivity, improvements in, 571, 599
Product lines, 568
Product market objectives, 570
Prototypes, 397
Publisher-Subscriber modeling pattern, 44
PutEvent, 125
put method, 117

Q

Quality Metrics for Object-Oriented Designs (QMOOD++), 606–611
Query interface tool, 545–547

R

Reactor pattern, 429
ReadyQ, empty, 126–128
Real time frameworks, and Simula, 119–130
REBBOOT project, 56
Recipes, 498–499
Recoverability, 170
Reenskaug's framework conditions, 311
Refactoring, 57, 75, 311, 315–317
Reference manuals, 500
References, 90, 93, 158
Reference variables, 93
Refinement, 452–453
   collaboration, 454
Reflective architectures, 342
Regis Orb Implementation (ROI), 345
Regulatory pressures, on markets, 574
Release criteria, 67
Requirements analysis, 67
Research, future topics, 617–619
reset methods, 160

Resource allocation frameworks, 61, 72, 445–446
Resource allocators, 117
Resume primitive, 96–97
Retrievals, 452
Reusability, 8, 573
Reuse, 3, 13–16, 29
of built-in tests, 488–491
through extension, 468
of framework style, 442–443
and hooks, 219–220. *See also*
Hooks
strategic options of, 567. *See
also* Value-Based Reuse
Investment (VBRI)
traditional approach, 442
types of, 496–497
Reuse Capability Model,
568–569, 579
risk management levels, 577
upper levels, 581
Reuse cycle, 544
Reuse Maturity Levels, 568
Risk management, 576–577
Role-Object pattern, 405–406
Role objects, 405
Role playing, teaching with,
508, 513
incremental, 515–519
Role Playing Pattern, 520
Roles, 482
Run method, 292–293
specifying, 296–298,
302–305
RWG, 395

S

Scalability, 526, 530
Scenarios, 391, 397, 501. *See
also* Use cases
Schrader, Joachim, 519
Searchability, 526–527
Searching frameworks,
545–547, 556
Select-Sort, 195
Self-education of users,
505–506
Self-modifying software, 417,
423
use-case map representa-
tion of, 435
Semantic networks, 173
Semaphores, 116
in GPSSS, 112, 113
in SimIOProcess, 128–129
Sensitivity analyses, 584–585

SeQuencing Set (SQS), 107
Serializability, 170
Shared behavior affected by
shared state problem,
185
Shaw, Alan, 114
Sherlock, 211–214
Shutdown behavior, class
participation in, 255–258
Signature matching, 545–550,
556
SIMDBM, 130
SimIOProcess, 123–130
Simset, 98, 100–103
example of, 102
Simula 1, 67, 89, 91
combining frameworks,
133–134
concepts of, 89–90, 92–98
DEMOS, 131
DISCO, 130
frameworks with, 98–109
garbage collectors of, 120
history of, 91–92
inheritance in, 94–95,
131–133
input/output of, 120
versus Java, 134–136
nested classes in, 95–96
operating system modeling
with, 114–119
for real time, 119–130
SIMDBM, 130
syntax of, 96
Simulation, 98, 103–109
example of, 105–106
implementation of, 107
Simulation classes, versus
threads, 136
Simulation for Real Time,
120–122
Simulation frameworks,
109–119. *See also* SimSet;
Simulation
Simulation system (SS)
framework, extending,
533–535
Size Engineering Application
Framework (SEAF) proj-
ect, 220
hooks in, 225–232
worksheets and data,
225–228
Sleep, 121
Smalltalk 80 environment, 5
Class Controller, 6–7

class library, 7
Class Object, 7
ClassView, 6
dependency mechanisms,
552–553
dynamic interactions in, 512
incremental teaching example, 510–515
Model class, 7
Standard SystemView, 6
static layout of, 511
subview hierarchy, 6
user-interface framework,
57
Software architecture, 29–30
abstractions, use of, 29. *See
also* Abstractions, architectural
Software artifacts, 191
Software connectors, 551
Software development, 59.
See also Development
Software Engineering Institute, 568
Software Engineering
Research Laboratory,
225
Software product metrics,
600–601
class architecture metrics,
606–611
framework architectural
metrics, 603–608
interaction characteristics,
603–604
Software Productivity Consortium, 568
Solitaire framework, documentation of, 562–564
Solution domain analysis,
199, 201–203
Source code:
access to, 478–479
packaging, 552–555, 557
Specification:
of framework behavior,
295–305
framework design tech-
niques for, 444, 447
Spiral development cycle,
374
Stability, framework, 601–602
and upgrading decision,
623
Standards, for framework
design, 12–13, 618–619

State-driven factories, 335–336
Statements, class, 92–93
Statistical analysis framework, 469–470
Steiger, Roger, 519
Storages, 109
    in GPSSS, 110
Strategic options:
    of software reuse, 567
    value of, 582
Strategic planning, 569
    objective of, 569–571
    risk management, 576–577
Strategic value, option pricing model determination of, 580–582
Strategy patterns, 182–183
Structural characteristics, 31
    metrics for, 603–604, 607–608
Subclasses, 17, 58, 259
    creating, 4
    declaration of, 94
    minimizing, 154
Subclassing, 405, 444, 448, 483
    and legacy components, 472–473
Subject-Observer framework, 458
Subject-Observer pattern, 456–457
Subject orientation, 484
Subsystems, 415
Subviews, 5–6
SUCC pointer, 100
suc function, 100
Superclasses, 4
Supervisor mode, 115
Supplier pressures, 574
Support, vendor, 622–624
SwapSort, 195
Synchronization. *See also* GPSSS
    in SimIOProcess, 128–129
Systematic generalization development cycle, 374–375
System infrastructure frameworks, 9
Systems, 415
    requirements of, 460–461
    self-modifying, 417
    structure of, 416

Systems architectures, heterogeneity, 83. *See also* Architecture
System view, 397, 416–419

T

Tailorability, 573
Taligent approach, 57, 309, 319, 408
Task class, 206–207
Task descriptor, 201, 206
Task knowledge, 173
Task list, 202
Task management framework design, 203–208
    implementation, 208
    object model, 208
Task manager, 201, 206
Tasks:
    concurrent, 202
    dependencies of, 209
    disposition, 203, 204, 209
    domain object associations, 202
    initialization and activation, 203, 204, 209
    interaction, 203, 204
    navigation among, 203, 204
Teaching techniques, 506–509
    combining, 509–515
    guidelines for, 514–515
    incremental role play pattern, 515–519
    incremental teaching, 509, 514
    pedagogical patterns, 515–520
Teams, 425
Technical kernel layers, 400, 401
Technology books, 500
Teledyne Fluid Systems-Farris Engineering, 220, 225
TeleLarm AB, 60, 470
Template classes, 40–41
Template-hook combinations:
    recursive, 390–391
    separation of, 382–384
Template Method pattern, 384
Template methods, 5, 40–41, 381. *See also* Hook methods
Templates, image, 174–175
TerminalProcess subclass, 121
TerminalQueue, 121

Test applications, 63, 66–67
    built-in tests, 488–491
Threads (Java), 134–136
    versus simulation classes, 136
Three Bears Pattern, 520
Three-tier application architecture, entity functionality, 73–74
Time threads, 501
Tool-construction framework, 401
Tools, 402
TotalOrder framework, 458
Traces, 290, 296, 299
Trader framework, 458
Traders, 340
Training, of users, 68–69, 506
Transaction blocks, 173–174
Transaction class, 110
Transaction framework, 170–171
    constraints and adaptability space in, 180
    dynamically changing implementations in, 182
    implementation of, 188
    knowledge domains in, 176–177
    top-level knowledge graph in, 173–174
Transactions, 109
Transport mechanisms, 254
Trees, merging, 97–99
Two-Way-Link framework, 458
Type matching, 546–547
Type models, 450, 454
Type object pattern, 228, 279–281
Type parameterization, in development, 66
Types, 450–452
Type system, 90
Typing conflicts, 472–473

U

UMxx framework series, 114–119
Unidraw, 408
Uniformity, 14–15
Upgrading, 623–624
Usability, guidelines for, 153–160
Usage problems, 67–71

Use-case assortment,
309–310, 312–318
analysis technique for,
315–317
background of, 310
modeling heuristics for,
313–315
Use-case explosion, 318
Use-case maps (UCMs),
417–419, 424–428,
430–433, 435
map notation, 426
versus Petri nets, 436–437
Use-case modeling, 316–317
model size, 317–318
Use-case paths, 434
Use cases, 391, 501
User class, 207
User interface frameworks,
557
User interfaces, for hypermedia applications, 275
User mode, 115
User object, 202
User profiles:
node views of, 273
points of view of, 272
Users:
educating, 505–506. *See also*
Teaching techniques
and vendors, expectation
mismatch between,
620–622
User tasks, analyzing, 397
Uses relationships, 313, 318

V

Validation, of frameworks, 12
Value, creating, 570, 577, 584

Value-Based Reuse Invest-
ment (VBRI), 567,
569–593
deferring investment,
588–591
investment valuation,
578–592
market economics,
574–576
risk management, 576–577
strategic planning,
569–571
Value framework, 401
Variables, and participants,
constraints on, 536
Variables slot, 536
Variants, 211–212
Variation points, 211–213
Velocity of business, 83
Vendors:
customer feedback for,
621–622
and customers, expectation
mismatch between,
620–622
Vendor support, 622–624
Verifiers, documentation for,
497
Very large scale integration
(VLSI) routing algo-
rithms, 7
Viewpoints, 163–165
Views, 5, 146, 540
in architectural specifica-
tion, 346
multiple, 185, 202
Views-a properties, 164
Virtual methods, 90
Virtual procedures, 98

Visual builders, 57, 143–160
classes versus parts,
145–147
class standards, 147–148
designer support, 147
interface complexity and,
149
methods, multiargument,
148–149
name change protection
from, 148
parts, connecting with, 145
Volatility, market, 584–585,
588, 591

W

Wait_Class object, 118
WaitEvent, 125
Wait_Until statement, 117
Welcome banners, 254
Whitebox framework, 10, 17,
48, 58, 169
hot spots in, 357–358,
379–381
Whitebox interfaces, 200
Whitebox teaching, 507–509,
511–514
Williams, John B., 578
Wirth, Niklaus, 123
Wizards, 225
Workflow management, 66, 84
Workplace context, 396, 398
Worksheets, 225–228, 230
Wrapper frameworks, 401
Wrappers, 474, 478–479, 481,
482

Z

zAPP, 7